SOVIET IMAGE OF CONTEMPORARY LATIN AMERICA

A Documentary History, 1960–1968

Publication Number Three
Conference on Latin American History

Soviet Image of Contemporary Latin America

A Documentary History, 1960-1968

Compiled and Translated from Russian by

J. GREGORY OSWALD

With an Introduction by Herbert S. Dinerstein

EDITED BY ROBERT G. CARLTON

PUBLISHED FOR THE CONFERENCE ON LATIN AMERICAN HISTORY

BY THE UNIVERSITY OF TEXAS PRESS, AUSTIN AND LONDON

Conference on Latin American History Publications

This series is issued under an arrangement between the Confer-
ence on Latin American History, Inc., and the University of
Texas Press. It includes works approved by the Publications
Committee of the Conference and the Faculty Board of the
Press. Publication funds are furnished by the Conference from
a Ford Foundation grant.

Type set by W.O.S. Typesetting, Austin, Texas
Printed by Malloy Lithographing, Inc., Ann Arbor, Michigan
Bound by Universal Bookbindery, Inc., San Antonio, Texas

FOREWORD

The Conference on Latin American History is pleased to present this third title in its series of publications. As the Preface to the first publication states, volumes in the publication program are "devoted primarily to works of general importance for the improvement of training and research in the United States related to Latin American history." Specifically authorized for the publications are source materials, "including those translated from languages not generally read by Latin American specialists," of which the present volume is an example. It is viewed as a supplementary teaching aid rather than as a tool for specialized research.

The compilation of translated excerpts from recent Soviet writings on Latin America is designed to make students aware that the problems of the area can be assessed differently from the more familiar presentations by what Soviet writers usually label U.S. "bourgeois historians" of Latin America. It also seemed worthwhile to expose both teachers and students to a corpus of writings often couched in the characteristic polemic terms seldom absent from the Marxist-Leninist context, and to provide such materials to which readers can apply the established canons of historical criticism, winnowing fact from unsupported testimony or undocumented assertion and testing implicit assumptions. It was also hoped that a selection of documents such as these might prove useful in various university courses on comparative topics and areas related to Latin American or Soviet matters.

All readers at the outset should be acutely aware that Soviet research and writings on Latin America are intimately linked to a basic, unchanging policy of the USSR: to promote socialist revolution leading to communism. It is held as a tenet that one major function of Soviet scholarship is to aid the achievement of that aim. Within the framework of Marxist-Leninist methodology, investigators are expected to show how other societies evolved and are developing today and to document credible theories to explain how developments in such societies do and will conform to Marxist-Leninist doctrine. Scholarship is directly and indirectly linked with analysis and interpretation of that doctrine, and thus to the formulation of "correct" national and international policies. To these ends, Soviet specialists probe the past and the present, sorting out and evaluating those elements favorable or unfavorable to establishment of socialism and its evolution to communism on the Soviet model. Responsibility to the state, and to the ruling communist party, are elements organically linked to investigations of Latin America by Soviet scholars and publicists. Worth repeating here is Professor Cyril Black's statement that, "in short, the historians are called upon to make a vital contribution in the realm of scholarship to the continuing propaganda campaign in which the [Communist] party is engaged."[1]

[1]Cyril E. Black, ed., *Rewriting Russian History* (N.Y., 1962), pp. 31–32.

The present volume initially developed from conversations between the writer and Professor J. Gregory Oswald in 1963. Its contents have gone through a number of outline changes and revisions since that time. An earlier phase was reported in some detail by Dr. Oswald in 1966, when it was thought that writings from 1945 through 1965 would be included.[2] Subsequent continuing review of Dr. Oswald's excellent selection of materials by various specialists on Soviet and Latin American affairs led to a later addition of some excerpts and deletion of others to provide a relatively recent, focused group of translated Russian materials, which for balance would also include some general Soviet policy statements. In the course of the review process, it was agreed that interpretative materials originally scheduled for inclusion at the beginning of various sections should be omitted as inappropriate to a source book.

Because of his familiarity with both the Soviet and Latin American aspects, and his editorial experience in these matters, the services of Robert G. Carlton were enlisted in 1968 to provide these editorial changes.[3] He also reviewed the translations (providing some for newly inserted selections), and prepared the requested minimal headnotes to place the selections in context. To guide readers in their use of these raw materials, Dr. Herbert S. Dinerstein, another specialist conversant with Soviet and Latin American matters, generously agreed to write some brief introductory remarks.

Support and help for Dr. Oswald's initial research and his selection and translation activities came from various sources, all overt. These included the University of Arizona and the Mershon Foundation of the Ohio State University. The Hispanic Foundation in the Library of Congress provided him with several hundred pages of photoreproduced materials from which he, aided by Gordon O. Packard, Jr., as University of Arizona graduate assistant in research, made provisional selections. These were translated under Dr. Oswald's supervision. The staff of the Slavic and Central European Division in the Library of Congress advised on a number of technical and bibliographical questions. Funds from the Ford Foundation also partially supported these tasks and have made it possible for the Conference on Latin American History to publish the results.

Grateful appreciation is herewith tendered for all these aids, as well as to various area and subject specialists who gave freely of their counsel and time at many points. The compiler, Professor Oswald, and the editor, Mr. Carlton, however, accept full professional responsibility for the volume.

On behalf of the Conference, the undersigned has undertaken a very minor role in the administrative coordination of this interesting and significant project. Enthusiastic cooperation by all concerned was universally forthcoming when he asked it, for which he records his sincere thanks.

Howard F. Cline
Chairman, Committee on
Activities and Projects
Conference on Latin American History

[2] J. Gregory Oswald, "Contemporary Soviet Research on Latin America," *Latin American Research Review*, I (Spring 1966), 77–96, esp. pp. 80–87.

[3] Robert G. Carlton, ed., *Latin America in Soviet Writings: A Bibliography, 1917–1964*, 2 vols. (Baltimore: The Johns Hopkins Press, 1966).

CONTENTS

IV. THE CATHOLIC CHURCH AND CHRISTIAN DEMOCRACY

V. CONSERVATISM

VI. LABOR AND TRADE UNIONISM

VII. THE RURAL AND URBAN MILIEU

VIII. ECONOMIC PROBLEMS

IX. Economic and Ideological Rivalry

X. The Cuban Revolution

INTRODUCTION

This book presents samples of Soviet writing on Latin America in order to furnish to students of the Soviet Union and of Latin America, in convenient form, source materials for the study of Soviet policy in Latin America. Like most Soviet discussion of sensitive political subjects these materials do not explain Soviet policy in themselves but, rather, constitute raw data to be analyzed. This introduction will seek to provide some guides for the conduct of such an analysis.

Since the Soviet expectations for successful revolution in Latin America were, until the Cuban revolution, rather low, Soviet scholarship was meagerly financed for the study of this area. However, individual historians, such as M. S. Al'perovich, did highly creditable work. But the quality of communist party political personnel assigned to work with Latin Americans was very low. In one of the few authentic accounts of the training of foreign Communists in Soviet secret schools, a Brazilian ex-Communist, Osvaldo Peralva, gives an amusing account of the egregious ignorance of A. M. Sivolobov.[1] Samples of Sivolobov's writings appear in this volume, and the reader can usefully compare their content and style with that of academically trained writers. The party writer, having received his directive, elaborates and repeats the official line in the insistent manner all too familiar to those forced to earn their living by reading communist party materials. By contrast, the academic analysts draw upon source material from the Latin American press to make a case that is often at variance, as we shall see, with the official line.

The first task the Cuban Revolution presented to the Soviet party writers was to find a major role for the proletariat as represented by the Cuban Partido Socialista Popular, the Communist Party. Since the Communists had opposed Castro until shortly before his entrance into Havana, facts to support the case are difficult to adduce and only bald assertion remains. A. A. Guber, in the foreword to a book written for the Higher Party School attached to the Central Committee of the Communist Party, says that the Cuban party adopted the correct Leninist line of forming a national front, glossing over the fact that such a line was not adopted until just before the Batista regime fell (Item 7). Guber then claims that "had the People's Socialist Party of Cuba not followed such a correct line, the Cuban Revolution would have been unsuccessful and the hegemony of the working class, which assured Cuba's transition to the socialist path of development, probably never achieved." Sivolobov, whose background has already been referred to, in a book written under the imprint of the Patrice Lumumba University, an

[1] Osvaldo Peralva, "O Chefe (russo) do PCB," in *O Retrato* (Belo Horizonte: Itatiaia, 1960), pp. 43–55.

institution for the indoctrination of students from underdeveloped countries, stresses, correctly enough, the importance of the Communist Party in the worker's strike of January 1, 1959, but then, quite incorrectly, gives the impression that the workers played the major role by listing them before the peasants and the intelligentsia as the driving forces of the revolution (Item 44). The reader will note that elsewhere the weakness of the Batista regime and the armed struggle led by Castro are emphasized and the role of the party downgraded (Item 46).

After disposing, at least to their own satisfaction, of the question of which class was responsible for the Cuban Revolution, Soviet writers turned to the question of whether the revolution could be replicated elsewhere in the hemisphere. The official party press was very optimistic on this score until the Cuban missile crisis. Some academic writers, such as A. F. Shul'govskii in a book published in 1963 and delivered to the printer in May of that year, continued to retain their optimism even after the setback the Soviet Union suffered in the Caribbean in October 1962. Shul'govskii wrote, "Cuba demonstrated that practically any country in the world, under favorable internal conditions can achieve a profoundly national revolution and launch the construction of socialism . . ." (Item 46), But this optimism was soon to be officially proscribed. In 1964, S. S. Mikhailov, the head of the Latin American Institute of the Academy of Sciences, labeled as dangerous the "tendency toward a mechanical projection of the experiences of the Cuban Revolution onto all the other countries of Latin America . . ." (Item 5), a warning that has been repeatedly offered since then.

If Cuba was not the model for future revolutions in Latin America, what then were the prospects? The Soviet leaders fell back upon a theory first enunciated at the Tenth Congress of the Communist Party in 1920. The national bourgeoisie were designated as the ally of the proletariat in the creation of a revolution. This designation of the middle class as obligatory members of a coalition forced the Communist Party to find a way of co-operating with them, and by that token constrained the party to give up genuine revolutionary activity. In the 1920's the Indian Communist Roy drew that conclusion, objected, and was ejected from the Communist International. Since 1966 Castro has been saying much the same thing. Interestingly enough, we find an echo of this dissatisfaction in an article by A. F. Shul'govskii on the national bourgeoisie (Item 10). Here the case is made, drawing carefully on statements by Latin American businessmen and industrialists, that the latter are really very closely tied to American capitalism and that often they voice complaints merely to get better bargaining terms from the United States. The really revolutionary classes are the students and the middle sectors of the population. Since the latter were essentially the elements Castro relied on, a rather thinly veiled case is being made for a revolution on the Castro model rather than dependence on collaboration with the national bourgeoisie. Such materials suggest persistent differences of opinion among various elements of the Soviet scholarly and party specialists on Latin America.

Another connected issue has been the attitude to be adopted toward guerrilla movements in Latin America. In the first years after he came to power, Castro tried to stimulate guerrilla movements by landing small bodies of exiles and some Cubans in various Caribbean countries. These attempts failed, and after the Cuban missile crisis the Soviet Union began to reassess the role of guerrillas. The Soviet position has always been consistent on this issue: Revolutions can be promoted by violent or peaceable means. Neither course is obligatory and a judgment must be made on the basis of the objective situation. The Soviet record of judgment, however, has not been very impressive. Quite frequently the moment for revolutionary violence was judged to be propitious when it was not, and the Soviets were surprised by the early success of the Chinese Communists and by Castro's voluntary conversion to communism.

In 1963 and 1964 the Soviet leaders were uncertain of the prospects of the guerrilla movements. In July 1964 an article in the authoritative organ of the Communist Party of the Soviet Union, *Kommunist,* charged that "attempts at artificially 'speeding-up' the revolution, 'at bringing it closer,' regardless of local conditions, are destined to failure . . ." (Item 4). The failures in Peru and Ecuador were specifically mentioned. A month later the ubiquitous Sivolobov in the same magazine spoke favorably of the peasant movement in Peru and in general adduced examples of successful guerrilla operations (Item 21). Obviously a change had taken place in the CPSU's estimate of the situation, which was reflected in an agreement made in Havana in December 1964 among all the communist parties of Latin America, with the participation of the Soviet party to support revolutions in those countries where the local communist party approved of it or was instructed to approve of it.

Another important subject dealt with by Soviet writers is agrarian reform. The reader will note the repeated advocacy of agrarian reform as a necessary step on the road to the development of a revolutionary situation, since only agrarian reform can create the internal market that will provide an outlet for an expanded domestic industry. Such a line contradicts the emphasis on guerrilla warfare, which recruits personnel from, and depends for support on, the peasantry. Castro and Guevara have publicly insisted that the Cuban Revolution was an agrarian insurrection led by true revolutionaries. From the Cuban evidence it is hard to tell whether these bearded gentry consciously created a myth or themselves fell victim to its appeal. The Soviet emphasis on agrarian reform, however, suggests that Soviet analysts were able to distinguish between myth and reality.

A particularly striking evidence of sober Soviet assessments is to be found in E. Kovalev's article on agrarian reform in Bolivia, which appeared in *Mirovaia ekonomika i mezhdunarodnye othnosheniia,* probably the best academic journal dealing with contemporary foreign affairs (Item 25). Instead of the usual undifferentiated criticism of Latin American agrarian reform programs as unsuccessful, the Bolivian reform is described as having reduced the power of the landlords and increased the role of the peasantry and contributed both to a modest growth in the standard of living and to the subsequent improvement of agricultural production. Either the Cubans did not share this pessimistic estimate of the revolutionary situation of the Bolivian peasants, or they felt that they had to try to make another successful revolution, even if the chances were slim.

The Soviet party and scholarly writing on the problems of Latin America as represented in this volume are not sufficient in themselves to give a satisfactory picture of Soviet policy in Latin America. The student of the subject must familiarize himself with the developments in the country or area under discussion in order to place the Soviet literature in the proper perspective and to judge to what extent the Soviet writer understands the situation. In some cases he may decide from the tone that the particular situation in Latin America is well understood, but that the writer for specifically Soviet reasons is skirting critical issues. To make this judgment he will have to familiarize himself with the situation in the Soviet Union. For the scholar the world is full of books yet to be opened. It is to be hoped that this collection of excerpts will bring some of these yet unread books to the attention of its readers.

Herbert S. Dinerstein
The Johns Hopkins University
School of Advanced International Studies

SOVIET IMAGE OF CONTEMPORARY LATIN AMERICA

A Documentary History, 1960–1968

I

Objectives and Achievements of Soviet Research on Latin America

The first two selections in this section illustrate the principle of "division of labor" as applied to Soviet research on Latin America. On the one hand, as pointed out by S. S. Mikhailov, are scholars working on "composite research on the problems of contemporary Latin America" in the Latin American Institute of the Academy of Sciences. The basic goal of the Institute—established only in 1961—is declared to be "the systematic, multifaceted, and thorough study of the economic and political problems of contemporary Latin America."

On the other hand, the history of Latin America is the special province of the Latin American Sector of the Institute of History of the Academy. Marxist periodization and the problem of evaluating the struggle for independence are considered by M. S. Al'perovich in the second selection as topics warranting special attention. Note also that Al'perovich appears to stake out a claim to evaluation of the national-liberation movement as a task for the Latin American Sector of the Institute of History—a subject Mikhailov declares to be within the scope of the Latin American Institute.

Item 3—by V. V. Vol'skii, the present director of the Latin American Institute —recounts Soviet interest in Latin America, indicates the principal directions of current research, and lists a number of publications on Latin America.

Other bibliographical materials that could not be included here but are of interest to students of Soviet *latinoamericanística* are the following:

M. S. Al'perovich, *Sovetskaia istoriografiia stran Latinskoi Ameriki* (Moskva: Nauka, 1968).

E. S. Dabagian, "50 let sovetskoi latinoamerikanistiki; bibliograficheskii ocherk," in *SSSR i Latinskaia Amerika, 1917–1967* (Moskva: Mezhdunarodnye otnosheniia, 1967), pp. 176–209.

1. Studying the Problems of Latin America*

S. S. MIKHAILOV

Latin America is acquiring ever greater significance in international affairs. The struggle of the Latin American peoples for freedom from foreign oppression is on a new upsurge. The peasant movement for the implementation of democratic agrarian reforms and for the elimination of the vestiges of feudalism is expanding. The labor movement is growing, becoming more solidary, and workers' parties—in the lead in the peoples' national-liberation struggle and striving to achieve unity of action of the working class—are steadily increasing.

The Latin American peoples are not alone in their struggle. On their side lies the warm sympathy and solidarity of the peoples of the Soviet Union and the entire socialist camp, and the peoples of the Asian and African nations who have only recently thrown off the yoke of colonialism. Expressing the feelings of all the Soviet peoples, N. S. Khrushchev declared at the Twenty-Second Congress of the CPSU, "We consider it to be an inalienable right of peoples to put an end to foreign oppression, and we shall support their just struggle."[1]

It is a debt of honor of Soviet social science scholars to supply a profound Marxist analysis of the economic and political processes presently occurring in Latin America. Even though our scientific literature of Latin America contains a number of works of known interest, completely inadequate attention

has been paid until recently to do research in the field of the economics and politics of contemporary Latin America. Such pressing problems as the development of the national-liberation movement, the labor movement, and other progressive social movements in Latin America are being inadequately studied. Not enough research is being done on problems connected with the colonial policy of the imperialist powers—above all the United States. There is inadequate analysis of the foreign policy of the Latin American countries and of the contradictions among the imperialist powers whose interests clash in Latin America. The relations of the Soviet Union and other socialists states with the Latin American countries have not been summarized. There is no clarification of the potentials and prospects for economic, scientific-technical, and cultural collaboration between the countries of the socialist camp and those of Latin America.

The themes of historical research are often not related to our times, though it is clearly obvious that the treatment of subjects having something in common with the burning problems stirring Latin America today would be of great in-

---

* "Izuchenie problem Latinskoi Ameriki," *Vestnik Akademii nauk SSSR*, 5:54–59 (1962).

[1] N. S. Khrushchev, *Otchet Tsentral'nogo komiteta Kommunisticheskoi partii Sovetskogo Souiza XII s"ezdu partii* (Moskva, 1961), p. 23.

terest. The research published to date does not reveal to the required extent the specific features of this or that Latin American country. The majority of the studies are limited to very narrow chronological frameworks, on the order of three to five years, which does not make it possible to follow the development of events in broader perspective and to supply an analysis of the profound historical, economic, and political processes now occurring in Latin America.

The still unsatisfactory status of our study in this area of the world is to a considerable extent due to the fact that until now there has been no unitary scientific research center in the Soviet Union devoted to composite research on the problems of contemporary Latin America. Now such a center has been established. The Presidium of the USSR Academy of Sciences has decreed the establishment of a Latin American Institute as part of the division of economic, philosophical, and juridical sciences of the Academy. The creation of this Institute answers a long urgent need in the Soviet Union and opens a new important stage in serious scientific research into Latin American problems.

Life and practice require in the first place the systematic, multifaceted, and thorough study of the economic and political problems of contemporary Latin America. This, in fact, is the basic goal of the Institute.

The contemporary status of Latin America and its place in international affairs are characterized above all by the immense breadth of the national-liberation struggle of the peoples of Latin America. Following the triumph of the people's revolution in Cuba, this struggle has entered a new, higher stage. As a result of this ever more intensified struggle, the position of imperialism in Latin America grows less tenable from day to day. The peoples of Latin America are step by step winning their right to freedom from imperialistic oppres-

sion and from exploitation, as well as their right to liberty, happiness, and social progress. The Latin American countries do not wish to remain the patrimony of the imperialists any longer. The peoples of these countries desire to be masters of their own fate, the masters of the wealth that is being plundered by the imperialists. They are also struggling with the forces of internal reaction and the traitorous oligarchy of capitalists and powerful latifundists who get rich from the sweat and blood of the millions of workers whom they keep in medieval feudal serfdom, poverty, and ignorance.

The anti-imperialist, antifeudal revolution unfolding in Latin America is developing in accordance with the action of the general laws that are inherent in the entire contemporary national-liberation movement. Yet, this revolution has its own peculiarities, stemming from the traditions of the past and the distinctive historical development of the Latin American peoples.

An important feature of the contemporary national-liberation movement in Latin America is the fact that it is guided by the rich experience of past revolutionary struggles. The peoples of Latin America are waging the "second war of independence"—now against contemporary colonialism—aided by the historical experience of the liberation wars of 1810–1826 against the Spanish and Portuguese colonialists, and the experiences of the heroic battles against imperialists that the peoples of Mexico, Cuba, and other Latin American countries have waged more than once in the past.

A second important peculiarity lies in the fact that the peoples of Latin America have to wage their struggle for independence directly against the most powerful imperialistic power—the United States, which today is the gendarme of the world.

There exists yet another important peculiarity of the contemporary Latin

American national-liberation movement: its peoples are waging this struggle after lengthy development along the path of capitalism. Even though this growth went very slowly, encountering many obstacles and in many cases assuming misshapen forms, it led to the formation of an urban proletariat—the most reliable militant strength of the national-liberation movement. At present, the steadfast vanguard of the proletariat in all the Latin American countries is comprised of the Communist and workers' parties—which have had long experience in difficult class struggle and have endured stern trials.

Taking all this into account, it is obvious that special attention in the scholarly research plans of the Institute will be given to the national-liberation movement, the labor movement, and other progressive movements in Latin America. There are still many problems that have been inadequately investigated and analyzed in this field. The importance of their study—a task for the social sciences—has been emphasized by the new program of the CPSU. Among them are such questions as the nature of the motivating forces of the national-liberation movement in Latin America and the nature of the class forces comprising the movement; the role of the working class, peasantry, and national bourgeoisie and the unique characteristics of the national-liberation movement in various Latin American countries; the experience of the Cuban people's revolution and the protection of its gains by the Cuban people; the influence of the victorious Cuban people's revolution on the upsurge of the Latin American national-liberation movement; and many other problems.

The economic basis of the national-liberation movement in Latin American countries lies in the struggle of their peoples for economic independence and for independent economic growth in opposition to the expansion of foreign monopolistic capital, above all, that of the United States. In this regard, there are many problems that have not been studied. Specifically, there is a need for a profound interpretation of the paths of current economic development in the Latin American countries, especially questions related to industrialization, for example, primary capital accumulation, the role of state capitalism in the Latin American countries, and the agrarian problem. It is important to shed light on the prospects for economic and technical aid to the Latin American countries from the USSR, other nations of the socialist camp, and others. Along with this, of course, special attention is merited by such problems as the penetration of private foreign capital and its negative influence on the economy of the Latin American countries; the problem of their economic integration and the establishment of "common markets"; the effect of the European Common Market on the economy of the Latin American countries; and problems of Latin American foreign trade, particularly the question of nonequivalent exchange.

The basic essence of the foreign policy problems of contemporary Latin America stems from the effort of the imperialistic powers to re-establish their former rule, to strengthen their tottering positions, and to retain the possibility for continuation of the policy of colonial looting at any cost and by any means. To achieve this the imperialists, especially U.S. imperialists, seek to stifle the national-liberation movement in Latin America. They intervene rudely in the internal affairs of Latin American countries, enter into deals with their reactionary forces, use military force, and employ diplomatic and economic pressures. To achieve their ends the imperialists use the Organization of American States — the "U.S. Colonial Office," as it has been referred to by Latin Americans — and the entire web of political, economic, and military obligations in which they have entangled the countries of Latin America. They resort to bribery, terror, their agents in all spheres of the social-political life of Latin American countries, the Catholic Church, and the reactionary military, and they actively attempt to influence public opinion with their propaganda by blackmailing Latin Americans with the alleged danger from the socialist countries.

The imperialists are mounting a united assault against the aspirations of the Latin American peoples for freedom and for political and economic independence. However, this does not mean there are not deep-rooted antagonistic contradictions among the imperialist powers. The United States, England, France, West Germany, Japan, and the Netherlands are waging a stubborn struggle among themselves for spheres of influence in Latin America, for capital investment spheres, and for the monopolistic right to squeeze out enormous profits from the various Latin American countries. This struggle is being waged in Latin America proper as well as outside its borders.

Life bears witness to the fact that the insolent imperialistic policy of the Western powers is running up against increasing resistance from the Latin American countries. This resistance is being manifested chiefly by the peoples of Latin America and sometimes by the governments, which under their pressure demand a stop to imperialistic plunder, to interference in internal affairs, and to all the intrigues of foreign imperialism and its agents.

Finally, the foreign policy situation in Latin America is characterized by the desire of its peoples to rely on the support of the Soviet Union and the countries of the socialist camp in their anti-imperialist struggle. Despite vehement resistance from U.S. imperialists and all reactionary forces, the governments of a number of Latin American countries, under the influence of the masses, are ever more often expressing a desire to establish trade relations with the USSR and the countries of the socialist camp and to utilize the economic and scientific-technical aid of the socialist camp to strengthen their independence and defend their national interests.

There are other aspects of the foreign policy struggle in Latin America, such as relations among the Latin American countries themselves (in particular, the rivalry among the powerful countries of Latin America and their struggle to gain influence over the small countries), their relations with the countries of Africa and Asia, the aspiration of the Latin American countries to develop regional economic cooperation, the problems of neutralism and Pan-Americanism, and the significance of the historical ties between Latin American countries and certain European countries, primarily Spain and Portugal.

All these and many other problems in the realm of Latin American foreign policy and international relations require theoretical elaboration, analysis, and elucidation. They naturally come within the scope of the problems with which the Latin American Institute will be concerned.

It is impossible to exclude the fact that in the future, as the Institute develops its work and establishes its position as a scientific research organization primarily concerned with contemporary problems, its nature in imparting general education will be expanded. In such a case the Institute would include in its sphere of activities the study of the history and culture of Latin America, in addition to research into current economic and political conditions. At present these problems are the concern of specialized sectors of the Institute of History and of the N. N. Miklukho-

Maklai Institute of Ethnography of the USSR Academy of Sciences.

Of course, the scientific research work of the Latin American Institute has to be closely associated with the demands of life and with the practice of political, economic, and cultural relations of the Soviet Union with the countries of Latin America. The Institute trusts that it will be able to establish fruitful working relations with the Soviet governmental and social organizations that have ties with the countries of Latin America, and it hopes that the scientific research conducted by the Institute will be useful in some degree to these organizations. In this way the Institute's work will contribute to the strengthening and development of the friendly relations between the USSR and the Latin American countries.

One of the tasks of the Institute must be to facilitate the coordination of the scientific research activities of Soviet Latin Americanists and also the coordination of their work with that of colleagues of other countries of the socialist camp. That activity will be implemented by the Institute both directly and through the scientific councils recently established by the Presidium of the Academy of Sciences of the USSR for the study of two complex problems: "the economic competition of two systems and the underdeveloped countries," and "the history of the workers' and national-liberation movement."

The Institute expects to draw to its work specialists in related fields of knowledge, particularly economic geographers, philosophers, and sociologists. It expects to establish contacts with Latin American scholars, and it will support relations and initiate book exchanges with scientific and cultural organizations of Latin America.

An extremely important task of the Institute is the training of highly qualified cadres of Latin American special-ists. To this end, a postgraduate study program will be established at the Institute. The Academic Council will have the authority to judge candidates' and doctoral dissertations on themes appropriate to the program of the Institute.

We might add that the problem of training Latin American specialists is especially pressing, since their training has been given little attention, and even now—it must be confessed—does not receive proper attention. In this regard, the number of advanced institutions teaching Spanish and Portuguese has, for obscure reasons, decreased in recent years. The faculty of history of Moscow University has cut back the number of students specializing in the modern and contemporary history of foreign countries, including that of the countries of Latin America. The programs of higher educational institutions training specialists in the modern and contemporary history, economics, and culture of foreign countries are in serious need of revision. These programs must give greater attention to Latin America, which would facilitate the specialization of graduates of these schools in their postgraduate training at the Latin American Institute, not to speak of satisfying the needs of those institutions that have relations in practice with Latin American countries.

Therefore, considering the significance of the problem of contemporary Latin America, it is to be hoped that the USSR Ministry of Higher and Secondary Education will extend the proper attention to the training of Latin American specialists proficient in the Spanish and Portuguese languages.

The plans of the Institute include the publication in the next few years of a series of major monographs and collections of articles. Planned for publication in 1962 are works on state capitalism in Latin America (with Mexico as the example) and on the common market in

Latin America, and also collections of essays on the present stage of the national-liberation and workers' movement in Latin America, on the successes of socialist construction in Cuba and on contemporary Brazil.

To satisfy the tremendous interest in Latin America that exists in the Soviet Union, the Institute proposes to publish as much important material as possible on Latin America's political and economic situation in its periodical and reference publications. In particular, a series of reference works on Latin America is planned for publication in conjunction with other institutes of the USSR Academy of Sciences and with the publishing house Sovetskaia Entsiklopediia. Initially, a large two-volume reference encyclopedia on the history, politics, economics, and culture of the Latin American countries is being planned for preparation and publication.

The Institute is now preparing for the general public a pamphlet with a survey of the political situation in Latin America for the year 1961, a popular work that unmasks the imperialistic essence of the new form of U.S. "aid" to Latin America —the so-called Alliance for Progress, and other programs.

Our tasks are clear, and all necessary conditions have been prepared for their solution. The elimination of the cult of personality and the overcoming of its consequences have assured social science workers very favorable conditions for further courageous, principled Marxist-Leninist research into the new phenomena that have occurred in the world. Soviet scholar-specialists on Latin America must assume an active role in the task of elevating the study of the problems of contemporary Latin America to a new, higher plane.

2. Marxist-Leninist Methodology and Problems of Latin American History*

M. S. AL'PEROVICH

The study of Latin America—a vast continent with a population exceeding 200 million and a continent whose peoples are waging a heroic struggle to liberate themselves from the yoke of imperialism and domestic reaction—is now acquiring a scholarly and political significance of exceptional magnitude. Research into the problems of this area is now concentrated primarily in the Institute of History of the Academy of Sciences of the USSR. In past decades certain successes have been registered in the development of this important branch of Soviet historical science.

In prior years, research on problems of the history of Latin American countries did not have any kind of planned or systematic nature. Only a few journal articles were devoted to the past history of these countries, along with chapters of a textbook on the modern history of colonial and dependent nations, written by the late V. M. Miroshevskii and designed for use by departments of history (1940). There were also two monographs by Miroshevskii, one of the pioneers in the study of Latin American history in our country, and L. I. Zubok.[1] The range of research topics undertaken was extremely limited. Works that were published dealt with the history of only a

few Latin American nations, and they were aimed primarily at exposing the imperialist expansion of the United States. For all practical purposes, almost no study was made of the internal civil history of even these countries, while the majority of Latin American states were completely ignored by the researchers.

The insufficient attention paid to questions of Latin American history and the one-sided approach to them resulted to a considerable degree from the dissemination of dogmatic and sectarian postulates throughout our historical literature, under the influence of Stalin's cult of personality. As we know, Stalin arbitrarily declared the Latin American countries to be the "aggressive nucleus of the UN," and included the national bourgeoisie of Latin America in his characterization of the entire bourgeoisie as the principal enemy of the lib-

* "Issledovanie problem istorii Latinskoi Ameriki," *Vestnik Akademii nauk SSSR*, 12:24–26 (1964).

[1] V. M. Miroshevskii, *Osvoboditel'nye dvizheniia v amerikanskikh koloniiakh Ispanii ot ikh zavoevaniia do voiny za nezavisimost'* (1492–1810 gg.) (Moskva–Leningrad, 1946); L. I. Zubok, *Imperialisticheskaia politika SShA v stranakh Karaibskogo basseina, 1900–1934 gg.* (Moskva–Leningrad, 1948).

eration movement, denying totally its capacity to fight for national independence and sovereignty. All this caused our historians to lose their proper bearings, hindered them from dealing objectively and distinctively with the evolutionary problems of different Latin American states, and made it difficult for them to evaluate correctly the character, features, and prospects of the national-liberation movement.

After the Twentieth Congress of the CPSU, these barriers to a penetrating and objective Marxist-Leninist analysis of the history of mankind, including the history of the peoples of Latin America, were finally removed.

Since the middle of the fifties, our Institute has been engaged in the preparation of comprehensive works summarizing the histories of the largest Latin American states. Surveys of the history of Mexico, Argentina, and Brazil have followed one another in publication.[2] These collective works present a systematic exposition of the most important events in the history of these countries for the first time not only in Soviet historiography, but in Marxist historiography in general. Special attention is paid to the history of the liberation movement against the Spanish and Portuguese colonizers, against feudal reaction and foreign — chiefly American — imperialists. Sharing this focus of attention is the struggle waged by progressive elements for freedom, for democracy, and for socioeconomic and political reforms — the problems that as a rule have been either ignored by bourgeois historiography or discussed in a distorted manner.

The aforementioned works by Soviet historians give a scientific Marxist periodization of the histories of the largest Latin American states, based on a painstaking analysis of the peculiarities of development of each of them and taking the general laws governing the overall historical process into account. While most bourgeois historians limit themselves largely to the recounting of political history, the [Soviet] authors of these essays in contrast devoted considerable attention to socioeconomic questions, tracing the emergence and subsequent growth of the system of capitalist relations and the formation of the bourgeoisie and the working class. They described the role of latifundism and the position of the peasantry in the countries indicated, and they shed light on the process of formation of nations, the increasing expansion of foreign capital, and the transformation of Mexico, Argentina, and Brazil into countries economically dependent on imperialism. Naturally, the researchers found their attention drawn particularly toward problems in the history of the class struggle at different stages in the evolution of these countries. Their books contain much factual material on revolts by Indians and Negro slaves, as well as on the workers' and peasants' movement.

The essays expound on the most recent historical events, down to the beginning of the 1960's. The facts presented by Soviet scholars testify to the enormous influence of the October Socialist Revolution upon the countries of Latin America, and they describe the activities of the Communist parties.

U.S. imperialist expansion in Latin America has grown especially intense in recent years, and the contradictions in Latin American society have become more acute. Under such circumstances, an objective analysis of the position and role of the national bourgeoisie, of the social nature of such phenomena as the Vargas regime in Brazil and Peronism in Argentina, and research into the many forms of struggle of progressive forces against imperialism and reaction ac-

[2]*Ocherki novoi i noveishei istorii Meksiki* (Moskva, 1960); *Ocherki istorii Argentiny* (Moskva, 1961); *Ocherki istorii Brazilii* (Moskva, 1962).

quires special significance. In describing the upsurge of the national-liberation movement after World War II, the authors of the essays trace its indissoluble link with the democratic and worker's movement, using numerous examples.

At the present time, the Latin American Sector of the Institute of History of the USSR Academy of Sciences is preparing a joint work of an analogous kind — essays on Chilean history.

Among the diverse problems of the history of the liberation movement of the Latin American countries, the problems of the wars of independence, which occurred in the first quarter of the nineteenth century (1810–1826), attract great attention from researchers. The scientific and political urgency of these problems is redoubled by the necessity for a critical revision of certain incorrect ideas and evaluations that have been disseminated in our historiography in the past.

Although the progressive significance of the liberation struggle of the Latin American peoples against the colonizers has been generally recognized in various Soviet publications, a tendency long prevailed to regard this struggle not as a broad national movement, but exclusively as the cause of a small group of "Creole separatists" who did not enjoy the support of the popular masses. Dogmatically accepting and mechanically reproducing the negative characterization of the outstanding leader of the liberation movement in South America, Simón Bolívar, which was given in his own time by Marx (who, as we know, had only extremely tendentious sources

at his disposal and did not have many important facts available),[3] a number of Soviet authors have been inclined to extend it to other leaders of the war of independence (San Martín, O'Higgins) and even to the movement itself as a whole.

The inadequate examination by Marxist historiography of the major problems of the struggle of the Latin American peoples for independence required the implementation of a series of scholarly investigations in the field. Some of the preliminary results of this research were announced at the May 1960 special enlarged session of the Academic Council of the Institute of History, devoted to the 150th anniversary of the beginning of the war of liberation of the Spanish colonies in America.[4] A collection of articles was compiled on the basis of these reports and other materials that sheds light upon both the general problems of the war of liberation and its course in individual regions of the continent (La Plata, Chile), on the revolutionary movement of the first quarter of the nineteenth century in Cuba, and on the history of the struggle for Brazilian independence, and that describes the policy of the United States and the European powers with respect to the liberation movement in Latin America. It also contains a critical survey of the works of bourgeois historians.[5]

---

[3]See n. 231 of Karl Marx's "Bolívar y Ponte," in Karl Marx and F. Engels' *Sochineniia*, 2nd ed., vol. 14, pp. 753–754.

[4]See *Vestnik Akademii nauk SSSR*, 7: 113–114 (1960); *Voprosy istorii*, 8:172–174 (1960).

[5]*Voina za nezavisimost' v Latinskoi Amerike (1810–1826)* (Moskva, 1964).

3. The Study of Latin America in the U.S.S.R.[*]

VICTOR V. VOL'SKII

Economic and political relations of the Soviet Union with the countries of Latin America are on the increase. Annually expanding cultural and scientific relations serve to stimulate the growing interest of the Soviet people in Latin America's rich historical background, its distinctive culture, and the present-day problems of that part of the world. Russian interest in Latin America extends over a long period of time. I should like to emphasize, therefore, that this interest in Latin America and the life of its people is not a passing fancy and did not develop overnight. This interest has its own history. Permit me to recount a few facts.

The first word of the New World in Russia dates back to 1530, and is recorded in the manuscript of the learned monk, Maxim Grek, who came to Moscow at the invitation of the Russian Tsar Basil III. In one of his commentaries, Maxim Grek makes special mention of Cuba, and this is the first geographic reference to the New World known in the Russian language. In the latter part of the eighteenth century, during the years 1782–1784, Feodor Karzhavin, the Russian writer and translator, visited Cuba. All available evidence indicates that he was the first Russian to have spent some time in Latin America. One of the first Latin Americans to visit Russia, during 1786–1787, was the distinguished leader of the liberation movement of the peoples of Latin America, Francisco Miranda, who sought support of European governments.

The study of Latin America by Russian researchers begins in the first quarter of the nineteenth century. From 1821 to 1828, an expedition to Brazil was undertaken by the Russian scholar, academician G. I. Langsdorf. The expedition produced a major study of the indigenous population of the Amazon River basin.

The struggle for liberation by the peoples of the colonies of Spain and Portugal gained great sympathy in the progressive circles of Russia. Trade relations evolved between Russia and Latin America in the 1830's and 1840's, and cultural relations were established in the last half of the century. At that time,

[*]*Latin American Research Review*, 3/1:77–87 (Fall 1967). This paper was prepared to be presented at the Conference on Latin American History, 1967, in the name of the USSR Academy of Sciences Latin American Institute by its director, Victor Vatslavovich Vol'skii, Ph.D. Translated by Professor J. Gregory Oswald, Department of History, University of Arizona, with the assistance of Ann Montano and Shelby L. Sheehy. Footnotes refer to original Russian titles of works cited.

diplomatic relations between Brazil, Argentina, Mexico, Uruguay and Russia were also established.

The growth of scientific interest in the study of problems of that part of the world and research on the life, customs, and culture of its peoples expanded apace with the broadening ties between Latin America and Russia. In the second half of the nineteenth century and in the beginning of the twentieth century, many Russian scholars visited Latin America to study its natural phenomena, climate, fauna, and flora. Among them was the founder of Russian climatology, Alexander Voeikov, the geographer and ethnographer, Veniukov, and the botanist, Al'bov. A clear indication of the interest of Russian researchers in the countries of Latin America was the complex expedition of 1915, composed of five young Russian scholars joined to study different scientific aspects of this region of the world. Their purpose was to study the natural life of South America, the material and spiritual culture of the Indians, and to compile ethnographic and zoological collections.

Direct ties and contacts between scientific institutions of Russia and the countries of Latin America were established before World War I. In 1910, for example, the Physiological Institute of Moscow University sent its scientific works to Caracas, Montevideo, Havana, the Museum of Natural History in Valparaiso, and others. The Naturalist Society of St. Petersburg exchanged publications with the National Museum of São Paulo and with the scientific societies of Montevideo and Santiago. The National Library of Rio de Janeiro exchanged books with the public libraries of St. Petersburg, Odessa, and the library of Moscow University.

The bases for research on Latin America and ties between institutions and individual scholars were thereby established in Russia. Established in our country, at the same time, were the

foundations for the systematic study of this part of the world and for the development of Latin American studies as an independent branch of science.

Soviet science continued the tradition of Latin American studies after the October Revolution of 1917.

The First Steps

Soviet Latin American studies may be said to have begun in the autumn of 1918, when the Society for the Study of South America was initiated by a large group of distinguished Russian scholars. From the outset, the Society planned to organize a complex scientific expedition to South America. Their plans were not realized, however, due to the hostile attitude of the imperialist powers and the start of the intervention against Soviet Russia.

One may justly state that Soviet scientific research on problems of Latin America dates from the mid-1920's. Included among the works of that time which retain a distinct scientific value to our day are V. Sviatlovskii, *The Communist State of Jesuits in Paraguay in the 17th and 18th Century* (Petrograd, 1924);[1] A. Vol'skii, *The History of Mexican Revolutions* (Moscow, 1928);[2] I. A. Vitver, *South America* (1930)[3] and *Countries of the Caribbean* (1931)[4] in the series *Universal Economic Geography;*[5] and M. Kogan, *Economic Crisis in Latin America* (Moscow, 1930).[6]

In the early 1930's, a department for the study of the Caribbean and South America was established in the Colonial Section of the Institute of World Economy and World Politics in Moscow. In the pre-war period it became the center of Latin-American studies in the USSR.

[1]*Kommunisticheskoe gosudarstvo v Paragvae v XVIII stoletii.*
[2]*Istoriia meksikanskikh revoliutsii.*
[3]*Iuzhnaia Amerika.*
[4]*Karaibskie strany.*
[5]*Vsemirnaia ekonomicheskaia geografiia.*
[6]*Ekonomicheskii krizis v Latinskoi Amerike.*

Related to the activities of this department were the more serious studies of the problems of Latin America, and the broadening themes of research. Appearing at this time were the works of G. Iakobson, *Aspects of the Indian and Negro Problem* [n.p.] (1933);[7] A. Sokolov, *Pizarro* (Moscow, 1935);[8] and the symposium, *Problems of the Caribbean and South America* (Moscow, 1934).[9]

A number of works of the pre-war period emanated from the pen of the talented Soviet Latin Americanist V. M. Miroshevskii, who died in the Great Patriotic War. It was Miroshevskii who prepared the first scientific, systematic Marxist interpretation of the basic problems of Latin American history. These are published as chapters of *The Modern History of Colonial and Dependent Countries*, I (Moscow, 1940).[10]

The foundation for Soviet Latin American studies, as a separate science, was doubtless established before the war. At that time a cadre of scholars began an overall Marxist evaluation of the problems of Latin America.

WHY WE STUDY LATIN AMERICA

The continuation of this study was somewhat interrupted during the course of the war with Hitler's Germany. Thereafter, greater opportunities for the development of Soviet Latin American studies presented themselves. The extension of economic and cultural ties and the establishment of diplomatic relations between the USSR and most of the countries of Latin America in the years 1942–1946 contributed greatly to the continuation of these studies.

Interest in the life of the peoples of Latin America has grown in our country. It became apparent there was a need to be informed and to encompass the increasing flow of information received by the Soviet people from this part of the world which was no longer distant in our times; and to begin a systematic, more serious study of the processes taking place in the countries of Latin America.

To achieve this Soviet researchers followed two main paths. By the first, there is popularization and dissemination of knowledge about Latin America to the broad masses about the life and customs of its peoples, their achievements, and so forth. With this goal in mind, a large number of books and pamphlets are printed in editions of tens of thousands of copies. To illustrate this, one might point to the series, "Latin America Today,"[11] which includes *Mexico* by R. Tuchnin, [12] *Panama for Panamanians* by S. Gonionskii,[13] *Uruguay Today* by K. Khachaturov, [14] and *The Struggles and Daily Life of Brazil* by A. Aglin.[15] More than a few of these brochures popularizing Latin America are issued by the publishing house, "Znanie." They include *Bolivia: Revolution and Counter-revolution* by Iu. Fadeev,[16] *The Soviet Union and the Countries of Latin America* by A. Sizonenko, [17] and others.

The Latin American theme is also broadly represented in the Soviet popular scientific series, *Maps of the World*,[18] and *Governmental Structures of Countries of the World*.[19]

Another aspect of Soviet scholarly activities is the scientific research in depth of the fundamental problems of Latin America. Our Communist Party and our scholars are seriously concerned

[7]*K postanovke indeiskoi i negritianskoi problemy.*
[8]*Pisarro.*
[9]*Problemy Iuzhnoi i Karaibskoi Ameriki.*
[10]*Novaia istoriia kolonial'nykh i zavisimykh stran.*
[11]*Latinskaia Amerika segodnia.*
[12]*Meksika.*
[13]*Panama dlia panamtsev.*
[14]*Urugvay segodnia.*
[15]*Bytvy i budni Brazilii.*
[16]*Boliviia: revoliutsiia i kontrrevoliutsiia.*
[17]*Sovetskii Soiuz i strany Latinskoi Ameriki.*
[18]*U karty mira.*
[19]*Gosudarstvennyi stroi stran mira.*

with comprehending and revealing the processes of the development of history, economics, and culture from the viewpoint of the Marxist methodology.

BASIC THEMES AND ORIENTATION

At the present time, the following is the main orientation of research pursued by Soviet scholars in their study of Latin America.

a) Research in the colonial period, the liberation struggle of the peoples of Latin America against Spanish and Portuguese rule. Also, problems in the modern and contemporary history of that continent;

b) The emergence and development of workers' and national liberation movements in Latin America;

c) Natural and human resources, the economic development of countries of Latin America;

d) The foreign policy and international relations of Latin American countries;

e) The culture, science, ideology, and ethnography of Latin America;

f) Literary criticism and literary translations.

In the elaboration of each of these themes Soviet scholars, having completed a number of major works, have achieved clear-cut results which I would like to briefly characterize.

Of the works related to the first research theme, one must include those of V. M. Miroshevskii, *The Liberation Movement in the American Colonies of Spain from the Conquest to the Wars of Independence* (Moscow-Leningrad, 1946);[20] I. P. Magidovich, *History of the Discovery and Exploration of Central and South America* (Moscow, 1965);[21] M. S. Al'perovich, "The Character and Forms of Exploitation of Indians in the American Colonies of Spain during the 16th-18th Centuries" (*Novaia i noveishaia istoriia*, 1957, No. 2);[22] and a symposium on *Bartolomé de las Casas* (Moscow, 1966).[23]

The Wars of Independence of the colonies of Spain and Portugal in the first quarter of the nineteenth century

represent a most important event in the history of the western hemisphere. This subject has always attracted the fixed attention of Soviet researchers. The symposium *The War of Independence in Latin America, 1810–1826* (Moscow, 1964)[24] was published in the U.S.S.R. in commemoration of the 150th anniversary of the Wars of Independence. Likewise published in 1964 were the works of M. S. Al'perovich, *The War of Independence in Mexico, 1810–1824,*[25] and L. Iu. Slezkin, *Russia and the War of Independence in Spanish America.*[26] Along with these major studies, Soviet Latin Americanists published a number of articles broadly illuminating the national liberation struggle of the people of Brazil, Chile, Argentina, and other countries. In Soviet historical science, more and more credence is attached to the view that the liberation wars of the colonies are part of an unfinished bourgeois revolution of national character, occurring with the active participation of broad sectors of colonial society. A number of works by Soviet historians are dedicated to an evaluation of the lives, deeds, and historical roles of prominent leaders of the wars of independence, such as Simón Bolívar, Francisco Miranda, José Artigas, Miguel Hidalgo, and José Morelos.

One of the questions most extensively studied by Soviet historians is the bourgeois democratic Mexican Revolution of 1910–1917. Writing on this subject have

[20]*Osvoboditel'noe dvizhenie v amerikanskikh koloniiakh Ispanii ot ikh zavoevaniia do voiny za nezavisimost'.*

[21]*Istoriia otkrytiia i issledovaniia Tsentral'noi i Iuzhnoi Ameriki.*

[22]"*O kharaktere i formakh eksploatatsii indeitsev v amerikanskikh koloniiakh Ispanii XVI–XVIII vv.*"

[23]*Bartolome de Las Kasas.*

[24]*Voina za nezavisimost' v Latinskoi Amerike, 1810–1826.*

[25]*Voina za nezavisimost' Meksiki, 1810–1824.*

[26]*Rossiia i voina za nezavisimost v Ispanskoi Amerike.*

been N. M. Lavrov, M. S. Al'perovich, B. T. Rudenko, and E. V. Ananova. Some of their works, such as the volume by Al'perovich and Rudenko, *The Mexican Revolution of 1910–1917 and the Policy of the United States* (Moscow, 1958),[27] have been translated in Mexico into Spanish, and granted great recognition by the Mexican people.

The period of World War II is characterized by the significant rise of the worker, peasant, and national liberation movements in Latin America. These matters received the attention of Soviet science in both collective works and monographs. Included among the former are *The Present Stage of the National Liberation and Workers' Move-America* (Moscow, 1961),[28] *The Liberation Movement in Latin America* (Moscow, 1964),[29] and *The Struggle for a United Workers and Anti-Imperialistic Front in the Countries of Latin America* (Moscow, 1963).[30] Monographs worthy of note include V. I. Ermolaev, *The National Liberation and Workers' Movement in the Countries of Latin America After the Second World War* (Moscow, 1958),[31] and M. V. Danilevich, *The Working Class in the Liberation Movement of the Peoples of Latin America* (Moscow, 1962).[32]

Studies of the natural resources and of the economic geography of Latin America are found in E. N. Lukasheva, *South America* (Moscow, 1958),[33] Ia. G. Mashbits, *Mexico* (Moscow, 1961),[34] A. A. Dolinin, *Chile* (Moscow, 1952),[35] and his *Peru* (Moscow, 1965),[36] and others.

Economic development matters are dealt with in such works as the symposium, *Economic Problems of Latin America* (Moscow, 1963),[37] O. G. Klesmet, *Industrialization Problems of Latin America* (Moscow, 1966),[38] and A. M. Sivolobov, *Agrarian Relations in Contemporary Brazil* (Moscow, 1958).[39] These and other works on the economy of Latin America examine a wide range

of problems such as those related to problems of industrialization, sources of financing, problems of planning, the role of the state sector, foreign capital, economic integration, the development of agriculture, agrarian relations and the conduct of agrarian reforms.

Soviet Latin Americanists pay considerable attention to foreign policy and international relations, as in N. V. Korolev, *The Countries of Latin America in International Relations, 1898–1962* (Moscow, 1962).[40] Various aspects of U.S. policy in Latin America from the time of the Spanish-American War to the present are examined in such works as L. S. Vladimirov, *U.S. Diplomacy During the Spanish-American War of 1898* (Moscow, 1957),[41] L. Iu. Slezkin, *U.S. Policy in South America, 1929–1933* (Moscow, 1956),[42] and S. A. Gonionskii, *Latin America and the U.S.A. Essays in the History of Diplomatic Relations, 1939–1959* (Moscow, 1960).[43]

Another group of studies is concerned with problems related to the origins and character of the Monroe Doctrine, as

---

[27]*Meksikanskaia revoliutsiia 1910–1917 gg. i politika SShA.*
[28]*Natsional'no-osvoboditel'noe dvizhenie v Latinskoi Amerike na sovremennom etape.*
[29]*Osvoboditel'noe dvizhenie v Latinskoi Amerike.*
[30]*Bor'ba za edinyi rabochii i antiimperialisticheskii front v stranakh Latinskoi Ameriki.*
[31]*Natsional'no-osvoboditel'noe i rabochee dvizhenie v stranakh Latinskoi Ameriki posle II mirovoi voiny.*
[32]*Rabochii klass v osvoboditel'nom dvizhenii narodov Latinskoi Ameriki.*
[33]*Iuzhnaia Amerika.*
[34]*Meksika.*
[35]*Chili.*
[36]*Peru.*
[37]*Ekonomicheskie problemy Latinskoi Ameriki.*
[38]*Problemy industrializatsii Latinskoi Ameriki.*
[39]*Agrarnye otnosheniia v sovremennoi Brazilii.*
[40]*Strany Latinskoi Ameriki v mezdunarodnykh otnosheniiakh, 1898–1962.*
[41]*Diplomatiia SShA v period amerikano-ispanskoi voiny 1898 g.*
[42]*Politika SShA v Iuzhnoi Amerike, 1929–1933.*
[43]*Latinskaia Amerika i SSha; ocherki istorii diplomaticheskikh otnoshenii, 1939–1959.*

well as other foreign policy doctrines of the U.S.A., and the meaning of present-day Panamericanism, and of modern aspects of U.S. policy related to the announced program of the Alliance for Progress in Latin America. Books in this category include: N. N. Bolkhovitinov, *The Origins and Character of the Monroe Doctrine* (Moscow, 1959),[44] M. V. Antiasov, *Contemporary Panamericanism* (Moscow, 1960),[45] B. I. Gvozdarev, *The Organization of American States* (Moscow, 1960),[46] and *The Meaning of "The Alliance for Progress"* (Moscow, 1964),[47] by the same author.

Increasing attention is given in the works of Soviet scholars to the history of relations between the nations of Latin America and our country. This is evident in the works of L. A. Shur, *Russia and Latin America* (Moscow, 1964),[48] K. S. Tarasov, *The Soviet Union and the Countries of Latin America,* (Moscow, 1958),[49] and A. I. Sozonenko, *The Soviet Union and Latin America.*[50]

Study of the ancient and contemporary culture, art, and literature of the peoples of Latin America is another concern of Soviet Latin American studies. The greatest achievement in this realm is that of Iu. V. Knorozov, in deciphering the written language of the ancient Mayas. The results of his research efforts, which have received international recognition, may be found in his major work, *The Writings of the Ancient Maya Indians* (Moscow-Leningrad, 1963).[51] The importance to world culture of the indigenous population of America is studied in the collective work, *The Culture of the Indians* (Moscow, 1963),[52] and in the monograph of R. V. Kinzhalov, *The Art of Ancient America* (Moscow, 1962).[53] The rich and unique art of Mexico is discussed in I. A. Karetnikov, *The Art of Contemporary Mexico* (Moscow, 1960),[54] and L. A. Zhadova, *The Monumental Painting of Mexico* (Moscow, 1965).[55]

Among the most important works of literary criticism are the monographs of V. N. Kuteishchikova, *The Twentieth Century Novel of Latin America* (Moscow, 1964),[56] and I. A. Terterian, *The Brazilian Novel of the Twentieth Century* (Moscow, 1965).[57] Aside from these, there are studies of the creative efforts of the greatest writers of Latin America, such as Pablo Neruda, Jorge Amado, and Nicolás Guillén, studies of the role of J. C. Mariátegui regarding the development of Peruvian national culture, works on the social motifs of Cuban poetry, and studies on the influences of Leo Tolstoi's writing upon the social literary life of Latin America.

The best writings of many of Latin America's poets, scientists, novelists, and cultural exponents are translated and published in massive editions in the Soviet Union.

Studies by Soviet Latin Americanists of the major social-economic and political processes of Latin America have led us to the conclusion that the development of Latin American countries occurs within the same general framework as that which applies to the historical development of all mankind, and that the laws of social economic development discovered by Marxist Leninist science operate in Latin America with the same force as they operate in other parts of the world.

[44]*Doktrina Monro; proiskhozhdenie i kharakter.*
[45]*Sovremennyi panamerikanizm.*
[46]*Organizatsiia amerikanskikh gosudarstv.*
[47]*"Soiuz radi progressa" i ego sushchnost'.*
[48]*Rossiia i Latinskaia Amerika.*
[49]*Sovetskii Soiuz i strany Latinskoi Ameriki.*
[50]*Sovetskii Soiuz i Latinskaia Amerika.*
[51]*Pis'mennost' indeitsev maiia.*
[52]*Kul'tura indeitsev.*
[53]*Iskusstvo drevnei Ameriki.*
[54]*Iskusstvo sovremennoi Meksiki.*
[55]*Monumental'naia zhivopis' Meksiki.*
[56]*Roman Latinskoi Ameriki v XX veke.*
[57]*Brazil'skii roman XX veka.*

MAJOR CENTERS FOR THE STUDY OF LATIN AMERICA

The study of Latin America in the U.S.S.R. is conducted at the present time in the Academy of Sciences, in universities, and in other advanced educational institutions of our country.

Within the U.S.S.R. Academy of Sciences, these studies are conducted in Moscow at the Institute of History, Institute of Ethnography, Institute of World Economics and International Relations, the Institute of World Literature, the Institute of Philosophy, and finally the Latin American Institute, which same I have the honor to represent here.

The Institute of History has within it a department of Latin American history, with a group of scholars who do research in that field. Among them are M. S. Al'perovich, L. Iu. Slezkin, and N. M. Lavrov. This department has completed and published a number of collective works on the history of the major Latin American states: *Essays in the Modern and Contemporary History of Mexico* (Moscow, 1960),[58] *Essays in the History of Argentina* (Moscow, 1961),[59] and *Essays in the History of Brazil* (Moscow, 1962);[60] soon to be completed is a similar work on Chile. The department has plans to prepare such books on most of the countries of Latin America. These works are the first in Marxist historiography to present a scientific periodization and a systematic presentation of the most important historical events based on a careful analysis of the peculiar development of the separate states and consideration of the general laws of the universal historical process.

The American department of the Institute of Ethnography has a group of scholars studying the ethnic structure, customs and culture of the contemporary population of Latin America, the development of Indian civilization prior to the European conquest, the characteristics of Spanish and Portuguese colonization, and the process of the formation of Latin American nations. Among these scientific researchers are: Corresponding Member of the USSR Academy of Science, A. V. Efimov, S. A. Gonionskii, I. R. Grigulevich, and E. L. Nitoburg, who have written the major works, *Peoples of America* (Moscow, 1959),[61] *Indians of America* (Moscow, 1955),[62] *Nations of Latin America* (Moscow, 1964),[63] and *Cuba: Historical-Ethnographic Essays* (Moscow, 1961).[64]

Another group of Latin American ethnographers, including Iu. V. Knorozov and R. V. Kinzhalov, work in the Leningrad division of the Institute of Ethnography.

In the Institute of World Economics and International Relations is a group of Latin America researchers among whom the best known are M. V. Danilevich, O. G. Klesmet, and K. S. Tarasov. M. V. Danilevich, the author of two monographs on the working class of Latin America, is also editor of *Problems of Contemporary Latin America* (Moscow, 1959).[65]

V. N. Kuteishchikova, I. A. Terterian, and others pursue problems of Latin American literature in the Gorky Institute of World Literature.

THE LATIN AMERICAN INSTITUTE

Permit me now to refer to the activities of the Latin American Institute. The Institute was founded by decree of the Presidium of the U.S.S.R. Academy of Sciences in 1961. Before discussing the activities of the Institute, I would like to digress historically to observe that the

[58]*Ocherki novoi i noveishei istorii Meksiki.*
[59]*Ocherki istorii Argentiny.*
[60]*Ocherki istorii Brazilii.*
[61]*Narody Ameriki.*
[62]*Indeitsy Ameriki.*
[63]*Natsii Latinskoi Ameriki.*
[64]*Kuba; istoriko-etnograficheskie ocherki.*
[65]*Problemy sovremennoi Latinskoi Ameriki.*

study of foreign lands and study of the life and culture of distant peoples has been traditional in Russia. May it suffice to merely refer to such internationally known Russian scholars as the ethnographer M. Miklukho-Maklai, who devoted his entire life to the study of Polynesian aborigines, the geographer and explorer of Asia, N. M. Przheval'skii, and others, in order to point out the broad interests which have long been pursued by leading representatives of Russian science and culture. The research of separate scholars indicated that in time there might be a better concentration of effort, and this led to the creation in our country of regional institutes as centers for the complex study of various parts of the world. The first of these centers was established in the mid-nineteenth century, as the Lazarevskii Institute of Oriental Languages, later renamed the Institute of Oriental Studies, and in more recent times incorporated into the U.S.S.R. Academy of Sciences Institute of the Peoples of Asia. There existed in the U.S.S.R., before the war, the Pacific Ocean Institute. The U.S.S.R. Academy of Sciences African Institute was established in Moscow in 1958, and finally, as I have stated, the Latin America Institute, established in 1961.

The establishment of the latter was the logical consequence of the development of Soviet Latin American studies, increasing interest of the Soviet peoples in the life of the peoples of Latin America, and expanding ties between the U.S.S.R. and that region of the world. Our Institute was destined to become the scientific research and coordinating center for the complex study of the problems of contemporary Latin America. Permit me to present a more detailed account of the activities and the organization of the Institute. It comprises seven departments: Economics, Foreign Policy and International Relations,

Workers' and National Liberation Movements, Agrarian Problems, Cuba, History, Culture, and Geography.

A large number of leading Soviet Latin Americanists are concentrated in the Institute. Among them are the economists I. K. Sheremet'ev and Z. I. Romanova, the international historians A. N. Glinkin and B. I. Gvozdarev, specialists of the history of the labor movement, V. I. Ermolaev, A. F. Shul'govskii, B. I. Koval', and S. I. Semenov, and specialist of the agrarian problems Iu. G. Onufriev. At present there are about 100 scientific workers in the Institute. In the course of the past five years, the Institute published a series of collective work, monographs of individual authors, brochures, articles in various Russian and foreign scholarly journals, reviews, notes, and so forth. Among them might be noted such collective works as *The Liberation Movement in Latin America* (Moscow, 1964),[66] *José Carlos Mariátegui: In Honor of the Seventieth Anniversary of His Birth* (Moscow, 1966),[67] *Political Parties of the Countries of Latin America* (Moscow, 1965),[68] the handbook *Economics of Latin America in Figures* (Moscow, 1965),[69] as well as the monographs of B. I. Gvozdarev, *Evolution and Crisis of the Inter-American System* (Moscow, 1966),[70] A. N. Glinkin, *A Contemporary History of Brazil, 1939–1959* (Moscow, 1961),[71] Iu. M. Grigorian, *The Economic Expansion of the Federal Republic of Germany in Latin America* (Moscow, 1965),[72] B. M. Merin, *Free Cuba* (Mos-

---

[66]*Osvoboditel'noe dvizhenie v Latinskoi Amerike.*
[67]*Khose Karlos Mariategi; k 70-letiiu so dnia rozhdeniia.*
[68]*Politicheskie partii stran Latinskoi Ameriki.*
[69]*Ekonomika Latinskoi Ameriki v tsifrakh.*
[70]*Evoliutsiia i krizis mezhamerikanskoi sistemy.*
[71]*Noveishaia istoriia Brazili, 1939–1959.*
[72]*Ekonomicheskaia ekspansiia FRG v Latinskoi Amerike.*

cow, 1964),[73] M. S. Nikitin, *Chile* (Moscow, 1965),[74] Z. I. Romanova, *Problems of Economic Integration in Latin America* (Moscow, 1965),[75] G. K. Seleznev (in English), *International Trade: The Path to Peace and Progress* (Moscow, 1966), and I. K. Sheremet'ev, *State Capitalism in Mexico* (Moscow, 1963).[76]

Fulfilling its role as coordinating center, the Institute, jointly with other scientific institutions, participated in the preparation and publication of the symposia, *Brazilia* (Moscow, 1963),[77] *Five Years of Cuban Revolution* (Moscow, 1963),[78] and *Chile* (Moscow, 1965).[79] Foreign scholars were enlisted to participate in the writing of these works. In preparation at the present time are similar publications on Venezuela and Mexico.

The Latin American Institute likewise organizes scientific conferences in cooperation with specialists of other research institutions of the U.S.S.R. Academy of Sciences. Conferences which have been held in the Institute include, "The New Stage of the National Liberation and Workers' Movement in Latin America" (1962), "Latin America in Contemporary International Relations" (1965), and "The Agrarian Question and Problems of the National Liberation Movement in Latin America."

Our Institute maintains ties with various scientific centers, institutions, and universities of Latin America, the United States, and Europe. Ties are manifested by exchanges of scientific literature, joint preparation of publications, and mutual exchanges of scholars. In 1966 the Latin American Institute maintained contacts with scientific centers of more than twenty-five countries. We propose to strengthen and expand these ties. My present visit to the United States is evidence of our intentions.

Plans of the Institute for the near future include the publication of a three-volume encyclopedic handbook on Latin America, major collective works on

the themes of "The Path of Friendship and Commercial Collaboration" (the U.S.S.R. and Latin America, 1917–1967),[80] "The Countries of Latin America in Contemporary International Relations,"[81] "Problems of Ideology and Culture in the Countries of Latin America,"[82] "The Proletariat of Latin America,"[83] "The Peasantry of Latin America,"[84] "Tendencies in the Economic Development of Latin American Countries,"[85] and "Problems of Industrial Development in Latin American Countries."[86] Likewise, in preparation for publication are the monographs of A. F. Shul'govskii, *Mexico at A Sharp Turning Point in Its History,*[87] B. I. Koval', *The Working Class of Brazil,*[88] A. S. Koval'skaia, *The Colonies in Latin America in the Struggle for Independence,*[89] B. N. Brodovich, *The National Income of Latin American Countries,*[90] and others.

THE PREPARATION OF SPECIALISTS

As I have already noted, the study of problems of Latin America is also being conducted in the universities and other scholarly institutions of the U.S.S.R., located in the cities of Moscow, Leningrad,

[73]*Svobodnaia Kuba.*
[74]*Chili.*
[75]*Problemy ekonomicheskoi integratsii v Latinskoi Amerike.*
[76]*Gosudarstvennyi kapitalizm v Meksike.*
[77]*Braziliia.*
[78]*Piat' let kubinskoi revoliutsii.*
[79]*Chili.*
[80]*Na putiakh k druzhbe i delovomu sotrudnichestvu (SSSR-Latinskaia Amerika 1917–1967 gg.).*
[81]*Strany Latinskoi Ameriki v sovremennykh mezhdunarodnykh otnosheniiakh.*
[82]*Problemy ideologii i kul'tury v stranakh Latinskoi Ameriki.*
[83]*Proletariat Latinskoi Ameriki.*
[84]*Krest'ianstvo Latinskoi Ameriki.*
[85]*Tendentsii ekonomicheskogo razvitiia latinoamerikanskikh stran.*
[86]*Problemy promyshlennogo razvitiia latinoamerikanskikh stran.*
[87]*Meksika na krutom povorote svoei istorii.*
[88]*Rabochii klass Brazilii.*
[89]*Kolonii Latinskoi Ameriki v bor'be za nezavisimost'.*
[90]*Natsional'nyi dokhod stran Latinskoi Ameriki.*

Kiev, Voronezh, Alma-Ata, Frunze, Dushanbe, Chernovtsy, and Kalinin. The scholarly publications of these institutions regularly include a large number of articles, notes, and other works on the Latin American theme.

Yet, the main purpose of these institutions is not to do research but to prepare cadres of specialists. For example, in the universities of Moscow and Leningrad, Latin Americanists are being prepared in history, geography, economics, and philology. And incorporated into the course work of many disciplines are aspects pertaining to the study of Latin America.

In addition, small numbers of students specialize in advanced courses studying Latin America in greater depth, that is, studying physical and economic geography, economics, history, international relations and foreign policy, literature, and art. Students in the above groups study Spanish and Portuguese. They prepare two modest scientific papers in the course of two years, and in the final course of university study they prepare a more thorough graduation thesis which they defend before an authoritative committee of specialists.

Specialists of more advanced qualifications, namely, Candidates of Sciences, pursue post-graduate preparation in the appropriate faculties of the universities, the Latin American Institute, or in other institutes of the U.S.S.R. Academy of Sciences.

II

THE NATIONAL-LIBERATION MOVEMENT

The lead article in this section (Item 4) appeared in the theoretical journal of the Communist Party of the Soviet Union, *Kommunist*. It consists basically of a call for the unity of all "democratic" and anti-imperialist forces in a broadly based national front. The forms that the struggle for "national liberation" may take are declared to depend on the concrete conditions in a given country. Implicit herein is a denial of the applicability of the Cuban experience on a continent-wide scale, and explicit is an attack on the "divisive" intrigues of the Chinese Communist Party.

S. S. Mikhailov's second selection (Item 5) is notable for his defense of the participation of the national bourgeoisie in the liberation movement. Mikhailov declares that the inconsistency and vacillation shown by the national bourgeoisie indicate the weakness of the working class rather than the inherent incapability of the national bourgeoisie to take part in a united front. On the other hand, the third selection (Item 6) —

from a collectively written book — appears to be less optimistic on the prospects of participation by the national bourgeoisie.

In Item 7, A. A. Guber assigns to the various classes their roles in the liberation struggle, starting from the premise that "in Latin America, as everywhere else, the working class and its parties are the most consistent fighters for nationwide goals." Guber quite frankly acknowledges that correct united-front tactics call for "exhaustive use of anti-imperialist potentials . . . including those forces that did not desire to, and by their class nature could not, proceed further with the people toward socialism under the leadership of the working class."

The two concluding sections in this chapter (Items 8 and 9) discuss the possibilities for communist cooperation with Socialists and the position of students in the Latin American liberation struggle.

4. The Liberation Movement in Latin America*

M. KUDACHKIN AND N. MOSTOVETS

I

Events in recent years have proved that the Latin American countries, which the imperialists regarded as their reliable rear guard, are being turned into a scene of anti-imperialist struggle and a reserve for the forces of peace and democracy. An anti-imperialist democratic revolution is now in progress over a vast territory stretching from the Rio Grande on the north to Tierra del Fuego in the south, from the Atlantic to the Pacific, an area embracing over twenty countries and 200 million people. The struggle waged by the Latin American people for their liberation is not an isolated phenomenon. It merges in a single stream with the struggle of all progressive forces against imperialism, with the international revolutionary workers' movement represented today by the world socialist system and the Communist parties in capitalist countries.

In 1959, the national-liberation movement in Latin America was marked by a great event that inaugurated a new era in the history of the peoples of the Western Hemisphere — a people's democratic anti-imperialist and antifeudal revolution took place on the island of Cuba, ninety miles away from the United States. Subsequently, it developed into a socialist revolution. The Cuban Revo-

lution became a tremendous stimulus in the struggle waged by the Latin American people for their national liberation.

The Latin American revolutionaries well understand that it is precisely the successes of the world socialist camp and the struggle of the workers' class in capitalist countries that created improved conditions for the development of the liberation movement in their countries.

The national-liberation movement of the peoples of Latin America is a structural part of the world revolutionary process; it has a great deal in common with the anti-imperialist movements of Asia and Africa and it also has its own peculiarities. The latter stem from the fact that most Latin American states achieved their independence at the beginning of the nineteenth century as a result of the wars of liberation waged against Spanish and Portuguese colonialism. This fact influenced the socio-economic development of the Latin American countries. Many of them have a comparatively well-developed capitalist economy. The workers' class has a rather high level of organization and

* "Osvoboditel'noe dvizhenie v Latinskoi Amerike," *Kommunist* (Moscow), 11:121–130 (July 1964).

class consciousness. The proletariat has become the main leading force in the national-democratic revolution. Communist parties exist in all Latin American countries. Some of them appeared immediately after the October Socialist Revolution.

The second war of independence, as the Latin Americans call the current stage of their liberation war, is unlike the liberation movement of the peoples of Latin America during the nineteenth century and at the beginning of the twentieth (Mexico, for example). Then, it was a question of a revolution aimed at clearing the path for capitalism and it was headed by the developing bourgeoisie, interested in attaining that goal. Now, due to new domestic and foreign circumstances, the Latin American revolution has reached a higher stage. It is a national-liberation, people's anti-imperialist and antifeudal revolution. Its main force is not the bourgeoisie but the working class.

The degree attained in the socioeconomic development of Latin American countries is not identical, which calls for different methods and means in the struggle based on different correlations of class forces. Still, common historical fate and the existence of a common enemy—American imperialism and geographical proximity—have helped to develop similar traits in the liberation movements of the various countries and presented them with coinciding tasks. In their programs, the Communist parties of the Latin American countries state that the basic tasks in the current stage of the revolution are:

1. Economically, the elimination of the domination of foreign, mostly American, monopolies, restoration of the national riches to the people, radical agrarian reform, and many other measures aimed at reaching total economic independence and a rise in the living standards of the masses.

2. Politically, the elimination of the dominance of imperialist monopolies and their allied financial-agrarian oligarchies, the establishment of truly national governments capable of carrying out radical revolutionary democratic changes in the interest of the majority of the populations of these countries.

II

As we know, the conquest of political independence by the Latin American countries 150 years ago did not lead to real independence. Foreign capitalism occupied the key economic positions in these countries, as they became suppliers of raw materials and cheap manpower, sources for the tremendous profits of the foreign monopolies. In the postwar years, under the banner of the so-called financial and economic aid to the Latin American countries, the United States tried, and is trying, to retain its old, and acquire new, positions and to broaden its social support by strengthening its alliance with the local bourgeoisie inclined toward conciliation.

The domination of the imperialist monopolies has a severe effect upon the economy of the Latin American countries. Thus, in the past decade, the growth in the per capita national income was an average of 1 percent per year. This average figure, eloquent all by itself, conceals the horrible picture of the economic situation of the working people. The Mexican writer Carlos Fuentes wrote: "There are 200 million people living in Latin America. Of these, 140 million work, in fact, as slaves. Seventy million do not know what money is. One hundred million are illiterate and 100 million are ill. One hundred and forty million are permanently undernourished."

Such is the situation of the Latin American people as a result of the plunder of the imperialist monopolies. The overall sum of direct capital investments by American monopolies exceeds 10 billion dollars. Monopolist profits from direct private capital investments alone totaled about 1 billion dollars in 1962. U.S. private capital investments in Latin America are concentrated mainly in industrial branches that bring the highest profits — oil, ores, electric power, light industry, and the processing industries. Thus, the profits of U.S. monopolies from capital investments in oil and iron ore mining in Venezuela frequently exceed 50 percent.

As a result of the predatory foreign trade policies of imperialist monopolies, the prices of goods exported by Latin American countries to the United States are continuously dropping, while prices of imported goods are rising. Every year, the Latin American countries lose about 1.5 billion dollars from nonequivalent foreign trading.

If we add to the losses from nonequivalent trade the interest paid on enslaving loans and other ways of plundering the national wealth, the total sum extracted by the American monopolies from Latin American countries would reach 5 billion dollars per year.

The new methods of colonial enslavement used by U.S. imperialists with a view to restricting the national-liberation movement in Latin American countries and keeping these countries within the capitalist system include military undertakings, such as the imposition of unequal treaties, the drawing of these countries into military-political blocs, the conclusion of bilateral military treaties, and the establishment of military bases on their territories.

The imperialists rely on the latifundist system, the retention of which leads to the fact that only a total of 5 percent of the arable land is under cultivation, and under which 1.3 percent of all landowners own 71.6 percent of all arable land, whereas 4 percent of small landowners owning up to five hectares each

own 0.9 percent of the cultivated land. The Latin American countries also have a tremendous mass of landless peasants and agricultural workers.

The objective development of the economic and political progress of the Latin American countries is the basis for the need to carry out in them radical socioeconomic changes — elimination of the domination of imperialist monopolies, radical agrarian reform, establishment of democratic governments. Interested in such changes are the broad people's masses: the working class, the peasantry, and the petty, middle, and even big bourgeoisie not connected with monopolistic capitalism. Such changes are opposed only by a small handful of representatives of the local financial and landowning oligarchies allied to the American monopolies.

III

The interests of the national-liberation movement challenge its participants with the task of unifying all forces interested in radical changes in a single national-liberation front. Under present circumstances, necessary revolutionary changes may be achieved only if all national anti-imperialist forces are united. The achievement of unity is a difficult and lengthy process depending upon the concrete situation of one country or another. Attempts at artificially "speeding-up" the revolution, at "bringing it closer," regardless of local conditions, are destined to failure and will lead to the opposite — a split in the national forces and a weakening of the anti-imperialist movement.

Thus, the peasant armed rebellions, organized by extremist elements in Peru in 1963, ended in the defeat of that movement. The mass of the workers' class and the peasantry was not ready for armed struggle. Reaction used the peasant rebellion as a pretext for repressive measures against the Communist Party, the trade unions, the national-liberation front, and other democratic organizations. A similar situation occurred in Ecuador as well, where a group of antiparty leaders of Trotskyite persuasion issued, in the summer of 1963, an appeal for immediate armed rebellion against the government, even though conditions in the country were not ripe for such an action. This facilitated a *coup d'état*, as a result of which, in July 1963, a military junta took power. The Communist Party had to go underground and its leaders — Secretary General Pedro Saad, Second Secretary Enrique Gil Gilbert, and others — were arrested. Trade union, democratic youth, and other social organizations' activities were suppressed.

The characteristic trait and particularity in the current stage of the national-liberation movement of the Latin American countries is precisely the fact that in many of them an anti-imperialist, national, and democratic front is being formed.

The current scope of the national-liberation movement in the Latin American countries is due, to a considerable extent, to the activities of the Communist parties, which have raised slogans around which the masses are rallying and national fronts are being set up. The growth of the Communist parties in Latin American countries is very indicative. In 1939 the Communist parties of these countries numbered a total of 90,000 people, in 1957, 200,000, and in 1962, 300,000.

Conditions under which Communist parties operate in Latin America are quite varied. Some of them are banned and operate in deep clandestinity (for example, in Argentina, Paraguay, Venezuela, Brazil [from April 1964], the Guatemalan Labor Party, the CP of Honduras, the Dominican Popular Socialist Party, the National Unity Party of Haiti, the Socialist Party of Nicaragua, and the CP of Ecuador and Salvador). Others

are semilegal (the CP of Mexico, the People's Vanguard Party of Costa Rica, and the CP of Colombia and Bolivia). Others are in the open, enjoying the rights of a political party and participating in political campaigns (the Communist parties of Chile, Uruguay, Martinique, and Guadeloupe). The characteristic common to all of them is that they have expanded their influence, strengthened their ties with the masses, and increased their membership. For example, in seven years the Communist Party of Argentina rose from 80,000 to 140,000 members; the Brazilian CP, from 5,000–6,000 to over 60,000; and the CP of Uruguay from 3,000–4,000 to 15,000.

Also growing are the People's Vanguard Party of Costa Rica, the CP of Salvador, and the People's Party of Panama. The National Unity Party of Haiti, which was recently formed, operates under the difficult circumstances of the fiercest terrorism and persecutions. Its ranks number over 1,000 members. Coming out of clandestinity in 1958, after the overthrow of the Pérez Jiménez dictatorial regime, the Communist Party of Venezuela numbered 700 members; two to three years later it numbered 35,000. In the past two years, following the banning of the party and arrests and persecutions for party membership, its ranks have decreased. However, even now it numbers up to 20,000 members. In many countries the Communist parties have become powerful and authoritative political forces.

The increased influence of the Communist parties among the masses and their successes in the national-liberation movement are the result of following the Marxist-Leninist general line of the international communist movement, drafted at the conferences of representatives of Communist and workers' parties in 1957 and 1960. The Communists of Latin America are united in their evaluations of important problems of the strategy and tactics of the revolutionary movement and in determining the nature and moving forces of the liberation revolution. They base their activities on a deep, creative Marxist-Leninist analysis of the concrete reality prevailing in their countries.

The Communist parties of Latin America consider the current stage of the struggle of their peoples not as a goal in itself but as the beginning of the struggle for the final objective—socialism. Thus, the program of the CP of Argentina speaks of the "democratic, agrarian, anti-imperialist revolution with a socialist future." The theses of the Brazilian Communist Party state the following on this subject, on the occasion of its Fourth Congress: "The national-democratic revolution, a revolution of a new type developing under the conditions of the growth of the world socialist system and collapse of capitalism, being a part of the world socialist revolution and led by the proletariat, is the 'form of transition or approach to the proletarian revolution' most acceptable to the broad people's masses."

The attempts of the leadership of the Chinese Communist Party to impose upon the other Communist parties its "general line," to split the communist movement and thus weaken the national-liberation movement on the Latin American continent have failed. Colliding with the firm Marxist-Leninist position of the Communist parties of the Latin American countries as regards modern world development and the international communist movement, the leadership of the CCP undertook the creation of the so-called independent antiparty groups. They succeeded in the establishment of such groups in Brazil, Peru, and Ecuador. These include various antiparty, factionalist elements expelled from the ranks of the fraternal parties. The so-called general line of the CCP leadership of "pushing the revolution" basically blends with the line of Trotskyite groups operating in the Latin

American countries. In the foreword of the book *Documents of the Chinese Communist Party on the Chinese-Soviet Dispute,* published in the summer of 1963 in the name of the Fourth International, one of the Trotskyite leaders in Latin America, J. Posadas, wrote that the Trotskyites hail the actions of the leaders of the CCP and express the hope that soon they will be able to agree with them "on all points." The agreement between the Chinese leadership and the renegades of the Latin American workers' movement did not and will not lead to success, for all logic of the struggle is against it, and so is life itself.

IV

Struggling for the establishment of national fronts, the Communist parties devote their primary attention to the working class as the main force, the leader, in the national-liberation revolution. The working class holds the most consistent position in the struggle against imperialist enslavement. The experience acquired in the struggle of the Latin American Communists clearly refutes the anti-Marxist thesis of the leaders of the CCP to the effect that the decisive force in such countries as those in Latin America is only the peasantry and even the urban petty bourgeoisie.

Today, the working class of Latin America is an imposing force. Up to 20 million people are employed in its mining and manufacturing industries and transportation, as compared with 6.4 million in 1940. To this one should add many more millions of farm workers. The intensification of the strike movement is proof of the growth in the activities of the working class. Thus, in the period 1950–1952, 3.4 million workers went on strike, whereas 21 million went on strike in 1961. In some Latin American countries, the strike movement assumed a scope unprecedented in the history of the labor movement of these countries.

The growth in the political activities of the workers and the upsurge in the strike movement have led to a regrouping of forces in Latin American trade unions. By the end of the fifties the trade-union movement in these countries was split and suffering a crisis. No single trade-union center existed on the continent. The Confederation of Latin American Workers, set up in 1938, had for some time ceased playing that role.

Of late, united and militant trade-union centers have been established and operate, fighting for national liberation, in Argentina, Brazil, Bolivia, Uruguay, Chile, and Costa Rica. The unity of the workers' movement is strengthening on a continental scale. A major step in this direction was the Continental Trade Union Unity Congress, held at the end of January 1964, attended by 387 delegates from eighteen Latin American countries, and representing 25 million working people. The trade unions in the USSR, France, Czechoslovakia, and Italy sent observers to the congress. The establishment of a coordination committee of trade-union unity and the adoption of resolutions in defense of unity, against the domination of imperialist monopolies, for the protection of the social and economic rights of the workers, and for strengthening solidarity with Cuba constitute serious successes achieved by the workers' movement of the Latin American countries. The attempts of leaders of the Inter-American Regional Labor Organization and of its American sponsors represented by Meany, Reuther, and others, at preventing the organizational strengthening of the Latin American workers' movement ended in failure.

An important factor in the revolutionary liberation movement of Latin America is the adoption of program documents by many Communist parties in these countries that determine their position concerning the peasant problem. The drafting of agrarian programs by the Communist parties marks the beginning of a new stage in the peasant movement and determines the way for resolving the agrarian problem, thus strengthening the union between the working class and the peasants.

The peasant movement in Brazil, Peru, Ecuador, Colombia, Chile, and many Central American countries has assumed a broad scope. During the first postwar years the peasant movement in the Latin American countries was spontaneous, whereas now it is becoming better and better organized. The fight of the peasant masses for a radical resolution of the agrarian problem is related to the struggle against foreign imperialist domination and for independent national economic development.

More and more actively participating in the anti-imperialist movement in the Latin American countries are the petty and middle bourgeoisie and even representatives of the big national bourgeoisie, not related to American imperialism and among whom the plundering policy of U.S. monopolies creates greater and greater discontent.

Thus, the Latin American countries are acquiring the objective prerequisites for the establishment of solid coalitions among the national anti-imperialist and democratic forces fighting for radical changes in the interest of the broad working masses.

V

The changes that the future national governments will have to make are aimed at the gradual and profound transformation of the entire socioeconomic structure of the Latin American countries. They will be of a revolutionary nature, since they will be aimed at the elimination of imperialist domination and the financial latifundist oligarchy and the removal of the most reactionary forces from political power. The struggle for such reforms is an important step in the development of the revolutionary process and in bringing it to a successful conclusion. The aims of the anti-imperialist and antifeudal revolution are directly related to the aims and tasks of the socialist revolution. They are a definite stage in the revolutionary process that is taking place in the Latin American countries.

Naturally, the rates of transition from anti-imperialist and antifeudal to socialist revolution will depend not only on objective, but also on subjective, conditions: on the ability of the leftist forces to achieve the isolation of the antinational reactionary elements and the creation of a broad single front of national forces against imperialism and the latifundists, and on the capability of the working class and its political parties to achieve recognition from the people's masses of the vanguard role they play.

Soon, many Communist parties will advance in their programs economic and political measures, which, by their nature, correspond to tasks facing national-democratic governments. This is a natural coincidence; the national-democratic state is a state free from the domination of foreign monopolies and local financial and landowning oligarchies, and promoting an independent foreign policy based on relations of equality with all countries and preparing the material and political prerequisites for further social progress. Therefore, in many Latin American countries, the completion of anti-imperialist and antifeudal revolutions may, under certain conditions, lead to the creation of national-democratic or similar states.

A study of the programs of the Communist parties indicates that Communists do not absolutize the form of struggle, and that such forms may change depending upon circumstances prevailing in one or another country.

The Latin American Communists are consistently in favor of the line entered in the program documents of the international communist movement and re-ject the position of the Chinese leaders who try to impose upon all parties the strategy and tactics they have developed for the specific conditions of their own country. "The revolutionaries," stressed the Secretary General of the Central Committee of the Communist Party of Chile, Comrade Corvalán, "cannot arbitrarily select one or another road, one or another way of assuming power. They must adopt only that path and that form which stem from a concrete set of conditions within which they operate." The statement of the Communist Party of Salvador stresses that, rejecting the position of the Chinese leaders and their attacks against other Communist parties, the Salvadorian Communists emphasize that "the choice of revolutionary tactics, forms and means of the struggle is, in every case, a matter for the Marxist-Leninist party of a given country to decide."

VI

In Chile there is currently firm unity among the leftist forces united in the Popular Action Front, which includes the Communist, Socialist, and National Democratic parties, the National Vanguard of the People, and many other small parties. In addition to this, the United Trade Union Center of the Working People and the National Federation of Peasants and Indians offer real prerequisites for the victory of progressive forces, the establishment of a people's progressive government, and the implementation of radical social changes.

The Communist Party of Chile, the leading force in the Popular Action Front, sets out from the possibility of achieving major democratic changes peacefully. The Communists realize that the victory of the people's forces in the forthcoming September 1964 elections requires a broad mobilization of the masses headed by the working class.

However, the Chilean Communist Party does not relate the struggle for a people's government and radical changes only to the forthcoming presidential elections, but is aware of the possibility of changing the form of struggle in the case of a sharpened domestic political crisis. "The working class and the people," said the report of the Central Committee to the Twelfth Congress of the Chilean Communist Party, "striving to assume power without armed struggle, must consider the fact that the enemy may impose such a struggle. Therefore, they must prepare to meet any eventuality."

The Communist Party of Argentina is operating in a complex atmosphere of acute political and economic crisis. The expanded plenum of the Central Committee of the Party held in July 1962 reached the conclusion that favorable circumstances have been shaped for merging the struggle for the direct economic, social, and political aims of the working class and the people with the general struggle for the assumption of power. This may take place by peaceful or nonpeaceful means, depending on concrete circumstances. However, whatever the circumstances, it must be achieved on the basis of expanding and deepening the activities of the masses. The solution of such a task is favored by a new phenomenon represented by the "turn to the left" of Peronism (a movement founded in the past by the former president of Argentina, Perón, and that includes many workers). The Twelfth Congress of the Communist Party, held clandestinely at the end of February 1963, clearly stated the necessity of waging a struggle for the unification of the leftist forces and organizing the actions of the broad masses into a single anti-imperialist and antioligarchic front for the assumption of power and the creation of a government of a new type, truly democratic and national.

Great successes in the unification of leftist forces have been achieved by the Communist Party of Uruguay: a Leftist Liberation Front and a United Trade Union Workers Center of Uruguay have been created.

Different again are the circumstances in Central America and the Caribbean countries, dominated almost everywhere by military dictatorships. In the summer of 1963, military coups took place in Honduras and in the Dominican Republic. Guatemala is dominated by a military dictatorship that was established after the overthrow of President Jacobo Árbenz in 1954. The Somoza family has dominated Nicaragua for over thirty years. The democratic forces of Venezuela are in difficult conditions. As a result of the terroristic and anti-communist policies of the Betancourt government and its successor, civil liberties have been abolished and the political opposition parties operate clandestinely. Salvador and Haiti are also under dictatorial regimes. The dictatorships in the Caribbean countries give the Communists of these countries grounds to believe that a peaceful path to democratic revolution has been closed to them and that armed struggle is the only possible form of change.

The policy of naked anticommunism and the suppression of democratic freedoms in Venezuela have led to increased discontent of the entire population. However, broad unity among all opposition forces has not yet been achieved, and this is one of the reasons for the weaknesses in the democratic movement of the country. On the eve of the December 1963 elections, the Communist Party of Venezuela turned to the left-wing parties with the appeal to act in a single front and support a common candidate. However, the party appeal was not answered. The left-wing democratic forces remained split, thus facilitating the assumption of power by

Leoni, a protégé of the American monopolies. Naturally, other factors as well influenced these events: repressions against those who did not wish to vote for Leoni, juggling of election results, forgery and substitution of ballots. The struggle in Venezuela is continuing. The leftist forces, which derived serious lessons from the elections, are rallying around the national-liberation front created as a result of the military collaboration between the Communist Party and the Leftist Revolutionary Movement.

VII

The growth of the national-liberation movement in Latin America causes apprehension and unconcealed hatred in U.S. imperialist circles. American reaction tries to use all possible means in order to retain its domination in the Latin American countries. It is becoming more and more certain of the fact that now no promises, small handouts, or Alliance for Progress demagogy could guarantee the achievement of this goal. More and more frequently, it is abandoning the play at democracy and sweetness, trying, with the help of the military and the domestic oligarchies, to defeat the left-wing democratic forces and establish obedient reactionary regimes. Washington is talking more and more openly of the next switch in U.S. policy as regards Latin America — the abandonment of the Kennedy Doctrine proclaiming nonrecognition of military-dictatorial regimes.

Leaning upon domestic reaction — the military, the comprador bourgeoisie, and the powerful latifundists — the North American imperialist monopolies promote military *coups d'état* and implant dictatorships favorable to them. The military *coup d'état* in Brazil is a proof of the incapacity of U.S. monopolistic circles and their agents to cope, with the usual means, with the growing revolutionary movement. In recent years, the Brazilian democratic forces have achieved considerable successes in the struggle for independence. A united national patriotic front of leftist forces has developed in the country in the course of the fight against reaction. The Brazilian Communist Party played a major part in this process. It has worked for the creation of a so-called solid, democratic national government that, with the support of the masses, would be able to ensure an independent national development of the country and achieve radical changes in the interests of the majority of the people. At the beginning of January 1964, the party supported President Goulart's proposal to create a Nationalistic Patriotic Front, based on a program envisaging the implementation of radical changes. The united leftist forces had also to fight against the conspiratorial activities of reactionary circles headed by the agents of the American monopolies — the governors of the state of Guanabara, Lacerda, and of São Paulo, de Barros — who were against any changes and were awaiting the time for overthrowing President Goulart and dealing with the democratic forces. The Nationalistic Front was being formed rapidly and the Brazilian Communist Party was attempting to solidify unity among democratic forces and raise the masses to fight. However, when an attack was launched by the reaction, frightened by the upsurge of the democratic movement, these efforts failed as a result of the organizational weaknesses of the front.

Together with this, the dissident policy of the leadership of the Chinese Communist Party played a sharply negative role during that important period in the activities of the Brazilian left-wing democratic forces. It attacked the Brazilian Communist Party and its Central Committee for their participation in the united Nationalistic Front and for supporting the progressive measures of President Goulart, denigrating the leaders of the CP and labeling them "traitors to the Brazilian people." Meanwhile, it gave thorough support to and praised the factioners expelled from the party, calling them true patriots. Instead of promoting the unity of leftist forces and unmasking the reaction, the Graboes-Amazonas factional antiparty group did everything possible to promote dissidence and weaken the leftist forces. It listened to the voices of its advisers from Peking, repeating after them the thesis of immediate armed rebellion and overthrow of Goulart, regardless of the fact that under the circumstances Goulart was the figure around which the people rallied and who was attacked by the American monopolists and Brazilian reactionary circles. Indeed, the overthrow of President Goulart's government played into the hands of only foreign imperialism and its agents within the country. Thus, the antiparty, factional, and pro-Chinese elements directed from Peking in fact turned out to be in the same camp as Lacerda and company.

Under those circumstances, the domestic oligarchy, following plans drafted in Washington and profiting from the organizational weakness of the nationalistic democratic forces, carried out a military *coup d'état* at the beginning of April 1964. Power was assumed by right-wing reactionary forces – the army clique, the most aggressive latifundist circles, and a group of the powerful comprador bourgeoisie. Cruel reprisals were instigated against the democratic elements, against the Communists. The reactionary coup will, undoubtedly, intensify the struggle of the Brazilian people for national liberation. Discussing the Brazilian coup, the French newspaper *Liberation* wrote, at the beginning of 1964: "The oligarchy of landowners, industrialists, and officers who have come out of their ranks will be unable to retain for long the order to which it clings. The contrast between luxurious wealth and tragic poverty will reach a degree at which explosion will be unavoidable, as is clearly shown by the Cuban example. Closing the gates to peaceful evolution, the Brazilian rightwing forces and their allies may find themselves wiped out by an irresistible explosion."

The advent to power of the reaction in Brazil was welcomed with unconcealed joy by the Pentagon and the State Department. In is an inspiration for the reactionary circles of other Latin American countries – Bolivia, Uruguay, Argentina, and Chile. Such methods, however, cannot stop the upsurge of the national-liberation movement, for the contradictions between imperialism and the peoples of these countries are sharpening even further, and the struggle for radical changes, for elimination of the domination of U.S. monopolies, and for social progress and democracy is intensifying.

The experience of the Communist parties in the Latin American countries and of the national-liberation movement in these countries confirms the correctness of the general line of the international communist movement, jointly drafted and accepted at the 1957 and 1960 Moscow conferences. They refute the anti-Marxist theories of the leadership of the CCP, which are aimed at alienation of the national-liberation movement from the common struggle of the peoples for peace, democracy, and socialism.

5. Determining Factors in the National-Liberation Movement of Latin America[*]

S. S. MIKHAILOV

The national-liberation struggle of the peoples of colonial and dependent countries is an integral and inalienable part of the world revolutionary process. The powerful new upsurge of the movement of the oppressed nations to obtain their freedom and independence is playing an enormous role in the revolutionary transformations that mankind is experiencing in our time. Next to the creation of a world socialist system, the second most important historical occurrence in the evolution of human society is the downfall of the system of colonial slavery.

An inseparable organic connection exists between the development of the forces of world socialism and the downfall of colonialism. The prerequisite conditions for liquidating the colonial system of imperialism were established only after the great October Socialist Revolution and the formation of the world socialist system. The complete collapse of colonialism, which has become inevitable in this new historical situation, represents one of the most important factors in the new third stage of the general crisis of capitalism.

Characteristic of this stage is not only the national liberation of the peoples of Africa, Asia, and Oceania, which is taking place at an accelerated pace, but also the transformation of Latin America into an active front in the revolutionary struggle against imperialism. In the words of N. S. Khrushchev, Latin America "has entered into a new stage in its history—the stage of struggle for genuine national independence."[1] The revolution in Cuba serves as an especially striking example. As a result of its victory, the heroic Cuban nation has unshackled itself from the chains of imperialist oppression and has been able to proceed toward the successful building of a socialist society. Its establishment of the first socialist state in the Americas was an important event in modern world history.

The Cuban popular revolution achieved victory within a framework of complex domestic and international political circumstances, because of the presence of the necessary objective and subjective conditions. This victory, as well as the rapid transition to socialist construction, was facilitated by the

[*]"Osnovnye cherty natsional'no-osvoboditel'nogo dvizheniia v Latinskoi Amerike na sovremennom etape," in *Osvoboditel'noe dvizhenie v Latinskoi Amerike* (Moskva: Izdatel'stvo Nauka, 1964), pp. 5–19.

[1]*Pravda*, December 13, 1962.

strength and the grandiose achievements of the world socialist system, the general upsurge of the labor and democratic movements, and the sudden proliferation of national revolutions in dependent and colonial countries. The forces of imperialism proved to have been so weakened that they were not able to prevent the Cuban people from expressing their will freely. In this respect, the solidarity shown by the sister states of Latin America also played a considerable role. Socialist Cuba in turn has begun to exert the strongest kind of revolutionizing influence upon the entire course of the national-liberation struggle of the Latin American people.

The development of revolutionary processes in Latin America as an integral part of the world revolutionary process is proceeding according to the general laws governing the transition of mankind from capitalism to socialism that were discovered by Marxism-Leninism. This does not mean that the revolutionary processes going on in the Latin American countries do not possess their own special characteristics. Their socioeconomic basis differs in many respects from conditions existing in, for instance, Africa and Asia, where, with rare exceptions—such as Japan—capitalism has not reached the level of development attained in Latin America.

Over the last few decades, the nations of Latin America have taken a significant forward step in their industrial development. The greatest advances in this respect have taken place in Brazil, Mexico, Argentina, Chile, and Uruguay. A working class has arisen in connection with this, with a considerable proportion concentrated in huge enterprises. There are also a great many agricultural workers. Thus, the most revolutionary class of modern society has gained in strength, a fact that has had a strong influence on changes in the disposition of class forces in most of the Latin American republics.

The capitalist development of Latin America is taking place within the context of a backward socioeconomic structure, under conditions of the retention of vestiges of feudalism and under imperialist oppression. Although this development has led to a certain increase in productive forces, the backward, semifeudal structure of the economy has not been abolished. This can be explained by the fact that Latin America has not undergone "a normal capitalist development, such as occurred during their respective periods in the economic evolution of the capitalist countries,"[2] according to an observation by Rodney Arismendi. Thus, capitalism has demonstrated its historical bankruptcy in its inability to solve the basic socioeconomic problems of the Latin American countries, which still remain economically dependent on and are mercilessly exploited by the imperialist powers, particularly the United States.

The peoples of Latin America are paying dearly for this. As the Second Havana Declaration justly pointed out,

The death toll in Latin America from starvation, curable diseases, and premature old age amounts to four persons every minute, 5,500 per day, 2 million per year, 10 million in the course of each half-decade. These deaths continue despite the fact that they could easily be prevented. Two-thirds of the population of Latin America have a very low life expectancy; the constant threat of death hangs over them. Their mortality for a fifteen-year period was twice that of the entire First World War, a situation that remains unchanged. Meanwhile a steady stream of money flows from Latin America to the United States—almost $4,000 a minute, $5 million a day, $2 billion each year, $10 billion every five years.[3]

[2]*Estudios*, August 21–22, 1961, p. 44.
[3]*Pravda*, February 6, 1962.

This truly tragic situation in which Latin America finds itself is rooted in the fact that the key positions in the principal branches of its economy are occupied by U.S. monopolies. They get rich from inequitable trade with the Latin American countries and dictate their will to them. Each dollar invested in Latin America yields a return profit of $3.17, but the U.S. capitalists leave the Latin American countries only $1.00 — and even this primarily in the form of reinvestment. The remaining $2.00 is exported to the United States.[4] Thus, from 1946 through 1961, the U.S. monopolies invested 5,467 million dollars in Latin America, while they exported profits amounting to 12,166 million dollars.[5] This kind of robbery is augmented still further through the medium of unequal trade. The financial losses incurred by the Latin American countries because of a deteriorating price relationship between raw materials and industrial products amounted to 722 million dollars in 1958 and reached the sum of 1,800 million dollars in 1960.[6]

Besides U.S. imperialism, the chief hindrance to the advancement of the peoples of Latin America is the institution of latifundism. Omitting Cuba and, to a certain extent, Mexico and Bolivia, where land reforms were carried out, the latifundists in Latin America, who comprise only 5 percent of the population, have concentrated possession of half the available land area in their own hands. Latifundism is primarily responsible for the monoculture system in Latin America, for its feeble economic progress, its backwardness, and its political stagnation. These find their manifestation in the absence of democracy; in the ignorance in which the overwhelming mass of people are kept, with access denied them not only to education in general, but even to elementary literacy; and in the enormous social gulf separating the majority, doomed to horrifying poverty, from a handful of privileged persons who belong to the ruling classes and boast unabashedly of their wealth.

Foreign monopolies, domestic latifundists, and the proimperialist portion of the bourgeoisie — these are the forces that block progress for the Latin American countries. Of course, many differences still exist from country to country in the correlation of class forces, in the composition and forms of the united democratic front, in the alliance policy, and in the methods of struggle. For this reason, one can only note the most common features of the liberation movement, those shared by nearly all the Latin American republics. The working class is playing an ever greater role in the common front of the national-liberation struggle of the peoples of Latin America.

What are the characteristic features of the Latin American workers' movement at the current stage?

First of all, in recent years the working class of Latin America has been gradually freeing itself from the influence of reformist theories, from the ideological and political influence of the upper bourgeoisie and imperialism. Anticommunism as the principal weapon for dividing the workers' movement is revealing its groundlessness ever more.

Second, the movement to achieve the trade-union unity of the working class has been making rapid strides forward. For instance, consolidated trade-union centers have been established in Chile, Bolivia, and Uruguay, while unity of trade-union action has been assured in Argentina, Ecuador, Costa Rica, Panama, and other countries. Substantial advances have taken place in the direction of coordinating trade-union activity on a South America–wide plane.

[4]R. Arismendi, "Latinskaia Amerika vykhodit na avanstsenu," *Kommunist*, 5: 77 (1961).
[5]Z. I. Romanova, *Ekonomicheskaia ekspansiia SShA v Latinskoi Amerike* (Moskva, 1963), p. 67.
[6]See Document ECLA E/C N 12/659, p. 9.

Third, the upsurge of the strike and general democratic struggle of the working class is assuming a more patently political character and anti-imperialist hue. The movement in defense of the Cuban Revolution bears graphic witness to the growing class consciousness of the proletariat of Latin America.

Fourth, cooperation between the proletariat and other sectors of the population is steadily increasing.

Fifth and finally, the vanguard of the proletariat—the Communist parties—is growing in influence among the workers and all toiling people. The successes achieved by the working class of Latin America would have been impossible without the unselfish activity of its political vanguard—the Communist parties. Guided by the great teachings of Marxism-Leninism, the Communist parties of Latin America are waging a vigorous struggle for the unification of all patriotic forces.

Cooperation between Communists and Socialists represents an important link in this struggle. Within the Socialist parties of Chile, Uruguay, and Argentina, there has been a strengthening of those elements which are anti-imperialists, which support the Cuban Revolution, and which favor joint action with the Communists. The Socialists in Chile have long worked together with Communists in the trade unions and in the ranks of the Popular Action Front, a situation that has a beneficial effect upon the progress of the liberation movement.

Indicative of the growing communist influence among the broad masses of the population are the party congresses that have been held in many countries — in Argentina, Venezuela, Guatemala, Honduras, Colombia, Mexico, Peru, Uruguay, Chile, and Ecuador. Attending these meetings, which have acquired the status of important political events in the lives of these countries, were representatives of other democratic parties, labor and peasant organizations, and popular organizations, as well as delegations from fraternal Communist parties.

Inspired by the documents of the conferences of representatives of the world communist movement and by the historical decisions of the Twentieth and Twenty-second Party Congresses of the Communist Party of the Soviet Union, the Latin American Communists adopted new party programs reflecting the changes that had occurred in the world and in which the goals of the revolutionary liberation movement are defined more fully. In threshing out the theoretical problems connected with an analysis of the contemporary situation in their respective countries and in determining the political line of the Communist parties, Latin American Communists turned their attention to the question of utilizing on the plane of practical activity the fundamental laws of our modern era and, in every possible way, took into account the basic contradiction of modern times.

An important feature of these new party programs is the fact that they accurately diagnose the complex make-up of the bourgeoisie in the different countries of Latin America and spell out the policies to be followed by the Communist parties with regard to the various bourgeois groups. In particular, it is pointed out that the domestic monopolistic bourgeoisie and the upper bourgeoisie, tied as they are to foreign monopolies, may be counted among the principal foes of the liberation movement.

Naturally, the conditions governing the struggle waged against this bourgeoisie in Latin America differ from the antimonopolist movement in economically more advanced countries dominated by large-scale capital. It is also pertinent to note that broad segments of the population can be united in the fight against monopolies in Latin America — including the national bourgeoisie, which is distinct from other capitalist groups primarily because it is engaged in a continual state of conflict with imperialism and is thus compelled to advocate each country's independent economic development. It is these sectors of the bourgeoisie which feel acutely the weight of foreign competition and whose interests are seriously prejudiced by the powerful circles of the great domestic bourgeoisie and the latifundists.

Defending itself from the assaults of foreign and domestic large-scale capital of the monopolistic type, the national bourgeoisie is advancing a number of progressive anti-imperialist demands attuned to the requirements for independent development of the Latin American countries. These requirements include effective protection of national industrial enterprises from foreign competition, regulatory action by the state in the area of foreign capital investments, creation of favorable conditions for the accumulation of domestic capital, making more credit available to domestic entrepreneurs, and an expansion of commercial ties with all the nations of the world. The national bourgeoisie favors protection for nationalized industry and advocates the development of several branches of industry, especially heavy industry, with government support and supervision. The reason for this stand is not only that the national bourgeoisie lacks sufficient means of its own and is not able to develop these branches easily by itself, but it lies also in the desire of this group to prevent important economic levers from passing into the hands of large-scale monopolistic capital, which strives to utilize key positions in industry to ruin and swallow up the national bourgeoisie.

At the same time, it is necessary to bear in mind that the dichotomous position of the national bourgeoisie often impels it to seek compromise and reconciliation with both imperialism and the domestic upper bourgeoisie. As a result, its representatives, while quite sharply critical of the United States, simultaneously harbor delusions regarding the notorious Alliance for Progress formed by Washington; they count on being able to use this "new United States policy toward Latin America" as a basis for initiating a more profitable kind of collaboration with foreign capital.

The chief weapon in the hands of the national bourgeoisie is nationalism, represented as the ideology of the whole nation. However, along with a certain democratic quality inherent in the nationalism of all economically backward and oppressed countries, this nationalism of the Latin American national bourgeoisie possesses its class aspect as well, reflecting the essential nature of the bourgeoisie as an exploiter group. Of course, when the national-liberation movement is on the rise and the national bourgeoisie, finding itself engaged in fairly bitter conflict with imperialism and internal reaction, tries to get the masses of the people to follow its lead, the reverse side of the coin of bourgeois nationalism remains hidden for the time being. Frequently, unable to see through the veil, some segments of the working people are held captive by their nationalistic delusions.

Yet the whole experience of the national-liberation movement—in particular, the very convincing examples of Mexico and Guatemala—shows that the national bourgeoisie is unable to wage a consistent and resolute struggle against either imperialism or internal reaction. Handing over complete leadership control of the anti-imperialist struggle to the national bourgeoisie means placing the successful progress of the liberation movement in jeopardy. Genuine accomplishments can be realized in this struggle only if there exists a powerful peoples' movement and if the workers' movement maintains its independence of the national bourgeoisie. Then the participation of certain circles of the latter in a single front acquires greater stability, while their possibilities for conniving with imperialist and domestic reactionary circles behind the backs of the people are reduced to a minimum.

The numerous instances of inconsistency and vacillation by the national bourgeoisie still do not justify the conclusion that it is incapable of taking part in the liberation movement. They indicate rather that the working class has not been strong enough to draw its allies along in a single front and to impose upon the national bourgeoisie that solution which corresponds to the interests of the people.

First, there has been lacking a solid alliance between the working class and the peasantry, which is the guarantee for the success of a democratic, agrarian, national revolution. The experience of the last decade demonstrates how contrived and groundless is the attempt to foist upon the working class the dilemma of either a single front together with the patriotically motivated national bourgeoisie or an alliance with the peasantry.

These last years have witnessed certain advances in the peasant movement of the Latin American countries. Independent peasant organizations calling for radical agrarian reforms have been established in Brazil, Chile, Venezuela, Mexico, and other republics. It is worthy of note that the Indian masses, who comprise an overwhelming proportion of the peasant population in several Latin American countries, are participating in these organizations. This testifies to the fact that the oppressed Indian masses are becoming aroused and, moreover, that they are overcoming their centuries-long isolation and alienation from the rest of the peasantry.

Clearly indicative of the growth in organizational ability of the peasantry as a whole in Latin America are the national and regional congresses of representatives of its organizations that have been held in Brazil, Peru, Chile, and other countries. The militant spirit exhibited in the speeches made at these congresses shows that the political level of the peasant movement in Latin America has risen immeasurably. The formation of independent peasant organizations is the result of expanded cooperation between urban and rural workers and is an indispensable prerequisite for building a united front of democratic and patriotic forces.

Until recently, the urban middle class in many countries was under the demagogic influence of reactionary circles and followed the lead of the parties of the oligarchy. Now, however, elements of this class are beginning to take an active part in the anti-imperialist movement. Among these sectors are the urban petty bourgeoisie – including craftsmen and small tradesmen – along with some of the salaried workers, intelligentsia, and students. Demonstrations by small tradesmen and craftsmen, and strikes by bank employees, teachers, doctors, and technicians and engineers of state enterprises and institutions, for example testify to the significant shifts in attitude that have occurred among these population groups. Such demonstrations have recently become a more and more frequent occurrence in Argentina, Peru, Brazil, Mexico, Uruguay, and other countries. The fact that government employees and the proletariat can engage in a joint struggle proves clearly that they are not separated from each other by some kind of Chinese wall; it shows that the basis for their rapprochement derives from their common position as labor for hire in a bourgeois society. Nor is it difficult to perceive what great prospects this cooperation opens up for the further development of the national-liberation movement.

Special reference should be made to the important role of students and the progressive intelligentsia in the national-liberation movement. The active struggle being waged by the young people is a strong indication of the deep crisis besetting the entire socioeconomic structure of the Latin American countries. Further confirming the invincible force of the new ideas is the fact that many young people from the privileged classes, such as Fidel Castro and several of his comrades-in-arms, are breaking with the old world and joining the side of the revolution. In this respect, the progressive youth of Latin America — to draw a historical parallel — bears a close resemblance to the heroic revolutionary youth of tsarist Russia, who underwent enormous privation and sacrifice while fighting for a better future for their motherland. Many times in recent years the whole world has witnessed mass political demonstrations by the students of Argentina, Mexico, Uruguay, Colombia, Guatemala, Venezuela, the Dominican Republic, Peru, Brazil, and other countries. Considerable casualties have been suffered by Latin American youth as they courageously step forward in the ranks of those who are fighting for freedom and democracy and against U.S. dictation in the political and economic life of their nations.

What is happening among the Latin American intelligentsia also merits our attention. The fact that an ever increasing number from their ranks has been showing a growing interest in Marxism and a recognition of the leading role of the working class is an important indication of the leftward trend among sections of the middle class. The transfer of more and more representatives of this part of the population to the side of Marxism and the working class strengthens the united anti-imperialist front of the struggle in which the peoples of Latin America are engaged.

This front assumes the most diverse forms, depending upon the concrete political circumstances, the historical traditions of the country, and the international position. Though the composition of those engaged in this front is constantly changing and at times lacks organization, experience has shown that the latter aspect is not at all mandatory for the existence of a united front. In the final analysis, what guarantees unity of action in practice is not so much the conclusion of paper agreements at the top as the ability of the vanguard to mobilize the broadest masses of the people behind the kind of demands that express their vital interests and correspond to the level of political consciousness attained by them.

In this connection, tactical questions arising in the course of the struggle by the patriotic and democratic forces take on considerable importance. The choice as to which path the revolutionary process will take in any given country — peaceful or nonpeaceful — depends to a large degree on the breadth and flexibility of the united front and on the organizational capabilities of the working class and its vanguard.

In accordance with the constructive Marxist-Leninist statement of aims contained in the declarations of the conferences of representatives of Communist and workers' parties in 1957 and 1960, the Latin American Communist and workers' parties point out that the working class and its vanguard, the Marxist-Leninist parties, are striving to achieve a peaceful development of the popular, democratic, liberating revolution free of civil war and its subsequent conversion into a socialist revolution. This peaceful path of revolution in Latin America, which corresponds to the vital interests of the working class and of the entire people, is facilitated by the radical change in the relative correlation of forces in the world arena and by the increasing attraction of the broadest masses of the people to socialism.

Inasmuch as the choice here does not depend solely upon the working class and its parties, the Marxist-Leninists do not postulate the peaceful path of development as a *sine qua non;* they point out the necessity of being prepared for any attempt by the exploiting classes to force a nonpeaceful course upon them. What is needed, therefore, is the ability to combine all the forms of struggle — both peaceful and nonpeaceful — with the choice between them being determined by the concrete conditions and the correlation of class forces within each country, as well as its situation in the world arena.

V. I. Lenin wrote, "If we do not master all the means of waging the struggle, we may suffer an enormous — sometimes even decisive — defeat, if changes beyond our control in the situation of other classes bring to the fore a form of activity in which we are particularly weak."[7] Regardless of the form in which the transition from capitalism to socialism is accomplished, it goes without saying that such a transition is possible only through a socialist revolution and the dictatorship of the proletariat in its various forms.

In the course of discussions among the participants in the liberation movement as to the ways in which the revolution should be conducted, incorrect views have been expressed — connected primarily with the tendency toward a mechanical projection of the experience of the Cuban Revolution onto all the other countries of Latin America, without taking their specific peculiarities into account. The gist of these views was that the only possible way to achieve revolution in all the Latin American states was via the path of armed struggle. Such a point of view, which in fact ignores the specific nature of the Cuban Revolution and the conditions — both objective and subjective — that made it successful, leads to underestimation of other forms of struggle, to the neglect of them and, consequently, to impoverishment of the arsenal of revolutionary resources. Furthermore, exclusive reliance on the path of armed struggle is fraught with the danger that the vanguard may become alienated from the entire revolutionary army and, thus isolated from the masses, be routed and destroyed.

In a speech at the Twelfth Congress of the Communist Party of Argentina, the party chairman, Victorio Codovilla, characterized the dialectical relationship of peaceful and nonpeaceful paths, with respect to conditions in his own country, in the following manner:

As we have already said on several occasions, the task of organizing, mobilizing, and supervising the mass struggle in the difficult conditions in which our party must function is hard and monotonous work, and it does not always yield immediate and striking results. For this reason, some comrades are of the opinion that an armed struggle will accomplish our goal sooner. We must bear in mind, however, that an armed struggle cannot be waged unless an open revolutionary situation has first been created. Though, as regards our country, it can be said that the revolutionary situation is indeed maturing, there still do not exist the subjective conditions that would assure the victory of the revolution.[8]

The decision as to which path of revolutionary struggle should be followed is made by the Communist and workers' parties on the basis of their own evaluation of the existing political situation, and not in accordance with any ready-made formulas. In arriving at such a determination, they consider, above all, the actual conditions in the country, the true correlation of class forces, and the

[7]V. I. Lenin, *Poln. sobr. soch.* vol. 41, p. 81.
[8]Victorio Codovilla, "Por la acción de masas. Hacia la conquista del poder." Informe rendido en nombre del Comité Central ante el 12 Congreso del Partido Comunista (Buenos Aires, 1963), p. 24.

degree of acuteness of contradictions in domestic and international politics at a given time.

The complex and diverse problems that arise in the course of development of the national-liberation movement bring to the fore the enormous role of the progressive, revolutionary ideology of Marxism-Leninism. The Communist and workers' parties of Latin America stress the fact that under the new conditions, as never before, class-conscious proletarian ideology must be defended and promoted, with ever new sectors of the people being won over to its side. While favoring alliance with the broadest circles of the population and demonstrating a maximum of flexibility and good will, the Communists at the same time make no concessions whatsoever in questions of principle or ideology. What makes this particularly important is the fact that the Latin American masses are under the very strong influence not only of reactionary ideology, engaged in justifying the economic backwardness and dependence of Latin America, but also of bourgeois nationalism.

Defending the purity of Marxist-Leninist theories, the Communist parties are fighting resolutely on two fronts: against revisionism, on the one hand, and against dogmatism and sectarianism, on the other. Indeed, both revisionism and dogmatism are products of the bourgeois-nationalist influence on the working class and are aimed at isolating the liberation movement, separating it from the world revolutionary process. Meanwhile, the liberation movement in Latin America is bound by integral and indissoluble ties to the global anti-imperialist movement, to world socialism, and to the struggle in defense of peace. Any attempt to separate the national-liberation movement in Latin America from similar movements on other continents, from the revolutionary struggle of the working class in Europe and North America,

from the world socialist camp, from the struggle to prevent war—any such attempt means objectively helping the enemies of the revolution and playing into the hands of the imperialists.

Marxism-Leninism has precisely defined the place and role of the national-liberation movement as an important component of the global revolutionary process and has also indicated the indissoluble connection between this movement, on the one hand, and world socialism, the international workers' movement, and the fight to stabilize and preserve the peace, on the other. The national-liberation movement does not represent a reserve or auxiliary force in the socialist revolution, but rather a powerful instrument for undermining the pillars of imperialism and—as the program of the CPSU points out—"a revolutionary force for the destruction of imperialism."[9] A most important prerequisite, however, for its ultimate success is that it be closely allied with and derive support from victorious socialism, since the national-liberation movement alone is not capable of destroying imperialism as a socioeconomic system. It cannot even hold onto its own gains unless it relies upon the entire invincible strength of the camp of victorious socialism and of the world revolutionary workers' movement.

For it is the world socialist system that protects newly liberated peoples against the menace of exported counterrevolution, and guarantees their existence and future development along the path of socialism by forestalling the danger of armed intervention by the imperialists. The world-wide national-liberation movement is therefore vitally interested in the preservation of peace, in the prevention of war, and in peaceful coexistence as a guarantee of its success

[9]*Materialy XXII s"ezda KPSS* (Moskva, 1961), p. 352.

and continued progress. Peoples fighting for their freedom and those who have already acquired it can make a most valuable contribution to solving the central problem of our time—the prevention of a new world war—by joining the peoples of the socialist states and the international workers' movement in their struggle against the danger of war. As the program of the CPSU notes, such a consolidation of effort represents a peace factor of the greatest significance, a powerful front expressing the will and strength of two-thirds of all mankind and capable of forcing the imperialist aggressors into retreat.[10]

This situation was brilliantly confirmed in the case of Cuba, where the socialist revolution and all its achievements were protected by the power of the Soviet Union and the entire socialist camp. This power checked imperialist agression and compelled the imperialists to fall back.

In our time, when there exists the great and powerful camp of peace and socialism headed by the Soviet Union and when the colonial system of imperialism is crumbling into the recesses of the past, the working people of Latin America are awakening more and more to the realization that it is possible to get rid of all the forms of oppression and exploitation only via the path of socialist revolution. A new day has dawned for Latin America. It is moving inexorably in the direction of the achievement of complete national liberation. And there can be no doubt that Latin America will achieve this legitimate and lofty aspiration in a quite brief space of history, thanks to the will of its freedom-loving peoples and with the support of the powerful camp of socialism and the entire world revolutionary movement.

[10]*Ibid.*, p. 357.

6. The International Revolutionary Labor Movement in Latin America*

In distinction from the overwhelming majority of the Asian and especially the African countries, the positions of the powerful domestic bourgeoisie have become more favorable and stronger in Latin America. Today, this bourgeoisie determines the nature of the entire capitalist class, which is a conciliatory and even an actively counterrevolutionary proimperialist force.

The national bourgeoisie in Latin America is inconsistent and inclined toward conciliation, notwithstanding the fact that it has serious contradictions with monopolies and that its anti-imperialist potentialities have not disap-

*Mezhdunarodnoe revoliutsionnoe dvizhenie rabochego klassa. 3rd ed. (Moskva: Izdatel'stvo politicheskoi literatury, 1966), pp. 333–343.

peared. The nationalistically and radically inclined urban and rural middle sectors are a real and serious force that could take part in the battle with imperialism and the oligarchy. However, only the proletariat, which is faced with arousing the peasant masses and leading them into battle, is capable of guaranteeing the success of the revolution with its determination and steadfastness. It does so by carrying out a tenacious struggle for the unification of all anti-imperialist forces. The level of consciousness and the degree of organization of the Latin American proletariat, which has gone through a long period of class struggle, are quite high.

Complex and responsible problems now lie before the working class of Latin America. This volcanic continent has become one of the most important fronts of the world-wide anti-imperialist struggle. The struggle has now entered a new stage of its history in the Latin American countries – a stage of struggle for genuine national independence. The profound crisis of the traditional socioeconomic structure of the countries of the continent has now become so acute that emergence from it can be found only on the path of revolution, on the path of basic socioeconomic and political transformation. The frequent surface reforms and compromising combinations and deals of the domestic bourgeoisie with the more farsighted imperialist circles cannot change the inexorable course of history. The revolution must sweep away the domination by monopolies and the latifundia, and the best representatives of the people must lead this revolution. In the countries with more developed economies, the guiding force of the revolution is the proletariat.

U.S. imperialism is forced to seek new paths for retaining its domination in Latin America as a result of the bankruptcy of its traditional support – the openly reactionary feudal-bourgeois sectors, which now retain power only in small and more backward countries. However, as it endures the failure of the Alliance for Progress program, the United States is now putting the "big stick" into operation again and is attempting to change the course of events by force. American imperialism is the bulwark of the latifundists and of all archreactionary and military-fascist regimes. The strategy of the U.S. monopolies consists of preserving the agrarian oligarchy as long as possible, in buying off and intimidating the bourgeoisie, and in strengthening the ugly semicolonial capitalism tied to it all over the continent.

The basic force that lies in the way of American imperialism is the working class. The aggregate power of the Latin American working class is huge. It it were organized into a single force under the leadership of a conscious vanguard and directed against the common enemy, it would be invincible. Hatred for the oppressors, which fills the hearts of the Latin American workers, unites the ranks of the working class and calls the workers into the struggle against any difficulties whatsoever in the name of their liberation. However, only the introduction of a conscious beginning into the struggle of the working class will give it a purposeful and organized nature. On the other hand, in places where the struggle of the Latin American proletariat is being conducted spontaneously, without any awareness of its class objectives, it cannot yield positive results for the workers. It will lead them into the blind alley of disillusionment or drive them onto the path of desperate actions, which in the end will lead to defeat.

In order to withstand the growth in the strength and influence of the working class of the Latin American countries, the domestic and foreign bourgeoisie are conducting an active offensive against the toiling masses of Latin America, above all, against the working class itself.

The bourgeoisie attempts to influence the working class through its political parties and through trade unions obedient to it. Characteristically, the basic bourgeois parties in the Latin American countries even have names that are aimed at penetration of the working class. Thus, there are bourgeois parties in Brazil called the Social Democratic and the Trabalhista ("labor") parties. The ruling bourgeois Institutional Revolutionary Party of Mexico has a special labor sector. The bourgeois parties of a number of other countries also call themselves workers' parties.

Leaders of anticommunist bourgeois organizations of the ilk of APRA in Peru and the supporters of Figueres in Costa Rica also continue to operate among the workers. Flaunting their nationalism and openly criticizing the expansionist activities of the United States, Figueres and Co. appear as champions of a certain third path—one in between "communism and imperialism." They declare that the U.S. monopolists are on the threshold of a path of "correction" and that, with good will, they can allegedly understand the needs of the peoples of Latin America.

In recent years, the ruling classes have been attempting to step up their influence among the working class with the aid of the so-called Christian Democratic movement. The Christian Democratic parties of Latin America are carrying out major work in labor districts, operating in particular through the Latin American Confederation of Christian Trade Unions (LACCTU), which enjoys well-known influence among the workers of the most economically and politically backward countries of Latin America—Peru, Bolivia, Ecuador, and Paraguay. In Chile, the Christian Democrats proclaimed a program of social reforms and, taking into account the peoples'

eagerness for a change in the backward social structure, they won an election victory and attained power.

Finally, the state apparatus, the agencies of coercion, and huge financial resources are at the disposal of the ruling elite, who use them for enslaving and pressuring the Latin American proletariat. Thus the labor movement in Latin America constantly clashes with the far-flung system of coercion of the broad masses of workers by the ruling classes.

On the other hand, the working class of the Latin American continent must also overcome the influence of petty bourgeois ideology. The history of the labor movement in Latin America has witnessed many occasions when the various pseudorevolutionary parties and organizations have attempted to draw the Latin American workers along with them, without taking into account the dialectic of the class struggle or the logic of revolution. They passed quickly from the scene, but in many cases they caused direct harm to the proletariat with their adventures. The Latin American labor movement has suffered especially severely from Trotskyite adventurists and the "leftist" anarchists who have willingly or unwillingly joined with them, and who at the first defeat have gone over to the camp of the most inveterate opportunists. It is sufficient to refer to the history of the Mexican labor movement in this connection. Adventurists of the Trotskyite type are doing great harm to the labor and democratic movement in Ecuador, Peru, and certain other Latin American countries.

The Communist parties of the Latin American countries are the vanguard force uniting the working class on the basis of a unified political platform, and they are helping it to become aware of its role in the national-liberation movement.

The Communists in the Latin American countries must exert huge efforts to oppose the subversive work of the bourgeoisie in the midst of the workers' organizations themselves — the trade unions. Having learned from the experience of past years, when the unity of the working class was the basic obstacle to the offensive of reaction, the ruling classes exert every effort to strengthen the schism in the trade unions of Mexico, Venezuela, and Colombia, and also toward preventing the unification of the working class in Argentina and other Latin American countries.

Making extensive use of the state apparatus, the bourgeoisie has registered definite successes in this respect. In many Latin American countries, the trade unions are under the control of the government and are even affiliated with the ruling bourgeois parties — as, for example, in Mexico. The ruling circles have established an entire network of coercive measures on trade-union leaders and have achieved their subservience and departure from the principles of proletarian policy. This is the most dangerous manifestation in the contemporary organized labor movement in Latin America.

The very worst aspects of U.S. trade-union traditions have been transferred to the trade unions of many Latin American countries: bossism, gangsterism, the absence of democracy and genuine elections, and the squandering of trade-union resources. The Communists are presently conducting a serious struggle against all these manifestations. However, eliminating them is not easy, since they are cultivated and stimulated by the ruling circles every day and every hour.

A certain part of the workers still follow the renegade trade-union leaders and join progovernment trade unions, in an effort to retain their jobs and housing and to protect themselves from police and employer persecution, which does not stop with badgering, but even extends to the physical annihilation of the most outstanding and conscious workers. Such persecution, baiting, and murders are quite common occurrences in certain Latin American countries, especially in Central America and in Mexico.

The increase in the influence of the working class on the economic and social-political development of Latin America and the battle for the establishment of trade-union, student, peasant, women's, and other mass organizations have strengthened the connections of the Latin American proletariat with other democratic sectors of the population and have established the prerequisites for rallying broad sectors of the people about it on an anti-imperialist basis.

At the Eighteenth Congress of the Communist Party of Uruguay, R. Arismendi spoke as follows about conditions in his country:

Only a national-democratic government is capable of implementing the essential radical transformations, consisting of the economic and political liberation of our homeland from the domination of American imperialism.

To establish such a government, it is essential to have a broad front that would unite a majority of the population: the working class, the peasants, the urban petty bourgeoisie, the intelligentsia, and the national bourgeoisie. The unification of these classes and social sectors in a broad bloc directed by the working class in association with the peasantry — this is a front of national liberation.[1]

The Twelfth Congress of the Communist Party of Argentina also has operated under the slogan "For mass actions directed toward winning power." V. Codovilla said at the congress:

The dilemma that faces our people is one of reactionary coalition or democratic coalition. No third choice of any kind exists. This is the reason why, even though the opposition

[1]*Estudios*, 25:66 (1962).

of certain leaders might block the formation of a broad democratic front, it is not in a position to prevent unity from being forged from below, in unitary committees of struggle for specific demands of the workers, peasants, students, etc. Only mass actions will decide the outcome of events in the struggle for power.[2]

The Thirteenth National Congress of the Communist Party of Chile has become an important landmark in the struggle for the establishment of a united front of all anti-imperialist, anti-feudal, and antimilitary forces in Latin America. The congress was held under circumstances characterized by the fact that the bourgeois-reformist Christian Democratic government had come to power in Chile. That government is influenced considerably, on the one hand, by leftist trends, and, on the other hand, it is feeling increased pressure from imperialism and the oligarchy, which are making use of the restricted class nature of Christian Democracy. Under these circumstances, the line of the Communist Party consists of implementing a change to the left in national policy and putting a stop to the slide to the right, which could lead to militarist adventurism and a reactionary *coup d'état*, and of opening the way to a successful battle for the satisfaction of the most pressing demands of the people and for changes that would lead to the satisfaction of revolutionary yearnings.

Setting out from this point, the Chilean Communists have formulated tactics consisting essentially of unification of the progressive forces of the opposition and of the government in a struggle against the reactionary forces of the government and of the rightist opposition. This means, in the first place, a general strengthening of such an outstanding gain for the Chilean people as the Popular Action Front, and, in the second place, the cooperation of the Popular Action Front with the new po-

litical trends that are assuming anti-imperialist and antioligarchy positions.

The unification of the anti-imperialist forces in the countries of Latin America is possible on the basis of their joint actions for strengthening the political independence of the countries; for the implementation, with the participation of the entire peasantry, of agrarian reforms that are in its interests; for the elimination of the vestiges of feudalism and the exclusion of foreign monopolies from the economy; for industrialization and an increase in the standard of living of the people and the democratization of public life; for the implementation of an independent, peace-loving policy; and for other general national objectives, that is, on the basis of a program promoted by the working class.

A solid union of the working class and the peasantry is the basic foundation for a front of national and social liberation. A substantial change has taken place in recent times in relations between the working class and the peasantry. The question of the role of the peasantry and unity with it has been especially discussed at trade-union meetings and at congresses of the Communist and Socialist parties.

The degree of organization of the peasant masses has been raised in recent years in many Latin American countries as a result of the work of the Communists among the peasantry. A multitude of revolutionary peasant organizations are being established in the countryside. Representatives of the working class are participating in the preparations for and the work of peasant gatherings and conferences. In Chile, for example, mining workers and metal workers played an especially active role in the preparations for a peasant congress; in Peru, miners and metallurgical workers; in Brazil, textile workers, met-

[2] *Problemy mira i sotsializma*, 6: 42 (1963).

allurgical workers, railway workers, and construction workers; in Venezuela, oil workers, construction workers, and metallurgical workers from the capital. Representatives of the textile, metallurgical, construction, and railway workers took part in the work of the Fourth Congress of Agricultural Youth in Argentina.

The revolutionary-inclined middle urban sectors, which in the Latin American countries are distinguished by their large numbers and political activity, are also an ally of the proletariat of the Latin American countries in its anti-imperialist struggle. These sectors include students, teachers, physicians, people in the free professions, white-collar workers, small businessmen, and street vendors. They constitute the mass support of many petty bourgeois parties, which are heterogeneous in their composition and often come up with extremely radical programs.

The experience of the Cuban Revolution has shown that the middle urban sectors, which are petty bourgeois in their situation and outlook, can play an important role in the Latin American countries, and not just in the anti-imperialist stage of the revolution. This conclusion is extremely important for countries with a proletariat limited in numbers.

Consequently, the Communist parties of the Latin American countries constantly give a great deal of attention to work among the middle sectors in the cities. These sectors have become quite revolutionary lately due to the fact that, on the one hand, their position has worsened, there having been an increase in the difficulties experienced by the petty and middle urban bourgeoisie, government employees, intelligentsia, and students because of increased oppression by foreign monopolies and domestic ruling circles, and, on the other hand, the Cuban Revolution, the national-liberation movement in Asia and Africa, and the growth of the world-wide forces of socialism are having their influence on them.

The movement to the left by the middle sectors is expressed in their more active participation in the national-liberation movement, in the struggle against the aggressive policies of the United States and against treacherous antinational bloody dictatorships, in the movement for solidarity with Cuba, and in the search for an independent, peaceful foreign policy on the part of their countries.

A definite place in the united anti-imperialist national front shaped under the leadership of the working class belongs to that sector of the national bourgeoisie which is concerned with the struggle against foreign monopolies. The working class is the force that is concerned to the highest degree with overthrowing the domination of the U.S. monopolies and domestic reaction, and it has real prospects for doing this. Historical experience shows that a limited half-way bourgeois revolution in Latin America is not capable of crushing imperialist and feudal reaction. The revolution in Bolivia, which ended in a blind alley, testifies particularly to this. Only a thorough smashing of the socioeconomic structure can open the way for progress in the Latin American countries.

The prospects for the implementation of a national, people's, and consistently democratic revolution, which in the event of its successful evolution would inevitably be transformed into a socialist revolution, have been appearing ever more distinctly in recent years in a number of Latin American countries.

The Cuban Revolution once again has shown that only the support of the broad masses and their attraction into conscious political struggle are capable of ensuring the success of revolutionary manifestation. The Cuban experience has shown that the toiling masses will follow revolutionary catchwords only if they understand their essence and purpose and the direct advantages for them. A people's revolution differs from revolutionary manifestations led by the bourgeoisie in that it is profoundly hostile to "revolutionary" phraseology about freedom and democracy without genuine material guarantees.

However, that same Cuban Revolution also emphasized very strongly that an indispensable condition of successful revolutionary activity is a strict reckoning of the specific national characteristics of the country.

The conditions for the development of the revolutionary process in the Latin American countries are varied. Consequently, a scheme that is divorced from reality can be frustrated by life itself. "On the basis of the fact that the revolution in Cuba broke ground for itself with the aid of arms," Luis Corvalán has commented, "it is sometimes concluded that this is the only path for all the countries of the continent." The leader of the Chilean Communists emphasized that this is a completely incorrect statement of the question. Such inclinations can lead to the result that many other real possibilities would not be utilized, especially the possibility of development of the revolutionary process along the peaceful path.

Even more, genuine prerequisites for the peaceful path of development of the revolution already exist right now in certain countries on the Latin American continent. In a number of countries, where the peaceful path for the entire revolutionary process is less probable, there also exists the possibility of making extensive use of the legal forms of mass struggle at various stages of the revolution. The maximum utilization of this possibility in complete form responds to the interests of the peoples, permitting reliance on constitutional legality (and, perhaps, on a broader social base), even in cases where the conduct of reaction in later stages of the

revolutionary struggle forces the masses to take up arms.

The Latin American Communists set out from the fact that the revolution and armed struggle are not synonymous. The most important thing in the revolution is the transfer of power and ownership of the basic plant and means of production from one class (or classes) to another. This can be achieved either peacefully or nonpeacefully, depending on the conditions. The Communists, who place the interests of the masses above all else, and to whom the life and struggle of the masses are their happiness, always will prefer the peaceful path of development of the revolution if the other conditions are equal.

The Thesis on the Peaceful Path — written into the program of the Communist Party of Chile — is not a tactical formulation. It is a programmatic demand of the communist movement. The proletariat and its party will never resort to violence for the sake of violence. We stand for the path that is associated with the least number of victims, in order that bloodshed and violation of material and cultural values might possibly be avoided. This corresponds fully to the interests of the movement ahead to socialism and to the profoundly humanistic nature of the theory of Marxism-Leninism.[3]

In its struggle, the proletariat of Latin America resorts to the most varied forms of peaceful and nonpeaceful actions. Its struggle has a mass nature, and the actions of the workers are ever more often becoming converted into acts of nationwide significance.

The increased role of the working class in the national-liberation struggle of the peoples of Latin America leads to the result that such forms of struggle of the proletariat as political strikes and anti-imperialist demonstrations are be-

[3] *Programmnye dokumenty kommunisticheskikh i rabochikh partii stran Ameriki* (Moskva, 1962), p. 324.

ing used by other democratic forces on the Latin American continent.

The varied forms and methods of the struggle of the proletariat depend on the situation in each individual country and in Latin America as a whole. In the presence of many forms that are characteristic to some degree for all capitalist countries, there are specific features in the development and organization of the struggle of the workers in Latin America. One of the most active forms for a long period of time has been the strike, as shown in Table 1.

The strike movement for the entire postwar period constitutes proof of the imperialist exploitation. The liberation of the oppressed peoples has been the result not only of their own heroic efforts, but also of the basic changes in the relationship of forces on the world scene, the decisive factor in which is now the world socialist system.

As Lenin predicted, the national-liberation movement of the oppressed peoples is not limited to the achievement of political independence, but is taking on the character of a social, anti-capitalist revolution. The achievement of the historic task that stands before the peoples who have been freed from colonialist oppression—the liquidation

Table 1. The Dynamics of the Strike Movement in the Latin American Countries
(Numbers of Strikers in Millions)

1949	1950	1951	1952	1953	1954	1955
c. 2.5	3.0	2.5	4.5	5.6	7.4	9.1

1956	1957	1958	1959	1960	1961	1962
9.7	8–9	11.8	20	20	21	13

1963
14

growth in the activity of the working class of Latin America, its consciousness, and the possibilities for its conscious vanguard to find correctly the necessary forms and methods of struggle responding to the circumstances that have been formed.

The history of the national-liberation movement confirms the profound correctness of the Leninist theory of world revolution. Life has shown that it is precisely the confluence into a single current of the great contemporary movements—socialist and communist construction, the proletarian revolutions, national-liberation revolutions, and the struggle of the international working class against capitalist exploitation and for democracy and socialism—that ensures the collapse of the entire system of

of centuries-old poverty and backwardness—cannot be done on the path of capitalism. A break with capitalism in the name of the progressive development of the liberated countries has become the chief trait of the new stage in the national-democratic revolution. In our times, it has gone beyond the bounds of bourgeois democracy. Profound social-economic transformations in the former colonies will in the end lead them onto the path of struggle for socialist development.

Consequently, the collapse of the colonial system and the rise of new states in place of the former colonies does not signify a "rejuvenation" of world capitalism or an expansion of its rule to the "third world." On the contrary, this collapse—along with the world system of socialism and the international labor and democratic movement—will become one of the factors leading to the weakening and collapse of imperialism and capitalism. The working class is acting on a worldwide scale as the vanguard of world revolution, the channel of which is now much broader than ever before with various currents merging into it. A number of countries under revolutionary democracy have set out on the path leading to socialism. Under these circumstances, the world socialist system plays the role of shield against imperialist counterrevolution and the role of source of material aid and moral inspiration. The socialist inclination of the revolution being developed there will be increased to the degree of the growth and development of the working class in the countries that have shaken off colonial oppression.

The most important task for the progressive anti-imperialist forces in our times is to guarantee the inviolability of the union with world socialism. Therein lies a guarantee of victory over imperialism, a guarantee of successful implementation of the historic objective—the elimination of the centuries-old backwardness of the countries of Asia, Africa, and Latin America.

7. The Role of the Various Classes in the National-Liberation Movement of Latin America*

A. A. GUBER

The tremendous significance of the Twentieth Congress of the CPSU is generally known. On the basis of a profound analysis of the contemporary processes of the national-liberation movement, the congress showed the motive forces of the national-liberation movement and put an end to the sectarian and dogmatic approach to it. This congress gave to the working class and its parties in all countries a powerful ideological tool for consolidating all forces capable of participating in the national-liberation struggle. The examples of many Asian and African countries permit assessment of the benefits of the resolute struggle of the working class and its parties against the dogmatic approach to the problem of a united national front and against the dogmatic denial of any possibility that the national bourgeoisie could take part in the national-liberation

* Foreword to Bor'ba za edinyi rabochii i anti-imperialisticheskii front v stranakh Latinskoi Ameriki (Moskva: Izdatel'stvo VPSh i AON pri TsK KPSS, 1963), pp. 7–15.

struggle, or even lead it, under certain circumstances.

Of course, we cannot mechanically apply to Latin America conditions of development in the colonial countries of Asia and Africa. Nor can we forget that the great majority of Asian and African countries only recently threw off the political domination of imperialist mother countries. Latin American countries meanwhile, having recently observed the 150th anniversary of their political independence, have developed differently in many respects. Their transformation into semicolonies was accompanied by the formation of oligarchies composed of a domestic feudal-latifundist and bourgeois upper crust in the service of foreign monopolies.

The concept of a national bourgeoisie in reference to some Asian or African country requires supplementary definition in every case, that is, the middle bourgeoisie, the industrial, that not connected with monopolies, or others. Similarly, the concept of comprador bourgeoisie has in our day increasingly become a synonym for the reactionary, proimperialist bourgeois elements and is losing its original meaning. Definition of the different bourgeois categories as applied to Latin America requires even more careful analysis for each specific country, in order to establish precisely what the local bourgeois strata are and to what degree they are capable of participating in the anti-imperialist struggle.

In contrast to the experiences of Asian and African states, historical peculiarities in the 150 years' development of the Latin American countries as formally independent political states resulted generally in the inability of the Latin American bourgeoisie not only to lead national-democratic renascences in their own countries but even to lead the first general national and democratic stages of the anti-imperialist struggle.

In the Latin American countries, imperialists have the support not only of the latifundists—who may be compared, with certain reservations, to the semifeudal landowners of Asia—and of the comprador bourgeoisie but also of the bourgeois upper crust, which has coalesced with the large landowners and often even originates from the hereditary aristocracy. The presence of a large-scale monopolist bourgeoisie allows use of the term *financial oligarchy* in some of these countries—a fact noted in party documentation of communist and labor parties in a number of Latin American countries.

However, the inability to lead the revolution does not at all mean that the Latin American bourgeoisie is totally incapable of fighting against imperialism. Of course, its anti-imperialist potential is weak, because the bourgeois stratum that is vitally interested in the elimination of imperialist domination and the numerous remnants of feudalism has only minor economic and political influence, while the stage of bourgeois participation in a national-democractic revolution is relatively brief. As a result, during the development and deepening of revolution, differentiation of the national front occurs more rapidly and is accompanied by a faster change in the components of the anti-imperialist front and by formation of popular unity in the country's struggle to achieve all the goals facing its transition to socialism. The Cuban Revolution graphically demonstrates such acceleration.

Setting out from the premise that the general-national and general-democratic problems of revolution can be solved only with the guidance of the working class—a point that was very clearly formulated in the Second Havana Declaration as a crystallization of the experience not only of Cuba but also of other Latin American countries—we must particularly stress the importance of making general and skillful use in the national front of all, even minimal, anti-imperialist potentialities existing among a large part of all the propertied classes of Latin America, not only among its national bourgeoisie.

In Latin America, as everywhere else, the working class and its parties are the most consistent fighters for nationwide goals. Only under the guidance of the working class can genuine national independence be won and fundamental democratic reforms implemented.

Nevertheless, leadership cannot be acquired by declarations and invocations. Only by active participation in the consolidation of national forces and in the emerging united front — even when the latter arises from the initiative of the national bourgeoisie and envisages quite limited aims — can the working class assume its leading role and free large numbers of people — especially the peasantry — from the influence of bourgeois ideology. In the course of the struggle for national liberation from imperialist domination, the ground is inevitably prepared for the growth of nationalistic movements and for the growth of that bourgeois-nationalistic ideology which the bourgeoisie tries to convert into the banner for the national-liberation struggle. Keeping the masses under its ideopolitical sway in this way, the bourgeoisie counts on perpetuating its class hegemony in the liberated country in the future.

Bourgeois nationalism is alien to the proletariat. The working class conceives the solution of national problems and the realization of the aspirations of its people — whose real spokesman is the proletariat — as lying on the route of international solidarity with the progressive forces of the entire world. However, it is extremely dangerous nihilistically to deny the natural presence of bourgeois-nationalistic influence upon broad sectors of the workers in those countries where national liberation still remains to be achieved and where general all-national goals still exist. Marxist-Leninist understanding of nationalism in subjugated nations — of its inner dialectic nature and its duality — is indispensable in overcoming the influence of bourgeois nationalism on the masses and in awakening them to the indisputable truth that it is precisely the working class which is the most consistent exponent of the nation's interests.

The problems of nationalism, of nationalistic ideologies, of nationalistic organizations, and of attitudes toward them are becoming acute in all the colonial and dependent countries that are struggling for genuine independence. V. I. Lenin always underscored the need to support nationalistic movements directed against imperialism and toward the achievement of independence.

It goes without saying that bourgeois-nationalistic ideology serves the bourgeoisie as a means of keeping the masses under its own influence and of restricting the democratic forces. With the aid of such ideology, not only the bourgeoisie but also the other propertied classes and petty-bourgeois strata often try to limit the national-liberation movement to a quite narrow framework, to prevent independent action by the popular masses, and — particularly important for all these forces — to block the struggle of the working class for hegemony. However, unmasking these ideologies and eradicating their influence upon the masses is inconceivable without separating out the general and objectively anti-imperialistic element contained in nationalistic programs, which directs large segments of the population — including workers, and especially peasants — away from the antidemocratic and ultimately antinationalistic purposes for which nationalism systematically uses the bourgeoisie. It is extremely important to consider this situation in connec-

tion with the struggle for a united national front in the Latin American countries.

Thus, with respect to such a reactionary ideology as Peronism, for instance,
we cannot limit ourselves to stating that
it is reactionary and that it characteristically combines demagogy and terror,
while ignoring its anti-imperialistic
aspect. It must be remembered that
precisely this anti-imperialistic facet of
Peronism assured it support not only
by the national and petty bourgeoisies,
but also by a certain portion of the
workers. And if Peronism today still
exerts considerable influence among
Argentina's working class, this very
fact is the reason. Discounting this
consideration, it is impossible not only
to create a broad national anti-imperialist front, but also to overcome many
difficulties in the struggle for working-
class unity. When we were fighting
bourgeois-nationalistic ideology—and
this task is always a timely one not to be
separated from that of winning the leading role for the working class—we
would often forget this side of the
matter. Suffice it to remember the
harm caused by an incorrect appraisal of
Gandhi and Gandhism and the way this
error actually retarded the struggle of
the Indian working class and of the
Indian Communist Party to liberate the
broad Indian masses from Gandhist influence—the people who, because of
many specific reasons, were especially
strongly influenced by this form of
bourgeois ideology.

The services rendered in all the Latin
American countries by the working
class and its vanguard, the Communist
parties, are quite important in the consolidation of all forces for genuine independence. It is impossible to understand the successes already achieved on
the path of the struggle for national
unity without taking into account the
unselfish and day-to-day efforts of the
Latin American Communist parties

under both legal and extralegal conditions and often under conditions of
harshest terror. It is precisely the Communist parties that are facilitating the
consolidation of national forces for the
struggle for general democratic goals
by tireless exposure of American imperialism and its Latin American allies—the latifundists, the reactionary
upper bourgeoisie, the right-wing socialist agents of imperialism—penetrating more and more deeply into the
popular masses in this work.

The growing influence of Marxist
ideology upon the Latin American intelligentsia is of undoubted, although
often underestimated, influence. Its
great importance in political life; the
role that the intelligentsia plays in all
dependent countries; the peculiarities
of its situation in these countries, where
only a relatively small part of them have
an opportunity to join the exploiting
classes, and even fewer of them to join
the proimperialist oligarchy; where the
nonpropertied sector of the intelligentsia is constantly growing—all of this
not only makes the intelligentsia an
active and instigating force in the struggle for national independence, but also
transforms it into a receptor for revolutionary socialist ideas. This condition
becomes especially apparent during the
era of world-wide socialistic conquests,
the era of the formation and growth of
the world socialistic system.

In countries where from 70 to 80 percent of the population is illiterate, the
propaganda and the work of Communist
parties naturally reach the advanced
proletarian strata and the revolutionary
wing of the intelligentsia first of all.
Winning the nucleus of the intelligentsia over to revolution is tremendously
important in spreading revolutionary,
anti-imperialist ideas.

Along with the favorable conditions
for the Communist Party, one must also
consider the many difficulties customarily encountered in the Latin Ameri-

can countries. The influence of traditional bourgeois parties, of course, is one of these.

Despite the fact that throughout Latin American history many traditional parties have repeatedly demonstrated their inability to lead the struggle for genuine national independence while many of their leaders now and again exposed their antipopular nature, "periods of harsh reaction have the amazing effect of restoring the prestige of fallen leaders who have suffered defeat in revolution."[1] Parties defeated and removed from power and replaced by others with a still more reactionary policy retain and regain their influence, including influence on part of the working class. By their oppositionist attitudes and various demagogical tactics, they once more garner support and reappear in the political arena, often as a result of the next "revolution."

Such a situation permitted the experienced demagogue Grau San Martín to advance once more to the forefront of political life. And Batista—a young army sergeant whose name was linked to the hopes of very broad Cuban democratic sectors when he first appeared on the scene—again achieved power, even after his real face had been unmasked, and could only be unseated by the victorious Cuban Revolution.

The revolutionary forces of Latin American countries must carry on a serious and systematic resistance to the poisonous weapon of anticommunism, which internal and foreign reaction in many of these countries still succeed in using to fight the democratic movement. For decades, elaborate, mendacious anticommunist propaganda has been combined with praise for the glories of western "democracy" and the "free world" as well as with unbridled slandering of the socialist countries, the Communist parties, and the leadership of the young revolutionary organizations in the Latin American nations.

Under the guise of democratic and "socialistic" covers and using any means—religious survivals, chauvinism, racism—reaction tries to frighten the backward strata of the people with talk of "communist atheism" and to cause dissension among the working people and their organizations. The odious role of anticommunist exploiters is played by the swordbearers of American imperialism—the reactionary and venal labor leaders of the United States. The repulsive results of their activity are still affecting the democratic and labor movements of most Latin American nations.

The struggle to take advantage of the steadily increasing objective premises favoring the growth of the anti-imperialist national-democratic movement and to overcome the serious obstacles on this path requires extreme steadfastness of principle and at the same time flexibility on the part of the working class and its party. Indispensable conditions for victory are skillful use of and assimilation with those elements which may be temporary and inconsistent but which yet are capable, at a given stage, of participating in the anti-imperialist struggle.

Study of the Cuban Revolution—the history of victory by a broad national front—is exceptionally important and instructive for any Latin American country. It is particularly important regarding the overcoming of dogmatic sectarian errors by the party of the Cuban proletariat, the People's Socialist Party. All fraternal Communist parties solve this problem on the basis of their own revolutionary struggle and that of the experience of the entire world communist movement. Without eradicating the sectarian-dogmatic approach and without uncompromisingly resisting revisionism, realization of the great

[1] Karl Marx and Friedrich Engels, *Sochineniia,* vol. 10, p. 376.

and noble aims of the parties of the working class is impossible.

We have traced the forging of the correct Leninist line in the struggle for the formation of a national front and the correct strategy and tactics that will assure to the working class the leading role in the liberation struggle. Had the People's Socialist Party of Cuba not followed such a correct line, the Cuban Revolution would have been unsuccessful and the hegemony of the working class, which assured Cuba's transition to the socialist path of development, probably never achieved.

The correct tactics of the united national front assured the opportunity for exhaustive use of anti-imperialist potentials drawn into the patriotic front of forces, including those forces which did not desire to, and by their class nature could not, proceed further with the people toward socialism under the leadership of the working class.

Thus, the naming of Urrutia as pro-tempore president in the first government following the flight of Batista and the victory of united government forces conformed to the goal of preserving the broadest possible front and of retaining these forces within the front until the democratic unity of the nation and the basis of a people's state—unity within the proletariat and its alliance with the peasantry—became strong and indestructible.

The sight of Urrutia, quite conservative in his political convictions, occupying the presidential chair awakened imperialist hopes—confirmed by many statements in the imperialist press—that the United States would easily reduce and tame the Cuban Revolution. Through the long years of their aggressive interference with Latin American domestic affairs, the imperialists had accumulated sufficient experience not only in organizing "revolutions" in their own interests but also in attracting to their side presidents who succeeded American figureheads overthrown by the people.

But as soon as the imperialists understood the popular character of the Cuban Revolution, reactionary forces began trying to strangle the young republic by every means. People's Cuba regularly received support from countries of the socialist system, especially from the Soviet Union.

All expedients were thrown into the battle against the Cuban Revolution—from sabotage and economic blockade to open intervention. Foreign imperialists employed not only the defeated Cuban reactionaries, but also those who had participated in the struggle against Batista, had withdrawn from the revolution, and had become the most determined opponents of the national-democratic revolution and the transition to socialism. Cuban counterrevolutionaries found asylum in the United States, where they were trained and armed for war against the Cuban people. Yet the imperialists had to be convinced by direct evidence that all their hopes for a defeat of the popular revolutionary regime had been built on sand.

8. Disruptive Socialist Activity in the National-Liberation Movement and Possibilities for the Movement's Future Cooperation with the Communist Party*

M.V. DANILEVICH

The upsurge of the national-liberation movement in the Latin American countries and the victory of revolution in Cuba have led to a sharp differentiation of political and social forces and a radicalization of the broad masses. As a result of this revolutionary process, a regrouping inside political parties is occurring—new leaders come forward, new programs and parties emerge. Changes within the Latin American Socialist parties are of particular interest in this complex process.

Not for the first time must the Socialists of Latin America determine their stand toward a united national front. In the past, reformist policies in the labor movement (such as economism or parliamentary liberalism) made the Socialists hostile to unity of action with Communists, and this in turn left a powerful impression on all their decisions on questions of a national front and hampered its formation, particularly in Chile, Uruguay, and Argentina.

Particularly instructive is the history of the labor movement in Chile, where the Popular Front twice—in 1938 and 1942—was victorious in elections and created its government but subsequently suffered defeat because of lack of unity between Socialists and Communists. The arguments that Socialists used in trying to justify their divisive activities were of a clearly anticommunist character and not essentially different from the phraseology of West European social democrats. In addition, in replying to the appeal of N. S. Khrushchev to the Socialist and labor parties of the West, they even referred to the Second International's resolution concerning refusal to cooperate in any form with "dictatorial parties." Here was the same old slander against Communist parties, which were declared to be the tool for penetration by "Soviet imperialism." As for the Popular Front, reformists depicted it as a "maneuver" by Communists aimed at strengthening their positions in the labor movement.

Every time the Communists have proposed cooperation based on common

*Osvoboditel'noe dvizhenie v Latinskoi Amerike, ed. S. S. Mikhailov (Moskva: Izdatel'stvo Nauka, 1964), pp. 144, 170–180.

political and economic demands to the Socialists, the latter have felt constrained to expose this supposedly subversive action. For instance, during the preparations for the 1958 elections in Argentina, the party, having advanced a broad program of action entirely acceptable also to the Socialists, appealed to them to overcome the obstacles to a joint struggle. The subsequent reply read: "We are not forgetting that all popular fronts help to weaken Socialists, disorganize labor unions, and strengthen the Communists."[1] Frugoni, the leader of the Uruguayan Socialists, replied as follows in 1956 to the Communist Party's offer: "We do not oppose union of the political forces of the working class in developing action of benefit to the working people . . . , but unity of action between adversaries would be harmful."[2]

Such an attitude toward Communists was characteristic of the period of ascendancy of the right wing in the Socialist parties. Anticommunism was the ideological platform that underlay their entire practice with respect to a united national front. This drove the Socialists on more than one occasion to betray the interests of the working class and effect a direct split.

Not to be overlooked is the fact that such a situation was sometimes aggravated because the Communists themselves were not always correct in their attitude toward Socialists. Not infrequently they took as their point of departure only those things which separated the two groups and transferred their appraisal of the activity of right-wing leaders to the entire party, thereby insulting and repelling honest Socialists devoted to the working-class cause. Nearly every one of the Communist parties of Latin America at one time or another viewed Socialists as adversaries and, protecting themselves from "infection," avoided contact with them. This important misconception was eliminated after the Twentieth Congress of the CPSU, which, as we know, exerted tremendous influence upon the worldwide communist and workers' movement. In subsequent years, the Communist parties of Latin America conducted an uncompromising struggle against sectarianism, revisionism, and dogmatism, revising their programs and bylaws. This had favorable repercussions on their contacts with Socialists.

On the other hand, this amelioration was facilitated by the Socialists' repudiation of anticommunism as the basis of their ideology and policy. Of course, the process of ridding themselves of their prejudices against Communists is still slow among the Socialists, a fact that constitutes one of the fundamental causes of the difficulties that characterize the process of building and developing a united-action front. But, just as in other matters, the different Latin American socialist groupings express themselves differently on this matter.

The experience of cooperation between Chilean Socialists and Communists is of considerable interest. In the past, cooperation had been sporadic, but in 1951 an agreement was made for joint political action. Coordination of the labor-union, parliamentary, and ideological struggle against domination by American imperialism made it possible to develop unity of action in labor unions and in the leadership of the peasant movement. It also united all the leftist democratic parties about the Socialists and Communists. In February 1956, the Frente de Acción Popular, or FRAP, was established. It formulated a detailed program of democratic, anti-imperialist, and antifeudal struggle.

[1]*La Vanguardia*, July 8, 1957.
[2]*Estudios* 8:1 (1958).

The force and influence of the FRAP are shown by the fact that as a result of its energetic action, supported by the masses, the reactionary law for "the defense of democracy" was revoked and the Communist Party obtained legal recognition. This influence is also shown in the steadily growing success of the FRAP in elections to Parliament and to local governmental bodies. Thus, in the presidential elections of September 1958, the socialist Salvador Allende, who ran on the FRAP ticket, received only thirty thousand fewer votes than the candidate of the reactionary parties' bloc. Further strengthening of unity in the democratic forces and their ties with the masses will undoubtedly guarantee future success in the struggle for the establishment of a people's government.

In the course of joint action, the Socialists and the Communists of Chile achieved mutual understanding and respect. Their cooperation is based on common goals and on a Marxist-Leninist ideological foundation. In the labor unions and in Parliament, close personal and organizational contacts were formed between the two groups. Communists and Socialists give each other opportunities to appear in their press, congresses, and conferences. Among other things, the then secretary-general of the Socialist Party of Chile, Solomón Corbalán, in speaking at the Twelfth Congress of the Communist Party of Chile in March 1962, said: "Here in this country, in this corner of the world, Communist comrades, the Communist and the Socialist parties are stepping together. This is proper because both parties are parties of the working class. Both parties believe in the same ideological principles and in Marxist teaching, and have common goals in the development of the Chilean and American revolutions."[3] In appraising the results of the joint struggle, he emphasized:

"We wish to continue this experiment, since our leaders and our rank-and-file members have come to know each other and since our parties no longer contain members who would like to cause a split between us."[4]

All of this does not mean, however, that divergence of principles between Socialists and Communists in Chile vanished at once. On the contrary, differences were quite significant during the first stage of united action, even though the discussion that developed was amicable.

Thus, in March 1962, when the leaders of the two parties exchanged letters on points of contention, the socialist leader Ampuero expressed disagreement with the Chilean Communist Party's stand regarding the role of the CPSU in the international communist movement. In replying to his incorrect stand, Luis Corvalán wrote: "The rise to power of FRAP depends greatly upon unity between Socialists and Communists, upon mutual understanding between these parties in the field of international politics, and upon their stand toward the socialist camp. If anti-communist and anti-Soviet feelings should develop in the Chilean popular movement, we would be in danger of making our revolution similar to the one in Bolivia rather than to the Cuban one." In speaking of the unity of the international communist movement, he stressed that the CPSU "occupies a vanguard post corresponding to the principle of mutual aid and brotherhood, without interference in domestic affairs and without infringement upon the sovereignty of other states."[5]

This important principle was completely confirmed in the practice of

[3]XII Congreso del Partido Comunista de Chile, p. 86.
[4]Ibid.
[5]El Siglo, March 29, 1962.

joint action by Communists and Socialists, which compelled the latter to refrain resolutely from asserting that wherever there is "leadership" there is also "subordination." Ampuero was forced to acknowledge that "all the decisions of the Communist Party of Chile have been adopted here by its own leadership. If this were not so, our alliance would have no moral foundation."[6] And Solomón Corbalán, speaking at the Twelfth Congress of the Communist Party of Chile, noted that "divergencies that had existed between parties are being effaced and obliterated from day to day. There is virtually complete accord between the parties in interpreting the characters of the American and Chilean revolutions. And this coincidence is founded and flourishes on the experience and practice of recent years."[7]

Successes obtained by joint work have strengthened the influence and the numbers of both the Communist and the Socialist parties. As noted at the Twelfth Congress of the Communist Party of Chile, ten thousand persons joined its ranks from May to November 1961, and 456 new cells were formed. For its part, the Socialist Party accepted seven thousand young men and women into its youth section in April 1962.

The fruitful results of united action by the Socialists and Communists of Chile are not accidental. They are closely bound up with the acute character of the internal struggle within the Socialist Party itself and with the sharp division between left and right. The pressure exercised from below by the working class is significant in this regard. Also apparent here, without any doubt, are the facts that the Chilean Socialists have always been less subject to the influence of social-democratic theory and practice and have never been connected even formally with the Second International.

An entirely different situation prevails in Uruguay, where political unity of the two proletarian parties has not yet been achieved. The effect of this fact on the struggle of the working class and the destinies of the democratic movement is seen to a greater degree here than perhaps in any other country in Latin America. Precisely for this reason, as Rodney Arismendi noted in his interview to the correspondent of Unità, "unity with the Socialist Party is the main goal of the Communist Party of Uruguay."[8] He also stressed the presence of important bases for such unity. The secretary-general of the Communist Party of Uruguay stated: "The Socialist Party has opposed the policy of the Socialist International. It has abandoned its former social-democratic positions and assumed anti-imperialist ones, stating its support of the Cuban Revolution, and it has adhered to its own course of development. We consider that conditions have emerged for lasting unity of Communists and Socialists within the framework of the general democratic, anti-imperialist movement."[9]

The Communist Party even earlier had repeatedly called for joint action with the Socialists. At its Sixteenth Congress in 1955, it proposed unity of action with the Socialist Party in questions "of defense of peace; of joint moves against American colonialization; and of the struggle for the economic and social demands of the toiling and popular masses, for unity of the working class, and for strengthening of the labor unions." In 1956, as well as in 1958, the Communist Party of Uruguay proposed joint action to Socialists three times, pointing out the objective coincidence in the goals of the two parties in many

[6]*El Sol*, June 1, 1962.
[7]*XII Congreso del Partido Comunista de Chile*, p. 386.
[8]*Unità*, January 18, 1952.
[9]*Ibid.*

areas of social struggle and political activity. Finally, in October 1960, the Communist Party appealed to all progressive democratic, anti-imperialist forces—including primarily the Socialists—to create an alliance of all leftist organizations; to promote a project of constitutional reform jointly; and to obtain a plebiscite on such political and social problems as an independent foreign policy, agrarian reform, economic development, the defense and extension of democracy, and a program of economic, social, and cultural demands.

Though these ideas were received favorably by workers' and democratic organizations, the Socialist Party leaders declined all proposals for unity made by the Communists and later by other political groups. They based their action on disagreement with the Communist Party stand on international problems and the party's appraisal of the revolutionary possibilities of the national bourgeoisie. Aware that these arguments were weak, since they were refuted by experience—for instance, in Chile, where similar divergencies did not block unity of leftist forces—certain Socialists resorted to attacks upon the Communist Party, accusing it of dogmatism, sectarianism, schematism, affiliation with "nonnational forces," "totalitarianism," and similar things. In addition, the Socialist Party decided to join with nationalist-minded bourgeois groups who demanded that the party abstain from joining a bloc with the Communists. The Socialists thus caused a split in a broad alliance of working people that had actually already been formed in the streets during class battles and demonstrations in defense of Cuba, in which the Communists took part, as one of the most active motivating forces.

In describing the true causes of such a policy by the Socialists, a resolution of the Eighteenth Congress of the Communist Party of Uruguay in June 1962 stated: "They actually reflect a tendency to prevent the proletariat and its Marxist-Leninist ideology from playing the principal role in revolutionary progress. Concessions in this respect, regardless of intent, will mean the strengthening of the political and ideological influence of those social strata which in the end are conduits of bourgeois ideologies. These concessions contain germs of future defeat for the revolutionary movement. There are many examples of this, including some in Latin America itself."[10]

The course of events could not have confirmed more the correctness of the policy of the Uruguayan Communist Party. Acting as a bloc with other leftist groups in the elections of November 17, 1962, it garnered nearly twice as many votes as did the Socialist Party with its allies. At the same time, election results again convincingly confirmed the need for uniting the forces of the left, since their divided participation was unable to withstand the traditional bourgeois parties, which then attained victory. Thus, no matter how much the Uruguayan Socialists speak of a sharp turn in their policy, their refusal to conclude an agreement with the Communist Party reduces to nothing the results of the broad ideological struggle of recent years, which had allowed the Socialists to work out a program for their participation in the national-liberation movement.

Relations between Socialists and Communists in Argentina have taken a peculiar form. Essentially, this problem, directly connected with the choice of the path for the national-liberation movement, was one of the principal problems in the sharp struggle that produced distinct dividing lines between Argentine Socialists.

[10]*El Popular*, July 18, 1962.

After the split of the Socialist Party in 1958, the main mass of its membership joined the struggle of the working class and of all workers and progressive forces in an insistent demand that the unity that existed in actuality be confirmed by the creation of a political alliance. This demand became even stronger under the influence of the Cuban Revolution. Nevertheless, the previously mentioned fear of uniting democratic forces, and fear of joint action with Communists, drove the rightists to an overt diversion. They conducted a ferocious campaign against the left majority in the executive committee of the party, accusing it of "procommunism" and "Fidelismo." A new split in May 1961 followed under conditions of a generally prevailing tendency for unity of democratic forces; those Socialists grouped around the newspaper *La Vanguardia* began to seek ways for joint action with the Communist Party. At their congress in October 1961, this question was one of the basic ones and was directly connected with renunciation of reformism and anticommunism by the left socialists.

A new position toward unity of progressive forces was expressed in the following statement from an article by Elías Zemía published in *La Vanguardia* after the congress:

After its last liberation from reactionary and anticommunist elements, Argentine socialism has understood the necessity to base its practice on unity of popular forces. The policy of splitting and opposing unity has been abandoned. . . . The Argentine Socialists now understand the role played by the communist parties in national liberation processes, the role of aid given by socialist countries, and the function of anticommunism in defending imperialism. . . . The Socialist Party of anticommunist tendency died the moment Socialists understood that under Argentine conditions they cannot attack Communists in the name of abstract conceptions only. . . . We recog-

nize the prospects for our socialism in Argentina and Latin America, and we open the doors for a new policy with regard to the Argentine Communist Party.[11]

This was the first article in the Argentine socialist press to contain an attempt at objective analysis of communist activity and a statement of readiness to collaborate with the Communists. During the subsequent period, the Partido Argentina Socialista de Vanguardia stated that it had no ideological differences with the Communist Party. In fact, the Socialists and Communists of Argentina reached complete accord on all the basic problems of the current stage of the revolution and of international relations. However, the pact of unity has not yet been achieved. To understand the reasons, we must turn to the characteristics of the present situation of the Socialist Party.

The fact is that the processes going on within the party testify to the birth of an essentially new party that renounces its reformist past and announces a "qualitative transformation," the refutation of liberalism, and the aim of becoming a genuinely revolutionary organization. Thus, it is still in the process of formation. In this process, the youth sector of the party, whose militant moods were long contained by the preceding opportunistic leadership, characteristically wish to demonstrate their "advantages" over the Communists. For this purpose, they employ a theory, which has gained some acceptance among young Socialists, to the effect that the Communist Party of Argentina has outlived its usefulness and completed its historic mission. This viewpoint is based on an erroneous interpretation of the nature of Latin American Communist parties, which purportedly "arose as a weapon to defend

[11]*La Vanguardia*, October 30, 1962.

the first socialist nation, persecuted by a capitalist encirclement. Their birth was thus determined by the Russian revolutionary process, and they have remained—in origin and development—alien to the experience of the working class and the popular movement of their own countries."[12]

It follows that the Argentinian left Socialists in practice have not yet cast off social-democratic influence in their appraisal of the role of the Communist Party, which is the vanguard of the country's working class and the organizer of its struggle for the accomplishment of national as well as social ideals. The Declaration of the Conference of Representatives of Communist and Workers' Parties in 1960 states that "the objectives of Communists respond to the highest interests of the nation."[13]

The erroneous stand of the left Socialists leaves a sharp imprint on all their negotiations about collaboration with the Communist Party. The following is approximately the sequence of their argumentation: first, the Socialist Party has radically revised its own positions and therefore is now guaranteed against making errors in evaluating current reality, and, second, as a young party, precisely it and none other is entitled to the leading position in "Argentine revolutionary socialism." For instance, Guisani writes in his article "The New Left": "What divides us from the Communist Party is not the ideological differences but the conviction that we have a clearer image of the concrete tasks of our revolution because we are a younger party."[14]

The Communists of Argentina, fighting persistently to build a united front composed of the country's progressive forces, take into account a certain immaturity in the ideological stands of the leftists, and they patiently explain their position in talks. As an editorial in the political and theoretical organ of the Communist Party, *Nueva Era*, states:

The problem of hegemony must not and cannot be solved as a prior condition of organizing the Front, because of the following considerations: the Front can be established only on the basis of equality among all parties and organizations. To establish prior conditions for granting hegemony to one or another party means to place the parties in unequal conditions, a policy that would be undemocratic and would result in narrowing the framework of the Front.[15]

Despite divergent opinions, the Communist Party of Argentina continues to develop collaboration with Socialists. This has an advantageous effect on the struggle for uniting the working class. Thus the Communists played a large part in organizing joint action by all the basic trade unions in preparing for the general strike of August 1–2, 1962, in which up to 3.5 million people took part. Moreover, an accord between the youth organizations of the Communist and Socialist parties has already existed for several years. The Communists of Argentina, like those of the other Latin American countries, believe that the logic of events and the entire development of the national-liberation struggle of the popular masses are leading to strengthening the unity of the working class and its parties.

Thus the changes that have taken place in the ideology, policy, and practice of the Latin American Socialist parties prove that only the resolution of internal contradictions and the determined renunciation of reformism and anticommunism can assure viability to these parties and their conversion into a meaningful force in fighting for national liberation.

[12]*Ibid.*, August 3, 1961.
[13]*Dokumenty Soveshchaniia predstavitelei Kommunisticheskikh i rabochikh partii* (Moskva, 1960), p. 38.
[14]*La Vanguardia*, August 3, 1961.
[15]*Nueva Era*, 1:8 (1962).

9. Students in the Liberation Struggle of the Peoples of Latin America*

M. I. Byl'skaia

State universities occupy a special position in the sociopolitical life of Latin American republics. As a rule, they are the scientific and technical centers of their countries, around which the most eminent domestic cultural figures and representatives of the creative intelligentsia are grouped. However, the universities do not merely train the cadre of diploma-holding specialists — physicians, engineers, agronomists, teachers, and others. Their significance does not rest solely in the scientific research indispensable to overcoming economic backwardness. Latin American universities are one of the most militant sectors in the front of the battle for the revolutionary transformation of society and for the liquidation of the oppression of foreign monopolies.

A majority of the students and many instructors are advancing toward democratic development. The most progressive teachings of the age have found and are now finding advantageous conditions here. Young students are in a hurry to convert these revolutionary ideas into life, to test them in practice, to translate them into the language of concrete action that often takes the form of demonstrations and strikes and,

occasionally, of armed insurrections against dictatorial regimes.

Students of the state universities of Latin America have added many glorious pages to the history of the national-liberation movement. Their activities have been highly praised, for example, by the Communist Party of Venezuela, which has declared: "The glorious traditions of battle for democratic liberties and against foreign oppression, battles against Gómez and Pérez Jiménez, the movements in 1936 and 1937 against López Contreras, and constant political activity of the students have converted them into a social nucleus from which the leadership of the petty bourgeois parties has drawn its forces, and from which the founders of our party emerged."[1]

The first quarter of the twentieth century is distinguished by sharp changes in the social composition of the popula-

* "Studenchestvo v osvoboditel'noi bor'be narodov Latinskoi Ameriki," in Osvoboditel'noe dvizhenie v Latinskoi Amerike, ed. S. S. Mikhailov (Moskva: Izdatel'stvo Nauka, 1964), pp. 236–239, 265–268.
[1] Programmnye dokumenty kommunisticheskikh i rabochikh partii stran Ameriki (Moskva, 1962), p. 64.

tion of the Latin American countries. The working class, having created its own revolutionary parties, grew and matured. The petty and middle bourgeoisies moved out onto the proscenium of political life. In several republics the landowning oligarchies were forced to share political power with them. Along with this, there were increased aspirations by the bourgeois and middle classes of the population—as well as by the workers—for guaranteed access to state institutions of higher education.

The social composition of the students began to be democratized, but university statutes still reflected old colonial systems, structures, and teaching methods, which did not respond to the new national objectives. These dogmatic scholastic methods of instruction, the predominance of professors in the humanities, the routine in the fields of socioeconomic and technical education—all conflicted with the spirit of the times. The appointment of rectors and professors by the government without provision for removal excluded the possibility of open competition, which would have permitted deliverance from the reactionary instructors and the introduction of vitally needed new subjects.

The first demands of the progressive circles of students were precisely formulated in the university of the city of Córdoba, Argentina, and were reflected in the "Córdoba Manifesto" of 1918. The battle to put these demands into practice—begun in Argentina and called the Movement for University Reform—quickly enveloped almost all of Latin America, for the solution of the problems of higher education was dictated by life itself. One of the fundamental demands was for university autonomy. This autonomy would be expressed primarily in the creation of an all-powerful administrative council—to include certain parts of the student body

—which would direct the educational process and the scholarly activities of the university.

Under these conditions, the movement acquired a sociopolitical character at its very inception. Its leaders understood that the universities could obtain their goals only under a democratic government enjoying the support of all the people. On the other hand, twentieth-century events indicated that the dictatorial regimes perceived in university autonomy a threat to the ideological and political principles behind their power. They tried to maintain control over the national intellectual centers at any cost, resorting to extremely cruel repression and arbitrary acts. For example, in 1928, Venezuelan dictator Vicente Gómez closed the Central University in Caracas for three years, in order to put an end to "student disorders."

As far back as 1927, one of the founders of the Communist Party of Cuba and the organizer of the Cuban Federation of University Students, Julio Antonio Mella, remarked:

Of the three fundamental postulates of the university revolutionary movement—democracy in the university [that is, autonomy], the right to re-elect professors, and the right to voice social demands—the most importance is vested in the latter. The university revolutionary movement is characterized by its aspiration to become a social movement, to reflect the hopes and needs of the unfortunate, to dissociate itself from reaction, to cross this "no-man's land" and unite boldly and nobly with the forces of social revolution, with the vanguard of the proletariat. This remarkable movement, which has seized the entire continent and has been a gigantic reverberation of the Argentine movement [for university reform] born in Córdoba's university, can be described as one of the fronts of the great class struggle that mankind has entered.[2]

[2]*La Reforma de la enseñanza superior en Cuba* (La Habana, 1962), p. 5.

The Second World War increased still more the political and militant activity of the basic mass of Latin American students. The victory of the Soviet Union in the war with Hitlerite Germany and the growth of the strength of the socialist camp significantly increased the interest of Latin American students in Marxist-Leninist ideology and in the culture and life of the socialist countries. Most of the student federations are becoming more progressive, and are consolidating ever more often with other national democratic organizations and joining the movement of supporters of peace.

The Cuban Revolution facilitated the solidarity of the democratic forces of Latin American students. In July 1960, the First Congress of Latin American Youth was held in Havana, attended by representatives of young political, professional, and student organizations from all the countries of the continent. Among them were delegates not only from the federations of state universities of Cuba, Argentina, Brazil, Colombia, Chile, Honduras, Peru, Mexico, Panama, Puerto Rico, El Salvador, Uruguay, and Venezuela, but also from student organizations of some private colleges in various countries. The participants in the congress unanimously adopted a resolution condemning the "political and economic interference of the North American imperialists in the internal affairs of the Latin American countries."[3]

The congress demonstrated the intense desire of the democratic youth of Latin America to be in the front ranks of fighters for national independence and against the armaments race and the establishment of U.S. military bases on Latin American territory. It became the first important milestone on the road to the unification of the youth and students of Latin America, and it also demonstrated their growing solidarity with the embattled youth of Asia and Africa.

Though in a social sense the Latin American students, of which the worker and peasant youth comprise only 2 percent,[4] do not reflect the overall disposition of class forces, the leading role in the movement for university reform is played by those participants who are closely associated with the anti-imperialistic and antifeudalistic aspirations of their peoples. For them, university reform is not an end in itself, but one of the elements in the basic transformation of society. For this reason, they aspire to a close union with the working class, the peasants, and all patriotic circles. The war cry of the Uruguayan students is, "Workers and students together—forward!"

Among the supporters of university reform more and more authority is being won by the young Communists and the members of the Young Communist League who, notwithstanding terror and suppression, actively propagandize the ideas of Marxism-Leninism. B. Kleiner, one of the leaders of the Communist Youth Federation of Argentina, has observed: "We Communists at the university are propagandists of dialectical and historical materialism. . . . Our ideology is the greatest achievement of the mind of man because it is a science that can be of aid in understanding not only professional matters, but also all manifestations of contemporary life."[5]

The Communist parties of Latin America are trying to unite all the students on the basis of a broad platform that includes the goal of the revolutionary transformation of society as a whole, as well as the solution of those concrete problems standing before the young

[3]*La juventud latino-americana de pie en defensa de la revolución cubana* (Buenos Aires, 1960), p. 6.

[4]See *Vsemirnye studencheskie novosti*, 1:7 (1962).

[5]B. Kleiner, *El humanismo y la universidad* (Buenos Aires, 1960), p. 3.

Latin Americans. The Communists see this as the means of drawing the mass of students into the working-class struggle for national liberation and social progress. The Political Resolution of the Fifth Congress of the Brazilian Communist Party says: "The unification of students of various philosophical and political tendencies is an important factor in the strengthening of college and university student organizations—the bulwark of the nationalistic and democratic front. In order to strengthen this unity and give an even broader, more massive character to the student movement, political activity must be combined with the struggle for satisfaction of specific student demands and the struggle for solution of the cultural, economic, and social problems disturbing young people."[6]

The politically active nucleus of this movement consists of members of the young communist organizations together with many socialist students and followers of other worker or petty bourgeoisie nationalistic parties. In Argentina, for example, these include a significant number of young Peronistas, as well as people without party affiliation. They are frequently joined by Catholic students who share anti-imperialistic convictions and who denounce the anti-Cuban activity of the Church.

This more conscious sector of the students is sweeping the ones who limit themselves to defense of their own specific rights and interests along with it.

In 1962 and 1963, a large number of mass student demonstrations under anti-imperialist slogans and with the demand for university reform took place in Columbia, Venezuela, El Salvador, Argentina, Paraguay, and Uruguay. In Brazil, 100,000 students went on strike during a two-week period. A significant number of university organizations—among them, those of Peru, Brazil, Venezuela, Ecuador, Colombia, and other republics—announced support of the Latin American Congress of Solidarity with Cuba. In Venezuela, the Federation of University Centers, which united 18,000 students, published a declaration with appeals for intensification of the struggle for "a democratic, patriotic, and nationalistic government." Almost one-sixth of the students of the University of Mérida began to fight against the reactionary regime in the ranks of the guerrilla movement, with weapons in hand.[7]

A large part of the contemporary students of Latin America are characterized not only by increased revolutionary activity, but also by an aspiration for unity. The students are responding to the offensive launched by reaction with a strengthening of the overall youth front.

The solidarity of the democratically inclined part of the students with the workers on the basis of common sociopolitical demands is leading to still greater revolutionizing of the movement for university reform and is facilitating the achievement of unity of the democratic forces of Latin America in the struggle for economic and social liberation.

[6]*Programmnye dokumenty kommunisticheskikh i rabochikh partii stran Ameriki*, pp. 29–30.
[7]*El Universal*, August 7, 1962.

III

THE FORCES OF REFORM

A. F. Shul'govskii's efforts in Item 10 to distinguish three clearly separated sectors of bourgeoisie in Latin America seem strained. He heaps special scorn on those Socialists who have asserted that no national bourgeoisie exists in Latin America and on the theorists of national capitalism. Shul'govskii clearly places little faith in the revolutionary potential of the national bourgeoisie, however, since he believes that the major efforts of that group are directed toward the defense of capitalism.

Shul'govskii also authored the second selection in this Section (Item 11), which analyzes the ideology of "national reformism." He reserves particularly harsh invective for Victor Raúl Haya de la Torre, Rómulo Betancourt, and José Figueres and asserts that the aim of national reformists is to "subordinate the national-liberation movement to their influence and to distort its true aims and purposes."

Finally, M.V. Danilevich in Item 12 examines the situation and revolutionary potential of the petty bourgeoisie, concluding that, while it "never plays and independent role," still the class has revolutionary potential and must be drawn over to the side of the working

10. The Proimperialist, Conciliatory, and National Bourgeoisies and Their Attitudes toward Economic Independence*

A. F. SHUL'GOVSKII

The bourgeoisie of the Latin American countries is characterized by an extremely complex differentiation, the presence of various groupings, and high mobility and variability. With all of this, however, three basic groups stand out most prominently, and their characteristics should be examined in detail.

In the first of these groups belong those circles of the bourgeoisie with strong proimperialist trends within their ranks. This group is characterized by the fact that it includes not only the direct agents of U.S. monopolies—consisting of various kinds of figureheads in foreign companies—and representatives of the biggest domestic commercial, financial, and industrial capital linked in some degree with foreign monopolies through participation in "joint companies" and various types of intermediary and other operations, but also their clientele: certain strata of the petty and middle bourgeoisies.

This group cannot, however, be called comprador, because the term, as the Latin American Marxists have repeatedly indicated, is much too nar-

row and specific to reflect fully the nature of the proimperialist bourgeoisie, at least of its strongest groupings. As a matter of fact, its nucleus consists of the old commercial and banking circles, which in the last few decades have substantially altered their activity and have been transformed from a commercial intermediary bourgeoisie into a bourgeoisie of an industrial type, linked with the domestic market and striving to control key positions in the country's economy. A growth in monopolistic tendencies has begun to appear.

Monopolistic groupings have already begun to emerge in Argentina, Brazil, Colombia, Mexico, Chile, and Uruguay. In Brazil, some of them—for example, the Matarazzo concern, the Votorantim and Jafet groups, and others—enjoy great influence. Forty-six percent of all capital belongs to 6,818 joint-stock companies and 66 firms,[1] whereas 2.5 percent of the total

* *Osvoboditel'noe dvizhenie v Latinskoi Amerike,* ed. S. S. Mikhailov (Moskva: Izdatel'stvo Nauka, 1964), pp. 98–121.
[1] Franclin de Oliveira, *Revolucāo e contrarevolucāo no Brasil* (Rio de Janeiro, 1961), p. 37.

recorded industrial enterprises in the country account for 41 percent of the value of production. The largest enterprises are increasing their production a great deal faster than the multitude of small enterprises. Thus, from 1947 to 1959, the value of production in enterprises with more than 500 workers increased almost eightfold; whereas, in small- and medium-scale enterprises, employing from 6 to 100 workers, it increased less than fourfold. In Colombia, a group of 411 men who own 217 million shares or approximately 56 percent of total capital invested, has been singled out among the large property owners. Three percent of the owners in the manufacturing industry and 7 percent of owners in commerce have concentrated in their hands 52 percent and 68 percent of the shares, respectively.[2]

In Chile, monopolistic trends are being manifested quite distinctly. There, 4.2 percent of all firms own 59.2 percent of the total capital. Intensive concentration is also taking place in the sphere of trade, in which 5 percent of all enterprises are carrying out more than 50 percent of all commercial operations. In the field of insurance, 62.8 percent of invested capital is controlled by four monopolisitc groups.[3] The merging of industrial and banking capital can be traced very easily in Chile. A group of 40 shareholders controls more than 50 percent of the total capital of the largest banks and enjoys the greater part of credits granted. More than 65 percent of all bank credits are controlled by 850 firms, less than 5 percent of the total number.[4] In addition to the North American monopolies, big monopolistic combines, such as the Alessandri, Bulnes, Edwards, de Castro, and other groups, are the chief exploiters of the Chilean people.[5]

The process of establishment of a financial oligarchy in Mexico is becoming ever more evident. The four largest private banks there control hundreds of financial, commercial, and industrial enterprises. Eighty-five different firms are controlled by the Banco de Comercio alone. The posts of director in many joint-stock companies are occupied by big bankers, such as Aníbal de Iturbide, Salvador Ugarte, Carlos Troalle, and others. Linked with foreign capital along many channels, this financial oligarchy has concentrated enormous wealth in its own hands and is brazenly robbing the toiling population.[6]

The growth of monopolisitic trends in the ranks of the domestic Latin American bourgeoisie intensifies its collaboration with foreign capital and its hostile attitude toward the forces of national liberation still further. At the same time, it must be noted that the dialectics of interrelations between foreign monopolistic capital and the powerful domestic bourgeoisie, as well as rapprochement between them, create objective prerequisites for contradictions to arise. They will undoubtedly expand as the economic positions of the domestic bourgeoisie become stronger and its "modernization" increases. This appraisal also applies fully to those circles of the proimperialist bourgeoisie—for example, the commercial intermediary bourgeoisie—that have, it would seem, nothing in common with foreign companies and every reason to be actually apprehensive of them. Thus, the critical pronouncements by representatives of these bourgeois circles with respect to

[2]Gilberto Vieira, *Organicemos la revolución colombiana* (Bogotá, 1961), p. 42.

[3]Ricardo Lagos Escobar, *La concentración del poder económico* (Santiago de Chile, 1961), pp. 166–167.

[4]See *XII S"ezd Kompartii Chili* (Moskva, 1963), pp. 39–40.

[5]*Principios*, 67:34–36 (1960).

[6]Adolfo López Romero, *Plan México* México, 1958), pp. 275–280.

the Alliance for Progress have been provoked by the unconcealed fear that the U.S. monopolies would use the Alliance to strengthen their own positions in Latin America still more.

These apprehensions are entirely natural, inasmuch as North American private capital investments in recent years have been pouring not only into extractive industries but also largely into the manufacturing industry, as well as into the financial and commercial spheres of the Latin American states. As a result, many traditional ties between the proimperialist bourgeoisies of these countries and the U.S. monopolies are undergoing considerable changes, some of them fading away altogether. In particular, the desire of these monopolies to gain control over distribution of their own products on the Latin American market makes them reject the services of certain groups of the commercial intermediary bourgeoisie as unnecessary. It is not at all surprising that under these conditions ardent supporters of foreign capital investments suddenly become "patriots" and declare that the Alliance for Progress is an insult to Latin American feelings and that it turns them into "international beggars."[7]

Undoubtedly, this is also a case of political blackmail, since the proimperialist bourgeoisie wishes to extract as many concessions and "guarantees" as possible from the American monopolies in return for its support of the Alliance for Progress. However, temporary dissensions arising between American monopolistic capital and the proimperialist bourgeoisie are of minor import. The most important characteristic of their interrelations is the close alliance and collaboration for the suppression of the revolutionary mass struggle. As the Latin American Communist parties emphasize, the domestic upper bourgeoisie of the monopolistic type and its imperialist allies are at present the chief enemies of the national-liberation movement. Not only the toiling masses, but also large segments of the petty and middle bourgeoisies, whose interests are being trampled underfoot by big capital, are concerned with the struggle against this oligarchy.

The question of the creation of a united antimonopolistic front is becoming ever more pressing, because the upper bourgeoisie is now bent on seizing power and is striving to impose its control on the governmental apparatus and the state sector of the economy. Precisely for this reason the monopolies, in contrast to their former position, now agree to state intervention in the economy but at the same time demand that private initiative determine the aims and extent of this coordination and that a barrier thus be erected to stop the advance of "dangerous" socialist trends. The powerful monopolistic bourgeoisies of Chile and, particularly, of Mexico are the closest to this goal.

Along this course, however, the monopolies enter into a contradiction with another capitalist group, which has been termed the "wealthy conciliatory bourgeoisie" by Latin American Marxist theoreticians in a number of their writings.[8] This group arose in the last few decades and, upon gaining strength in the postwar period, now occupies key positions in the governments of a number of countries. It is distinguished by the fact that it grew up and was strengthened with the help of the state sector, which transformed it —for example, in Mexico, Uruguay, Colombia, and, particularly, in Argentina, Brazil, Costa Rica, and certain other countries—into the basis of its

[7]*Excelsior*, August 15, 1962, p. 11.
[8]An especially comprehensive description of this bourgeois group is given in the recently published fundamental work of the Secretary of the Uruguayan Communist Party, Rodney Arismendi. Cf. R. Arismendi, *Los problemas de una revolución continental* (Montevideo, 1962).

own strength and power. It includes individuals from the ranks of the petty and middle bourgeoisies and from certain groups of the highest government bureaucracy, a sizable substratum of officials of various state-capitalist commercial, financial, and industrial enterprises and combines. This group also includes representatives of the wealthy private property owners, closely linked with the state sector via receipt of credits and licenses for forming enterprises.

In order to strengthen their influence, the representatives of this sector of the bourgeoisie surround the state sector with a "belt" of private enterprises allegedly complementing the production cycle and expanding the sphere of activity of the nationalized branches of the economy. In Mexico, for example, private petrochemical enterprises are grouped around the oil industry belonging to the state. That country serves as the most striking example of the wealthy Latin American bourgeoisie's use of the state sector as an effective tool for controlling the country's economic and political life.

The transformation of a part of the middle domestic bourgeoisie, resting on the state sector, into the wealthy grand bourgeoisie may also be traced very clearly in Mexico. This process was convincingly demonstrated by Encarnación Pérez, one of the leaders of the Mexican Communists, in his interesting article, "The Question of the Level of Economic Development of Contemporary Mexico." In his opinion, the rise of the wealthy conciliatory bourgeoisie became possible precisely as a consequence of the establishment of a strong state sector and the introduction of agrarian reform. These changes made it possible for quite large strata of medium-scale property owners to utilize the expanding domestic market; to receive subsidies, cheap fuel, and means of transportation from the state; and thus

to become the wealthy conciliatory bourgeoisie that "has benefited from imperialist credits, especially those coming from the United States."[9]

The strong positions that the wealthy conciliatory bourgeoisie holds in the government apparatus and the control it exercises over the state-capitalist enterprises have brought into its services numerous political figures, economists, sociologists, and other representatives of the intellectual elite. With their help, the ruling circles are trying to subject the popular masses to their influence also, by pretending to be bearers of progress and supporters of socioeconomic reforms.

The peculiar characteristics of the origin and development of this group of the ruling class predetermine its attitude toward foreign capital and the local proimperialist bourgeoisie and also predetermine the antagonisms that arise between them from time to time. Inasmuch as this group of the bourgeoisie is interested in accelerating the economic development of Latin American countries with the aid of so-called elements of planning and the coordinating role of the state, it insists on eliminating the price scissors between exported raw materials and imported mechanical equipment, which benefits the foreign monopolies. It frequently endeavors to make use of foreign loans for the purpose of concentrating the financial resources in its own hands, in the name of strengthening the state-capitalist sector, and thus to establish control over other bourgeois groups.[10] This control is exactly what the American monopolies do not wish. Since they do not wish to strengthen the positions of some possible competitors with their

[9]*Voz de México*, January 15, 1963.

[10]At the same time—for example, in Mexico—the proimperialist bourgeoisie has unleashed a fierce campaign against concentration of foreign loans in the hands of the state, declaring that it inhibits the expansion of "private initiative."

own money, they prefer to do their financing "from hand to hand," that is, bypassing state channels.

However, even these very pressing antagonisms do not stop the conciliatory bourgeoisie from actively advocating close collaboration with the ruling circles of imperialist powers and from setting out from the policy of foreign aid in their plans to industrialize Latin America. It is not by accident that the conciliatory bourgeoisie supports the Alliance for Progress, declaring that the economic development of the Latin American countries can be achieved only with its aid.

This interlacing of antagonisms and trends toward rapprochement is also characteristic of the relations between the groups of the domestic bourgeoisie —the proimperialist and conciliatory bourgeoisies.

As to their dissensions, obviously they are engendered above all by the competitive struggle. The proimperialist bourgeoisie is trying hard to dominate the state sector. But, since this control might lead to denationalization of many enterprises and might weaken the positions of the conciliatory bourgeoisie, the latter fights just as stubbornly in order not only to retain its own control over the state sector but also to control the supporters of "private initiative."

These dissensions are, however, devoid of sharp antagonisms. On the contrary, there is a rather obvious trend toward rapprochement between the two above-mentioned groups, on the basis of the "harmonious" coexistence of private and state interests. The conciliatory bourgeoisie, for instance, calls upon the representatives of proimperialist capital to make certain concessions for the sake of strengthening the positions of the entire capitalist class. The representatives of proimperialist capital strive in turn for compromise. This accounts, for example, for the proposal of the proimperialist bourgeois circles of Mexico toward the end of 1962—that private capital be allowed to take part in formulating the government's economic policy. They promised in return to be "more tolerant" of state intervention.[11]

Curiously, the Mexican government representatives did not reject the possibility of this kind of compromise, though they reaffirmed once again the coordinating role of the state in the economy. Taking all these trends into account, the Latin American Marxists especially stress that the line between the proimperialist and conciliatory bourgeoisies cannot be drawn too sharply. In this connection, the draft program of the Communist Party of Mexico states: "We distinguish between these two groups of the bourgeoisie essentially for tactical reasons, inasmuch as in the general scheme both groups oppose the radical reforms required for the progressive development of Mexico. The democratic revolution of national liberation will bring about the removal of both the proimperialist and the conciliatory bourgeoisies from power."[12]

Yet there is an intermediate stratum within the domestic bourgeoisie that occupies a special position in the socioeconomic structure of the Latin American countries and that, in some degree, fights for national interests. This largest group is customarily called just the national bourgeoisie. It includes petty and medium-scale merchants and industrialists—who own not less than from 80 percent to 90 percent of all enterprises—and certain groups of the rural bourgeoisie.

This group, which has a nucleus composed of industrial enterprise owners, increased especially intensively at certain periods between the two world wars, but chiefly during and after World War II, when a certain decrease in foreign competition had created more

[11]*Industria*, October 1962, p. 25.
[12]*Nueva Época*, 3:13 (1962).

Table 2. *Capital Investments and Manufacturing Income in Mexico*

Enterprises	Share of Yearly Income (percent)					
	Food	Textiles	Chemical	Metallurgy & Metal Processing	Shoes & Clothing	Other Branches
Small (with capital investments up to 300,000 pesos)	52.2	13.7	4.4	14.3	—	36.1
Medium (from 300,000 to 3 million pesos)	11.4	48.3	76.2	34.6	81.8	31.1
Large (over 3 million pesos)	36.4	38.0	19.4	51.1	18.2	32.8

favorable conditions for national industrial growth. Precisely at that time, numerous small- and medium-scale enterprises serving the domestic market and lacking traditional ties with foreign capital sprang up. For example, their number in Brazil increased from 13,565 in 1920 to 92,350 in 1950; 79.3 percent of these enterprises had no more than ten workers each.[13]

There also appeared a rather large number of medium-scale shops and factories[14] having more up-to-date equipment and using modern methods of production. They sprang up not only in the traditional branches of the manufacturing industry but also in such new branches as the chemical, metallurgical, and others. Their place and importance in the economy of the Latin American countries are shown in Table 2 by comparative data on capital investments and income of the manufacturing enterprises of Mexico.[15]

As the table shows, medium-scale enterprises occupy a highly important place not only in production of textiles, shoes, and clothing but also in the metallurgical, metal processing, and, particularly, the chemical industries. The high relative importance and modern nature of many of these enterprises make the owners of medium-scale enterprises the leading force of the national bourgeoisie in whose name they speak.

There are other factors, however, which adversely affect the position of the national bourgeoisie. Its attempts to strengthen its own influence encounter resistance on the part of the entire system of economic domination, which the proimperialist bourgeoisie has been erecting over many years in alliance with foreign capital and the great landowners. The monopolistic trends, which have increased in the last few years, and the aspiration of the domestic capitalist oligarchy for total domination of the domestic market restrict the national bourgeoisie's opportunities to develop still further.

As a rule, its combines belong to confederations controlled by the wealthy

[13] *O Observador Economico e Financiero*, December 1960, p. 29

[14] It has become customary in Latin American economic literature to regard enterprises as medium scale if they have between 50 to 100–150 workers each. Often the amount of capital invested and the costs of production are also taken as criteria. In Mexico, for instance, enterprises with investments from 300,000 to 3 million pesos are considered medium scale. At the same time, a great deal depends on the nature of production and the degree of mechanization. Therefore, it is not unusual for an enterprise to be listed as medium scale even though it is large, and vice versa.

[15] *La industria mediana y pequeña de México*, Banco de México (México, 1961), p. 47.

industrial, financial, and commercial bourgeoisies. In such a state of direct dependence upon the latter are such organizations of the national bourgeoisie as the Chamber of the Manufacturing Industry in Mexico, the Federation of Commercial and Industrial Chambers and Associations of Venezuela, the Association for Factory Development in Chile, and many others. Finally, the power of the wealthy conciliatory bourgeoisie places the national bourgeoisie in a subordinate position in a number of Latin American countries in which the ruling circles control the state sector and the system of financing. In this respect, Mexico serves as the most typical example.[16]

It should be emphasized that the national bourgeoisie also has not escaped dependence upon foreign capital. The fact that a significant part of Mexico's chemical industry is controlled in one way or another by North American monopolies is instructive in this respect. It is not by accident, therefore, that certain enterprise owners of that branch of industry either vacillate in their attitude toward the independent development of the national economy or openly support collaboration with foreign capital.

The precariousness of the national bourgeoisie's positions and its dependence on other, economically more powerful capitalist circles engender erroneous theories proclaiming the national bourgeoisie as virtually nonexistent. Utterances are heard to the effect that it is no longer possible to distinguish objectively between the various bourgeois strata of Latin America. In particular, certain functionaries of Latin American socialist parties declare that capitalism is a single whole and that there is no essential difference between the representatives of foreign and domestic capital.

Such views do not stand up under criticism, inasmuch as their adherents essentially confuse the concept of production relations, which are the same in any country under capitalism, with the character of interrelations between different bourgeois groupings under conditions of domination of economically weak countries by imperialist powers. Of course, the exploitation and private property basis of the national bourgeoisie links it by many threads with other capitalist groups—including foreign capital—and establishes its trends toward compromise and conciliation. However, this does not warrant speaking of the national bourgeoisie's disappearance.

Other arguments from supporters of the above theory are likewise unconvincing. For example, Vivian Trías, the leader of the Uruguayan Socialists—in referring to the fact that 74 percent of the country's capital is concentrated in the hands of the 3.6 percent of the industrial firms controlled by foreign capital and the domestic oligarchy—considers the bulk of enterprises, estimated at nearly 30,000, to be a sort of clientele of "the mighty of this world." He asserts on that basis that Uruguay does not have, so to speak, a national bourgeoisie "capable of resisting imperialism and latifundism."[17] But, as is generally known, concentration of capital does not signify by any means that the country lacks the economic foundations necessary for the existence of a national bourgeoisie. On the contrary, a profound differentiation between individual capitalist groups creates a basis for antagonisms between them.

Hence, the existence of the national bourgeoisie in Latin America is a fact. Moreover, facts bear out not only that it exists there, but also that it operates as a political force. The upsurge of the anti-imperialist liberation struggle has intensified the aspiration of the national bourgeoisie to gain control of the move-

[16]*Nueva Epoca*, 3:13 (1962).
[17]*El Sol*, June 22, 1962.

ment and to take advantage of it to resolve its own antagonisms with imperialism and its domestic allies.

Here we must point out another peculiarity of the Latin American national bourgeoisie. In the course of its somewhat lengthy history, it has not succeeded in actually forming a political party of its own in any country, primarily because it was not able to consolidate its own positions and demarcate itself politically from other bourgeois groups. An important role has also been played by tradition, according to which the Latin American bourgeois political parties have always comprised the most varied bourgeois groupings. The absence of bourgeois political parties is a weakness of the national bourgeoisie and impedes it in spreading its influence among the broad masses of the population. Nonetheless, the prolonged experience gained by the national bourgeoisie in the course of its political struggle has equipped it with certain methods for influencing the popular masses ideologically, methods it has employed most persistently, especially during recent years.

The national bourgeoisie's extensive propaganda of its own ideology is based on the desire to utilize the upsurge of the anti-imperialist liberation struggle in its own interests. The "national capitalism" theory has become the ideological weapon employed to this end. Its substance lies in its declaration that the principal contradiction at the present stage of Latin America's development is the one between the national bourgeoisie, on the one hand, and imperialism and latifundism, on the other. From time to time, more abstract concepts than these terms are counterposed, such as either "national industrial development" or "national industrialization," on the one hand, and "regressive forces" impeding the attainment of these aims, on the other.

In this manner, an attempt is being made to prove that the task consists of creating a progressive "national capitalism" in place of the old semifeudal society. Arguments used in defense of this theory by the influential Brazilian weekly, *O Semanario*, are typical. "Imperialism and latifundism," the weekly declares, "are the two most serious and most powerful barriers along the path of development of national capitalism. Our capitalist revolution, i.e., national industrialization, is being fully realized under the influence of these two negative factors."[18] Another article in the same weekly stated: "Brazilian capitalism has a clearly pronounced progressive character and, therefore, the people—the toiling masses—support it and protect it from the subversive activities of the imperialist forces and the internal forces that personify precapitalist relationships."[19]

Calling upon the popular masses to support "national capitalist development," the ideologists of the bourgeoisie declare that their aim is to build a capitalist society of a "special type" in Latin America without exploiters and exploited, without the sins of the "traditional" monopolistic capitalism of the highly developed industrial powers. They identify "national capitalism" with independent economic development and assert that it will ensure a sharp rise in public well-being and will abolish the abyss between the handful of rich and the bulk of the population. "The national industrialists," declares the prominent Venezuelan entrepreneur Alejandro Hernández, "insist that they be given credit and state aid, since they favor independent economic development—a source of jobs and wealth for everybody."[20]

The "theory of national capitalism" is inseparably linked with the ideology of nationalism. Essentially, they are two

[18]*O Semanario*, July 22, 1961.
[19]*Ibid.*, July 29, 1961.
[20]*El Nacional*, December 23, 1960.

sides of the same coin, since nationalism reflects the bourgeoisie's desire to
pass off its struggle and its interests as a
nationwide movement transcending
class barriers and its ideology as the
only acceptable system of views in the
dependent and economically underdeveloped countries of Latin America.

The link between the ideology of
bourgeois nationalism—a complex and
contradictory phenomenon—and the
immediate interests of the national bourgeoisie is, of course, neither direct nor
mechanical. We must keep in mind that
rather broad strata of the population are
under the influence of nationalism and
yet are essentially alien to the bourgeois
interests they reflect. This contradiction gives rise to a number of curious
phenomena and lends some originality
to the ideology of nationalism. Quite
often representatives of the nationalist
ideology even criticize the national
bourgeoisie and call on it to join the
liberation movement for the sake of its
own ends. Thus the Brazilian weekly *O
Semanario* has stated that the national
bourgeoisie must take an active part in
the struggle for implementation of "a
revolution of social reforms," lest it
otherwise "lose the only remaining
chance of influencing the fate of the
nation and be thrust away from leadership by other more radically minded
forces."[21]

Like the ideologists of the national
bourgeoisie, the theoreticians of nationalism envisage the future development of Latin America as the implementation of "national capitalism." At the
same time, as has already been pointed
out, an attempt is made to prove complete identity of the interests of the
national bourgeoisie with the hopes of
the other popular strata. In this manner,
according to the prominent Brazilian
sociologist Helio Jaguaribe, the ideals
of nationalism unite "the most dynamic
sector of the bourgeoisie" acting in

support of the "industrial revolution,"
on the one hand, and the proletariat,
whose "rate of consumption will increase as industrialization progresses,"
on the other. Furthermore, Jaguaribe
declares, the technical and administrative cadres adhere to the positions of
nationalism, as well as "the intelligentsia from the ranks of the middle class,"
all of whom are concerned with "the
process of economic development and
the internal and external consolidation
of the state."[22]

Aguinaldo Marques, another Brazilian public figure of nationalist inclination but one who takes a more democratic position, says: "Nationalism is a
complex of ideas and practical measures
aimed at gaining economic and political
independence in the struggle against
imperialist aggression and achieving
the country's moral, material, and cultural progress. Nationalism is the property not only of the Brazilian people in
their struggle for well-being and happiness, but also of the other peoples
struggling to achieve the same aims."[23]

Obviously, such talk is always merely
a propagandistic trick, aimed at convincing the masses that the "nationalistic
stage of the anti-imperialist movement
is indispensable. The idealization of
nationalism in one form or another is
especially dangerous for the revolutionary struggle, since the program advanced by the national bourgeoisie
generally coincides with the aims and
tasks of the struggling progressive
forces and therefore is in a favorable
position for dissemination among the
broad masses. Herein lies one of the
characteristic features of the national
bourgeoisie's policy, which strives to
seize leadership of the people's strug-

[21]*O Semanario*, May 24, 1962.
[22]Helio Jaguaribe, *O nacionalismo na atualidade brasileira* (Rio de Janeiro, 1958), p. 35.
[23]Aguinaldo N. Marques, *Fundamentos do
Nacionalismo* (São Paulo, 1960), p. 10.

gle under the banner of nationalism.

However, the dialectics of the development of the liberation movement and of the class struggle gradually relegate to secondary importance the contradictions between the national bourgeoisie, on the one hand, and imperialism and latifundism, on the other, as compared with the tasks and aims of the revolutionary forces of Latin American society. Whereas the national bourgeoisie is trying to restrict the aims of the liberation movement within the framework of the capitalist society, in one way or another the vanguard of the anti-imperialist front sets for itself broader goals that open up possibilities for a noncapitalist course of development.

The national bourgeoisie's desire to stop half-way greatly influences its ideology and policy and predetermines its relations with other social forces as well as its approach to the fundamental problems of the liberation movement.

In order to understand the nature of the contradictions between the national bourgeoisie and imperialism, one must take into account the fact that representatives of this bourgeois group point to changes occurring in the world and the struggle going on between the two systems for the purpose of corroborating their own thesis that economic independence can be achieved. Characteristic of the national bourgeoisie is its effort to resolve the contradictions with imperialism in its own favor by using the strength and power of the world socialist system: its policy of disinterested aid and mutually beneficial collaboration with underdeveloped countries. It sees favorable opportunities for achieving these aims in the elimination of a united world capitalist system and the rise of new types of international economic ties.

We can say without exaggeration that the ideologists of the national bourgeoisie interpret the basic content of the present epoch in their own way. Besides the struggle between two social systems, they declare, a struggle is being waged for economic liberation and consolidation of independence by the peoples of the dependent countries, under the banner of nationalism. A thesis has also been advanced to the effect that, as a result of the liberation movement, the peoples of the underdeveloped and dependent countries will build their own special social order, different from the social order existing in either the socialist or the capitalist countries.

Such are the general tenets of the theory, but they fall far short of explaining its substance. They do not answer such questions as the manner in which the contradictions between imperialism and the dependent countries will be resolved, or whether the national bourgeoisie is capable of combining its allegiance to capitalism with a struggle against the latter's highest and ultimate stage—imperialism—or, finally, which role the world socialist system is destined to play in this contest.

Let us examine these questions more closely.

As a rule, representatives of the national bourgeoisie reason that, while the rise of the socialist world has substantially altered relations between highly developed capitalist countries and economically backward, dependent ones, new circumstances make it immeasurably easier for dependent countries to find more effective ways of achieving liberation. To this deduction is linked a demand that is common to the national bourgeoisie of all Latin American countries—that fatalistic allegiance to "capitalist metropolis" in the field of commercial ties be renounced and that new markets be sought.

In this connection, the point of view of Masa Zavala, a well-known Venezuelan economist, is of interest. In criticizing the theory of geographic and economic fatalism, he declares: "Venezuela's commercial ties are not confined to the narrow limits that North American imperialist geopolitics is trying to impose upon the country. There is a profound contradiction in the imperialist system, which we must take advantage of in the interests of our economic development." Zavala speaks in support of representatives of the private sector, who aspire to seize "leadership at this moment of the progressive national bourgeoisie's advance to forward positions and are struggling to end fear, prejudices, and a feeling of submission, which strongly affect the character of our economic relations with the outside world."[24]

No less typical are the arguments of Sergio Magalhães, the prominent figure of the Brazilian nationalist movement. In *Problems of Economic Development*, he writes that the presence of socialist countries in Eastern Europe and Asia has opened tremendous prospects for economic collaboration to the underdeveloped countries and that, therefore, "any Brazilian policy of industrialization must undoubtedly proceed from an appraisal of the changes that have occurred in international relations."[25] In the development of manifold relations with socialist countries, representatives of the national bourgeoisie perceive, not without good reason, an opportunity to eliminate the old forms of servile dependence on imperialist powers and to establish relations based on equal rights with all the countries of the world. While pointing out that no political considerations can justify opposition to the establishment of economic ties with socialist countries, the nationally oriented Chilean journal, *Panorama Económico*, declares that only through development of a broadly based trade can the foundations for genuine independence be laid.[26]

At the same time, the ideologists of "national capitalism" urge the bourgeoisie of the industrial powers to take into account the fact that two social systems are linked in struggle and to reconstruct the entire policy in relation to "the periphery of capitalism" in accordance with this factor. This demand clearly corroborates the fact that the representatives of the national bourgeoisie regard imperialism as a special sort of policy which can be replaced by a more effective policy that sets out from the interests of defense of capitalism on a world-wide scale. This point of view also figures invariably into the polemics of the ideologists of the national bourgeoisie with the spokesmen for the interests of foreign monopolies. Whereas the latter speak of the beneficial effect of "the export of capitalism" on underdeveloped states, their nationalistic opponents call on the industrial capitalist powers to renounce it because it leads to retention of the country's backward structure, and, instead, to give utmost support to the development of national capitalism in order to strengthen the positions of the entire capitalist system.

In other words, everything is staked on achieving the coexistence of national capitalism with monopolistic capital within the framework of the world capitalist system, with the help of imperialism, and on reconciling independent economic development with an accelerating integration process in a world of capitalism. Thus, José Domingo Lavín, a prominent ideologist of the Mexican national bourgeoisie, has urged the U.S. monopolies to realize that their policy in Mexico contradicts their own interests, since it leads to the elimination of the national capitalists

[24]*El Nacional*, May 10, 1959.
[24]Sergio Magalhães, *Problemas do desenvolvimento econômico* (Rio de Janeiro, 1960), p. 25.
[26]*Panorama Económico*, September 1961, p.24.

and by so doing undermines the positions of capitalism on a world-wide scale. Furthermore, Lavín makes a highly typical remark to the effect that certain "farsighted representatives of American business circles" are, apparently, beginning to understand this situation.[27]

This peculiar position of the national bourgeoisie in relation to imperialism predetermines its support of the trend in the policy of U.S. monopolistic circles that allegedly has the goal of laying the foundations for new mutual relations with Latin America. Opportunity for collaboration with North American capitalism is perceived, for example, in the Alliance for Progress, even though a number of serious objections are voiced against it. Thus, the influential Venezuelan journal, *Mundo Económico*, reflecting the interests of the nationalistically minded bourgeoisie, expresses approval of the program of the Alliance for Progress, which, as it says, makes it possible for Latin America "to remain faithful to the cause of the Western world." Then there follows a highly significant admission that the national bourgeoisie supports this program out of concern not only for the future development of Latin America but also for "the stability of the capitalist system and its political form—representative democracy."[28]

The Chilean journal *Panorama Económico* has also supported the fundamental aims and tasks of the Alliance for Progress,[29] as have the representatives of the national bourgeoisie of Mexico and of other countries, who have declared that their aspirations coincide with the basic principles of the "new" Latin American policy of the United States.[30]

Since the Alliance orients itself, as mentioned earlier, primarily toward collaboration with the wealthy conciliatory bourgeoisie, the national bourgeoisie, fearful of being reduced to the status of a poor relative—a hanger-on— is particularly stubborn in insisting that aid under this program reach it directly without intermediaries. Only in that case, it declares, can the preservation of the "economic independence" of the Latin American countries be guaranteed. Demands of this type were expressed particularly in late 1961 by the Venezuelan bourgeoisie, united in an Association in Defense of Venezuela, in a communication to the U.S. government. In this document, praise for the Alliance for Progress alternates with persistent requests for more "reliable guarantees" of the national bourgeoisie's participation in the aid program.[31]

We are confronted here with a classic example of the duplicity *sui generis* of the national bourgeoisie. The long and quite deplorable experience of its attempts at collaboration with monopolistic capital has made the national bourgeoisie react with distrust to all advances by North American ruling circles. At the same time, however, the national bourgeoisie has not renounced all hopes of extracting concessions from imperialism and of compelling it to recognize the "peaceful coexistence" of national capital with foreign monopolies. It must be emphasized that trends of this kind have gained strength in connection with the socialist revolution in Cuba and the great changes in the disposition of the class forces of the antiimperialist liberation movement.

Yet whatever the future relations between U.S. monopolies and the Latin American national bourgeoisie, it is already obvious that the latter will remain a highly reliable ally of the former in implementing the program of the Alliance for Progress. This program

[27]José Domingo Lavín, *Las inversiones extranjeras en México* (México, 1954), p. 5.
[28]*Mundo Económico*, July–August 1961, pp. 4–5.
[29]*Panorama Económico*, August 1961, p. 209.
[30]*Política*, September 16, 1961.
[31]*El Nacional*, December 16, 1961.

is not only incapable of wiping out the contradictions between them but objectively—that is, independent of any subjective inclinations on the part of any representatives of the national bourgeoisie—it gives rise to new, more acute contradictions.

The fact is that the industrial development of the Latin American republics and the intensification of the struggle for economic liberation by the patriotic forces are compelling U.S. monopolistic capital to pursue a policy directed toward disruption of the economies of these countries through seizure of dominant positions in key industries. Characteristically, such intrusion can be observed even in the existing branches. It is accompanied by dislodgment of the national bourgeoisie, which confronts a dilemma in this connection—whether it should give up the struggle and accept crumbs off the table of foreign capital or collapse under the blows of competition.

Having chosen the lesser of the two evils, certain circles of the national bourgeoisie are becoming the clientele of foreign capital. This fact is borne out by numerous splits within their complexes, by sudden changes in orientation in the case of some of them who have changed from ardent adversaries of imperialism into protagonists of collaboration with it. Typical in this respect is the situation in the Mexican Chamber of the Manufacturing Industry, from which certain groups of entrepreneurs have already withdrawn and have linked their fate with American capital—for example, those in the chemical industry.

However, this trend is, nonetheless, not typical of the position taken by most of the national bourgeoisie, which understands the danger that threatens it in "mixed" companies and various "systems of participation" and sharply criticizes the "new" forms of foreign penetration.

Manuel Hernán Parrá, one of Mexico's outstanding economists, analyzes the mechanics of mixed enterprises most convincingly. He is opposed to any type of joint participation of foreign and domestic capital, even if the latter holds an equal or greater number of shares. According to Parrá, mixed enterprises are the most dangerous form of penetration of foreign capital, since they are veiled and particularly "subtle" and therefore less controllable. At first the large foreign corporations confine themselves to buying, let us say, 49 to 50 percent of the shares in small enterprises, leaving the management positions to the Mexicans. Soon the newly formed companies begin to take over the domestic market by dislodging and swallowing up the domestic enterprise owners with interests in the same branches of the economy. In time, the activity of the mixed companies expands and capital requirements grow. Then the Mexican enterprise owner, lacking the means for further investments, is compelled to issue new shares. But since he is not in a position to acquire them, his "share in the company comes to not more than 1 percent" very soon. Hence, "whatever the form of 'mixed' enterprises, the result is the same—total destruction of the national bourgeoisie's independence."[32]

Sergio Magalhães, who was mentioned above, speaks just as positively on this matter. "It is a question," he writes, "of implementing a policy that would lead to replacement of the national bourgeoisie by a corporation of managers, consisting either of Americans or individuals of some other nationality." This, the author continues, will in turn inevitably entail the loss of influence by "the national groups" over the state apparatus and the strengthening of the positions of "American man-

[32]*Problemas agrícolas e industriales de México,* 1–2:94 (1957).

agers in determining national policy."[33]

The problem of mixed enterprises is only one aspect of the antagonisms between the national bourgeoisie and the monopolies in defining the role of foreign capital in the economic development of the Latin American countries. It manifests itself with particular sharpness in the theory of the inevitability of the stage of Latin American dependence on foreign capital. The authors of this thesis, U.S. monopolists, declare the struggle for economic liberation to be "nationalist extremism" and call it unjustified, because in the end the Latin American countries, they say, will automatically gain their "economic autonomy."

This theory, calculated to gild the shackles in which the imperialist monopolies wish to confine the countries of Latin America, is receiving a quite unanimous rejection from the national bourgeoisie, the nationalistic circles. The well-known Brazilian nationalist, Oswaldo Costa, has called it "a great lie circulated among the people by the economists of Standard Oil," adding that the development of the country is determined not by foreign capital, as has also been proven by the experience of the United States, but by national accumulations, an independent economic structure.[34] Incidentally, the representatives of the national bourgeoisie of Brazil draw a rather pointed contrast between the independent development of a country and "the Canadian path" of industrialization, as they have termed foreign economic domination and "association" of domestic capital with North American monopolies.[35]

As we can see, protection from foreign competition is one of the basic demands of the national bourgeoisie. In struggling to achieve it, the national bourgeoisie appeals to the popular masses, mounting an extensive propaganda campaign under the slogan "Use only prod-

ucts of domestic industry." The Venezuelan bourgeoisie, for instance, has been quite active, having set up an Association in Defense of Venezuela.[36] The national bourgeoisie obviously is objectively interested in expanding the domestic market and increasing the purchasing power of the population. But since it is compelled at the same time to heighten the exploitation of the workers in order to withstand foreign competition, it attempts to solve this contradiction by impressing on the popular masses the need for sacrifice for the sake of the country's economic progress.[37]

These appeals, however, do not lessen the proletariat's struggle for its own class interests. It is not an accident that all attempts at establishing "social peace" end in failure and that the objective development of the class struggle invariably makes headway. To a considerable extent this situation can be explained by the fact that the national bourgeoisie lacks a clear perspective of the battle with imperialism, that it substitutes efforts toward coexistence with foreign capital for a genuine and radical solution of the problem. Essentially, it is prepared to give equal rights to foreign capital and endeavors merely to equalize opportunities and to deprive it of the privileges that place domestic entrepreneurs in a subordinate position. At the base of the national bourgeoisie's entire policy regarding imperialism in the international arena as well as inside the country lies not an effective struggle against plunder and predominance by foreign monopolistic capital but a

[33]Sergio Magalhães, *Problemas do desenvolvimento económico*, pp. 15–16.

[34]*Brasilieros contra o Brazil. Antologia nacionalista* (São Paulo, 1960), pp. 224, 225–229.

[35]Sergio Magalhães, *Problemas do desenvolvimento económico*, p. 5.

[36]*El Nacional*, December 23, 1960.

[37]Aguinaldo N. Marques, *Fundamentos de Nacionalismo*, pp. 123–124.

search for compromise and the creation of conditions for "honest" competition. Thus, private property serves as a stumbling block that makes the struggle of the national bourgeoisie against imperialism half-hearted and inconsistent.

This shortcoming is no less pronounced in agrarian reforms, which the national bourgeoisie has tried or is trying to put into effect. It should be noted that the national bourgeoisie goes farther in this direction than the wealthy conciliatory bourgeoisie and much farther than the proimperialist circles, which at best agree to the settlement of idle land. As for the national bourgeoisie, it advances the "social function of property" theory, according to which expropriation of surplus land may be carried out in the interests of society, under the condition of compulsory payment of compensation.

However, the history of agrarian reforms carried out under the leadership of the national and petty bourgeoisies is limited to two examples only: rather profound agrarian reforms in the 1930's in Mexico, which undermined the positions of the semifeudal latifundists, and similar but unsuccessful attempts in Guatemala at the beginning of the 1950's.[38]

Incidentally, the agrarian question is far from being solved even in Mexico. Right now there is a critical situation in the rural economy of that country, one that the patriotic forces have labeled "agrarian counterrevolution."[39] The status of the bulk of the peasantry is deteriorating ever more, and, at the same time, a rapid concentration of landed property is taking place. The predatory agrarian bourgeoisie, which has seized vast areas of the best land, has come to replace the latifundist class. Calls for the development of "private initiative" in the rural economy through expansion of property owned by the most "enterprising" peasants are becoming ever more persistent. The rest of the peasants are destined to fill the ranks of agricultural workers on large capitalist farms.[40] The situation of the peasants is so grave that even Mexico's national bourgeoisie, driven out of power at the beginning of the 1940's, is now advocating renewal of the agrarian reform.[41]

All these factors attest to the fact that in Mexico, as in the other Latin American countries, the only way to resolve the contradictions racking the rural economy lies in a noncapitalist solution of the agrarian question. As for bourgeois reforms, even the most radical ones lead only to a partial allotment of land to the peasants and, in doing so, facilitate the rebirth of big private landholdings and consequently a new offensive against the interests of the peasant masses.

The national bourgeoisie not only is incapable of bringing forth any positive program of agrarian reforms, but also opposes progressive ideas in that regard ever more stubbornly. The general upsurge of the revolutionary movement in Latin America and the growing influence of socialist ideology and of the noncapitalist path of development intensify the conservative mood of the national bourgeoisie and its desire to solve the agrarian question by means of "moderate" reforms. Objectively, this means that the national bourgeoisie, fearing revolutionary "surprises," consents to economic development that would ensure its subordination to imperialism and the wealthy domestic bourgeoisie.

Consequently, the theory and prac-

[38]In Guatemala, the implementation of the agrarian reform was discontinued as a result of the overthrow of the Árbenz government.

[39]Cf., for example, Jesús Silva Herzog, El agrarismo mexicano y la reforma agraria. Exposición y crítica (México, 1959).

[40]Ramón Fernández y Fernández, Ricardo Acosta, Política agrícola (México–Buenos Aires, 1961).

[41]Política, September 1, 1962.

tice of national capitalism are displaying increasing vulnerability in the face
of the most vital problems of Latin
American reality.

11. Imperialism and the Ideology of National
Reformism in Latin America*

A. F. SHUL'GOVSKII

The upsurge of the national-liberation movement in Latin America is bringing about an intensification of the ideological struggle and a clash between different theories and conceptions regarding the paths of development to be followed by the Latin American countries.

Seeking to preserve their economic and political positions in this area, American monopolistic circles recently have sharply accelerated their campaign against the revolutionary movement of national liberation. Whereas, formerly, principal reliance was placed on the practice of implanting dictatorial regimes and providing them with every measure of support, this situation has been changed by the overthrow of dictatorships in a number of countries and by the victory of the Cuban Revolution. Now attempts are being made to apply other, more subtle methods. In particular, the American ruling circles are making wide use of economic and political means in order to achieve their aims, striving to convince the Latin American peoples of the earnest desire on the part of the United States to facili-

tate the development of "democracy" in Latin America and to contribute to its economic progress.

American propaganda has recently been giving wide publicity to the Kennedy administration's "new program" with respect to Latin America. This program was spelled out in a message from the President of the United States to the Congress on March 14, 1961,[1] bearing the resounding title "Alliance for Progress." Although it confirms the necessity of a radical change in the United States' approach to Latin America, it is directed essentially toward isolating revolutionary Cuba from the other Latin American countries and counterposing "evolutionary," "democratic" reforms to those revolutionary Cuban methods of the national-liberation struggle that are increasingly winning the hearts of the masses in Latin America. In brief, screened behind the camouflage of

*"Imperializm i ideologiia natsional-reformizma v Latinskoi Amerike," *Mirovaia ekonomika i mezhdunarodnye otnosheniia*, 8:45–59 (1961).
[1]*New York Times*, March 15, 1961.

these new words is the far-from-new intent of U.S. monopolistic circles to prevent the independent development of Latin America by all possible means.

It is therefore no accident that American imperialism is seeking and finding a base of support for itself among the national reformist circles of certain Latin American countries, encouraging in every way their attacks upon the communist movement and upon Marxist-Leninist theory.

The viewpoints of so-called national reformism are held by quite influential groups within a number of political parties in Latin America; among these are the People's (Aprista) Party in Peru, Democratic Action in Venezuela, the National Revolutionary Movement in Bolivia, National Liberation in Costa Rica, the Febrerista Party in Paraguay, the Guatemalan Revolutionary Party, the People's Democratic Party in Puerto Rico, and several others.[2]

The national reformists uphold the theory that the role of American monopolistic capital is a "positive" one for their countries and that there are no "fundamental" contradictions between the national-liberation movement and imperialism. At the same time, they not infrequently appear attired in the garb of "revolutionaries," arming themselves with liberation slogans that are popular among the masses of the people —but emasculating their revolutionary, anti-imperialist content.

The social base of national reformism is composed principally of certain petty bourgeois elements and of those representatives of the middle strata of the population who have been subject in one degree or another to the influence of American monopolistic capital. It should be noted that this base is extremely unstable and is becoming smaller and smaller with each passing year, due to the steady growth of revolutionary sentiments among the middle strata of the population. It is already

beyond question that Latin America is undergoing an acute process of radicalization of its urban petty bourgeoisie, students, and intelligentsia, and that they feel increasingly drawn toward collaboration with the working class. This trend toward a change in basic attitudes is creating new potential opportunities for the further advancement of the anti-imperialist revolution in Latin America. This process has been affected tremendously by the triumphant experience of the Cuban Revolution, which for the first time in the Western Hemisphere provided a practical example of how to put a complete end to dependence on American monopolies. The national reformists are able to derive support only from an inconsistent upper portion of the middle strata, those who are inclined toward compromise and conciliation with reaction and imperialism.

As early as the 1920's, when the danger that reformism posed for the liberation movement was just becoming apparent, the Latin American Marxists stressed the necessity of determining the social causes of the rise of reformism, of exposing its roots and showing the role of imperialism in the spread of reformist views. The founder of the Communist Party of Peru, José Carlos Mariátegui, gave a vivid description of the relationships of certain petty bourgeois circles in Latin America to American capital—a description that even now retains its essential significance. He observed, in particular, with respect

[2]This article examines only national reformism —the specific manifestation of petty-bourgeois reformism under Latin American conditions. With respect to the ideology of the Socialist parties of Latin America (they are most influential in Chile, Argentina, and Uruguay), reformism of the European Social-Democratic variety did not spread greatly in their ranks, because of a number of historical reasons. The leftist forces in the socialist parties are now coming out ever more resolutely against American imperialism and for solidarity with the Cuban Revolution.

to the economically backward countries of Latin America, that:

The establishment of big enterprises, despite the fact that they engage in the monstrous exploitation of their local salaried personnel, nevertheless always entails an increase in remuneration for this group and is therefore looked upon with favor by the members of the middle class. American enterprises provide higher salaries, opportunities for advancement, and freedom from the scurry after jobs within the government apparatus, where prospects open only to the artful. This factor acts as a decisive force upon the mind of the petty bourgeois who is seeking some position or is already occupying one.[3]

Another Latin American Marxist, Julio Antonio Mella, the founder of the Cuban Communist Party, noted in his characterization of the social roots of reformism that one of the determining causes in the appearance of this phenomenon was the effort of the petty bourgeois elements to "earn their living in a bourgeois society."[4] In a draft outline of political thesis published by the Central Committee of the Venzuelan Communist Party on the occasion of its Third Party Congress, in late 1960, special reference was made to the social base of national reformism: "Because of their economic position, some of the upper strata of the petty bourgeoisie are inclined to make a deal with the bourgeoisie and to support its compromise with imperialism."[5]

The recent surge of activity on the part of the Latin American reformists is due in large part to their desire to "coexist" with the upper, domestic, conciliatory bourgeoisie and oligarchy and to share state power with them. Reformist elements participating to some degree in the control of a state—in Venezuela, for example—"forget" about their clamorous declarations and act like fervent defenders of so-called representative democracy, which in reality

is nothing more than a disguised form of the rule of the privileged classes and imperialism. Thus, the national reformist leadership is merging more and more closely with the upper, conciliatory bourgeoisie and objectively expresses and defends the interests of the latter.

Typically, a number of the present leaders of reformism underwent training in various kinds of international economic and social organizations under the influence of the United States. Bourgeois theories about "global integration," variants of technocratic concepts, theories with respect to "interdependence"—these exerted a great influence upon the prominent figures of Latin American national reformism. Their "concepts" represent an eclectic mélange of diverse bourgeois idealistic theories, into which certain falsified Marxist theses torn speciously out of their general context have been interwoven. Speaking of the struggle against the reformists, Julio Antonio Mella emphasized, "We fight against them because their views contradict American reality, are without foundation, are reactionary, and are utopian."[6]

The national reformist concepts are based on the premise that imperialism fulfills a "special" role in Latin America. One of the most pretentious ideologists of national reformism, Haya de la Torre, the leader of the Peruvian Aprista Party, attempts to play the part of an iconoclast demolishing the teachings of Marxism-Leninism concerning imperialism. He upholds the relativistic point of view in his assertion that, whereas in the most advanced capitalist countries imperialism represents the

[3]*El movimiento revolucionario latinoamericano* (Buenos Aires, 1929), p. 151.
[4]*Amauta*, June–July 1930, p. 48.
[5]*Tribuna Popular* (Venezuela), November 4, 1960.
[6]*Amauta*, August–September 1930, p. 26.

highest and final stage of capitalism, in the economically underdeveloped countries of Latin America, on the other hand, "imperialism is the first or lowest stage of capitalism."[7] He substantiates this by saying that the penetration of imperialism into Latin America "stimulates economic development." In consequence, imperialism is supposed to be fulfilling the same role in these countries that European capitalism performed during the period of the demise of feudalism and the industrial development of the European nations.[8]

Claiming, as it were, sociological substantiation for his "discovery," Haya de la Torre proposes an idealistic, relativistic theory of historical "time and space," artificially dividing the history of human society into isolated zones and regions, each governed, supposedly, by its own unique laws of development.[9] To formulate this image, Haya de la Torre emasculates its socioeconomic content from the concept of imperialism. Imperialism, he affirms, signifies the inevitable, inexorable expansion of the industrially more advanced nations into those regions and countries that are economically underdeveloped. In carrying out this incursion, imperialism creates the most technically advanced sector of the economy and helps eliminate backward forms of production. The conclusion follows that imperialism, apparently, plays a "progressive" role in Latin America and represents an absolutely indispensable stage in the development of the Latin American countries.[10] The whole course of arguments employed by the ideologist of Aprismo is designed to prove that, in point of fact, there are no forces in Latin America capable of transforming the backward, semifeudal socioeconomic structure without the "revolutionizing" assistance of American capital.

The attempt on the part of Haya de la Torre and the other theoreticians of national reformism to prove the inap-plicability to Latin America of the Leninist theory of imperialism is an attempt utilizing worthless means, a sophistic misrepresentation of the objective processes of the development of the Latin American countries. It is certainly true that the penetration of monopolistic capital into the Latin American states brings with it a definite degree of development of capitalistic relationships, some industrial growth, and a rise in employment in certain branches of the economy. But the crux of the matter is the scale on which foreign capitalists are pursuing this activity and, above all, their purpose in doing it.

Let us take as an example the Venezuelan oil industry, dominated by foreign monopolies. There is no denying that its development has definitely contributed to breaking up the old, semifeudal relationships existing in the country. But this "progressive" role of the oil industry—the disruption of semifeudal relationships—manifests itself only to the extent and on the scale considered advantageous and necessary by the imperialist companies for in-

[7]Haya de la Torre, *Treinta años de aprismo* (México–Buenos Aires, 1956), pp. 145–146.

[8]*Ibid.*, p. 151.

[9]A detailed analysis of this theory is outside the scope of this article. It represents an eclectic mishmash of the views of Spengler, Toynbee, certain elements of Hegelism, and a mechanical transference of Einstein's theory of relativity to social phenomena. Let us note in passing that even many of the people who share Haya de la Torre's "theory" with respect to imperialism regard his "philosophical" theory skeptically. The "philosophy" of the Aprista leader was subjected to annihilating Marxist criticism in a book by the leader of the Uruguayan Communist Party, Rodney Arismendi: *La filosofía del marxismo y el señor Haya de la Torre. Sobre una gran mistificación teórica* (Buenos Aires, 1946). In an article entitled "Haya de la Torre—a Secret Enemy of Revolution," the Cuban newspaper *Noticias de Hoy* wrote on February 28, 1961, that the Aprista leader is an old enemy of the Latin American revolutionary movement and that the American imperialists are using him in their anti-Cuban campaign at the present time.

[10]Haya de la Torre, *Treinta años de aprismo*, pp. 125, 143–144*ff.*

creasing the output of petroleum, for the rapacious exploitation of the country's natural resources, because oil monopolies get along "peacefully" with the landowner latifundists, from whom they lease a large amount of land. Thus, the oil sector in Venezuela's economy has not only failed to effect the abolition of the old relationships but has actually served to "perpetuate" the rotten conditions of the nation's backward economic structure.

During the postwar period, foreign monopolies stepped up their penetration of the manufacturing industry in Latin America, establishing branch operations in the different countries. At the same time, they did not fail to strengthen their positions in extractive industry—their traditional sphere of capital investment.

As a rule the foreign enterprises are supplied with modern equipment and possess a substantial store of productive capacity. According to the latest available data, the output of American enterprises constituted 10 percent of the total combined gross national product of the Latin American countries.[11] A considerable portion of this production is accounted for by American firms engaged in extractive operations and is exported from Latin America. In fact, American enterprises account for about one-third of all Latin American exports.[12] By far the major share of production in the manufacturing industry remains in Latin America, but this is in no way a "blessing" for it. The increased tendency on the part of monopolistic capital to set up its own enterprises in Latin America is due primarily to the fact that the U.S. monopolies are anxious to circumvent the customs barriers established in some Latin American countries, to further consolidate their positions in Latin American markets, and to camouflage their competition with domestic industry.

The American magazine Survey of

Current Business wrote that U.S. companies engaged in manufacturing are most active in the economically advanced Latin American nations—Argentina, Brazil, Mexico—allegedly to satisfy the demand of "growing domestic markets."[13] Concealed behind these seemingly innocent words is the unattractive picture of relentless competition by the American monopolies, who are undermining the domestic manufacturing industry—which, given favorable conditions, could amply supply the domestic market with its own production.

The ideologists of American monopolistic capital and the national reformists assert that U.S. enterprises comprise an integral part of the economic structure of the Latin American countries and that, allegedly, existing distinctions between domestic and foreign enterprises are being obliterated: it's all the same to the Latin Americans, they say, as long as there's work to be had. The imperialists and national reformists also like to allude to the fact that the establishment of American enterprises helps promote the introduction of modern technology and of the latest production methods into the Latin American countries. In actual practice, however, these foreign enterprises hinder the development of productive forces in Latin America. This situation must inevitably result in further aggravation of the contradictions between the national interests of the peoples of Latin America and the imperialistic plans of the foreign monopolies. A visible manifestation of these contradictions is the increased momentum of the struggle of the Latin American countries for economic independence.

As a counterpoise to the struggle for economic liberation, which they reject

[11]Survey of Current Business, September 1960, p. 22.
[12]Ibid.
[13]Ibid., January 1957, p. 8.

as supposedly incompatible with "Latin American reality," the national reformists advance a thesis of "mutuality of interests" between the United States and Latin America. While, according to their scheme, Latin America's own interests are served by the activity of North American capital, they maintain that Latin America is also vitally needed by the United States as a source of raw materials. From this argument follows the conclusion that, in order to supply the needs of its "northern neighbor," Latin America's task is to develop in every way possible the "traditional" branches of its economy by concentrating on "industrialization" of these particular sectors.[14]

Exposing reformist contortions of this kind, Rodney Arismendi writes: "This constitutes the essence of Pan Americanism and represents one of the manifestations of global capitalist reality in the era of imperialism. The same ideas are championed by Morgan and Rockefeller but from a different standpoint. To be sure, their presentation is less muddled than that of Haya de la Torre, who talks about 'democratic Inter-Americanism without empires'— but they endow it nevertheless with the same practical meaning."[15]

So obvious is the evidence of the pernicious effect of American monopolies on the Latin American economy and so numerous are the instances of open intervention by U.S. ruling circles in the internal affairs of the Latin American countries that the national reformists are unable to pass over this question in silence. They advance the thesis that imperialism possesses a dual nature. From one standpoint, declares Haya de la Torre, imperialism is progressive, while from another standpoint it represents a menace. But this threat, according to him, arises only in the event that economic imperialism is joined to political imperialism. Haya de la Torre concludes that one must indeed

fight against political imperialism, while making a distinction between it and economic imperialism—the latter, if an expansionist policy is eschewed, can form the basis for collaboration between the United States and Latin America. He has given currency to the following intricate formula: "democratic Inter-Americanism without imperialism."

The national reformists are prepared to acknowledge the necessity of the anti-imperialist struggle, but the anti-imperialism they advocate is of a different type—"constructive" in nature, they say, directed only against political imperialism and designed not to "split" Latin America from the United States, but to "unite" them.[16] The reformists are vigorously promoting the idea of "interdependence" precisely to add substance to these "theoretical" formulations, supplementing it with geopolitical arguments.[17]

One of the most active figures of Latin American reformism, Luis Muñoz Marín, leader of the Popular Democratic Party of Puerto Rico, expressed his views in an article appearing in the journal *Combate* (published in Costa Rica under the editorial direction of Haya de la Torre, Betancourt, and Figueres). He states that the countries of the Western Hemisphere have become so "interdependent" that the underdeveloped nations of Latin America, if they are to progress economically,

[14]Haya de la Torre, *Treinta años de aprismo*, pp. 161–162.
[15]*Problemy mira i sotsializma*, 6:34 (1959).
[16]Haya de la Torre, *Treinta años de aprismo*, pp. 163, 190, 191.
[17]The advancement of the theory of "interdependence" is generally characteristic of bourgeois-reformist conceptions under contemporary conditions. The peculiarity of Latin American national-reformism is that it makes extensive use of geopolitics, with the help of which it attempts to justify its thesis about the "impossibility" under Latin American conditions of such a national-liberation struggle as the peoples of the colonial and dependent countries all over the world are conducting.

must become closely integrated with the United States and must refrain from "antiquated" notions of national sovereignty.[18] An essentially analogous point of view is held by the leader of the Venezuelan reformists, Betancourt, who asserts that "troubled times" are ahead for the Latin American countries if they base their policies on the principle of absolute sovereignty.

The national reformists promise the peoples of Latin America the glowing prospect of the disappearance of imperialism, an end to conflicts of interest, and "harmonious" collaboration with U.S. monopolistic capital. Similar views were subjected to scathing criticism during the First World War by V. I. Lenin, who demonstrated the reactionary nature of Kautsky's ultraimperialist theory. In exposing Kautsky's theoretical "revelations," which separated imperialist policy from its economic basis, Lenin characterized the theory of ultraimperialism thus: "Instead of an exposure of the deep-seated nature of the most basic conflicts inherent in the latest stage of capitalism, what we have here, in effect, is an obscuring, an attenuating of such conflicts; instead of Marxism, we get bourgeois reformism."[19] Performing this task of exposure himself, Lenin showed how the ultraimperialist theory stood refuted by the actual course of social development.

In their arguments regarding "interdependence," the national reformists try to prove that imperialism is disappearing and is being supplanted by "collaboration" among the countries of the Western Hemisphere. Actually, the latter are in a state of "interdependence" under the aegis of American imperialism. But also in existence and becoming active—as exemplified by Cuba —are powerful forces of national liberation that are undermining this "interdependence," countering it with a struggle for the strengthening of national sovereignty and for economic libera-

tion. In light of the tremendous changes that have taken place in the world, in the context of the powerful upsurge of the national-liberation struggle of the Latin American peoples—the efforts of the Kautsky-imitating national reformists to construct a new "ultraimperialist design" for Latin America are truly pitiful.

A central position in the ideas of national reformism is occupied by the premises relative to the beneficial role of U.S. enterprises in increasing employment in the Latin American countries, in the improvement of Latin American living conditions, and in the general economic progress of Latin America. Betancourt, for instance, declared in a speech of November 1958 that the oil workers could better their living conditions through negotiations with the foreign companies, while the state would obtain from these companies the necessary resources for industrial development.

The national reformists reply to criticism of their views by maintaining that it is not that they have ceased to be anti-imperialistic, but that the foreign companies have ceased to be imperialistic.[20] These demagogic fabrications, however, are conclusively refuted by the facts. The meager improvement registered in the position of workers in the Venezuelan oil industry, a circumstance to which the reformists like to refer, is actually the result of

[18]*Combate*, January–February 1960, p. 9. American monopolistic circles make intensive use for their purposes of Luis Muñoz Marín and his National Democratic Party, which is led by a bureaucratic upper layer coming from the middle sectors of the population. Marín attempts to play the role of an "intermediary" between the "nationalistic movements" in Latin America and the United States. The "freely associated state" (this is the title borne by the colonial regime imposed on the Puerto Rican people by U.S. ruling circles) is advanced by Haya de la Torre and other reformists as an example of the "new," "democratic" inter-American relationships.

[19]V. I. Lenin, *Sochineniia*, vol. 22, p. 257.

[20]See, for example, *La Nación* (Bolivia), December 16, 1958.

many years of self-sacrificing struggle by the workers, who were finally able to wrest some concessions from the foreign monopolies. The imperialist companies make up for their "losses" a hundredfold, however. In a relatively short time, the number of oil workers in Venezuela was reduced substantially (from 61,000 in 1948 to 45,000 in 1957), while the oil production rose.[21] Here is direct evidence of relentless intensification of labor, of increased exploitation of the workers, while the availability of a reserve army of unemployed in the oil regions gives the monopolies possession of an effective additional instrument for "putting in their place" those workers who make "excessive" demands.[22] As a result, oil-company profits climb steadily upward. One of the largest American companies, Creole Petroleum, increased its profits in 1959 by 20.7 percent over the corresponding figure for the previous year.[23] All in all, the profits made by the oil companies average in excess of 30 percent relative to the amount of capital invested.

For many years, the foreign companies have been hampering the training of domestic cadres of specialists in every possible way. Typically, only 10 percent of the engineers and technicians employed in the Venezuelan oil industry are native Venezuelans. Moreover, they receive considerably less pay than do the foreign specialists and are required to know English.[24] The question of the position of domestic salaried workers within the oil industry even came under discussion in the Venezuelan Congress. A number of deputies demanded the immediate creation of a national oil company, which would make it possible for Venezuelan specialists to work for the benefit of their people, instead of being "second-class" persons in foreign enterprises.[25]

A favorite theme of the national reformists is their reasoning with regard to the beneficial role of U.S. aid for

the countries of Latin America. What is the true function of this "aid"? Let us take Bolivia as an example. Indeed, the national-reformist ideologists proclaim this country to be a convincing illustration, supposedly serving to confirm their theory of the "beneficial" role of American "aid" for Latin America. An article in the journal *Combate*, for instance, stated that American "aid" would make possible the creation of a class of small landowners in the country, provide impetus for the formation of a "middle class," and lead to a "spiritual rebirth" of the toiling masses.[26] The actual effect of this "aid," however, was to undermine the social gains already achieved by the Bolivian people, to sabotage Bolivia's struggle for economic liberation, and to institute rapacious capitalist methods of exploitation. The American adviser Eder proposed a plan for "stabilization" of the economy, a plan clearly aimed at undermining the state-controlled sector and encouraging increased activity on the part of American monopolies in Bolivia. Acceptance of this "aid" resulted in an acute deterioration of the Bolivian workers' situation.

Similar results stem from an activity of U.S. monopolies that is carried out through the Inter-American Agricultural

[21]*Tribuna Popular*, November 4, 1960.
[22]Characteristically, the oil companies, which were forced to make some concessions to the oil workers in the collective agreement concluded in February 1960, categorically refused to include in the contract one of the major demands of the workers—job security, elimination of dismissals of workers.
[23]*Tribuna Popular*, August 22, 1960.
[24]The American journal *World Petroleum* came out for an increase in the numbers of lower and middle employees—"proletarians and white-collar workers"—from among the ranks of the Venezuelans, thereby creating the impression of a "national character" of the Venezuelan oil industry. However, it emphasized that the higher, leadership positions must be retained in the hands of "qualified foreign specialists" (*World Petroleum*, 7:93 [1957]).
[25]*El Nacional* (Venezuela), August 21, 1959.
[26]*Combate*, 9:77 (1960).

Service. This agency establishes organizations that compete with government institutions and execute policies contrary to the interests of the country. Called upon to cooperate with the Bolivian peasantry, the Inter-American Agricultural Service in reality helps the large capitalist farms, ignoring the needs of the peasant communities. It has taken over control of the government "mechanization service," which was originally intended to help the peasants with agricultural equipment. Now, however, the only "help" extended by the "mechanization service" is to those who are able to make quick and punctual payment. Consequently, only the large-scale agricultural capitalists derive any advantage from it.[27]

The national reformists attempt to justify such a situation by saying that it represents the cost of the "industrial revolution" that allegedly is being accomplished in Bolivia with the assistance of American capital. They declare, in particular, that, as a result of the country's technical and economic progress, splendid prospects of "full employment" and of a "leading role" are now opening up before the Bolivian intelligentsia. Gradually, as a result of progress, Bolivians will displace the foreigners and occupy management posts in all areas of the economy—such is the major theme of their assertions. Our attention is drawn to yet another fact: the reformists are trying to set the middle strata of the population and the intelligentsia against the working class and all the toiling people, declaring that the middle strata must seize control or else risk losing everything, since the proletariat might come to power.[28] Meanwhile, say the reformists, one must do everything possible, with the aid of foreign capital, to encourage the growth of capitalism and utilize its potential for developing the nation's economy to the maximum.

It is precisely at this point, however, that the petty bourgeois essence of the reformist theory is revealed with ample clarity—this theory with its fetish worship of technology, its technocratic tendencies, and its fatalistic-objective approach to reality. Relying on the national reformists, American monopolistic capital is trying to consolidate its positions in Latin America and has no intention of yielding them to the Latin Americans. While it is doubtless true that a small portion of the Latin American population, including some of the uppermost sections of the petty bourgeoisie, do obtain definite advantages from such "collaboration" with American capital, the overwhelming majority of the people suffer terribly from exploitation by the monopolies.

In their efforts to impart some coherence to their theoretical formulations, the national reformists advance their concept of the so-called anti-imperialist state,[29] which, they say, can radically alter existing relationships between foreign capital and the Latin American countries. These are resounding words, but there is nothing revolutionary or anti-imperialist in this theory. However paradoxical it might seem, the fact is that the reformists, in putting forward their concept of the "anti-imperialist state," are concerned most of all with creating "favorable conditions" for activity by foreign capital. In their own words, it is the mission of the "anti-imperialist state" to do away with the detrimental consequences of political imperialism without, however, opposing economic imperialism.

[27]El Sol (Uruguay), March 11, 1960.
[28]La Nación, March 3, December 12, and December 20, 1958.
[29]The term "anti-imperialist state" was advanced by Haya de la Torre. National-reformist theoreticians from other countries usually do not use this terminology, but the essence of their reasoning is exactly the same.

According to Haya de la Torre, if foreign capital is not provided with "reliable guarantees," it suffers a kind of inferiority complex. As a result, it resorts to illicit methods, often turning to Latin American dictators for help.[30] "We are in urgent need of foreign capital," reiterates Haya de la Torre, "and one of our most revolutionary ideas is to give foreign capital a voice in the management of our national economy."[31]

While the peoples of Latin America struggle against domination by foreign capital, the reformists feverishly seek loopholes for retaining the positions of the imperialist monopolies. Haya de la Torre proposes establishing a fourth power in Latin American countries—as a supplement to the legislative, executive, and judicial powers—in the form of a so-called economic congress, in which, along with representatives of labor, government, and capital, the representatives of foreign capital would also participate as members with full and equal rights.[32]

The reformists declare that this economic congress, as one of the chief instruments of the anti-imperialist state, would be in a position to put an end to contradictions between the national interests of the Latin American peoples and foreign capital, to eliminate "political imperialism," and to open up "unlimited" prospects for progress in Latin America. In practice, therefore, the "anti-imperialism" of the reformists is nothing more than an attempt at state "regulation" of the commanding heights secured by foreign capital, with the latter recognized as an "equal" partner in the economies of the Latin American countries. It is not surprising that the attitude of the reformists toward the genuine anti-imperialist struggle is one of unconcealed hostility.

The opposition to the nationalization of property belonging to the imperialist monopolies is particularly bitter. Nationalization represents one of the most

radical forms for the resolution of the contradictions between the Latin American peoples and imperialism. The accomplishments of the nationalization program in Cuba have shown what tremendous positive results can be achieved by a people, once it embarks upon a path of resolute struggle against any form of dependence on the American monopolies.

One of the most widely disseminated reformist arguments on the impossibility of nationalization is allusion to the concept of interdependence. Nationalization is termed an unrealistic, antihistorical action that disrupts established world economic ties. Betancourt writes, for instance, that Venezuela cannot isolate itself from its international economic links, since it has become a world center in the production of oil. Interdependence, he concludes, renders any nationalization of the Venezuelan petroleum industry impossible.[33] Betancourt is working for "harmonious" collaboration between Venezuela and foreign capital.

Setting themselves in opposition to nationalization, the reformists advance the thesis that it is possible to use the power of the state as a means for obtaining major concessions from the foreign monopolies—without any accompanying "upheavals." This would be a step toward "nationalizing" them but without deprivation of property rights. For

[30]Haya de la Torre ignores the active participation of American monopolistic circles in the establishment of military-dictatorship regimes in Latin America. In his opinion, the ones chiefly responsible are the Latin American peoples themselves, who do not know how to maintain "order" in their own houses. And, in resorting to support of military dictatorships, foreign capital is acting quite "logically," since there is no other guarantee of protection of its interests—such a conclusion is actually drawn by Haya de la Torre, appearing as an advocate for foreign capital (*Seminario Peruano*, March 27, 1959, p. 14).

[31]*La Nación*, December 16, 1958.
[32]*Combate*, January–February 1960, p. 24.
[33]Rómulo Betancourt, *Venezuela, política y petróleo* (México, 1956), p. 741.

example, the idea of the Venezuelan government's "partnership" with the foreign companies in the exploitation of petroleum resources is being propagandized in Venezuela. But what kind of "partnership" can there be if all controls over the oil industry are in the hands of the foreign companies, with "participation" by the Venezuelan government relegated exclusively to the receipt of taxes from the production of oil? Moreover, it is actually the oil companies themselves who determine the amount of taxes to be paid by them to Venezuela, while, unhampered by controls, they carry out their operations in the world market. These foreign-owned oil companies not only do not fulfill the role attributed to them by the national reformists—as a unique sort of accumulator of the capital required for the economic development of the country—but, on the contrary, they are becoming more and more of a hindrance to national progress, a kind of state within a state. They are siphoning riches out of the country on an enormous scale. In 1957 alone, the profits of the oil companies in Venezuela represented 55.7 percent of the sum total of profits earned by the American monopolies in all Latin America.[34]

The example of Bolivia, one might add, is no less convincing. The reformists claim that an "anti-imperialist state" has virtually been established in Bolivia already, one which is successfully carrying out a policy of "collaboration" with the American monopolies. Defining the principle that serves the government as a guide, La Nación, the Bolivian government newspaper, wrote that "national liberation" could be accomplished in Bolivia by having the state maintain an equilibrium between the "public" and "private-enterprise" sectors of the economy.[35] The latter term, in effect, means the American monopolies.

How is this "collaboration" translated into actual practice? In the Bolivian petroleum industry, American companies (in recent years the Bolivian government has granted oil concessions on a wide scale) and the state petroleum enterprise "coexist." The American oil companies are steadily extending their sphere of influence and getting their hands on more and more oil-bearing lands. They are striving to undermine the position of the state company and to implant private enterprise in the petroleum industry. Romero Losa, one of the directors of the state company, stated that there were "very large resources of petroleum" at the company's disposal but that "these could not be exploited because of insufficient capital." Furthermore, he emphasized, foreign interference made it impossible to obtain the necessary means.[36]

"Regulated" capitalist development in Bolivia has had the effect of further consolidating the position of American capital and impeding socioeconomic reforms. The reformist theoreticians and politicians attempt to combine a fatalistic acceptance of the inevitability of the penetration of American capital into the Latin American countries with the voluntaristic propagation of their policy of the "anti-imperialist state." Such an unnatural combination is bound to lead to deplorable results.

The national reformists also declare that nationalization is inexpedient, since, they say, it throws the Latin American countries backwards, because nationalization undermines the most "advanced" sector of the economy.

Basing their theory on the fetish worship of technology and ignoring the problems involved in the socioeconomic development of Latin America, the national reformists substitute an abstract, purely quantitative conception

[34]Universidad Central, Boletín Informativo (Venezuela), March 10, 1960.
[35]La Nación, December 16, 1958.
[36]Unidad (Bolivia), February 25, 1960.

of increasing production for the question of nationalization. For instance, one of the most active figures of Latin American reformism and the leader of the Costa Rican party of "national liberation," José Figueres, asserts that at present nationalization has lost its meaning and that the important thing now is to "produce more, distribute equitably, and accumulate the capital required for development."[37] Figueres is critical of the "dogmatic" U.S. approach to the various forms of private property, but his purpose here is to provide a basis for his theory on the necessity of "organic coexistence" of the American monopolies with the "anti-imperialist state," with the latter exercising overall control of the national economy in the interests of "international unity." There is nothing anti-imperialist in this theory, nothing undermining the positions of the foreign monopolies. His "attacks" on the "dogma of private property" alternate with criticism of the "dogmas of public property."[38] Naturally, such a striving for "balance" brings him to the conclusion that what is important is not one form of property or another, but rather the principles governing relationships between the countries of Latin America and the United States.

It is hardly surprising that such "subversive theories" cause the American monopolies no anxiety. In April 1960, the Second Inter-American Congress in Defense of Democracy and Freedom took place in Caracas. Joint proposals and recommendations were presented to this assembly by Figueres and former U.S. Assistant Secretary of State Adolph Berle, one of the ideologists of monopolistic capital currently serving as President Kennedy's special emissary. A good deal was said in these proposals about the need for increasing U.S. aid to Latin American countries for their economic development, as well as for bringing to an end the existing disparity between the underdeveloped and the industrialized countries. However, the authors of these proposals took particular pains to convince those participating in the congress that foreign capital, once integrated into the economic structure of the Latin American countries and thereby acquiring a "national" identity, would become an even more effective factor for progress in these countries. All this effort was accompanied by abundant recommendations to foreign capital that it display an understanding of the interests of Latin American states, that it fullfill a "social function" in their development, and so on.[39] There is no point in speculating as to which "contribution" to these proposals came from Berle and which from Figueres. One thing is clear: both the representatives of the American monopolies and the Latin American national reformists subscribe readily to these recommendations.

The masses of Latin America are coming more and more to realize the groundlessness of the theory and practice of national reformism, which repudiates the struggle for economic liberation and strives for accomodation with imperialism. Important new processes are at work among the petty bourgeois elements, on whose support the reformists set their primary hopes. Of particularly fundamental importance are the changes that have transpired in the attitudes and opinions of a substantial proportion of the middle strata in Cuba, a circumstance that has had a great influence as well on the views of the middle strata in other Latin American countries. The progressive elements of the Cuban people, waging an unyielding ideological struggle, have inflicted a defeat upon the opportunistic, conciliatory right wing of the petty bourgeoisie, which was attempting to paralyze the revolutionary move-

[37]*Combate*, July–August 1959, p. 9.
[38]*Ibid.*
[39]*Ibid.*, July–August 1960, pp. 11–12.

ment, thwart the anti-imperialist policy of nationalization, and prevent the creation of an independent economy. More and more members of the petty bourgeoisie and the intelligentsia are now becoming convinced that only in the context of a free and independent Cuba can they have maximum opportunity for applying their creative energies and their knowledge.

One of the principal tasks facing Cuba is to achieve higher production, to raise labor productivity. "Cuba has begun a campaign to increase labor productivity, and the triumph of the revolution on the economic front depends to a considerable extent on fulfillment of this goal," wrote the Cuban newspaper *Noticias de Hoy*.[40] It is not difficult to perceive the vast difference between this objective, expressed by revolutionary elements, and the outwardly similar catchword used by reformist ideologists of the Figueres type!

The example of Cuba and the growth of the national-liberation movement are having an ever increasing influence as well on the struggle against the ideology of reformism in the other Latin American countries and are leading to a constantly greater polarization of social forces. In Venezuela, for instance, a split in the ranks of the Democratic Action Party has occurred. Its leftist groups quit the party and, in 1960, formed a new political organization, the Leftist Revolutionary Movement. This new party opposes the reformist ideology of the Democratic Action Party's leadership, cooperates with the Communists, and propounds an anti-imperialist program for the implementation of basic socioeconomic reforms in Venezuela.

The new party's newspaper, *Izquierda*, has written:

Setting out from the basic premises of our program, we must recognize that there can be no prospect of revolution in Venezuela without a clear and unambiguous position in regard to nationalization of the Venezuelan oil industry. All attempts to avoid bringing to the fore this problem—one of such vital importance for the future of our country—are a manifestation of capitulationist theories of economic and geographical fatalism; they represent advocacy of the idea of "capitalism as a partner," a concept that finds its most repugnant embodiment in the existence of the Puerto Rican Associated State.[41]

Characteristically, the Leftist Revolutionary Movement affirms its acknowledgment of the leading role of the working class. The new party is carrying on a determined fight against rightist and capitulationist elements in the liberation movement.

The struggle against reformism is being accelerated also in such countries as Peru and Costa Rica, where leftist elements in the ranks of the Aprista and the National Liberation parties are opposing their leaders' conciliatory, reformist policies. True, many progressively minded persons in the Aprista Party, even after forming their own political organization—an "insurgent APRA"—have still not rid themselves of their illusions about Haya de la Torre, but consider him the "anti-imperialist" leader of Latin America. Nevertheless, the importance of attacks against reformism originating in the ranks of the Aprista Party can scarcely be exaggerated. As was noted by the Peruvian communist newspaper, *Unidad*, the changes taking place within the Aprista Party are a "sign of the times" and are in keeping with the goals of the anti-imperialist revolution in Peru. Wrote *Unidad*, "We extend our hand to the democratic elements in the Aprista Party, and we express the hope that we shall travel together along the difficult path of the liberation movement."[42]

[40]*Noticias de Hoy*, August 14, 1960.
[41]*Izquierda*, June 24, 1960.
[42]*Unidad*, November 7, 1959.

No less significant are those changes going on in the Costa Rican National Liberation Party, whose left wing is gaining in strength. An immediate impetus for stirring the leftist elements into activity was provided by the anti-imperialist strike of agricultural workers on the plantations of the United Fruit Company, from December 1959 to January 1960. At that time, many members of the National Liberation Party, overcoming bitter resistance by the rightist leadership, established wide-scale cooperation with the Communists and other democratic forces. Indeed, the united front of patriotic forces was the deciding factor in winning the anti-imperialist strike. The experience of this struggle convinced many members of National Action of the treacherous, capitulationist policy being practiced by the rightist, reformist elements, who in their efforts to prevent the strike from spreading tried to intimidate the people with the threat of American intervention. At the beginning of 1960, Gonzalo Facio, one of the most violent anti-Communists and a lackey of imperialism, was expelled from the party. The Venezuelan newspaper *Tribuna Popular* laid stress on the fact that removal from the party of Facio, a supporter of Figueres, inflicted a heavy blow upon the position of the latter and intensified the intraparty ideological struggle.[43]

The ideological conflict in Bolivia merits close attention. The artificiality and baselessness of reformist "theories" about the necessity of undergoing a "special" capitalist stage of development, which would derive its stimulus from American monopolistic capital, have been revealed with particular clarity in that country. The growing discontent of the masses, including petty bourgeois elements as well, has been manifested in the split of the governing party, the Nationalist Revolutionary Movement. Quitting its ranks were the rightist, reformist elements, who then proceeded to establish their own party, the Authentic Nationalist Revolutionary Movement. The results of the presidential election in Bolivia in 1960 bear witness to the rising dissatisfaction of the broad masses of the people with the policies of the reformists. Victory at the polls was won by those elements which advocated restricting the activity of American monopolies in the country and developing an independent economy. Characteristically, criticism of American "aid," which was undermining the national economy of Bolivia, increased greatly during the period. In regard to the election results, the Venezuelan newspaper *Izquierda* wrote, "The people voted for revolution and not for reformism."[44]

For the progressive forces of Bolivian society, the decisive battle lies ahead. Illusions with regard to American "aid" are still quite strong in that country. Some elements of the population are still under the influence of reformism. In our opinion, however, one should emphasize the main point—one that is applicable in one degree or another to the other Latin American countries as well. The realization is growing in Bolivia that it is impossible to achieve progress in building a free and independent country by pursuing the path of capitalist development. The Bolivian people are learning from experience what American "capitalist progress" brings to the toiling people. It is no accident that there is increased interest in socialism in the country; inseparably linked with this fact is the spread both of Marxist ideas and of the truth about the Soviet Union and the other countries of the world socialist system, making it easier to discern the true nature of various reformist ideas regarding "industrial revolution," "technical pro-

[43]*Tribuna Popular*, February 26, 1960.
[44]*Izquierda*, June 24, 1960.

gress," and American "aid." Hence the great enthusiasm with which the Bolivian working people greeted the news that the Soviet Union was prepared to assist Bolivia in the construction of a tin-smelting plant and in the development of a national petroleum industry. Speaking at a mass meeting, Federico Escobar, the leader of the miners from the Twentieth Century mine, said: "We cannot accept American handouts because they pursue ends that are alien to us. The Yankees want to enslave us further. This is why we say, 'Long live the disinterested help of the USSR!'"

In the Declaration of the Conference of Representatives of Communist and Workers' Parties, the following is stated: "The masses of the people are becoming convinced that the path of non-capitalist development is the best way to put an end to their age-old backwardness and improve their living conditions. Only by choosing this way can the peoples rid themselves of exploitation, poverty, and hunger. The working class and the broad masses of the peasantry are destined to play a most important role in the resolution of this fundamental social problem."[45] The situation in Latin America fully corroborates their conclusions.

Facing the progressive, revolutionary forces of Latin America in the not-too-distant future is an even more intense ideological struggle with reformism. It must not be forgotten that, while the national-revolutionary wing of the liberation movement is growing stronger, the reformists are feverishly stepping up their campaign to consolidate their own forces. For instance, in August 1960, in the Peruvian capital of Lima, a conference was held in which, besides the Aprista and the Febrerista parties, the parties of Democratic Action, National Liberation, and the Nationalist Revolutionary Movement participated.

As might have been expected, the resolutions adopted on all fundamental questions by the conference were clearly in the spirit of the "thinking" of Haya de la Torre and the other ideologists of reformism.

Of course, since the top leadership of the parties assembled at Lima could not entirely ignore the feelings of the Latin American masses, the conference resolutions did include some criticism of the United States. Completely in the spirit of the reformist notion of "constructive anti-imperialism," however, it was given unequivocally to be understood that the existing contradictions between the United States and Latin America had been completely eliminated and that the advent of a new era of "inter-American democratic interrelationships" was possible. At the same time, the resolutions of the conference were marked by violent anticommunism and hatred toward the socialist countries.[46] Not a struggle against imperialism, but a struggle against revolutionary ideology and Marxism-Leninism—this, in point of fact, is the "latest pronouncement" of the Latin American reformists. In 1960, the national reformist leaders established a so-called International Institute of Political Education in Costa Rica, designed to train cadres for fighting the "communist ideology." This institute is directed by José Figueres and Haya de la Torre. Harry Kantor, the reactionary American Sociologist, was invited to serve as one of its directors.

As we can see, the national reformists are unflagging in their efforts to subordinate the national-liberation movement to their influence and to distort its true aims and purposes. Nevertheless, it can be said that in this conflict, the revolutionary ideology and the

[45]*Programmnye dokumenty bor'by za mir, demokratiu i sotsializm* (Moskva, 1961), p. 67.
[46]*Noticiero Obrero Interamericano*, no. 40 (September 1960).

practical experience of the struggle for national liberation are already inflicting palpable blows on reformism, exposing both its theoretical and practical baselessness and its inability to solve the fundamental problems of Latin American reality.

A conclusive refutation of the national reformists' views regarding "attenuation" of the anti-imperialist struggle in Latin America and the advent of an era of "interdependence" was furnished by the March 1961 Latin American conference for national sovereignty and independent economic development and peace. A declaration adopted unanimously by the conference stated:

The principal force obstructing progress in Latin America is North American imperialism. By its close alliance with the oligarchies in our countries and the pernicious consequences of its economic and cultural penetration, it is the chief cause of that universal backwardness which characterizes the present situation in the Latin American countries. The defeat of imperialism is the most important and the indispensable precondition for any program of development in our countries.[47]

The declaration bears witness to the great gains already achieved by the national-liberation movement of Latin America in consolidating its forces and in defining the general goals of the anti-imperialist struggle.

No reformist strategems or sophisms are capable of stemming the historically inevitable process of political, economic, and social liberation of the peoples of Latin America.

[47]*Problemy mira i sotsializma*, 5:48 (1961).

12. The Deteriorating Economic Position of the Petty Bourgeoisie*

M. V. DANILEVICH

The intensification of the fundamental contradictions of capitalism is leading not only to greater absolute and relative impoverishment of the working class, but also to the ruin of the urban petty bourgeoisie, the craftsmen, the small merchants, the peasants, the intelligentsia, the salaried employees—in effect, to the impoverishment and ruin of the majority of the population in the capitalist countries, especially in the colonial and dependent ones.

The urban and rural petty bourgeoisie in Latin America is extremely numer-

*Rabochii klass v osvoboditel'nom dvizhenii narodov Latinskoi Ameriki (Moskva: Gosudarstvennoe izdatel'stvo politicheskoi literatury, 1962), pp. 49–51, 53–55.

ous. In Uruguay, this sector comprises up to 30 percent of the gainfully employed population,[1] while its proportion in Argentina is even higher—35 percent. The figure for Chile is the same as that for Uruguay. For Brazil and Mexico, it is 15 percent.[2]

The petty bourgeoisie in the cities and large towns is represented by a large group of craftsmen and by small merchants who do not use hired labor. There is widespread peddling carried on by "itinerant tradesmen" who earn barely enough to live on. The situation of the small craftsmen is extremely difficult. They can hardly make ends meet, even with the most strenuous labor by the craftsman himself and by his entire family.

Despite their wretched standard of living and the ruinous competition from the manufacturing industry, these craftsmen and small merchants do everything possible to cling to and preserve their unprofitable "business." Because of the slow rate of industrial development, the ruined craftsmen and small merchants, along with their children, end by filling the ranks of the labor reserve; only a portion of them find work in industry or in construction.

The extent of displacement of craft labor serves as one of the indexes used for measuring the growth of the manufacturing industry and, consequently, the level to which capitalism has developed. The craft and domestic handicraft industries show relatively greater stability in the economically backward countries of Latin America.

In all the Latin American states, an important and constantly increasing stratum consists of low-paid government employees, the personnel of private offices, banks, and various small institutions, and of people engaged in the so-called service occupations. The number of persons employed in government agencies has especially risen in Argentina, Colombia, Venezuela,

Mexico, and Chile. This stratum is of heterogeneous derivation. A large proportion of its members belong to semi-proletarian elements, while another significant percentage stems from the petty bourgeoisie. Comprising a special group are the officials of the government bureaucracy and its agencies that perform repressive functions in the interests of the ruling classes. Of 6,000,000 people of hired-labor status (75 percent of all the gainfully employed) in Argentina in 1959, salaried personnel accounted for 2,750,000. Among the latter, 700,000 worked in commerce, banks, insurance companies, and offices, while no fewer than 1,100,000 were employed in administrative agencies of the government. Included statistically in the category of salaried personnel are 650,000 service employees in hotels and theaters, as well as those employed as domestic servants.[3]

Teachers in the urban and rural schools, medical assistants, and other members of the rural intelligentsia are in a disastrous situation. Their salaries hardly suffice to make ends meet. Particularly hard is the situation of rural teachers, whose pay is so low that it frequently approximates the wages earned by agricultural workers. In order to live, they are compelled to seek supplementary sources of income—whatever may be available.[4]

In the report of the Central Committee of the Mexican Communist Party to the Twelfth Party Congress, particular

[1]The following categories belong to this group: low-echelon state employees—more than 115,000 people; employees of banks and private offices— 20,000; small merchants and trade employees— approximately 130,000; workers in hotels, restaurants, and various entertainment businesses— some 20,000; and several tens of thousands of artisans and other low-paid workers (Curso de Economía, 1958, p. 65).
[2]John Johnson, Political Change in Latin America (Stanford, 1958), p. 2.
[3]See Problemy mira i sotsialisma, 4:63 (1961).
[4]El Popular, June 17, 1953.

point was made of the fact that the salaried employees and the intelligentsia, like the working class, are being detrimentally affected by the plunder of their country by the American monopolies. "The living conditions of these sectors of the population are in many instances identical with those of the working class; just like the workers in industrial plants, they too receive wages and pensions that doom them to a life of hunger, they have no job security, and they lack many of the rights set forth in the labor code and the constitution of the republic."[5]

The problems of unemployment, housing, and inflation are just as acute for lower-echelon government and private salaried personnel, for teachers, and for other representatives of intellectual labor as they are for labor.

Specialists in the field of technology, engineers, professors, instructors in institutions of higher learning, lawyers, writers, and journalists—such persons may be divided into bourgeois, petty bourgeois, or proletarian intelligentsia, depending upon which class they serve.

The majority of the intelligentsia are patriotic in attitude, taking an active part in the fight for democratization of political life and for the economic independence of their countries. A considerable portion of the technological intelligentsia links its destiny with the development of the national economy, particularly with the creation and strengthening of domestic industry.

Due to the enormous difficulties faced by the Communist parties in working under illegal conditions, substantial sectors of the petty bourgeoisie have long been and still are under the influence and leadership of ruling, reactionary, rightist parties in a number of countries. Wherever the Communist parties have been able to extend their influence to the petty bourgeoisie, the role of the bourgeois parties has been correspondingly lessened.

In parties that have a considerable membership from the petty bourgeoisie, but in which the leadership has been seized by representatives of the powerful conciliatory and reactionary bourgeoisie, the latter have been able to paralyze temporarily any revolutionary activity by the petty bourgeois masses. The vacillations and inconstancy of the petty bourgeoisie, as well as the spread within its milieu of anarchist and even fascist ideology, often lead it into the reactionary camp. In this connection, the party program of the Communist Party of Ecuador states: ". . . they—the petty bourgeoisie and the intelligentsia—not infrequently succumb to the demagogy of the ruling classes. During election campaigns, we can see how they follow reactionary scheming politicians who have succeeded in deceiving them with demagogic promises."[6]

It is no accident that various reactionary, nationalistic organizations—such as the Peronista Party of Argentina—often entice the urban petty bourgeoisie into their ranks.

The experience of the Russian proletariat and of the international workers' movement has shown that, though the petty bourgeoisie—comprising a considerable part of the population, especially in the colonial and dependent countries—is of no small significance in political life, the fact remains that it never plays an independent role. It either falls under the influence of the powerful bourgeoisie and becomes a tool of it, or it leans to the side of the working class. Lenin pointed out that, with the development of capitalism, the middle strata undergo a process of erosion and decomposition:

While the bourgeoisie crushes and disperses the peasantry and all the elements of

[5]*La Voz de México*, November 5, 1955.
[6]*Democracia, independencia y paz para el pueblo del Ecuador. Lineamientos programáticos del Partido Comunista del Ecuador, aprobados por su VI Congreso* (Quito, 1957).

the petty bourgeoisie, at the same time it solidifies, unites, and organizes the proletariate. Only the proletariat—by virtue of its economic role in large-scale production—is capable of leading *all* the working people and the exploited masses who, though often exploited and oppressed no less and even more rigorously than the proletariat by the bourgeoisie, are nevertheless incapable of waging an *independent* struggle for their liberation.[7]

The working class cannot win either in the struggle for socialism or in the anti-imperialist, antifeudal struggle unless it detaches the urban and rural petty bourgeoisie from the influence of the bourgeois-landowner parties and draws them into a joint liberation movement.

Since the war, bourgeois sociologists have been widely disseminating the theory of the "middle classes" as the determining force in the social development of modern capitalism.[8] According to the pronouncements of these theoreticians, the proletariat is acquiring the characteristics of the bourgeoisie, and, in the course of this process, the "middle class" is expanding by "absorbing" certain elements of the proletariat and the bourgeoisie. This process is supposed to culminate in the elimination of class antagonisms and the formation of a classless society.

The "theory" of "middle classes" serves the bourgeois apologists as a basis for their premises regarding the transformation of modern capitalism into a "classless society," into a "people's capitalism." The supporters of this "theory," misrepresenting the actual state of affairs, try to deny the sharpening of class antagonisms and the deteriorating situation of the petty bourgeoisie, white-collar workers, and the toiling masses in general. The "theory" of "middle classes" is refuted by reality, which vividly reveals the destitution of the proletariat, the ruin of the petty bourgeoisie, and the rise of the powerful bourgeoisie.

The process of capitalist development brings the situation of white-collar workers and petty bourgeois masses closer to the conditions of life and work of the working class, converting the former into a revolutionary element and drawing them into the liberation struggle. The revolutionary potential of the petty bourgeoisie and the intelligentsia was especially graphically demonstrated in their active participation in the Cuban people's struggle.

[7] V. I. Lenin, *Sochineniia*, 4th ed., vol. 25, p. 376.

[8] Arbitrarily discussing the concept of classes (as distinctions in line of business, people's professions, amount of income, living conditions, type of housing, area of residence, and even in the biological "value" of people), these sociologists include in the "middle class" the most diverse social strata and class groups, up to well-to-do farmers, officers, a significant portion of skilled workers, landowners, and even various businessmen, and representatives of the upper and middle bourgeoisie.

IV

The Catholic Church and Christian Democracy

This section consists of four selections on two major subjects: the position of the Catholic Church in Latin America and the nature of the spreading Christian Democratic political movement.

In Item 13, N. A. Koval'skii rehashes some of the differences between Catholicism and communism and asserts that the Church finds itself in an increasingly difficult position in Latin America. In the succeeding selection, the same author examines Catholic activities among labor in Latin America. He concludes that in the effort to retain the allegiance of that part of the working class still under its influence, the Church is being forced to combine anticommunism with a flexible policy of accommodation.

Item 15, by S. I. Semenov, traces the history of Christian Democracy in Latin America. Semenov considers that the Christian Democrats will inevitably move farther to the left, in line with the "new course" of the Catholic Church in Latin America and under the pressure of socioeconomic changes presently taking place.

In the concluding selection (Item 16), I. R. Grigulevich analyzes the significance of the 1964 Christian Democratic electoral victory in Chile. Unlike Semenov, Grigulevich unhesitatingly applies the term "clerical party" to the Chilean PDC. He concedes that President Frei has carried out his pre-election promises quite consistently in foreign relations, but maintains some reservations on the PDC's willingness and ability to implement the structural reforms that were to lead to the promised "revolution in peace."

13. The Political and Economic Strength of the Church in Latin America and Its Efforts to Contain the Revolutionary Movements*

N. A. KOVAL'SKII

Although it was deprived of part of its stolen riches as a result of the revolts against the Spanish colonizers, the Church nevertheless even today is one of the largest landholders in Latin America. It owns almost 6 million hectares in Argentina, 1 million hectares in Brazil, 100,000 hectares in Colombia, 70,000 hectares in Peru, and 50,000 hectares in Venezuela.[1]

The Catholic Church officials widely exploit Indian labor on their landholdings. Just what the concern of the Church for Indians' souls is based upon is demonstrated in a report of the Ecuadorian Institute of Anthropology and Geography. It states:

"The Indians not only work to increase the income of the employer-owner or tenant— but, in addition, they must look after the welfare of the priest of their parish. As things stand, the parish priest loses no opportunity to aggrandize his own position. All of the religious rites from christening to burial cost the Indian dearly. When a marriage is contracted, the priest from Cajabamba demands that the bride remain with him for one month under the pretense of converting her to Christianity and preparing her for the wedding ceremony. The future husband is required to fulfill various obligations: to transport church belongings, to plow the land belonging to the parish, or to pay a "qualification tax."[2]

Luis Felipe Ángel, the secretary of the National Liberation Front of Peru, maintains that exploitation of the Indians by the Church is not restricted to Ecuador. He says: "The Indians live under vigilant surveillance of the Church. The Church owns gigantic agricultural latifundia in Peru. The Indians perform all of the work on the land, and for their labor they receive nothing except the promise of salvation. The Church teaches the Indians "patience" and "obedience"; the courts systematically repudiate all of their claims; the landowners openly dominate their lives and their wives; and the army cruelly suppresses any attempts at protest."[3]

In Latin America the Church controls not only colossal landholdings, but also

*Vatikan i mirovaia politika (Moskva: Izdatel'stvo Mezhdunarodnye otnosheniia, 1964), pp. 202–204, 208–209, 211–212, 214.
[1]A. Tondi, "Der kirchliche Kolonialismus in Lateinamerika," Deutsche Aussenpolitik, 1961, Sonderheft 11, pp. 121–122.
[2]Quote from "D'iavol s krestom," Za rubezhom, May 19, 1962, p. 27.
[3]Quote from Pravda, March 6, 1963.

significant capital investment in various branches of the economy. It cooperates, in particular, with U.S. monopolies and has shares in the United Fruit Company, American and Foreign Power Company, Light Company, and others.[4]

The Catholic Church in Latin America plays a significant role not only in the economic sphere, but in the political sphere as well. In the opinion of some specialists, such as Professor K. Silvert of the United States, the Catholic Church is a major power behind the scenes in the countries of Latin America.[5] Even if this is an exaggeration, it is in any case very typical.

In one group of Latin American countries the church is separated from the state: in Brazil, Chile, Ecuador, El Salvador, Guatemala, Honduras, Mexico, Nicaragua, Panama, Uruguay, and Cuba. In the others such legislative delineation has not been accomplished. However, in the majority of cases, in both groups of countries (excluding socialist Cuba, of course) the Catholic hierarchies and the ruling classes have the same goals.

The clergy of Latin America intervenes extensively in the internal affairs of states. It actively participates in conspiracies against those states which, for some reason or other, do not satisfy it. For example, in the Dominican Republic many Catholic clergymen participated in organizing a *coup d' état* that resulted in the overthrow of the Juan Bosch government in 1963. Bosch himself remarked, "The first to accuse me of being a Communist was a Catholic priest."[6]

The Catholic clergy of Latin America attempts to exert pressure during election campaigns in order to promote its representatives. It tries to make the Catholic vow of obedience a weapon for the attainment of goals of a political character. A pastoral letter of the Bishop of Chile announces that the participation of Catholics in elections is considered an obligation to the Church. "All Christians are obliged to vote," the message says, "and to participate in politics to a degree commensurate with their profession and responsibilities."[7] During the elections in October 1962, the higher clergy in Brazil assumed the same position. Three days before the election they published a list of candidates for whom the Catholics were required to vote. At the same time they forbade Catholics to vote for progressive candidates.

The Catholic Church has maintained its strong position in Latin America over the course of hundreds of years despite several anticlerical movements—in particular, attempts of the young bourgeoisie of the nineteenth century to limit its power. However, since the spread of revolutionary tendencies throughout the world, especially since the Great October Socialist Revolution in Russia, support for the Catholic Church in Latin America has been somewhat shaken. This process has been particularly intensified since the Second World War. Under the influence of the world revolutionary processes and the changes in the correlation of forces in favor of the socialist system, the upsurge of the national-liberation movement—the struggle of the peoples of Latin America for national independence and against imperialism—has reached new heights. The peoples of Latin America have increasingly come to regard communism as the only doctrine that can lead their countries to prosperity and progress.

Under these conditions the leaders of the Catholic Church regard the fight against communism as the primary

[4]See A. Tondi, "Der kirchliche Kolonialismus in Lateinamerika," pp. 121–122.
[5]See *The United States and Latin America* (New York: The Assembly, Columbia University, 1959), p. 77.
[6]*Paese Sera*, October 3, 1963.
[7]*El Mercurio*, September 23, 1962.

issue. In 1957 Pius XII expressed alarm at the growing influence of the Communist parties in Latin America. He remarked that "Marxism is being manifested very actively in the universities and now controls most of the workers' organizations."[8]

The Latin American Council of Bishops examined the question of the struggle against communism during its session of 1959. Its concluding declaration noted that clergymen must assume a hard and uncompromising position in relation to communists.

Aspiring to neutralize the effects of the Cuban Revolution on the masses, the Catholic Church heirarchy of Latin America has directed a vast propaganda campaign against Cuba. Attacks on the Cuban Revolution are contained in the statement of the thirty-eight bishops of Central America, in the pastoral letter of the episcopate of the Dominican Republic in early 1962, and in many other addresses to believers.

In Cuba itself, the reactionary Catholic clergy had openly engaged in subversive activities against the revolution for a long time. This is to be explained in particular by the fact that the vast majority of the clergy in Cuba consists of Spanish Franciscans. They opposed the agrarian reform and fought against relinquishing control of all education to the state. Trying to undermine the influence of the peoples' government, they organized openly counterrevolutionary actions: they provoked strikes by students in private schools, encouraged antigovernment demonstrations in the streets of Havana, and incited the activities of terrorists. During the time when the American mercenaries tried to land at Playa Girón, the reactionary clergy sharply stepped up its antigovernment activities. Thus, it is not accidental that the Cuban radio declared at the time that the Catholic Church "is an accomplice in the aggression against our homeland."

The government was forced to take measures against the counterrevolutionary clergy. Many foreign priests were deported. As a result, openly counterrevolutionary activities by the Cuban Catholic clergy declined. The more realistically disposed priests began to support the Cuban Revolution.

Aware that the growing influence of communist ideas in Latin America was caused by objective circumstances—including causes of a socioeconomic character—leaders of the Catholic Church were forced to support partial reforms in the economic and social life of the Latin American countries. An acknowledgment of the need for social and economic reforms is contained in the declaration of the Latin American bishops at the International Eucharistic Congress held in Rio de Janeiro in 1955, which stated that "rapid and equitable change in the social structure of Latin America is a necessity." It also noted that in this connection the Church should "exert influence on social development, that is, teach and instill a sense of social responsibility in Catholics, and, finally, act in this field."[9] The declaration of the 1959 conference was written in the same spirit.

The statements of the clergy in favor of reforms have been dictated not by concern with the workers' welfare, however, but by the fear that this wave of national rage would turn into a revolution that would sweep the clergy out of Latin America along with the capitalists, latifundists, and foreign imperialists. Recognizing the strength of the revolutionary working class and its ally, the peasantry, they supported the institution of reforms from above in order to prevent revolution from below.

In the field of practical activities, the leaders of the Catholic hierarchy of

[8]*Informations Catholiques Internationales,* October 15, 1957, p. 28.
[9]*Informations Catholiques Internationales,* February 15, 1961, p. 26.

Latin America are trying to create the impression that they are prepared to institute appropriate reforms immediately, and to take concrete measures to raise the standard of living of the masses. In an attempt to obtain the maximum propagandistic effect, they are distributing among the peasants of various countries separate plots of land that form an insignificant part of the huge amount of property belonging to the Catholic Church. This operation was carried out with extraordinary pomposity and widespread publicity.

The same sort of ballyhoo was raised about the following activities: the establishment in Peru of two hundred "people's banks," which were to extend credit to small landowners for modernization of their farms; the creation in Brazil of the Catholic Agrarian Front for carrying out a "just agrarian reform"; the activities of Acción Misionaria Argentina in developing a cooperative system in the agricultural regions of Argentina; and other similar measures.

In spite of the large number of Catholic Church members and the considerable activity of Church leaders, the Catholic Church in Latin America is experiencing great difficulties. Statements of many of the clergy testify to this. "The tragic discovery of the last few years is that the traditionally Christian areas, particularly Latin America, are risking becoming witnesses to the complete collapse of the Church," writes the prominent Catholic A. Daniel-Rops, a member of the French Academy.[10]

This crisis is expressed in the fact that the leaders of the Catholic Church are not able to prevent the spread of the ideas of communism nor the increasing sympathy toward the socialist bloc countries, especially Cuba.

In the eyes of the masses, the Church is frequently identified with "Yankee imperialism."[11] This leads to reduction of Church authority, to growth of anticlerical feelings, and in many cases to massive anti-Church demonstrations.

[10]Daniel-Rops, *Vatican II*, (Paris, 1961), p. 160.
[11]See *Informations Catholiques Internationales*, May 1, 1961.

14. The Nature and Motives of Catholic
Reform in Latin America*

N. A. KOVAL'SKII

The ideology that Catholicism is trying to instill in the working class of Latin America is based on the thesis that only the Catholic social doctrine makes it possible to solve urgent problems. Under these circumstances, the Church considers the Communist parties as its primary opponent. The parties present clear-cut sociopolitical programs and enjoy considerable influence among the masses.

Clergymen and their agents in the social organizations of the workers are taking into account the great strength and realism of communist ideas. "The working class knows," admitted the leader of the Latin American organization, Young Christian Workers, "that communism offers not only theoretical but also practical solutions to social problems."[1] In this document, obvious anxiety over the increasing class consciousness of the workers is apparent. "Awareness of their mission came quickly to the workers," it says, "as a result of the consequences of rapid industrialization. Unfortunately, this evolution is being manifested independently of the Church and is slipping away from its influence. History testifies to the fact that the first ones interested—not in

theory alone—in the condition of the working class were enemies of the Church."[2]

Realizing that the Communists and all progressive society of the Latin American countries are interested primarily in gaining economic independence, in guaranteeing national sovereignty, in the democratization of the political system, and in instituting basic socioeconomic reforms, Catholic leaders are searching for alternatives that would be acceptable to them and to their secular partners and at the same time would appeal to the workers. It is exactly in this way that Catholic ideologists hope to win the battle for the mind of the working class.

Propagandizing their renovated social doctrine and trying to strike a pose as defenders of the workers' interests, the clergy do not hesitate to criticize capitalism superficially. They express the matter as if the Catholic Church had always sided with the exploited and had

*"Politika katolicheskoi tserkvi v rabochem dvizhenii Latinskoi Ameriki," in *Osvoboditel'noe dvizhenie v Latinskoi Amerike*, ed. S. S. Mikhailov (Moskva: Izdatel'stvo Nauka, 1964), pp. 191–206.

[1]*Jeunesse dans le Monde*, May 1960, p. 36.
[2]*Ibid.*, p. 35.

never cooperated with the exploiting classes and had never received material advantage from this cooperation. Such an attempt to declare spiritual affinity with the working class is contained, for example, in the declaration made by the Latin American bishops in 1959. "The Church," they contend, "has always defended human individuality from those who would exploit the weakest and has backed a more equitable distribution of wealth in accordance with the demands of Christian social justice."[3]

Many other Church declarations reflect this same line—that the Church is the advocate of interests of the working class and of bold social reforms. Thus an acknowledgment of the necessity of social and economic reforms was made by the Latin American bishops in their statement to the International Eucharistic Congress of 1955 in Rio de Janeiro. "A rapid and equitable change in the social structure of Latin America is a necessity," they said, and they further contended that the Church should "exert influence on social development, that is, teach and instill a sense of social responsibility in Catholics and, finally, act in this field."[4]

The high Latin American church officials expressed similar thoughts in their conference in Fómeque, Colombia, in 1959. The question of reforms in Latin America was reflected also in the speeches of the Latin American bishops and cardinals at the Ecumenical Council in Rome. As reported by the Mexican journal *Política*, they spoke of the necessity of social reforms and "expressed concern about the wretched position of believers and their exploitation by capitalists."[5] The leaders of the Latin American organization Young Christian Workers have also called for economic reforms. In 1959, they said: "According to data from the experts of the UN Economic Commission for Latin America, the population in this area will

increase by one hundred million by 1957 [*sic*] and this fact makes it necessary for all countries to increase the rate of their industrialization, because this is the only way to solve their problems."[6] Catholic trade unions have made similar declarations. For example, the congresses of the Latin American Confederation of Christian Trade Unions in 1957 and 1959 advocated the institution of economic reforms, eradication of discrimination in labor, institution of agrarian reforms, and removal of the dictatorial regimes.

The contemporary social doctrine of the Catholic Church was presented in its most complete form in the papal encyclical *Mater et Magistra*, published in July 1961. It is considered the ideological weapon of the clergy of the entire world, including the countries of Latin America. Catholic propaganda has been widely popularizing it among various levels of the population, presenting it as a program for raising the standard of living of the masses without a class struggle. Special attention has been called to those points in the encyclical which consider "national capitalism" as a means to transform society, which suggest acknowledgment of "the desire of the workers to participate more actively in the operation of businesses" as lawful, and which recommend that capitalists" give shares of the business on credit to their hired hands, especially those whose wages do not exceed the minimum."[7]

The encyclical's appeal for an effort toward "effective and just distribution of the wealth" is echoed in the pastoral letter of the Chilean episcopate.[8] And the Argentine Catholic journal *Criterio*,

[3] *Informations Catholiques Internationales*, February 15, 1961, p. 26.
[4] *Ibid.*
[5] *Política*, January 1, 1963.
[6] *Jeunesse dans le Monde*, May 1960, p. 35.
[7] *La Documentation Catholique*, August 6, 1961, p. 958.
[8] *El Mercurio*, September 23, 1962.

for example, has assured its readers that the encyclical "presents to Catholics and all people of good will a method for analyzing contemporary social problems and a way to influence existing reality."[9]

At the same time, a very careful examination reveals that the actions of the princes of the Church with regard to the institution of reforms have been dictated primarily by the fear that a wave of national anger could turn into a revolution that would sweep them out of Latin America along with the imperialists who support their bourgeois-landholding cliques and the reactionary militarists. Therefore the Church adheres to the principle that it is better to institute reforms from above than to wait until they are brought about by the masses from below. This was hinted at in the memorandum delivered to the President of Brazil by the Brazilian episcopate on July 14, 1962. In discussing the so-called threat of communism, they implored the ruling classes to agree upon instituting reforms, explaining that any other decision would actually be "suicide."[10] In that same year, it was noted in a pastoral letter of the Guatemalan episcopate dedicated to "social problems and communism" that one could "expect the very worst" if the necessary reforms were not introduced to raise the living standards of the population.[11] The journal *Informations Catholiques Internationales* expressed this line even more succinctly in one of its articles about the situation in the Latin American countries. "If important social reforms are not implemented in a short time," the journal stated, "if this crying social injustice is not eliminated, the present rulers are risking provoking the masses to despair and throwing them into the arms of communism."[12]

Thus, no matter how the clergy propagandizes their "new" social doctrine among the masses, its true character is quite clear. Thus, it is no accident that the encyclical mentioned above, which was directed toward the preservation and strengthening of the dying capitalistic order, was favorably regarded by a significant part of the ruling cliques of Latin America. Many large capitalists recognized the "expediency" of its tenets, particularly K. Loren, one of the leaders of the Catholic Association of Business Managers of Argentina, and V. Xacaxa, a representative of the Argentine Union of Catholic Industrialists.[13] Finally, Pope John XXIII himself remarked that his encyclical *Mater et Magistra* was "warmly received by the businessmen" of the countries of Latin America.[14]

Reforms urged by the clergy are half-measures, and their implementation would not resolve the complex social problems stirring the workers of Latin America. The Communist Party of Colombia, discussing the "agrarian reform" plans proposed by the powerful bourgeoisie and supported by the clergy of that country, noted in the political resolution of its Ninth Congress in June 1961, that the matter was a "pitiful concession" meant to hinder the peasantry's struggle for land.[15]

The stand taken by the clergy on the institution of reforms from above is closely connected with their support of the Alliance for Progress. So the Chilean Jesuit, Cifuentes Grets, regards this North American imperialistic program as one of the means of "peaceful implementation of revolution." Argentine

[9]*Criterio*, July 27, 1961, p. 534.
[10]*Informations Catholiques Internationales*, August 1962, p. 14.
[11]*La Croix*, January 6–7, 1963.
[12]*Informations Catholiques Internationales*, September 15, 1962, p. 20.
[13]*La Prensa*, December 5, 1962.
[14]*La Documentation Catholique*, April 1, 1962, p. 420.
[15]*Programmnye dokumenty kommunisticheskikh i rabochikh partii stran Ameriki* (Moskva, 1962), p. 159.

cardinal Caggiano, speaking in one of the Catholic congresses in Mexico in 1961, also did not stint on the glorification of the Alliance for Progress. Specifically, such a position is conditioned by the fact that part of the financial resources received by the Latin American governments on the basis of this program falls in many cases into the hands of the clergy. For example, the clergy received a large sum for "education" in Colombia, where the educational system is Church-controlled.

While agreeing to limited reforms, the Catholic leaders at the same time adjure the peoples of the Latin American countries not to accept the socialist method of development in any case. And the deeper the ideas of socialism penetrate into the masses, the more furiously the campaign of slander against this most progressive social system is conducted. "Young Christian workers," for example, states the bulletin of that organization, "are refusing to support those demands which lead to radical socialism—a tendency that is becoming particularly widespread at factories.[16]

Catholic propaganda asserts that this path is not acceptable to the countries of Latin America, because it is incompatible with the supposed special devotion of the population to Christianity and to "individualism." The clerics proclaim themselves proponents of a "third way," which in the long run is the same as "people's capitalism." Actually, all the arguments of the clerics lead to declarative censure of the "old" capitalism and a demagogic appeal to replace it with the "new," more "democratic" way, which would supposedly lead to the creation of a "state of general prosperity."

Working in the interests of the ruling cliques, the Church advocates repudiation of the class struggle and regards strikes as "undesirable." In this regard the Argentine journal *Criterio* wrote:

"One should never consider work stoppage as the first and normal method of solving labor conflicts. A strike has economic consequences. Work stoppages affect production and paralyze economic mechanisms. . . . A strike even has social consequences. . . . It aggravates the mutual distrust between the workers and industrialists and intensifies the class struggle."[17]

The scope of the democratic movement on the continent and the aspiration of the workers to attain basic changes in all areas of social life makes not only the Church hierarchy in Latin America but also the leaders in the Vatican uneasy. In a series of epistles, speeches, and addresses, they summon Latin American Catholics to "moderation" and "prudence" in instituting reforms in social and economic areas and let it be understood that nationalization and the battle against Yankee imperialism should not be speeded up.

In the Vatican it is thought that, if these reforms are inevitable, they should be carried out on the basis of the social doctrine of the Church. In January 1962, for example, in his address to the bishops of Latin America, the Pope expressed concern over "the serious problems of civil, social, and economic character" and urged their solution "with complete delicacy and necessary wisdom within the framework of God's law and the rules of morality." The general lines of action of the clergy are laid out in the address as follows: "To disseminate as broadly as possible a Christian social doctrine and awaken the believers . . . to the existence of it in practicality, being aware at the same time of false doctrines and prejudices, which are so destructive to the prosperity and freedom of nations and the eternal salvation of souls, and guarding against the insinuations of the

[16]*Bulletin de la JOC Internationale*, 11:4 (1959).
[17]*Criterio*, November 23, 1961, p. 844.

Church's enemies, according to whom the Church should not be concerned about the needs of this world."[18]

Thus, the Catholic Church calls for repudiation of the socialist method of development—the only way that can guarantee the Latin American peoples rapid economic success and prosperity. It backs the implementation of limited reforms within the framework of the social doctrine of the Church, the basis of which is the sacred principle of private ownership of the means of production. This means that the half-measures proposed by the clergy can lead only to a certain variation in the form of domination by the North American imperialists and bourgeois-landholding cliques in the countries of Latin America. The path along which the Catholic Church wants to lead the peoples of these countries is in fact the path of capitalism embellished with demagogic phraseology.

In the last few years, the practical activity of the Catholic Church in Latin America has been distinguished by an apparent flexibility in masking its actual essence. If the clerics earlier openly supported the ruling classes, denounced the workers' demonstrations against foreign capital and latifundists, and closed their eyes to the monstrous exploitation of the masses, racial discrimination against the Indian population, and existence of the remnants of feudalism—they are now trying to create among the masses an impression that supposedly the clergy itself and the organizations associated with it are the true spokesmen for the workers' interests. This tendency reflects the aspiration to strengthen the position of clericalism and re-establish its former influence in these countries. In order not to find itself bypassed by history, the Church hierarchy adjusts by all possible means to the present stage of development in Latin America, now that it has become necessary to solve the problems of the anti-imperialistic and antifeudal

revolution. It is precisely for this reason that the Catholic hierarchy is spuriously proclaiming its love for the people and is concealing its ties with reaction.

One of the tactics to which the clergy are resorting to win the trust of the workers is the effort to create an impression of maximum affinity with the masses of the population, a superficial "democratization." To do this, the Church from time to time even makes material sacrifices, in spite of which, incidentally, her riches do not dwindle. Thus, there have been some occasions of transfer of Church land to the peasants in Latin America. For example, in 1962 the press reported that the archbishop of the city of Medellín, Colombia, Tulio B. Salazar, relinquished all his riches for the use of the workers and transferred the ownership of his luxurious estate to them as a school for the preparation of leaders of Catholic social organizations. Such measures, designed for outward effect and testifying to the fact that it is becoming ever more difficult for the clergy to retain their influence among the masses, are utilized immediately for the creation of extensive propaganda campaigns designed to demonstrate that the Church is supposedly another "have-not."

However, having chosen this course, the leaders of the Catholic Church clashed with the necessity of defining their attitude to the social struggle that is being led by the workers. This problem is even more acute for the Catholic trade unions and other organizations created specifically to strengthen the position of the clergy within the labor movement. As a result, they have worked out flexible tactics that allow them to retain control over certain sectors of the masses.

Although, as mentioned above, the

[18]*La Documentation Catholique*, April 1, 1962, p. 419.

Catholic hierarchy and its agents among the workers condemn strikes—the great weapon of the working class in its struggle for its rights—nevertheless, in a number of instances Christian trade-union leaders had to assume the role of strike leaders, as organizers of demonstrations of the workers against employers. In 1957 they participated in the large strike of the Argentine bank workers. Later, in Chile, several thousand members of a Catholic trade union undertook a "hunger march" in the capital, Santiago. In Panama, some of the unemployed headed by Catholic trade-union leaders burst into the parliament building demanding changes in the government's economic policies. In Montevideo, Uruguay, workers who were members of a Catholic trade union and their leaders occupied a building belonging to General Electric and held it for a month.

However, in all such incidents the Christian trade-union leaders, as a rule, were responding exclusively to pressure from below and to fear of losing their influence on the working class. Moreover, participation of the clergy in the strikes gives them an opportunity to control the scope of the demonstrations and hold them within prescribed limits. The higher clergy readily acts as an intermediary between strikers and employers, putting into practice the policy of "class peace." For example, Cardinal Caggiano assumed such a role when the Argentine railroad workers went on strike in 1961.[19]

In all this activity, the Catholic hierarchy not only accentuates in every way possible the "revolutionary actions" of the clerical trade unions, but also tries to create the impression that it is becoming the most consistent fighter for realization of the hopes of the workers. To this end it uses in particular the disputes that spring up periodically between the clergy and various industrialists. For example, in Brazil the em-

ployers—who were perturbed by the fact that a Catholic lawyer, Mario Carvalho, led a two-month strike in Santo André near São Paulo, which was supported by Bishop De Oliveira—threatened to stop making deductions for the Church, describing the leaders of the strike as "Communists."[20]

However, these actions of the Catholic circles, which are heralded as concern for the welfare of the workers, are actually protection of the interests of the bourgeoisie. This fact is frequently disclosed by the clergy itself. It has happened this way, for example, in Guatemala, where the employers have accused the clergy of playing a double role, receiving money from the capitalists and at the same time supporting the workers in their fight against owners. Such a "misunderstanding" of the meaning behind the activities of the clergy in the labor movement on the part of their shortsighted partners irritated the clergy. The archbishop of Guatemala, Rosselli Arellano, frankly acknowledged that the clergy had acted in the interests of the employers and spoke with indignation of those who "call us Communists—we who are defending their rights."[21]

The Catholic workers' organizations use the Church openly for political objectives. At times they do so to implement their plans in connection with one or another group of the ruling bourgeoisie. Because of this, the participation of the clergy in anti-imperialistic demonstrations and in the battle against dictatorial regimes in an overwhelming majority of instances has nothing in common with those problems which the democratic forces are confronting. Usually the Church only tries to wrest compromises from the

---

[19]*Criterio*, December 24, 1961, p. 937.
[20]*Informations Catholiques Internationales*, September 1, 1960, p. 10.
[21]*Ibid.*, February 1, 1961, p. 10.

dictatorial regimes, but when it sees that the regimes' days are numbered, it quickly joins the future victors. That is how it was in Argentina, for example, when the Christian trade unions took part in the sixty-day strike of 300,000 metallurgical workers that played a crucial part in the fall of Perón, and also in Venezuela and Paraguay, where the Catholic trade-union leaders, E. A. González and F. V. Rodas, took part in the fight against the dictatorial regimes of Jiménez and Stroessner.

The basic purpose of the Catholic Church's participation in the labor movement is to undermine its unity and its revolutionary efforts and the growing influence of the vanguard of the proletariat, the Communist parties. The reactionary essence of these efforts, of the clergy appeared most distinctly after the victory of the people's revolution in Cuba, where a part of the Catholic trade-union leaders embarked on a counterrevolutionary path and cooperated with the armed provocations of U.S. imperialism against the Cuban people. As a result, the people's government had to halt the subversive activities of these accomplices of clericalism.

The Church regards labor unity as a major danger to it, and the struggle against unification as a basic part of the battle against communism. The offensive of the clericalist forces in the labor movement is proceeding, for the most part, in two directions. The Catholic trade-union leaders either try to reorganize the existing trade unions into reformist organizations by means of seizing control of their administration, or by separating part of the workers from the unions and founding new ones. The reactionary clergy gives special attention to efforts to weaken the democratic federations of the working class, which are the consistent champions of the interests of the masses. They repeatedly attack the Confederación de Trabajadores del Ecuador and the Cen-

tral Única de Trabajadores de Chile with the goal of dividing them. This has succeeded in Colombia. As was noted in the political resolution of the Ninth Congress of the Communist Party of that country, the ones guilty of undermining trade-union unity in this case were "powers alien to the working class.... We mean the struggle between the bourgeoisie, who are predominant in the leadership of trade-union centers, and Church ideology, on the one hand, and proletarian ideology, on the other, which breaches its way into the toiling masses."[22]

The policies of the reactionary clergymen with regard to the working class are therefore divisive and in total contradiction to the interests of the toiling masses, including Catholic workers.

The Communist parties of Latin America are fighting for the unity of all patriotic, democratic forces. They set out from the fact that North American imperialism is the main enemy of the working class and of all the workers of the Latin American countries, and that all of the latter are interested in completing the struggle against foreign domination, the latifundists, and the antinational, proimperialist bourgeoisie. In the interests of the anti-imperialist, antifeudal revolution, the Communists call for unity also from those Catholics who, in spite of differences over the basic goals or methods of achieving them, are ready to work jointly for the good of the working class. In so doing, the Communist parties are displaying the maximum good will and the desire to reach an agreement in the highest interests of all the workers alone, without tying their partners to the communist ideology.

Thus, the Twelfth Congress of the Communist Party of Chile, affirming in its program approved in March 1962

[22]*Programmnye dokumenty kommunisticheskikh i rabochikh partii stran Ameriki*, p. 167.

that "the basis for an anti-imperialistic coalition and its primary condition is the unity of the working class," declared: "The Communist Party leads the struggle for the organization, strengthening, and development of anti-imperialistic unity in order to achieve patriotic collaboration among all classes, sectors, groups, and persons to whom the peace, freedom, independence, and progress of Chile are precious. In addition, we Communists are ready to enter into agreement, even temporary agreement, on all or any part of our program, even point by point. We are prepared to consider with equal interest the opinions of all other factions and to formulate jointly a program in the interests of the nation."[23]

Declarations similar in spirit and character are contained in materials of congresses and plenums of leading organs and in speeches of responsible leaders of other Communist parties of Latin America. The Brazilian Communist Party called for unity of action at its Fifth Congress in September 1960, and emphasized: "Trade unions and other professional organizations must not serve the cause of divisions within the working class. On the contrary, they must be an instrument for unity of action of the workers and all ideological and political trends banded together in trade unions, as well as nonorganized and nonparty workers. Communists must fight to see that the trade-union movement is not limited to the activity of the upper leadership, but that the workers actively participate in it."[24] The Communist Party of Venezuela also considers that the policy of united action and ties with organizations influential with the working class and toiling masses is essential. Its Third Congress called for closer ties with those sectors in the Christian Socialist Party which "regardless of their vacillation and weakness, are willing to conduct talks

and find points of agreement with the left and to make a stand against the old capitulationist policy, a policy of betraying the interests of the country to imperialism."[25]

The position of the overwhelming majority of leaders of Catholic parties, trade unions, and other clerical organizations in regard to the program of unity of action proposed by the democratic forces is nevertheless determined by the spirit of anticommunism that is supported by the upper heirarchy of the Church in Latin America. For a long time the Catholics were categorically forbidden to cooperate with Communists in any manner; only in very recent times has there been a more flexible approach to the problem. This may be explained by the fact that life itself has frustrated the prohibitions of the reactionary Church leadership. The presence of the common enemy—North American monopolies and powerful domestic capitalists and latifundists—gives rise to a community of interests among workers of all religious and political beliefs. As a result, ordinary worker members of Catholic trade unions ever more frequently participate in strikes and anti-imperialistic demonstrations along with their own class brothers— the Communists, Socialists, and radicals. This has occurred in Brazil, Argentina, Chile, Peru, and other Latin American countries where the social conflicts have become acute.

The leadership of Catholic trade unions cannot neglect the workers' insistent efforts for unity. Under pressure from below, definite improvements in this regard have occurred in a number of Latin American countries. In recent

[23]*Ibid., p.* 322.
[24]*Ibid.,* pp. 27–28.
[25]*Ibid., p.* 74.

years distinct advances toward working-class unity have been noted in Bolivia, Chile, Uruguay, Ecuador, and Haiti, where single trade-union centers have been established. In Chile, for example, three leaders of the Christian Democrats joined the Communists and Socialists in the executive council of CUTCh. The trade-union conference of the Confederación de Trabajadores de América Latina (CTAL) in September 1962 was a success in the struggle for unity. Attending were representatives of various political and ideological views in the labor movements—Socialists, Communists, Peronistas, and Christian Democrats. Participating in its sessions were 120 delegates representing 22 million workers.[26]

It is evident from the above that some of the Catholic trade-union leadership, forced to take note of the mood of the masses, is displaying a trend toward partial and not always consistent withdrawal from its former position of militant anticommunism, toward a search for mutually satisfactory solutions to the problem of the unity of the working class in the struggle for its interests.

The upper clergy has also begun to maneuver. In a pastoral letter of 1962, the episcopate of Chile, though it defined communism as a "delusion," nevertheless could not refrain from admitting its avant-garde role in the transformation of society. The letter reads: "Communism contains something of the truth. It seeks to improve conditions of the working class, destroy existing abuses, and achieve a more just distribution of wealth. Furthermore, it is true that it has, in large measure, contributed to the awakening of people and institutions from a deep, age-old inertia and has among its assets undeniable material and scientific achievements."[27]

Along with the fears that "should communism achieve victory in Chile, the Church and its children may expect only persecution, blood, and tears" and categorically forbidding Catholics to engage "voluntarily" in any form of contact with Communists, the Chilean episcopate still does not exclude the possibility of making such contacts with the approval of Church authorities. "In this delicate realm, more than in any other," the letter says, "caution and filial submission to the directives of the Church are recommended."[28]

The Catholic hierarchy is pushed into these maneuvers by the not unfounded fears that, under circumstances of an irresistible demand of the workers for unity, the Church could lose influence among the people and be cast aside by evolving events. This pressure of the masses on the policy of the upper hierarchy will no doubt increase to the degree that political, economic, and social contradictions in the countries of Latin America are aggravated, and the anti-imperialist, antifeudal struggle is developed.

The Catholic leadership, closely linked with North American imperialism and semifeudal elements, basically implements the reactionary policy of supporting conservative forces, promoting anticommunism, and persecuting democratic organizations. Church leaders strive to weaken the working class, to hinder its unity, and anesthetize the consciousness of the laboring masses with social-democratic demagogy.

Despite this situation, the Catholic workers, experiencing the same joys and sorrows as their class brothers and suffering from exploitation as much as Communist, Socialist, Peronista, and radical workers, are deeply interested in the realization of a social-economic transformation. Such circumstances

[26]Vsemirnoe profsoiuznoe dvizhenie, 11:5, 9 (1962).
[27]El Mercurio, September 23, 1962.
[28]Ibid.

create the prerequisites for solidarity of the labor movement and for the establishment of single trade-union centers and a common, anti-imperialist, antifeudal struggle.

Consequently, the leadership of the Catholic Church in Latin America, striving to retain the allegiance of that element of the working class under its influence, attempts to combine its anticommunist posture with a flexible policy of accommodation to new situations. In the face of the powerful upsurge of the liberation movement, the Church hierarchy propagandizes the same old social doctrine of Catholicism, but now adjusted to the requirements of the ruling classes in the contemporary stage of the general crisis of capitalism.

15. The Evolution of the Christian Democratic Movement in Latin America*

S. I. Semenov

As the experience of Cuba has shown, revolutionary change is taking place in the Ibero-American republics in a more favorable international situation than was present earlier in Eastern European and even in many Asian and African countries. Capitalism has so discredited itself in the eyes of society that only a few individuals still act as apologists for it, the more so since in Latin America the overwhelming majority of the population knows only too well the delights of the "free enterprise" system, from its own experience.

Since the population of each Latin American republic remains basically under the influence of Catholic ideology, the attraction toward political life of great masses who had earlier stood aloof from politics, their turn toward the socialistic ideal, and the search for ways to attain it are producing an internal upheaval in the traditional Catholic movement. Individual voices of Catholic Democrats, which even in the early twentieth century were rather easily muffled by the conservative Church hierarchy, now begin to sound like a united chorus and are starting a whole new trend. The Catholic Church, compelled to take into account changes in the social situation and the world outlook of its flock, is relinquishing its dogma of single-party Catholicism and disciplining political action by Catholics, and is sanctioning the formation

*Osvoboditel'noe dvizhenie v Latinskoi Amerike, ed. S. S. Mikhailov (Moskva: Izdatel'stvo Nauka, 1964), pp. 207, 208–217.

of such political parties as would advance programs of moderate social reform. However, having once allowed the spirit of inquiry and independent thinking to emerge from the narrow container stuffed with thousand-year-old dogmas, the Church now finds it difficult to control that spirit. In the new parties, which usually adopt the Christian Democratic label, a radical democratic trend is emerging. These processes leave a quite singular impression on the entire progress of the liberation struggle in the Ibero-American countries.

It goes without saying that in most of these countries it would be unthinkable to build anything like a broad united front, to organize revolutionary action, and to transform the social structure and the political system without the participation of Catholics. To achieve unity of action with Catholic-patriots and with Catholic-Democrats, to involve them in the working people's day-to-day struggle is one of the fundamental problems of the revolution in the countries of South and Central America. The issue here is not only and not so much to attract progressive leaders who openly break with the Catholic Church and carry with them a number of parishioners. Where Catholic political parties are really mass parties, the problem arises of how to defeat the common enemy despite ideological differences with these parties and how gradually to lessen the breach between their respective positions on the basis of revolutionary program.

It must be remembered that the Christian Democratic movement began later in the Ibero-American countries than in Europe. The Catholic Church, which has maintained and in many Latin American areas still maintains spiritual sway over the population—particularly the rural element—has inherited from colonial times vast land-holdings and wealth. It has often acted as the unseen organizer of conservative landlord parties, assuring them votes and sometimes soldiers drawn from the fanatical and benighted mass of peasants, hired farm workers, urban mixed classes, and lumpen proletariat.

However, it was precisely the fact that the masses served as the base for the conservative parties, while the landowner elite was leading them, which caused democratic trends to appear among these parties. Moreover, in trying to secure popular support in their struggle against the liberal parties, especially after the secularization of church and monastery estates, individual conservative leaders resorted to preaching feudal socialism. This preaching often went along with the ideological-political trend known as Hispanism, which came alive particularly as a reaction to pressure by the imperialist United States after the Spanish-American War of 1898 and during the First World War. No matter how reactionary it was with its dream of returning to the colonial "golden age," its rejection of "industrialization," and its contrasting of the "Spanish" spiritual principle to "Anglo-Saxon" materialism, Hispanism nevertheless sounded some anti-imperialist and even democratic notes.

In Brazil, the movement for the spiritual and political renewal of Catholicism—which, according to the acute observation of João Cruz Costa, appeared like "Catholic reaction to the spread of socialist ideas after the First World War"[1]—had a strong nationalistic anti-Portuguese tinge. But even this movement, the ideological leader of which was the philosopher and

---

[1]João Cruz Costa. *Contribução a historia das Ideias no Brazil* (O desenvolvimento da Filosofia no Brazil e a evolução historica nacional) (Rio de Janeiro, 1956), p. 416. See also Pedro Motta Lima, "Marksizm-leninizm i kul'turnaia zhizn' Brazilii," *Problemy mira i sotsializma*, 10:22 (1962).

writer Jackson de Figueiredo, seemed to have the world outlook of a freed slave of the colonial middle ages, harking back to the lost patriarchal paradise.

The thought of the emerging ideologists and leaders of the Christian Democratic parties, such as the Uruguayan jurist and diplomat Dardo Regules, was shaped by the very strong influence of Hispanism. In their works written in the 1920's and 1930's, a generally conservative and paternalistic conception of Christian Democracy was developed, and they repeatedly referred to its creator, the Italian Giuseppe Toniolo.[2] The opinions of the Brazilian Alceu Amoroso Lima, who is known under his pseudonym, Tristão de Athayde, carried the stamp of strong influence by the French neo-Thomist philosopher, Jacques Maritain.

The active eruption of the working class and its parties into the political life of their countries, especially during the years of the world economic crisis, caused ideologists of the Social-Christian tendency to shift from propagandizing their convictions to political action. This was also aided by the papal encyclical *Quadragesimo Anno,* which appeared in 1931.

The first arena in which the Christian Socialists tested their doctrine was the universities. When the movement for university reform began (Argentina, 1918), the students emerged as the vanguard in the revolutionary battles. The slogan of a united workers' and students' front enjoyed great popularity in Latin America. By way of the student movement, the Christian Socialists hoped to find a mass audience, to forge their own cadres of political activists, and to penetrate into "the people."

The National Alliance of Catholic Students of Mexico, founded in late 1931, took the initiative in convoking the American Catholic Student Con-

gress. It laid the beginning of the Ibero-American Confederation of Catholic Students, comprising student leagues from Chile, Uruguay, Mexico, Peru, Ecuador, Colombia, Costa Rica, Cuba, Puerto Rico, and Spain.[3] At first it was directly subordinated to Church authorities, but in 1941 it acquired a degree of independence. This confederation was a kind of forge preparing future organizers of Christian Democratic parties. For example, one of the founders of the Chilean Christian Democratic party, E. Frei, was at one time chairman of the University Catholic Association of Chile, and secretary-general of the American Congress of Catholic University Students in Rome (1931–1933).

The framework that held the declining conservative parties, which had too definitely linked their destinies with the landed oligarchy and big capital, proved too confining and prevented the Christian Socialist leaders from establishing connections with urban middle strata and workers.

It was not by accident that independent Christian Democratic parties first emerged in countries where the traditions of a labor movement and class struggle were strongest. After the proclamation in Chile—for the first time on the American continent—of a socialist republic, short-lived as it was, and after Chilean Socialists and Communists had joined in a single bloc, the Christian Democratic elements in 1935 founded their own organization within the Conservative Party. The triumph of the popular front in Chile in 1938 and the orientation of Conservative Party leaders toward fascist Germany caused the Christian Democratic

[2]Tristão de Athayde, *Introducción a la sociología* (Buenos Aires, 1958), p. 126.
[3]*Handbook of International Organizations in the Americas.* Prep. by Ruth D. Masters (Washington, D. C., 1945), p. 75.

organization to break completely with the Conservatives and to form into an independent antifascist party that they named National Falange. However, the influence of the latter spread mostly among the petty-bourgeois Catholic intelligentsia and a portion of the student body. A somewhat similar social base underlay the oldest of the existing Christian Democratic parties of Latin America—the Uruguayan Civic Alliance, founded in 1912.[4]

Attempts to form a Christiam Democratic party in Argentina were unsuccessful. The groups that acted here at different times—the Christian Democratic League (1902), the Christian Democratic Alliance (1911 and 1920), and the People's Party (1927–1932)—unsuccessfully attempted to transplant onto Argentine soil the experience of the Italian Christian Democrats. The presence of a military dictatorship that securely protected estate landownership and the privileges of big capital caused the Catholic Church to nip in the bud any tendencies toward creating a mass Christian Democratic party in Argentina.

In the other Latin American republics, only scattered Christian Socialist circles were active, usually within the limits of the traditional rightist parties. Thus the Christian Democratic trend played no outstanding part in the political life of the Ibero-American countries, either before or during the Second World War. As the Colombian political leader Belisario Betancur said: "For long years, years of Christian humility, we existed in destitution and waited in vain—sometimes at the sacrifice of dignity—for heavenly manna that some outside protector, some monopolist power greedy for our resources, would bestow on us, in view of our backward condition. Meanwhile, the landed aristocracy's conspicuous consumption increased and the purchasing power of the proletarian masses declined."[5]

During the 1940's, the Christian Democratic trend in Latin America often suffered attacks from the official representatives of the Catholic Church for its radicalism and for collaborating with progressive forces. The upper hierarchy of South America, closely bound up with the great landowners was hostile to it.[6] Thus, for example, the leader of the Catholic Action Organization in Chile rudely attacked the National Falange Party. The senior Catholic hierarchs of Brazil took a similar stand.

Perhaps the only exception in this matter was the Costa Rican archbishop, Sanabria, who supported the Communists in their struggle to introduce progressive labor legislation. The Partido del Vanguardia Popular of Costa Rica, after it became an impressive national power, managed to secure a united front with progressively minded members of the Catholic Church, which undoubtedly aided its struggle for peaceful development of that country along a democratic course during the 1930's and the Second World War. A direct result of this struggle was the adoption of a labor code, the first in that country's history, which confirmed the gains of the Costa Rican working class.

[4]To be sure, this organization differs substantially from other Christian Democratic parties of Latin America in that it came into being in a country where the influence of the Catholic Church is minimal.

[5]Belisario Betancur, *Colombia cara a cara* (Bogotá, 1961), p. 189.

[6]Generally speaking, the social doctrine of the Catholic Church has always been viewed by the conservative upper hierarchy of the Latin American countries as a dangerous innovation and sometimes as a suspicious heresy. In Mexico, for example, the encyclical *Rerum Novarum* did not become known until after the 1910 revolution. The influential Catholic newspaper of Chile, *Diario ilustrado*, refused for a long time to publish the encyclical *Quadragesimo Anno*. The encyclical *Mater et Magistra* also met with hostility in these spheres. A conspiracy of silence enveloped the encyclical *Pacem in Terris*.

The rise of the liberation movement in Latin America from 1943 to 1946, the dynamic growth of the Communist parties, the perspective of profound social-political reforms that opened before many states as a result of the defeat of the fascist powers by the Soviet Union and its allies, and the serious weakening of the world capitalist system led to a regrouping of forces in the Latin American countries.

The crisis of the Pan American system was reflected, among other things, in the collapse of the traditional parties that had secured the stability of the Ibero-American states' social-political structure. Changes in the population structure caused by the industrial transformation led to the loss of a social base by the traditional parties, primarily the conservative ones. Among the ruling classes themselves, noticeable shifts are occurring, and the groups that formerly governed are gradually fading from the political scene. Their former position became the object of competition, basically between two groups: on the one hand, the reformist parties, which ideologically are close to European Social Democracy; and, on the other, the Christian Democrats. It may be said that the social bases of both, in spite of differing ideological sources, were about the same, as even their basic programs were similar.

The beginning of the "cold war" and the shift to the right of the Christian Democratic parties of Italy and France coincided with increased political activity among South America's Christian Democrats. It is noteworthy that the initiative in this matter came from the Uruguayan Dardo Regules, known for his ties with North American monopoly capital and a most energetic participant in the formation of the military-political bloc of the American states under the aegis of the United States.

In 1947, almost simultaneously with the visit to Washington of de Gasperi, the Italian Christian Democratic Party leader, Regules arranged a meeting of the Christian Democrats in Montevideo, where he represented Uruguay; Eduardo Frei represented Chile; Alceu Amoroso Lima, Brazil; and Manuel Ordóñez, Argentina. This was how the "Montevideo Movement" came into being. Its participants gathered again in 1949, when the Christian Democrats from Peru joined them. The result of this meeting was the formation of the Organización Demócrata-Cristiana de América (ODCA),[7] which is of a closed nature; any party desiring to join it must show proof of its devotion to the common ideal, and the question of accepting new members can be decided only by the organization's congress.

The members of the ODCA are the Christian Democratic parties of Argentina, Brazil, Uruguay, Chile, Panama, and Peru, and the Christian Socialist parties of Bolivia and Venezuela.[8] Christian Democratic parties, movements, and groups from the following countries maintain connections with it as sympathizers: Colombia, Costa Rica, Ecuador, El Salvador, Guatemala, Mexico, Nicaragua, Panama, Paraguay, the Dominican Republic, Puerto Rico, Curaçao, and British Guiana, as well as one of the Cuban counterrevolutionary groups. All these parties are not clerical (confessional) ones in the proper sense of the word. In other words, they are not directly subordinated to the clergy and may include persons who are not Catholics.

The unfolding of revolutionary processes in many Ibero-American coun-

[7]For practical purposes, this organization in its modern shape began activity after the meetings of 1955 and 1957, which since then have come to be called "congresses."

[8]The latter is better known under the name of Committee for the Introduction of Independent Policies in Elections (COPEI).

tries, along with the irrefutable evidence of the advantages of socialism over capitalism, have led the Christian Democratic parties in Latin America to break officially with conservative traditions and declare themselves to be a revolutionary and anticapitalist force. The congresses of their representatives take place under commensurately corresponding slogans. "Christians who share the principles of this conference," states a resolution of the first congress of 1947, "must resolutely break with the practice of constantly defending the capitalist system in any domain."[9] Their duty, in the opinion of the participants of the Montevideo Movement, is to help the worker and peasant masses to achieve their rights and their participation in economic, political, and cultural life.[10]

Inasmuch as not a one of these parties has full power[11] and all of them, with the exception of the Christian Democratic Party, are in opposition to the existing governments,[12] it is not, on the whole, too much of a burden on them to stigmatize capitalism and the existing order. The sincerity of these speeches, however, appears doubtful, since, for instance, the Third Congress of Christian Democracy in South America established official connections with such zealous defenders of capitalist ramparts as the West European Christian Democratic leaders. It seems noteworthy too that on the invitation of this congress, the first world-wide Christian Democrat conference took place in Paris in 1956. And as the result of the two subsequent conferences that took place in Brussels in 1958 and in Santiago in 1961, the Christian Democratic parties of Latin America and Western Europe joined in a single organization. The drawing-in of the Christian Socialist parties and groups of the Caribbean zone, which are distinguished by their conservatism, also

does not fit revolutionary and anti-capitalist concepts. Nevertheless, as one of the prominent leaders of the Belgian Christian Socialist Party admitted, "the Christian Democratic parties of Latin America stand much farther to the left than their confreres in Europe."[13]

On one hand, this is explained by the "new course" of the Catholic Church in Latin America,[14] worried by the so-called de-Christianization of the population.[15] On the other, changes in the structure of the population, displacement of great masses of former peasant believers and hired rural workers who have gone to live in the cities, increasing numbers of Catholic workers and urban middle strata who do not give up religion—all these factors cannot help but revolutionize the political and ideological views of honest leaders of the Christian Democrats in Latin American countries. Thus, the Catholic masses, who only yesterday were illiterate and did not have the right to vote—especially the women, who received that right only recently—are being drawn into political life and struggle by the Christian Democrats, who talk a language and advance slogans these people can understand.

[9]*Congresos Internacionales Demócrata-Cristianos* (Santiago de Chile, 1957), p. 25.

[10]*Ibid.*, pp. 3, 7.

[11]The Christian Democrats put up their own candidates for presidential elections in Argentina, Venezuela, Chile, Peru, and Guatemala, but invariably suffered defeats.

[12]The following have their own representatives in parliament: the Christian Democratic parties of Brazil, Chile, Peru, Uruguay, and Venezuela; and their analogous groups in Ecuador, Costa Rica, El Salvador, and—until dissolution of the parliament—in Guatemala.

[13]Raymond Scheyven, *De Punta del Este a La Havane. L'Amérique Latine et le Monde.* 2nd ed., p. 11.

[14]Jean Gaçon, "Pacem in Terris," *Democratie Nouvelle*, 6:13 (1963).

[15]Raymond Scheyven, *De Punta del Este a La Havane*, p. 116; *Social Change in Latin America Today: Its Implications for U.S. Policy* (New York, 1960), pp. 53–54.

16. The Significance of the Christian Democratic Electoral Victory in Chile*

I. R. GRIGULEVICH

Leaders of the Partido Demócrato-Cristiano (PDC) emphasize that their party will pursue the policy of the European Christian Democrats, with whom they are developing and strengthening ties in every possible way. After World War II, there sprang up in Latin America the Organización Demócrata-Cristiana de América (ODCA), which—along with the Chilean PDC—was joined by other clerical parties of Latin America. The ODCA, in turn, became a component part of an international organization uniting all other Christian Democratic parties. In this way the Chilean clerics achieved political "maturity" and found their place as a part of the world clerical movement. This facilitated their reconciliation with the church hierarchy and still closer cooperation with the followers and leaders of the former Falange.

Advocating widely disseminated "reformist slogans," the PDC was able to unite within its ranks the national bourgeoisie, churchmen, and the petty bourgeois masses—civil service officials, storekeepers, a section of the professional intellectuals, students, and the lower popular strata. On the political plane, they are also joined by such diverse elements as fascistic conservatives, liberals, and even Catholic supporters of Fidel Castro.

Can the PDC be called a clerical party, considering that even nonbelievers are admitted to it and that the PDC leaders themselves reject such a designation? Unquestionably, in our opinion, for the ideology is a variation of Christian socialism and its major ideologists are theoreticians of Catholic Church "renewal."

Transforming their party into a respectable clerical party, the Chilean clergy began to think seriously of rising to power. In the 1958 elections they nominated a candidate for president for the first time—party leader E. Frei. The struggle that developed around his nomination demonstrated that there were several trends within the party: the rightist, which stood for more complete submission to the Church hierarchy and for an openly anti-Communist policy; the leftist, inclined toward closer cooperation with leftist forces; and the centrist, maneuvering between the right and the left—joining the right, and then

*"Tserkov' i klerikalizm v Chili posle Vtoroi Mirovoi Voiny," *Voprosy istorii*, 11:85–89 (November 1965).

the left, depending upon circumstances. Frei is the leader of the latter trend.

In the 1958 elections, the PDC received 295,769 votes, or 20.4 percent. Though for an initial test of strength this amount was more than sufficient, the election results as a whole proved that the PDC could hardly dream of coming to power by campaigning independently. It became apparent that the party had to maneuver in such a way that in the next elections its presidential candidate would have the support of one of the two large political blocs controlling the country's political life: either the coalition of the rightist parties—conservatives, liberals, and their allies, the radicals; or the bloc on the left—the Frente de Acción Popular (FRAP). On the one hand, the Christian Democrats were flirting with FRAP: They favored implementation of "structural" reforms—especially agrarian reform—observance of democratic liberties, a limitation on the activity of American monopolies, restoration of diplomatic relations with the socialist countries, and noninterference in the internal affairs of Cuba. Promising enactment of these reforms, the clerics seemed to be saying to the left, "If our candidate becomes President, he will carry out your program better than the leader of the Socialist Party, Allende, already nominated twice for the presidency by the FRAP and twice defeated." Simultaneously, the clerics were flirting with the pro-American bloc of conservatives, liberals, and radicals. The clerics supported the Alliance for Progress and the foreign policy of President Kennedy, especially his idea of a "peaceful revolution." To the capitalists they promised to carry out "a revolution in conditions of freedom," that is not to disturb their basic interests, and they opposed nationalization of the property of the American monopolies in Chile. To the right they said, "Support us and we will save you from the communist revolution." Regarding this tactical line of the Christian Democrats, Allende wrote, "They say 'revolution'—winking with one eye to the people; they then say 'in conditions of freedom' and with the other eye wink to the exploiters."[1] Striving to please both "God and mammon," the leader of the clerics, Frei, as Orlando Millas said, was "like a man who was simultaneously trying to get to the presidential chair astride a horse galloping forward and a mule stubbornly straining backward."[2]

Trying to bar Allende's way in the 1964 elections, the bloc of rightist parties announced the candidacy for president of an extreme reactionary anti-Communist, the radical Durán, for they hoped that the combined vote of these parties would give them a considerable lead over the FRAP candidate, who once more was Allende.

The Christian Democrats nominated Frei as their candidate. In the beginning Frei tried vigorously to win the leftist forces to his side. The Church hierarchy, generally, did not exclude such a possibility. Symptomatic was the 1962 message to the faithful by the bishops of Chile, entitled "Political and Social Duty," in which, although with reservations, the important role of Communist teachings on the transformation of society was acknowledged. The authors of the message did not preclude contact with the Communists if Church authorities consented.[3] Just the same, according to

[1] S. Allende, "La encrucíjada de Chile," *Aurora*, 12:12 (1964).
[2] See O. Millas, *Los communistas, los católicos y la libertad* (Santiago, 1964), p. 37.
[3] See N. A. Koval'skii, "Politika katolicheskoi tserkvi v rabochem dvizhenii Latinskoi Ameriki," in *Osvoboditel'noe dvizhenie v Latinskoi Amerike* (Moskva, 1964), p. 205.

observers, the chances of Frei in presidential elections were slim before March 1964. Durán and Allende were considered favorites.

The partial elections for Parliament held on March 15, 1964, in the district of Curicó introduced radical changes in the disposition of these forces. The election district of Curicó has long been considered a stronghold of conservatives. This time, however, the majority voted for the FRAP candidate. The FRAP victory in the Curicó elections created real panic in the ranks of the Democratic Front—the label under which the conservative, liberal, and radical bloc campaigned. It became apparent that with three candidates running, Allende had a chance to receive, if not an absolute majority, then a plurality of the votes and to become president. Such a prospect aroused antagonisms to the breaking point within the Democratic Front. Durán withdrew his candidacy. Many radicals and even liberals switched to Allende. Under such circumstances, the leadership of the conservative and liberal parties decided to break with the radicals and to support the candidacy of Frei as a "lesser evil" than Allende. Thus, from a candidate of the "democratic left," as he had styled himself till now, Frei became a candidate of the conservative, liberal, and clerical bloc. The Church hierarchy, forgetting their repeated promise to remain neutral in the election fight, opposed Allende, depicting him before the faithful as a stooge of the "Reds." The right radicals also supported the candidacy of Frei.

In his speeches, Frei, the leader of the PDC, continued to promise implementation of progressive reforms. Appearing on June 21, 1964, at a pre-election meeting in Santiago, he said,

The country knows that it can no longer exist under a regime that has brought it to poverty

and despair . . . I am deeply convinced that, just as the epoch of feudalism and aristocracy has passed, so has the bourgeois epoch outlived itself. And today we are witnessing the birth of civilization founded on labor in which the human personality will find its full expression. Thus capitalism as a social philosophy with communism as its antidote has become obsolete. . . . Now no one in the world doubts that, in our America and in Chile, a revolutionary process is taking place.[4]

Frei spoke in defense of private schools, promising to make them tuition free, as are state schools, and to establish fifty thousand scholarships for primary pupils and three thousand grants for university students. He promised to give the voting franchise to illiterates, to incorporate "the rights of workers" into the Constitution, and to fight for the political and economic integration of Latin America as a counterweight to the inter-American system controlled by the United States.

Of great interest is the "programmatic summation of the Frei administration, which should serve as a guide for persons directing the election campaign."[5] This document expounds the basic postulates of the PDC. The Frei government promised to conduct a policy of "active pacifism," to establish broad economic relations "consistent with the national interests of Chile" with all countries, and to fight "imperialism and any form of exploitation of one country by another." Noting that the Alliance for Progress was ineffective, the document proposed to change the Inter-American military pacts from bilateral to collective ones. It promised to implement an agrarian reform and establish three kinds of land ownership—family (plots owned collec-

[4] E. Frei, *Chili: 1964–1970* (Santiago, 1964), pp. 16, 45–46.
[5] *El Gobierno Nacional y Popular* (Santiago, 1964).

tively by all members of the family), cooperative, and private. It promised to see that all smelting of copper be done in Chile but without nationalization of the mines, which are the property of American monopolies. A special chapter was devoted to the solution of the housing problem. Frei gave assurance that within six years his administration would build 360,000 homes. The program promised establishment in Chile of a "communal society," in which there would coexist in peaceful collaboration workers and capitalists; peasants and landowners; domestic and foreign capital, which aided the economic development of the country; and all parties—from Communists to the extreme reactionaries. If one puts aside the patently utopian projects to establish "a communal society," then the rest of the Frei program differed from the FRAP program in the following matters: refusal to nationalize the property of American monopolies, in particular the copper industry; the pledge to support the Alliance for Progress, with the condition that it extend proper aid to the Frei administration; denunciation of the Cuban Revolution; and implementation of a limited agrarian reform.

In the closing stage of the election campaign, the Chilean reactionaries developed a murderous campaign against Allende, asserting that his election would mean the establishment of a "communist dictatorship." Playing upon the psychology of the "man in the street" and the most backward elements of the population, they threatened them with the "horrors" of communist domination. If Allende were victorious, asserted the reactionaries, the opponents of communism would be subjected to repressions, children taken from their mothers and sent to the Soviet Union for re-education, priests put behind bars, churches closed, be-

lievers persecuted, girls raped, sons turned against fathers, daughters turned against mothers, theft and robbery encouraged, and so forth and so on. Many churchmen threatened to close the churches and leave the country if "Allende, the agent of the Communists" should win. Only individual churchmen, like the vicar of the Santiago diocese, Jorge Ramos Ugarte, spoke in support of Allende.[6] A few activists of Catholic organizations formed a Catholic movement for the Allende candidacy. Generally, however, churchmen and clerics teamed up for Frei. According to press reports, Belgian Jesuits received 60 million dollars for propaganda against Allende from West German banks.

The U.S. embassy in Santiago, American and British monopolies, and West German firms operating in Chile spent no small sum of money in the campaign against the FRAP candidate. The vast propaganda against Allende, no doubt, influenced the vacillating sectors of voters, who quite concertedly voted for Frei. There is also no doubt, however, that the hundreds of thousands of votes cast for Allende could not help but influence the subsequent policy of the Frei administration. In his first statement after the election, on September 5, 1964, Frei said that Chileans do not want a "democracy" that would mean freedom only for the few to eat, to obtain an education, and to improve one's self and to find work.

For the many [said Frei] as we know so well, such a democracy in Chile means freedom to live in poverty, without the means to provide for their children's education, without work or a roof over one's head. A considerable sector of the population that voted for me, that supported my candidacy, is convinced that the democracy we have is extremely limited in its present form. It gives

[6]*Revolución*, June 19, 1964.

the people little opportunity for education, job security and housing, a part in cultural development and national life in general. If anyone should claim that our victory means the continuation of things as they are, without advancement, it would be a violation of the will of the people.

Frei affirmed the need to carry out basic social reforms in Chile, to do away with conditions in which "foreign capital can be a state within a state," and he came out for industrialization of the country. He stated that he favored good relations with all countries on the basis of mutual equality. Replying to a question by a correspondent of the American newspaper *Los Angeles Times* regarding the incoming government's attitude toward Cuba, the new President declared that on this question it was necessary to find a "peaceful solution consistent, above all, with the principle of respect for the right of peoples to self-determination and the principle of noninterference in their internal affairs."[7]

In November 1964, the governments of Chile and the USSR re-established diplomatic relations. This important event was received with great satisfaction among all circles of Chilean society and was also hailed by the people of the Soviet Union. The Chilean government also re-established diplomatic relations with other socialist countries of Europe. The Frei government condemned the criminal armed intervention of the United States in the Dominican Republic and refused to participate in the "inter-American armed forces," which were called upon to serve as a screen for this intervention and which the ruling circles of the United States intended to utilize for suppression of the national-liberation movements in other countries of Latin America also.

And so it may be said that in the sphere of foreign relations the Frei government is carrying out its pre-election promises quite consistently. The complications involve "the structural reforms" situation, the implementation of which was to lead to "the peaceful revolution" promised by the Christian Democratic leaders. The Frei administration is preparing agrarian and other reforms. It should be noted that there is a good chance for the Frei administration to bring about these reforms. It commands an absolute majority in the Chamber of Deputies, not to speak of the fact that the realization of social reforms will have the support of the overwhelming majority of the Chilean people. In the meantime, the economic situation of the country continues to worsen, while the American monopolies continue their enrichment at the expense of the Chilean people.

The contemporary history of Latin American countries is replete with cases of radical leaders who, enjoying the trust and support of progressive forces, once in power betrayed the national interest and became tools in the hands of imperialists and domestic reactionary groups. Such were R. González Videla in Chile and Arturo Frondizi in Argentina. There are other examples of leaders of a quite moderate tone who, once in the Presidential chair, carried out progressive, anti-imperialist policies. Such sharp "changes of course" are possible under a type of government that endows the President with nearly unlimited power with which he, supported by certain social forces, can exercise tremendous influence on the course of political events.

No matter how political events develop in Chile, one fact remains clear: the 1964 presidential elections have opened a new page in its history.

[7]See *Za rubezhom*, 37:18 (1964).

How it will be written will depend on the degree of unity of the Chilean progressive forces, their political maturity and wisdom, and the determination, courage, and political awareness of the Chilean people.

V

CONSERVATISM

The essence of the single selection by M. V. Danilevich comprising this section—an analysis of "internal reactionary and imperialist bloc forces" —is contained in the following excerpt from it: "In Latin America a contemptible coterie of wealthy men utilizes the government apparatus and an entire system of compulsive measures against the oppressed and exploited mass of workers, peasants, and petty bourgeoisie, for its own interests and those of the American monopolies."

Danilevich not unnaturally sees no revolutionary potential in the conservative forces. Curiously enough this prominent Soviet scholar has not mastered Spanish usage in names: Marcos Pérez Jiménez is referred to as Jiménez, and Gustavo Rojas Pinilla as Pinilla.

17. The Make-up of Internal Reactionary and Imperialist Bloc Forces*

M. V. DANILEVICH

Army leadership in the great majority of Latin American countries is in the hands of representatives of the agrarian oligarchy, high officialdom, and various political adventurers—all of whom comprise a reactionary military clique in the service of the American imperialists. The military circles composed of high-ranking officers have always served as the force for carrying out military coups and for issuing their famous *pronunciamientos*, which

*Rabochii klass v osvoboditel'nom dvizhenii narodov Latinskoi Ameriki (Moskva: Gosudarstvennoe izdatel'stvo politicheskoi literatury, 1962), pp. 22–35.

reflect the struggle for power by the different ruling cliques. English, American, and—during the prewar years—German imperialists, have stood behind the military circles.

At the present time the domestic reactionary elements of Latin America are making widespread use of their armies, equipped with American artillery, tanks, and aircraft, against the strike and the national-liberation movement, as well as for organizing acts of progressive governments.[1] In a document outlining the party program, the Communist Party of Ecuador has characterized its domestic situation as follows: "The Ecuadorian army has been subordinated to the military missions of the United States and to the aggressive aims of imperialism. With each passing day, our army is losing more and more of its national character."[2]

In many countries those who represent the reactionary military circles are "elected" to the post of president. In Argentina, from 1943 to 1958 the presidents were all army generals, while half the ministers and 45 percent of the state governors belonged to the top military command. Generals are heading the governments of the Dominican Republic, Haiti, Nicaragua, Paraguay, and other countries of Latin America; this situation until recently also existed in Chile, Colombia, Venezuela, and Cuba. During the postwar years, the military clique has further increased its wealth in landholdings, especially in countries with dictatorial regimes. The army commands are not homogeneous in their composition. In many countries, military men of petty bourgeois origin and lower-echelon commanders stand in opposition to those who comprise the top army leadership. This situation is best exemplified in the Brazilian army, the largest in Latin America. There have been instances in the past in which

the officer class of this army came out in favor of instituting certain, albeit limited, bourgeois-democratic reforms. At the present time, a significant proportion of officers of the lower and middle ranks, as well as some from the highest level of command, are opposed to the antinational policies of the reactionary circles. Worthy of note are the statements by many military men urging protection of their countries' national wealth. In 1945, groups of young officers in Venezuela participated in the overthrow of the reactionary regime of General Medina, while in January 1958 they staged an uprising against Pérez Jiménez.

On the whole, however, the top command of the armed forces rests in the hands of a reactionary military caste.

Thus, the principal reactionary force that determines both domestic and foreign policy in most of the countries of Latin America is the agrarian oligarchy of the big landowners, which is supported by clerical and military circles. The agrarian oligarchy has in large measure retained its political power, sharing it in most of the countries with the upper bourgeoisie. Many of the leading political figures—presidents, ministers, and leaders of the government parties, as well as representatives of the lower houses of the legislatures and senators—are members of the group of biggest landowners. The latifundists are interested in preserving not only the semifeudal forms of exploitation, but also the agrarian nature of the economy.

---

[1] The Ambassador of Costa Rica to the United States, Gonzalo Facio, speaking in January 1958 at the Overseas Press Club, gave the following description of what occurs in many Latin American countries: "As it is, each country is occupied by its own army."

[2] *Democracia, independencia y paz para el pueblo del Ecuador. Lineamientos programáticos del Partido Comunista del Ecuador aprobados por su VI Congreso* (Quito, 1957).

Another reactionary force in Latin America consists of those who form the upper stratum of the commercial and industrial bourgeoisie. The economic and political interests of this group are tied to both foreign imperialism and the agrarian oligarchy. This stratum of the domestic reactionary bourgeoisie forms a common bloc with the imperialists and pursues antinational, proimperialist policies.

The origins of this reactionary bourgeoisie are rooted deep in the historical past. In the nineteenth century there emerged a stratum consisting of the semifeudal, so-called comprador class of the bourgeoisie engaged in developing intermediary commercial ties as middlemen with the capitalist countries. The functions of this bourgeoisie became more complex and their sphere of activity broadened with the increasing accumulation of wealth and, as the era of imperialism appeared, their profits grew and their position became generally strengthened because of their direct connection with foreign monopolies, British and American. The reactionary strata of the domestic bourgeoisie have played an enormous part in the enslavement of Latin America by foreign imperialists. The large-scale commercial bourgeoisie went about buying up agricultural produce from the peasants, carried out export operations, and acted as middlemen for marketing industrial products imported by foreign companies. These merchant middlemen and moneylenders, like the members of the agrarian oligarchy, were interested in preserving the semifeudal agrarian structure and in consolidating the status of Latin America as an agrarian appendage and an assured source of raw materials for the imperialist powers. This upper domestic bourgeoisie was transformed into a direct agency of imperialism.

The national bourgeoisie took shape and grew as capitalism and the forces of production evolved and new branches of industry appeared. The national bourgeoisie consists of those strata of the industrial, agricultural, and commercial bourgeoisie whose basic economic interests were bound up with the development of national industry and the national economy as a whole, and who found themselves in conflict with the interests of the imperialist monopolies that were holding back the industrial progress of Latin America. A quite numerous but economically unstable middle-scale national bourgeoisie was created. As time went on, a part of this bourgeoisie developed into a big industrial bourgeoisie in a number of countries.

Parallel with the process of formation of the national bourgeoisie, the middleman bourgeoisie and a certain portion of the agrarian oligarchy underwent significant structural changes. The process of formation of stock corporation, banks, and joint enterprises financed by both domestic and foreign capital tended to draw the middleman bourgeoisie and the large landowners into capitalist industrial production. In a number of countries, there was formed a stratum of the upper bourgeoisie that became rich by supplying strategic raw materials, foodstuffs, and the products of light industry. During the first and second world wars, this part of the bourgeoisie joined the large landowners in speculating on the basis of the hunger of the masses and plundered the population of not only the warring countries, but also their own. A portion of the upper bourgeois, including the industrial bourgeoisie, developed in close association with foreign monopolies and became a proimperialist, antinational bourgeoisie (in Brazil, Argentina, Venezuela, Mexico, Chile, Cuba, Peru, and Colombia).

The effect of the wars, with their

attendant intensified demand for agricultural raw materials and food-stuffs, was to accelerate the process of drawing the landowning oligarchy into the general stream of capitalist development and to tie it to large-scale domestic and foreign capital, to the imperialist monopolies. Some of the large landowners became agrarian capitalists, entrepreneurs engaged in the preliminary processing of agricultural products intended for export. Frequently these people became monopolistic exporters, fulfilling the functions of the commercial bourgeoisie, and consequently they were receiving not only income from their land, but also commercial and industrial profits. The big landowners, the cattle ranchers, and the owners of cotton and sugar plantations, deriving enormous profits from the sale of their products, invested a considerable portion of their capital in banks, securities, and stock corporations, as well as in national and foreign industrial enterprises, particularly American.

At the same time, the upper bourgeoisie was not always able to make use of its accumulated capital for the development of industry because of the difficulties entailed in buying machines, equipment, and raw materials, and for that reason applied its resources to the acquisition of land.

Thus, certain strata of the industrial and commercial bourgeoisie, primarily of the upper bourgeoisie, simultaneously became landowners and owners of cattle ranches and plantations.

The intertwining of the economic and political interests of foreign monopolies with the interests of the reactionary apex of the bourgeoisie and the agrarian oligarchy became sharply evident in the more advanced countries of Latin America. In Argentina, for instance, enormous areas of land in the southern part of the province of

Buenos Aires belong to the large Tornquist family. The Tornquists—powerful cattle ranchers, sugar refiners, and industrialists—are closely connected with American and Belgian companies. This family owns twenty-five companies with a capital value exceeding 500 million pesos. The Tornquists are directors of chemical and metallurgical enterprises, construction and credit firms, banks, and even companies engaged in the business of colonization.[3] Members of this family are on the boards of directors of twenty-one stock corporations, including the American electrical company, C.A.D.E.

There is in Argentina a huge joint company called Bunge y Born. This company owns flour mills and twenty-nine other enterprises and companies. One of the directors of these companies is the representative of the English concession La Forrestal, García Victorica, who is also a director of three other companies. The Bunge y Born Company, together with the American company Duperial, controls the entire chemical industry of the country. This firm is tied to American and British capital and also to the great landowners and cattle ranchers who produce agricultural products for export to European countries, especially to England. The company has branches in other countries of Latin America, and in Brazil half the milling and sale of wheat is concentrated in its hands. In the case of this gigantic company and of others, the interests of foreign capital, large landowners, and industrialists are closely interwoven.

Certain big industrialists are directors and large shareholders of foreign companies. Local stock companies do not utilize their capital for the development of the domestic economy, but rather invest it in American enter-

[3]*Neuva Era* (Buenos Aires), 4:42 (1955).

prises, forming large joint concerns.

In his book, *Los trusts yanquis contra la Argentina,* the progressive Argentine economist Jaime Fuchs writes: "There will always be a cozy little niche in the management of American imperialist enterprises for certain members of the agricultural oligarchy and big capital."[4] Providing numerous examples to support this premise, the author comes to the conclusion that these social strata, interested as they are in the preservation of latifundism, are exploiting the national resources and hindering the development of Argentina as an independent country.

In the largest countries—Argentina, Brazil, and Mexico—there is taking place an intensification of the process of integration and fusing of the interests of a small top layer of the ruling classes and the large local magnates of the agrarian oligarchy with the U.S. monopolies. A bourgeoisie of the monopolistic type is being formed.

In Brazil, the last twenty years have seen the creation of influential groups of local, upper-industrial monopolistic-type bourgeoisie controlling various branches of industry. A typical feature in Brazil, and one which exists in many other countries of Latin America, is the formation of "family" stock corporations belonging to a single family. (According to Brazilian law, seven members are sufficient for forming a stock corporation.) The largest stock corporations of this type, called *industrias reunidas,* belong to the families of Matarazzo, Votorantim, Jafet, Abdalla, Clabin, Mochnias, Santistas, and others. These are the leading representatives of Brazilian monopolistic capital. For instance, in 1934 Matarazzo formed a stock corporation that included his father, the Senator Andrea Matarazzo, and four brothers. At present this family owns three hundred different enterprises—textile,

chemical, cellulose, cement, and other companies, as well as railroads and a merchant fleet. Branches of this firm exist not only in neighboring countries, but also in the capital cities of a number of European states. According to the press, there is no sector of Brazilian national life into which this industrial complex has not penetrated.

The *industrias reunidas* of the Votorantim group owns enterprises in the textile, metallurgical, and chemical industries, as well as plants for the production of wire, cable, pipe, and various aluminum products. This group holds in its hands 40 percent of the entire cement production of the country.

The Abdalla group owns a great many enterprises in the textile industry and factories that manufacture synthetic silk, cement, and other products. Many thousands of workers are employed in the enterprises of this group.

The President of Peru, Manuel Prado, who came to power in 1956, is one of the richest men in his country—the owner of many firms, "stock companies," and banks. The President of Chile, Alessandri, is a major capitalist. He controls thirty-six stock corporations and sixteen insurance companies.

A prominent figure in the communist movement of Latin America, Rodney Arismendi, writes with respect to the big reactionary bourgeoisie: "In many Latin American countries, this stratum of domestic big bourgeoisie—in whom may be discerned the cosmopolitan outlook and manners, as well as the predilection for luxury typical of the big bourgeoisie in the advanced capitalist countries—has now concentrated in its hands the major portion of all commercial, banking, and industrial capital."[5]

---

[4] Jaime Fuchs, *La penetración de los trusts yanquis en la Argentina* (Buenos Aires, 1959), p. 53.
[5] *Problemy mira i sotsializma,* 6:31 (1959).

In the most backward countries of Latin America, where there is almost no great industrial bourgeoisie, the top layer of the commercial bourgeoisie continues to exhibit traits of the comprador class. In these countries, those who belong to the middleman bourgeoisie have themselves become large landowners. Together with the agrarian oligarchy, this bourgeoisie possesses control of political power and serves as a base of support for American monopolies.

Dictators, the lackies of American monopolies, open wide their gates to the entrance of American capital and as a rule themselves become active participants in the plundering of their countries.

Utilizing the power of the state, the dictator of the Dominican Republic, Rafael Trujillo, became one of the richest men in Latin America. The state monopolies of tobacco, salt, and cement were turned into monopolies of the Trujillo family. He was the owner of extensive sugar, cotton, rice, and jute plantations, of an enormous quantity of livestock, dairy farms, municipal slaughterhouses, and sugar refineries. To Trujillo also belonged manufacturing firms for the production of cement, industrial oils, clothing, footwear, and china, a marble mining company, a shipbuilding firm for constructing ships for local navigation, an insurance firm, flour mills, and many other enterprises.

A monopoly over the export of cocoa, rice, and coconuts, plus a number of other agricultural products, was concentrated in Trujillo's hands. He was the owner of the principal newspaper of the country, *La Nación*, as well as of the publishing house El Caribe. According to information supplied by the Latin American press, the total value of enterprises, plantations, and land seized by him exceeded 70 million dollars, and his annual profits exceeded 10 million dollars.[6] Although in May 1961, Rafael Trujillo was killed under extremely dubious circumstances, his relatives and the people who were formerly around him continue to direct affairs in the country, assuring both their own personal interests and the key position enjoyed by the United States.

The family of the Nicaraguan dictators, the Somozas, serves as another typical example. Having seized power as early as 1936 with the aid of the United States, the Somoza family owns many dozens of coffee, sugar cane, and banana plantations, and gold and silver mines. This dynasty exploits a huge army of peasants in a state of near-serfdom, as well as agricultural workers and miners, shackled by a system of peonage (debt slavery). The Somoza clique ships everything it produces to the United States.

The dictators, along with the military cliques and high officials who support them, everywhere employ the power of the state for their own enrichment. The former Colombian dictator Rojas Pinilla and his entourage of generals helped themselves to enormous wealth in the form of land and "accumulated" capital holdings in domestic and foreign banks. Pinilla became the richest man in Colombia while he was in power, and was considered to be a multimillionaire. According to the Mexican newspaper *Excelsior*, Pinilla has on deposit in various banks about 80 million dollars acquired in all kinds of shady deals (by the smuggling of coffee and platinum, by buying up for trifling sums huge sugar plantations and livestock, by issuing credits to companies belonging to members of his family, and the like). The same can be said in regard to such former

[6]*Mañana*, No. 11 (1957).

dictators as Jiménez of Venezuela, Batista of Cuba, and others, along with their "associates."

However, the main thing is not the personal aggrandizement of individual dictators or prominent members of the growing bureaucracy (also typical of Latin America), but the increasing significance of the process of merging and fusing together of the capital holdings and interests of different groups of the bourgeoisie, the large landowners, and the bureaucratic elite of the state apparatus and army, on the one hand, with foreign monopolies, on the other.

The magnates of Wall Street are bent on harnessing the upper bourgeoisie of Latin American countries to their chariot and using it for the purpose of reinforcing their domination. This is being done by different methods, one of which is the creation of joint companies. By establishing joint companies, the American monopolies, besides serving the purpose of camouflage, set themselves still other far-reaching political aims. The U.S. imperialists are anxious to tie the monopolistic upper bourgeoisie of Latin America more firmly to American capital by creating joint companies and associations. By yielding a portion of the surplus value to the domestic upper bourgeoisie, American capital to a certain extent contributes to the growth of the upper bourgeoisie and to the strengthening of its class hegemony within the country. At the same time, American capital is concerned lest the bourgeoisie grow too strong and be able independently, without any help from U.S. imperialism, to assure its ruling position. To a certain degree, the strengthening of the upper bourgeoisie, allied as it is with imperialism, is advantageous to the latter, since it can be utilized by the imperialists for suppressing the democratic anti-imperialist movement.

A distinctive feature employed by the American monopolies in ensuring the strengthening of their position in the countries of Latin America is the bribing of various political figures, members of the government, senators, deputies, leaders of the governing parties, and also representatives of the bourgeois intelligentsia, enlisted as legal consultants and lawyers for American firms and generously compensated for their services by the American monopolies. Many of these lawyers and directors, having proved their fidelity to their American masters, have been helped by the latter to become leading government figures, pursuing policies that conform to the interests of the American monopolies. Instructive in this respect is the case of a former lawyer for a subsidiary of Standard Oil who became President of Colombia after attaining power through the support of Wall Street—the leader of the Conservatives, Laureano Gómez. Turning up as members of the Colombian government that was established after suppression of the spontaneous popular uprising of April 1948 were the following employees of American oil monopolies: the Minister of Internal Affairs, Urdaneta, a lawyer for the Colombian Gulf Oil Company; the Minister of Communications, Dávila, a lawyer for the Richmond Petroleum Company; and the Minister of Finance, Pérez, who served the Tropical Oil Company in the same capacity.

In Brazil, the Minister of Finance of the Vargas government, Horacio Lafer, a major owner of sugar plantations in the state of Pernambuco, is a director of the national Companhia de Mineração Sulba and of the American company Orkima, which is interested in getting its hands on Brazilian monazite and other important raw materials of military strategic value. This man is the Dupont Corporation's protégé in the Brazilian government.

Thus, as capitalism finds itself undergoing a period of intensifying crisis, the ruling classes, composed of the great landowners and the reactionary upper echelon of the large-scale industrial and commercial bourgeoisie, have formed a reactionary bourgeois-landowner bloc. It is from this bloc that U.S. imperialism derives its basic support as it carries out its penetration of Latin America. Allusion has been made to this situation in a number of the party programs of the Communist parties of Latin America. For instance, the Communist Party of Ecuador has emphasized the fact that American imperialism in that country "relies for its support not only on a group of feudal lords and on the Catholic clergy, but also on an extremely powerful large-scale commercial and financial oligarchy tied to that imperialism. These groups subject the people to dual exploitation."[7]

In the overwhelming majority of the Latin American countries, down to the years 1957 and 1958, representatives of the reactionary bourgeoisie and the agrarian oligarchy, allied with American imperialism, were in power. Moreover, in many countries they came to power as a result of military coups supported by the United States. Among such dictators were Laureano Gómez and Rojas Pinilla in Colombia; Pérez Jiménez in Venezuela; Odría in Peru; Ramírez, Farrell, Perón, and Aramburu in Argentina; Batista in Cuba; Castillo Armas in Guatemala; and others brought to power even earlier in Paraguay, Haiti, the Dominican Republic, and Nicaragua.

The reactionary upper bourgeoisie of Latin America, closely associated with the agrarian oligarchy, has sanctioned the continued penetration of their economies by American imperialism, the further seizure of national resources by the Americans, and the concluding of inequitable, enslaving treaties. This upper bourgeoisie accepted without reservation the infamous American Western Hemisphere Defense Treaty and affixed its signature to the anticommunist pact and other decisions of the Ninth Inter-American Conference in Bogotá, held in 1948, and the Tenth Conference in Caracas, in 1954. These ruling circles support the policy of bilateral military agreements and enslaving loans, and accept the conditions set forth by the International Monetary Fund. In the United Nations, most Latin American governments have made a practice of blindly following the diplomatic lead of the United States. During the early postwar years, at the dictate of the American magnates, the governments of Brazil, Chile, Colombia, Venezuela, and Cuba—to the detriment of their economic interests and in opposition to the will of the masses—broke off diplomatic relations with the USSR.

Fulfilling the will of the ruling classes, these governments pursued policies contrary to the interests of their peoples and lent their support to American aggression and to the militarization of the Western Hemisphere.

Certain sectors of the ruling classes perceive a source of further enrichment in following a policy of armament and formation of military blocs. In order to maintain their power and to assure themselves new accumulations of capital, these people, with the help of the United States, are stepping up their assault on the political and civil rights of labor and on the living standards of the masses.

In Latin America a contemptible coterie of wealthy men utilizes the government apparatus and an entire system of compulsive measures against the op-

[7]*Democracia, Independencia y Paz para el Pueblo del Ecuador.*

pressed and exploited masses of workers, peasants, and petty bourgeoisie, for its own interests and those of the American monopolies.

The governing parties in the majority of countries are reactionary bourgeois-landowner parties. They conduct a policy of alliance of domestic reaction with American imperialism, and they protect the interests of the agrarian oligarchy and the reactionary upper bourgeoisie. Typical of such parties are the National Democratic Party of Argentina, the Conservative Party of Chile, the Peruvian Democratic Movement, the Bolivian Socialist Falange, the Movimiento Revolucionario Nacional Ortodoxo of Bolivia, and others.

In Brazil, the União Democrática Nacional (UDN) is the party that most completely reflects the interests of the large-scale industrial bourgeoisie and the great landowners, with their close ties to U.S. monopolies. The leader of this party, General Eduardo Gómez, was the most prominent figure involved in the pro-American coup of August 24, 1954. The Partido Social Democrático of Brazil—headed by former President Juscelino Kubitschek, Gaspar Dutra, and Amaral Peixoto—unites landowners with the large-scale industrial and commercial bourgeoisie, and it follows contradictory policies. The decisions of this party reflect the interests of the oligarchy and the upper bourgeoisie. Within the party itself there exist differences of opinion between an "old wing," which believes in close cooperation with the United States, and a "young wing" concerned with defending the interests of the upper national bourgeoisie.

The interests of the ruling classes in Colombia are represented by the Conservative Party. The ideology of this party is close to that of Spanish falangism. With the development of capitalism, the reactionary bourgeois

wing of the party has become stronger. During the period of dictatorship, five rival factions sprang up in the party.[8]

In the Dominican Republic this bloc is represented by the so-called Partido Dominicano, the only legal party in the country, formerly headed by Rafael Trujillo. The governing parties of Nicaragua are the Liberal and Conservative parties.

Similar parties exist in the other countries of Latin America. The bourgeois intelligentsia and high officialdom comprise an important component of their membership.

Together with the traditional parties of long standing with their permanent leaders, every country has a large number of other reactionary (clerical, bourgeois-landowner) bourgeois parties. The majority of them are unstable and lack sharply defined programs and consistent membership. Quite often they are brought into being for the sole purpose of participating in elections. The programs and platforms of these parties are drawn up by the leaders, and the rank and file members are often unaware of their contents. The party program is subject to change at election time, when new democratic slogans are put forward and leaders who may have compromised themselves are replaced by new ones.

Political leaders cross over from one party to another, from opposing the government to supporting it. These men are often inveterate political schemers and adventurers who in a relatively brief space of time manage to dabble in several parties. In each party there are a number of groupings, tendencies, viewpoints, and trends. All these parties engage in a frantic struggle for power, for positions in the government and in various government-controlled organizations. Once

[8]*Documentos Politicos*, 13:17 (1959).

a party attains power, it seeks to settle accounts with its more dangerous rivals from the other bourgeois-landowner parties. The American monopolies turn this discord to their own advantage by making every effort to replace the less subservient, the unsuccessful and weak leaders with those who are more "dynamic." Endless conspiracies, *Putsche,* and coups are concocted and instigated.

Characteristic of the bourgeois-landowner parties of the continent are their subordination to American imperialism and their acute hostility toward the national-liberation movement and the implementation of agrarian reform.

Thus, as the economy of Latin America continues to advance, the upper reactionary bourgeoisie is no longer the former intermediary (comprador) bourgeoisie with its activity concentrated in the sphere of commerce. These people are now large-scale capitalists operating in the area of foreign and domestic trade, in finance, and in industrial and agricultural production. They have been transformed into a proimperialist, antinational bourgeoisie, forming a common bloc with imperialism and with the agrarian oligarchy.

VI

LABOR AND TRADE UNIONISM

Soviet analysts of the labor movement in Latin America are obviously concerned by the inroads being made there by such organizations as the Inter-American Regional Labor Organization (ORIT), the Agrupación de Trabajadores Latinoamericanos Sindicalizados (ATLAS), and the American Institute for Free Labor Development (AIFLD). In the first selection in this section (Item 18), V. G. Spirin presents what to him is a rather gloomy picture of the successes achieved by "schismatic" organizations—particularly the AIFLD—but concludes that the efforts are "doomed to failure."

M. V. Danilevich, in Item 19, does not appear to be so sanguine about the predestination of these efforts to failure. While she defines the ORIT as a "champion of reformist ideology among the working class," she nevertheless states that the CTAL (Confederación de Trabajadores de América Latina—the Latin American affiliate of the communist-dominated World Federation of Trade Unions) has "more than once approached the ORIT organizations and other trade unions with an appeal to reconsider the possibility of joint action."

The final selection, Item 20, is a Soviet view of the evolution of the labor movement in Mexico during the post–World War II period and the effective blunting of the class struggle there by the government.

18. The Enemies of Trade-Union Unity in Latin America*

V. G. Spirin

The course of political events in the Latin American countries—where the struggle of the masses for freedom and independence is being stepped up—arouses alarm among imperialist circles in the United States, which are the basic exploiters of the human and natural resources of these countries.

The ruling circles of the United States reply to the national-liberation manifestations of the peoples of Latin America with gross interference in their internal affairs, open support of reaction and the persecution of progressive forces, the organization of military plots, and the overthrow of democratic governments. Washington resorts to direct armed aggression in the struggle against the forces of democracy and national progress, as happened in the Dominican Republic.

Resorting to the old methods of direct pressure on the anti-imperialist movement in the Latin American countries, the United States at the same time is using more flexible tactics, something the victory of the Cuban Revolution prompted them to do. While relying on the traditional connections with feudal reaction, the comprador bourgeoisie, and the reactionary military, U.S. imperialism is attempting to broaden its social base. An ever more significant place in Washington's neocolonial arsenal is being occupied by attempts to implant and strengthen a reformist labor movement in Latin America to split the working class, establish control over trade-union organizations, stifle democracy in trade unions, paralyze the revolutionary anti-imperialist demonstrations of the workers, and ward off the formation of broad, anti-imperialist fronts.

The notorious "free" trade unions that the United States has been implanting hurriedly in Latin America have become a weapon for doing battle with nationalistic-progressive forces and a means for preserving the capitalistic system and—in the final analysis—the economic backwardness of the Latin American countries and their semicolonial dependence.

The line for the installation of bourgeois reformism in the labor movement of the Latin American countries, the splitting of this division, and its subjection to imperialist plans have been elevated in the level of U.S. state policy. It is conducted by the Department of State and the Department of Labor of

*"Vragi profsoiuznogo edinstva v Latinskoi Ameriki," in *Ot Aliaski do Ognennoi Zemli* (Moskva: Nauka, 1967), pp. 347–360.

the United States, which have special attachés for labor affairs attached to U.S. embassies in the Latin American countries. A great deal of attention is paid to these matters by the Agency for International Development, the U.S. Information Agency, and the leadership of the Peace Corps in their work. The American trade-union confederation—American Federation of Labor–Congress of Industrial Organizations (AFL-CIO), the Inter-American Regional Labor Organization (ORIT), and similar organizations—operate along the same lines.

The subversive activities of U.S. government and nongovernment organs in the trade-union movement of the Latin American countries is inspired and financed by the monopoly circles of the United States, which are interested in continuing their expansion there. George Lodge, the director of the School of Business at Harvard University and until recently an Assistant Secretary of Labor for International Affairs, has written that, for the U.S. business world under the conditions of the "developing Latin American revolution," the so-called responsible trade unions are "a necessary instrument of social stability in Latin America, a buffer against radical changes."[1]

The problem of penetration into the Latin American labor movement has become the subject of extremely close attention among U.S. ruling circles, which have proceeded to the formulation of a "new approach" to their neighbors to the south in connection with the victory of the Cuban Revolution.

On an assignment from the U.S. Congress in 1960, the University of Chicago prepared a special study under the title "American Business and Labor in Latin America," which argued for the establishment of "democratic cooperation between the United States and the labor movement in Latin America."

The authors of this study were forced to acknowledge that the working class of the Latin American countries has an anti-imperialist disposition and that the yellow U.S. company unions have no significant influence on them. "It would be unreasonable to expect," the document says, "that the labor movement in Latin America will follow the path of U.S. trade unionism in the future." With respect to the activity of the ORIT, the authors of the study commented on its loss of prestige among Latin American workers and ascertained that it "has extremely limited influence in South America."

Having reached such unfavorable conclusions, the University of Chicago recommended that the U.S. Congress take measures to see that the "progressive and liberal sectors" in the labor movement of the Latin American countries "do not side with communism and do not begin to offer it support," so that "the social changes the workers do achieve would be in conjunction with the development of democratic institutions."

To this end, it was proposed that the training of trade-union leaders be expanded both in the cities and in the countryside, that mutual exchanges and tours by trade-union personnel be increased and that "cooperation" between American and Latin American trade unions be strengthened.[2]

From the very beginning, the initiators of the neocolonialist Alliance for Progress program saw one of the goals of this program in the financing of subversive work in the trade-union movement of these countries and in the implantation of "free" trade unions and the formation of a labor aristocracy

[1]*Foreign Affairs*, January 1966.
[2]*United States—Latin American Relations*, in U.S. Senate, 86th Congress, 2d Session, Document No. 125 (Washington, 1960), pp. 373–374, 387–390.

as their direct agents in the Latin American countries.

The entire schismatic activity in the labor movement of the Latin American countries is directed and coordinated by the U.S. embassies in those countries. In a speech to the U.S. Senate in connection with the State Department appropriations for fiscal year 1962, Assistant Secretary of State for Administration William Crockett reported that the labor attachés at the U.S. embassies in the Latin American countries inform the Latin American trade unions about "the achievements and the democratic nature of trade unionism in the United States," exert a "personal influence" on their leaders and rank-and-file members, oppose "the penetration of leftists," utilize "every opportunity to direct the actions of these trade unions along democratic channels," and strive to achieve "the support of the labor organizations in the respective countries for the broad goals of the policy of the United States Government and the free world in general."[3]

The American labor attachés interfere quite unceremoniously in the internal affairs of the Latin American countries. For example, as reported by the Bolivian press, Attaché Boggs in Bolivia extended financial resources to the separatist labor confederation Central Nacional, which was formed in December 1963 in opposition to the Central Obrera Boliviana, the country's unified trade-union center. By mid-1964 these subsidies came to 57,000 dollars. To the end of introducing division in the labor movement, the newborn trade-union organization announced the holding of a so-called Congress for the Unification of Workers. In June 1964, the former Bolivian Minister of Labor Aguilar came out against "harmful foreign tutelage in trade-union organizations" and accused Boggs of having attempted to organize the con-

gress and establish control over Bolivian trade unions.[4]

The dispatch of special advisers on labor matters by the U.S. Information Agency to Brazil, Argentina, Mexico, Venezuela, Colombia, Bolivia, Chile, Peru, and Uruguay testifies to the activization of U.S. subversive activity in the Latin American labor movement, directed toward splitting the movement.

As noted in a USIA report, the USIA advisers, with the aid of the U.S. embassy labor attachés, established contacts with trade-union leaders of the above Latin American countries, which they intended to "expand and strengthen" to the end of aiding in understanding the goals of the program of the Alliance for Progress and explaining the "potentialities" of that program. It appeared from the report that the USIA advisers were given the assignment of propagandizing the "achievements" of U.S. trade unionism and slandering communism by reporting falsely about the situation of the workers in the socialist countries. These advisers were "well equipped" with the corresponding propaganda materials, which they sent to the local trade-union press, to radio stations, and to television stations. They distributed USIA pamphlets and arranged for the showing of propaganda films, among other activities.[5]

Similar subversive activity is also carried out by the American advisers attached to the Latin American missions of the Agency for International De-

[3]*Departments of State, Justice, the Judiciary and Related Agencies Appropriations, 1962, Hearings before the Subcommittee of the Committee on Appropriations,* U.S. Senate, 87th Congress, 1st Session. (Washington, 1961), p. 222.
[4]*Presencia* (La Paz), June 19, 1964; *Boletín Sindical Latinoamericano* (Santiago, Chile), No. 5–6, 1964.
[5]*U.S. Information Agency, 20th Review of Operations, January 1–June 30, 1963* (Washington, 1963), p. 18.

velopment, who "advise local trade-union leaders."[6]

In their attempts to split the trade-union movement in Latin America and to subordinate the labor organizations to imperialist influence, the ruling circles of the United States are resorting ever more to the services of the AFL-CIO, which has stepped up its efforts in the Latin American countries considerably.

In a letter to Thomas Mann, appointed U.S. Assistant Secretary of State for Inter-American Affairs, President Lyndon Johnson in December 1963 pointed out the need for maintaining "close contact" with the AFL-CIO and the U.S. nongovernmental organizations operating in Latin America. Speaking on the occasion of the fifth anniversary of the Alliance for Progress program on March 14, 1966, Johnson noted the "great contribution" that the AFL-CIO, cooperatives, and other organizations make in the formation of the "mechanism of cooperation" on the continent, and declared that the U.S. government is enlisting their support "in an ever greater measure."

Such an evaluation by the American President of the role of the AFL-CIO in the conduct of U.S. policy in Latin America is quite understandable. By taking root in the labor movement of the Latin American countries, the AFL-CIO is striving to subordinate the trade unions of these countries to its influence, to oppose their national-liberation forces, and to undermine the struggle of patriotic forces for national independence and social progress from within. "As a result of the stepped-up movement for the achievement of genuine independence in the Latin American countries and the increase of Washington's unpopularity among the masses," wrote the U.S. Communist Party newspaper *The Worker*, "Amer-

ican diplomacy has come to depend to a large extent on the aid of AFL-CIO leaders, who carry out extensive subversive and missionary activity in these countries through their fraternal trade-union channels."[7]

The entire activity of the AFL-CIO in the countries of Asia, Africa, and Latin America testifies to the fact that this trade-union confederation is a weapon of the State Department and other U.S. government agencies. Concerning the divisive activity of the AFL-CIO in Latin America, Dean Rusk publicly declared: "As the U.S. Secretary of State, I am particularly aware of the resolute support—for which I am grateful—which the AFL-CIO has extended to our foreign policy and to our efforts to make it more effective."[8]

The Inter-American Regional Labor Organization—the activities of which are widely known—has been operating as the traditional weapon for dividing the Latin American workers. The ORIT conducts a struggle with the progressive trade unions in Latin America, actively collaborates with American monopolies, and extends full support to U.S. foreign policy. It connects the AFL-CIO and those Latin American trade unions which are members of the proimperialist International Confederation of Free Trade Unions (ICFTU). From the very beginning the AFL-CIO has assumed the initiative in the formulation of the policy of the ICFTU and ORIT, and it finances them almost in their entirety.

Not content with the intrigues of the ORIT, the AFL-CIO, under conditions of the growth of the liberation movement in Latin America, has expanded its direct and active subversive activity

[6]Agency for International Development, *Alliance for Progress . . . an American Partnership* (Washington, 1963), p. 23.

[7]*Worker,* February 2, 1964.

[8]*Department of State for the Press,* No. 497, November 23, 1964.

there, establishing for that purpose the notorious American Institute for Free Labor Development (AIFLD).

The institute began operations in June 1962. Its president is the president of the AFL-CIO, George Meany; its executive director, Serafino Romualdi; and its treasurer, Joseph Beirne, who is a vice-president of the AFL-CIO and the president of the Communication Workers of America.

Just like direct accomplices of U.S. imperialism, the American trade-union hierarchy trains its agents at the institute. The agents then infiltrate into the Latin American trade unions. Through the AIFLD, the AFL-CIO finances a reformist "free" trade-union movement and implants it in the Latin American countries.

In the executive committee's report at the Sixth Congress of the AFL-CIO (December 1965), a considerable expansion of the scope of the "operations" of the AIFLD in recent years was noted. The institute is striving to strengthen "democracy" through the formation of "free" trade unions, it participates in the implementation of the neocolonialist program of the Alliance for Progress, and it helps the Latin American labor movement to become "an equal partner" of business and governmental circles in the accomplishment of the notorious "democratic social revolution" in this region.[9]

Thus, it is not accidental that the AIFLD has very influential protectors —U.S. monopolies and the U.S. government. The annual expenses of the institute for training students come to about two million dollars, and they are covered chiefly by the American government (80 percent of the sum comes from the U.S. Agency for International Development), as well as by the AFL-CIO and various U.S. monopolies and businesses.[10] According-

ing to its director, Bell, the Agency for International Development "finances the basic part of the operations of the AIFLD, which submits its draft budget to the Agency each year. That budget includes the institute's expenditures on both the training of trade-union cadres and on the extension of various credits to trade unions and cooperatives in the Latin American countries."[11]

The president of the AFL-CIO himself, Meany, does not conceal the fact that American businessmen extend financial aid to the AFL-CIO institute and thus act as partners of the AFL-CIO. The chairman of the AIFLD is Peter Grace, the president of W. R. Grace and Co., which owns steamship companies, sugar plantations, textile factories, and other installations in Latin America. Also members of the institute's council are the president of the Rockefeller Fund, Berent Freely (vice-chairman); the president of the Anaconda Co., Charles Brinckerhoff; the president of Pan American World Airways, Juan Trippe; the chairman of the United Corporation Co., William Hickey; and others. All of these monopolies have considerable interests in Latin America. One of the members of the council of the AIFLD, chairman of the board of directors of True Temper Corporation, Henry Woodbridge, said as follows with regard to the community of goals of the U.S. monopolistic circles and the AFL-CIO: "The support of this institute by American business can be explained by the following statement which Meany made not long ago: 'without free trade unions, free enterprise is impossible, and with-

[9]*AFL-CIO News,* December 11, 1965.
[10]*Nation,* July 5, 1965.
[11]*Foreign Assistance Act of 1965, Hearings before the Committee on Foreign Affairs, House of Representatives, 89th Congress, 1st Session,* Part 1 (Washington, 1965), p. 82.

out free enterprise, free trade unions are impossible.' "[12]

Some thirty-five to forty specially selected young trade-union leaders come from Latin America to the AIFLD in Washington for training every four months. As noted in a AFL-CIO publication, the students are instructed by AFL-CIO specialists, professors, and various "guests."[13] Every week the Voice of America broadcasts to Latin America a special program about the activities of the institute, prepared jointly with the AFL-CIO.

In addition to the Washington center, the AIFLD has opened its branches—schools and courses for trade-union workers in many Latin American countries that are also basically supported from funds of the Agency for International Development (in the Alliance for Progress program) and by U.S. monopolies. Such branches, with an eight-to-twelve-week course of instruction, have been established in Peru, Colombia, Brazil, Mexico, Venezuela, Ecuador, the Dominican Republic, Honduras (for the Central American countries), Argentina, Bolivia, Chile, Uruguay, and Jamaica (for the Caribbean basin). As a rule, the instructors at these courses are graduates of the AIFLD. As an example, one might mention the Uruguayan Institute of Trade-Union Instruction, opened in Montevideo in November 1963 with the aid of the U.S. Agency for International Development, which provided fifty thousand dollars for this purpose. The objective of this branch of the AIFLD is "to render aid in the accelerated preparation of responsible democratic leaders for the trade-union organizations of Uruguay." Jack Goodwin of the American Embassy and the representative of AIFLD for the Plata River area became treasurer of it. No fewer than three courses a year are given at it. The students at the institute are paid huge stipends, which

they receive from the National City Bank.

The AFL-CIO and the ORIT also hold two-week seminars in the Latin American countries. These are conducted in working-class districts by traveling groups of instructors of the AFL-CIO institute's branches.

What do the AFL-CIO bosses teach Latin American trade-union activists at the American Insitute of Free Labor Development in Washington and at its branches in the Latin American countries?

Among the subjects studied are the methods of trade-union work, the political system of the United States, the principles of economics, the history of the AFL-CIO and the international labor movement, the principles of "free" trade unionism, the program of the Alliance for Progress, a course in anticommunism, and other special subjects.[14] Anticommunism is the ideological platform of the entire system of trade-union instruction in the AFL-CIO. The program for one of the special courses intended for training students in a spirit of anticommunism was prepared by Jay Lovestone, who in his time was expelled from the ranks of the Communist Party of the United States for connections with the secret police and is now an adviser to the AFL-CIO on international affairs.

The students at the AIFLD and its regional branches are taught to establish yellow, schismatic trade unions, to expose "communist agents," to propagandize the American way of life, and to work toward strengthening "democratic society." Carrying out the order of imperialist circles, the AFL-

[12]*Nation*, February 10, 1964.
[13]"The Hands that Build America, by AFL-CIO," *New York Times*, Section XI, November 17, 1963, p. 6.
[14]*The AIFLD Report* May 1965 (Washington).

CIO strives to convert the graduates of the AIFLD into active defenders of the capitalistic system and, with their help, to draw workers away from the class struggle. The yellow trade-union bosses from the AFL-CIO impress on the students of the AIFLD and its branches that, in contemporary capitalist society, the interests of labor and capital allegedly do not contradict each other. The executive director of the AFL-CIO institute, S. Romualdi, considers the basic credo of the AIFLD to be "the conception of cooperation, and not hostility between the various economic elements of society." He declares that the period of class struggle is supposedly "overcome," that strikes are "superfluous," and that it is essential to work toward "cooperation with the government and with capital."[15] "We are a part of capitalist society," declares AFL-CIO President Meany. "American trade unionism is an inseparable part of American society, which is capitalistic. We have no differences with the capitalist system. It is precisely this which we teach Latin American students."[16]

In the years 1962 to 1965 the AIFLD ideologically treated and graduated 410 yellow trade-union leaders, while its regional branches in Latin America did so for 7,600 trade-union workers. In addition, 17,500 persons were embraced by seminars and lectures organized in the Latin American countries by traveling groups from AIFLD affiliates.[17] The disciples of the AFL-CIO institute immediately turn to subversive activities in the Latin American labor movement. They continue to receive stipends from Washington for nine months after completion of the course, sums they earn through genuine service to their masters. In the words of S. Romualdi, this stipend "continues to be paid to institute graduates in order that they will be able to devote all their time to the establishment of a broad free labor movement in their countries,"[18] or, in other words, to the establishment of reformist trade unions and the undermining of the trade union movement in Latin America that has come to the defense of the class demands of the workers and the general interest of the toiling people.

An open interference of the AFL-CIO in the internal affairs of the Latin American countries was the establishment by the American Institute for Free Labor Development—with the aid of its graduates—in Peru, Colombia, El Salvador, British Guiana, and other countries of "democratic" trade-union "alliances" for the unification of the notorious "free" trade unions.[19]

As an example of divisive activity of such "democratic" trade-union confederations, we might take the maneuvers of the General Confederation of Trade Unions of El Salvador, which were directed toward undermining the unity of the workers and betraying their interests. In January 1966 the text of a letter was made public in the national legislative assembly of El Salvador, in which the leaders of this confederation addressed themselves to the director of the AFL-CIO Latin American branch Andrew McClellan in the spring of 1965, and a copy of which was sent to the U.S. Ambassador in that country. The letter expressed gratitude for the pittances of dollars that the General Confederation of Trade Unions had received through McClellan.

[15]*Mañana* (Montevideo), March 26, 1963.
[16]*Winning the Cold War: The U.S. Ideological Offensive, Hearings before the Subcommittee on International Organizations and Movements of the Committee on Foreign Affairs, House of Representatives, 88th Congress, 1st Session,* Part II (Washington, 1963), p. 142.
[17]*AFL-CIO News,* December 11, 1965.
[18]*Mañana,* March 26, 1963.
[19]*The Hands that Build America . . . ,* p. 6.

The directing council of this yellow Salvadorean trade-union confederation promised its North American patrons in the letter to wreck the unity of the trade-union movement that had been achieved at the Second National Congress of Trade Unions in April 1965. Under the pressure of rank-and-file members of trade unions belonging to it, the General Confederation of Trade Unions was forced at the time to take part in that national congress, which worked out a joint program of action by the trade-union movement in El Salvador. However, the unity of action of the Salvadorean trade unions was soon violated. The bosses of the General Confederation of Trade Unions kept their promise to McClellan: in July 1965 they held a separate congress of their organization at which resolutions that brought about a new schism in the country's trade-union movement were adopted. It is extremely significant that the convening of this congress was preceded by the receipt by the trade-union bosses of the General Confederation of Trade Unions of Salvador of their regular monetary assistance from the AFL-CIO and ORIT.

The activities of the Department of Social Projects of the AIFLD, which is an important channel for financing divisive activities on the part of the yellow trade unions in the Latin American countries by the AFL-CIO, serve the objectives of establishment and strengthening of the proimperialist "free" trade unions in Latin America. In this activity, a great deal of attention is paid not only to the cities, but also to rural areas, where the level of organization of the agricultural proletariat and peasants into trade unions is still quite low.

The AIFLD Department of Social Projects, established in August 1962 and staffed basically by American specialists, has available to it tens, if not hundreds, of millions of dollars received from the Agency for International Development, the Inter-American Development Bank, and the resources of the AFL-CIO. Together with the reformist Latin American trade unions, the organization formulates plans in the fields of housing construction, the establishment of cooperatives and workers' banks, and extends credits to "free" trade unions for carrying out these projects within the framework of the Alliance for Progress. Representation of the Department of Social Projects of the AIFLD has been established in many Latin American countries, and these branches have become centers for subversive activity in the labor movement of those countries.

The recruitment by the U.S. government of the AFL-CIO for the implementation of the neocolonialist program of the Alliance for Progress in the Latin American countries quite obviously testifies to the sociopolitical nature of American aid to the Latin American countries, which is directed toward the creation of an appearance of "concern" for the interests of broad sectors of the population and to the weakening of the anti-imperialist manifestations of the peoples of these countries.

The financial pittances of the AIFLD have become a means for the assertion of imperialist control over the Latin American labor movement and a tool for gross interference in the internal affairs of the trade unions. Only those unions that are considered "worthy" and "democratic" can turn to the AFL-CIO institute. According to the statement of the director of the AIFLD Department of Social Projects, William Dougherty, the leadership of a number of trade unions in the Latin American countries has been replaced after the AFL-CIO institute reported a cessation in their "assistance" to those unions as long as "undemocratic elements" stand at the head of them.[20]

The "free trade-union movement" implanted in Latin America by American imperialism with the help of the AFL-CIO and ORIT makes extensive use of U.S. monopolies and the government in the fight against progressive national forces in Latin America.

A dismal renown was brought to the AFL-CIO by its gross interference in the internal affairs of British Guiana, directed against the progressive government of that country headed by the leader of the Progressive People's Party, Cheddi Jagan, who had come out for the national liberation of British Guiana and the institution of democratic reforms. The dismissal of the Progressive People's Party from power in December 1964 was a result of direct imperialist scheming.

From the very beginning, the United States and England set out on a course of subversive actions against the Jagan government. As the American newspaper *Evening Star* wrote, the ruling circles of the United States "refused to help British Guiana so long as Jagan was in power."[21] In return, they heavily financed Jagan's opponents—in the first place, their own trade-union agents in the country.

In a letter that he sent to the *New York Times* in June 1963, Cheddi Jagan remarked: "The local trade-union leaders, who are well known for their hostility to the present government of British Guiana, received their training in the American Institute for the Development of Free Labor for the purpose of undermining my government. Serafino Romualdi, the executive director of that institute, does not conceal his negative attitude toward my government." The trade-union leaders who had been trained in the United States seized control of the Congress of Trade Unions of British Guiana, which be-

came one of the centers of the imperialist plot against the progressive forces of the country.

In 1963–1964, the American trade-union leaders and agents of the CIA literally flooded British Guiana. During a period of eighteen months, more trade-union figures came from the United States with subversive aims than had come during the preceding eighteen years. American trade-union bosses William McGabe, Gene Meekens, and others carried out active antigovernmental activities in the country. Thus, Gene Meekens arrived officially in British Guiana in September 1963 as a representative of the American Federation of Newspaper Workers for the purpose of "helping the leaders of the Congress of Trade Unions set up their publicity apparatus." He went to work as the press secretary for the congress.

Nevertheless, the Jagan government immediately declared Meekens to be an undesirable immigrant and ordered him on January 15, 1964, to leave the country "for the conduct of subversive activity to the advantage of the U.S. government."

At the beginning of 1963, the Washington institute of the AFL-CIO hurriedly trained and graduated eleven leaders of anti-Jagan yellow trade unions in British Guiana, spending sixty thousand dollars on their training.[22] Included in the training of these graduates of the AFL-CIO institute was the overthrow of the legal government in British Guiana in order to hand power over to the opposition parties. The usual period for payment of the stipend from the institute (nine months) was extended five months for them, in order that they might take a more active part in the antigovernmental plot.

[20]*New York Times*, September 17, 1963.
[21]*Washington Evening Star*, December 13, 1964.
[22]*Worker*, February 2, 1964.

With the objective of undermining the positions of the Jagan government, the AFL-CIO, ORIT, CIA, and British intelligence in 1963 organized a strike of the trade unions that belonged to the Congress of Trade Unions of British Guiana. It lasted eleven weeks, had a clearly defined antigovernmental character, and was accompanied by a wave of violence, murder, and racial clashes.[23]

In view of these events, Cheddi Jagan disclosed in a statement to an Associated Press correspondent concerning the conspiratorial activity of the AFL-CIO against the legal government of the country, that the AIFLD had given the Congress of Trade Unions of British Guiana two million dollars and that an additional 1.2 million dollars reached the trade unions of British Guiana "from other sources" during the strike.[24]

In Honduras, the first graduates of the AIFLD seized the leadership of the trade union of workers in the American Standard Fruit Company by resorting to all kinds of provocations. The deputy director of the Agency for International Development, Frank Coffin, in an appearance on January 15, 1964, before a subcommittee of the U.S. House of Representatives, disclosed that the "knowledge" and "experience" received at the AIFLD permitted these graduates to return the trade union to "democratic principles."[25]

When the reactionary military of Honduras associated with the Pentagon overthrew President Ramón Villeda Morales in October 1963, the rank-and-file trade-union members and some trade-union leaders of Honduras demanded the call of a general strike of protest and of refusal to permit the installation of a dictatorial regime in the country. However, the local agents of the AFL-CIO and ORIT, who had worked their way into trade-union leadership positions, undermined a general strike. The AFL-CIO institute did not consider it necessary even to make a show of a judgment of the military dictatorship in Honduras by the United States and came out for an extension of the program of American economic aid in that country.

With respect to the military *coup d'état* in Brazil in April 1964, the director of the Department of Social Projects of the AIFLD, Dougherty, acknowledged that the graduates of that institute "operated so actively that they turned out to be closely connected with certain secret measures of the revolution before it had actually begun. . . . Many trade-union leaders—a considerable number of whom were actually trained in our institute—took part in the revolution and in the overthrow of the Goulart regime."[26] Many progressive labor leaders were then arrested, and the AIFLD graduates seized the leadership posts in a number of trade unions (those of machinists, metal workers, telegraphers, etc.). This reorganization of the Brazilian trade unions was directed by the secretary-general of the ORIT, Arturo Jauregui, who arrived in Rio de Janeiro immediately after the *coup d'état*.[27]

Toward the end of 1964, AFL-CIO President Meany sent a letter to Fred Sammerford, the attaché for labor matters at the U.S. embassy in the Dominican Republic in which he thanked him for his "distinguished contribution to the democratic trade-union movement in the Dominican Republic." For what did Sammerford receive such gratitude? In 1962–1963, he directed the subversive activities of the trade-union organization CONATRAL, established by the

---

[23]Cheddi Jagan, "Protiv reaktsii i rasizma, za demokratiiu i natsional'nuiu nezavisimost'," *Problemy mira i sotsializma*, No. 8, 1965.

[24]*Nation*, February 10, 1964.

[25]*Winning the Cold War . . . 2d Session*, Part VIII, p. 973.

[26]*Nation*, July 5, 1965.

[27]*Boletín Sindical Latinoamericano*, No. 5–6, 1964.

AFL-CIO in the Dominican Republic, activities that were directed against President Juan Bosch, who was accused of a "soft attitude toward communism." A few weeks prior to the *coup d'état* in the Dominican Republic that led to the overthrow of Juan Bosch, CONATRAL published an announcement in the press calling on the population to entrust their defense against "communism" to the "armed forces." As an acknowledgment of the services of the AFL-CIO in the struggle against progressive forces in the Dominican Republic, AIFLD executive director Serafino Romualdi was decorated with the Order of Duarte, Sánchez, and Mela by the leader of the pro-American junta, Reid Cabral.[28]

The gross interference of the AFL-CIO, ORIT, and their local trade-union agents in the internal affairs of other Latin American countries is also common knowledge.

Opposing the divisive subversive activity of the AFL-CIO, AIFLD, and ORIT in the labor movement of the Latin American countries are the efforts of the workers toward unity of action in the anti-imperialist struggle. A powerful step in this direction was the Congress for the Trade-Union Unity of Latin American Workers, held January 24–28, 1964, in Rio de Janeiro, Brazil.

Delegations representing 25 million urban and rural workers through the national trade unions and trade-union organizations of eighteen Latin American countries took part in the work of the congress. The congress saluted "the victorious socialist revolution in Cuba, which has ended the exploitation of man by man for all time, and which is an example and stimulus in the struggle of our peoples for liberation." In the program of struggle approved by the congress, which bears a class and anti-imperialist nature, there are de-

mands for the defense of general peace as well as a constant and active struggle for economic and social liberation; for the elimination of the latifundia and the implementation of profound agrarian reforms; for the elimination of the system of exploitation established by the imperialist monopolies, for higher wages and for improved social insurance; for struggle in defense of democratic rights and trade-union liberties; in defense of national sovereignty and the right of nations to self-determination; and in defense of Cuba and in opposition to the blockade of Cuba by the United States.[29]

The Congress for the Trade-Union Unity of Latin American Workers was declared to be "in standing operation." A permanent council to act as a regional trade-union organization was elected at it.

The meeting of representatives of the Communist parties of the Latin American countries, which was held toward the end of 1964, established the goals of the labor movement on the continent, confirmed the rise in the struggle of the working class and the strengthening of its political and anti-imperialist nature, and emphasized the enormous influence on the continent's labor movement of the Cuban Revolution, which opened the age of socialism in America.

A considerable part of the Latin American workers who take part in the trade-union movement are moving ever closer to the vanguard of the working class and are joining forces in the struggle for its rights and for social-democratic changes and against the aggressive imperialist policy of the United States.

The successful holding of a People's Congress in Uruguay in August 1965 testifies to the growing unity of action

[28]*Nation,* July 5, 1965.
[29]*Boletín Sindical Latinoamericano,* No. 3, 1964.

of the toiling masses. Participating in it were 1,376 delegates from 700 trade-union organizations representing over 800,000 people. Such progressive organizations as the following have been considerably strengthened: the Unified Trade-Union Center of Chilean Workers, which has over 1 million members; the Unified Trade-Union Center of Uruguayan Workers; the Unified Workers' Center of Venezuela, which is carrying out a struggle for the observance of legality and the cessation of repression in the country; the Confederation of Workers of Ecuador, which unites the democratic forces of the trade-union movement; the Trade-Union Confederation of Workers of Colombia, which takes in 200,000 workers who support unity of action by the various trade-union organizations; the Federation of Workers of Panama; and the Confederation of Workers of Costa Rica. In October 1965 a trade-union confederation was established in El Salvador grouping fourteen trade unions, which has opened the way to the establishment in that country of a new confederation of democratic orientation.

The intensifying movement of the Latin American workers for unity of action in the struggle for their rights, against imperialist oppression, and for the gains that have been achieved testify to the fact that all the intrigues of the trade-union agents of imperialism in the Latin American labor movement are doomed to failure, and that the national-liberation movement of the peoples of these countries will sweep away all barriers erected in its path by U.S. imperialists and their servitors from the AFL-CIO and the ORIT.

19. The Divisive Role of ORIT, ATLAS, APRA, and Catholic Trade Unions in the Latin American Labor Movement*

M. V. DANILEVICH

The creation of the Inter-American Regional Labor Organization, known in the Latin American countries as ORIT, was announced at a convention in Mexico in January 1951. It included the AFL, the CIO, and the state-controlled trade-union organizations of Cuba, Chile, and Peru. The trade unions of Brazil and Argentina had not been invited to the convention. Representatives from the Mexican unions controlled by the government party and

*Rabochii klass v osvoboditel'nom dvizhenii narodov Latinskoi Ameriki (Moskva: Gosudarstvennoe izdatel'stvo politicheskoi literatury, 1962), pp. 257–258, 260–273, 279–281.

connected with the AFL at first took an active part in the work of the conference. They hoped to play a leading role in the new organization. However, after they realized that the commanding position would belong to the trade-union bosses of the United States, they refused to join the new organization and left the conference. As a result, the seat of the ORIT was established in Cuba. To be sure, a number of Mexican federations and the CTM soon joined the ORIT.

Reactionary Latin American governments gave general support to the ORIT and compelled trade-union organizations to join.

The nature of the ORIT and the trend of its activity became particularly apparent at its second congress in December 1952, at Rio de Janeiro. This second congress, like the first, did not discuss vital day-to-day problems of the working class and of the Latin American nations as a whole. The words *imperialism* and *colonialism* were absent from the speeches. The ORIT leaders limited themselves to defending the State Department's policy in Latin America, eulogizing the "syndicalism of Vargas" and engaging also in endless reiterations of anti-Soviet slanders and the inciting of war hysteria.[1] The congress went on record in favor of the rearmament of Latin America under the leadership of the U.S. General Staff and adopted a resolution leading essentially to the complete economic and political subjugation of Latin America to the United States. The congress also censured those countries that had failed to send troops to Korea and had delayed ratification of the bilateral military pacts with the United States.

ORIT not only emerged as a champion of reformist ideology among the working class. It used every means, including ideological ones, to defend U.S. imperialist policy in Latin Amer-

ica. In such a vitally important area as the struggle for national independence, the ORIT leaders took the side of imperialism and of the local wealthy bourgeoisie connected with monopoly interests. They supported the foreign policy of American imperialism: the Marshall Plan, the North Atlantic Treaty, the arming of West Germany and Japan, the South Atlantic Pact, and other "plans" for imposing bondage and exploitation upon Latin America. They strove to implant the reactionary ideology of Pan-Americanism in the minds of working people by extensively propagandizing "continental solidarity," "continental citizenship," and the necessity of "defending the Western Hemisphere." In effect, their goal boiled down to defeating the anti-imperialist movement. ORIT portrayed expansionist policy of the U.S. monopolies in Latin America as a "good neighbor" policy of "disinterested aid" to brotherly republics of the Western Hemisphere, and so forth.

In describing the subversive activity of ORIT leaders the CTAL organ, *Noticiero de la CTAL,* and several other labor-union newspapers wrote that they were linked not only with the AFL leadership but also with the Department of State and that they were doing their work with financial aid from the latter.[2] ORIT failed to win either influence or authority among the working masses. Nonetheless, it officially represented the labor-union movement of most of the Latin American countries.

In April 1955 the third congress of the ORIT was held at San José, Costa Rica, where, according to official data of this organization, 25 million workers of the Western Hemisphere were re-

[1] Rubens Iscaro, *Origen y desarrollo del movimiento sindical argentino* (Buenos Aires, 1958), p. 193.
[2] *Noticiero de la CTAL,* 230:iii–iv (1953).

presented. Inasmuch as the ICFTU at that time numbered 50 million members, the Western Hemisphere should have one-half of this membership. The unions of the United States and Canada comprise more than two-thirds of the membership of the ORIT and define its policies. The ORIT membership from Latin American organizations numbers about 6 to 7 million.

According to official figures of the ICFTU, ORIT in 1957 included all trade-union organizations of Venezuela, (200,000 members), Cuba (1.5 million), Colombia (400,000), Paraguay (45,000), and Brazil (over 2 million).[3] Argentina was represented in the ORIT by the schismatic Independent Working Committee of Trade-Union Action, created by the Socialist Party. It was believed that this organization numbered 40,000 members (the Argentine Confederation of Labor [CGT] did not belong to any of the international centers). Approximately the same number of members were in the Uruguayan federation of unions. In Chile, five small federations belonged to ORIT, with a membership, according to official figures, of about 45,000.

Leadership of the ORIT is in the hands of reactionary U.S. trade-union leaders who support the aggressive colonization policy of the monopolies. A considerable portion of Latin America's union organizations came under the control of the reactionary leaders of the AFL-CIO. The ORIT essentially has taken the place of the former Pan American Federation of Labor.

The leaders of ORIT union centers in most cases were not elected but were appointed by the Ministry of Labor. In such labor unions there could be no question of internal democracy. Hardly any meetings were held and compulsory membership was practiced. Membership dues were withheld from wages by the employers themselves, regard-

less of whether workers wanted to join these unions. The dues were remitted to the Ministry of Labor. In some countries, such dues payments became a kind of labor-union tax.

To forestall strikes, the leadership of the ORIT organizations used a variety of methods, often joining with the police in exerting pressure upon individual unions. By various machinations, it blocked the expression of the will of the toiling masses, foiled meetings of workers, prevented unorganized workers from attending the meetings, scheduled meetings at inconvenient times for the workers (during hours when most of them were at work and so on).[4]

The political nature of the ORIT is revealed by its attitude toward events in Guatemala. The ORIT not only failed to support the Guatemalan people in their fight against aggression, but, on the contrary, it even engaged in a provocationist campaign of slander against the participants in that movement and particularly against the Confederation of Guatemalan Workers (CGTG). As soon as the U.S. puppet Castillo Armas seized power and perpetrated bloody reprisals against progressive leaders and activist workers, the ORIT representative Romualdi appeared in Guatemala with a proposal to replace the now-outlawed progressive trade-union organization with "free trade unions that understand their responsibility," that is, unions that would satisfy the requirements of the United Fruit Company. This ORIT proposal was in complete accord with the stand of the State Department. The then–Vice-President of the United States, Nixon, who visited Guatemala, also "appealed" to the workers to create a trade-union

[3]*Yearbook of the International Free Trade Union Movement, 1957–1958*, pp. 204, 209, 364.
[4]*Imprensa Popular*, November 2, 1955.

center similar to those belonging to ORIT, as the basis for recognition by United Fruit Company.[5]

"Assistance" to the pro-American dictator in "reorganizing the labor movement" took place under conditions of terror and reprisal. It was effected by such methods as raids on labor-union premises, the imposition of "governing boards" appointed by the government, repression of trade-union democracy, and complete destruction of the gains that had been made by workers.

It would be erroneous to believe that all workers and employees in ORIT organizations share its ideology, methods, and ways of action. Not only considerable numbers of members but even entire federations fail to agree with the trend of the ORIT's activity and are actually supporters of the CTAL and WFTU program. The struggle of workers in a number of countries has shown that, despite the policies and the will of their official leaders, the trade-union masses carry on a dedicated offensive based on working-class unity of action, that is, they are guided by slogans advanced by the WFTU.

Thus the union centers comprising the ORIT were created as a result of direct intervention by Latin American governments, while the ORIT itself was established on the initiative and with the support of ruling circles of the United States.

The ORIT organizations enjoy all manner of government assistance in fighting progressive unions. In many countries (Brazil, Cuba, Chile, Guatemala, Mexico), the leadership elected by the union masses has been forcibly removed, the leaders being either deprived of their legal powers or arrested and exiled. With the help of the police and army, appointed government officials have seized trade-union centers. Progressive unions have been deprived of legal recognition. The unions

established in Guatemala and led by agents of monopolies are, in the eyes of ORIT leaders, models of trade-union organization.[6]

ORIT sets up Latin American affiliate federations for branches of industry and conducts their conferences. A Textile Workers' Federation of Latin America, with headquarters in Mexico, has been created. It belongs to the World Federation of Textile Workers based in London. ORIT distributes agitational literature filled with anticommunist insinuations.

Leaders of ORIT organizations practice fascist methods of politically motivated discrimination among workers. They sanction (and sometimes even initiate) the discharge of Communists and generally progressive worker-activists from their jobs. The ORIT maintains the fight against communism as its principal goal.[7]

The work of ORIT is based on the principle of "class cooperation" and "class peace" between labor and capital. The leadership of ORIT therefore strives to increase labor productivity in the interests of foreign monopolies. The frankly cynical statement of Mujal, the former secretary of the Cuban Confederation of Labor (CTC), is characteristic of this scheme: "Workers should be ready to sacrifice for the sake of an increase in investments that further the development of new sources of employment. . . . Inasmuch as we live under capitalist conditions, it is the busi-

[5]*Justicia*, November 11, 1955.
[6]Speaking as a guest of honor at the Third Congress of the ORIT was the Minister of Labor of Guatemala, a bloody butcher of the proletariat of that heroic country. This fact aroused profound indignation among the workers. The trade-union delegations from Uruguay, Argentina, and Venezuela withdrew from the congress, stating that the workers of their countries repudiated dictatorial regimes and that they did not approve of similar actions by the ORIT (*Justicia*, November 11, 1955; *Noticiero de la CTAL*, p. iv [1955]).
[7]*Visión*, December 19, 1958.

ness of the Cuban Confederation of Labor to guarantee capitalist profits."[8]

ORIT and affiliated continental organizations are champions of bourgeois influence among the working class and struggle for subordination of the interests of the working class to those of the bourgeoisie. Their activity is aimed at preventing the development of proletarian ideology and the growth of socialist consciousness in the working class.

Argentine unions controlled by the government and the Peronista Party sowed dissension in the Latin American labor movement. Under the conditions of the Peronista regime, Argentine trade unions were established according to the principle of class cooperation and "community of interests between labor and capital." The Peronistas attempted to direct union work so as to contain and limit the independence of the labor movement. Finding support among the remnants of anarchist ideology and syndicalist traditions, they distracted workers from participating in political activity, leaving that to the Peronistas.

The mission of the Peronistas was to impose bourgeois ideology upon the proletariat, converting militant organizations intended to defend proletarian class interests into appendices of the government apparatus and the Peronista Party. The terms "state syndicalism" and "production syndicalism" were applied extensively in Argentina, meaning the creation of labor unions controlled by the reactionary dictatorship and of organizations that would work, according to Perón, "in accordance with instructions from the State."[9] Labor unions managed by government officials were included in the state apparatus. There could be no question of any democracy or independence for the unions. There existed a union hierarchy or, as the Argentine workers called it,

"the holy trinity" of union leaders, employers, and police.

The work of trade-union leaders amounted to glorifying the *justicialista* regime, "furthering harmony among all strata of the Argentine people," and preventing strikes. If strikes nevertheless arose, union leaders were obliged to support the government, recruit strikebreakers, and perform other cooperative tasks. There were cases, however, where Perón, seeking popularity among the workers, intervened in conflicts, forcing employers to satisfy some part of the workers' demands. It was necessary for Perón to do this in order to propagandize the "regime of greatest justice" in Argentina. The leaders concealed their antilabor activity by asserting that the workers of Argentina had already "received maximum satisfaction of their demands and achieved all that capitalism could grant them without impinging on the common interests

[8]Such cynicism is not surprising if one takes into account the fact that Mujal acquired a huge fortune by appropriating trade-union dues that were compulsorily deducted from workers' wages. He became the owner of the large Finca América property, with an area of 1,342 hectares and value of 4 million dollars. On it worked three hundred agricultural laborers whom Mujal prevented from joining trade unions and whom he paid less than workers on neighboring farms earned. The people's government confiscated his farm in 1959 and transferred it to the workers.

The leadership of the CTC was a supporter of the dictatorial regime of Batista and it fled to the United States with him. The ORIT extended all kinds of support to Mujal, considering the CTC to be "one of the most powerful and most effective trade-union organizations." One of the members of the CTC leadership, Ignacio Telechea, became chairman of the ORIT.

[9]In a speech delivered at the stock market on August 25, 1944, Perón notified the capitalists that there was no reason to fear his syndicalism. He said: "I want to organize the workers on a state scale in such a way that the state would lead them and supply their direction. In this way, the ideological and revolutionary sectors among them would be neutralized, sectors that could be a threat to our capitalist society in the postwar period. The workers must be given some improvements, and they will become a force that can be easily managed" (*La Hora*, December 12, 1945).

of employers and workers, and the general interests of the country."[10] They declared themselves to be partisans of "new forms" of labor-capital relations or of the so-called human relationships in production and preached the Peronist "theory" of *justicialismo* and "nonexploiting capitalism."

The union leaders hindered in every way the satisfaction of workers' demands. They delayed implementation of collective agreements, "froze" wages for lengthy periods, and forcibly imposed terms with employers on the workers without the workers' agreement. All this was embellished with the broad social demagogy of Peronism. Naturally, no protection of workers' interests could be expected from the leadership of these unions. Actually, they had been created for the purpose of paralyzing working-class activity, shackling its initiative, and grafting an alien ideology onto it so as to disarm the working class facing an employers' offensive.

The subversive demagogical propaganda by Peronist union leaders spread not only among Argentine workers but to neighboring countries as well. The Peronistas tried to exploit the hatred of the Latin American working masses for U.S. imperialism in such a manner as to deepen dissent among them; they agitated for the notorious slogan of "the third position" or "the third course."[11] In order to split individual labor unions in Latin American countries away from CTAL and the WFTU and extend their influence to neighboring countries, the Peronistas began to build up a continental labor-union central under the leadership of the Argentine CGT. They proclaimed that the new organization would carry on a "third force" policy and would "protect the interests of the Latin American working class against communism as well as against capitalism"[12]

With this purpose in view, a conference of the workers of La Plata was called in early 1952 in Paraguay, in which there participated representatives of government labor unions and small individual splinter groups of Paraguay and Uruguay and representatives from other countries in no way connected with the La Plata region— Honduras, Panama, Nicaragua, Costa Rica, and Peru. Also present was the well-known dissentient of the Mexican labor movement, Morones. The conference adopted a resolution to create a Latin American labor-union committee that was to prepare for the establishment of a continental central.

In its declaration of principles, this committee demagogically stated that the new organization intended to "facilitate the unity of the working class without discrimination as to political, racial, and religious views, so as to achieve a union of the toiling people of the Latin American continent."[13] The organization also proclaimed an anti-imperialist stand.

The mere fact of the creation of another labor-union central, at a time when deep cleavage in the working class existed, signified further splintering of proletarian forces and damage to their fighting capability and inevitably served the interests of imperialism and domestic reaction.

The next stage was a conference in Mexico in November 1952, which created the Agrupación de Trabajadores Latinoamericanos Sindicalizados (ATLAS). The new organization began work with a flurry of activity. ATLAS Secretary-General Fernando Pérez Vidal visited Mexico, Cuba, Canada, Guatemala, Nicaragua, Honduras, Costa Rica,

[10]V. Codovilla, *Nuestro camino desemboca en la victoria* (Buenos Aires, 1954), p. 292.
[11]Rubens Iscaro, *Origen y desarrollo del movimiento sindical argentino*, p. 199.
[12]*Noticiero de la CTAL*, 230:iii–iv (1953).
[13]*Nuestra Palabra*, January 27, 1953.

El Salvador, and Panama, establishing in those countries bases of support in the form of "national committees." Wherever such organizations emerged, dissent deepened within the workers' ranks. Thus, during the period of democratic government in Guatemala, agents of the Peronista movement tried in every way to prevent creation of a united class organization of labor unions. And when the General Confederation of Workers of Guatemala was nevertheless established, a representative from ATLAS initiated subversive schismatic activity to disrupt the unity that had already been achieved. A letter from the executive committee of the CGT of Guatemala to national labor organizations stressed that ATLAS "serves the interests of U.S. imperialism and tries to split the labor and democratic movement in order to facilitate overthrow of the progressive government of President Arbenz."[14]

ATLAS, however, was unable to develop its activity widely. It confined itself to Latin America without establishing connections with any of the international labor-union organizations. Principal members of the ATLAS were the CROM of Mexico, a small organization in Colombia, and minor union organizations in Central America and Haiti. To increase its influence, ATLAS planned to establish a labor confederation of Central American countries.

The following is typical of the political inclination of this organization's leaders: on the occasion of the ninth anniversary of Perón's access to power, the ATLAS leadership sent him a telegram of congratulation calling him the creator of a new Argentina, where "social justice, political sovereignty, and economic independence" had supposedly materialized.[15]

Thus, ATLAS and ORIT competed with one another. They differed on certain ideological points, but both of them were instruments of schism, striking the labor movement at the most vital point—the problem of working-class unity. This divisive work was conducted during one of the most difficult periods of the Latin American peoples' struggle, when the offensive of the imperialist bloc and domestic reaction reached unprecedented scope.

The subversive ideological work by the above-mentioned labor center was accompanied by radical organizational changes in the labor-union movements.

Subordination of labor unions to government control, daily interference by government labor ministries in the internal affairs of unions, appointment of reformists and sometimes simply government bureaucrats to the leadership organs—all resulted in the formation of a separate caste of "trade-union leaders." In several countries (Argentina, Brazil, Cuba, Mexico), a labor-union bureaucracy was created, bribed, and nurtured by employers and the state. Subordination of unions to the ministry of labor, obligatory membership, a system of employers withholding "union dues" from earnings and depositing them into a special fund controlled by the ministry of labor—all these methods increasingly converted union leaders into union bureaucrats or appendices to the ministry of labor. Within state-controlled unions the number of administrative employees unconnected with production increased. They were often transferred by the management from one union to another.

The labor-union bureaucracy grew especially powerful in the Peronista CGT in Argentina. The number of highly paid union leaders swelled incredibly. The governing apparatus of some unions contained so many administrative employees that a special

[14]*El Siglo,* July 18, 1953.
[15]*Ibid.,* November 9, 1955.

"trade union of trade-union workers" was created.[16] The lack of internal democracy, meetings, and free elections of governing boards, and the alienation of workers from the decision-making process in essential questions all converted the labor leaders and the apparatus of union management into something independent of the workers and dependent on the Ministry of Labor with its special organs, such as the "labor police." This labor bureaucracy, quite firmly supported by the top ranks of the labor unions and the government, disunited the labor unions of the several federations by isolating them from one another. At the same time this union bureaucracy grew further estranged from the masses. Union leadership ceased to express the interests of the workers. The latter began to leave unions or remained members only on paper.

Schismatic divisive activity within the labor movement was carried on by organizations other than the two we have examined. From 1944 to 1948, a considerable divisive role was also played by the Peruvian People's Party (APRA). It has its separate history. This party laid the foundation for a movement that came to be called "Aprista." It was used by the AFL in its divisive machinations not only in Peru but also in other Latin American countries, especially those with considerable Indian populations.

As early as the 1930's, Haya de la Torre and other APRA leaders extensively advanced anti-imperialist slogans and even advertised their party as "Marxist" and "Communist." In reality, the Apristas are conduits of bourgeois influence in the working class. They have denied the leading role of the proletariat in the national-liberation movement and have preached a "theory" of the "originality" and "exclusiveness" of Latin America.[17] The ideology of the "Aprista movement" presented a great danger to the labor and national-liberation movement. Attempting to direct the liberation movement, the Apristas viewed their party as an organization of several classes and considered the petty bourgeoisie as possessing hegemony over revolution in Latin American conditions.[18]

In connection with the growth of political activity on the part of the working class, the Apristas gave new impetus to propagandizing their "theory" to the effect that the working class of Latin America, because of its weakness and small numbers, was allegedly incapable of playing the leading role in democratic reforms and in uniting democratic, progressive forces.

For demagogic ends, the Apristas proposed a program of fighting for "social justice," in which, however, they asserted that they did not aspire to take wealth away from those who possess it, but merely promised to seek out new sources for improving the living conditions of the people.

When the United States after the Second World War stepped up its offensive against Latin America, the Apristas unleashed propaganda in the press about the progressive role of imperialism in the dependent countries. They assured their readers that "U.S. imperialism at present is not dangerous," that "the flow of capital from the United States will alleviate social and economic conditions in Peru." At the very time that the progressive forces of Peru were fighting to protect their national resources, the APRA leaders began to demand that the United States be accorded exclusive rights to the rich Sechura petroleum reserves, arguing that the raw-materials-producing countries of Latin America " 'complement'

[16]*Problemy mira i sotsializma*, No. 4:66 (1961).
[17]V. R. Haya de la Torre, *El antiimperialismo y el APRA* (Santiago de Chile, 1936), p. 118.
[18]*La Correspondencia Sudamericana*, May 1, 1930, p. 19.

the industrial might of the United States."[19]

In its activities, APRA paid special attention to Indian communes and agricultural laborers, striving to subject them to its influence and at the same time to block any collaboration between them and progressive trade unions belonging to the WFTU.

APRA attacked the trade unions belonging to CTAL and carried on divisive activities in various countries. It was hardly a coincidence that the first splinter organization to oppose the CTAL—the Inter-American Confederation of labor (CIT)—was established in Lima with the very active participation of the Apristas. It is clear from the foregoing facts why the Aprista movement is praised in every possible way in the trade-union press of the United States and why efforts are made to link the Apristas with the bourgeois and petty-bourgeois movements of other countries.

The Church and the leaders of those trade unions under its influence, as well as the leadership of the yellow, reformist trade unions, focus particular attention on the task of instilling in the minds of the workers social demagogy on the necessity of developing "humanitarian relations" within industry. They try to convince the worker that he is becoming a "social partner" of the employer, with equal rights, and that the worker and his employer share an equal interest in seeing their enterprise "prosper." And all this is said so that the worker will draw the intended inference: that I must not strike, and someday my zeal will be rewarded with some prize or, perhaps, with a microscopic share of the profits! Although arrayed in somewhat modernized dress, what is being advocated here is nothing more than the infamous paternalism of old.

Such catchwords as "a third way" and "social ideal" do not at all prevent the Catholic Church from presenting its anticommunist propaganda in order to undermine the unity of democratic forces that is being shaped. From the standpoint of the clergy, the growth of Church influence is tied directly to the struggle against the Communists and the spread of Marxist ideas. The Church openly declares itself as the most reliable opponent of communism, for which posture it enjoys the well-deserved support of imperialism. The secretary-general of the American Association of Peasant Farmers, Luigi Ligutti, gives the Catholic Church its due for its struggle against communism: "The Church in Latin America is the main obstacle in the path of communism. It is only the attachment of the peoples of Latin America to the Catholic Church that keeps them from going over to the side of the Communists."[20] The basic content of all meetings, congresses, and conferences by representatives of the Church and organizations controlled by them is that of struggle against communism and Communists— referred to by them as "enemies of Christianity and democracy."

In order to retain their influence over the masses, Christian-Democratic parties are forced occasionally to criticize colonialism and imperialism, while the Second Congress of these parties condemned dictatorial regimes, particularly that of Pérez Jiménez of Venezuela, as "leading to the unjust distribution of the vast riches of the country."[21]

In the realm of the trade-union movement, the Church opposes the creation of united national trade-union centrals, concealing its position in the demagogic cry for "freedom of association." Thus, for example, a declaration of the Argentine episcopate made a direct appeal to Catholics during the presi-

[19]Rodney Arismendi, *Vtorzhenie dollara v Latinskuiu Ameriku* (Moskva, 1948), p. 100.
[20]*Cahiers Internationaux*, 67:78 (1955).
[21]*La Prensa*, November 25, 1957.

dential election in which they were urged not to vote for candidates who supported the creation of united trade-union centrals, as these would "infringe on the principle of freedom of association." "Above all," states the declaration, "the Church proclaims the postulate of trade-union liberty."[22] What is really meant by this is freedom for reactionary Catholic trade unions and the suppression and restriction of the activities of progressive workers' organizations.

Touring Latin America with the intention of becoming acquainted with the trade-union situation, Vanistendael, the secretary general of the IFCTU (International Federation of Christian Trade Unions), justifies his opposition to united trade-union centrals in another fashion. He explains that the Christian trade-union movement "is not an advocate of unification, because that would lead to ideological confusion."[23] He defines "ideological confusion" as that which would stem from the creation of unions that would join workers of various political orientation and parties, forgetting that earlier he had restricted the activities of trade unions exclusively to the defense of economic interests.

Regardless of their adherence to different political parties, points of view, or religious denominations, workers joined in united trade unions have common general demands and goals: the struggle for their economic interests, for independence, democracy, and peace.

The goal of Church interference in the trade-union movement is to prevent the formation of new united trade-union centrals and, whenever possible, also to intensify the split in the labor movement.

The division of the working class, carried out by the leaders of ATLAS, ORIT, as well as the Christian, Catholic trade unions has posed very crucial and complex problems before the CTAL and all progressive trade-union organizations and their allies in those countries where such organizations had been destroyed. It has become necessary to advance common demands under new, more difficult conditions and to fight with united effort for their realization.

Under such circumstances, the struggle for the unity of the working class has become one of the most vital and acute problems of the labor movement. Despite the serious differences that exist between ORIT and the CTAL in program demands and methods of trade-union work, or the fact that ORIT did not lead the struggle against monopolies—and conducted a policy of politically motivated discrimination, expelling communists and worker activists, thereby deepening division in the working class—despite all this, the CTAL and its member organizations have more than once approached the ORIT organizations and other trade unions with an appeal to reconsider the possibility of joint action.[24] The progressive trade unions understood that in those organizations there were workers for whose interests a genuine workers' organization should conduct the struggle.

[22]*Ibid.*, June 9, 1957.
[23]*Labor*, 1:4–8 (1960).
[24]*El Siglo*, November 9, 1955.

20. The Subversion of Labor by the Bourgeois Government of Mexico*

O. KONSTANTINOV

During World War II, the upper bourgeoisie supplanted the petty and middle bourgeoisies and it now employs new slogans to exert its ideological influence on the masses.

The slogan of "national unity" about the "revolutionary government" has replaced the slogan of class struggle, heretofore formally recognized by nearly all Mexican trade unions and even inscribed in the program of the ruling party of the Mexican Revolution. There has been a revision of the entire bourgeois publicity campaign. The Mexican bourgeois historian Alfónso López Aparico, who devotes himself to problems of the labor movement, wrote:

Previously the most important labor organizations were based on a more or less concealed Marxist ideology and enthusiastically paid homage to the systems that were put into effect in the USSR. The new program of "national unity" has necessitated some radical changes in the theoretical aspirations of the labor movement. The attention of labor organizations has become focused primarily on effecting a material reconstruction of the country, eliminating quarrels between union locals, renouncing the idea of class struggle in its absolute sense, and promoting goodwill between the state and the capitalists in order to eliminate or forestall unnecessary conflicts between workers and employers.

The doctrine of class struggle began to yield to the idea of coexistence within the framework of legal procedure as an expression of the majority will. Proletarian class internationalism has been eliminated in the face of the categorical and inflexible declaration of the feeling of the Mexican nation, which found itself menaced by the war.[1]

In reality, however, the bourgeoisie has utterly failed to erase from the minds of the Mexican workers the ideas of class struggle and proletarian internationalism.

Yet the ideologists and agents of the bourgeoisie have continually strived to ensure the ideological domination of reformism, nationalism, and class collaboration within the labor movement. They relentlessly

talk about so-called peace between classes as a guarantee of the country's development and of improvement in the status of its masses; they extol before the entire world the slogan of patriotism, implying that the workers must dedicate themselves to productive and creative labor in order to avoid jeopardizing the interests of their homeland; they say that this struggle must be conducted by "lawful means," that is, through officially recognized trade-union leaders

*Voprosy mezhdunarodnogo rabochego i natsional'no-osvoboditel'nogo dvizheniia na sovremennom etape, ed. A. A. Guber and V. V. Lenin (Moskva: Izdatel'stvo VPSh i AON, 1963), pp. 91–94, 95–97.

[1] A. L. Aparicio, El movimiento obrero en México: Antecedentes, desarrollo y tendencias (México, 1958), p. 236.

who, naturally, enjoyed the benevolence of the government; at every step they intimidate by making false assertions to the effect that a wage increase inevitably entails a rise in prices, and so forth.[2]

The upper bourgeoisie under the pretext of an ideological campaign unleashed an offensive during the war against the working class for the purpose of completely subjugating labor to its own authority and depriving it of an opportunity to resist the policy of the ruling classes, which are becoming ever more reactionary. The bourgeois offensive against the economic and political interests of the working class became particularly unruly during President Miguel Alemán's administration. In that period the struggle between the working class and the bourgeoisie reached exceptional intensity. The government began to suppress the workers' strike movement by force, employing not only the police but also the regular army. The working class—disunited, inadequately organized, and betrayed by trade-union leaders—failed to defend its positions at the time. In the throes of an internal crisis, the Communist Party of Mexico made serious errors and was thus unable to provide leadership in the workers' struggle for their rights.

In March 1947 government agents within the trade-union movement—Fidel Velásquez, Amilpa, Rojas, and others—split the Confederation of Mexican Workers (CTM) and expelled from its leadership all those not wishing to carry out implicitly the will of the ruling circles, including those reformists, who had thought it necessary to mask to some extent the fact that the labor movement was subservient to the bourgeoisie. In December 1947 the CTM withdrew from the Confederation of Latin American Workers (CTAL) and the World Federation of Trade Unions (WFTU), and in 1949 it joined the yellow international trade-union center —the ICFTU.[3]

When a number of the largest trade unions—such as the unions of petroleum workers, miners, and railroad workers —had withdrawn from the CTM after its leadership was seized outright by government agents, the ruling circles chose the path of direct intervention in the affairs of labor organizations. Police and troops occupied the headquarters of recalcitrant trade unions and forcibly removed the labor leaders who were objectionable to the government, replacing them with their own puppets. In this manner, almost the entire Mexican labor movement found itself controlled by agents of the government and the employers during President Alemán's administration.

Neither the views nor the status of most Mexican labor leaders of today have anything in common with the working class, inasmuch as many of them have enriched themselves and have become wealthy bourgeois. They are direct representatives and officials of a bourgeois state apparatus and not only are in the pay of the employers and the government, but also are frequently appointed directly by them. In summation, this clique of trade-union bums makes up part of the bourgeois state apparatus. Many of the trade-union leaders are senators and deputies in the Mexican Congress and also occupy numerous posts in the administrative apparatus of the bourgeois state as state governors, chairmen, and counselors of local government. We can judge from the following facts what these "labor" functionaries are like. Fidel Velásquez, secretary general of the CTM, is a wealthy capitalist who has invested

[2]"Tesis sobre el trabajo sindical," p. 28.
[3]V. I. Ermolaev, *Natsional'no-osvoboditel'noe i rabochee dvizhenie v stranakh Latinskoi Ameriki posle vtoroi mirovoi voiny* (Moskva, 1958), p. 61.

large sums of money in a number of enterprises of the chemical industry. Together with another trade-union boss, Jesús Iuren, he controls several truck lines, is a landowner, and holds shares in a number of different companies.[4] In 1961 the press reported that the government had peremptorily appointed millionaire Jesús Robles Martínez, chairman of a construction company, as secretary general of the Federación de Sindicatos de Empleados del Estado.[5]

Dissension is one of the basic weapons employed by the bourgeoisie to subjugate the labor movement. It is difficult to imagine a labor movement more disunited than the Mexican one. The following data bear witness to the degree of disunity within the Mexican working class. In 1954 there were 7 national trade-union centrals in the country, 125 "independent" trade unions, and innumerable local unions belonging neither to any trade-union central nor to a national trade union.[6] In addition, there are contending groups and groupings in nearly every trade union that fight each other for union leadership. In many of the enterprises the owners have established reactionary strikebreakers' unions. A large number of Mexican workers have not been organized into trade unions at all. Thus in 1954 the trade unions had recruited only 864,656 of 1,475,593 industrial workers.[7] The schismatic and treacherous policy of the yellow trade-union bureaucrats greatly hampers the struggle of the workers for their vital interests and rights. The outrages committed against the trade unions by Alemán's government still further encumbered the struggle of the working masses and virtually doomed Mexico's labor movement to stagnation for many long years. Since the end of the 1940's, we can observe a sharp decline in the number of strikes. According to official statistics, in 1943 there were 569 strikes recorded by federal authorities; in 1944, 374; in 1945, 107; in 1946, 24; in 1947, 13; in 1948, 11; and in 1949, 9. The strike movement remained approximately at the same level up to the beginning of 1957.[8]

Though official statistics distort the real picture in that only those strikes are recorded which are recognized by the government as "legal," the strike movement declined and the struggle of the workers throughout those years became extremely difficult. To forestall strikes, the ruling circles made wide use of antilabor legislation. The federal labor law[9] now in force in Mexico was adopted in 1931 and at the time represented a certain achievement for the workers. But its chief purpose was to place the rising labor movement under state control by bringing it within the framework of bourgeois "legality." Subsequently, amendments and addenda were repeatedly incorporated into the the law, enhancing its reactionary nature. The Mexican worker is actually deprived of the right to set up his trade unions freely. According to the law, a trade union is recognized only after it has registered with the Ministry of Labor. Otherwise it is considered illegal and suffers the corresponding consequences. The government takes extensive advantage of this situation to depose those trade-union leaders it deems objectionable.

On the other hand, the labor law—in Article 3, paragraphs nineteen and twenty—permits compulsory deduc-

---

[4]*La Voz de México*, September 4, 1962.

[5]*Ibid.*, December 5, 1961.

[6]V. I. Ermolaev. *Natsional'no-osvoboditel'noe i rabochee dvizhenie v stranakh Latinskoi Ameriki posle vtoroi mirovoi voiny*, p. 62.

[7]"Situación de la clase obrera de México," *Frente Obrero* (México), 1957, p. 7.

[8]A. L. Aparicio. *El movimiento obrero en México*, p. 247.

[9]Victor Manuel Varela, *Ley federal del trabajo* (México, 1945).

tions of trade-union dues from workers' wages, in turn enabling the capitalists to maintain a mercenary bureaucratic trade-union machine, through which they exercise control over the labor movement. Furthermore, the law contains a so-called exclusion clause, or *clausula de exclusión* (Article 236), stipulating that an employer is obligated to discharge immediately any person identified by the trade union as a traitor to the interests of that labor organization. This clause was at first adopted at the demand of the workers themselves, who hoped in this manner to rid the trade union of real traitors to the workers' interests. However, since an overwhelming majority of trade unions are controlled by reactionary trade-union bureaucrats, the latter employ this clause to expel revolutionary workers—and, primarily, Communists—from the enterprises.

By imposing compulsory arbitration, the federal labor law reduces to the minimum the workers' right to strike. So-called mediation and arbitration juntas enjoy unlimited power over the trade unions. As stipulated by the law each consists of three representatives—one from the management, one from the government, and one from the trade-union leadership, the latter in most instances being servants of the first two. They are given the right to declare any strike "legal" or "illegal." If the junta declares a strike to be nonexistent, and the workers do not return to work within twenty-four hours, the employer has the right to sever the collective agreement with them and declare a lockout. To impede the workers' strike effort, Mexican legislation has gone so far as to subdivide strikes in a most ridiculous fashion into de facto (*de hecho*) and de jure (*de derecho*) strikes. According to this regulation, the government, when it declares a given strike to be de jure, requires the workers to return to work. Though formally de jure, the strike is not called off and the trade-union leaders must continue negotiating with the employers for a solution to the conflict. In this manner the effectiveness of the strike—this most important instrument of the workers' struggle for their own interests—is for all practical purposes nullified.

VII

The Rural and Urban Milieu

Leading off this section is an analysis of the peasant movement in Latin America by A. M. Sivolobov (Item 21). The author concludes that the basic peasant demands—for elimination of latifundia and for agrarian reform—can be achieved in some countries only with the aid of armed struggle, while in other countries a combination of the revolutionary movement in the cities with a mass peasant movement can achieve the desired result.

The next two selections (Items 22 and 23), by M. V. Danilevich, examine landownership and rental systems.

Agrarian reform on the continent is surveyed briefly by Iu. G. Onufriev in Item 24, while Item 25 is a rather detailed analysis of the agrarian reform in Bolivia by E. Kovalev. While Onufriev tends to disparage the Bolivian reform, Kovalev cautions against underestimating its effect and even points to a number of positive results.

Finally, in Item 26, Ia. Mashbits deals with a subject that has received scant attention in Soviet literature on Latin America—urbanization and its consequences.

21. The Peasant Movement in Latin America*

A. M. SIVOLOBOV

One of the most important questions of the national-liberation and anti-imperialist struggle by the peoples of Latin America is the agrarian question, which affects all classes of society. Problems connected with the elimination of the age-old backwardness of the Latin American countries are focused in it. The one-sided economy and process of capitalist industrialization, which is extremely retarding and extraordinarily difficult for the popular masses, the narrowness of the internal market, the sharpening of the foodstuffs problem, the impoverishment of the popular masses, the supremacy of the agrarian oligarchy in the economy and the politics of the state—all these are features closely tied in with the agrarian problem.

The characteristic peculiarity of agricultural production in Latin America is the dominance of latifundia and monopolistic ownership of land held by a small group of landowners and foreign monopolies. According to FAO figures, 1.3 percent of the landowners in Latin America—the largest landowners—hold 71.6 percent of the entire land under cultivation.

The last census showed that in Brazil 3.4 percent of the large landowners (latifundia with an area of over 500 hectares) have concentrated in their hands two-thirds of the entire land mass of the country. In Venezuela 1.5 percent of such farms with a land area of over 1,000 hectares control 78.6 percent of the land resources. In Mexico 0.7 percent of the farms control 76 percent of the entire land area. In Uruguay six hundred families—large estate owners comprising less than 1 percent of the landowners—control land comprising one-half of the territory of the country. Hundreds of thousands and even millions of hectares of land have been appropriated by foreign and, primarily, North American monopolies (Bunge and Born, United Fruit Company, Anderson, Clayton & Co., Sanbra, cattle-breeding companies, packing houses, and others). The official figures in the *Bulletin of the Inter-American Statistical Institute* for 1960 show that during the last twenty years foreign monopolies connected with agricultural production have acquired over 50 million hectares of land in Latin America.

An insignificant portion of the land area is available to the petty and average peasant. According to the *Bulletin of the Inter-American Statistical Institute,* more than 80 percent of the peasants in the majority of Latin Amer-

*"Krestian'skoe dvizhenie v Latinskoi Amerike," *Kommunist* (Moscow), 12:100–107 (August 1964).

ican countries do not own land and are forced to rent it from landowners under oppressive conditions. Thus, in Brazil 85.2 percent, in Venezuela 83 percent, in Paraguay 93 percent, and in Peru 81 percent of the farmers do not own their land.

The predominant system of land utilization is the semifeudal sharecropping system, where peasants barely make ends meet. Often they are completely without any money and equipment, and their status approaches that of the semi-proletarian. Such are the *colonos* and *agregados* in Brazil, Colombia, Guatemala, and Peru and the *inquilinos*—sharecroppers—in Chile. They pay the landowner from a third to a half of their harvest for the use of a plot of land.

Another feudal remnant is the system of paying by work, in which the landowners, usurers, and foreign and national monopolies allocate to the peasants a plot of land, stock, cattle, or credit, and the peasants must work on the farm of the landowner-creditor for one or several days a week in order to repay the amount of the loan. In many areas of Brazil, writes the well-known writer R. Faco in the book *Twentieth-Century Brazil*, peasants still work on the estate of the landowner, almost without pay, from two to four days a week for the use of a one-or-two-hectare piece of land.

Despite the strong feudal remnants in the Latin American countries, capitalist relations are developing, although slowly, and they breed differentiation and the ruin and proletarization of the peasantry. This is confirmed by the figures on the growth of the agricultural proletariat. While in the years 1937 to 1940 there were 9–12 million hired workers in agriculture, in 1960 their number had increased to 25–26 million). In such countries as Brazil, Chile, Venezuela, Argentina, Uruguay, and Mexico the number of hired workers in the countryside grew three to four times.

Agricultural workers, together with the basic mass of the peasantry and with the active support of the industrial workers, are fighting increasingly energetically for a revolutionary solution of the agrarian problem. Since the remnants of feudalism are hindering capitalist development, the national bourgeoisie is also interested in the solution of the agrarian problem. Under these conditions each class and each party is striving to determine its program, tactics, and course of action in the peasant problem.

In order not to fall behind the movement and not to lose influence among the peasant masses, the bourgeois leaders in the Brazilian Workers' Party (the party of former President Goulart), the Venezuelan Democratic Action Party, the Revolutionary Institutional Party of Mexico, the National Revolutionary Movement in Bolivia, and others have also begun to talk about agrarian reforms. However, they are not inclined to change the agrarian relations essentially. Their aim is to solve the contradictions not by revolutionary means, as the working class and peasantry propose, but by means of half-baked reforms that are supposed to avert a revolutionary explosion and give them political power, even at the cost of a deal with latifundists, as was stated in the resolutions of the Fourteenth Conference of the Communist Congress of Mexico, which was held in December of 1963. They advocate the maintenance of the basis of latifundist ownership: they are against the development of productive forces, for the retention of their countries in the orbit of the world capitalist system, and for only a little improvement in the situation of the workers and a slow formation of capitalist relations in agriculture.

The political figures in the bourgeois nationalistic parties have proposed a number of theories, the essence of which boils down to justifying the measures by the bourgeois-landowner governments, which are aimed not at the confiscation of latifundist estates but at the acquisition of state land that is barren and unusable for agriculture and is located far from industrial centers, ports, or major cities. These theoreticians introduce into the concept of agrarian reform only a technical-economic meaning (the modernization of large estates, the introduction of technology, and methods for working land). In addition they advocate the transfer of state land to the capitalists. It is true that sometimes under the pressure of the masses the ruling bourgeoisie come out with demagogic aims on the side of the slogan "the land to those who work it"; however, the practical results for implementing this slogan are insignificant. Thus, the government of Venezuela, under the pressure of the workers' and peasants' movement, is forced to carry out a "revolutionary act" by announcing the transfer to the state of lands from thirteen latifundists who had greatly compromised themselves by their ties with the former dictator. However, at the same time the landowners were well compensated for their land, and it was transfered to the peasants at a high cost.

In Brazil the former Goulart government attempted to withdraw part of the land, primarily unused land within the limits of a ten-kilometer strip parallel to the railroads, from the landowners and to transfer this to peasants for payment. These measures were regarded as a first step to a broader reform that would direct the agrarian revolution along a bourgeois course. However, the timidity with which these measures were implemented and the reluctance of the government to lean upon the broad popular masses evoked an unbridled attack by reactionary forces and, along with other causes, contributed to the fall of the regime.

The democratic forces in Latin America demand radical socioeconomic changes in the countryside. They advocate the elimination of large estates and other major landholdings, sharecropping, payment in kind, and lengthy servitude in favor of a free and accelerated growth of production forces in the interests of the workers. They are linking the struggle for a radical solution of the agrarian problem with the struggle against foreign imperialist domination, for an independent national economy, and for a noncapitalist way of developing their countries.

An important landmark in the revolutionary liberation movement in Latin America has been the adoption by the majority of the Communist parties during the last four or five years of new program documents, which determined their position on the peasant problem. The agrarian reform in Cuba helped the Communist parties define concretely their program demands and clear up their perspectives and the forms and methods for implementing them.

The programs of the Communist parties of Argentina, Chile, Colombia, Ecuador, Venezuela, Mexico, Brazil, and a number of other countries have common features, but they also take into account local conditions and the requirements of other parties that also participate in the united-front movement.

These programs stem from the necessity to eliminate the latifundia system; to confiscate land from latifundists, foreign and domestic monopolies, and other major landowners; and to transfer these lands to peasants with very little or no land. It is emphasized that peasant organizations and committees will take an active part in the implementation of the agrarian reforms, primarily in the confiscation and distribution of land on the spot.

The programs of the Communist parties state that the democratic government, which will be created in the course of the national-liberation and popular revolution, recognizes that the land taken away from the landholders should pass into the hands of the peasants, and it will issue corresponding documents. The democratic state specifically guarantees the right to land to those peasants who have taken and are working idle estates or state lands and who do not have titles for them. Peasants farming on rented plots will also be given titles for that land.

The Communist parties of Chile, Ecuador, Uruguay, Argentina, and a number of other countries provide in their programs, along with free transfer of confiscated lands to the peasants, for the acquisition of land by peasants for an established sum. The programs of some Communist parties (Venezuela, Chile, Colombia, and others) contemplate payment to landowners for the expropriation of their land in bonds to be paid in installments over a period of twenty to thirty years according to the capability of the state. Such a statement of the question permits the unification of more forces in the struggle against the latifundists and for the implementation of the agrarian reform.

The programs of the Mexican Communist Party and the Communist parties of Colombia, Venezuela, Argentina, and a number of others emphasize that land being held by foreign monopolies will be confiscated and become national property during the period of major revolutionary transformations.

Taking into account the presence in Latin America of a widely developed plantation system, the programs of the Communist parties envisage two methods of approach to the solution of the agrarian problem. On the one hand, many farms and plantations of foreign monopolies will be transferred to the state to be converted into state estates (people's farms) or state cooperative enterprises; on the other hand, the confiscation of land from the latifundists and its transfer to the peasants with ownership rights is contemplated.

The principle of the division of estate lands among the peasants does not signify rejection of the socialist perspective in the development of agriculture. The point is that the aspiration to become a landowner has become stronger in the minds of the peasants in Latin American countries. The majority of them do not look upon the agrarian revolution as anything else but a distribution of estate lands. Regarding the slogan concerning the nationalization of lands, the peasants view it with some mistrust, assuming that it can signify an attempt to take away their plots of land. The transition to socialist reorganization in agriculture will obviously take place gradually through intermediate stages.

Simultaneously with the elimination of latifundism and the confiscation of land from latifundists, the abolition of all forms of feudal exploitation—sharecropping and all types of payment by work, in kind, and lengthy servitude—and the establishment for all categories of agricultural workers of an obligatory payment of wages in cash at a level not lower than that of unqualified industrial workers are foreseen.

The programs of the Communist parties also contemplate other measures for providing material and technical aid by the democratic state to the peasants and for the creation, on a voluntary basis, of various forms of agricultural cooperation (credit, market, and production).

The work by Communists among the peasants is one of the central problems discussed during recent years at the congresses of the Communist parties of Latin America. Various demands that express the interests of the wide masses in the village were examined, and the basic propositions of the agrarian reforms were formulated. Thus, the Eighteenth Congress of the Communist Party of Uruguay discussed and developed a broad program of struggle by the peasants and agricultural workers and came out with an "appeal to the village poor" that set forth the demands by the various sections of the rural population.

The peasant congresses—the first conference in Venezuela (1959), in Peru (the first in 1960 and the second in 1963), the Congress of the National Peasant Assembly of Costa Rica (1960), the National Congress of Peasants in Chile (1961), the Congress of Agricultural Workers of Panama (1961), the Congress of the Peasant Union in Mexico (1963), the National Congress of Peasants and Agricultural Workers of Brazil (1961), the National Congresses of Peasants and Agricultural Workers of Colombia (the first in 1960 and the second in 1962)—as well as the formation of national peasant organizations for the leadership of the peasant movement have been major events in the life of the peasants in Latin America.

The congress of peasants is an extremely representative workers' forum. For instance, over 4,000 delegates from 1,200 local organizations attended the peasant congress of Venezuela; 920 delegates—peasants and agricultural workers, as well as delegations from industrial trade unions—took part in the work of the congress of the peasants of Chile; over 3,000 delegates from peasant leagues and trade unions of agricultural workers, who came primarily from regions with a peasant movement, were sent to the First Constituent Congress of the new peasant federation of Mexico—the Independent Peasant Center.

The importance of peasant congresses lies in the fact that the basic questions of the peasant movement—agrarian reform and the organization of the toiling masses in the struggle for the vital interests of the peasants—are discussed there. The second congress of peasants in Peru declared that if the government did not adopt a law in 1964 concerning agrarian reform, taking into account the demands of the peasant masses, they would take up arms and carry these out with their own forces. The peasant congress of Peru condemned the state draft law on land reform, which does not affect the interests of major landowners, and sent to parliament its draft for agrarian reform, which envisages the expropriation of land from latifundists, the abolition of feudal forms of exploitation, the reduction of rents, the abolition of lengthy servitude, and the granting of freedom to trade unions and peasant organizations. The second Congress of Agricultural Workers of Colombia discussed the problems of the organization of peasants and agricultural workers and the methods for the struggle by the peasants at the present stage.

At the invitation of the federation of peasants in Peru, tens of thousands of rural residents from various provinces arrived for a meeting in Lima in December 1963, at which they demanded from parliament an urgent examination of the draft law. The government of Peru, fearing that this manifestation might assume an undesirable nature, told the leaders of the federation of peasants that it was willing to examine their demands.

The trade unions do a great deal of work in the convocation of peasant congresses. Meetings of peasants are organized at which the status of the agricultural workers is discussed, instructions are worked out for the delegates elected to the congress, and appeals are prepared for the lawmakers. In Brazil, Chile, Colombia, Mexico, Venezuela, and Costa Rica, the trade unions provided funds and premises for the holding of peasant congresses, sent delegations of workers to them, took part in the preparation of the resolutions of the congresses, provided the delegates with transportation, and organized meetings between peasants and workers in enterprises. Leadership on the part of the industrial workers is of tremendous importance in the correct determination of the program of action by the peasants. Such aid by the working class assures the success of the peasant congresses and conferences, turns them into schools of political training for the peasant leaders, and promotes the strengthening of the political union of workers and peasants in the struggle against the common enemy—landowners and imperialists.

New forms of joint action by workers and peasants are appearing. The workers in industrial centers and various trade unions take over zones of the peasant movement and help the peasants create their organizations. The activities of the industrial workers of Chile are characteristic. They send to the countryside brigades of workers to aid in the creation of peasant organizations, and also doctors and lawyers who provide medical help for them and conduct their legal matters during collective conflicts and during strikes by the employed peasants. The industrial workers help organize cultural and educational work in the countryside; they build schools for eliminating illiteracy and set up libraries and sports clubs. This work promotes closer ties between the working class and the peasantry.

Mutual support in the struggle by workers and peasants is becoming more typical. Thus, in 1962 the trade unions in Argentina, which were united into MUCS (Union of the Movement for the Coordination of Trade Unions) supported the agricultural workers during the general strike. The government was forced to satisfy the demands of the agricultural workers. Conversely, when in 1962–1963 a difficult situation regarding food supplies arose in Argentina and general strikes by workers took place, the peasants and agricultural workers organized the collection of food, which they sent to the strikers. In Chile, during a sixty-seven–day–long strike, which was begun in March 1962 by the workers in the potassium mines, the peasants continuously supplied the strikers and their families with food. The general strike in Uruguay early in 1963 called forth a wide movement of solidarity among the peasants, who sent trucks loaded with food to the strikers. Analogous examples of the solidarity between industrial workers and peasants also are found in other countries. Thus, in the course of the struggle, the union between the workers and peasants becomes more solid, and the broad peasant masses are drawn into the all-national movement, the united-front movement.

In a number of areas in Brazil, Colombia, Chile, Mexico, Venezuela, Bolivia, and Ecuador, the peasants proceed from demands for reform to seizure and distribution of estate lands, drive out the latifundists, and implement the agrarian reforms in a revolutionary manner. Not awaiting the decisions of the government, they create agrarian commissions and committees and organize a struggle for the establishment of just prices for produce and for the allocation of credits and reduction in taxes. Such committees are converted into organs for the mobilization of the peasant masses, and the government is forced to reckon with them. In Bolivia, Colombia, and Venezuela the governments, under the pressure of the workers' and peasant movement, have adopted laws concerning agrarian reforms; some agrarian acts have also been adopted in Chile, Argentina, Guatemala, and Ecuador.

Depending on the disposition of political forces and the degree of organization of the working class and peasantry in various countries, the peasant movement for agrarian reform takes on various forms in different countries. Many peasant congresses and federations proposing agrarian reform set out from the possibility of implementing these peacefully, by means of pressure, on the parliament and government from the working class and the peasant masses.

The Communist parties and other democratic organizations acknowledge a definite positive importance of governmental acts on the agrarian question. Since laws concerning agrarian reforms have been adopted in a number of countries, the Communist parties and democratic organizations struggle for their consistent implementation and improvement and for the most active participation by peasant organizations in the expropriation and distribution of lands on the spot. The lawful nature of the movement permits the inclusion of quite extensive sectors of the peasantry. However, as long as the ruling classes attempt to frustrate the implementation of even these limited reforms, the peaceful forms in the struggle by the peasants (demonstrations, meetings, mass protests, and peasant marches) will change into direct action by the masses for the seizure of land. By supporting agrarian reform, the peasantry is gradually becoming involved in the political struggle and is being included in the all-national movement. The forms and methods of the struggle change quickly.

Setting out from the interests of millions of people whose happiness constitutes the purpose of their life and struggle, the Communists of Latin America prefer the peaceful road to revolution, when other conditions are equal. In some countries of Latin America there also exist objective possibilities for the peaceful development of the revolutionary process, the use of legal forms of mass struggle, the increase in the successes by the democratic and patriotic forces, and the unmasking and frustration of the antipopular plans of the reactionaries. At the same time, in those countries where dictatorial regimes rule, conditions for a peaceful way do not exist or exist only to a small extent. At some stage of the revolutionary process the reactionaries will probably force the masses to start out on the nonpeaceful path of realizing the cardinal social transformations.

The experience of the Cuban Revolution and the revolutionary movement in Guatemala, Colombia, and other countries shows that the peasant movement can develop successfully if it combines with the actions of the working class, with the development of the mass revolutionary movement, and with general economic and political strikes. At the proper time, general strikes can paralyze the activities of the reactionary forces and in this way support the struggle of the peasants.

In Peru, Paraguay, Brazil, Colombia, Venezuela, Ecuador, Mexico, Costa Rica, Guatemala, Honduras, and the Dominican Republic, major actions by the peasants are taking place. In order to crush the peasant movement the governments send military troops, punitive expeditions, aircraft, and tanks. In answer to the bloody repressions, the peasants are creating self-defense groups and detachments of partisans.

With the help of the mining workers employed at the American Cerro de Pasco enterprises, peasant committees were created in Peru in 1962–1963 that soon turned into organized centers for the peasant movement in the departments of Cuzco, Junín, and Pasco. Not having the strength to crush the peasant movement, the military junta government in Peru in January of 1963 resorted to trickery: it declared that it was in agreement with an agrarian reform and even published some of its conditions. However, the peasants, knowing the tricks of the ruling circles, did not lay down their arms.

The peasant movement in Venezuela was developed in 1960 during the dictatorship of Betancourt. The movement achieved the greatest successes in the states of Falcón, Lara, and Portuguesa, where large detachments of partisans appeared. In 1962 the partisan groups of Venezuela became a part of the Armed Forces for National Liberation. Soon they carried out a number of major military operations and frustrated many plans of the reactionary forces. Despite the fact that major parts of the regular army and police were thrown against the groups of popular resistance, the struggle by the people is taking on an ever more acute character, and the size of the detachments is constantly growing. The army of national liberation is being joined by patriotically minded officers from the government forces, and the movement for solidarity of the working class in the cities and industrial centers of the country is being stepped up.

The liberation movement in Guatemala is expanding. On November 13, 1960, a large group of the military, in which various political forces were represented, came out against the reactionary dictatorship. From the beginning of 1962 the struggle by the popular masses was stirred to greater activity, particularly in the northeast and the south of Guatemala. The press reports that three major partisan groups—"Alejandro de León," "13 November," and "20 October"—are active in these areas. Their actions are tied in with the struggle by the democratic forces in the cities and are directed by the Revolutionary Political Front of Guatemala.

The partisan movement in Venezuela, Guatemala, and other countries does not as yet shape the political situation by itself. In order for it to become effective in the sense of influence on the course of the revolutionary process, the declaration of the Guatemalan Labor Party states that it is necessary to create a broad antifeudal and anti-imperialist front that must be supported by the actions of the masses and by their growing consciousness and organization, and that the insurgent forces are called upon

to turn themselves into the armed forces of this front. That is why the Communists and other democratic forces are attempting to use to the maximum any legal opportunity to strengthen and build up the revolutionary forces and to draw the broad masses of the population into the struggle.

The peasant movement in Colombia is characterized by its broad scope. Major centers for the peasant movement have appeared in a number of the departments of the country. In answer to the government's repression, the peasants unite into committees, leagues, and unions, and new sectors of the agricultural population become included in the movement. The peasants are arming themselves and going over to active operations. National committees are being formed in the regions controlled by the peasants. The actions of peasants here are met with ever greater support by the working classes in the cities and industrial centers.

In Brazil the peasant movement is directed by a confederation of agricultural workers that was created in December of 1963 and has united 263 officially registered trade unions of agricultural workers in nineteen states and, in addition to that, approximately 500 trade unions that have not as yet been legalized. It was not by chance that the reactionary forces of Brazil, which carried out the *coup d'état* early in April of 1964, directed the first blow against the leaders of this confederation. They wanted to render the peasant movement leaderless. In various regions of the country the peasants were able to seize the lands that belonged to landowners and to divide it among themselves. In a number of places the peasants' struggle for land developed into an armed struggle. In the state of Goiás, for instance, the peasants forced the government to recognize them as the owners of the land for which they had conducted an armed struggle for several years.

Active militant action by the peasants also took place in Uruguay from 1961 to 1963. In February of 1964 many thousands of peasants and agricultural workers from the north of Uruguay carried out a march on the capital. They demanded agrarian reform and called upon the peasants to fight against the latifundists and against exploitation by them. This march evoked a broad surge of solidarity in the country. The industrial trade unions in the departments and the united trade-union center of Uruguay supported the demands of the peasants. The journey by the peasants was accompanied by meetings along their path of movement and ended at the parliament building in Montevideo in a meeting attended by many thousands. The march by the peasants laid the foundation for the creation of a peasant organization in Uruguay.

An analysis of recent events confirms the fact that, in the countries where dictators, puppets of the foreign monopolies, are in power, the development of a broad front in the struggle, including armed struggle, and the creation of partisan detachments combine to make a completely justified course. It cannot, however, be mechanically transferred to countries where the people in recent years have overthrown the military-police dictatorship and the governments that have ridden to power on the crest of revolutionary events have been forced —under the pressure of the national-liberation struggle of the peoples and primarily the struggle by the working class—to liberalize somewhat the regime and to restore law and some institutions of bourgeois democracy, where the democratic progressive organizations have come out from the underground and have begun open political activity. Under these conditions, only the combination of the mass revolutionary movement in the cities with the active movement of peasants can have a substantial influence on the political situation in these countries.

22. The Concentration of Landownership in Latin America and the Class Divisions within the Peasantry and Agrarian Proletariat*

M. V. DANILEVICH

The other side of the growing process of land concentration and centralization is the partition of peasant farmsteads, their ruin, and the creation in the countryside of a great mass of small landowners and landless peasants.

The majority of the rural population of the Latin American countries is de-

*"Zemlevladenie i zemlepol'zovanie v stranakh Latinskoi Ameriki," in *Latinskaia Amerika v proshlom i nastoiashchem* (Moskva: Izdatel'stvo sotsial'no-ekonomicheskoi literatury, 1960), pp. 79–84.

prived of land, the basic means of production in agriculture. In Ecuador 58 percent of the peasants are landless; in Chile, 74.4 percent; in Venezuela, 72 percent; in Colombia, 79 percent; in Guatemala, 80 percent; in Peru, 86 percent; in Paraguay, 94 percent.[1]

Under such circumstances, how does the process of joining manpower with the means of production—land—take place? There are actually two possibilities.

One form of uniting the means of production with labor is based on ancient precapitalist production relations, relations of a feudal nature in which the peasant becomes a small tenant-farmer-sharecropper or receives a small plot in return for work-off on the estate of the landowner.

The other form is based on capitalist production relations, wherein a landless peasant becomes a hired worker selling his labor and working on the estate of a landlord or a *kulak* (exploiting peasant) or on a capitalist plantation.

Both forms are widespread in the Latin American countries. Their relative ratio varies not only from country to country but within each country as well.

In the Latin American countryside a variety of outdated semifeudal forms of exploitation have taken root and act as a brake on the process of developing the productive forces and the class differentiation of the peasantry. This, in turn, preconditions the existence of a multitude of transitory forms, from independent farmer to proletarian.

In addition, modern methods of capitalist exploitation in the Latin American countryside are intertwined with forms of semifeudal exploitation. Along with the use of hired labor, big landlords, planters, and foreign companies widely practice sharecropping and the work-off system. These practices form the basis for an intricate system of oppression of the peasantry and include various forms of forced labor and debt enslavement (peonage) of farmhands and agricultural workers on sugar cane, cotton, and banana plantations, large estates, and cattle ranches.

Let us take a look at the condition of the peasantry in some of the Latin American countries.

Here, as in other capitalist countries, are the following groupings and strata of rural population in addition to the large landlords: the agricultural proletariat, semiproletariate or parcel farmers, small farmers, middle farmers, and big or prosperous farmers.

While it exists in all of these class divisions, the peasantry retains its distinct characteristics in each of them, which determines the prevailing method of production. With the penetration and development of capitalist relations, the peasantry, although the fundamental class of a feudal society, ceases to be a single class. A slow and agonizing process of differentiation takes place. On the one hand, a small sector of the well-to-do, forming the rural bourgeoisie, breaks away from a relatively homogeneous mass of peasantry; on the other hand, the sector of semiproletarians and proletarians of the countryside constantly expands and grows rapidly. Feudal and large peasant landownership is gradually transformed into capitalist ownership. However, in the majority of capitalist countries, particularly the underdeveloped ones, work-off and sharecropping are still preserved as forms of peasant bondage.

To the extent that the countryside retains its semifeudal relations, the peas-

[1] M. M. Fernández, *El problema del trabajo forzado en América Latina* (México, 1953), p. 41.

antry continues to be a class of the old society, but, as the feudal relations are forced out and supplanted by capitalist relations, the peasantry ceases to be a single class. At one pole stands the rural proletariat; at the other, the rural bourgeoisie and the *kulaks*, or exploiting peasantry.

The peasantry as a whole is waging a struggle against the semifeudal order. This is a reflection of the deep class antagonism existing between all the peasants and the big landlords allied with foreign imperialists. While resisting the oppression of big landlords, foreign exploiters, and the government that serves them, the peasantry yet continues to be a class, every sector of which—including the well-to-do—is interested in the eradication of feudalism and colonialism. However, the peasantry is not homogeneous.

The *kulak* owns land, implements, agricultural machinery, and draft animals. His personal labor on the farm accounts for only a part of his family's maintenance. The other means for his sustenance and enrichment comes from exploiting the labor of others, the labor of hired workers, and quite often from renting and sharecropping. Part of the *kulaks* exploit the peasants by letting their land on bondage terms whereby they receive half the crop or payment in labor. They lend money at high interest, seed, draft animals, and food to the village poor in return for the lion's share of the crop or for working-off. The *kulaks* own commercial and industrial enterprises, such as flour mills. They supply the market with a significant portion of its agricultural produce.

The prosperous peasantry, quantitatively, is not a significant part of the rural population. During the war years the *kulak* group grew somewhat in countries supplying the world market with produce and raw materials. *Kulak* farmsteads spread throughout Argentina, Brazil, Mexico, Uruguay, and Chile. In Argentina, the prosperous farms are found mainly among the suburban dairies and among tenant grain farms; in Chile, among truck farms and vineyards; in Uruguay, among dairy enterprises; in Brazil, among the farms of German colonists. In the last few years, there has been a considerable increase in the use of hired labor and in the amount of land cultivated on the *kulak* farmsteads of Brazil. The use of machinery and fertilizer has also increased.

The inadequacy of state agricultural credit combined with the high marketability of single crops have turned the *kulak* into a usurer and middleman through his connection with the big bourgeoisie and monopolist exporters. The policy of the ruling circles, anxious to preserve their position in the countryside, is to foster and support this sector by all possible means.

However, the existence of extensive latifundia and semifeudal privileges, as well as the domination of American capital in buying, processing, and transporting agricultural produce does harm to the interests of the *kulak*. Inequitable exchange, a characteristic feature of United States–Latin American trade, infringes upon the interests of the *kulak* group, which controls a great amount of marketable produce destined for the foreign market. The greater part of the surplus value of the farmhands' and small farmers' toil acquired by the *kulak* is expropriated by foreign monopolies and banks. For this reason, the *kulak* is forced to endorse the elimination of the latifundia and the curtailment of the activity of American capital.

The middle peasantry, not a large group but one under dual pressure from landlords and foreign monopolies and totally deprived of political rights, is on the downgrade, augmenting the ranks of rural semiproletarians and proletarians.

Only in rare cases can an individual peasant succeed in accumulating some savings that would allow him to enlarge his holdings, hire additional labor, and become a rural exploiter. While an insignificant number of this group become prosperous, the fate of the overwhelming majority of the middle peasantry is that of being converted from landowners who rent out land into sharecroppers, and in the end—ruin.

The proportion of the middle peasantry, as well as the proportion of their lands, is not increasing with the development of capitalist relations; on the contrary, it is decreasing. Nor is their role in producing marketable products great. The middle peasantry consists most often of farmers who have retained their own land, the amount of which ensures subsistence for their families and in good years might earn a certain profit. Some add to their land by renting a parcel from a landlord or a small peasant and by hiring labor seasonally for the harvest.

The agricultural proletariat, semiproletariat (or parcel peasants), and small farmers (petty peasant-owners and lessees) form a sector of the population that is incredibly beaten down, scattered, and doomed to a semiprimitive way of life in all capitalist countries, even the most advanced ones, and they represent the absolute majority of the rural population of Latin America.

While it is relatively easy to trace the semiproletarian and small farmer elements, it is much more difficult to define the middle and *kulak* strata. The main distinction between the middle and the prosperous peasant is the extent of their use of hired labor. But aside from this consideration, the definition depends on many concrete situations created by the specific historic background of the country—or even its separate regions, which in turn determine the standards of living and the needs and customs of the people (which are also variable quantities). It is necessary to take into account the kinds of agricultural production, the size of the landholding, and the monies invested. It is also important to bear in mind whether the land is irrigated or not and whether it is owned or rented. One must also consider the amount of livestock and machinery, the labor intensity, and such factors as distance to and conditions prevailing at the market.

Classification of farmsteads by the amount of land is less accurate for a correct breakdown of the various class groups of the peasantry, to the extent that the agriculture is intensive. However, since Latin American agriculture is of low productivity, except where irrigation is practiced, land-size classification presents an adequate basis for general conclusions in defining agricultural class groups.

According to information from the Latin American press, the small and middle farmsteads in Argentina, Brazil, Colombia, and Uruguay can be classified tentatively as those having up to 50 hectares and the prosperous farmsteads as those having up to 100 hectares (without considering the prevalence of individual crops and other peculiarities of production). A ranch may have been a larger spread if the land is used extensively as natural pasture.

At the Eighth Congress of the Communist Party of Colombia, the following data regarding the class strata of the countryside were presented: small land-owners, up to 5 hectares, 500,000; middle owners, from 5 to 50 hectares, 250,000; well-to-do owners, from 50 to 200 hectares, 15,000. In addition, there

were 500,000 farmsteads of sharecrop-pers, semiproletarian tenants, and poor and middle peasants in the country.[2]

[2]*Documentos Políticos* (Bogotá), 13:61 (January–February 1959).

23. An Analysis of the System of Land Rent and Forms of Exploiting the Tenant-Farmer Class*

M. V. DANILEVICH

The monopoly of private ownership of land, the concentration of land in the hands of large landowners, and the surviving traces of feudal relations and privileges convert millions of landless and virtually landless peasants into semiserfs and debt slaves.

The landless peasants are forced to rent land for work-off, to become share-croppers or "copartners," or to become farmhands. According to data from a number of researchers, two-thirds of the Latin American land is worked not by proprietors, but by tenants, sharecrop-pers, and farm laborers.

While the census figures for the individual countries of Latin America reflect the general number of farmsteads more or less accurately, the question of the forms of landownership is much more difficult to ascertain. In most countries the system of a plot of land in return for labor on the owner's land does not appear in the census at all. In many countries, including Brazil, the census

listed as tenants only persons who had written contracts, an insignificant minority. In addition, the census as a rule does not give the breakdown of farm tenants by groups, according to the size of the rented land. However, these figures, although far from being complete, do reveal the forms of landownership (see Table 3).

As shown in Table 3, the smallest percentages of private holdings are found in Panama, Honduras, Paraguay, Argentina, Cuba, Venezuela, Guatemala, and Uruguay; it is also here that tenant relationships and the most burdensome forms of land cultivation under conditions of bondage concealed in the columns of "others" and "squatters" are most widespread. The latter forms of landownership reach exceptionally

*"Zemlevladenie i zemlepol'zovanie v stranakh Latinskoi Ameriki," in *Latinskaia Amerika v proshlom i nastoiashchem* (Moskva: Izdatel'stvo sotsial'no-ekonomicheskoi literatury, 1960), pp. 90–94, 96–97.

large proportions in Panama, Paraguay, Venezuela, and El Salvador.

Landlords often encourage settlement of their vacant lands for two reasons: in countries where legislation has been adopted to settle landless peasants, the landlords assume that the state will buy their vacant land to parcel out among the peasants who have already settled on it. In the other case, the landlord, unwilling to go to the expense of clearing virgin land, does not prevent the squatters from occupying it. But as soon as the latter have made the necessary improvements, the landlord, aided by the authorities, drives them off the land.

ments are made only in special cases concerning government or community land. Verbal agreements, as a rule, are based on custom and semifeudal tradition.

Only a few countries have laws governing minimal tenant tenures (in Argentina and Uruguay, not fewer than five years; in Cuba, from three to six years). As a rule, they are rarely obeyed. In all other countries, short-term tenures—for instance, one year—are widespread. Laws protecting the tenant from arbitrary eviction by the landlord exist only in Argentina, Uruguay, and Cuba. In a number of countries the law as well

Table 3. The Number of Farmsteads According to Type of Holding in Some Latin American Countries (According to Agricultural Censuses)

Country	Date	Number of Farms in Thousands	Percentage by Type of Holding			
			Owners*	Tenants (incl. sharecroppers)	Squatters	Others
Argentina	1947	468.7	36.8	33.4	—	29.8
Brazil	1950	2064.5	80.8	9.1	10.1	—
Venezuela	1950	248.7	41.3	20.6	35.8	2.3
Guatemala	1950	341.2	48.3	16.4	3.9	31.4
Honduras	1950	156.1	21.3	12.6	11.0	55.1
Dominican Republic	1950	276.8	60.2	1.7	—	38.1
Costa Rica	1950	43.1	81.1	3.6	—	15.3
Cuba	1946	160.0	36.3	53.9	8.6	1.2
Mexico	1950	1365.6	98.7	1.0	0.2	0.1
Panama	1950	85.5	14.1	9.3	67.3	9.3
Paraguay	1943	94.5	15.9	6.6	63.0	14.5
Salvador	1950	174.2	62.9	18.1	19.0	—
Uruguay	1951	85.3	50.2	34.7	3.1	11.4

*In Brazil, Cuba, Guatemala, and Mexico, including managers

Only three countries—Argentina, Cuba, and Uruguay—codify, if only formally, the contents of agreements concluded between landowners and tenants of various categories and stipulate that these agreements be made in writing. In other countries entirely arbitrary rule prevails concerning the basic masses of peasantry who have no land of their own. Legislation regulating relations between tenant and owner is nonexistent. The peasant is left to the mercy of the landlord. Written agree-

as custom provides that all improvements of a permanent nature must be made by the tenant, and, after expiration of the term, they revert to the landlord.

With the development of capitalism and the growing domination of foreign monopolies, there occurs an acceleration of the process of peasant exploitation and of the transformation of owners into tenants and tenants into farmhands.

This process can clearly be seen in the juxtaposition of figures from Argentina's three censuses. Table 4 shows clearly the sharp drop in the volume of owner farmsteads and the rise in the various "other forms of landowner-ship," which assure greater dependence and exploitation.

Great changes have taken place with farmsteads not possessing their own land; their condition has deteriorated sharply and their relative volume has decreased. These farmsteads have shifted to the group of "other forms of landholding," which now embraces approximately 30 percent of all farm-steads. The relative volume of this group increased almost threefold from 1914 to 1947. Consequently, the num-ber of farmsteaders deprived of the right of ownership, lacking a rental agree-ment, and chained to various forms of bondage oppression (half-and-half crop-sharing, work-off, etc.) is growing. The latter, shown in the column "other forms," represent a variety of the cruel-est exploitation, prevailing primarily in areas remote from the country's center, especially in the northern and western provinces of Argentina, where the In-dian population is large and where the landowner is the omnipotent master.

In 1947 the farmsteads organized by landowners—36.8 percent of all farm-steads—amounted to only 22.2 percent of the arable land. The rest of the land was rented out or put on a sharecrop-ping basis. In other words, over three-fourths of the arable land belongs to per-sons not working on it but receiving income from it. The countryside is vic-timized by the yoke of the big landlords whose income amounts to 20 percent of the value of gross agricultural produc-tion.[1]

Land rent in Latin America is quite high, extending to 40–50 percent of the entire crop cash value, or its value before harvest. The rule for the rental scale is that it is increased as the size of the plot decreases. The smaller the rental plot, the more the tenant pays per

hectare. For instance, according to data of the Uruguayan Ministry of Finance, the rent per hectare for small plots up to 5 hectares in the provinces of Flores and Rincón del Piño was 24 pesos in 1951; for plots from 5 to 100 hectares, 13.5 pesos; from 100 to 300 hectares, 11 pesos; from 300 to 1,000 hectares, 9.5 pesos; and over 1,000 hectares, 7.5 pesos.[2]

Table 4. Change in the Relative Forms of Landholding in Argentina* (Percentage of the Overall Number of Farmsteads)

Date of Census	Owners	Tenants	Other Forms of Landownership
1914	50.5	38.4	11.1
1937	37.9	44.3	17.8
1947	36.8	33.4	29.8

*Compiled according to C. Taylor, Rural Life in Argen-tina (Baton Rouge: Louisiana State University Press, 1948), p. 191; L. Sommi, El Plan Prébisch y el destino argentino (Córdoba, 1956).

The small tenant paid three times more rent per hectare than the large ten-ant renting thousands of hectares. Here-in lies the economic basis of the forma-tion of a considerable element of power-ful middlemen between the direct pro-ducer and the landowner, and herein is the source of enormous incomes for the middlemen.

The rent is not only high but also con-stantly on the increase, a condition caused both by the demand for land of the growing army of landless and small landowning peasants and by the in-crease in investment and labor for cul-tivation of the land. Again in Uruguay, cash rent payments from 1940 to 1954, taking inflation into account, almost doubled.[3]

Besides cash payment of rent there is the widespread form of payment in

[1]The Landless Farmer in Latin America (Ge-neva: International Labour Office, 1957), p. 21.
[2]Justicia, January 20, 1956.
[3]Ibid., March 6, 1956.

kind, as well as such forms of semi-feudal relations as crop sharing and working-off. In Argentina, for instance, out of 200,000 farms operated on rented land, only 57 percent of the farmers were paying their rent in cash; the rest were paying in kind.

Rent payment in kind is convenient for foreign monopolies and the land-owners, who are the big suppliers of agricultural products. Hence, foreign financial capital, directly or through agents—buyers, landowners—utilizes this semifeudal type of rent payment and attempts to make it permanent.

All over Latin America one encounters subrental, a system aggravating the tenants' already deplorable situation. The middlemen—big buyers, exporters, special brokerage firms—take from the tenant 20–40 percent of his income. At times there are several middlemen between the landlord and the small tenant.

The monopoly of private landowner-ship, the extremely high cost of land and land rents, and the system of subrentals lead to an enormous diversion of capital from agricultural production; retard the development of productive forces in agriculture; and result in backwardness, a low technical level, low harvest yields, and extreme poverty in the countryside.

The precapitalist peasant rental system is widespread in Latin America. In this instance, rent received by the owner of the land reflects the production relations not of the three classes of capitalist society—the land proprietor, the capitalist tenant, and the hired laborer—but of two classes, remnants of the old feudal society—the peasant and the proprietor of the land. The big landowner, as a rule, appropriates not only the surplus but even part of the indispensable labor of the peasant, who is often reduced to a state of total economic dependence on the landlord. In the era of monopolistic capitalism, however, the precapitalist system of rent assumes a distorted shape. With the increasing stratification of the peasantry, production of food for export, and subordination of the productive activity of the peasant farmstead to imperialist monopolies, rent reflects precapitalist relations, complicated by the connections of contemporary capitalism.

Short-term rentals are the scourge of agriculture as well as one of the causes for its backwardness, the low harvest yield in the fields, and the seminomadic way of life of the peasants.

24. Agrarian Reforms in the Latin American Countries[*]

Iu. G. Onufriev

The entire process of the economic and political development of Latin America is predicated on the necessity of enacting radical land reforms as a prerequisite to solving the peasant problem and the related problems of building an independent economy based on the development of national industry and agriculture, strengthening national sovereignty, democratizing the internal political and social life, and raising the standard of living of the people.

The dead end into which Latin American agriculture has been driven makes the urgency of radical reforms so obvious that now no one dares to speak openly against them. However, only the Communist parties, trade unions, and peasant organizations are fighting stubbornly for the eradication of the latifundia and the vestiges of feudalism.

The upsurge of the peasant movement and the growing active struggle of the masses for land are forcing the ruling circles of Latin America to pose as advocates of land reforms and "defenders" of the peasants' interests. In many countries various projects have been drawn up or are in a stage of discussion regarding "agrarian reforms," colonization of land, or individual legislative acts, supposedly directed toward "infusing health" into the agricultural economy and improving the living conditions of the working masses in the countryside.

However, a close look at the official documents of the ruling circles reveals that, far from trying to satisfy the needs of the peasantry and the demand for economic development of these countries, these circles are pursuing the narrow, selfish interests of separate exploiting groups. The basic rationale of their "agrarian measures" is to split the peasantry so as to divert them from uniting with the working class and from revolution.

In declaring that within the framework of Latin American conditions the land problem can be solved by allocating state-owned vacant and uncultivated lands to the peasants, the rulers of these countries are attempting to sidetrack the toiling masses by any means possible from the problem of eliminating latifundia, to preserve landlord ownership as inviolate, and to assist the landlords in transition to capitalist methods of management. The ruling circles are planning to ease the land problem, particularly in areas of

*Ekonomicheskie problemy stran Latinskoi Ameriki, ed. V. Ia. Avarina and M. V. Danilevich (Moskva: Izdatel'stvo Akademii nauk SSSR, 1963), pp. 289–296.

acute land shortage, in a "peaceful, lawful, organized" manner, by recommending that the peasants purchase the uncultivated lands from the state.

At the eleventh Latin American seminar on land problems held in Montevideo in November 1959, it was emphasized that "the colonization of state-owned land is the present problem in Latin American agriculture."[1] Advanced as a basis for "colonization" is the fact that the state owns huge expanses of largely virgin land. Therefore, the needs of the peasants can be satisfied at the expense of the state-owned land without resorting to expropriation of estate holdings.

The United Nations Economic Commission for Latin America (ECLA) is an active conduit for the "colonization" idea. Presenting colonization as a remedy for solving the land problem, the ECLA is misleading not a few patriotically minded people in these countries and gaining their support. The experience of the Latin American countries, however, shows the class essence of "colonization." In actuality this amounts to plunder of the greater part of state lands by capitalists and the formation of a new stratum of rural bourgeoisie. The governments of Argentina, Colombia, Venezuela, and other Latin American countries are following this method of solving the agrarian problem.

"Colonization" of lands in Latin America under present conditions will serve as a means of fortifying the position of the landlords in the countryside and will facilitate strengthened domination by American monopolies. Politically, it is directed toward weakening the peasant movement, confusing the democratic forces, and sidetracking them from the revolutionary path of struggle for the elimination of latifundism.

Apportionment of land to the peasants, without eliminating large estates and the power of feudal landlords, retains the economic foundation of peasant exploitation by the big landowners.[2] Commenting on the difference between revolutionary changes in agrarian relations and "agrarian reforms" handed down from above, V. I. Lenin wrote, "We do not take the view that the peasant has little land and needs more. This is a common opinion. We say that landlord ownership of land is the basis of the oppression that crushes the peasantry and causes its backwardness. The question is not whether the peasant has little land. How to put an end to serfdom is the crucial question from the point of view of the revolutionary class struggle, not the way the bureaucrats are debating it, that is, how much land the peasant has and by what standard it should be divided."[3]

Some ideologists of the ruling classes use the term "agrarian reform" in a technical-economic sense without taking cognizance of the social aspect. In their opinion reform should concern itself primarily with increasing the productivity of the land. For this reason the ruling class advocates the following in the agrarian sector: allocating credit, furnishing the farmer with agricultural technology and fertilizer, building experimental farms, constructing irrigation systems, roads, and so on. In practical terms, only a few well-to-do in the countryside could afford to take advantage of these measures.

[1]*Mundo del Trabajo Libre*, March 1960, p. 23.
[2]In Venezuela, for instance, the agrarian reform law adopted March 6, 1960, specifies neither the maximum size of a landlord's estate nor any limits for foreigners. State lands are earmarked, first, for transfer to landless and small farmers. The uncultivated lands of landlords are taken over only in cases where state lands prove to be insufficient to satisfy the needs of the peasants. Two-thirds of all the land marked for partition (about 12.5 million hectares, mainly arid land, of which 7 million hectares are natural meadows and grazing lands) belongs to the government.
[3]V. I. Lenin, *Polnoe sobranie sochinenii*, vol. 31, p. 419.

In Latin American governmental documents on agriculture, as a rule, not a word is said about restrictions on the land rights of foreigners, though it is well known that the American monopolies inflict enormous harm on the national economy and agriculture.

The national bourgeois attitude toward agrarian problems is an indecisive and contradictory one. The course of the economic and political development of the Latin American countries impels the bourgeoisie, particularly the industrial bourgeoisie, to fight for the removal of obstacles to the further development of the productive forces of their countries. United with the democratic elements, the more progressive sector of the national bourgeoisie has actively campaigned for the eradication of the big semifeudal ownership of land.

Due to its class character, however, the national bourgeoisie is not interested in a radical break with the antiquated production relations in the countryside. In the relatively more developed Latin American countries (Argentina, Brazil, Mexico, Chile Uruguay) close ties exist between the bourgeoisie and the landlords, formed on the basis of mutual exploitation of the workers of the city and countryside. Sizable groups of the national bourgeoisie are at the same time large landowners.

With the intensification of the class struggle and the greater role of the working class in the economic and political life of Latin America, the national bourgeoisie dares not seriously infringe upon private property rights. Supposedly interested in the development of industry and expansion of the domestic market, it can venture to favor only those reforms which partially limit the ownership of land. The Second Havana Declaration states: "Under present historical circumstances, the national bourgeoisie of Latin America cannot lead the antifeudal and anti-imperialist struggle. Experience indicates that in Latin American countries this class, even when its interests conflict with those of Yankee imperialism, is incapable of leading the peasants, for it is petrified with fear of social revolution and dreads struggling with the exploited masses."[4]

In large measure this predetermined the fact that, in carrying out agrarian reforms in Mexico, Guatemala, and Venezuela, the problem did not involve the abolition of landlord ownership, as in Cuba, but only a certain limitation, the removal of the most objectionable features of feudal oppression. The manner of limitation of landlord property and the degree of deliverance of the countryside from feudal fetters were determined by national and historical conditions, including the acuteness of the peasants' struggle for land, the organizational strength of the democratic movement in general, and similar factors. Although the reforms in Mexico and Guatemala (to 1954) contributed to the development of productive forces in agriculture, helped to overcome the vestiges of feudalism in the countryside, and created tangible conditions for expanding the internal market, they did not and could not finally resolve the agrarian problem. The position of the great bulk of the population in the countryside, even in Mexico, remains as difficult as before; social inequality grows and the peasantry is being ruined ever more.

The reform in Mexico, which was of relatively radical nature, was carried out nearly half a century ago. The first agrarian law was adopted on January 6, 1915, amidst the raging armed struggle of the toiling masses against the oppression of the landed oligarchy and foreign imperialists.

From a socioeconomic standpoint,

[4]*Pravda*, February 6, 1962.

agrarian reform was an important prerequisite to general economic development and particularly to the industrial and agricultural development of
the country. It contributed to the rise in
agricultural production and to the satisfaction of the country's demand for raw
materials and food products, a demand
that grew in response to the acceleration
of industrial growth. Due to the agrarian
reform and a number of other measures
(the nationalization of railroads, expropriation of foreign oil monopolies,
creation of state credit agencies, and so
forth), the development of the national
economy of Mexico reached such a level
that it seemed possible to industrialize
the country despite the resistance of
foreign monopoly capital.

However, the land reform that
brought definite changes in the agricultural organization of Mexico did not
provide a definitive solution to the land
problem. Between 1915 and 1960, the
peasants were given 47.2 million hectares of land through the *ejido*[5]—that is,
a little over half the area they had lost
during the rule of dictator Díaz (1876–
1911). The arable amount of this land
was over 11 million hectares (about 20
percent). Along with 1.3 million *ejido*
families and over 1 million private farmsteads of less than 5 hectares each, there
are 2 million landless peasants and a
tremendous army of completely or partially unemployed farm workers in the
country. The great landowners, however, continue as before to retain control of two-thirds of the accountable
land area.[6]

The most telling blow to the great
landholders' properties was delivered
between 1935 and 1940 when, under the
pressure of the newly strengthened
antifeudal and anti-imperialist movement, Lázaro Cárdenas, a representative of the radical wing of the national bourgeoisie, came to power. However, even during that period many

landlords were able to retain their estates intact by utilizing privileges accorded large cattle ranches and "rationally managed" farm enterprises. Acting
in this same direction was the fictitious
division of estates into smaller parcels,
consolidating these in the hands of relatives and figureheads, to which the
landlords resorted in order to conceal
the size of their holdings. Consequently, the economic position of the landlord class was somewhat undermined
during these years, but not to the degree
that one might assume from the official
statistics.

Moreover, the socioeconomic measures of Cárdenas benefitted the bourgeoisie itself most of all. The various
state capitalist measures adopted during this period, which were intended to
raise the technical level of agriculture,
develop the credit system, improve
means of communication in rural areas,
and construct irrigation systems, presumably afforded an equal opportunity
for all the farming population. Actually, to a large degree, only a small handful of wealthy people in the countryside
who had accumulated both cash and a
considerable quantity of marketable
produce could avail themselves of all
these things. It was precisely in this
period that the rapid rise of the agricultural bourgeoisie began, especially
in regions where intensive agriculture
prevailed.

After 1940 the bourgeoisie once
again made a deal with the reactionary
forces. If the resurrection of the old-type
latifundia was not politically possible
(although in less developed parts of the
country, it had not been eliminated), a
clearly defined tendency toward land
concentration could be observed—but
concentration on a capitalist basis now.

The implementation of the agrarian

[5]*Noticias de Hoy*, November 3, 1960.
[6]*Tercer Censo Agrícola Ganadero y Ejidal*, pp.
215, 218 (1950).

reform in Bolivia—the law was issued in August 1953—took place under complex domestic political conditions of sharpening class conflict in the countryside.

In reply to the vacillating and contradictory policies of the government and the fierce resistance of the landlords, the peasants resorted to arms and began to occupy the estates of the landlords. A considerable part of the arable area came into the hands of the peasants. However, after obtaining the land, the peasant was not able to till it, since he had neither money nor tools. In addition, the formality of transferring the right of ownership of the land was hampered by bureaucratic runaround.

In the course of the agrarian reform the economic and political influence of the landlord in the village was not eliminated. Resorting to every kind of bureaucratic procrastination, corruption, and bribery of village judges and inspectors, the landlords quite often got decisions on the "lawfulness" of exemptions of individual estates. In the absence of state credit, the peasants, as before, were compelled to seek loans from the semifeudalist landlord. This circumstance gave the latter a chance to exploit the peasants with work-off, personal services, and taking part of the crop as exchange for rental of implements, livestock, and so forth.

The agrarian reform did not create all the conditions necessary for developing production relations in the countryside or for expanding the domestic market capacity, and it did not solve the food and raw material problems of the country. Except in isolated instances neither a landlord nor a peasant economy was capable of increasing agricultural production.

Partial abolition of the vestiges of feudal serfdom could not bring about fundamental changes in the nature of production relations in the countryside. Modern methods of production did not replace obsolete methods. The wooden plow and the hoe remained the basic tools on peasant farms and on the majority of those of the landlords, and this predetermined an extremely low labor productivity in agriculture.

Facts indicate that the Bolivian peasants who won the issuance of an agrarian reform decree are continuing their fight to achieve its practical realization. The imperative condition for a successful solution of the agrarian problem, however, is the establishment of a firm bond between the peasantry and the working class. In this respect the Bolivian example confirms the indisputable truth that, without the organizational and leadership role of the proletariat and its vanguard, the peasantry cannot achieve improvement of its social and economic status.

Granting that the resolution of the agrarian-peasant problem is an indispensable condition for securing economic independence, democratic forces and, above all, the Communist parties of Latin American countries urgently demand the elimination of medieval vestiges paralyzing the development of productive forces in agriculture and industry.

25. The Class Essence and the Significance of the
Agrarian Reform in Bolivia*

E. KOVALEV

The postwar period has been characterized by great quantitative changes in the development of productive forces in world agriculture. In the major capitalist countries, agriculture has acquired a number of characteristics that bring it close to industrial production. Nor has Latin America avoided this process.

The intensive development of productive forces in the agriculture of the Latin American countries has led to an abrupt sharpening of social contradictions. Intensified exploitation on the part of domestic and foreign monopoly capital has taken place in these countries along with the retention of large latifundist landholding and the semifeudal (and in some places, simply feudal) conditions of renting, leasing, and utilization of manpower that are based on it.

The predominance of large latifundia creates the conditions for an extreme polarization of the distribution of land in Latin America. Somewhat over 1 percent of the landowners own about 100,000 estates with areas of over 1,000 hectares each. They own 61 percent of all the agricultural land, while 3.5 million landowners who have plots of less than 5 hectares own 1 percent.[1] The Latin Americans themselves characterize the situation with the bitter aphorism, "People without land, land without people." Huge unopened areas, a limitless army of landless or virtually landless peasants, a low percentage of cultivated land, and an extreme shortage of food products—such are the direct results of the predominance of latifundism. The average annual growth of agricultural production in Latin America (2.6 percent) does not on the whole exceed the growth in population, which means stagnation or even a decrease in per capita agricultural production.

Along with this, the social changes that have been introduced into Latin America by the process of mechanization are more extreme and more erratic in comparison with the developed countries and, consequently, more distressing for the toiling masses of the countryside. The transition to modern technology is frequently accomplished not gradually—as it was, for example, in Europe—but all at once, from such primitive hand tools as hoes. By sharply in-

---

*"Agrarnaia reforma v Bolivii: klassovaia sushchnost' i znachenie," *Mirovaia ekonomika i mezhdunarodnye otnosheniia*, 6:56–64 (1966).
[1] A. Samper, "Atraso agrícola," *Progreso*, p. 166 (1964–1965).

creasing labor productivity, such a transition considerably decreases the number of workers engaged in agriculture and squeezes a large number of workers out of this sphere of production. Industry is not in a position to absorb them, which leads to a further increase in the relative overpopulation in the cities and countryside.[2]

Under conditions of increased exploitation in its contemporary technologically "progressive" forms with the retention of archaic economic and noneconomic dependence, the masses see their only salvation in the struggle for land. The activization of this struggle is a direct result of the sharpening social contradictions in the Latin American countryside. If we take into account the role that agriculture plays in the economy of Latin America, it becomes clear why agrarian reform has taken on the significance of the central question of the political struggle in the countries of this region.

Latin America differs from the developing countries of Asia and Africa in its higher level of economic development, which leaves its mark on the political positions of the ruling classes. The implementation of agrarian reform is in the interests of the upper and middle bourgeoisies of the Latin American countries, although their political calculations do not permit them to operate consistently against the landlord class. The latifundists are an extremely reactionary force both in economics and in politics. Utilizing their traditional influence in the army and police, they are, thanks to the retention of caste privileges, prepared to go to extreme measures, including the establishment of a terrorist dictatorship in the country and the sacrifice of national interests to foreign imperialism, especially to American imperialism. The latter in turn exerts extreme pressure to the end of retention of the domination of the latifundists and upper bourgeoisie in these countries and the prevention of changes in the nature of landownership.

The specific nature of agrarian reforms in the Latin American countries is determined by the sharply hostile position of the class of large landowners toward any reform that touches deeply on agrarian relations, and the support of this position by the upper and middle bourgeoisie as a whole, along with foreign imperialism. The toiling masses of the cities and countryside force the reforms on the ruling classes by means of armed struggle. It was precisely in this way—against the will and in spite of the resistance of the powerful landowners and upper bourgeoisie—that the agrarian reforms in Mexico, Bolivia, Guatemala, and Venezuela were carried out, reforms that deserve the title to a greater or lesser degree. The most extensive agrarian reform, one that responded to the interests of the masses, was carried out in Cuba, but it became possible only after the triumph of the socialist revolution. In Mexico and Bolivia, the bourgeoisie were forced to proceed to the implementation of agrarian reform in order to retain power in their hands after the actual victory of popular uprisings. In both countries, of course, they exerted every possible effort to limit the scope of the reform, to exclude the greatest possible number of latifundia from its effects, and to make its conditions easier for the landowners.

In the land question, the position shared by considerable sectors of the middle and even upper bourgeoisie and

[2]This is reflected in bourgeois statistics in the huge increase in the number of persons employed in services, but actually unemployed, existing on occasional odd jobs, personal services, or petty trade. The rate of growth of the actively employed population engaged in nonproductive services is greater than that in any other sector. In the period 1945 to 1960, it came to 4 percent as compared with 1.3 percent in agriculture, 1.2 percent in extractive industries, and 2.8 percent in manufacturing. *The Economic Development of Latin America in the Post-War World* (New York: UN, 1964), p. 30.

reflecting their specific interests has found its expression in the concept of "social function." Its meaning consists of coercing the large landowners, if possible without resorting to extreme measures, to shift from extensive land usage to intensive usage, from renting out land to farming it—in other words, to extract fulfillment of their "social function" by the big landowners. On the one hand, the bourgeoisie is interested in the elimination of large landholdings and the distribution of land to the peasants, which would facilitate the strengthening of bourgeois relations in the countryside and, most importantly, would increase the domestic market for industrial products. On the other hand, considerable sectors of the upper bourgeoisie, who came directly from among the large landowners, have retained landholdings. Many of them have acquired considerable real estate and are connected with the latifundists by thousands of threads. The bourgeoisie is deeply interested also in the retention of political unity with the large landowners. The principle of the "social function" of land is in fact a synonym for the landlord path to the implementation of bourgeois agrarian transformations.

The intensification of social contradictions in agriculture and the upsurge of the peasant struggle for land lend special meaning to the problem of agrarian reform. We may trace the principal features of agrarian reforms in Latin America by using the example of Bolivia.

THE PRE-REFORM SITUATION IN BOLIVIA

Notwithstanding a number of unique features, the agrarian reform in Bolivia may to a considerable degree be regarded as typical of the Latin American agrarian reforms carried out by the bourgeoisie.

The majority (63 percent) of the gainfully employed population of the coun-try is engaged in agriculture. Thus, the demands for the implementation of a reform were genuinely mass in nature. The distribution of landownership was characterized by extreme inequality: 90 percent of the agricultural population owned only 30 percent of the land, while the remainder belonged to 4.5 percent of the landowners.[3] A multitude of feudal traces were retained both in landownership and in the methods of renting land and in hiring labor. In the majority of the regions of the country, there existed a noneconomic dependence of the peasants on the large landowner that could hardly be described otherwise than as feudal dependence. In exchange for a small plot of land received from the landowner, the peasant had to work four days a week on the landlord's fields, look after livestock, and carry out a number of other obligations. As the progressive Bolivian public figure Raúl Ruiz González has noted, the price of land in the country depended not so much on its fertility and location as on the number of peasants working it. In the field of rental relations, an important place was occupied by sharecropping, in which the sharecropper paid the landowner half of the harvest and performed a number of services for him gratis. In the eastern part of the country, a semifeudal system of relations prevailed—peonage, in which the peasant was unable to leave the master without his permission.

The landowner-latifundist had economic and political mastery over the countryside. There were very few purely capitalistic enterprises based on the use of hired labor. There was a substratum of wealthy peasants who controlled considerable areas of land, used hired labor, and let out certain parcels on a sharecropping basis. In a number of cases, the wealthy peasants rented land

[3]F. Beltrán, J. Fernández, ¿Dónde va la reforma agraria boliviana? (La Paz, 1960), p. 18.

from the latifundists. In addition, there
was a sector of intermediate peasants
who had enough land to support a
family. The intermediate peasant did
not ordinarily use hired labor, and he
would take on day workers only during
planting and harvest time. Finally, the
basic mass of the rural population consisted of small and petty peasants, the
majority of whom could not exist and
support a family on the income from
their plots and who were forced to seek
supplementary income on the side. The
overwhelming majority of the small
peasantry were in Indian communities.

The revolution of April 1952 overthrew the mining and landlord oligarchy and brought to power the Nationalist Revolutionary Movement, which
expressed the interests chiefly of the
petty and middle bourgeoisie. Under
pressure from the armed people, the
government, headed by Victor Paz
Estenssoro, announced the implementation of two reforms of vital importance
for the country—the nationalization of
the mining industry (October 1952) and
agrarian reform (August 1953).

GOALS AND NATURE OF THE AGRARIAN REFORM

According to the law of August 2,
1953, the agrarian reform was to achieve
the following goals:

a. To provide arable land to the peasants who did not have any or who did
not have enough, with the requirement
that it be worked; to expropriate the land
of latifundists who illegally controlled
extraordinarily large areas for this purpose.

b. To return to Indian communes the
land that had been illegally seized from
them, and to cooperate with them in accomplishing production, respecting and
utilizing their collective traditions inso-
far as possible.

c. To liberate the peasants from feudal dependence by banning personal
dependence and free services.

d. To stimulate increased productivity and marketability of agricultural
production by facilitating the investment of new capital, respecting the interests of the small and middle peasants,
making agricultural cooperatives possible, extending technical aid, and facilitating the possibility of obtaining credits.[4]

The bourgeoisie believed that the
implementation of agrarian reform
would clear the way for an acceleration
of the capitalist development of the
countryside by eliminating a number of
traces of feudalism in agriculture. They
counted on taking the peasant masses
with them, after having separated them
from the working class and turning them
into their own political reserve. In addition, they counted on the fact that the
interests of the large landowners were
touched on to a minimal degree, so as
not to lose in them a political ally in the
struggle against the working class.

Although the goals proclaimed in the
law on agrarian reform expressed first of
all the class interests of the bourgeoisie,
the demands of the peasantry and of the
working class exerted great influence
on their formulation. Consequently,
they may be regarded in a certain sense
as general national goals.

The Bolivian agrarian reform had two
basic directions:

1. The acknowledgment of the peasants who received land from landlords
of the requirement to perform a number of obligations (work the landlord's
land, pasture cattle, and such) for the
owners of those plots.[5] Data from the

[4]Ibid., pp. 24–25.
[5]Article 78 of the decree-law on agrarian reform reads:
"Peasants who have been subjected to a feudal
system of exploitation as *siervos* [serfs], *obligados*
[under obligation], *arrimantes* [fixed], *agregados* [attached], *forasteros* [new arrivals], etc.,
who are over 18 years of age, as well as married
persons over 14 years of age and widows with
minor children—are declared by the provisions
of this decree to be the owners of the parcels
that they now hold and that they cultivate."
(M. Zambrana Yánez, *La distribución de tierras
en Bolivia* [La Paz, 1963], p. 39–40).

former president of the National Agrarian Reform Service, Ernesto Ayala Mercado, indicate that 324,355 peasants from all over the country were to become landowners according to Article 78, with the exception of the departments of Santa Cruz, Beni, and Pando, where the problem of servitude dependence did not exist.[6]

2. Giving peasants with no land or insufficient land enough for the support of their families.

The law acknowledged the legality of small and medium landholdings as well as landholdings by agricultural enterprises. Latifundist landholding was declared to be illegal. The expropriated land was to be paid for by the peasants over a period of 25 years at a rate of 2 percent a year.

A number of supplementary laws adopted in 1955 and 1956 were intended to intensify the process of alienating the land from the latifundists. Thus, the law of February 17, 1955, revised the matter of limitation of the maximum size of the middle-sized farm, which the reform had touched on only partially. Earlier, for example, the size of the average farm in the valleys near the city of Cochabamba was 50 hectares on irrigated land, 100 hectares on arid land, and 24 hectares in grape-growing regions, while now it was equal to 20, 40, and 6 hectares respectively.[7] The law of December 22, 1956, altered the procedure for confiscating land. The changes introduced in the 1962 law on agrarian reform shortened the period for review of claims regarding land confiscation and provided for a free allotment of land to peasants. The compensation for confiscated lands was now to be paid not by the peasants, as formerly, but by the government over a period of ten years.

According to the 1950 census, the overall number of farms in Bolivia was 83,599, while the number of farms subject to total or partial confiscation in accordance with the law on agrarian reform was 25,342, or 30.3 percent of the total number.[8]

The process of implementation of the Bolivian agrarian reform was not equal, but varied in accordance with the intensity of the peasant struggle for land and the correlation of political forces in the country. Consequently, the history of the transformation may be provisionally divided into two periods: the first, from the beginning of 1954 to the end of 1959, and the second, from the end of 1959 to the end of 1964.

During the first period, the effect of the agrarian reform encompassed only 806 farms, or 3.2 percent of the farms subject to confiscation. By August 18, 1959, 528,369.6 hectares had been divided up among 29,216 families as private and collective property. Such a rate of implementation of agrarian reform (assigning allotments to 6,000 families a year) did not even assure allotments of land to as many persons as the number by which the population increased naturally, which, according to data of the FAO, amounted to 60,000 people a year in Bolivia.[9]

A considerable acceleration of the tempo of implementation of the reform took place during the second stage. Nine times more land was distributed in four years than in the preceding six years. According to the data of Edwin Moller Pacieri, by June 30, 1963, 4,853,000 hectares of land had been distributed among 151, 500 families.[10] This can be explained chiefly by the intensification of the peasant struggle for land and by the intensification of the struggle between the bourgeoisie and the work-

[6]F. Beltrán, J. Fernández, ¿Dónde va la reforma agraria boliviana?

[7]Raúl Ruiz González, Boliviia—Prometei And (Moskva, 1963), p. 212.

[8]F. Beltrán, J. Fernández, ¿Dónde va la reforma agraria boliviana?

[9]Ibid., pp. 74–75, 79–80, 82.

[10]E. Moller Pacieri, El cooperativismo y la revolución (La Paz, 1963), p. 299.

ing class, in connection with which the bourgeoisie accelerated the implementation of the agrarian reform for the purpose of winning the peasantry over to its side. It succeeded in doing this to a certain degree, as witnessed by the frequent use of the peasant militia against the workers.

Notwithstanding the considerable acceleration of the progress of the agrarian reform during its second stage, the agrarian problem in Bolivia remained unresolved, even if we rely on the apparently somewhat inflated data of Moller Pacieri.

In the first place, the land distributed among the peasantry in accordance with the reform made up only 20 percent of the overall agricultural land of the country, which, according to the calculations of Bolivian economists, amounted to 23.6 million hectares.[11] Thus, 80 percent of the land remained in the hands of the former landowners.

In the second place, they retained the major part of the cultivated land. The basic quantity of the land received by the peasants was not cultivated land, but only land suitable for cultivation.[12]

In the third place, notwithstanding the fact that sizable sectors of the Bolivian peasantry received land or were recognized to be the owners of land they cultivated, the parcels of the majority of the peasants are not large enough to support a family. The law on agrarian reform provided that the average size of peasant plots after the implementation of the agrarian reform should be 6 hectares per family in the valleys and 50 hectares in the tropical zones.[13] Actually, the average size of the peasant parcel amounted to 3.61 hectares and in the principal agricultural areas, even less: in the department of Cochabamba, 1.54 hectares; in the department of Tarija, 3.2 hectares; in the department of La Paz, 2.06 hectares; and in the department of Chuquisaca, 2.13 hectares.[14]

In the fourth place, large landholdings and the class of latifundist landlords were not completely eliminated as a result of the introduction of the agrarian reform. State lands were widely used for distribution among the peasantry. This is accounted for by the fact that the process of expropriation of land of the large landowners lagged considerably behind the rate of assignment of land to the peasants.

In the fifth place, the lack of state aid in extending credits, seeds, agricultural technology, and equipment in sufficient scope prevented the peasants from clearing the majority of the land that they received in the agrarian reform.

The history of the Bolivian agrarian reform is a story about how a victorious people—victorious workers and peasants—were deceived by the bourgeoisie and gradually deprived to a considerable extent of the fruits of their victory. From the very beginning of the agrarian reform, proclaimed among masses of armed people on August 2, 1953, the bourgeoisie regarded it on the social and political plane as first of all a means of reducing the revolutionary activity of

[11]Raúl Ruiz González, *Boliviia—Prometei And*, p. 197.

[12]It is very simple to establish that the majority of the cultivated land was retained for the landowners. The number of farms subject to total or partial confiscation was 25,342. The overall amount of cultivated land in Bolivia, according to the data of the ECLA, was 654,000 hectares, while according to data of the FAO it was 570,000 hectares. According to Article 35 of the law on agrarian reform, the majority of the latifundia were not to be subject to total confiscation, but rather reduced to the size of a medium farm. If we presume that 20 hectares remained in the hands of each large landowner and that the number of latifundia subjected to total distribution approximately counterbalances the number of farms considered to be large agricultural enterprises and therefore remaining in the hands of the former owners, then the landowners must have retained 500,000 hectares of land (20 hectares multiplied by 25,000).

[13]*El movimiento sindical libre del continente y la reforma agraria* (México: ORIT, 1961), p. 34.

[14]F. Beltrán, J. Fernández, *¿Dónde va la reforma agraria boliviana?* p. 80.

the masses and as a means of struggle with the revolution. The Bolivian bourgeoisie was forced to begin the implementation of the agrarian reform from above in order to prevent its accomplishment from below by the peasant masses themselves.

The political immaturity of the masses and the ideological and organizational weakness of the democratic forces, which had suffered cruel persecutions from the dictatorial regimes, permitted the middle and petty bourgeoisie to make the reform a means of subjecting the peasantry to their influence and of accelerating the struggle against the working class.

At the same time, the exploiting classes—the bourgeoisie and the latifundists—attempted to turn, and to a certain degree succeeded in turning, public opinion in the cities against the peasants, to the advantage of the landowners who had been "harmed" by the agrarian reform and who had "suffered" from peasant demonstrations, from the seizure of estates, and from other acts. The bourgeoisie directed their efforts, on the one hand, toward emasculating the antilandlord nature of the reform, and, on the other, toward setting the peasantry up in opposition to the working class.

According to the law on agrarian reform, exempt from confiscation were small holdings, medium holdings (plots held by peasants among the latter could be recognized as their property and excluded), lands of large agricultural enterprises, and commune lands. Commune lands that had been illegally seized by large landowners were to be returned to the commune members. In this, however, the large landowners received compensation, something that did not occur in the case of the Mexican agrarian reform, for example, which returned gratis to communes lands that had been seized from them. Where peasants lived on lands returned to communes in Bolivia, the peasants had to leave the lands, and the compensation was paid not to them, but to the large landowners.

According to the legislation an agrarian reform, large latifundia were subject to total confiscation and distribution among the peasantry. During the course of the agrarian reform, the maximum permissible size of medium farms was considerably decreased, but nevertheless a number of provisions were retained in the legislation on agrarian reform that permitted the owners to keep a considerable part of their land. Thus, Article 35 of the law provided that farms on which the owner invested capital in the form of machinery or modern methods of cultivation with his own participation or that of his close relatives in working the farm would not be considered latifundia. In those areas where the topography prevented the use of machinery, only the second condition was to be considered obligatory. Such land was not subject to total expropriation, but was reduced to the size of medium farms. Landowners made extensive use of this provision to retain their lands.[15]

Finally, the large landowners retained their equipment and part of their livestock, which greatly hampered the consolidation of the newly organized peasant farms.

Articles 35 and 36, which were included in the law on agrarian reform, guaranteed the inviolability of agricultural enterprises using both hired

[15]In a number of cases, the court decided in favor of the owner on the basis of purely comical proof of capital investment on the part of the latifundist and of his personal participation in agricultural production. The progressive Bolivian scholars F. Beltrán and J. Fernández present in their book an instance where the participation of the latifundist in agricultural production was "proven" by the presence of a manor house with all its conveniences, which allegedly testifies to the presence of the owner on the farm during the period of agricultural work (*ibid.*, pp. 33–34).

labor and corvée (work by the peasants on the landlord's land in exchange for use of a plot of land). These articles created extensive possibilities for the protection of latifundist property. The bourgeois principle of "the social function of land" was expressed in these articles—that is, the greater the extent to which a large estate became a capitalistic enterprise, the less the owner suffered from the agrarian reform. The possibility for the owners to retain a considerable quantity of the cultivated land often meant defense of latifundia in practice, since the owners in Bolivia characteristically cultivated a small percentage of their land. On large estates, this amounted frequently to no more than 20 to 40 hectares of land.

The announcement of the inviolability of small and medium-sized farms closed the path for distribution of land to a considerable number of peasants who cultivated plots belonging to such owners. In a number of cases, the peasants were even forced to abandon these plots.

By forbidding tenant farming and sub–tenant leasing, the Bolivian legislation (particularly the decree of March 24, 1961) did not provide for an immediate transfer of leased land to the peasant lessees, but rather converted the latter into hired workers. Instead of tenant relations, the Bolivian agrarian reform is promoting relations involving direct hiring of manpower. The prohibition of leasing referred in the first place to small peasant leasing, while that on a large scale was retained, provided the landowner submitted a plan for introducing improvements on his property.

The same decree prohibited sharecropping, recommending in its place the engagement of hired workers or the organization of peasant cooperatives. This decree was one of the methods used by the government for the purpose of forcing the large landowners to conduct their operations more intensively.

Such an approach to sharecropping created conditions for the ineffectiveness of measures for its eradication. In a number of localities, especially in the Cochabamba valley, sharecropping has been retained in practice up to the present, although with a considerable deterioration in the position of the sharecroppers. The latter are prepared to accept even more difficult conditions for the sake of retaining their position, frequently as hired workers. A single prohibition is not enough for a genuine eradication of sharecropping and the elimination of its economic causes. To do this, it would be necessary to divide the land among the peasants both individually and as collective property, and particularly to transfer to the sharecroppers the lands they cultivate and to assure them of agricultural equipment and credits. The nature of the abolition of sharecropping in Bolivia proves once more that the edge of the principle of "the social function of land" is directed against the peasantry.

The effective implementation of the agrarian reform in Bolivia was hampered by the complex procedures for confiscating and distributing land and the cumbrous bureaucratic apparatus established for accomplishing it. A peasant seeking recognition of himself as the owner of a plot of land he cultivates has three stages to hurdle: the local courts, or the circuit courts introduced by the law of December 22, 1956; the national council of the National Service for Agrarian Reform; and finally, the President of the Republic.

In order to receive land, the peasants had to abandon their work for long periods in order to attend court hearings, confer with lawyers, negotiate with surveyors, and so on. The Bolivian peasants—the overwhelming majority of them illiterate and the bulk of them without any knowledge of the Spanish language (80 percent of the peasants are Indians)—had to bring suit for the confiscation of land from landowners individually in every case and had to appear against the owners in court.

The utilization by the bourgeois government of Bolivia of such a conservative institution of the bourgeois state as the judiciary as the basic weapon of agrarian reform was one of the principal reasons for the slowness in implementation of the reform. There is one case where the peasants began proceedings for the division of the Mamaota estate in Betansos (department of Potosí) on August 14, 1954, and which five years later were still locked in the Ministry for Peasant Affairs. [16] Some courts openly sabotaged fulfillment of the basic provisions of agrarian reform, protecting the large landowners in every possible way. Agrarian judge Enrique Pérez was removed from his post for systematic violation of the provisions of the agrarian reform.[17]

The bureaucratic machine established to implement the agrarian reform was not only complex and slow, but also very costly. The National Service for Agrarian Reform received 779,760,250 Bolivian pesos from the budget for implementation of the reform in 1956, for example, and during the course of that year it made land available to 3,431 families. Each parcel that was distributed cost the government 227,269 pesos.[18] These figures do not include the expenditures of the Ministry for Peasant Affairs, the office of the President, and other agencies that also participated in the implementation of the agrarian reform. And they do not include the expenses that the peasant had to bear in order to receive a plot! The peasant had to pay for the services of a lawyer, a surveyor, a judge, a secretary, and jurors, and had to pay for travel expenses for himself, for stamped paper, for court expenses, and such. In addition, for the first eight years, he also had to pay compensation for the land

received. This often meant that the plot cost the peasant as much as if he had simply bought it from the owner. As a result, the peasants actually were frequently forced to resort to direct purchase of land.

In the majority of cases, the judges—following the lead of the surveyors who provided the corresponding materials—declared as latifundia only those estates where the area of cultivated land (and not the area suitable for cultivation, as provided by the law) exceeded the maximum norm for a medium-size farm. By this means, a large number of latifundia were saved from distribution.

The bourgeoisie opposed the peasant resolution of the agrarian problem—an armed seizure of estates and their distribution—with a so-called legal route. Such a position on the part of the government permitted the owners to utilize the fact of peasant seizure of their land as justification for charging the peasants with "insurrection" and obtaining a court decision in their favor.

The landlords were generally extremely active, even though they were on the defensive side. In striving to retain their land at any cost, they promoted through their agents clashes between different groups of peasants and set Indians against non-Indians, small peasants against medium peasants, specialists, and physicians—all for the purpose of harassing the peasantry, diverting them from the struggle for land, and as a result obtaining suppression of peasant unrest from the government. The landlords made extensive use of the corruption that corroded the apparatus established for implementation of the agrarian reform.

[16]*Ibid.*, p. 70.
[17]M. Zambrana Yáñez, *La distribución de tierras en Bolivia,* p. 45.
[18]F. Beltrán, J. Fernández, *¿Dónde va la reforma agraria boliviana?* p. 62.

Landlord pressure on agrarian judges was facilitated by the fact that circuit judges carrying out their duties usually lodged with the landlords and spent a considerable amount of their time in the company of landowners. The landowners resorted especially frequently to bribing surveyors, on whose conclusions depended the declaration of a farm to be small, medium, or a latifundium. The surveyors also extorted considerable sums of money from the peasants. For example, one surveyor received 50,000 Bolivian pesos from each of the 320 peasants living on the Cocamarca estate in Arca (department of Cochabamba).[19]

The large landowners also used all kinds of machinations to retain their estates: sale of a part of the land, a fictitious division of a large estate among relatives so that each parcel would not exceed the maximum size for medium property, and other devious actions.

The presence of a huge number of small peasant plots after the conduct of the agrarian reform testifies to the urgent need for carrying the agrarian reform through to its conclusion, to the total elimination of latifundist landownership and of the landlords as a class, and to the need for the establishment of cooperation in Bolivian agriculture.[20]

SOME RESULTS

The agrarian reforms that have been carried out in Bolivia and other Latin American countries have not led and cannot lead to profound socioeconomic transformations, because of their limited nature. Nevertheless, they have exerted an undoubted influence on the economic and political position of these countries, and it would be a mistake to underestimate their significance and results.

Notwithstanding the fact that the Bolivian reform did not lead to the elimination of landlords as a class, it considerably decreased their role in the political and economic life of the countryside and increased the role of the peasantry. The reform struck a perceptible blow to the semifeudal forms of exploitation of the peasantry, although it did not extirpate them completely. It put an end to serfdom and other traces of feudalism, and the peasants have been freed from the odious corvée—the obligation to work gratis on the landowner's farm in return for use of a parcel of land—and from the humiliations associated with their dependent position. The standard of living of the peasantry has also increased somewhat. All of this has affected the growth of agricultural production in the country, although not immediately.

In the first years of implementation of the reform, there was even a considerable fall in agricultural production and a decrease in the area under cultivation. This can be explained by the intensification of the class struggle in the countryside, direct sabotage from the landowners, a decrease in the amount of agricultural machinery in use, and an outflow of monetary resources in connection with the fact that landlords transferred their capital into other spheres of social production. This was facilitated also by difficulties that arose before the peasantry in connection with clearing the land received, and also by the dumping of

[19]*Ibid.*, p. 69.
[20]Producer cooperatives in Bolivian agriculture have not been developed greatly. This fact determined the course of the bourgeoisie in establishing individual farms although the government took certain steps directed at the encouragement of producer cooperatives in agriculture and official spokesmen often declared themselves to be in favor of the formation of producer cooperatives. As of May 31, 1963, there were 244 cooperatives in Bolivia with a membership of 18,575, of which 139 with a membership of 7,005 were agricultural cooperatives (E. Moller Pacieri, *El cooperativismo y la revolución,* anexo 2).

American agricultural products, which were made available to the country as "aid." When the lands that the peasants had received were cleared, Bolivian agricultural production rose considerably (see Table 5).

Table 5. Growth of Agricultural Production in Bolivia

Product	Year	
	1950	1963
	(Tons)	(Tons)
Sugar cane	342,939	1,161,600
Rice	10,000	40,000
Corn	129,701	260,803
Wheat	45,652	78,400
Potatoes	189,384	700,000
Barley	44,247	126,759
Coffee	1,000	3,150
Citrus fruits	35,000	150,000
Bananas	63,712	150,000
Cotton	126	910

Source: E. Moller Pacieri, *El cooperativismo y la revolución* (La Paz, 1963), p. 299.

However, the technological level of Bolivian agriculture has remained virtually unchanged. The confession contained in the message of the President of the Republic to the National Congress on August 6, 1959, merits attention: "The problems of agricultural research into expansion of cultivated areas and revolutionary changes of working methods in the countryside were neglected. Agricultural machinery fell into the hands of intermediaries or of large landowners in the eastern part of the country, and not into the hands of the peasant communes or the producer cooperatives of Oruro or Cochabamba, La Paz or Potosí. Even the peasant communes bordering on experimental stations were not taught anything and did not receive any advantage from their machines and new equipment."[21]

Not wishing to implement radical agrarian transformations, but following the path of concessions to the landowner class, and also partly taking into account the overpopulation of a number of regions of the country (for example, along the banks of Lake Titicaca), the Bolivian government resorted to carrying out colonization plans in order to assure land to the considerable number of peasants who were left without parcels. Colonization was also essential to provide land for miners who had been left unemployed as a result of the closure of a number of mines. Efforts undertaken in the eastern part of the country resulted in the formation of a number of colonies and settlements in which somewhat over one thousand families were settled on newly cleared land. At the same time, colonization carried out by private individuals—the independent resettlement of peasants on new lands—acquired a larger scope than colonization conducted by the government.

It is reckoned that forty to fifty thousand peasants—chiefly Indians of the Quechua and Aymara tribes—have resettled on uncleared land in the province of Clapara in the department of Cochabamba, in the Caranava and Inquisava zones of the department of La Paz, and in many regions of the department of Santa Cruz over the course of fifteen years.[22] The increase in spontaneous resettlement of peasants on new lands is a result of the abolition of serfdom in Bolivia, which had prevented the free mobility of the peasant population.

During the course of the implementation of the agrarian reform in Bolivia, great masses of the peasant—and chiefly the Indian—population were drawn into the political struggle. They participated in militant actions for distribution of land, in demonstrations, in court proceedings, and in other activi-

[21]Cited by Raúl Ruiz González, *Boliviia—Prometei And*, p. 220.
[22]*El movimiento sindical libre del continente y la reforma agraria*, p. 36.

ties. This without any doubt has contributed toward raising the political consciousness of the masses and toward the acquisition of political experience by them. In a number of instances, the Communists were successful in leading the revolutionary movement of the masses, even though the ruling party—the Nationalist Revolutionary Movement—tried with all its efforts to remove Communists from leadership positions and did not hesitate to make use of persecution and arrest.

The implementation of the agrarian reform facilitated a decrease in the alienation and isolation of the Indians. The elimination of a number of traces of feudalism caused the process of levelling of differences between the Indians and the remaining part of the population to become more rapid, which facilitates the acceleration of the process of formation of a unified Bolivian nation. It can be noted only that the bourgeoisie who are leading this movement lend it a negative nature, attempting in particular to thrust Spanish on the Indians in place of their native language and to erode ancient customs and rites from their consciousness.

One of the most important results of the agrarian reform in Bolivia is the fact that it has cleared the path for capitalistic development in the countryside. The acceleration of the development of capitalist relations in agriculture simultaneously signifies (a) a rise of the separation of the peasantry into substrata and (b) acceleration of its impoverishment and proletarization, which the reform directly facilitated, since a considerable number of tenants and sharecroppers were converted by the agrarian reform law into hired laborers and extensive masses of the peasantry were forced to pay out huge sums of money.

By carrying out an agrarian reform, the Bolivian bourgeiosie was also able to a certain degree to undermine the union between the peasantry and the working class and to draw a considerable part of the peasantry over to its side and to follow it. This has allowed the bourgeoisie to strike a number of serious blows against the labor movement, to carry out a military coup, and to establish a reactionary military dictatorship.

The young Communist Party of Bolivia is fighting to strengthen the union between the working class and the peasantry against the large landowners and the reactionary sectors of the bourgeoisie. It supports a revolutionary deepening of the successes that have been achieved by the workers in the implementation of the agrarian reform, guarantees to the peasants regarding the land they have received, the adoption of effective measures to provide the peasants with agricultural machinery, equipment, and inexpensive credit, and also a general development of cooperatives in agriculture.[23]

[23]*Boletín de Información* (Prague), 1:43 (1965).

26. Latin America: Urbanization and Socioeconomic Development*

IA. MASHBITS

The growth of urban population and the development of the network of cities are characteristic of all regions of the world. From 1800 to 1960, the number of cities with populations of over 100,000 increased from 36 to 1,128, and their population increased from 11.5 million to 590 million.[1] Urbanization is extremely important for the progress of society. Cities—especially the largest centers—play a prominent role in the economic, political, and cultural life of all countries and all peoples.

Urbanization in the contemporary world is a many-sided and contradictory process. Its scope, nature, and results are conditioned by the concrete socioeconomic, historical-ethnographic, and geographic conditions of countries and regions.

SCOPE AND SOURCES OF URBANIZATION

In the extent of its urbanization, Latin America is behind the industrial regions of the capitalist world, but considerably ahead of Asia and Africa. Among other reasons, this can be explained by the higher level of economic development of Latin America in comparison with other regions of the Third World. According to the estimates of the United Nations Economic Commission for Latin America (ECLA), the urban population as a percentage of the region's total population was 34 percent in 1940, 39 percent in 1950, and 50.3 percent in 1965.[2]

Statistics for the Latin American countries do not permit a sufficiently precise estimate of the degree of development of urban life or the numbers of the urban population. The official criteria on this point differ greatly from country to country. The ECLA considers inhabitants of points with a population of over 2,000 to be urban residents. However, this is an extremely relative criterion.[3]

---

* "Latinskaia Amerika: Urbanizatsiia i sotsial'-no-ekonomicheskoe razvitie," *Mirovaia ekonomika i mezhdunarodnye otnosheniia*, 10:43–51 (1966).

[1] *Land Economics*, February 1966, p. 53.

[2] The average world figure for the proportion of urban population is about 33 percent, while that for Asia (less Japan) and Africa (less the UAR) is about 20 percent.

[3] Frequently agricultural population predominates in large cities, while nonagricultural functions (settlements near mines, etc.) predominate in small towns. Antonio Gramchi has noted the formal nature of dividing population structure "from the point of view of greater or lesser concentration. It sometimes truly paradoxically happens that a rural resident can be more progressive than an urban type." (A. Gramchi, *Izbrannye proizvedeniia*, v. 3. [Moskva, 1959] p. 378).

Data on the concentration of population in large and the very largest centers are more objective measures of urbanization. At the beginning of the 1960's, there were 227 cities in Latin America with populations of over 50,000. Their population was 62 million—25 percent of the population of the entire region. In 1965, there were 24 major cities in the Latin American countries with populations of over 500,000 (in Africa, there are 12 such cities). About one-sixth of all Latin Americans live in these major cities.

There are great differences in the degree of urbanization among the Latin American countries. According to estimates of the ECLA, the percentage of urban population in 1965 ranged from 14.7 in Haiti to 82.6 in Uruguay. Central America is the least urbanized, with about one-third of the population in cities. Almost 60 percent of the population of Mexico and somewhat more than two-thirds of the populations of Argentina, Chile, and Venezuela are considered urban. Of the Latin American countries that are most highly developed economically, only in Brazil does less than 50 percent of the population live in the cities—in 1965, 44 percent, in 1950, 31 percent.

The population of the cities in Latin America is growing more rapidly than that of the countryside. Until the world economic crisis of 1929–1933, the growth of the Latin American cities was determined to a large extent by European immigration. This was especially true in Argentina, Brazil, Uruguay, Chile, and Cuba. After the Second World War, the immigration had a certain significance in the growth of the urban populations of Argentina, Venezuela (a result of the oil boom), and partially in Brazil. In Latin America, as in other regions of the "third world," the rate of urbanization in the postwar period has been closely associated with the ever increasing flight of the peasantry to the cities, which has become the most significant direction of internal migratory currents. The following figures show the portion of the increase in urban population that can be attributed to internal migratory currents (chiefly the moves of peasants to the cities): 68 percent in Colombia during 1938–1951; 71 percent in Venezuela during 1941–1950; and 47 percent, 49 percent, and 42 percent respectively in Chile, Brazil, and Mexico during the years 1940–1950.[4]

During the period 1950–1960, the urban population of Latin America increased by 34 million, while the rural population increased by 16 million (growth rates corresponding to 5 percent and 1.5 percent per year). In the more developed countries, the average annual rates of growth for urban and rural population were as follows: in Brazil, 5.2 and 1.6 percent; in Mexico, 4.7 and 1.5 percent; and in Venezuela, 6.3 and 0.7 percent. There is a similar outlook for the future. According to the predictions of the ECLA, the annual growth rate for the entire population during the years 1960–1975 will be about 3 percent, while that of the urban population will not be less than 5 percent.[5]

In sociological literature on Latin American problems, a great deal of attention is devoted to the matter of the relationship between "the attraction of the cities" and the "push out from the countryside." The con-

---

[4]*La urbanización en América Latina* (New York: UNESCO, 1962), p. 113.

[5]The differences in rates of growth between urban and rural populations are very expressive, especially if one takes into account the considerably higher natural increase of population in the countryside in all the Latin American countries. In Mexico, for example, according to data from the 1950 census, the number of children over four years old per 1,000 women between the ages of 15 and 49 was as follows: in places with a population under 10,000, 668; in cities with a population range of 10,000–50,000, 569; and in cities with populations of over 50,000, 493.

stantly increasing scale of the flight of the peasants to the cities is connected above all with the "push out from the countryside." This is caused by the extremely difficult living conditions of the peasants and by the nature of landholding and land utiliziation. According to data of the ECLA, out of a gainfully employed agricultural population of 32 million of Latin America, 0.1 million control almost two-thirds of the agricultural land area. The reasons for the increasing "push out from the countryside" can be shown from the example of Colombia. According to data from the Colombian Institute for Agrarian Reform, 874 major landowners in that country controlled about one-third of the land in 1962–1963. At the same time, 500,000 peasant families had no land.

The number of persons employed in agriculture as compared to the total number of gainfully employed persons in Latin America fell from 59 percent in 1936 to 46.5 percent in 1962 (in Asia and Africa it is about 60 percent). Nevertheless, there is an annual increase of about five million in the rural labor force. In addition, the majority of the peasantry in Latin America is not employed over two hundred days a year. The gradual collapse of the backward consumption agriculture and the development of a capitalist sector within it add impetus to the "push out from the countryside."[6]

Internal migrations in Latin America are sometimes represented schematically as a flight of peasants to the large cities. It would appear that the migration processes are much more complex. Former peasants frequently settle first in small cities ("local centers"), and the residents of the latter in turn move to the large cities and the capitals. According to the data of the head of the Latin American Demographic Center of the UN, Carmen A. Miró, the following ratios apply to settlers in the capital of Chile: persons coming directly from the countryside, about 12 percent; settlers from cities with from 900 to 5,000 inhabitants, 18 percent; from cities with a population of 5,000 –20,000, 24 percent; and from cities with a population of over 20,000, 40 percent.[7] There occurs a distinctive "intermingling" of various social and ethnic groups of the population, which increases their mobility and gives impetus to the processes of consolidation of the Latin American nations.

The flight of peasants from the countryside has a powerful influence on the growth and sex structure of the urban population. Young people are in the majority in the stream of migrants.[8] There is a high ratio of women among them (while men predominate sharply in internal migrations in Asia and in Africa). Women are a majority of the urban population in almost all Latin American countries. This is connected with women being drawn into production. For example, the ratio of women among the gainfully employed in production in the Federal District of Mexico increased from 18 percent in 1930 to 30.3 percent in 1960.

The constantly increasing withdrawal of the population from agriculture sharpens socioeconomic problems both in the countryside and in the city. The employment situation of the new city dwellers is extremely complex, as they frequently do not have the necessary skills to obtain employment, and their adjustment to the new conditions of urban life is difficult.

[6]UN World Population Conference (WPC), Belgrade, August 30–September 10, 1965, A3/V/E-/111, pp. 1–2.

[7]Demography (Chicago), 1:27 (1964).

[8]In Greater Mexico City, where migrants from other regions of the country accounted for one-third of the overall increase in population for the period 1950–1960, 80 percent of the population is under forty years of age.

THE GROWTH OF THE CITIES
OUTSTRIPS INDUSTRIALIZATION

In distinction from the industrial regions of the developing countries of the world, the growth of cities considerably outstrips the tempo of industrialization. This important structural anomaly exerts a powerful influence on many facets of life in the Latin American countries. Rapid urbanization here is connected not so much with the development of production as with the rapid growth of the service sector. The limited nature of their industrial functions is characteristic of the overwhelming majority of Latin American cities. Administrative and intermediary commercial functions traditionally predominate in them.[9]

The development of the functional production foundation of the cities is particularly hampered by the narrowness of the internal market. For example, according to the estimates of the National Council for Economic Planning and Coordination of Ecuador, at least one-third of the population of that country is outside the money and commercial market.[10] The population, the production, and the major cities are concentrated in a comparatively small number of regions, which are separated from each other by huge, virtually unpopulated and virgin expanses. Half the population lives on one-eighth of the area of Colombia, on one-eleventh of the area of Brazil, on one-twentieth of the area of Chile, and on one-fortieth of the area of Argentina and Paraguay. Of the sixty-five Brazilian cities with a population of over 50,000, only nine of them are in the interior of the country.[11]

The structure of production in Latin America, which was shaped under the influence of the subordinate position of the region in the capitalist division of labor, does not facilitate the development of manufacturing industries. The peculiarities of the contemporary industrial development of the region also influence the nature of urbanization unfavorably. Its share of capitalist industrial production comes to about 4 percent, representing 3.7 percent of manufacturing production and 8.4 percent of extractive production.

Extractive production in Latin America cannot become the basis for urbanization based on the development of production. This can be demonstrated by the example of Venezuela, Chile, and Mexico, which provide 84 percent of the value of production in this branch for the entire region. According to the 1961 census, only 44,000 persons were employed in the most important branch of production in Venezuela—extractive production—out of a total of 1,957,000 gainfully employed persons. This represented eighteen times fewer persons than the number employed in various service industries. In 1960 in Chile, 90,000 persons were employed in the extractive industry—less than 5 percent of the gainfully employed. In 1961 in Mexico, 120,000 persons were employed in the extractive industry—less than 1 percent of the total gainfully employed.

---

[9]The majority of Latin American cities sprang up during the colonial period as administrative, commercial, political, and religious centers. They served territories with a predominantly feudal system of landholding. Sociologist José Medina Echavarria characterizes the nature of the Latin American city as follows: "In Latin America, for better or for worse, the large estates [haciendas] imparted material organization to broad expanses of territory. The city thus became an 'intermediary' of spiritual forces. And it has remained so to this day" (*Aspectos sociales del desarrollo económico en América Latina*, v. 2. [New York: UNESCO, 1963], p. 42).

[10]*Inter-American Economic Affairs*, 1:83 (Summer 1965).

[11]The sparse settlement of land in Latin America is reflected in the average distance of railway freight shipments. In 1962, it was as follows: in Argentina, 125 km.; in Mexico, 109 km.; in Chile, 86 km.; in Brazil, 75 km.; in Colombia, 69 km.; in Peru, 63 km.; and in Ecuador, 47 km. (*Economic Survey of Latin America, 1963*. [New York: UN, 1965], p. 98).

The rapid rates of growth of non-production branches also affect the nature of urbanization in the Latin American countries. The entire self-employed population of Latin America increased on the average 2.6 percent a year during 1945–1962, while the number employed in industry increased 1.9 percent and the number in service industries 5 percent. The proportion of the latter among the gainfully employed increased from 21 percent in 1945 to 30 percent in 1960. The proportion of small businessmen, servants, temporary auxiliary workers, and similar types is high in Latin American cities in comparison with cities in industrially developed countries. This is connected with the presence of cheap surplus labor. At the same time, about 6 percent of the population of Latin American cities is employed in the extractive industry. This indicator varies from 2 percent in Nicaragua to 8 percent in Argentina.[12]

The predominance of the service sector (the so-called tertiary sector) in the functional structure of the cities is constantly increasing. In one of the most developed countries of the region, Chile, the urban population increased 4 percent from 1950 to 1960 and the number of persons employed in industry decreased by almost 1 percent, but the number employed in services increased by 6.6 percent.

The calculations of D. Lambert on the relationship between persons employed in the service sector and the urban population are interesting. This indicator rose from 52 percent in 1935 to 72 percent in 1960 in Argentina. It reached 69.3 percent in Chile in 1960. It was about 59 percent in Brazil in 1950, and in Columbia was 56.2 percent in 1951.[13]

It should be emphasized that new characteristics can be seen in the functional structure of Latin American cities. It is becoming gradually more diversified, and, at the same time, the number of narrowly specialized urban centers is increasing. The development of capitalism in breadth and in depth and the expansion of the domestic market are gradually overcoming the isolation of certain regions and are facilitating the strengthening of internal economic ties.

The importance of the manufacturing industry is increasing in the major economic zones of the Latin American countries. Rather large manufacturing regions are being established about São Paulo, Buenos Aires, Mexico City, Rio de Janeiro, Santiago, Monterrey (Mexico), and Medellín (Colombia). City systems are being formed in them. Specialized industrial cities are also appearing. After the Second World War, major industrial centers sprang up in Mexico—Monclova (ferrous metallurgy), Ciudad Sahagú (machine building), Reynosa and Minatitlán (petro-chemicals), and a number of others. Similar processes are characteristic of Argentina, Brazil, and Chile.

The importance of local commercial distributional and organizational centers is increasing in connection with the growth of capitalism in Latin American agriculture. These are most often medium-sized cities (25,000–100,000 population), but larger centers are frequently found. In the northwestern Pacific-coast states of Mexico—where the production of cotton for export and of wheat for the domestic market is developing rapidly on irrigated land—the growth rate for the urban population is higher than the average for the country. A similar situation prevails in the new agricultural area on the northern coast of Peru. In Brazil during the years 1940–1960, the number of settlements

[12]*The Economic Development of Latin America in the Post-War Period* (New York: UN, 1964), p. 78; Rodolfo Quintero, *Antropología de las ciudades latinoamericanas* (Caracas, 1964), p. 195.

[13]*Civilisations,* 2:169 (1965).

with more than 2,000 inhabitants doubled (from 900 to 1.799), while the number of local centers (with populations of from 25 to 100,000) in agricultural area quadrupled (from 31 to 122).

HYPERTROPHY OF THE MAJOR CENTERS

The concentration of population and of economic power in the capitals and a few major centers is systematically increasing in Latin America. From 1930 to 1960, the population of these cities (each with over 500,000 in 1960) increased 3.5 times. The total population of Latin America doubled during the same period.

The capitals and the other major centers stand out as concentrations of the economic and spiritual life of the countries and regions. They are very important in the intrastate and international division of labor. However, under conditions of economic backwardness, the rapid development of a few centers intensifies the most important socioeconomic problems and aggravates irregularity and structural disproportions in the development of branches and regions.

As recently as the mid-1920's, only Buenos Aires in Latin America had over one million inhabitants. By 1960, there were eleven "million" cities, and the ECLA estimates that there will be no fewer than twenty by 1980. As in other areas of the world, complex systems of populated points—agglomerations—form about the largest centers. According to our calculations, there are about thirty urban agglomerations in the Latin American countries, and four of these are among the largest in the world. They are Greater Buenos Aires, with over 7 million inhabitants; Greater Mexico City (6 million); and São Paulo and Rio de Janeiro (5 million each).

With the exception of Brazil and Colombia, more people live in the capital cities in every country of the region than in all the other cities with populations of over 100,000.[14] The urban agglomerations of Buenos Aires, Montevideo, and Mexico City have approximately ten times as many inhabitants as the second largest cities in those countries. From 40 to 50 percent of the urban populations of the respective countries live in the capital agglomerations of Uruguay, Haiti, the Dominican Republic, Honduras, Nicaragua, Bolivia, Peru, and Chile, while in Costa Rica and Panama the figure is from 50 to 60 percent. In each of the countries of the region (except for Brazil, Colombia, and Ecuador) the population of the largest city comprises from 60 to 90 percent of the total population of the four largest cities of the respective country. Such a sharp predominance of the largest agglomerations over the remaining centers makes it impossible to put together urban systems whose sizes would be more or less proportional.[15]

The growth in population concentration in a few very large centers is accompanied by an increase in the cities' economic hypertrophy. According to some estimates, the capital regions of the Latin American countries concentrate about 25 percent of the national wealth of the region.[16]

The majority of the agglomerations are situated in a few relatively developed areas. The rapid growth of these agglomerations frequently hinders the development of both the territory of the cities themselves and, particularly, the

[14]A new capital—the city of Brasília—has been functioning in Brazil since 1960, while the two large cities of Medellín and Cali exist in Colombia along with Bogotá.

[15]Bourgeois literature on urban problems claims that proportional systems of cities of varying size ("a hierarchy of cities") can be established if the largest city is not more than twice the size of the second largest.

[16]J. P. Cole, *Latin America: An Economic and Social Geography* (London, 1965), pp. 410–411.

remaining surrounding areas. A few agglomerations—especially São Paulo, Mexico City, Buenos Aires, Lima–Callao, Montevideo, Rio de Janeiro, and Santiago—absorb a considerable portion of the imports of their countries, while their role in exports is extremely small. They "eat up" what other regions produce and export.

The materials of the symposium on Latin American industrial development (Santiago, 1966) testify to the fact that only three agglomerations—São Paulo, Mexico City, and Buenos Aires—account for one-third of the production of the region's manufacturing industry. In every Latin American country, a substantial amount of the production of the manufacturing industry comes from two major industrial centers. Two-thirds of the national production of the manufacturing industry comes from Buenos Aires and Rosario in Argentina, and the same percentage from Santiago and Valparaíso in Chile. In Mexico, the share of Mexico City and Monterrey is 45 percent, while that of Lima and Callao in Peru is 56 percent. The most extreme case of hypertrophy is that of Uruguay: 46 percent of the country's population lives in Montevideo, and it accounts for 75 percent of the country's industrial production.

Despite the efforts at population and economic decentralization in the Latin American countries, the concentration of the economy in the largest agglomerations continues to increase. This can be accounted for by the presence in them of a relatively extensive market, a developed transporation network and other elements of the infrastructure, a labor supply, and financial resources. The example of the agglomeration of Mexico City is instructive. Despite the absence of raw material and energy bases and the great difficulties in water supply and in selecting sites for new construction, this agglomeration accounts for 35 percent of the new industry and 40 percent of capital investment in industry in Mexico. In addition to the reasons named, the growth of the concentration of industry in Mexico City is facilitated by governmental subsidies and privileges, which bolster the position of capital-city industry in the markets of other Mexican areas and in the countries of the Latin American Free Trade Association. According to the estimates of Mexican economists, 10–12 million will live in Mexico City by 1980 (over 25 percent of the country's population) and it will account for up to 60 percent of the production of Mexican industry.

The most backward regions in the Latin American countries are becoming something like internal colonies of the largest agglomerations. The northeastern part of Brazil has become a distinctive colony of São Paulo. In Peru, the extensive eastern part of the country is an internal colony of Lima. In the presence of this situation, interregional antagonism aggravates competition for the domestic market by the major agglomerations. Every Latin American country has a few major centers, in which a considerable part of the national income is concentrated, and impoverished villages. For example, the average per capita income in Medellín and in the capital of Colombia was 32 to 34 times greater than in one-third of the subordinate political-administrative subdivisions of the country.[17]

The accelerated urbanization is leading to a sharpening of the foodstuffs problem in Latin America, where the per capita production of food is less than before the war. Food prices increase systematically in the large cities, where the population has low purchasing power. It has been calculated that if a Rio de Janeiro family of

[17]*Economía* 1 (1): 216–221 (1964).

four to five members spends 50 percent
of the established minimum wage on
food, the caloric value of the average ra-
tion will be only one-half the normal.[18]

"Belts of poverty" of extensive size
are characteristic of all the large cities
of the region. They lie on the outskirts
and usually have no roads, normal
water-supply, or other conveniences.
These hovels mounted helter-skelter
house a huge number of migrants from
the countryside seeking any kind of job.
They are sometimes called a "prein-
dustrial proletariat."[19] The "belts of
poverty" in the outskirts are growing
very rapidly. During the period 1947–
1960, the population of Buenos Aires
within the official city limits increased
by only 16,000. But the population of
the outlying areas of the capital metropolis increased by almost 2 million.
In 1964, there were 324 so-called
proletarian colonies in Greater Mexico
City, with a population of 1.5 million
(80 percent of them migrants from
other parts of Mexico). The population
of the outlying slums (*favela*) in Rio
de Janeiro increased from 400,000
to 900,000 in 1947–1961 (the latter
figure 38 percent of the entire population of the city). Not less than 50 percent of the population of Recife is concentrated in the *favela* zone. In Lima,
21 percent of the population lived in
slums in 1961, while the figure for
1940 was 10 percent.[20]

The rapid growth of the "poverty
belts" causes an expansion in the area
of the agglomeration and produces
great difficulties in the urban economy.
At the second general meeting of the
Inter-American Planning Association
(Lima, 1958), notice was taken of the
lack of regulation of construction in
the major Latin American cities. Since
that time, the situation has become even
worse, especially in Mexico City, Buenos Aires, Caracas, and Lima. The implementation of programs for housing
construction and the reconstruction of

the central and outlying areas in the
major cities of the region are proceeding
very slowly, with great difficulties
being encountered. Under present
conditions, the efforts of local authorities to improve living conditions in
Latin American cities produce a stream
of new migrants. And this brings the
results of the improvements to naught.

Prior to the Second World War, there
was formulated in American sociology—
which paid a great deal of attention
to urban problems—the "law of the
primate city." It established the special
importance of the largest city in the
life of any country and set up definite
ratios in the numbers of the population of groups of cities. Efforts have
been made in recent years to modernize
this law, in order to bring it more in
line with the actual conditions of the
developing countries. It is even being
claimed that the hypertrophy of the
major centers facilitates the progress
of countries and of regions.[21] The hypertrophy of a few major Latin American
centers reflects the contradictory and
unhealthy nature of capitalistic urbanization. "Capitalist production, by constantly increasing the preponderance of
the urban population that this production accumulates in large centers, by
this same process on the one hand
amasses the historical strength of society's march forward, and on the other
hand hinders the exchange of goods between man and the earth."[22]

URBANIZATION AND THE "POLITICAL CLIMATE"

The rapid growth of the urban population and of cities exercises a powerful
influence on the political life and the

[18]*WPC*, A.7/1/E/81, pp. 5–6.
[19]*WPC*, A.3/V/E/111, p. 3.
[20]*Economic Survey of Latin America*, p. 163.
[21]*Demography*, 1:147 (1964).
[22]K. Marx and F. Engels, *Sochineniia*, Vol. 23,
p. 514.

disposition of class forces in Latin America. The cities—especially the capitals and the major cities of the region—act as generators of ideas and accelerators of sharpened social processes. They are knots of contradiction between the national patriotic forces and domestic and internal reaction.

The importance of manufacturing and other "urban" sectors is increasing in Latin America. The portion of agricultural production in the total national product of the region fell from 31 percent to 21 percent between the prewar period and 1964, while the share of extractive industry remained at 1 percent and the share of manufacturing increased from 15 percent to 24 percent. United States direct private investments in Latin America increased 3.2 times from 1940 to 1963, while those in manufacturing increased tenfold and those in commerce elevenfold. The concentration of foreign capital increased especially in ports and in major cities in the interior.

However, these centers are an important base for the national bourgeoisie and also for the state-capitalistic sector. "Local" monopolies have sprung up and are gathering power in a number of countries. The substratum of powerful "local" employers and managers is growing in the large cities of the region, and they are playing an ever more active role in both economic and political life.[23] Several bourgeois investigations of Latin American problems assert that, in the future, "local" monopolies closely associated with foreign capital will become the main force in the region's development.[24]

The fact that urbanization is outstripping industrial development is leading to a rapid increase in the numbers of that part of the gainfully employed population which bourgeois sociology attributes to the so-called new middle sectors, including herein both true representatives of the group and new ranks of hired workers in the cities. Their proportion of the total population has increased from 8 percent to 20 percent during the past ten to fifteen years in Venezuela, owing chiefly to their rapid growth in the cities.[25]

Bourgeois-reformist authors assert very categorically that the rapid growth in numbers and in influence of this category of the population has become the most important factor in the political life of all the Latin American countries, one that allegedly is creating the prerequisites for an "industrial revolution" and that eliminates the possibility of profound revolutionary transformations. Unquestionably, this is an important factor in the contemporary political life of Latin America. In our time, however, the process of revolutionizing the middle classes themselves is developing steadily. Along with this, the ranks of the industrial and transportation proletariat—numbering about 15 to 16 million persons—are increasing quantitatively and strengthening their influence. There has also been a noticeable increase in the numbers of the intelligentsia and students in the Latin American cities.

It is extremely important to take note of the territorial concentration of the basic mass of the urban proletariat and of students in certain large centers— in Buenos Aires, Mexico City, São Paulo, Rio de Janeiro, Santiago, Lima, Montevideo, Caracas, and Bogotá. This concentration considerably increases

[23]The American author David L. Graham notes that a new factor in Mexican political life is the organizational capability of the powerful bourgeoisie and an increase in the influence of associations of industrialists, businessmen, and bankers (*The Yale Review*, October 1962, pp. 102–111).
[24]The American sociologist J. D. Harborn writes: "The new generations of industrial managers can establish a balanced economy in the Latin American countries in the future" (*Inter-American Economic Affairs*, 2:62 (Autumn 1965).
[25]*Social Science* (Winfield, Kansas), June 1963, p. 145.

the revolutionary potential and the role of the cities in the class struggles of the Latin American revolution.

Bourgeois governmental figures and scholars are ever more often reflecting a lack of concern with the possible social consequences of urbanization in developing countries. According to the words of the authoritative American specialist in urbanization problems, Philip M. Hauser, in the countries of Asia, Africa, and Latin America "cities are more a symbol of poverty and political instability than a triumph of man over nature." He notes that the accelerated urbanization in Latin America aggravates the "political instability" of the region.[26]

Bourgeois-reformist literature on Latin American problems claims that the morbid manifestations engendered by the rapid growth of cities can be neutralized by limited socioeconomic and technical programs. However, these cannot basically change the nature of urbanization in Latin America. This is shown particularly by the examples of Mexico, Brazil, Argentina, Chile, and Venezuela.

Of much greater interest is Cuba's first experience in solving urban problems on a planned and scientific basis. Effective measures are being taken in Cuba to overcome the consequences of the hypertrophy of Greater Havana. Serious attention is being given to small and medium cities, especially in the interior, and to the gradual development of a production base in them. Housing and medical-sanitary conditions are being improved for the Cuban workers in the cities. Regional plans for the rational location and development of populated places are being prepared for zones of new economic development (for example, the Northern Oriente plan).

Society and progressive personalities in culture and science in Latin America are demanding improvements in the living conditions of the urban population, especially the least well-to-do sector of it. These questions are very closely interwoven with the basic socioeconomic problems facing the Latin American countries.

[26]Philip Morris Hauser, *Population Perspectives* (New Brunswick, N.J., 1960), pp. 22, 24–25.

VIII

Economic Problems

Hardly any specialist would disagree with the general consensus that industrialization is highly desirable and even essential for Latin America. Soviet economists are no exception.

Items 27–29 present varying views of the problem. Iu. Grigor'ian in the first selection argues that real possibilities for industrialization can be created only by first implementing major socioeconomic transformations. In the following selection, I. K. Sheremet'ev stresses an alleged effort by the United States to block the way to Latin American industrial development. O. G. Klesmet in the third selection asserts that "economic growth under modern capitalist domination means the strengthening of monopoly capital power," and that "industrialization in itself does not assure economic independence." She concludes that Latin America must curtail investment in order to be able to accumulate the capital necessary for industrialization. In Item 30 the same author proposes a number of concrete measures that would facilitate this internal capital accumulation.

Other suggestions for promoting capital accumulation are advanced by I. K. Sheremet'ev in Item 31, in which the author defends "the progressive role of state capitalism in national economic development."

The section concludes with selections by O. G. Klesmet, Z. I. Romanova, and V. Zholobov, dealing with special aspects of economics—the structure of manufacturing, the attitude toward economic integration, and monetary problems, respectively (Items 32–34).

27. Latin America: The Industrialisation Problem*

Iu. Grigor'ian

Not many problems are given as much prominence in Latin American socio-economic research as that of industrialisation.

That is quite understandable, for al-

*"Latin America: The industrialisation problem," *International Affairs* (Moscow), 6:29–34 (June 1967).

though industry in Latin American countries has made some progress, the contradictions inherent in the capitalist economy are becoming increasingly manifest in industrialisation. Hence the search for new ways and means of achieving industrialisation, for financing it, and so on.

Enhanced interest in industrialisation was borne out by the Latin American Symposium on Industrialisation held in Santiago (Chile) in March 1966,[1] the discussion of industrialisation problems at the first session of the Inter-American Advisory Committee in Buenos Aires in September 1965, and the setting up of the Advisory Committee for Industrial Development under the Latin American Free Trade Association.

It is difficult indeed to overestimate the part industrialisation plays in the socioeconomic progress of the developing countries. Today, the economic level of most countries is determined chiefly by their degree of industrial development.

Industrialisation is therefore one of the most important factors for accelerating economic development and bridging the gap between the Latin American countries and the industrially developed capitalist states. Increasing employment by creating more and more jobs, industrialisation leads to a rapid rise of social labour productivity—the basic element of economic growth—and to an increase in per capita national income. There is a definite link between the national income and the share of the manufacturing industry that goes to create it. It is a well-known fact that the bulk of the national income in the industrially developed countries comes from industry, notably from its manufacturing branches.

Given the necessary conditions, industrialisation is capable of removing one of the most serious obstacles to Latin American economic development —the plunder of these countries in the world capitalist market. It can somewhat improve the conditions in which they are forced to trade and eventually put an end to their unequal position in the international capitalist division of labor in which they have been placed by the imperialist Powers.

The establishment of a modern national industry also enhances the Latin American countries' economic independence and works vast social changes. Industrial development directly influences the formation of the industrial proletariat and industrial bourgeoisie and, consequently, the realignment of class forces in Latin America.

Most of the Latin American countries set out to industrialise considerably earlier than the developing African countries and the overwhelming majority of Asian states.

Industrialisation became the basis of the economic policy of very many Latin American countries in the late 1930s, when they passed special laws to stimulate industrial development by granting a number of privileges to industrialists. These included taxation privileges (up to and including full exemption), preferential duties on imported machinery, equipment and materials, guaranteed supplies of raw materials, protection against external competition, granting of easy-term credits and other forms.[2] In Brazil, Mexico and Argentina, the state helped to lay the foundation of the iron and steel, chemical and engineering industries. Latin America now has its own atomic and radio-electronic industries.

It is only natural that the levels of industrial production, the methods of

[1]See official report of the *Simposio Latinamericano de Industrialización. Santiago de Chile, 14 al 25 marzo de 1966. Informe sobre los preparativos para los simposios sobre industrialización*. St. ECLA (Conf. 23), L. 10. Later referred to as *Simposio*.
[2]*Simposio. El proceso de industrialización en América Latina*, Vol. 2. St. ECLA (Conf. 23), L. 2, capítulo III.

industrialisation, and the extent to which it influences the economic pattern vary in the Latin American countries. The biggest Latin American countries (Argentina, Brazil, Mexico and Chile), which have turned from agrarian into agrarian-industrial, already have fairly developed branches of heavy industry and large modern enterprises. In other countries (Ecuador and Paraguay, for instance), there are only the traditional branches of light industry consisting predominantly of small enterprises.

In its level of industrial development, however, Latin America is ahead of the economically underdeveloped areas of Asia and Africa. Though accounting for only 15 per cent of the population of all the developing countries, Latin America produces about 40 per cent of the Third World's manufactures.

Latin America's share of world industrial output comes to about 3 per cent.[3] Nevertheless, in the rate of growth of industrial production it began to outpace some of the highly developed capitalist countries soon after the outbreak of the Second World War. This fact testifies to considerable progress, especially if one bears in mind that the rate of Latin America's industrial growth was below the world average in the 1930s.

The average annual increment of industrial output in Latin America between 1955 and 1965 was 6.7 per cent and that of the capitalist world in general—4.8 per cent.[4] Between 1938 and 1964 industrial output in Latin America increased by 300 per cent and that in the industrially developed capitalist countries by 240 per cent.[5]

The acceleration of Latin America's postwar industrial growth has been influenced by a set of internal and external factors due to the momentous changes in the world. Gradual elimination of industrial backwardness in Latin America is one of the symptoms of the weakening of imperialism under the blows of the liberation movement. Monopoly capital is no longer in a position to dictate the main direction of the economic development of the Latin American countries.

But however important the quantitative changes in the rates of Latin America's industrial growth may be, the qualitative indices are no less so. If these rates of growth are analysed by industries, substantial changes will be revealed in the manufacturing industry. At the end of the 1950s and the beginning of the 1960s, for instance, the rate of development of the heavy manufacturing industry was twice as fast as that of the light manufacturing industry (7.7 and 4.2 per cent).[6]

The rates of growth of the so-called dynamic branches (heavy and durable commodities) were higher than those of the mining industry. In the group of manufacturing industries, the ones to develop fastest were the important chemical, oil-refining, iron and steel, electrical engineering and automobile industries.

Speaking of these qualitative changes in Latin America's industrial development, one should stress that the engineering and chemical industries (that is, the industries which serve as criteria of industrial level in developed countries today) are the weakest links in Latin American industry. A considerable portion of the products of these industries is imported. Hence, while the industrial base is being enlarged, it is as yet insufficient for the reproduction of social capital in industry on a national scale.

---

[3]Ibid., Vol. 1, p. 2.
[4]CEPAL, Estudio económico de América Latina, 1965, New York, 1966, p. 21.
[5]See Monthly Bulletin of Statistics, November 1966, pp. xii, xiv.
[6]See The Growth of World Industry, 1938–1961: International Analyses and Tables, New York, 1965, p. 156.

Although the rates of growth of industrial output in Latin America were faster than in the rest of the capitalist world in the 1950s, they were not high enough noticeably to raise its relative industrial level, that is, its share in capitalist industrial production. This even dropped from 4.1 per cent in 1958[7] to 3.8 per cent in 1964,[8] i.e., the level of 1938.[9]

As for absolute volume of industrial output the gap between Latin America and the industrially developed capitalist countries is growing instead of narrowing, because the absolute magnitude of one per cent increase is several times greater in the leading capitalist countries than in the Latin American countries. It should also be stressed that the rates of industrial growth have slowed down since the end of the 1950s. Between 1955 and 1960 the average annual rates increased by 6.7 per cent, but between 1960 and 1965 they dropped to 5 per cent.[10] Nevertheless, the relatively high rates of growth of industrial output in Latin America (over the whole post-war period) have led to definite changes in its economic structure.

The share of industry in the aggregate social product has increased noticeably. In 1965 the share of agriculture came to 21.8 per cent and that of industry to 27.6 per cent (22.7 per cent in the case of the manufacturing industry)[11] and between 1936 and 1940 the figures were 31 and 19 per cent respectively.[12]

But however illustrative these figures may be, they have not brought about decisive changes in the pattern of Latin American economy.

It would be a mistake to gauge the degree of industrialisation of any country or area solely by the share of agriculture and industry in overall production. In 1965, for example, the share of Chile's agriculture in overall production was about 11 per cent, less

than in Italy, and in Venezuela it was approximately 8 per cent,[13] less than in the Federal Republic of Germany.

Consequently, one should take into account all sectors of the economy, and not only agriculture and industry on the whole. Chief account should be taken of the share of heavy industry, for it is the main indicator of the level of industrialisation. From this point of view, Federal Germany, Italy and the other leading capitalist countries are incomparably better off economically than the Latin American nations. Industry's relatively large share in the gross Latin American product is explained by the considerable shares of the mining (especially in Venezuela) and light industries.

Although heavy industry is developing faster than light industry and the disproportion between Departments I and II, which is inherent in industry, is decreasing, the biggest share in the Latin American manufacturing industry is still that of light industry, chiefly textile and food industries. In Britain, for instance, these two industries account for about 17 per cent of the output of the manufacturing industry, in the United States for 15 per cent, and in Chile for 28 per cent, in Peru for 44.5 per cent[14] and in Central America on the whole for 77 per cent.[15] And the share of engineering in the output of the manufacturing industry comes

[7]*Ibid.*, p. 332. The reference is to newly created values.

[8]Calculated from data given in the *Monthly Bulletin of Statistics*, November 1966, p. 10, and *The Growth of World Industry*, p. 332.

[9]*The Growth of World Industry*, p. 330.

[10]CEPAL, *Estudio económico de América Latina, 1965*, p. 21.

[11]*Ibid.*, p. 24.

[12]U.N. *The Economic Development of Latin America in Post-War Period*, New York, 1964.

[13]CEPAL, *Estudio económico de América Latina, 1965*, Primera parte, Santiago de Chile, 1966, p. 35.

[14]*Simposio. El desarrollo industrial del Perú*, St. ECLA (Conf. 23), L. 39, p. 24.

[15]*Wirtschaftsdienst*, Hamburg, 1964, No. 6, p. 239.

to only 17.3 per cent (including instruments and other small tools),[16] whereas in Britain it is almost 36 per cent, in Japan—34 per cent, and in Federal Germany—31 per cent.

All this testifies to substantial intersectoral disproportions in Latin American industry. Despite the high rates of industrial growth, the absolute volumes of production are very small in Latin America compared with industrially developed countries. In 1963, for instance, per capita output of steel was 38.6 kilogrammes in Brazil, 14 times less than in Belgium.

Consequently, despite their progress in replacing imported goods with their own, the Latin American countries still depend on imports for machinery and equipment as well as for many industrial materials (steel, chemicals, plastics, and certain non-ferrous metals). In 1964, means of production accounted for 30.8 per cent of total Latin American imports.[17] Even by 1957 Latin American industry will be meeting only 70 per cent of requirements in capital goods.

The process of industrialisation in Latin America is highly uneven.

The difference in the level of industrial development of Latin America may be gauged by the share of each country's manufacturing industry in the G.N.P. In 1965 the figure was 33.2 per cent in Argentina, 23.4 per cent in Brazil, 22.5 per cent in Mexico, 10.8 per cent in Bolivia, 11.5 per cent in Nicaragua, and 12.1 per cent in Guatemala.[18]

While considerable changes have occurred in the industrial pattern of the big Latin American countries, that of the other countries remains practically unchanged: light industry still plays the leading role there. This is due to their greater dependence on foreign capital and to the more destructive consequences of foreign monopoly domination.

One of the obstacles to the development of Latin American industry, especially the branches producing the means of production, is the absence of a big domestic market. In most of the Latin American countries some key branches of heavy industry (mining, for instance) work for export, and their links with the domestic market are weak. Reproduction in industry is largely controlled by foreign capital. Intersectoral ties are largely determined by foreign-trade ties with the imperialist countries.

The expansion of the domestic market is seriously impeded by survivals of pre-capitalist relationships in the countryside. Successful industrialisation is unthinkable without the industrialisation of agriculture. And Latin American agriculture still consumes a very small part of industrial output. This is evidenced by the figures for farm machinery. In the United States, for instance, there is a tractor for every 39 hectares of land cultivated, in the Common Market countries one for every 29 hectares, and in the Latin American countries one for every 274—in short, they have seven times as few tractors as the U.S.A. and nine times as few as the Common Market countries.[19]

This very low technical level is easily explained: the millions of poor peasants cannot afford the means of production, and the big farmers are not interested in mechanisation because labor is cheap. The low rate of mechanisation in agriculture restricts its basic capital requirements and this naturally retards industrial development.

Stressing the negative consequences

[16]CEPAL, *Los principales sectores de la industria Latinoamericana: Problemas y perspectivas, México,* 1965, p. 223.
[17]CEPAL, *Estudio económico de América Latina 1965,* Primera parte, p. 44.
[18]*Ibid.,* p. 35.
[19]*Estructura. Revista Empresaria Latinoamericana,* Buenos Aires, 1966, No. 1, p. 44.

of the disproportions in the development of Latin American agriculture and industry, Prof. Alberto Baltra Cortés, the well-known Chilean economist, rightly said: "It is impossible to introduce new techniques in some sectors of the economy without damaging the country's interests while other sectors remain in the grip of obsolete, anachronistic methods of production and institutions conforming to these methods. The existence of industry and related branches in conditions in which agriculture remains technically backward is costly for society, since agricultural backwardness upsets the economic balance and hinders overall development."[20]

The expansion of the Latin American internal market is seriously hindered by low living standards and the low purchasing power of the population.

The purchasing power of the population grows very slowly and this holds up the development of light industry which, in turn, keeps down light industry's requirements of equipment and other capital goods.

The growth of the domestic market is also hampered by the Latin American economy being dominated by foreign monopolies, which meet a major part of the local demand for goods and thus retard the development of national industries. In 1964 U.S.-controlled enterprises sold $5,100 million worth of goods (as against $2,400 million in 1957), considerably more than the value of all U.S. exports to Latin America.

Another negative factor in the development of Latin American industry is the shortage of skilled workers, engineers, and technicians. In Peru, for instance, more than half the people employed in industry in the mid-1960s were unskilled workers. While West Germany has 70 engineers per 10,000 of the population and France 62, Brazil and Mexico have seven, El Salvador three, and Honduras two.

These and certain other factors are responsible for the relatively low labour productivity in industry, especially when it is compared with labour productivity in the United States. In 1961, for instance, one North American worker produced about $11,000 worth of goods and one Latin American worker only $2,200 worth, or five times less.[21]

The low level of labour productivity in industry is one of the main reasons why Latin America remains the exploited element in the system of the international capitalist division of labour. It is precisely because of their low labour productivity, especially in industry, that the Latin American countries are suffering from the discrepancy in prices and unequal trade.

A very active part in the industrialisation of Latin America is played, along with local capital, by foreign—particularly North American—monopolies, which to a large extent determine its character. While the Latin American countries are industrialising themselves to overcome their backwardness and building the foundation of their economic independence, foreign monopoly is "helping" in the industrialisation to strengthen its position.

Most of the big private enterprises in the key sectors of industry are controlled by foreign capital. But it is not only a question of its direct control over a part of Latin American industry. In analysing the positions of national and foreign capital, it is essential to bear in mind such factors as foreign capital's domination in the credit and finance system and in trade, the dependence of local entrepreneurs on imports of capital goods, etc.

Foreign investments in the iron and steel, chemical engineering, electri-

[20]*Simposio. El desarrollo industrial del Perú*, St. ECLA (Conf. 23), L. 39, p. 11.
[21]*The Growth of World Industry*, pp. 218–221.

cal engineering and automobile industries have increased considerably
in the past decade or so. In 1949,
for example, private U.S. investments
in the Latin American manufacturing
industry constituted only 14 per cent
of all investments, and in 1965 they
came to 29 per cent.[22]

This trend in foreign investments
is due primarily to the Latin American
people's struggle for the establishment
of their own industrial base. The imperialist monopolies realise this and
have been trying from the very start
to subordinate the new branches to
their control, especially those which
offer favourable conditions for deriving high profits. Foreign capital's
heightened interest in the Latin American manufacturing industry may also
be explained by the intensification of
the inter-imperialist struggle in this
part of the world.

In short, the imperialist Powers are
forced to help the Latin American countries in their industrial development,
but their assistance in no way shows
that the monopolies are interested in
hastening industrialisation of the area.

It is perfectly obvious that industrialisation based on large-scale foreign
capital assistance means intensification of imperialist domination in new
forms and not consolidation of economic
independence. Therein lies the inconsistency of the industrialisation policy
pursued by the Latin American ruling
elements.

The foreign-monopoly domination of
the economies in the Latin American
countries makes them all the more
dependent on foreign capital, since the
pumping out of their national wealth
in the form of profits, interest and dividends complicates accumulation and
slows down the rate of economic development.[23] Hence, the question of finding sources capable of financing the Latin American countries' plans for further
industrialisation is one of the important

problems confronting them at present.

Foreign assistance could undoubtedly be one of these sources. But the
bulk of the funds allocated by the imperialist Powers under different programmes of "aid" to Latin America
goes into other sectors of the economy.

One of the clauses of the Alliance
for Progress programme drawn up in
Washington in fact stresses the need
to devote greater attention to industrialising Latin America. But while the U.S.
ruling quarters purportedly advocate industrialisation, they do everything to
hamper it. The total U.S. allocation for
the industrial development of the Latin
American countries between 1961 and
1965 was but 4 per cent of the sum earmarked for the Alliance for Progress programme. What is more, this "aid" is distributed in such a way that it delays the
expansion of the key sectors of industry.
Of the $483 million granted in loans to
Latin American industry in 1960–
1964 by the Inter-American Development Bank, the Agency for International
Development, the International Bank
for Reconstruction and Development,
and the Export-Import Bank, only
$6 million (1.3 per cent) were allo-
cated for the expansion of the engineering industry, and as much as 13 per cent
was allotted to the paper industry.

In such conditions, Latin American
industrial progress depends a great
deal on how the local sources will
be used for financing it and what part
will be played in this by the state,
which can ensure large sums by redis-
tributing the national income. At present, the government share in total investments in Latin America comes to no
more than 33 per cent. The long-term

[22]*Survey of Current Business*, January 1954,
p. 6; September 1966, p. 34.
[23]Even according to official U.S. data, profits
from direct U.S. private investments in Latin
America add up to $1,100–$1,200 million a year.
Survey of Current Business, September 1966,
p. 35.

development programmes of the Latin American countries attach much importance to state investments, which they call a "stimulating factor." Much depends of course on what this factor will really be like and whether or not these state investments will grow sufficiently fast.

Latin America has the necessary potentialities to accelerate industrial development. Nevertheless, some countries have failed to achieve the level of industrial output envisaged by their programme. While Brazil, Mexico, Argentina and Chile have turned from agrarian into agrarian-industrial countries, most of the states in this area are still agrarian.

On the whole, the process of Latin American industrialisation is still in its beginnings. It is beset with huge difficulties and contradictions engendered chiefly by foreign monopoly domination and capitalist relations of production.

The main contradiction of the policy of industrialisation followed by the Latin American ruling quarters is that while it calls for the development of their countries' industrial potentialities, it does not aim at putting an end to their dependence on foreign monopolies. Besides, it is the foreign imperialist quarters, and the sections of the local bourgeoisie and landowners dependent on them that constitute the force hampering the implementation of socio-economic reforms which could eliminate the obstacles to industrialisation.

The profound crisis in the economic pattern and the industrial development of the Latin American countries resulting from these contradictions leads to the aggravation of class antagonisms there. The progressive forces of Latin America are demanding major socio-economic transformations (such as radical agrarian reforms, eviction of foreign monopolies, nationalisation, all-round expansion of the state sector) which would create real possibilities for the industrialisation of the Latin American countries and for the improvement of living standards.

28. Latin America's Thorny Path of Industrial Development*

I. K. Sheremet'ev

Latin America has entered a complicated and deeply contradictory stage of economic development. The striving of the Latin American peoples for genuine national freedom and better conditions impels wide sections of the public, including some members of the ruling parties and groups, to seek new ways and means to accelerate

°"Latin America's thorny path of industrial development," *International Affairs* (Moscow), 12:21–26 (December 1966).

economic growth rates and modify the structure of social production in line with the requirements of the local market and national development. Particularly popular in Latin America is the idea of programming (planning) economic growth, efficiently utilising material, financial and manpower resources, building up industry and pooling efforts within the framework of the economic integration of Latin American countries.

The progressive character of these ideas is obvious, but it is not easy to put them into practice, that is, to lay the economic foundation for national independence. It is extremely difficult to achieve this because of the lack of national financial resources, technical knowledge and experience and industrial capacities, which make it necessary to import machines and equipment on a large scale. This is a result of the prolonged domination of the imperialists, U.S. imperialists above all, who have been plundering Latin American countries for decades and who bear responsibility for their lopsided economic development.

Now that these countries are straining every effort to cope with some of these economic difficulties, a paradoxical situation arises. Objective circumstances press them to resort to foreign financial, technical and economic aid. It would seem that they can expect this aid from those who derived and continue to derive enormous profits from capital exports to Latin America. But aid under the notorious Alliance for Progress programme most frequently turns against the national interests of the Latin American countries.

The Alliance for Progress programme is obviously used in the selfish interests of the most powerful and aggressive imperialist groups, whom the U.S.A.'s neighbours know only too well through their bitter experience over the past decades. Imperialist mo-

nopolies, capitalising on the economic difficulties, needs and hopes of the Latin American countries, strive to establish there a new system of dependence, oppression and control, sugared with handouts of subsidies under the name of "grants."

The reminder of the danger of neo-colonialism, contained in the Report of the C.C. to the 23rd Congress of the Communist Party of the Soviet Union, fully applies to the situation in this part of the world. "It should be borne in mind that to this day many of the newly-free countries are subjected to economic exploitation and political pressure by imperialism, which has not reconciled itself to its defeats. It is doing everything it can to preserve the possibility of exploiting the peoples and is resorting to new and craftier methods."[1]

NEW TRENDS IN FOREIGN INVESTMENTS

A comparison of the present-day structure of direct U.S. and other foreign investments in Latin America with that in the early 1950s shows the following characteristic changes.

On the one hand, the share of foreign investments in some "traditional" branches of economy (municipal enterprises and mining industry) has substantially dwindled; on the other, the share of investments in the manufacturing industry and trade has sharply grown. For example, in 1950, the first group of branches accounted for 35 per cent of U.S. direct investments in Latin America, and the second, for only 23 per cent, while in 1964, the ratio was reversed: only 18 per cent of the investments went to the "traditional branches," and 39 per cent, to the new

[1] *23rd Congress of the C.P.S.U.*, Moscow, 1966, p. 36.

spheres, including 26 per cent to the manufacturing industry.[2]

What explains this striking change in favour of new spheres of capital investment? Does it mean that the foreign monopolies have voluntarily abandoned their positions in the former key branches of economy (transport system, power industry, extracting and primary processing of raw materials)?

Some of the reasons for this change will be shown below, but in the meantime it is important to stress that the imperialist monopolies have not curtailed their activity in their former main sphere of business of their own free will or due to any loss of economic interest. This change was chiefly the result of the stubborn and persistent struggle of the peoples for the establishment of control over the exploitation of natural resources and over the big communal service enterprises.

The struggle against the imperialist monopolies in their traditional spheres of expansion and domination assumes many forms, including the gradual expansion of state participation in various industries and the creation of so-called mixed enterprises. For example, mining companies in Mexico are being "Mexicanised" and copper industries in Chile, "Chileanised." Besides, both countries take measures to change the structure of the mining industry and set up capacities for processing mineral raw materials on the spot.

Although this branch of economy as a sphere of foreign capital investment has become relatively less important, the absolute volume of the capital invested in it by imperialist companies has grown considerably as compared with 1950, and has remained stable in recent years. The imperialist monopolies tenaciously hold on to Latin America's mineral resources. Wherever conditions permit, they strive to crush national enterprises, take the sting out of state control and consoli-

date their positions. This is strikingly demonstrated by the sad fate of the Bolivian tin industry, which was nationalised in 1952. Deliberately aggravating the difficulties of the state-owned company COMIBOL (particularly its tin-marketing difficulties), the U.S. monopolies first tried to discredit its business activity and then, "coming to its aid," placed it to all intents and purposes under their control.

Besides non-ferrous metals, the valuable chemical raw materials found in many Latin American countries (natural sulphur in Mexico, for instance), high-grade iron ore, raw materials for the atomic industry and others have now become an object of great attraction of the U.S. and other foreign monopolies.

But the increasing striving of the U.S. companies to monopolise the Latin American raw material sources is perhaps most vividly demonstrated in the expansionist activity of the oil companies. Despite the legal restrictions operating in many of these countries (wide rights and privileges of state-owned oil companies), foreign monopolies cleverly evade these obstacles and entrench themselves in the most important sphere of the oil industry (processing and marketing), and thus succeed in pocketing enormous profits.

From 1950 to 1964, U.S. capital investments in the Latin American oil industry increased by more than 120 per cent, while their share in the total amount rose from 28 to 35 per cent. The U.S. oil monopolies have consolidated their positions in Colombia, Peru, Bolivia and some other countries, not to mention Venezuela, their main stronghold in Latin America.

[2]Here and elsewhere, unless otherwise specified, data on U.S. private investments in Latin America are from *Survey of Current Business* for 1966 and earlier years.

INDUSTRIALISATION PROBLEMS

Priority development of industry is typical of the economic policy of many Latin American countries today. The reason is not hard to see. The creation and development of their own industry, one that would correspond to the economic, geographical and socio-demographic features of the Latin American countries, is an essential prerequisite for strengthening their economic independence, eliminating the one-sidedness of production and export, increasing labour productivity, and improving the national social structure.

The conditions in Latin America favour all-round industrial development. Huge resources of hydropower, oil and gas, abundant mineral deposits and agricultural raw materials, a large and rapidly growing population—are all factors which objectively facilitate the creation of a powerful industry there and hold out great prospects for economic advance in this part of the world.

To promote industrialisation on a national basis, the Latin American countries encourage the investment of national private capital. This policy consists in protecting local markets from foreign rivalry, granting low-cost credits and tariffs, granting a rebate or complete exemption from taxes for new enterprises for a number of years. These measures ensure higher profits on capital invested in the manufacturing industry.

But due to the lack of national resources and technical know-how, as well as constant pressure by the U.S.A. and other imperialist Powers on local business circles and governments, who are only too ready to agree, since they profit from co-operation with foreign financial capital, many privileges and advantages reserved for national enterprises are actually extended to firms affiliated to foreign capital. The inconsistent and contradictory nature of the bourgeois industrialisation policy is best seen from the fact that it does not draw a clear distinction between national and foreign capital.

It is only natural that the manufacturing industry of the leading Latin American countries has now become a profitable sphere of capital investment for the U.S. and other monopolies. In the 1940s, the manufacturing industry accounted for 10–12 per cent of total U.S. direct investments in Latin America, while in 1964, this figure rose to 26 per cent. The U.S. and West European companies are penetrating primarily into the chemical, power engineering, automobile and food industries. In 1964, these industries accounted for over 60 per cent of total U.S. capital investments in the manufacturing industry of the Latin American countries.

Imperialist propaganda widely advertises these investments as a contribution by foreign monopolies to the industrialisation of the United States' southern neighbours. It cannot be denied, of course, that the foreign, including U.S., investments promote the industrial growth of Latin American countries to a certain degree and that they cause some changes in the structure of industrial production. But it should not be forgotten that the present changes in the policy towards foreign investments must be attributed mainly to the intensifying struggle of the peoples of that continent for economic independence and social progress.

This struggle in one way or another restrains the imperialist monopolies' freedom of action, forces them to manoeuvre and adapt themselves to the prevailing situation. This explains the movement of foreign capital from one branch of the economy to another (the more so as it is guaranteed higher profits in the manufacturing industry). This is also the reason for the changes in the form of foreign capital investments: affiliates of foreign firms are being replaced by mixed companies, in which private national and state capital participates. Therein lies the concession the imperialist monopolies are compelled to make to national economic interests.

Yet facts prove that there is no reason to think that the present industrial development of the Latin American countries is determined to any decisive degree by their national interests. Imperialist monopolies, and above all the most powerful U.S. monopolies, taking advantage of the many vulnerable spots of the Latin American economy and the inconsistent industrialisation policy, are striving to extend their control over local industry, to channel its further development in the direction they want, and to profit from the Latin American countries' dire need of financial and technical aid.

When official restrictions make it impossible to penetrate into national enterprises and firms openly, the foreign monopolies resort to underhand manoeuvring: they render "technical aid," sell patent rights and licences, "assist" in technical projects, supply and install basic plant on credit, etc. The Latin American countries naturally have to pay hard cash for these services. Their indebtedness avalanches, bringing with it new forms of heavy dependence on the imperialist creditor countries, as will be seen below. Meanwhile one thing should be stressed here: the imperialist "benefactors" use all aid allegedly intended for the industrialisation of Latin America as a springboard to expand their influence, consolidate their control and secure profits.

National capital often holds a controlling interest in the newly emerging mixed companies, at least in the initial stages of their organisation, but this state of affairs is usually short-lived. The foreign companies use the lack of capital or the need to expand or modernise production as a means for increasing their share holdings in the mixed companies. Thus, it is quite possible that predominantly national companies may in actual fact become branches or daughter companies of foreign monopolies. We refer the reader to the instructive data in the book written by José Luis Ceceña, a prominent Mexican economist.[3]

He shows that out of the 400 biggest Mexican enterprises of various types, 160 are directly controlled by foreign, predominantly U.S., capital (51–100 per cent of the joint-stock capital of each of them is in the hands of U.S. monopolies). In 73 more of the biggest enterprises foreign capital has a considerable, though not formally dominating share (25–50 per cent). In other words, the U.S. monopolies, directly or indirectly, control the 233 largest Mexican enterprises, which account for more than 40 per cent of the total income made by the 2,000 economically most important enterprises in the country.[4]

Similar conditions prevail in the other Latin American countries. The share of foreign capital in various Brazilian industries in the early 1960s was: in metal-working—70 per cent; in chemical manufacturing—50; in automobile construction—90; and in the pharmaceutic industry—90 per cent.

Foreign private monopolies are not interested in all branches of Latin America's manufacturing industry. Cases when foreign monopolies are willing to set up industrially important complexes, producing finished goods, are exceedingly rare and can be explained

[3]José Luis Ceceña, *El capital monopolista y la economía de México*, México, 1963.
[4]*Ibid.*, pp. 106–109.

mainly by reasons of prestige (more often to oust competitors, notably in the state sector).[5] Foreign monopolies invest their capital primarily in those industries and enterprises which promise a quick return of capital and high net profits, which are repatriated from the Latin American countries. These include mainly the production of consumer goods for home sale at prices considerably higher than world market prices because of the state protection extended to national enterprises. Typical in this respect is the rapid development of the local automobile industries with the participation of the biggest U.S. and West European companies.

Initially many foreign companies limited their activity in this sphere to assembling machines from imported parts and units with the aim of employing capacities at enterprises in the U.S.A. or Western Europe to the greatest possible extent. And only the prospect of higher profits and the fiscal-economic measures of the Latin American governments impelled some of the foreign monopolies to organise or participate in organising local complex plants, without relinquishing their control over local markets.

Apart from Venezuelan oil, which yields exceptionally high profits, the manufacturing industry is the most profitable sphere of foreign capital investment in Latin America. In 1964, the U.S. monopolies made a gross profit amounting to $229,000,000, or over 35 per cent of all profit on direct investments in Latin America, excluding revenues from oil.

It should be noted that these figures, taken from the summarised official accounts of U.S. companies, operating in Latin America, minimise the actual profits the U.S. monopolies derive from their participation in the industrial development of those countries. In estimating the total volume

of their profits, the interest from portfolio investments, loans and credits given to local enterprises, profits from sales of patent rights and licences at higher prices, etc., should also be taken into account.

However, no summarised data are available on such profits, which amount to dozens or, probably, hundreds of millions of dollars. But the monopolies are not interested in publishing figures on the enormous contribution the Latin American countries have to pay for their efforts to overcome the obsolete technological and economic structure being imposed on them.

STRUGGLE OVER U.S. AID

Five years ago, the U.S. ruling circles raised a hue and cry about the Alliance for Progress programme. It was advertised as a turning point in U.S. policy toward Latin America, as a sign of the United States' readiness to help the Western Hemisphere solve its vital economic and social problems. Washington assured the Latin American countries that from now on they would receive from the Unites States extensive financial and economic aid not only in the form of private investments, but also in the form of state credits and subsidies. It also promised to direct a large part of these credits to the financing of national programmes of economic and social development.

Different sections of the Latin American public reacted to the new U.S. promises in different ways. Being well aware of U.S. imperialism's true intentions the spokesmen of the democratic public insisted on a cautious approach to the new programme, seeing

[5]Such a rare case is the construction of the metallurgical complex Corporación Venezolana de Guayana, Matanzas, Venezuela, whose produce goes to meet national requirements.

it as an ordinary imperialist manoeu-
ver aimed at disorganising and splitting Latin America's national-liberation
movement.

The bourgeois reformists and the ruling elements of these countries adopted
a different attitude to the programme.
They were inclined to see in U.S. aid
a generous act and a sign that understanding of the necessity to heed the
voice of its southern neighbours was
growing in the U.S.A. They believed
that the Alliance programme would facilitate economic development.

True, in the 1960s Washington increased the volume of state credit and
subsidies to Latin America. Its help
through the specialised "international"
crediting organisations—the International Bank for Reconstruction and
Development and the International
Monetary Fund[6]—also grew.

The ratio between U.S. direct private
investments in the economy of Latin
America and long-term loans, credits
and subsidies has changed considerably
in favour of the latter. Whereas from
1951 to 1955, yearly Latin American
receipts averaged $325 million from
direct private investments (including
re-investments) and $281 million from
long-term state loans and credits and
private credits, in 1961–1964 these
figures were respectively $293 million,
and $1,841 million.[7]

It is quite obvious that, other conditions being equal, capital investment in the form of state credits has a
number of advantages for the Latin
American countries as compared with
private investments. State credits are
given for a definite period of time
and the interest paid is fixed before-
hand (moreover, as a rule, it is much
lower than the profit on direct investments). The recipient state is able
to distribute the funds thus received in
accordance with the country's needs.

Because the recipient Latin American countries prefer long-term state

credits to private capital investments
by imperialist monopolies, the latter
are opposed to them. Private capital
very often regards the export of state
capital as "unfair" competition which
undermines its interests.

This explains the constant striving
of U.S. monopoly capital to cut the
Government's aid programme for the
Latin American countries to a minimum, particularly for the state sector of
the economy, which is its most dangerous competitor. This also explains its
own political and economic purpose,
to make it promote private capital expansion and to use it as an effective instrument to control the national economy and secure maximum profits.

A case in point is the intense struggle
around President Kennedy's aid programme for Latin America which broke
out in U.S. business and political
circles soon after his death.

This programme was opposed first
of all by the powerful groups of the U.S.
monopoly bourgeoisie who have taken
a firm grip on Latin America and know
well what profits they can get from
exploiting her raw material and manpower resources. These groups succeeded in changing the underlying
principles of the Alliance for Progress.
Today U.S. economic policy in Latin
America is being increasingly subordinated to the idea of promoting
the private capital's expansion and

[6]The policy of these international organisations
is subordinated in practice to the interests of a
small group of imperialist Powers, and above
all the U.S.A., who have the largest share in the
capital of these organisations.

[7]Calculated according to data in the study of
the U.N. Economic Commission for Latin America
(*Estudio económico de América Latina*, 1965,
Mexico, May 1966, p. 206, tables 1–57). It should
be noted that what we have in mind here is the
ratio between the annual new investments, not
between the absolute figures of direct private
investments and the state credits received by
Latin America for the whole past period. In the
total amount of foreign investments in Latin
America, private capital continues to dominate.

creating there a favourable investment climate.

A favourable investment climate means a lot of things. It means the inviolability of foreign property, the right to free business and commercial secrecy (nondeclaration of profits), new financial and economic privileges, boosting profits, the right to repatriate profits, etc. The meaning of such importunity on the part of the Washington "benefactors" and their demand for "political stability," i.e., a stern police system, are becoming increasingly evident even for those Latin Americans who only yesterday pinned their hopes on the Alliance for Progress programme. The following fact is indicative in this respect.

Early in May, a group of prominent Latin American economic experts from the Alliance for Progress ostentatiously retired. The representatives of Colombia, Brazil, Argentina, Costa Rica and some other countries declared that their decision was dictated by the U.S. Government's refusal to consider the economic needs of the Latin American countries and their development programmes, when deciding aid questions.

To assess this retirement correctly it should be recalled that when the Alliance for Progress was set up it was insistently recommended that the participant countries draft national plans of economic and social development. These plans, considered and approved by the Alliance's experts, were to become the basis for applications for foreign financial aid.

However, after Washington's de facto abandonment of its initial principles, political considerations closely connected with the interests of U.S. monopolies again began to play the main role in determining the direction, volume, forms and terms of the aid rendered. The needs of the Latin American countries themselves, as reflected in their national programme, are actually ignored.

It is quite natural that such aid creates conditions in which a considerable part of the loans and credits is used irrationally, is wasted and pocketed by those who are not interested in the national progress and welfare of the people. But irrespective of who used these loans and credits and for what purposes they were expended, they have to be paid off with the interest accrued.

THE BURDEN OF FINANCIAL DEPENDENCE

A major result of foreign "aid" is the increasing financial dependence of the Latin American republics on the creditor countries. According to various estimates their total foreign debt reaches $10,000–15,000 million. If we take the data of the summary balance of payment of the Latin American countries (Cuba excluded), this debt increased in 1951–1964 alone by $12,400 million; in Argentina it rose by $2,200 million, in Brazil—by $3,900 million, in Mexico—by $2,400 million, and in Chile—by $1,300 million.[8]

Currency and financial credits are very often given to debtor-countries to enable them to pay out the profits of foreign monopolies and to repatriate them. These credits also serve to clear debts to foreign banks (Brazil, Argentina and other countries). So-called stabilisation currency credits issued by the International Monetary Fund, renowned for its pro-imperialist activity in Latin America, are used for this purpose.

Table 6 shows that the payments made by the Latin American countries to foreign, and above all U. S., capital

[8]The calculation is based on data in the *Estudio económico de América Latina*, 1964, vol. I, p. 63, tables 1–11; *Estudio económico de América Latina*, 1965, p. 171, tables 1–43.

have greatly increased in the last ten years. Today they absorb almost 30 per cent of the total currency receipts of Latin America, including the revenue from exports.

Politically, the U.S.A. and other imperialist Powers use the economic bondage of Latin American countries to exert pressure on the ruling circles and the local bourgeoisie of those coun-

Table 6. Payments to Foreign States as a Percentage of Total Current Receipts of Latin American Countries (excluding Cuba)*

Year	Profits from Direct Investments	Interest	Payments on Credits and Loans		Total Payments
			Clearing of Basic Debt	Clearing of Credits and Loans	
1951–1956	10.5	1.2	3.9	5.1	15.6
1956–1960	11.4	2.1	9.5	11.6	23.0
1961	11.0	3.3	14.3	17.6	28.6
1963*	10.0	3.2	15.3	18.5	28.5
1964**	10.5	3.5	12.6	16.1	26.6

*The calculation is based on data in the Estudio económico de América Latina (1964), Vol. 1, Chapter 1, p. 80, tables 1–18; Estudio económico de América Latina (1965), p. 197, tables 1–54.

**Estimates

The payments for profits on direct investments (in absolute figures) amounted in recent years to over $1,000 million on the average, the payments for interests on credits and loans—to $400 million; and payments for the basic debt on credits and loans —to $1,500 million. Thus, the total annual payments reach $3,000 million, which amounts to almost one third of the total value of Latin American exports. This sum by far exceeds the gains of the Latin American countries from new direct private investments and from new credits and loans.

The consequences of the enormous currency and financial dependence are tragic for the Latin American countries. Economically, this dependence forces them to intensify development of the traditional export branches, even though the extraction and export of raw materials in conditions of a falling market often run counter to national economic interests.

tries. Using methods of financial blackmail, these Powers intervene in the domestic affairs of the Latin American countries and make their social and economic efforts serve the ends of the imperialist Powers.

Table 6 also shows that the national-liberation struggle in Latin America is acquiring a new quality. Greater importance is attached to economic and social changes that will ensure a really independent national development.

The economic progress of the Latin American countries is seriously hampered by the constant interference of foreign imperialism and its tenacious efforts to keep Latin America's further development in check. Taking advantage of its vital needs, capitalising on the confidence or the selfish interests of some influential local groups and holding out promises of aid, the U.S. imperialists are striving to suppress or weaken the will of the Latin American peoples for freedom and independence. When they fail to succeed by means of financial and economic pressure, they resort to armed force.

The future of the bulk of the Latin American countries still hangs in the balance. An intense struggle is proceeding in all spheres of social political and economic life. Its outcome will largely depend on the active participation of the popular masses in the nation-wide movements, the unity of action of all democratic and patriotic forces, and the consistency of their programme for consolidating the economic basis of national independence.

29. Paths of Economic Development in the Countries of Latin America*

O. G. KLESMET

The question of the reasons for and the means of overcoming economic backwardness in the countries of Latin America preoccupies a majority of Latin American economists. Several monographs of the United Nations Economic Commission for Latin America have been written on the matter. The works of bourgeois writers generally reflect the opinions of the pro-American and conciliatory bourgeoisie of Latin America, and they have two points in common. First, they skirt the question of the social causes of Latin America's economic backwardness. They either pass over it in silence or they attempt to gloss over the fact that this backwardness is the consequence of imperialist domination and the systematic plundering of the peoples of Latin America by U.S. monopoly capital. Second, in considering the prospects for Latin America's further development, they set out from the premise that the Latin American countries are incapable of developing their economy independently with their own efforts and that they need the aid of the United States.

Latin Americans are told that they can reach a high level of economic development within the framework of the capitalist system, that the predominance of imperialism is no obstacle to attaining economic independence, and that the capitalist path of development can assure a high and steadily rising standard of living for the toiling masses.

Nevertheless, there are significant differences among bourgeois economists, and these reflect the increasingly

*"Voprosy ekonomicheskogo razvitiia stran Latinskoi Ameriki," in Ekonomicheskie problemy stran Latinskoi Ameriki, ed. V. Ia. Avarina and M. V. Danilevich (Moskva: Izdatel'stvo Akademii nauk SSSR, 1963), pp. 39–48.

sharp conflicts between imperialism and the national interests of Latin American countries. Even at present the antiquated theory of so-called comparative advantage or comparative costs of production is still current in Latin America. Supporters of this theory defend the present international division of labor among capitalist countries under which Latin America provides the industrially developed countries with raw materials and food. These theorists cite the fact that in this branch of production Latin America has the "comparative advantage," that is, it produces goods at comparatively lower costs. The Latin American countries, on the other hand, should permit the free import of manufactured goods, in the production of which the industrialized countries have a "comparative advantage." These economists assert that the Latin American countries should not build up their own industry, because their production costs would be higher than those of the industrially developed states.

This theory of "comparative advantage," as applied to under-developed countries, is directed at perpetuating their position as a raw-material appendage of the industrially developed capitalist countries. Yet, during recent decades, the steady deterioration of Latin American trade conditions (the price decline of export goods accompanied by a constant or even rising cost level of imported and industrial goods) serves as an obvious refutation of the theory of "comparative advantage," and points up its unsoundness.

This theory is advanced not only by U.S. monopolist groups that try to preserve Latin America as a consumer market but also by some Latin American economists and statesmen who represent the interests of some of the large landowners and the reactionary upper bourgeoisie connected with American capital. Among them is a group of Brazilian economists led by Professor Otavio Guveita de Bulhois, Eugenio Gudin, the former Minister of Finance in the reactionary government of Café Filho, and others. In arguing the necessity of intensifying the growth of agriculture—"the only sphere of economic activity in which we have shown ourselves capable of producing at a profit, that is, for export,"[1] Gudin definitely opposes the development of industry. To combat inflation he demands that capital investment be limited. His position coincides with the policy of the International Monetary Fund, which, in making "recommendations" for the economic "normalization" of certain Latin American states, requires first of all curtailment of capital investment in the economy of the country; in other words, halting its process of economic development.

A considerable segment of the Latin American ruling classes is becoming discontent with the worsening conditions of Latin American trade in the world capitalist market. In particular, this discontent was expressed in the theory of so-called peripheral economic development of the Argentine economist Raúl Prébisch. In essence, this is a refutation of the theory of "comparative advantage." In his work *Economic Development of Latin America and Its Basic Problems*, Prébisch critically analyzes the existing system of the international division of labor that has placed Latin America in an extremely unfavorable position.

He points out that, in the first place, Latin America's specialization in the production of raw materials and food for industrially developed countries has resulted in a lopsided development of

[1] A. da Cunha Xavier, "O Governo Atual e os Interêsses da Indústria Nacional," *Revista Brasiliense*, 35:47 (May–June 1961).

her economy. Second, as the result of steadily declining prices of raw materials and foods exported by Latin American countries, their export profit is systematically declining. Third, the cycles of boom and bust in industrial countries (Prébisch calls these countries "industrial centers") have repercussions in the "periphery" countries of Latin America. In this process the profits received by "periphery" countries from increased prices of the raw materials they export during boom periods do not compensate for the losses they suffer as a result of declining demand and lower prices during recession periods. Moreover, demand for Latin American export products increases very slowly, since, as a result of technical progress, raw materials are used more economically by the industrial countries, and many of them are being replaced by synthetic materials.

At first these assertions seem to be correct; however, they are centered on the superficial side of phenomena, and when it is a question of the reasons for this, the facts become entirely distorted. Prébisch points out that technical progress and increased labor productivity have occurred to a large degree in the manufacturing industry; consequently, prices of finished goods should have declined more than prices of raw materials. But this has not happened, presumably because wages have increased as the real cost of production in industrial countries has declined. The deduction one would make is that declining trade conditions in Latin American countries are caused both by technical progress and, chiefly, by the workers in the industrial countries, who presumably arrogate to themselves the advantages resulting from technical progress at the expense of the underdeveloped Latin American countries. Actually, the situation of the Latin American countries and under-developed countries in general with respect to trade with highly industrialized countries is deteriorating because the prices of raw materials furnished by the underdeveloped countries are dictated by monopolies, which also fix the high prices on finished goods they sell to those countries. By maintaining high prices at levels that exceed the value of the goods, the monopolies (and not the workers) appropriate the benefits of increased labor productivity and lower production cost.

Writing on the problem of industrialization in the Latin American countries, Prébisch has expressed the opinion that Latin America should develop her export branches of industry (i.e., production of raw materials) and the consumer goods branches, but not basic industrial production, which, as he has pointed out, should come into these countries in the form of foreign investments "within the framework of the general program of development."[2]

Meanwhile, in a number of Latin American countries, certain branches of heavy industry (even though in embryonic condition) have been developing at quite a fast rate for over ten years. Moreover, the demand for industrialization and development of national industry has become one of the slogans of the growing anti-imperialist national-liberation movement that is supported by the broad masses, including the national bourgeoisie.

Unable to halt the progress of historical development, the imperialists and the Latin American ruling classes allied with them strive to assure themselves key positions in this process. They no longer come out openly against industrializing the Latin American countries, but rather support the call for

[2]*Economic Development of Latin America and Its Principal Problems* (New York: ECLA, 1950), p. 58.

"industrialization," which would be under the control and would serve the interests of, and would enrich, the foreign monopolies and lead to an even greater subjugation of the Latin American economy. As they pursue these aims, they try to prove that the Latin American countries lack sufficient capital, technical knowledge, and cadres and thus are not in a position to industrialize with their own efforts. They need aid from industrially developed countries mainly in the form of private foreign investments and mainly from the United States. The Latin American countries must then attract foreign capital by creating "a favorable climate," that is, by granting various accommodations and advantages.

The conciliatory upper bourgeoisie holds the same viewpoint. Theoretically, this viewpoint is founded on the so-called theory of economic growth, which has gained fairly broad acceptance among Latin American bourgeois economists.

According to this theory, "economic growth" is understood as increased real per capita national income (a development rate that lags behind the rate of population increase is not acknowledged as economic growth). This theory, formed mainly in the 1930's, was later developed by some economists as it applied to underdeveloped countries. Its general purpose is to cast a veil over the contradictions of the capitalist mode of production and to create illusions with respect to the future development of capitalism. It completely ignores any connection between material production and production relations and sets out from the premise that all strata of the population are equally concerned with the results of economic growth. In reality, economic growth under modern capitalist domination means the strengthening of monopoly capital power. In the Latin American countries this growth is

accompanied by further penetration of foreign, chiefly American, monopolies. As applied to underdeveloped countries, the theory of "growth" ignores the plundering of these countries by foreign capital, the persistence of feudal remnants in the countryside, and so on.

The theory of "growth," as noted by the Secretary General of the Communist Party of Uruguay, Rodney Arismendi, "evades the study of Latin American social-economic structure, fails to take into account the existence of imperialist oppression and the latifundia, and reduces everything to the increase of the 'norms of production per capita of population,' representing this process as simple quantitative development of productive forces without destruction of the old production relations and ties."[3]

The theory of "growth" is also expressed in the works of the United Nations Economic Commission for Latin America (ECLA). Much stress is placed on calculations of production, conditions of trade, and so-called import capacity; but due attention is not given to the obvious, systematic siphoning from Latin America of newly created capital in the form of profits, dividends, and interest; and the increasing penetration of foreign capital into the most important branches of industry is almost completely ignored. The ECLA defends the constructive role of direct private foreign investments and sees the penetration of foreign capital into the Latin American economy as a desirable phenomenon.

A similar attitude underlies the policy of several Latin American governments who would "industrialize" at any cost, chiefly by attracting foreign capital by granting all kinds of privi-

[3]R. Arismendi, "Latinskaia Amerika vykhodit na avanstsenu," *Kommunist* (Moscow), 5:81 (1961).

leges that lead, in the long run, to further bondage and increased exploitation.

In attempting to answer the question of what could be the result of such an "industrializing" policy, certain Latin American economists assert that this policy does not in the least threaten further subservience for Latin America. Thus Brazilian economist Helio Jaguaribe writes that Brazil has reached a level of development where the "colonizing influence of foreign capital" can be reduced to a minimum by "regulating" it.[4] Another Brazilian economist, the president of the Department of Development of Northeast Brazil, Celso Furtado, believes that import of foreign capital in the form of patents and equipment is "the means for the speediest possible assimilation of technology," and that technological dependence will be overcome as industrial development increases.[5]

Increasing anti-American feeling, clearly expressed in popular demonstrations during the trips of U.S. statesmen to the Latin American countries and in the widespread movement in defense of revolutionary Cuba, is impelling the U.S. imperialists and their accomplices to use new propaganda methods. The new twist in their tactic is that, unable openly to defend North American imperialism, which has compromised itself sufficiently in the eyes of Latin America, they offer a critique of U.S. policy, while at the same time justifying the bases of imperialist expansion.

In this respect there are instructive statements in print by the former president of Costa Rica, José Figueres.[6] In his articles in the journal *Combate* in 1959 and 1960, Figueres hurls a series of reproaches at the United States. The United States, states Figueres, opposes the establishment of fair prices for the exports of "proletarian" (as he puts it) countries, which find it "difficult to save

and accumulate capital," and supports dictatorial regimes in Latin America. At this point, however, he comes to the defense of American imperialism by declaring that the intervention in Guatemala, organized by the United States, was a "defensive measure," and that in general the United States "is interested in avoiding imperialism" and that its foreign policy is "less imperialistic than that of any other power at any time in the past."

Figueres and Berle[7] assume the pose of defenders of the national interests of the Latin American countries. They even speak against direct private foreign investments in Latin America. "The continuing presence of foreign property . . . is a new form of colonialism," the authors exclaim. In their opinion, it is necessary "to facilitate the gradual transfer of foreign investments to local ownership," and also "to put political and moral restraint on the ruling classes." It would seem that a demand for nationalization of foreign companies would follow these rather radical statements. But not at all!

Additional "recommendations" by Figueres and Berle demand not infringement on the interests of foreign companies but, on the contrary, facilitation of their further penetration into the Latin American economy. Foreign companies should reinvest part of their

[4] H. Jaguaribe, *O nacionalismo na atualidade brasileira* (Rio de Janeiro, 1958), p. 212.

[5] C. Furtado, *Perspectivas de economia brasileira* (Rio de Janeiro, 1958), p. 51.

[6] J. Figueres, "La América de hoy," *Combate*, 7:11 (July–August 1959).

[7] J. Figueres and A. A. Berle, "Países ricos y países pobres," *Combate*, 11:11 (July–August 1960). It is significant that the second article is a rendition of the report given by Figueres, jointly with the former U.S. Assistant Secretary of State for Latin American Affairs, Adolf Berle, Jr., to the Second Inter-American Conference for Democracy and Freedom held in April 1960, in Caracas. Such "collaboration" of a Latin American political figure with a champion of Washington policy needs no comment.

profits and thus "serve the development of the country."

Figueres and Berle further recommend that Latin American governments "encourage the purchase of foreign enterprise shares by local private parties and by such organizations as pension funds, social security, and other national institutions," in other words, transferring to foreign (more correctly, North American) monopolies the funds accumulated by deductions from workers' and employees' wages, that is, to finance the exploiters at the expense of the exploited.

Demands for limiting the activities of foreign capital and for stopping its further penetration into the economy are being voiced ever louder in Latin America. These demands are also being made by the national bourgeoisie, which is suffering defeat in its competition with foreign companies.

It is interesting in this connection to note the viewpoint of Raúl Prébisch, director of the Latin American Institute for Economic and Social Planning, who undoubtedly influences the various projects of the ECLA. In 1949 Prébisch advocated expanding the role of Latin America as supplier of raw materials to the United States; a little over ten years later he points out the need for industrializing Latin America and remarks with alarm that private national enterprises "are in an unfavorable situation as they try to resist private competition." As a result, "enterprises that originally were national property have now fallen into foreigners' hands."[8] Prébisch immediately adds that he does not oppose the influx of private foreign capital but that the Latin American countries first of all need loans from government or international credit institutions for reinforcing the private capitalist sector. This, of course, means the United States and the International Bank for Reconstruction and Development, the International Monetary Fund,

and the Inter-American Development Bank, all of which the United States controls.

In advocating expanded "aid" from the United States to private—and not state—enterprises, Prébisch in essence is approving the U.S. policy of financing private national enterprises in Latin America. The United States expects in this manner to expand its base of social acceptance in the face of the growing national-liberation movement, to link itself more firmly to the developing economies of Latin America, and to obtain new concessions from the governments of these countries. These loans and credits are also used to finance enterprises controlled by U.S. monopolies, which operate behind the label of national firms.

Secretary General of the Communist Party of Chile Luis Corvalán noted in his report to the Twelfth Party Congress in March 1962 that "obtaining new loans leads into a vicious circle because new loans bring higher interest payments."[9] It is well known, Corvalán says, that "American loans bring no advantages to Chile but on the contrary are a way of getting profits for foreign investors and a tool for pressure and interference in domestic affairs."[10]

Many bourgeois economists view Latin America as a U.S. appendage that in the future may develop only with U.S. "aid" in one form or another. Thus they emphasize the dependence of the Latin American countries on the United States and their inability to overcome economic backwardness by means of their own resources. These bourgeois economists generate a lack of faith in the creative forces of the Latin American countries.

[8] R. Prébisch, "Producir i vivir dependen de Latinoamérica," *Combate*, 14:28 (January–February 1961)
[9] *Cuba Socialista*, June 1962.
[10] *Ibid.*

Different views on the matter of the paths and possibilities for Latin America's economic development are advocated by Latin American economists who represent the progressive elements of society, including the national bourgeoisie. The economists of this school are characterized by their anti-American orientation and a negative attitude toward direct foreign capital investments. They recognize the need for freeing Latin America's economic and political life from the predominant influence of the United States, for discovering a force that could help them become free of this influence, and for understanding the great role that the USSR and other socialist countries can play in this respect.

Brazilian economist Aristotle Moura writes that Brazil must not force her raw material exports on the United States,[11] since this would increase her dependence on the United States. Brazil must search for other markets, particularly in the socialist countries.

Chilean economist Alberto Baltra Cortés writes that the Latin American countries should stop exporting raw materials, and that they should process these materials themselves. Industrialization should be achieved not by attracting private foreign capital, but by mobilizing national resources.[12]

Industrialization in itself does not assure economic independence, writes Venezuelan economist Salvador de la Plaza.[13] If an underdeveloped country industrializes by using imperialist capital, this can lead to the greater subjugation of the underdeveloped country by the imperialist power. The decisive factor is not the existence of natural resources and skilled labor, but rather who controls the capital in the long run. If the product of labor is siphoned off by foreign investors in the form of profits, dividends, and interest, the accumulation of national capital for independent economic development becomes impossible.

[11]A. Moura, *Inostrannyi kapital v Brazilii,* IL, 1961.

[12]A. B. Baltra Cortés, *Crecimiento económico de América Latina* (Santiago de Chile, 1959), pp. 74, 144.

[13]S. de la Plaza, *Estructuras de integración nacional* (Caracas, 1959), p. 23.

30. Capitalistic Sources for Financing Economic Development in Latin America[*]

O. G. KLESMET

The problem of financing—that is, mobilizing and distributing funds to assure expanding production—is of primary importance to the Latin American and all underdeveloped nations. The future structure of the Latin American economies, their rate of development, and consequently their future position in the international division of labor will be determined by whether internal or external sources (foreign loans, direct private foreign investments) provide the means of financing and to which branches of the economy these means are allocated.

It is obvious that mobilizing domestic financial resources and distributing them among the branches of economy that are vitally important for the country, as well as receiving aid from the socialist countries, facilitate attainment of economic independence. On the other hand, an influx of foreign capital from imperialist countries (especially in the form of direct private investments), usually in the interest of monopolies, perpetuates the role of the Latin American countries as suppliers of raw materials and increases their dependence on imperialism.

The opportunities for domestic financing are determined by the extent of capital accumulation, that is, the size of that share of newly created wealth which can be converted into productive capital. Under conditions of exploitation by large imperialistic monopolies that make tremendous profits, the accumulation of capital for economic development becomes exceedingly difficult for the Latin American countries. They are compelled to make huge annual payments to foreign monopoly capital, returning a considerable part of foreign currency receipts (mainly earnings on exports) in transfer of profits, dividends, interest payments, costs of patents and licenses, and so on. Foreign currency is particularly important for the Latin American countries, since it allows them to import machinery, equipment, and those raw materials and semimanufactured goods that Latin America does not produce.

The situation is further complicated by the fact that currency receipts from exports are subject to very intense price fluctuations in the world market. This fact, as well as the constant deteriora-

*"Voprosy ekonomicheskogo razvitiia stran Latinskoi Ameriki," in *Ekonomicheskie problemy stran Latinskoi Ameriki*, ed. V. Ia. Avarina and M. V. Danilevich (Moskva: Izdatel'stvo Akademii nauk SSSR, 1963), pp. 49–50, 56–59.

tion of trade conditions and the systematic siphoning off of foreign currency, greatly limits the opportunities to use export earnings for the expansion of production. Quite often foreign currency is used to import luxuries and also to purchase foodstuffs and other consumer goods that easily could have been produced domestically. All this reduces the capacity to accumulate capital. Capital accumulation is also hampered by a low level of labor productivity.

When speaking of insufficient capital accumulation in the Latin American countries, various bourgeois economists point out that to accelerate accumulation by curtailing consumption does not seem possible, because per capita national income is very low. This argument is customarily used to prove the necessity of attracting foreign capital. It is a fact that per capita income in Latin America is extremely low. But it must be remembered that average figures conceal to a great extent the exceedingly unequal distribution of income among various classes. The overwhelming majority of Latin America's population ekes out a half-starved, beggarly existence while a small group of capitalists and landlords have enormous incomes.

The extent of self-financing may be estimated only in the case of joint stock companies, which are required to publish their accounts. In Brazil an annual summary of stock companies' business is published from announced profit-and-loss statements. Data from 7,104 stock companies for 1959—of which 3,657 were industrial—and 5,587 stock companies for 1960—2,642 of them industrial—in various branches of the economy (manufacturing, transportation, commerce, banks) allow one to conclude that an exceedingly high profit rate exists in Brazilian business. Profits of industrial companies in 1959 amounted to 26.1 percent of invested

capital; in 1960, to 27.7 percent (in trade, correspondingly, 24.8 percent and 25.4 percent).

A large portion of the industrial profit was retained by the enterprises: 72.2 percent in 1959 and 73.7 percent in 1960;[1] 63.6 percent of all investments made in 1960 by these industrial companies from their own resources was reinvested. Net investments of capital in 1960[2] were made at the expense of reserves and undistributed profits (30 percent), new issues of stock (22 percent),[3] and borrowed funds (38 percent).

As indicated above, one of the ways to stimulate the reinvestment of profits is to free from taxation completely or partially that portion of profits not distributed among shareholders and stock owners. In Mexico about 20 percent of the reinvested profits of industrial and agricultural enterprises are exempted from the 15-percent tax on profits, while enterprises that use accumulated reserves to increase basic capital are entirely free of the 15-percent tax. Moreover, some medium-term bank loans are granted to companies on condition that they pledge not to distribute dividends during the term of the loan.

To obtain this kind of tax relief in Chile, companies must present proof to the financial authorities that undistributed profits have actually been used for reinvestment.[4]

The greatest portion of investment (about 75 percent) is in the private sector (including foreign capital) and is attributable to the profit motive. One consequence is the disproportionate

---

[1]*Conjuntura Económica*, February 1961, pp. 131, 135; February 1962, pp. 152, 154.

[2]*Ibid.*, February 1962, p. 135.

[3]A new issue of stock does not always reflect an actual increase in capital but is often due to watering.

[4]*Economic Survey of Latin America, 1955* (New York: UN 1956), p. 150.

development of production and the preponderance of those branches that
assure fast capital turnover and high
profit rates; another result is the presence of surplus production in some
branches and unused capacities or insufficient development in others.

The under-capitalized industrial bourgeoisie of Latin America is unable by
itself to assure the building of expensive
up-to-date enterprises that could resist foreign competition. Latin American industry is faced by powerful imperialist monopolies that possess large
amounts of capital, a great deal of technical experience and qualified technical
and administrative cadres. The Latin
American industrial bourgeoisie, while
it agrees to collaborate with foreign
companies through the organizing of
"joint companies," is at the same time
concerned with strengthening its own
economic base, and thus seeks assistance from the state.

The average proportion of state investments in the economy for all Latin
America during 1950–1956 was somewhat over 25 percent. The remaining
75 percent was private, including foreign capital investment. The situation
varies greatly from country to country.
Not all state investments represent an
actual increase in material value.
Some data on these investments reflect transfers of private enterprises
to the state with payment of compensation; the transfers appear as new
capital investments, although they are
actually payment for obsolete, long-
amortized property, such as the railways purchased in Argentina and Brazil after World War II.

State investments come not only from
national but also from foreign capital:
intergovernment loans, loans from international financial organizations, and
loans from private banks. These loans
are granted to Latin American governments and used either directly by them
or for financing private enterprises
through state credit establishments.

It must once again be emphasized
that one of the main obstacles to rapid
accumulation of capital in Latin America is the systematic siphoning off of
an important part of newly created
value through the transfer of profits
and dividends, lowering of prices of
exported raw materials, and other measures. The increase of foreign monopoly profits is further enhanced by the
Latin American governments' policy
of attracting foreign capital by granting numerous privileges: tax and tariff
relief, huge state loans, lowered railway tariffs, and the sale of low-cost
electric power from state power plants
to foreign electric power enterprises
that resell it to consumers at higher
prices (as in Brazil and, until 1959, in
Mexico). Essentially, these privileges
make it possible for foreign capital to
acquire an additional portion of the
national income of the Latin American
countries.

One of the primary tasks of the Latin
American countries is to mobilize the
resources that assure economic development. An important step in this
direction would be such measures as
the prohibition of luxury imports and
the substitution of local products for
imported goods. However, as long as
the systematic bloodletting of the Latin
American economy continues in the
form of the exporting of profits by
foreign companies, it is difficult to see
how the Latin American countries can
increase their capital accumulation to
any considerable extent and thereby materially accelerate their rate of economic development.

31. The Attitude of the Latin American Economic Classes toward State Capitalism*

I. K. SHEREMET'EV

State capitalism has now become an important economic force in the Latin American countries. In Brazil, Mexico, Argentina, Chile, Uruguay, and several other countries, the state holds a number of economically important, commanding positions that could be used under certain conditions as effective means for transforming the national economy. Determining who controls these commanding positions, therefore, becomes extremely important, that is, which class and political forces should control and determine the activity of the state apparatus and its economic organs. The class that holds power determines whether state capitalism will develop along a course of limiting and expelling foreign capital from the nation's economy, thus developing productive forces and strengthening the economic independence of the Latin American countries, or whether the country's development will take the course of adapting the activity of state economic organizations and enterprises to the interests of foreign and domestic monopoly capital. The class in power also determines the foreign or domestic sources and the classes and social groups that will contribute to the development of the state sector and of the national economy.

To understand the essence of the acute and complex class struggle that is being waged about state economic policy and that ultimately determines the degree of its effectiveness in defending Latin American national interests, it is necessary to examine the causes and motives that impel the different classes to act in support of state capitalism. This examination also enables us to form an opinion on certain common interests of democratic forces and certain local bourgeois circles in the development of the national economy.

STATE CAPITALISM AND THE NATIONAL BOURGEOISIE

The economic dependence of Latin America on foreign monopolies causes important difficulties in the development of national capital. These foreign monopolies make a tremendous effort to preserve the unnatural, lopsided character of the economy of the Latin American countries. This results in making the generation of national capital in these nations exceedingly

*Ekonomicheskie problemy stran Latinskoi Ameriki, ed. V. Ia. Avarina and M. V. Danilevich (Moskva: Izdatel'stvo Akademii nauk SSSR, 1963), pp. 398–401, 404–408.

dependent on the unstable condition of the foreign capitalist market. Even insignificant fluctuations of demand or prices on the world market seriously affect the economic, currency, and financial conditions of these countries, the level of the so-called business activity, and the speed with which national capital can be accumulated. When the economic situation of the basic exports of the Latin American countries fluctuates more seriously, during crises in the main capitalist countries, their economies frequently suffer near-collapse. Many national enterprises, particularly the small and middle-sized ones, are forced to cut back production or stop work completely.

By infiltrating the Latin American economy and developing the export branches of the countries' economies, foreign capital hampers in every possible manner the growth of domestic heavy industry, which furnishes the means of producing national capital. The lack of domestically produced machinery and equipment is particularly felt today, when development of national capital in Latin America has made significant progress and the need for means of production and industrial equipment has increased. However, satisfying these demands by means of imports is becoming increasingly difficult because of foreign exchange problems and sometimes even because of the sabotage of equipment deliveries by foreign companies.

Having infiltrated the mining industry of Latin America, foreign monopolies hamper the access of national capital to sources of raw material and power. They also slow down the development of domestic transport. Monopolies limit the opportunities for investing national capital in more advantageous areas of activity. And, finally, using its privilege as the stronger partner, foreign capital appropriates an important share of the excess value created by the Latin American workers, thereby reducing national capital's share of the profits and limiting opportunities for its accumulation.

The economic interests of the Latin American bourgeoisie clash with the interests of foreign monopolies. This conflict is the basic cause of the anti-imperialist feelings among a certain part of the domestic bourgeoisie. This same conflict also causes the national bourgeoisie to ask the state for financial economic support and to demand that the state as the "representative of national interests" (but actually the representative of the governing bourgeois landlord classes) should take measures to eliminate certain of the more onerous consequences of the dominance of foreign capital in the national economy.

The growing tendency of the Latin American bourgeoisie to use the state and its treasury as a means of eliminating certain obstacles to the development of the national economy does not mean that there is full unity of opinions and interests among the different bourgeois groups on questions of developing state capitalism. The lower and middle bourgeoisie, being most sensitive to those "inconveniences" which foreign monopolies create by having their way in the national economy, take a more radical stand on the question of limiting the activity of these monopolies, as well as on the question of the methods, forms, and limits of state interference in the economy.

The upper bourgeoisie, which enjoys much greater financial economic power and has some support from foreign capital, however, tends to define and limit state participation in the economic development of their countries as much as possible. Extracting as it does large profits from certain individual state capitalist measures, the bourgeoisie also prevents in every way the realization of any radical reforms that might really aid a more rapid and independent development of the national economy. It tries to neutralize as much as possible the anti-imperialist trend of state capitalism and to convert it from a means of defending the genuine national interest to a means of reconciling its own narrow class interests with those of foreign capital at the expense of the workers and other weaker groups of the domestic bourgeoisie.

STATE CAPITALISM AND THE DEMOCRATIC FORCES OF LATIN AMERICA

The increasing penetration of the Latin American economies by foreign capital, and attempts by foreign monopolies to subjugate to their own interests all state-run activity, lend even greater significance to the struggle of the democratic and patriotic forces to achieve a course of development for state capitalism in Latin America that will be consistently progressive and anti-imperialist. This struggle is now considerably abetted by the fact that the Communist and labor parties of Latin America (and even of other economically underdeveloped countries outside Latin America) have taken a proletariat-defined attitude toward state capitalism.

State capitalism is a complex socioeconomic and political phenomenon. It is a higher form of organizing public production than private-economy capitalism. Even with the bourgeoisie politically predominant, and without impinging on the foundations of private capitalist property, state capitalism still affords greater freedom for developing the productive forces of the Latin American nations than does private-enterprise economy. This is confirmed by the now well-known data on the more rapid growth of those branches of Latin American production that are

in the state sector, for example, the oil, electric power, and iron and steel industries.

The progressive role of state capitalism in national economic development is especially apparent where its development is accompanied by elimination of the foreign imperialist hegemony in the corresponding spheres of the national economy. On this aspect of state capitalism, the Mexican Communist Party declares that state capitalism "on the whole, plays a progressive part, since it is expressed in nationalization of foreign property and since it is a step forward in comparison with private economy capitalism."[1] However, both the Mexican Communist Party and the Communist parties of other Latin American countries are far from exaggerating the progressive role of state capitalism in the modern economic and political conditions prevailing in most Latin American countries. These conditions are characterized by intensive penetration of foreign capital and subordination of the state apparatus to the interests of the reactionary upper bourgeoisie. The Mexican Communist Party flatly asserts that state capitalism is not independent of foreign monopolies and that often "state enterprises are formed in order to facilitate the conditions for the operation of private enterprises, foreign as well as Mexican; they are used to considerably increase the profits of Mexican and foreign capitalists."[2]

The democratic and patriotic forces of Latin American countries are waging a relentless struggle against the basic evil of this phenomenon—the dependence of state capitalism on foreign monopolies and on powerful domestic capital. This dependence makes it difficult to use state capitalism as an effective means of strengthening and

[1] *La Voz de México*, June 15, 1961.
[2] *Ibid.*

developing the national economy and of reducing its dependence on foreign imperialist powers.

It is not accidental, therefore, that one of the most important economic and political demands of the Communist and labor parties of Latin America is their call for nationalizing all key branches of the economy that have been seized by foreign monopolies. A draft program of the Communist Party of Argentina provides for expropriation without compensation and for nationalization of foreign capital and facilities in oil, meat packing, metallurgy, mining, and several other branches of the economy. At the same time this program emphasizes that there would be no expropriation of foreign capital that might aid in the independent development of the national economy under Argentine law. It also proposes nationalization of foreign banks and insurance companies, taking into account, however, the interests of private organizations and persons whose money is deposited there. Bank capital would be invested in branches of industry that are important in developing the national economy. The program further states that exporting and importing would be conducted directly by the democratic state or by cooperative or private organizations under its control. The Communist parties of Mexico, Chile, Brazil, and other Latin American countries also favor the nationalization of enterprises and companies belonging to foreign monopoly capital. These demands are the basis for the formation of a broad democratic front of national liberation.

The working class and other democratic forces of Latin America also attribute great importance to the question of sources for financing state capitalist measures.

It is known that the ruling circles of the Latin American countries, guided as they are by the interests of big national capital, engage in a financial economic policy that places the burden of intensified national economic development on the shoulders of the poorest strata of the population. The principal method of realizing such a policy is direct taxation of workers, along with deficit-budget financing of state expenditures with its contingent inflation. However, since the opportunities for an overt offensive by state capital against the living standards of the people through increased taxes are limited by exceedingly low personal incomes, the bourgeois governments of these countries are attempting to make extensive use of a second method, that of mass redistribution of national income in favor of the state and the governing classes.

Such a policy is justified by bourgeois economists and statesmen by references to a "shortage" of capital and to the "financial poverty" of Latin American countries. The untenable nature of these arguments is obvious. It is a known fact that the Latin American nations are characterized by a tremendous inequality in the distribution of national income. The meager incomes of the overwhelming majority of working people exist side by side with the fabulous incomes of the landed oligarchy, a multitude of usurers, big merchants and financiers. Only a pittance of the immense amounts of money concentrated in the hands of these exploiter groups is used to expand production; the vast majority is used for speculation and parasitic consumption.

By the introduction of just one radical tax reform it would be possible to solve to a great extent the problem of the so-called shortage of capital and to give the state considerable additional means to develop the national economy.

All economic aspects of the state capitalism problem in Latin America are indissolubly linked to the important political aspect. By political aspect we mean that the further development and reconstruction of the economic activity of the state—as applied to the true national interests of the Latin American countries—presupposes a struggle for democratizing both the political life in these countries and the entire state apparatus. The significance of this aspect of the problem of state capitalism in economically retarded countries is stressed in the following statement of the Moscow Conference of Representatives of Communist and Labor Parties, of November 1960: "Especially important in these countries is the formation and expansion on democratic bases of the state sector of the national economy—especially in industry—a state sector that is independent of foreign monopolies and consequently becomes the determining factor in the economy of the country."[3]

The state sector and the various forms of state control over economic life already practiced in the Latin American countries are powerful levers for exerting pressure on the national economies. Presently these levers are in most instances little used in the interests of the socioeconomic progress of these nations. Real opportunities for decisive and consistent use of the state sector and for state intervention in economic affairs—in the interests of strengthening and developing the national economy, freeing the economy from imperialist plunder, and raising the living standards of the masses—are possible only under conditions of a genuine popular democratic state guided by the interests of the nation's majority instead of by a handful of powerful exploiters.

[3]*Programmnye dokumenty bor'by za mir, demokratiiu i sotsializm* (Moskva: Gospolitizdat, 1961), p. 66.

32. The Tempo of Industrial Growth and General Structure of Manufacturing in Contemporary Latin America*

O. G. KLESMET

Considering Latin America as a whole, the following characteristics of industrial development may be noted. Food and textile production predominate in the manufacturing industry. According to 1955 data, the relative value of production of individual branches of manufacturing among the ten largest produ-

cers of Latin America was as follows:[1]

*"Razvitie obrabatyvaiushchei promyshlennosti," in *Ekonomicheskie problemy stran Latinskoi Ameriki*, ed. V. Ia. Avarina and M. V. Danilevich (Moskva: Izdatel'stvo Akademii nauk SSSR, 1963), pp. 163–165, 212–214.

[1]*Economic Survey of Latin America, 1955* (New York: ECLA, 1956), p. 60.

Food products, beverages, and
    tobacco............... 34 percent
Textiles................. 16 percent
Metallurgical and machine
    tools................. 15 percent
Chemical and pharmaceutical
    products.............. 6 percent
Footwear and clothing.... 7 percent
Rubber.................. 2 percent
Cement, glass, ceramics... 4 percent
Other branches...........16 percent

Shifts have taken place in the structure of the manufacturing industry in individual Latin American countries. In the more economically developed countries, the relative size of the metallurgical, machine tool, and chemical industries has increased, but foods and textiles have retained the lead.

Total industrial production in the Latin American countries increased in 1960 to twice that of 1948; this includes production in the mining industry, which increased by 105 percent (mainly because of a 113-percent increase in production of oil), and production in the manufacturing industry, which increased by 100 percent. The average yearly increase of industrial growth in the Latin American countries in the years from 1948 to 1959 was 4.9 percent, which includes 6.1 percent for mining and 4.7 percent for manufacturing.

Latin America is outstripping the United States in its rate of industrial development. However, this rate cannot be judged as satisfactory when we consider that the underdeveloped Latin American countries are far behind the industrially developed countries in their absolute production levels, and that it is precisely their rate of economic progress that is important for them. While the general growth of production in Latin America is slow, heavy industry is progressing at a somewhat more rapid rate than light industry.

The industrial development of Latin American countries is adversely affected by their heavy dependence on imported fuel, many raw materials (mainly industrial), semimanufactured goods, and various kinds of machinery and equipment.[2] The inability to equip national industry from internal resources, and the chronic shortage of foreign currency for buying machinery and equipment abroad, help explain the low value of Latin American capital. This also explains the severe lag in labor productivity and the small cadres of skilled workers, engineers, and technicians.

Of the total amount invested in machinery and equipment from 1954 through 1956, the proportion of investments in Latin American–produced equipment was as follows:[3] agriculture, 17 percent; industry, 5.3 percent; transport, 13.0 percent; average for all other branches, 9.0 percent.

In Mexico, there is a relatively high proportion of private capital investment in domestic production; yet, even this amounts to less than 50 percent (not including construction costs):[4] in 1953, it was 46 percent; in 1954, 45 percent; in 1955, 38 percent; in 1956, 39 percent; in 1957, 40 percent; and in 1958, 43 percent. The proportion in Chile is very insignificant: 7.2 percent in 1954, 6.1 percent in 1955, 6.3 percent in 1956, and 6.4 percent in 1957.[5]

While mentioning the dependence of

[2]An important share of raw materials and semimanufactured goods could well be produced by these countries at home (e.g., many chemical products, caustic and carbonate soda, sulphuric acid, pulp, cellulose, superphosphates, petrochemicals, primary aluminum).
[3]Computed from *La influencia del mercado común* (Panamá, 1959), p. 48.
[4]For the period 1953–1957, *Revista de Economía*, 5:156 (June 15, 1958); for 1958, *Three-monthly Economic Review, Mexico*, May 1959, p. 8.
[5]*Economic Survey of Latin America, 1957*, Santiago de Chile: 1958) UN, Mimeographed edition, Part 2, p. 271.

Latin American countries on the import of raw materials, and principally on machinery and equipment, we should not fail to point out certain facts that contradict the thesis advanced by apologists of American imperialism—namely, that the Latin American countries are allegedly incapable of organizing industrial production by their own efforts and that this task must be assumed by foreign private capital.

In a number of cases, it was precisely national capital that created new industries, which foreign monopolies then infiltrated when production had already been somewhat organized and had become profitable. Foreign monopolies with greater economic power then either crowded out the local producers or assigned them roles of voteless "junior partners." For example, the foundations of the automobile industry in Argentina and Brazil were laid by national enterprises organized and controlled by the state (DINFIA in Argentina and Fabrica Nacional de Motores in Brazil). During the Second World War national industrialists alone started production of automobile parts and primary aluminum in Brazil, and of synthetic fibers in Mexico.[6] Subsequently, these undertakings were crowded out by American monopolies that built sister enterprises on these original foundations. The production growth of state-owned automobile works in Argentina (one plant) and in Brazil (one plant) is hampered by the competition of foreign firms that have gained a foothold in these countries.

On the basis of the above data, the following conclusions can be made regarding industrial progress in Latin America:

1. Development of industry in Latin American countries takes place to a great extent on other than an independent basis. Imperialist monopolies that occupy commanding positions in the world market have seized important positions in the economy of the Latin American countries, have subjugated them to their influence, and are attempting to direct the economic development of these countries in accordance with their own interests.

2. Many of the presently exploited sources of mineral wealth, including the richest oil fields, are in the hands of foreign monopolies, chiefly American. The major quantity of ore is exported raw or after only preliminary processing and so does not help in developing the Latin American countries' own industry. Measures taken by several Latin American governments to protect their national resources are of a partial, halfway character and therefore insufficiently effective. Cuba alone has put an end to the exploitation of her natural wealth, by carrying out nationalization of foreign enterprises.

3. During the postwar years some progress was made in the more economically advanced Latin American countries (Argentina, Brazil, Mexico, Chile) by such branches of heavy industry as ferrous and nonferrous metallurgy, railway-car building, tractors, electronics, chemicals, certain kinds of machinery, and lathes. Nevertheless, these countries depend on importation of machinery, equipment, and many industrial materials (chemicals, plastics, primary aluminum, steel, nonferrous metals).

4. National capital in the extractive and manufacturing industries is represented mainly by many small and medium-size enterprises. However, there also exist large local monopoly groups that maintain close ties with foreign capital along lines of joint participation in industrial undertakings. Most new industrial branches are dependent on foreign companies to a very great extent not only for investments but also for production technology.

[6]S. A. Mosk, *Industrial Revolution in Mexico* (Berkeley and Los Angeles, 1950), p. 236.

5. Industrial development in the Latin American countries is accompanied by infiltration of foreign capital, primarily North American, in important new branches. As a rule, large plants in key branches are under the control of foreign capital. Such industrial progress is considerably aided by the policy of Latin American ruling circles that grant easements in taxation, custom tariffs, and currency exchange to foreign companies that will establish enterprises in certain branches. This kind of industrial development cannot secure economic independence for the Latin American countries. On the contrary, it leads to increasing the exploitation of workers by foreign monopolies and enables the latter to have decisive influence on the whole industrial structure; it limits the field of action for national capital and leads to still further siphoning of profits from Latin America.

6. The Latin American countries face the task of building a durable industrial base capable of assuring free development of the national economy. Democratic and progressive opinion in the Latin American countries demands the complete liquidation of the economic base of imperialism, that is, nationalization of the natural wealth that has been appropriated by foreign monopolies and of the industrial enterprises controlled by them. Only in this way is it possible for the Latin American countries to lay a foundation for the free development of their economy. Carrying out these tasks under democratic political conditions will assure accelerated economic progress, social progress, and improved living standards for the popular masses. The existence of a powerful socialist camp that is always ready to extend disinterested aid to underdeveloped countries greatly facilitates the achievement of this goal.

33. The Faults of Latin American Economic Integration under Capitalism and Why the Latin American Bourgeoisie Supports the Common Market Idea*

Z. I. ROMANOVA

Economic integration is one of the most important processes of today, not only for the advanced capitalist countries, but also for the countries of Latin America. It is a part of official policy of the majority of the Latin American countries.

*Problemy ekonomicheskoi integratsii v Latinskoi Amerike (Moskva: Izdatel'stvo Nauka, 1965), pp. 243–250.

The growth of the industrial bourgeoisie, the increasing concentration of production and centralization of capital, and the expanded scope of present business enterprises form the material base for integration. Its political aim is to strengthen the capitalist economic system in Latin America and to resist the growth of the national-liberation movement. In struggling to preserve the capitalist foundations in Latin America, the bourgeoisie is trying in every way to retard and undermine the revolutionary process and to confront it with a united front of domestic and foreign big capital. It is not by accident that the establishment of a "common market" in Central America is being accompanied by military-political measures.

The peculiar feature of economic integration in Latin America is that it represents predominantly a development of capitalism in breadth, that is, an expansion of the sphere of capitalist production to new territories, concomitant with a relatively weaker development of capitalism in depth, that is, a growth of capitalist production in a given territory.

An intense struggle has broken out within the framework of economic blocs among different strata of the bourgeoisie in Latin America about the interpretation of the essence of integration, the concrete definitions of its aims and tasks, and its political orientation.

The upper bourgeoisie—especially the bourgeoisie with monopolistic tendencies—regards economic integration simply as a means for an abstract growth of production and trade. The Latin American bourgeoisie secretly aims to force its way into the ranks of the international financial oligarchy and to become a full-fledged member. To achieve this end, all means are acceptable; it can and must form an alliance with foreign capital.

The middle bourgeoisie has its own interpretation of economic integration, perceiving it as a means of strengthening its own position in the Latin American market and as a defensive measure against the inroads of foreign imperialism. The national middle bourgeoisie would like to make use of the established alliances to expand national industry and to increase the national intrazonal transport system. At present, however, the middle bourgeoisie does not play a leading or decisive role in the integration structures. It finds itself compelled to follow the lead of the upper, conciliatory, and proimperialist bourgeoisie.

It should be noted that in the early 1960's the growth rate of industry was relatively high in Brazil, Mexico, and Colombia, and partially in Chile. It was especially high in Brazil, reaching 10 percent in some years. This comparatively high industrial index had its effect on the position of both the middle and the petty bourgeoisie, which together form the nucleus of the national bourgeoisie, and planted in the latter the illusion of the possibility of independent development. Under conditions of industrial growth, the national bourgeoisie expected to strengthen its own position. This assumption explains why the national bourgeoisie initially accepted economic integration rather cheerfully. But, as it became more evident that economic integration in the form in which it was being introduced in Latin America could not ensure relatively high rates of industrial growth, the attitude of the national bourgeoisie became ever more guarded. Its criticism was aroused particularly by the clear realization that integration would bring an unprecedented intensification of competition with big capital, primarily of powerful foreign enterprises.

The Latin American bourgeoisie is united in purpose only concerning the formulation of the overall aim of economic integration, namely, strengthening capitalist forms of economic management, keeping the countries of Latin America "on the side of the West," and preventing the emergence of socialist methods of economic development.

The results of integration, which are more than modest, compel the national bourgeoisie to seek some other trade reforms and to inject a still broader meaning into economic integration. The ideologists of the national bourgeoisie understand objectively that the "common market" cannot resolve the complex economic problems confronting Latin America. Thus, in the opinion of Alberto Baltra Cortés, "structural reforms constitute a necessary preliminary condition for the establishment of a common market. Without them, the regional market cannot resolve the basic problems that threaten and worry the peoples of Latin America."[1]

A lowering of customs barriers leads inevitably to the acceleration of competition. As a result, industrial establishments that experience the effect of intensified competitive struggle strive to lower the costs of production. This decrease, however, is accomplished chiefly by a reduction in wages. Economic integration does not promise to alleviate the toiling masses' condition. Even now it entails grave economic consequences for many groups of toilers, primarily, the working class. Even the urban middle strata are beginning to suffer its consequences.

Economic integration calls for new forms of class struggle. The majority of agreements concluded within the system of economic integration are intergovernmental in character and their conclusions often are preceded by a broad public discussion. The significance of the class struggle is increasing. At the same time, the struggle against big capital and the economic integration being implemented by it transcends the national framework and acquires an international character. The unity of action of labor forces—primarily, trade-

union organizations—is beginning to play an especially big role. Within the framework of economic integration, the united action of the workers must become a barrier to the offensive unleashed against their living standard. International proletarian solidarity will be the primary force capable of withstanding the consolidation of big capital.

The present forms of economic integration in Latin America have been determined by economic, political, and military factors in the development of capitalism at the new stage of its general crisis. In Latin America the following objective natural factors promote economic rapprochement: strengthening of the wealthy bourgeoisie, development of productive forces, expansion of economic territories, transcendence of national boundaries, and acute aggravation of the marketing problem. Capitalist integration, however, is unable to do away with the economic and political, class and national, internal and external contradictions in the capitalist economy.

The hopelessness of either solving or reducing the existing contradictions impels the upper bourgeoisie to transfer the center of its interest to the external economic sphere. In the opinion of the American economist J. Viner, "many people see at least a partial solution of major economic and political problems in the international field."[2] The old bourgeois slogan of so-called free trade, around which bitter arguments had revolved in the last century, has now been revived.

The question of two basic orientations in foreign trade policy—protectionism and free trade—is not new. In themselves, these orientations are not dia-

[1]Alberto Baltra Cortés, *Ekonomicheskoe razvitie Latinskoi Ameriki* (Moskva, 1963), p. 310.
[2]J. Viner, *The Customs Union Issue* (New York, 1960), p. 3.

metrically opposed. V.I. Lenin pointed out that "the question of protectionism and free trade is a matter *between* enterprise owners—sometimes between owners in different countries, sometimes between different factions of enterprise owners in the same country."[3] In Latin America, the industrial bourgeoisie traditionally has acted as an advocate of protectionism. It has tried to defend itself against disastrous foreign competition by means of a customs tariff system. Protectionism has helped the national bourgeoisie resist foreign monopolies and gain strength against them.

Characteristically, U.S. monopolies for some time have expounded "free trade" in Latin America. They needed this "freedom" to disarm the Latin American countries in the face of their foreign economic expansion. Now, while foundations are being laid for a future Latin American market, American monopolies are particularly energetic and eloquent in their advocacy of "freedom" of trade. In recent years the capital investment of the United States in the industry of Latin American nations has grown rapidly because of the U.S. desire to entrench itself in "integrated Latin America" and to take advantage of the privileges offered by the "common market" now being formed. By establishing new subsidiaries, the United States intends to expand substantially the sale of its products on the Latin American market. Therefore, Latin American integration is by no means regarded by U.S. monopolistic capital as an economic threat. Moreover, the U. S. monopolies not only foresee large economic gains for themselves from this integration but also regard it, not without good reason, as a political necessity—particularly now, when the national-liberation movement in Latin America is growing stronger. Recently published program documents of U.S. foreign policy stress the importance of Latin America in U.S. economic and

political plans and the necessity of strengthening capitalist economic forms in Latin America and turning it into a reliable ally in the struggle against the "Communist offensive." In the opinion of the United States, a "united" Latin America capable through collective efforts of preventing a "penetration by communism" could be such an ally.

Under conditions of rivalry between two systems, in a period of upsurge of the national-liberation movement in Latin America, one of today's major questions—the direction of Latin American development—is becoming ever more acute. Thus, the central political task of the ruling circles of Latin America and of U. S. monopolistic capital is to keep Latin America on the side of the West and to strengthen the capitalist mode of production in it.

The U.S. ruling classes cannot fail to recognize that any strengthening of industrial production in Latin America, any expansion of foreign trade ties, may cause a rise in competition and an aggravation of antagonisms in foreign markets. They understand that under certain conditions even an unstable, disproportionate industrial development of the Latin American countries could weaken the position of American capital.

However, the general interests involved in the struggle against the liberation movement and the fear of revolutionary outbursts prevail, and they are compelling the United States to act in support of integration.

Born of the continued development of productive forces, economic integration per se is a historically sound and progressive tendency. It is the expression of the countries' objective longing for reciprocal economic ties, for an opportunity to internationalize their economic life and to merge their produc-

[3]V. I. Lenin, *Polnoe sobranie sochinenii*, vol. 2, p. 190.

tive resources. Under existing conditions in a Latin America divided by national boundaries, economic integration signifies an objective trend to eliminate dissociation.

Economic integration, if introduced under different sociopolitical conditions, produces different socioeconomic results, lends a different character to unions, and leads to diametrically opposite goals. In a commercial economic union within the socialist world economic system, a rapprochement occurs between countries having equal rights, possessing proportional planned economics, and striving to render each other the maximum possible aid. In a commercial economic union within the capitalist world economic system, there inevitably develops a bitter competitive struggle, a desire on the part of each participant to resolve his own difficulties at the expense of others and to use the union in his own interests. Capitalist integration entails an intense rivalry, an accentuation of deep-seated antagonisms, and an even more erratic development of countries. Under existing Latin American conditions—that is, in a

period of a rapidly growing national-liberation movement—integration also signifies an attempt on the part of both domestic and foreign big capital to unite the disparate Latin American countries and to reconcile developing productive forces with an obsolete economy of backward production relations.

Today, the substance and aims of general, democratic reforms objectively mesh with those of a socialist character. Concerning the democratic alternative to economic integration as it is being practiced, we must recognize that genuine economic integration, with equal rights for all countries and mutual gains for all participants, can be achieved only under conditions of socialist relations. By fighting for real freedom of economic ties and by waging a decisive struggle against domination by foreign monopolies, against the upper pro-imperialist and the upper conciliatory bourgeoisies, against discrimination in reciprocal economic relations within integration as well as outside its limits, the toiling masses are taking an important step in the direction of genuine democratic integration.

34. The Monetary Problems of Latin America*

V. ZHOLOBOV

The monetary problems of Latin America serve as a distilled expression of the economic difficulties that the countries of the continent are experiencing. To

overcome these difficulties presupposes

*"Valiutnye problemy Latinskoi Ameriki," Mirovaia ekonomika i mezhdunarodnye otnosheniia, 5:79–88 (1966).

the introduction of profound structural changes in the economy—agrarian reform and industrialization—and dictates the need for deliverance from the predominance of foreign capital and for changes in the Latin American position in the international division of labor. The achievement of these objectives requires huge financial resources. However, the basis for accumulation in the Latin American countries remains extremely small because of the backward nature of their economies, and this forces them to use the methods of deficit financing, one of the chief causes of inflation.

Another important result of the economic backwardness of these countries is the heavy dependence on the foreign market. With the urgent need to import machinery and equipment and the one-sided direction of the export economy, profits from exports are becoming a vital factor in accumulation and in overall economic development. However, the situation of the Latin American countries in this respect has deteriorated over the past decade, and this, together with other factors, has had a negative effect on the balance-of-payments situation. Inflation and balance-of-payments deficits have been the basic causes for sharp deterioration of the Latin American monetary situation in the postwar period.

The countries of the continent have sought a way out of the difficulties along the path of strengthened currency restrictions. This trend has been expressed chiefly in a system of a variety of rates of exchange, which is hardly suitable for Latin American conditions. Only relatively recently and in connection with economic integration have the Latin American countries begun to seek solutions in a number of measures on the establishment of a system of mutual accounts on a multilateral basis.

INFLATION, BALANCE OF PAYMENTS, AND RATE OF EXCHANGE

The currency systems of the Latin American countries show a great variety —from such strong convertible currencies as the Mexican peso and, to a certain extent, the Venezuelan bolivar and the Peruvian sol, to the Brazilian cruzeiro, the catastrophic drop of which has been unprecedented, even for Latin America. As a rule, however, the majority of the Latin American countries encounter very serious difficulties when they attempt to put their rate of exchange on a stable basis. The falls in rates are shown by the following data: from 1950 to 1964, the Venezuelan bolivar as compared to the dollar fell 25.6 percent; the Ecuadorean sucre by 19 percent; the Peruvian sol by 44.2 percent; and the Uruguayan peso by 91 percent.

The greatest depreciations have been suffered by the currencies of the leading countries of the continent. The rate of exchange of the Argentine peso in 1950 was 14.02 to a dollar, while it was 150.9 to a dollar in late 1964. During that same period, the Brazilian cruzeiro fell from 18.5 to a dollar to 1,850 to a dollar. Chilean currency fell from 72.5 pesos to a dollar to 3.26 escudos (the new monetary unit introduced into Chile in 1960 and equal to 1,000 of the old pesos). In other words, Argentine currency in 1964 was worth only 9.3 percent of what it had been worth in 1950, while Brazilian was worth 1 percent and Chilean 2.2 percent. Even for Latin America, where sharp currency depreciation invariably accompanies economic development, the extent of the fall in the purchasing power and rate of exchange of the cruzeiro and escudo are rarities.

Almost all the currencies of the Latin American countries have been devalued in recent years, some of them several times.[1] Thus, in mid-1965, the Argentine government announced the fourth devaluation since the end of 1963, as a result of which the peso fell from 151 to 171 pesos to a dollar. During that same period, the Brazilian cruzeiro was devalued four times, depreciating by approximately two-thirds.

The Uruguayan peso has been devalued twice since the beginning of 1964. As a result of the devaluations, it has fallen in value by about one-third in comparison with late 1963, and, if we consider the sizable fall in the exchange rate of the peso during 1963, it was depreciated by about 65 percent during the two years. Chilean currency is also in a difficult position. Its rate of exchange at present varies between 2.9 and 3.3 escudos to the dollar, as compared with 2.1 to 3.1 at the end of 1963 and 1.6 to 2.4 at the end of 1962. The decline in the rate of exchange of the Colombian peso has been concealed to a certain extent by the multiple rates of exchange. However, there is no doubt that its real rate of exchange fell considerably. The same thing may be said for the Venezuelan bolivar.

An observer of the *Financial Times*, Lombard, wrote as follows: "The new wave of devaluations which is sweeping through the Latin American countries serves as a gloomy reminder of the fact that the hopes for saving the countries of the continent from chronic inflation have decisively failed." And chronic inflation is the principal cause of declines in the exchange rates of Latin American currencies. It leads to constant decreases in the domestic purchasing power of national currency and creates a situation in which the rate of exchange becomes unreal. As we know, the situation in currency circulation depends not only on the amount of currency outstanding, but also on the quantity of goods turned

over and the level of their prices. This premise, which stems from a formula of Marx, is the key to understanding the complex inflationary processes that are taking place in the Latin American economy. It was possible during a short period of time to combine the printing of surplus paper currency with relatively high rates of economic growth. During the past few years, the situation with respect to currency circulation had deteriorated sharply. This in turn has checked the rate of increase in production in Latin America and encouraged inflation even more, since increased issues of paper money coincided in a number of cases with a decrease in the volume of production and goods turnover.

The amount of money in circulation has increased by dozens and hundreds of times in the past fifteen to twenty years in certain Latin American countries, but this bears absolutely no relationship to the dynamics of such indicators as gross national or social product and goods turnover. Naturally, this signifies negative results for the domestic purchasing power of the Latin American currencies.

The reasons for inflation in the Latin American countries are complex and varied. However, the most important of them has its roots in the difficulties connected with the elimination of the backward economic structure that is a direct result of the many years of domination of foreign capital. Even the conservative English newspaper *The Times*—in posing the question not of

---

[1]An exception is the Mexican peso, which has remained at a stable level of 12.5 pesos to the dollar since 1954. Also stable are the currencies of a few Central American states, a fact that nevertheless is of a purely nominal nature. Characteristic in this respect is the example of Panama, where the American dollar is legal tender along with the national currency—the balboa. Moreover, the overwhelming majority of Panamanian payments turnover is conducted in dollars.

a superficial but of a more profound understanding of the nature of inflation in the Latin American countries, especially in Argentina, Brazil, and Chile—was forced to admit that "these countries are victims of circumstances, for which the rich [that is, the imperialist] countries are responsible, and inflation is nothing other than the result of poor management of credit and monetary policy, speculation, and unreasonable plans."

The financing of economic growth, which requires huge expenditures from the state budget, was incompatible with the real prospects of the Latin American countries and led to chronic budget deficits that were concealed by issuing more paper money. In the past few years, inflationary processes have literally been sweeping the continent like a fever, exerting a negative effect on all facets of the generation of social product. Such is the internal economic side of the question. Along with that, serious inflationary results bring with them a deterioration in the balance of payments and particularly in trade. A negative balance sharply reduces the possibilities for accumulation. In the belief that a considerable part of the profits made in the economy stem from the mechanism of export prices, national capital prefers the sphere of circulation to that of production. Of course, this increases the shortage of capital, which is compensated for at the expense of budgetary financing (chiefly deficit financing) with all the inflationary results stemming from it. The constant decrease in profits from exports leads to curtailed revenue, of which taxes on foreign trade are a part. This also leads to deficit financing and inflation.

The influence of inflation on the currency situation of the Latin American countries is manifested in the following directions:

1. A decrease in the purchasing power of currency brings with it the need for a decrease in the exchange rate, which in turn provokes an increase in domestic prices and further depreciation of the national currency.

2. There is an increase in speculation based on the foreign exchange situation.

3. Counting on further devaluation of the national currency, exporters prefer to maintain their profits abroad.

4. There is increased flight of capital abroad, which has a negative reflection on the balance of payments.

While inflation facilitates the undermining of the currency position, the recurring monetary crises in the Latin American countries in turn step up inflation.

Let us look at the second factor that determines the currency situation of the Latin American countries—their balance of payments position. A negative balance of payments causes a fall in the rate of exchange, which immediately raises the prices of imports. However, in distinction from the developed capitalist countries, where a lowering of the exchange rate brings with it an increase in ability to compete and an increase in internal prices on imported goods serves as motivation for increasing domestic production, Latin America cannot utilize this responsive measure, because of the one-sided structure of the economy and the still weak industrial development.

During the Second World War, the Latin American countries had a basically favorable balance of payments and trade. This was to a certain degree associated with the fact that the United States—their basic partner in foreign trade—accelerated its purchases of Latin American goods, especially of strategic raw materials. The unhealthy basis of the temporary improvement in gold reserves in connection with the wartime economic situation was fully revealed at the end of the "Korean boom" of the years 1950–1953. The difficulties being experienced now are shown clearly in the balance-of-payments situation of the Latin American countries (see Table 7).

Notwithstanding the favorable trade balances that certain Latin American countries have managed to attain in individual years (of the largest countries on the continent, Argentina in 1963, Brazil in 1964 and 1965, and Chile in 1962 and 1964), an overall surplus of exports over imports for the entire continent was last noted in 1956. The unfavorable development of foreign trade relations for the Latin American countries not only curtails the amount

Table 7. Balance-of-Payments Situation of the Latin American Countries (in millions of dollars)*

Country	Year	Balance of Payment on Current Operations	Movement of Private Short-Term Capital	Movement of State Capital and "Aid"	Movement of Other Capital, and "Errors and Omissions"	Balance of Payments	Movement of Gold Reserves
Brazil	1961	-292	269	159	-87	49	-49
	1962	-408	33	112	-125	-388	388
Chile	1961	-280	93	84	-9	-112	112
	1962	-157	83	136	-82	-20	20
Colombia	1961	-142	-9	4	18	-129	129
	1962	-119	10	80	-13	-42	42
Dominican Republic	1961	41	-30	—	-27	-16	16
	1962	12	—	15	-15	12	-12
Mexico	1961	-82	169	127	-249	-35	35
	1962	64	131	135	-316	14	-14
Peru	1961	18	—	-2	18	34	-34
	1962	-22	-12	41	-1	6	-6
Uruguay	1961	-16	4	-5	-9	-26	26
	1962	-40	—	—	—	-40	40
Venezuela	1961	375	-247	-94	-71	-37	37
	1962	331	-226	-89	-18	-2	2
Others	1961	-757	291	253	43	-170	170
	1962	-471	272	94	-263	-368	368
Total	1961	-1135	540	526	-373	-442	442
	1962	-810	291	524	-833	-828	828

*This table, compiled on the basis of the latest yearly reports of the IMF, gives only a general impression of the balance-of-payments situation of the Latin American countries and does not show a number of important factors in the balance-of-payments situation. The selection of these data as the basis for the compilation of the table was conditioned by the fact that they give one the rare possibility of presenting the balances of the Latin American countries as computed by a common methodology.

of monetary profits, but also decreases its purchasing power. In analyzing the results of the deterioration of the Latin American foreign trade, the Colombian newspaper *El Tiempo* noted that "the relationship between prices for imported goods and those of exported goods has become a sword of Damocles hanging over the economies of the Latin American countries." The foreign trade deficit has increased to more than 9 billion dollars in just the past three years. If this level is maintained during the years 1965–1970, the deficit in the Latin American foreign trade balance will amount to 18–20 billion dollars.

However, the foreign trade balance is not the only factor that determines the level of the exchange rate. It would be pertinent to recall here that the exchange rate fluctuates not only under the pressure of foreign trade, but also under the influence of the entire aggregate of foreign relations, "since this produces payments abroad in cash."[2]

An examination of the other items in the balance of payments of the Latin American countries with respect to current transactions shows that they are accompanied by a chronic negative balance. Expenditures for freight, insurance, payments of interest and dividends, and expenditures on other "invisible items" of the balance of payments are especially large. These sums, which come to billions of dollars, are mostly not taken into account by official sources. The materials of the International Monetary Fund (IMF) publish only obviously favorable data on the scope of the outflow of capital from the Latin American countries. According to the estimates of certain progressive economists, the overall total of profits, interest, and supplementary proceeds received by the imperialist powers in Latin America has amounted to 2.4 billion dollars a year for the past decade.

Liabilities in current transactions are concealed by foreign credits, that is, at the expense actually of a further deepening of imperialist servitude and a direct loss of gold reserves. These trends are clearly manifested in an examination of such a part of the balance of payments as the "movement of capital and credit." The deficit in the balance of payments on current transactions is compensated for by an influx of private, short-term capital. As we can see from Table 7, the amount of such capital came to over 1 billion dollars in Latin America in the years 1961–1962.

The policy of limiting credit expansion, which the majority of the Latin American countries have followed in recent years as part of the struggle with inflation, compounds the difficulties connected with the shortage of financial resources. Under these conditions, the large Latin American industrialists have become ever more interested in receiving resources from abroad, basically in the form of financial deals called "swaps."[3] However, the negative results of such monetary deals for the balance of payments was quickly revealed, and the volume of such deals has begun to decrease in recent times.

The second important source for concealing the current deficit is state credits and foreign "aid." The scope of these operations for the same period is estimated at 1.5 billion dollars. It would be in order here to recall the vaunted program of the Alliance for Progress. Not a trace of the former optimism with respect to it can now be

---

[2] K. Marx and F. Engels, *Sochineniia*, 25, pt. 2, p. 140.

[3] This is a name for agreements on the extension of mutual, short-term reserve credits in national currency, which ensure the possibility of automatic receipt of credit to a certain level.

found in Latin America.[4] The total of the profits that foreign monopolies squeeze out of the area every year considerably exceeds the credits granted to these countries by the United States and Western Europe. The fact that this places a heavy burden on the balance of payments of the Latin American countries requires no explanation.

The ultimate equalization of the balance of payments occurs by means of decreasing the reserves of the Latin American central banks and the shipment of gold abroad. Due to the factors mentioned above, Latin American currencies, like those of other developing regions of the world, are quoted on foreign markets at discounts or are not quoted at all. Consequently, the Latin American countries are deprived of the possibility of utilizing their own currencies for foreign trade accounts, services, and capital movement. Thus, they are forced to use their gold and currency reserves not only to equalize the balance of payments, but also to finance their foreign trade activity.

Along with other factors, such a strained and unbalanced situation in balance of payments makes constant currency devaluation necessary, patently proving the weak positions of the Latin American economy in the world capitalist economic system. The Mexican journal *Comercio Exterior* points out that "devaluation and the existence of a multitude of rates of exchange appear as an external manifestation of illness of the economic organism."[5] The diagnosis of illness holds no secret. The monetary difficulties of the Latin American countries are a result of a dependent position in the international capitalist division of labor and are a direct consequence of the rapacious activity of international monopolies.

Doubtless the experience of the struggle these countries are waging to strengthen their monetary situation

is of no little significance. As we have already noted, the most important efforts in this field are connected with the policy of exchange limitations expressed in the system of a multitude of rates of exchange.

THE MULTIPLICITY OF RATES OF EXCHANGE

The appearance in the Latin American countries of a multiplicity of exchange rates relates to the period of the world capitalist crisis of 1929–1933. The reasons lie in the deterioration of the general economic situation, the collapse of the monetary system based on the gold standard, and the growth of monetary financial difficulties throughout the capitalist world.

After the war, the system of multiple exchange rates became widespread throughout almost all the Latin American countries. The majority of them used this type of monetary restriction as a weapon for the defense of their internal market and for activization of their foreign trade policy, for the improvement of their balance of payments, and as a means of struggle against depletion of their gold reserves.

The complex system of multiple exchange rates has existed throughout the postwar period in Argentina and Brazil, the two largest Latin American countries. In Argentina, up to the 1959 currency reform, there existed, along with the central-bank official rate of 18 pesos to the dollar in the purchase and sale of foreign exchange, a large number of fluctuating rates, the levels of which varied

[4]In 1964, a well-known Uruguayan journalist published a book on the results of the activities of the Alliance of Progress under the symbolic title *Anatomy of a Dead Horse*. Badano begins his book as follows: "We invite the reader to be present at the autopsy on the horse on which American imperialism promised to carry Latin America to unprecedented progress."

[5]*Comercio Exterior*, October 1963, p. 738.

from 18.5 pesos to the dollar in accounts for the export of crude oil and lumber to 76.9 pesos to the dollar for the import of automobiles and spare parts, sporting goods, and other merchandise. The Argentine government used this system to encourage exports, particularly of agricultural goods, and also to conceal the true scope of the peso's loss of value.[6]

In Brazil, the exchange rate for the cruzeiro for import operations was based on two elements: the official rate of 18.5 cruzeiros to the dollar plus the price paid for foreign-exchange certificates at weekly auctions. This price varied in accordance with supply and demand for foreign exchange. There were also several exchange rates. Notwithstanding many amendments to it, this system remained the basis for the Brazilian exchange system throughout the 1950's. The various rates were established by the Currency and Credit Office (SUMOC), an official organ responsible for the country's monetary and credit policy.[7] A similar situation existed in Bolivia, Chile, Uruguay, and other Latin American countries.

About the middle of the 1950's, Latin American attitudes toward multiple exchange rates began to change. During this same period, a trend toward unification of exchange rates arose and gradually began to be put into practice. This was usually accompanied by corresponding reforms, which were carried out in the majority of the Latin American countries: Chile and Bolivia (1956), Paraguay (1957), Argentina (1959), Uruguay (1959–1960), Brazil (1961), and Venezuela (1964). A gradual abolition of multiple rates took place in Nicaragua, Peru, and Ecuador. However, it must be emphasized that both here and later on, we are speaking not of a total rejection of the multiple rates, but only of alterations of the system and its adaptation to changing economic conditions.

Let us examine the motives that impelled the Latin American countries to reject the old system of multiple rates. The basic reason must be sought in the fact that by the mid-1950's the ineffectiveness of the multiple rates had been demonstrated, which was a result of inflation. The progressive currency depreciation nullified the advantages of specific monetary restrictions.

The ruinous effect of inflation on the multiple exchange rate system was associated first with the fact that the sharp depreciation of money required the establishment of the corresponding rate of exchange—that is, a lowering of that rate even in cases where the balance of payments was favorable. Thus, inflation curtailed, and in some cases totally eliminated, the possibility of influence on the rate of exchange. In the second place, under the conditions of inflationary growth of domestic prices, the periodic raising of premiums to Latin American exporters for the purpose of guaranteeing the competitiveness of their goods began to have little effect and did not save Latin American exports from marketing difficulties.

The basic factor affecting the dimensions of monetary profits was the world market. At the same time, in carrying out a policy of industrialization, the Latin American countries were constantly forced to expand the amount of the merchandise for which importers received foreign exchange at advantageous, preferential rates. This

[6]For more detail on the system of multiple exchange rates in Argentina during the postwar period, see A. V. Evreiskov, *Krizis valiutnoi kapitalizma* (Moskva, 1955).

[7]In early 1965, the Brazilian congress approved legislation to convert SUMOC into a central bank. The Bank of Brazil, which together with SUMOC and the treasury carried out the functions of a central bank, remains a state credit institution.

also undermined the idea of multiple exchange rates.

The ineffectiveness of this system in Latin America as the result of inflationary processes can be proven in a variety of examples. Thus, in Venezuela, the foreign oil companies, which play a key role in the economy of the country, were basically free from currency regulation. Nevertheless, these companies were required to acquire Venezuelan currency at a rate unfavorable to them—3.09 bolivares per dollar—for such operations as paying taxes, paying wages, acquiring the products of Venezuelan industry, and so on. Under the conditions of an officially free market in the country, where one could obtain 4.5 bolivares for a dollar, the foreign companies actually chose that method of obtaining Venezuelan currency. They also were permitted to acquire all necessary merchandise abroad. All of this created a situation in which, while the rate of 3.09 bolivares to a dollar existed, it was virtually never applied.

Along with inflation, the abandonment of the system of multiple exchange rates was dictated to no small degree by the growth of the foreign trade ties of Latin America with the countries of Western Europe, whose currencies began to compete more actively with the American dollar. Latin American trade with Western Europe, which in the early postwar years was often conducted on a clearinghouse basis, began gradually to be based on freely convertible currency accounts. The Latin American countries were thus faced with the necessity of abandoning the system of multiple rates, since retention of it under conditions of elimination of currency restrictions in Western Europe and even in certain Latin American countries would have had a serious effect on their foreign trade relations.

In this connection, it should be noted

that it was just at this time when detailed discussion of plans for the economic integration of Latin America began, something that Western economists—F. Collings, for example—associate directly with abandonment of multiple rates of exchange.[8]

A single, freely fluctuating rate—which as a rule was considerably lower—was introduced in almost all the Latin American countries. Along with this, the activity of free currency markets was permitted, at which the quotations could not differ essentially from the official rate, since the central banks support the rate quoted by them in case of need. In Bolivia, for example, all profits in foreign exchange from exports are subject to surrender to the central bank, which has a monopoly on the purchase and sale of foreign currency. Since 1959, there has been relative freedom of monetary transactions in Argentina, where the central bank also makes active use of monetary policy to defend the peso exchange rate that it has fixed.

The stability of a freely fluctuating exchange rate actually depends on the determination of official monetary agencies to defend that rate and, naturally, on their actual ability to do so, both conditions being determined by the balance of payments and foreign exchange–gold reserve situations. The growth in these reserves in certain countries permitted the central banks to support a stable exchange rate notwithstanding the increased demand for foreign exchange. Later on, the situation deteriorated and the exchange rate fell. Such systems have been called "temporarily fixed rates" in practice.

The basic form of transition of the Latin American countries from multiple exchange rates to a single fluctuating rate has been the stabilization pro-

[8]See, for example, the opinions of IMF expert F. Collings in *IMF Staff Papers*, 2:286 (1961).

grams carried out on the initiative and with the participation of the IMF. In its recommendations on monetary matters to the Latin American countries, the IMF actually sets out from the view that the solution of all the other problems of economic development should be subordinated to the achievement of a stable exchange rate. Calling inflation the basic cause of the depreciation of Latin American currencies and expenditures on industrialization the source of inflation, the IMF has recommended a slow-down in rates of economic growth as an anti-inflationary measure. Thus, under the pretext of a struggle for stable state finances and currency circulation, a program of conservatism and consolidation of economic backwardness is offered.

Of course, this does not mean that all recommendations of the IMF in the monetary field should be disregarded, but there is no doubt about its one-sided proimperialist orientation. The effort of IMF officials to squeeze the economic problems of Latin America into the Procrustean bed of a program of monetary financial stability is also meeting with many objections from official representatives of the Latin American countries. The credit policy of the IMF is subjected to especially justifiable criticism. In a speech delivered to the annual meeting of IMF directors in 1963, Brazilian Finance Minister C. Pinto reproached the IMF management for the fact that it "suspends the extension of loans and credits to underdeveloped countries during a period of substantial deterioration of their financial situation, that is, at the very time when these countries particularly need help."[9] As a result of IMF neglect of important Latin American economic problems, the stabilization programs frequently end in total failure.

The example of Argentina is especially instructive in this respect. The introduction of the stabilization plan that was begun in 1959 only worsened the economic difficulties of that country. The policy of "frugality and sacrifice" recommended to the Argentine government by the IMF took the form of returning a considerable part of state enterprises to private hands, curtailing the imports that were needed for the development of domestic industry, and lowering the exchange rate of the peso, which led to increases in domestic prices and a considerable deterioration in the standard of living of the masses. In the monetary field, the 1959 reform had only temporary success. Over a period of three years, the Argentine exchange rate (82–83 pesos to a dollar) could be retained unchanged thanks only to the support of the Central Bank of Argentina, which intervened periodically to support the established peso rate. By 1962, however, increased inflation and the deterioration in the balance-of-payments situation had so deepened the contradiction between the internal and the external value of the peso that devaluation of the Argentine currency was the only way out. Following a series of devaluations in late 1964, the exchange rate was left at 151 pesos to a dollar. Such were the results of one of the most widely publicized IMF stabilization programs.

In Brazil, where at one time it seemed possible to combine inflation and multiple exchange rates with a sizable growth of industry, the situation deteriorated sharply, and it has not been possible to correct it over the course of the last five years. The rate of industrial growth fell, inflation assumed a "galloping" character, and a certain increase in exports in 1963–1964 turned out to be unstable and temporary.

[9]*Bank of London and South America,* November 2, 1963, p. 924.

In 1961, the IMF also put pressure on the Brazilian government for elimination of the multiple exchange rates. The Currency and Credit Office issued a directive on decreasing the preferential import rate from 100 to 200 cruzeiros to a dollar and eliminating the system of foreign exchange certificates. Importers who previously had had to acquire certificates began to buy foreign exchange to pay for imported goods at the free market rate. A few months later, the preferential import rate and the export rates were lowered to the level of the cruzeiro on the free currency market. However, the measures put into effect at the insistence of the IMF did not approach a solution of the primary problems of the economic development of the country, and they immediately provoked a number of negative consequences. Increasing the amounts that importers had to pay the Bank of Brazil for foreign exchange led only to a rise in domestic prices, since the importers hurried to pass their costs on to the consumer. In the subsequent years, the increased inflation brought to nought the efforts of the government in the field of stabilizing the exchange rate of the cruzeiro. Consequently, the Brazilian government in recent years has shifted its efforts in the field of credit and monetary policy to the battle against inflation and the regulation of the currency market.

The example of unification of exchange rates in Venezuela is of interest because the process took place without any special interference from the IMF, and because, in spite of the existence of multiple exchange rates, the Venezuelan bolivar had been a relatively stable currency during the entire postwar period. In January 1964 the Venezuelan government carried out a currency reform that abolished the multiple exchange rates and fixed the official value of the Venezuelan currency at 4.5 bolivares to a dollar. As in other Latin American countries, the currency reform resulted in a sharp increase in the prices of "essential" imported merchandise. The advantage of the devaluation of the bolivar fell to U.S. monopolies, which could now purchase Venezuelan raw materials, merchandise, and other goods cheaply and pay taxes and wages to Venezuelan workers in depreciated bolivares.

In abolishing the multiple exchange rates, the governments of the Latin American countries had reckoned on influencing the balance-of-payments situation and on retaining the previous possibilities of obtaining budgetary resources with the help of differential taxes on foreign trade. For example, all export operations in Argentina are conducted at the free market rate. However, a tax ranging from 10 to 20 percent, depending on the category of the merchandise, is levied on Argentine exporters when they exchange their monetary profits. Most imported merchandise is subject to import taxes, which range from 20 to 230 percent. In Chile, the amount of the import tax varies from 0.1 to 200 percent of the value of the merchandise, and in Uruguay, from 20 to 300 percent.

In addition, there is a kind of import operation in which the importer, prior to purchasing goods abroad, is required to make a preliminary deposit in the central bank in amounts that vary according to the monetary legislation of the respective country. For example, in Argentina, the amount of this deposit is 100 percent for most goods. In Uruguay, the amount of the preliminary deposit is as high as 200 percent for goods bearing an import tax of more than 150 percent. A particularly broad range of preliminary deposits is in effect in Chile, where there are eight categories of such levies with a huge range of fluctuation—from 5 percent to 10,000 percent.

Actually, these practices represent an altered form of the system of multiple exchange rates, since they pursue the same goals and utilize the same methods of influencing the economy, especially the balance of payments. A supplementary effect of the transfer of this mechanism from the monetary sphere to the field of domestic currency circulation is that the new form is an important instrument for establishing control over inflation.

Monetary difficulties are forcing certain Latin American countries to seek salvation to this day in multiple exchange rates. Multiple rates were reintroduced in Brazil in 1963, for example, although without revival of the practice of foreign exchange auctions. Notwithstanding the repeated exhortations of the IMF, a number of countries on the continent maintain as before that the old system of monetary restrictions best answers the requirements of economic development.

LATIN AMERICAN INTEGRATION— A NEW ROUND OF MONETARY PROBLEMS

The problems associated with the economic integration of the Latin American countries have already been repeatedly examined in Soviet economic literature. From the point of view that we are investigating, it is necessary to emphasize that interregional trade is on a comparatively small scale as compared with total foreign trade, and that not a single one of these countries—not even the most developed ones—can satisfy its own requirements for production consumption. Latin America remains dependent on the import of industrial goods from the developed capitalist countries, and trade with them requires hard currency in large amounts. This situation greatly hampers Latin America in the solution of the already complex problem of international balance of payments.

In discussion of the problems of Latin American economic integration, an important position is given to the implementation of a number of specific measures in the monetary field. The most important one is the proposal for establishment of a system of mutual accounts on a multilateral basis. This prospect was first discussed in late 1956 in Santiago, when the problem was submitted to the trade committee of the United Nations Economic Commission for Latin America. The representatives of the committee proposed the formation of a working group of experts that was directly charged with the task of "studying the possibility of establishment of a system of mutual accounts on a multilateral basis."[10] At the meetings of representatives of Latin American central banks in Montevideo (1957) and Rio de Janeiro (1958), agreement was reached on standardization of accounts on a bilateral basis as the first step in transition to the new system. At Montevideo, a model draft agreement was worked out that established a unified system of payments on a bilateral basis. A proposal on the adoption of an accounting unit was first advanced here. During the period 1958–1960, in connection with the organization of the Central American Common Market and of the Latin American Free Trade Association (LAFTA), discussion of the problem of liberalizing payments was relegated to somewhat secondary status, but it was precisely then that the Latin American countries took a number of practical steps in this direction. Thus, out of fourteen bilateral payments agreements that had been functioning in 1958, only one remained by the end of 1962 (between Argentina and Uruguay).

[10]*Problemas de pagos en América Latina* (México: CEMLA, 1964), p. 108.

However, the most important thing in connection with the agreements signed by the central banks was the formation of a clearinghouse in July 1961 for the Central American countries —El Salvador, Costa Rica, Guatemala, Honduras, and Nicaragua. The clearinghouse, located in Tegucigalpa, Honduras, makes payments on a multilateral basis using an accounting unit—the Central American peso —that is on parity with the American dollar.[11] The capital of this organization consists of 1.5 million dollars, since the quota of each member country is 300,000 dollars.

The problem of currency unification was discussed early in 1965 at a meeting in San Salvador, since five different national monetary units are in circulation on the small area of the five states with a population of only 10 million. The establishment of a unified currency is now being studied by leading banks in the countries of the Central American Common Market.

The significance of such a measure as the establishment of a payment union in Central America lies not merely in the event itself. It is a kind of prototype of future organizations that will embrace the member countries of the LAFTA. Naturally, this problem acquires even more significance in connection with the new plans for implementation of integration on a continent-wide scale.

The establishment of a new system of accounting and the coordination of monetary credit policy were the basic themes at the regular meeting of representatives of the central banks in Rio de Janeiro in October 1963. Specific agreement was reached at this session on the basic principles of the future organization. The objective of the payments union being established was the introduction of accounting in interzonal trade and the extension of mutual credits to the member countries of the

zone. The establishment of a permanent agency for the coordination of monetary and credit policy—which is what the clearing house would be—is destined to influence the development of Latin American integration in the field of currency circulation and international payments. It was noted at the session that the system being established cannot hope to achieve total centralization of accounting. It was emphasized that no account system is capable of achieving a total balance of payments within the zone, and so the system and rules for extending credits were discussed at the meeting.

Accounts for foreign trade among the Latin American countries are now handled in dollars through American banks located principally in New York, San Francisco, and New Orleans. These banks credit the accounts of exporters in the Latin American countries, discount bills of exchange, grant loans in foreign currency, and conduct other routine banking operations. Although many banks in the Latin American countries have corresponding relationships with each other, these are nevertheless not accompanied by mutual opening of accounts, and the usual method of payment is through American banks. This fact again confirms the dependence of the Latin American countries in the monetary and credit field on American imperialism and illustrates the extensive expansion of the dollar into Latin America.

The establishment of a clearing house in Latin America is regarded as an important step in strengthening cooperation among the Latin American countries, since this measure will help

[11]The exchange rates of the currencies of member countries in terms of the accounting unit indicated are as follows: for one Central American peso, 1 Guatemalan quetzal, 2 Honduran lempiras, 2.5 Salvadorean colones, 6.625 Costa Rican colones, and 7 Nicaraguan córdobas.

them to eliminate many of the obstacles in international accounts. The transition from accounting in dollars to payments in local, clearinghouse currency "directly, rapidly, and economically"—as business circles in Latin America are convinced—will facilitate the development of intercontinental trade.[12] The establishment of a clearing house will also be of aid in reclaiming from the United States and mobilizing considerable monetary resources that the Latin American banks handling accounts on foreign trade are forced to maintain in accounts in U.S. banks.

The initiator of the establishment of a payments union in these countries is the Latin American Center for the Study of Monetary and Credit Problems, which is headquartered in Mexico City. The center's economists have prepared several draft plans for solving the problem. On the request of the center's management, the well-known American economist Robert Triffin in late 1962 prepared a report entitled "The Latin American Clearinghouse and Payments Union." In the report, he explained his understanding of the matter and proposed a plan for establishment of a trade payments mechanism within the framework of the LAFTA. The basic position of the plans of the Latin American Center and of Triffin's report may be summarized as follows:

1. The central banks of the Latin American countries establish a clearinghouse, which would conduct accounts on a multilateral basis, using for this purpose a monetary accounting unit (the name of which has not yet been definitively established).

2. The extension of mutual credits at the end of an established period and within previously stipulated limits is provided for the purpose of balancing payments.

3. The clearinghouse will have a fund of convertible currency to which all the member countries will contribute. For example, Triffin proposes to establish a contribution to the fund by each country in the amount of 3 to 10 percent of its gold reserves. In addition, the central banks of the Latin American countries can maintain in the accounts of the clearinghouse a part of their gold reserves above the minimum amount established above. The purpose of the fund is to ensure conditions for immediate payment to the accounts of creditor countries.

Equalizing the debit and credit balances that will inevitably arise in interzonal trade is a difficult problem. The essence of the plans that have been prepared lies in having the credit balances of the LAFTA member countries credited within the zone itself and not assigned for payment to a third country. On the other hand, as the well-known Argentine economist Raúl Prébisch has pointed out, "It is important for the proper functioning of a common market for none of the member countries to attempt to assume the role of permanent creditor, exporting more goods and services to all the other countries than it imports from them."[13]

These measures in the Latin American credit and finance field, which are now in the discussion stage, represent attempts to solve—even if only partially—the problem of international accounts abruptly facing the countries of the continent. Of course, it is impossible not to see the limited sphere of accounting on the new basis. It sets

[12]*Problemas de pagos en América Latina*, p. 132.

[13]Alberto Baltra Cortés, *Ekonomicheskoe razvitie Latinskoi Ameriki* (Moskva, 1963), pp. 306–307.

objective limits to the possibilities of trade expansion among the Latin American countries. Thus, a total solution of this problem is tied in with the development of national industrial production as the basis of increased trade and a change in the dependent position of Latin America in the international division of labor.

Consequently, it is not coincidental that great importance is being attributed in the countries of this continent to the development of economic and trade relations with the Soviet Union and with the other socialist countries. The expansion of these ties by means of conclusion of bilateral trade, payment, and credit agreements will aid the Latin American countries to ease the strain of the balance of payments and simultaneously will ensure fulfillment of programs for importing the machinery and equipment that are vitally necessary for the development of their economies.

IX

ECONOMIC AND IDEOLOGICAL RIVALRY

This section begins with an analysis of "Latinidad" by Iu. A. Zubritskii, who opines that recent attempts to revive the theory reflect intensified economic rivalry and constitute proof of the inability of bourgeois ideologists to construct new theories.

In the second selection (Item 36) Z. I. Romanova presents a Soviet view of the tactics used by American capital to penetrate Latin America, stressing that the weakness of the Latin American economy invites foreign domination. In Item 37 the same author assesses international credit-distributing agencies, asserting that their basic purpose is to promote the interests of world capitalism.

B. I. Gvozdarev examines the program of the Alliance for Progress in the fourth selection (Item 38). The author believes that the program is destined to fail, and that stabilization of prices for export commodities would benefit the Latin American economy much more.

Pan-Americanism is surveyed from a Marxist point of view in Item 39 by M. V. Antiasov. The author declares that "the ideology of Pan-Americanism stands in complete contradiction to the democratic development of the Latin American nations, and that the Pan American 'community' is a check on that development."

Proceeding from theory to specific recommendations, M. A. Grechev presents in the sixth selection (Item 40) a program for Latin American economic independence, emphasizing in totally unsubstantiated form that the latter is "inseparably connected with political independence and the democratization of internal political life."

Item 41 reviews postwar political and cultural ties between the Soviet Union and Latin America, and the concluding selection (Item 42) expounds on the potential benefits for Latin America implied by the existence of a socialist camp.

35. A Critical Analysis of Latinidad*

Iu. A. Zubritskii

In 1957, on the occasion of Peruvian independence day (July 28), the President of the Republic of Peru, Manuel Prado, delivered a speech devoted mainly to the need for rapprochement between the peoples "of Latin origin" who, according to Prado, should form " a bond of politically allied nations."[1] "The Latin nations," the President asserted, "possess common culture, traditions, and origin."[2]

Prado's statement provoked a lively response. Subsequently, under the banner of rapprochement between "Latin" countries, there took place a visit to Peru by the French Minister of Foreign affairs, the laying of the foundation in Lima of the French Alliance building, the opening of a French exposition in Lima, and in this connection a visit by the head of the French government. Many newspapers in Peru gave generous space to an apologia of "Latinidad," of "the Prado Doctrine," as the theory of "the unity of Latin countries" came to be called. Ministers and other highly placed persons from more than ten countries spoke in support of it. Declarations on the cultural unity among all "Latin nations," their unity of origin and spiritual makeup, poured as if from a horn of plenty.

In this article, we intend briefly to examine the essence of this "new"

theory. It is not by accident that we placed the word *new* in quotes. Latinidad already has a history of some length behind it. In the second half of the past century there emerged in Latin America the concept of Latinity as a certain unity of the "Latin" peoples of the globe. At that time, this concept harbored a certain progressive element: against the imperialistic expansion of the United States (economic, ideological, and military), it proposed an alliance of Latin American nations with the best, foremost carriers of West European culture. And indeed, the best examples of French, Spanish, and Italian culture exerted a definite positive influence on the cultural formation of several Latin American nations. Yet, even at this time, Latinidad as a theory had one very vulnerable spot: it neglected the great role played by the Indian and Negro cultures that developed in specific local conditions. In the course of time, the reactionary

---

*"Latinidad i ego sushchnost'," *Vestnik istorii mirovoi kul'tury*, 25/1:112–117 (January–February 1961).

[1] *Afirmación de la Latinidad: Dos discursos históricos* (Lima, 1957), p. 14.

[2] If the question here were only of certain common elements of culture and of only some common moments of ethnogenesis, we would not, of course, call special attention to this idea. [Iu. Z.]

side of Latinidad came to predominate definitely over the progressive side, and by the 1920's the leading cultural figures of Latin America opposed the Latinidad theory. An outstanding part in this struggle was played by the prominent Peruvian social leader and founder of the Peruvian Communist Party, José Mariátegui, who unmasked the fictitious nature of Latinidad—Latin culture and Latin spirit—as applied to the Latin American countries. He wrote, "Let us thoroughly understand that we are not Latins and that historically we are no relation of Rome."[3]

In fact, despite the extensive spread of "Latin" languages (Spanish, Portuguese, French), the population of the majority of the Latin American countries was not formed by emigration from Spain, Portugal, and France (the solid Latin image of these countries is also, to put it mildly, more than doubtful). These populations are the result of complex ethnic processes—in particular, the interaction of various components, among which the Indian and the Negro played and continue to play not by any means the last role, and often the first. And if we look at Peru itself, the truth of this assertion becomes quite evident. More than half the population of Peru in the 1920's, as in our day, were the Quechua and Aymara Indians and the so-called Forest Indians, who speak their own languages. This fact alone is a weighty enough refutation not only of the "Latin" but even of the "Spanish" character of the Peruvian population. As for the remainder of Peru's population, its language is basically its only bond with "Latin" Spain and Rome.

The culture, psychological traits, customs, and ethnology of most Spanish-speaking Peruvians were formed on the basis of an Indian substratum and are inseparable from it.

Mariátegui—himself a "white," Span-ish-speaking Peruvian, who had lived for a long time in Italy—uses a curious reasoning, which we think not superfluous to repeat here. He writes:

While on Latin soil, I felt the whole emptiness of that lie which attempts to bind us spiritually to Rome. The baby blue sky of Latium, the sweet grapes of the Roman earth, the golden honey of Frascati, and the sentimental landscape poetry of the eclogue intoxicated my senses. In my soul, however, I felt far from the Latin stem. Italy, beautiful Italy, italianized me slightly, but did not latinize or romanize me. One day, when we representatives from all the so-called Latin nations held a banquet in the ruins of the Paolo Emilio baths celebrating the foundation of Rome, I understood to what degree we Spanish Americans were outsiders at this event . . . Spanish America has the mixed blood of various peoples, various races.[4]

Mariátegui also actively opposed Latinidad because he saw in it an ally of fascism, which at that time was taking its first ominous steps under the leadership of Mussolini. Wrote Mariátegui: "Reactionism is seeking spiritual and ideological weapons in the arsenal of Roman civilization. Fascism intends to restore the Empire. Mussolini and his Black Shirts have restored the hatchet of the lictors, the decurions, centurions, consuls, and so forth in Rome."[5]

Mariátegui lived only a short time after writing his articles on Latinidad, but he succeeded in dealing a staggering blow to this profascist ideology, after which the advocates of Latinidad remained silent for a long time. Three decades have passed since then. Mussolini's Italy and Hitler's Germany have suffered defeat. The military debacle of these powers signified the defeat of misanthropic theories of racial

[3] J. C. Mariátegui, *Ensayos escogidos* (Lima, 1956), p. 106.
[4] *Ibid.*, pp. 107–108.
[5] *Ibid.*, p. 108.

and national conceptions. Advocates of Latinidad did not again begin to raise their voices until these theories became reborn, with the blessing of imperialism, especially its American variety, done up in "democratic" finery and singing old racist songs—only in a new key.

Has the essence of Latinidad changed in the thirty years since the death of Mariátegui? Undoubtedly some details have changed, but, as for the essence of the movement, its reactionary character has remained the same. Even a brief analysis of the basic premises of Latinidad convinces us of its reactionary and antiscientific nature. The corner stone and point of departure of the theory is the claim "that cultural ties are stronger and more effective than those conditioned by geographic position and economic ties."[6] The number of persons in the whole world (we do not dare, in this case, to use the word "scholars") who would subscribe to such an unscientific statement is small. The assertion is too absurd to need refutation. The worst part of it—and of the entire Prado Doctrine—is that it sets out from recognizing a nonexistent "all-Latin culture, all-Latin blood, all-Latin spirit" and the presence of all these "all-Latin virtues" in Peru and other Latin American countries. We often come across expressions to this effect in the statements of Prado and the followers of his doctrine. In other words, this is another denial of the culture, language, history, psychology, and ethnology of the Indian populations; of the history, culture psychology, and ethnology of mestizos and Creoles; of the importance of the Indian and Negro components in the formation of the modern Latin American Spanish-speaking nations and nationalities, and of Brazilians and Haitians.

The example of Peru—and we could take other countries as examples—makes it obvious that after thirty years this denial has become even less well founded and tenable. During this period in the history of Peru, the process of ethnic consolidation of the Peruvian Indians, especially the Quechua, has become intensified. Written literature has developed in the Quechua language, particularly poetry. The Peruvian poet Alencastre invokes images from the distant and glorious past of the Incas, linking them with our times and with popular aspirations. The Indianist movement is growing steadily and becoming stronger, and its progressive and most active wing is taking active steps toward the resurrection and development of the language and culture of the Indians. Ernesto More, Indianist leader and deputy in the Peruvian Parliament, succeeded in introducing regular radio broadcasts in the Aymara language. Such examples are numerous. Could we possibly speak of a predominance of "Latin spirit" in an author of Quechua poetry or his readers, or in a radio announcer in this language and his audience?

Just as far from the "Latin spirit" are the Spanish-speaking mestizos, who are only one step removed from Indians in the direct as well as in the figurative sense. Also just as alien to the "Latin spirit" are the Peruvian poets, composers, sculptors, and artists who speak and think in Spanish but whose creations mirror the life and aspirations of the people who gave them not only life but also Peruvian taste, Peruvian traditions, Peruvian temperament, and Peruvian national consciousness. And yet, in spite of everything and contrary to obvious facts, Manuel Prado claims that "Peru lives in accordance with the great edifying virtues bequeathed us by Spain together with her race, language, and religion."[7] The above example and similar statements show us that the partisans of Latinidad

[6]*Afirmación de la Latinidad*, p. 8.
[7]*Ibid.*, p. 12.

have already reached the point of proclaiming the existence of a separate Latin race.[8]

Thus, the essence of Latinidad (here we limit ourselves to Latin America only) comes down to an unfounded and antiscientific denial of the distinctive ethnic traits of all the nationalities that populate the immense territory from the Rio Grande to Tierra del Fuego. To be sure, in one of the speeches eulogizing Latinidad, the Peruvian Minister of Education, Jorge Basadre, devotes one sentence—literally one—to the Indians and mestizos ". . . we must not and cannot forget our aboriginal and mestizo population."[9] Exactly how do the partisans of Latinidad intend to remember the Indians and mestizos? Not a word about it. However, to some degree an answer to this question may be found in a photograph taken at one of the banquets in honor of "harmonious action by Latin nations." Next to French guests and Peruvian creoles, we see faces of Indians and mestizos present at the banquet as servants. It could not be more symbolic!

Let us note here that the destiny of being servants to "the white Latin race," according to the Latinidad theoreticians, awaits not only Indians. "France," says Manuel Prado, "in her endeavor to spread to the entire globe the advanced culture she inherited from ancient Greece and Rome, from apostles and lawgivers, has brought her administrative and political forms to other latitudes as well . . . and if today she is fighting in defense of these territories and of their inhabitants' existence, she does so in the assurance that in so doing she is rendering invaluable service to the defense of the West and to these peoples' own freedom."[10]

The Peruvian President had tried to clothe his far-from-elegant idea in elegant dress. Alas, this is an impossible task. And so France defends the Algerians by exterminating them just as she recently exterminated the Vietnamese. And in doing all of this, she is defending the interests of the West? Whoever so desires may try to make heads or tails of this, but a clear-thinking person will not find it easy. Incidentally, if we do not talk about the "West" but about Western imperialism, the final statement quoted above elicits no doubt.

While tracing the ideas of Latinidad, we have imperceptibly strayed from Latin American soil and have come out on the international arena, but here again we become convinced of the reactionary essence of Latinidad.

We see here that Latinidad assumes the task of justifying plundering colonial wars and the enslavement of some nations by others and eulogizes the "cultural mission" of the imperialist powers, which, in practice, always wind up as the stiflers and destroyers of the culture of the enslaved peoples.

And how about such a pearl as the claim of the "advanced culture" of Greece and Rome? In comparison with which culture of which peoples and in which ages can this culture be called advanced: If we compare the culture of German or Iberian contemporaries to ancient Rome, this assertion is correct. So was the culture of the Incas and Mayas an advanced one in comparison with the culture of other tribes that populated the American continent. In Asia, there flowered the cultures of ancient China and India, the foremost ones of their time. It would

---

[8]*Ibid.*, p. 15.
[9]*Acción armónica de las naciones latinas* (Lima, 1957), p. 18. It must be noted that Jorge Basadre is a historian who has done much work in investigating and popularizing the culture of Indians. His participation in an apologia for Latinidad seems more than strange.
[10]*Afirmación de la Latinidad*, p. 13.

hardly be correct to pose and decide the question as to which of these slave-owning civilizations was the most advanced. It is quite clear, however, that when he spoke of the "advanced culture of Greece and Rome," Prado had in mind not the ancient cultures of the primitive communes and slave-owning societies but the culture of modern nations. His words were addressed to modern times and, in this case, they again revealed amazing ignorance or else the intentional ignoring of certain generally recognized moments of the historical process. The culture of slave-owning societies—including the ancient Greek and Roman ones—represents a very definite, historically conditioned type of culture. Therefore, in spite of the great development of this culture's individual aspects—first of all, art (in ancient Greece and Rome, this concerns mainly epic poetry, the theatre, sculpture, and architecture)—in spite of the inclusion of individual elements of it into the world's treasury of civilization, the feudal and capitalist types of cultures stand undoubtedly higher than the slave-owning one. It would be difficult to deny that in spite of the relative independence with which the arts develop, they are determined in the final analysis by the degree of development of productive forces and the nature of production relationships. The flowering of the socialist, truly advanced culture of the USSR and of the entire socialist camp is the best proof of this.

Advocates of Latinidad often like to display their successes in achieving international recognition of their theory. We may dwell on this point also. Let us see which countries have most actively supported the Latinidad theory. They are, first of all, Spain, Portugal, Belgium, Nicaragua, France, and England. What, then, attracts these coun-

tries—to be more exact, the governments of these countries—to the Latinidad doctrine? It seems to us that the fascist regimes of Franco and Salazar and of today's Nicaragua sought and continue to seek support in it for their fragile and unenviable domestic and international situations. Fascist regimes see in Latinidad their direct ally. And how could it be otherwise, with the outstanding leaders of Latinidad slandering the world of socialism and the communist movement and prophesying that "Latinidad will be the indestructible rampart"[11] against the mythical expansion of the Soviet Union? It is precisely this aspect of Latinidad that suits the other "Latin" and "non-Latin" governments of the imperialist camp. Not in vain did the British Foreign Office declare that the Prado Doctrine "might become an important and influential contribution in the cause of defense of the Western world."[12]

Let us note that this declaration of the "cause of defense of the Western world" cannot hide the fact that Latinidad, while remaining a reactionary theory within the framework of imperialist ideology, also reflects the actual imperialistic contradictions of our day. France, Italy, and England do not intend to accept as immutable the fact that a colossal share of the profits extracted from Latin America is drifting away into the safes of Wall Street. They, too, wish to bite off a good-sized piece, and "Latin unity" is a convenient screen to cover up their sharp competition with the stronger partner.

There is still another side of Latinidad, which cannot be passed over in silence and which in its reactionary character can well compete with the other aspects of the Prado Doctrine.

Latinidad pleads for a united "Latin"

[11]*Ibid.*, p. 14.
[12]*Ibid.*, p. 7.

world and a single "Latin" culture, for the "harmonious unity of all Latin countries and nations," and for their political unification. This is not a new song. As we know, "Pan-Germanism" also laid claim to a similar unity of the "Germanic" nations. To us, however, the thought of unity between popular-democratic Rumania and Franco Spain, or of free Cuba after the expulsion of Batista and Salazar's Portugal—which gave Batista shelter—seems absurd and archreactionary in every respect.

In summary, we cannot help but think of how pathetic and helpless is this bourgeois ideology, which, incapable of conceiving a really new theory, is compelled to revert to old forms in its reactionary conjectures. Latinidad is a brilliant example of deliberate falsification of the laws and facts of historical development.

36. The Forms and Methods of Penetration Employed by American Capital in Latin America*

Z. I. ROMANOVA

Thus far, we have discussed the quantitative side of U.S. capital investment in Latin America, its volume, dynamics of growth, and departmental structure. It is also important to analyze the manner in which American capital succeeds in becoming entrenched in the Latin American economy, the methods that U.S. monopolies employ to export capital, and the conditions established for that purpose.

Above all, it should be noted that the weakness of the Latin American economy invites domination by foreign capital and is a major prerequisite for its penetration. The almost total absence of competition from the national bourgeoisie, the shortage of domestic capital, the unbalanced development of industry, and the obsolete technological equipment all create favorable conditions for the export of American capital. At the same time, the rise of the national-liberation movement in the countries of Latin America puts certain barriers in the way of U.S. export capital. This condition forces American monopolies to be flexible and to search for certain ways to invest capital.

For some time, as the advance of American capital has progressed, opposition to it has developed and grown in the Latin American countries. Not infrequently, American goods have

*Ekonomicheskaia ekspansiia SShA v Latinskoi Amerike (Moskva: Izdatel'stvo sotsial'no-ekonomicheskoi literatury, 1963), pp. 54–61.

been boycotted by Latin American customers who refuse to buy merchandise labeled "Made in the U.S.A."

The methods used by some U.S. businessmen to win the Latin American market at the very dawn of U.S. expansionism included giving their companies the names of Indian fighters against Spanish colonizers, outstanding Latin American public figures, and Latin American national symbols. Thus, the Mexican affiliate of the American trust American Tobacco Company was named El Aguila, or "The Eagle," since that bird is the basic element on the Mexican coat of arms. The largest U.S. meatpacking firm in Uruguay bore the name of Artigas, a national hero of the Uruguayan people of the time of the struggle for independence.

It must be stated that Latin American laws recognize any firm organized according to the laws of a given country as a domestic company, although the owners or the management organs of the firm may be located abroad. As a result, the prevailing form of Latin American companies has become the *sociedad anónima*, or corporations usually issuing common stock. This means that the actual identity of the owner or owners can easily be concealed.

As a result, many companies may have among their titles words like "Argentina," "Brasileira," "Chilena," "Ecuatoriana," but they belong to American capital. Thus the great oil refining company in Argentina, Diadema Argentina, is controlled by the international oil trust, Royal Dutch Shell, in which U.S. capital is involved. Another oil refining company, Esso Petrolera Argentina, is under the control of the American monopoly, Esso Standard Oil. The same monopolies control the oil-refining companies of Brazil: Shell Brazil and Esso Standard do Brasil.

In Brazil, notwithstanding the na-

tionalization of some of the American electric power stations in 1962—Rio Light and São Paulo Light, and others —the major part of electric energy is in the hands of two U.S. monopolies that prefer to hide behind Brazilian names. One is called Brazilian Traction, Light, and Power; the other, Companhia Auxiliar de Empresas Electricas Brasileiras.

U.S. monopolies not only utilize national symbols but also attract the participation of native investors. Such joint enterprises are universally prevalent in Latin America and at present have become one of the main tools of American capital for penetration of the Latin American market and for seizing it from within.

A company with a national trade name and with the participation of domestic investors has become the most dependable source for investment capital. It provides protection from the increasing nationalization of foreign property in Latin America and creates additional opportunities in the competitive struggle.

In creating mixed companies, American investors do not always insist on 51 percent stock ownership. Moreover, it is even more profitable for them if their share is from 20 percent to 40 percent, at times even less. In that case they can place more national capital under their control and can conceal their domination. On the U.S. side stands a mighty monopoly with technical know-how, based on a great financial network capable of putting up the necessary industrial equipment, while on the side of national capital are numerous scattered investors. In most instances, they can offer only capital, and it is often in deflated national currency. Despite this drawback, they bring with them knowledge of the domestic market, the support of the domestic consumer, and, quite frequently, government aid.

U.S. monopolies need national owners who at the same time, being relatively weak technically and financially, are no real threat to the American investors. That is why the new Mexican legislation of 1960—the so-called Mexicanization of industrial enterprises—which stipulated that 51 percent of the stock of industries in the most important fields must be in Mexican hands, was received quite calmly in the United States. Some measures to encourage national capital were worked out in Brazil, Venezuela, Chile, and Uruguay, but these, too, were met with no protest from the mercantile-industrial circles of the United States.

Of some interest in this respect is a book by American Senator William Benton, who, with Adlai Stevenson, visited a number of Latin American countries in 1960 and championed a "new look" at Latin America. Describing the sociopolitical changes taking place in Latin America, Benton writes: "For Latin Americans, the word 'industrialization' does not mean merely Anaconda Copper or Mercedes-Benz or American and Foreign Power. It means Paz-del-Rio, a steel mill in Colombia; it means Huachipato in Chile, and El Caroní—an electric power and metallurgical combine in Venezuela."[1] Taking into account the new spirit in Latin America, Benton recommends that American investors change their tactics. "If they want to export capitalism and protect their investment in Latin America, U.S. companies must extend the opportunity for the citizens of those countries in which they operate to acquire stock in Latin American enterprises and increase their participation in profits and dividends.This is one of the great problems of the future."[2] As an example, Benton cites a number of companies in Argentina in which national capital controls 51 percent of the shares.

At present, mixed enterprises in Latin America have spread everywhere. They evidence particularly strong growth in new fields of industry.

While in mining and oil companies the United States prefers, with few exceptions, to adhere to the "old" methods and to retain their exclusive domination, in the manufacturing industries (enterprises of the future) they seek to join with domestic capital. Mixed enterprises are particularly widespread in the pharmaceutical, chemical, synthetic rubber, and electrotechnical branches of industry.

Holding companies as well as purely industrial companies assume the form of mixed companies. These holding or financial companies control enterprises in various industrial fields. The New York banking firm of Kuhn, Loeb, and Company and the National Bank of Mexico are partners in one such holding company—Inversiones Latinas, founded in Mexico by American bankers.

By using the form of mixed companies, the U.S. companies are able to attract the capital they need from Latin American businessmen. With relatively modest resources, American operators control and make use of enormous sums of Latin American capital. For example, according to data compiled by the Argentine economist Jaime Fuchs, there were 283 American companies in Argentina in 1956 whose total published balances came to 4.3 billion pesos. However, through the system of partnership in Argentine enterprises, the U.S. monopolies controlled capital of over 10 billion pesos.[3] Since then, especially after 1958, when Argentine President Arturo Frondizi threw open

---

[1]W. Benton, *The Voice of Latin America* (New York, 1961), p. 43.
[2]*Ibid.*, p. 44.
[3]See J. Fuchs, *Proniknovenie amerikanskikh trestov v Argentinu* (Moskva, 1959), pp. 120, 122.

the doors to American capital, the number of mixed companies has grown.

Just as in industry, there are mixed companies in agriculture that facilitate the exploitation of the rural economy of Latin America. Thus, in Brazil, in the state of Mato Grosso, a Rockefeller group owns 40 percent of the stock in a million-acre cattle-breeding company in partnership with former Brazilian ambassador to Washington Walter Moreira, now director of the large Brazilian bank, Banco Comercial.[4] Mixed companies have become widespread in agriculture in Argentina, Chile, and Uruguay.

The sharpening of the competitive struggle on one hand and the weak technological facilities of Latin America on the other have prompted U.S. monopolies to resort more often and more actively to camouflaged forms of seizure of markets, the most important of which is the patent agreement. These agreements make it possible to overcome trade, custom-tariff, and currency restrictions and also to compete successfully with local industry, even in fields supported by the state. Patent agreements allow profit to be made from the sale of goods under a national trademark—goods produced by local firms, but under American patents.

The American monopoly press keeps completely silent on the matter of U.S. patent agreements. If by chance information about foreign-affiliated U.S. monopolies is published, the facts regarding the nature and magnitude of patent agreements are virtually absent. Nothing, perhaps, is as diligently concealed by U.S. corporations as information about patents. After all, the sale of a patent represents no transfer of tangible value, and the United States does not invest any capital. The disclosure of sums paid for patent agreements would show how much the Latin American countries must pay for their backwardness.

As a rule, patent agreements are made with enterprises controlled by national capital. By the same token, they become an added way of subordinating those branches of industry and individual companies which are not yet dominated by American monopolies. In addition, patent agreements give U.S. monopolies an opportunity to drain enormous profits out of Latin America. Patent agreements require not only high royalties, but sometimes even monthly or annual payments. Often a charge is added for technical service connected with the use of a patent.

The Philco Corporation, a large American company that produces household appliances, has become very active in Latin America. The company has concluded a number of patent agreements in Argentina, Brazil, Uruguay, Chile, and Mexico for the manufacture of refrigerators, washing machines, electric appliances, and dishwashers. A number of patent agreements have been made by Coering Overseas Corporation, a U.S. machine-building company. In mid-1961, the latter made an agreement with the large Brazilian company Fabrica Nacional de Vagões, of the state of São Paulo, for the construction of railroad rolling stock.[5]

According to the figures of the first conference of scientists and businessmen of Venezuela in 1962, deductions for the use of patents in the country amount to 3 percent of the total value of industrial production. Inasmuch as the national industry is poorly equipped technologically, it was noted at the conference that "the volume of foreign exchange transfers abroad as compensation for the use of patents in the manufacturing industry alone was valued at 250 million bolivars annually." As a result, if the projected 8

[4]*Time*, June 20, 1960, p. 62.
[5]*Foreign Commerce Weekly*, June 12, 1961.

percent annual rate of growth of industrial production should be maintained during the next twenty years, Venezuela by 1980 will have to pay out 2,350 million bolivars abroad for the use of patents.[6]

Payments for patent agreements by Brazil are enormous. While in 1955 the payments of Brazil to the United States for the use of patents amounted to 196 million dollars, in 1956 they approached 275 million dollars and in 1957, 350 million dollars.[7]

To secure high profits, U.S. monopolies stop at nothing. Counterfeit, bribery, bookkeeping machinations—these are usual things in the practice of American companies. The Latin American press is full of stories about the many violations of Latin American laws by American companies, especially stories of tax evasion. In this respect, wide publicity has been given to the notorious United Fruit Company, famous for its lawlessness not only in relations with workers and farmers but also with the Latin American governments to whom it refuses to pay taxes. Many mining and oil companies are not far behind. An American concern, Hanna, acquired an iron ore mine in Brazil in 1958. By the middle of 1961, it had become indebted to the Brazilian government for back taxes totalling 203 million cruzeiros.[8]

United States monopolies have mapped out definite lines of attack upon the Latin American economy. These would not only facilitate the acquisition of strong positions in important categories of the economy but would also maintain them. In the present situation, the American monopolies prefer not to advertise their dominating role in various spheres of activity in Latin America, but choose to remain behind the scenes. Meanwhile, they are not squeamish about using old means and methods to assure high profits.

[6]*Mundo Económico*, March-April 1962, p. 4.
[7]*Viçao*, January 16, 1959.
[8]*O Semanario*, July 1, 1961.

37. An Assessment of International Credit-Distributing Agencies in Latin America and Their Role in Serving the Interests of World Capitalism*

Z. I. ROMANOVA

The export of capital, especially to underdeveloped countries, is one of the economic pillars of imperialism. The imperialist state is assuming the function of capital exporter as a result

*Ekonomicheskaia ekspansiia SShA v Latinskoi Amerike (Moskva: Izdatel'stvo sotsial'no-ekonomicheskoi literatury, 1963), pp. 87-96.

of the socialist system's undermining of the economic and political roots of foreign monopoly–capital domination in underdeveloped countries, and because of the immense growth of the internal forces of national liberation. The primary purpose of the export of state capital is to shore up the shaky system of international exploitation and to strengthen existing social and production relations in the underdeveloped countries, thereby preserving the foundation for the export of private foreign capital.

The distinguishing feature of contemporary U.S. credit policy is the ever-expanding role of state loans and credit.[1] Before World War II, state loans and credits were of small consequence, comprising less than 10 percent of all U.S. investments abroad. Their role at present has grown immeasurably. State loans account for one-fourth of all U.S. foreign investments, and the export of government capital is proceeding steadily and systematically.

Such strong government support of foreign economic expansion is a sign of the general crisis of capitalism and a reflection of the inability of the monopolies to compete for markets with the usual old methods. With a constantly broadening national-liberation movement throughout the underdeveloped world, particularly in Latin America, the mercantile-industrial monopolies place on the government the basic risk for the export of capital into important but low-income fields of the economy. The basic task of government credit is to encourage private investment, not to replace it. Government credits and loans are used to engender a favorable political and investment climate in Latin America. They prepare the conditions and clear the road for the subsequent flow of private capital.

In contrast to private investment, the importance of government loans goes far beyond the limits of the profits they secure. Using its credit mechanism, U.S. monopoly capital pursues the following aims: (a) to give capital investment a direction that would predetermine and strengthen the semi-colonial economic structure of Latin America; (b) to promote the export of American goods; (c) to facilitate the drain of valuable raw materials; (d) to exert pressure on the economic policy of the Latin American countries; and (e) to create the illusion of aid to Latin America.

The peculiar characteristic of the postwar export of state capital is that more and more often it hides behind the screen of international banking organizations. Before World War II, U.S. government loans and credits proceeded chiefly according to patterns set by the U.S. Export-Import Bank. After the war, they were made through the International Bank for Reconstruction and Development, the International Monetary Fund, the International Finance Corporation, and the International Development Association, in which the United States plays the leading part.

In an atmosphere of growing hostility to the export of American capital, even when it takes the form of government loans and credits, the American monopolies are making every effort to disguise it, giving their capital the more acceptable coloring of "international" funds. This, however, is an indication not of the strengthening, but of the weakening of American monopolistic capital and the deepening of the general crisis of capitalism.

In the first postwar decade, credits and loans of the Export-Import Bank, on the one hand, and of the International Bank for Reconstruction and

---

[1]The first of the large government loans by the United States were made during the First World War. They were of a purely military character and with the end of the war were discontinued.

Development and the International Monetary Fund, on the other, were about equal. By the end of the 1950's, when new international banking organizations were created, the latter had clearly gained precedence. At present, the greater part of the export of U.S. government capital into Latin America is transacted through the so-called international banks into which the United States deposits its grants, while the role of such an old banking instrument of U.S. monopoly capital as the Export-Import Bank has not been weakened.

The distinctive feature of U.S. credit policy in Latin America today is that large private American banks have begun to furnish their credits and loans to Latin America not directly but via government and international banks. Short-term commercial credits, as a rule, are the only exception.

For example, in 1961, the International Bank for Reconstruction and Development extended Venezuela a credit of 45 million dollars. The fundamental role in this transaction, however, was played by the following American private banks: The Chemical Bank, New York Trust Company; the First National City Bank of New York; the Girard Trust Bank of Philadelphia; and the Grace National Bank of New York.[2] Thus, the World Bank is assuming the centralized direction of capital export of private American banks.

The first bank to regularly export government capital to Latin America was the Export-Import Bank (EIB), founded in 1934. It differed from any other leading credit institution operating in Latin America in that it was owned entirely by American capital. The original purpose of this bank was to increase the competitive potentialities of American merchandise on the Latin American market, where the European countries, especially Germany, were staging an aggressive attack. Later the horizons widened, though, as before, the principal aim continued to be promotion of the export of American goods.

Latin America occupies first place among economic areas of the world in the volume of loans received from banks. Of 10,238 million dollars loaned by the EIB from 1934 to 1959, Latin America's share amounted to 3,809 million dollars, or 37 percent.[3] In the next two years, its proportionate volume increased further. In 1961 the Latin American share was 490 million dollars, or 44 percent of a total of 1,114 million dollars.[4]

The bank's activity in the postwar period expanded without interruption. Its credit resources were increased from 700 million dollars in the first postwar years to 4.5 billion dollars in 1951, and to 7 billion dollars in 1958. In the years 1934 to 1945, the EIB extended credits of 500 million dollars, but in the 15 postwar years the total credits amounted to over 10 billion dollars.

The EIB does not substitute for the activities of private capital; on the contrary, it cooperates with it in every way. In a special message to the national conference of the American Association of Bankers EIB President Harold Linder stated: "We are called upon to supplement and stimulate private capital, not compete with it . . . While fulfilling the bank's first function —providing aid to U.S. exporters— we have an additional bright and noble task, since ours is the unique position of promoting our national goals and of making profit for Uncle Sam without competing with private interests."[5]

[2] *Fortnightly Review*, December 30, 1961.
[3] *Export-Import Bank of Washington. Report to the Congress, June, 1959* Part 1 (Washington, D.C. 1959), p. 193.
[4] *Foreign Commerce Weekly*, January 29, 1962, p. 146.
[5] *Ibid.*, p. 145.

A large role in supplying credit to Latin America is played by the International Bank for Reconstruction and Development (IBRD). The charter of its incorporation became effective in December 1945, and it commenced operations in June 1946. However, the hopes that the Latin American countries had originally built on it were not justified. They expected that the IBRD would become a powerful tool for the increase of government capital investment, which would change the character of Latin American foreign financing. Is it not the bank's purpose to help underdeveloped countries? Surely these countries, bled white by foreign private capital, are in need of government investment. However, the rules and bylaws of the IBRD maintain that one of its aims is cooperation with private foreign capital investment and that the bank is not competing with private investment. The rules provide that the IBRD may furnish credit only in cases where private credit investment is unobtainable or not feasible.

Nor did the International Monetary Fund (IMF), founded simultaneously with IBRD, justify Latin American hopes. The Latin American countries assumed that the IMF would help them strengthen their foreign exchange and financial situation and support their currency regulations. However, Article VIII of the IMF charter specifically provided for the gradual elimination of foreign exchange restrictions and the systems of multiple currency valuation that are used to safeguard the developing industries of Latin America.

The organizational structure of the IMF and IBRD are similar, each with an executive council and a board of directors. Participation of countries in the IBRD presupposes simultaneous participation in the IMF, since only members of the IMF are eligible for credit in the IBRD. The difference between these two institutions lies only in the form by which they issue loans. While the IMF furnishes short-term credit to cover balance-of-payment deficits, the IBRD extends long-term credit.

A special place is occupied by the International Finance Corporation (IFC), created in July 1956. According to its rules and by-laws, the purpose of the corporation is to issue loans only to private (domestic and foreign) concerns, without demanding government guarantees. This purpose was frankly stated in the corporation's charter. It discloses the real aims that both the purely American and the international banks have. The existence of previously established international banking institutions relieves this corporation of the necessity of resorting to the support of national, including government, capital to justify its activities.

The methods of the IFC coincide to a large degree with the dealings of private financial establishments. For instance, the Corporation may sell its capital investments to private investors. In case of any threat to the investment or bankruptcy of an enterprise, the Corporation may adopt "any measures." Through agreements with a number of Latin American companies, the IFC reserved for itself the right to acquire stock of the given enterprise equal to the amount of its credit during the period the agreement is in force. Quite often the IFC reserves for itself the right to participate in profits. Thus, according to a 1958 agreement with the Brazilian company DLR Plasticos do Brasil, IFC received the right to 10 percent of the profit of that company.[6]

The charter of the IFC provides that the corporation issue loans only to "profitable" private industrial, agricultural, and mercantile concerns of

[6]See *BIKI*, June 3, 1958.

medium size. It specifically provides that IFC should not invest in the building of costly heavy-industry undertakings. Curiously, the IFC does not issue credits for the building of schools, hospitals, and enterprises for public use, since such outlays are "too big" for it.

A recently formed international banking institution is the International Development Association (IDA). The incentive for creating IDA was the growth and consolidation of the world socialist system, the increasing aid given to the underdeveloped countries by the socialist states, and the stronger gravitation of the young sovereign states toward new forms of financial and economic cooperation. The great response with which the unselfish aid of the socialist countries has been met in the underdeveloped countries forced the imperialist states not only to cover up their real neocolonial foreign economic policy carefully, but in some cases to make concessions concerning the export of government capital . The IDA was founded in October 1959 and began to function in January 1961.

The purpose of the IDA is stated in its charter as "the promotion of economic development, increase in production, and a higher standard of living in the underdeveloped areas of the world." On closer observation, however, it is apparent that this new institution differs very little from earlier ones. True, the charter states that the under-developed countries will be extended the "necessary financial means on conditions more flexible and less burdensome for their balance of payments than ordinary loans issued for these purposes by the International Bank for Reconstruction and Development." However, in the preamble to the charter it is again emphasized that the economic development of the underdeveloped countries and the improve-

ment of the standard of living of the population "will be facilitated by the increased flow of foreign capital— state and private."

In addition, the IDA can grant credits and loans both on favorable terms and on the terms drafted by the IBRD. Underdeveloped countries will receive "aid" only after a thorough investigation of their economic and political situation, and those which are "ineligible" will be rejected.

The Agency for International Development was created in 1961 to regulate the "aid" the United States is extending to foreign countries through its own chain of banks as well as through international banking houses. Actually, its function is to determine U.S. credit policy and to channel the export of American state capital.

The basic international credit institutions—the International Monetary Fund, the International Bank for Reconstruction and Development, the International Finance Corporation, and the International Development Association—can be called international only with reservations. One need merely to examine their organizational structure to see that behind the international facade is the United States.

In the middle of 1961, the United States controlled 29 percent of the votes in IBRD, while all of Latin America controlled only 8 percent. The post of president of the IBRD is invariably occupied by a representative of major U.S. finance capital. At present it is held by Eugene Black, a member of the board of the Rockefeller financial empire. The vast personnel of the bank is mainly American. The activity of the American delegates in the IMF as well as in the IBRD is directed by the U.S. National Advisory Council on monetary-financial problems, whose members include the Secretary of State and other representatives of the govern-

Table 8. Participation by Country in IBRD

Country	1959*		1961	
	Deposits in Million Dollars	Votes in Percent	Deposits in Million Dollars	Votes in Percent
United States	3,175	28.43	6,350	29.23
Great Britain	1,300	11.77	2,600	12.04
France	525	4.89	1,050	4.93
Federal Republic of Germany	330	3.15	1,050	4.93
India	440	3.78	800	3.79
Canada	325	3.11	750	3.56
Japan	250	2.44	666	3.17

*As of June 30

ment as well as the director of EIB. The share of various countries in the capital formation of IBRD and the allocation of their votes are shown in Table 8.[7]

Thus, the purely American EIB and the IMF and IBRD act in close cooperation. In mid-1959, the United States increased its share in the IMF by 1,375 million dollars and in the IBRD by 3,175 million dollars. The United States thus plays a predominant role in the IBRD, and its importance not only is not diminishing but, on the contrary, is increasing, in spite of the entrenchment of West European and other exporters of capital.

The International Finance Corporation is an affiliate of the IBRD, although it is considered a specialized agency of the United Nations and was originally planned as a banking institution, subordinate only to the United Nations.[8] The chairman of the IFC is also the president of the IBRD. The most important organizational and financial questions related to the activities of the IFC are reviewed at the annual meetings of the Board of Governors of the IBRD and IMF. In the IFC, as in the IBRD and IMF, decisions are made by a vote wherein each member country has 250 votes, and an additional one for each share of stock. The U.S. share is 33 percent of the vote, or more than 6 times that of all the Latin American countries together.

The International Development Association is also an affiliate of IBRD. As in previously formed international banking institutions, the number of votes of IDA members is proportional to the size of their deposit, that is, their financial strength. The number of IDA votes is distributed approximately the same as in the IBRD—the U.S. share is 32 percent, and top positions are held by officials of the IBRD. Thus, in spite of the "international" label, the decisive role in these banking institutions is played by the United States.

[7]Deutsche Wirtschaftsinstitut, 8:17 (1962).

[8]This information explains precisely the cool attitude of the United States toward IFC in its first stage of formatory negotiations begun in 1951.

The intensification of the national-liberation movement in the underdeveloped countries, including those of Latin America, has prompted the United States to seek the cooperation of other imperialist states in its offensive against these underdeveloped countries. In October 1961, a special International Organization for Economic Cooperation and Development (OECD) was formed, uniting the United States, Canada, and the countries of Western Europe. The aim of OECD, as stated in its charter, is "to cooperate in the economic development of economically underdeveloped countries." As a matter of fact, it was created to coordinate the activities of the major exporters of capital.

38. The True Nature of the Alliance for Progress*

B. I. GVOZDAREV

The authors of the Alliance contemplate that with its help they will be able to exert an overall economic, political, and ideological influence upon the people of Latin America to keep them in the world capitalist system. One of the basic concepts from which the ideologists of the Alliance set out is that of the "developing revolution," which, according to the authors, must eventually bring the Latin American republics wealth and prosperity under the guidance of the United States. It is precisely here, however, that one finds the irreconcilable ideological contradictions of the Alliance. Although they advertise the "developing revolution," they are in fact committed to preventing basic social reforms in Latin America, to disarming the Latin American people ideologically, and to mobilizing internal counterrevolutionary forces to fight the national-liberation movement.

What, then, are the initiators of the Alliance offering the Latin American workers as a counterbalance to the attraction of communism? First of all, in their trite and hackneyed bourgeois propaganda, they offer the "doctrine" of anticommunism. President Kennedy did not deny the direct link between the Alliance for Progress and the policy of anticommunism. Criticizing the decision adopted by the U.S. Congress in the fall of 1962, to reduce the foreign "aid" program somewhat, he declared: "It is perfectly senseless to make speeches against the spread of communism, to voice regrets over the instability of Latin America and Asia . . . and then to vote for a reduction of spending for the Alliance for Progress, to put up roadblocks in the way

*Soiuz radi progressa i ego sushchnost' (Moskva: Izdatel'stvo Nauka, 1964), pp. 118–122, 134–136.

of the Peace Corps, and to undermine the efforts of those who are trying to stop communism's influence in the vital areas of the world."

The imperialist ideologists attempt to falsify communist teachings, to distort the true meaning of world events, to sow disunity among peoples in their struggle for national independence, and to conceal from them the truth of the successes of socialist countries.

The ruling circles of the United States and their henchmen in Latin America made extensive use of anticommunism even before the founding of the Alliance. However, under present conditions anticommunism is being spread by Yankee imperialists in Latin America in a more subtle and skillful manner. In an article entitled "The Misadventures of Anticommunism," the Brazilian public figure Pedro Motta Lima writes:

It must be said that modern anticommunism —for instance—the Alliance for Progress —is different from the anticommunism of John Foster Dulles. Although the strategy of imperialism actually has not changed, the Kennedy government does use a more flexible approach and employs new forms of propaganda in certain countries, such as Brazil, Mexico, and Chile. This is reflected particularly in the appointment of new ambassadors to these countries. These are no longer the "dinosaurs" of the old State Department, nor are they slick operators. Now Washington is resorting to the services of professors, economists, and sociologists.[1]

With the aid of the new propagandists of anticommunism, efforts are being made to convince and win over the scientists, students, intellectuals, and entire peoples of Latin America. But neither the old nor the new angles of the champions of anticommunism, within the framework of the Alliance for Progress or outside it, can conceal the reactionary essence of this imperialist "doctrine" from the workers of Latin America.

Propaganda about the "American way of life" and advertisement of the phantom blessings that the Alliance allegedly will bring to the people of the Latin American countries are regarded by the masters of the Alliance as the most potent antidotes against communist ideas. The aim of the "American way of life" propaganda is to convince the Latin American people that only in a system of world capitalism under U.S. leadership can they obtain genuine prosperity. The fable of the "American way of life" camouflages and distorts the real conditions of the American workers. It conceals the increasing exploitation of the working class and the sharpning internal contradictions between the American bourgeoisie and the proletariat. The sponsors and ringleaders of the Alliance are not stingy with cheap promises. The Latin American workers are promised literally everything: elimination of illiteracy, free health care, low-cost housing, democratic freedom, and many other advantages—but all in the "course of time," perhaps in ten years or more. In the meantime—patience and still more patience. Or, as the American adage goes, "You'll have pie in the sky when you die."

The fact that not the welfare of the Latin American workers but entirely different aims are being pursued is at times acknowledged by the Alliance architects themselves. Thus, the zealous advocate of the Alliance, Senator Robert Sykes, speaking on plans for housing construction in Latin American countries, stated: "We must never forget that a man who owns a home or is buying one is a solid citizen and is the least likely to risk his property in exchange for the promises of communist agitators."[2]

[1]*Problemy mira i sotsializma*, 9:75 (September 1962).
[2]*Congressional Record*, August 28, 1961.

The building of a few homes, hospitals, and schools is not at all intended to relieve the lot of millions of slum dwellers in Caracas, Lima, Rio de Janeiro, and other large cities of Latin America but to mollify their discontent and to fence them off from the "influence of communist agitators."[3] But the authors of the Alliance obviously err. Evidence of this fact lies in the irreversible process of a growing revolutionary movement on the American continent. The gravitational force of communism lies not only in the fact that it brings a wealth of material blessings, but also in the fact that it creates conditions for an all-round, harmonious development of society and eliminates exploitation of man by man in all its manifestations. The authors of the Alliance for Progress, generous as they are with promises, could not make such promises to the Latin American people. All the efforts of the Harvard professors and the "brain trust" notwithstanding, they could not succeed in creating an ideological machinery that would be in the interests of the monopoly groups and at the same time be accepted by the Latin American people, who do not want their countries reduced to semicolonial status.

According to a characteristic admission of the American journal *Time*, the Alliance failed in trying to create an appropriate "political ideology" that could compete with communism and revolutionary thought. Nevertheless, U.S. ruling circles do not cease in their efforts to win over the masses of the Latin American republics ideologically by every means possible.

Seeking to attract the broad strata of Latin American workers to the Alliance, the ideologists of the "new course" strenuously disseminate the idea of "peaceful revolution." Yesterday's patrons of Batista, [Pérez] Jiménez, and other Latin American dictators hypocritically declare themselves to be heirs to the democratic traditions of the revolutionaries of the nineteenth century: Bolívar, San Martín, Artigas, and even José Martí. Why should the ideologists of the monopolies pose as "revolutionaries"? They do so because with the aid of the "peaceful revolution"—which would be under full Washington control—they hope to ward off impending social upheavals in Latin America. "Revolution" from above to avoid a revolution "from below" and interference with the Latin American people's pursuit of the heroic Cuban example—such is the basis of the reasoning about a "peaceful," "regulated" revolution. "Unable to prevent the establishment of a communist regime in Cuba in the 1950's," regretfully remarks Dean Rusk, "the United States and its allies in the Western Hemisphere were faced with a more difficult problem—how to find a cure."[4] U.S. ruling circles consider the Alliance for Progress to be such a cure. With its aid they actually intend to bring about the "peaceful revolution of hope"—that is, to replace radical resolution of Latin American socioeconomic problems with palliatives; deep-seated revolutionary transformation, with curtailed reforms under the control of U.S. monopolies; and the class struggle, with a reactionary and utopian idea of the "harmony of class interests."

THE ALLIANCE FOR PROGRESS AND THE DOCTRINE OF SELF-HELP

So-called self-help is given an im-

[3]According to information of ĬBR, for the first year of operation of "aid" by the Alliance for Progress, 55 million dollars was allotted for the construction of houses—a sum guaranteeing the building of only 15,000 small suburban type homes—while Argentina alone is in need of 500,000 urban dwellings; Mexico, not less than a million; and Brazil, eight million (*Newsweek*, August 27, 1962, p. 36).

[4]*The Department of State Bulletin*, March 4, 1963, p. 313.

portant place in the Alliance for Progress charter. The treatment of it constitutes one more insoluble inner contradiction of the Kennedy Plan. The U.S. ruling circles estimate that to fulfill the aims set for the Alliance, the Latin American countries would have to earmark the amount of not less than 80 billion dollars by 1970 for it. This sum would be gathered from the "maximum effort" of the Latin American governments.

In the absence, however, of radical socioeconomic reforms, mobilizing such great resources is practically impossible, since, even according to the official data of the OAS and the ECLA, the economy of the Latin American countries is in a state of "near-stagnation." The report prepared by these organizations for the meeting of IESS in Mexico in October 1962 stated that in the overwhelming majority of Latin American countries the situation is characterized by a shortage of capital, unemployment, a drop in consumer goods demand, and decreased purchasing power of the population. Agriculture is in a particularly grave condition.[5] The amount of foreign indebtedness of many Latin American countries increases from year to year. For example, in the beginning of 1962 the indebtedness of Brazil reached 2,357 million dollars, out of which 1,587 million dollars are to be paid by 1965. The foreign debt of Argentina reached 1,800 million dollars, out of which 1,260 million dollars are to be paid in the next five years.

The systematic dwindling of gold reserves can be observed in a number of countries. For the period 1958 to 1962, these reserves fell from 160 million dollars to 122 million dollars in Colombia; in Mexico, from 372 million dollars to 326 million dollars; and in Venezuela, from 1,058 million dollars to 477 million dollars.[6] There has been a deficit balance on current

items of balance of payments in several countries of Latin America during these years (see Table 9).[7]

Table 9. Current Items of Balance of Payments (in millions of dollars)

Country	1957	1958	1959	1960	1961
Argentina	-301	-256	-14	-198	-572
Brazil	-275	-267	-337	-538	-250
Uruguay	-123	-4	-44	-79	—
Mexico	-220	-202	-46	-176	-62

At the same time the "flight' abroad of national capital continues. Representatives of the landowning oligarchy and large mercantile-industrial bourgeoisies, terrified by the upsurging national-liberation movements, prefer to transfer their assets to banks in the United States and the West European countries. According to figures of the subcommittee on Inter-American Economic Relations, headed by Senator J. Sparkman, transfer of domestic capital from Latin America to foreign banks in the last few years amounted to a sum of from 5 billion to 15 billion dollars.[8] The mass drainage of national capital naturally intensifies the problem of providing indigenous financial resources.

Another important factor complicating the economic situation in Latin America is the systematic drop in prices for traditional export commodities. As a result of inequivalent foreign exchange, the Latin American countries lose each year enormous sums, exceeding by several times receipts of foreign "aid." This loss is precisely the reason for the widespread opinion among Latin Americans that stabilization of prices on their products would

[5]Newsweek, October 15, 1962, p. 27.
[6]International Financial Statistics, January 1963.
[7]Ibid.
[8]Economic Developments in South America. Hearings before the Subcommittee on Inter-American Economic Relations of the Joint Economic Committee, Congress: 87th session (Washington, D.C., 1962), pp. 4, 53.

bring them immeasurably greater benefits than aid from the program of the
alliance.

Prevailing economic conditions in
Latin America fully justify the skep-
ticism of many economists regarding
the possibility of raising 80 billion dollars by "self help" out of internal resources without changing the social or
economic structures of their countries.
However, assuming that even the above
means could be found, this amount
would still be insufficient to solve the
vitally important problems of the countries of Latin America. And with expenditures like those mapped out by the

United States, it would take tens or
even hundreds of years for the Latin
American republics—with the exception of Cuba—to achieve the level of
industrial development of the capitalist
countries. According to calculations by
Soviet economist I. K. Sheremet'ev,
in order to raise the economic potential of Latin America to the U.S.
level, the absolute amount of capital
investment would have to be 1,700 to
1,800 billion dollars.[9]

[9] I. K. Sheremet'ev, "Posuly S.Sh.A. i deist-
vitel'nost'," *Mezhdunarodnaia zhizn'*, 4:86–87
(1963).

39. A Critique of the Concept of Spiritual Brotherhood in the Pan American Movement*

M. V. ANTIASOV

After Blaine, the idea of a "spiritual
unity" among the American countries,
in opposition to Europe, temporarily
vanished from the ideology of Pan-
Americanism, since it no longer had
any meaning. While in the early and
middle nineteenth century it had been
possible to some extent to picture the
American countries as a sort of contrast to Europe where the Holy Alliance was ruling, on the threshold of
the twentieth century such a comparison became too difficult even for
the ideologists of Pan-Americanism.

Both in the European countries and

in the United States, one and the same
class became the dominant force: the
imperialist bourgeoisie. The result was
that the political differences dividing the republican United States from
monarchist Europe gradually became
extinct. V. I. Lenin wrote: "Comparison between, say, the republican
American bourgeoisie and the monarchist Japanese or the German bourgeoisie shows that their strong political divergence becomes much weaker

Sovremennyi panamerikanizm (Moskva:
Izdatel'stvo Instituta mezhdunarodnykh otnoshenii, 1960), pp. 196–209.

during the imperialist epoch . . . because in all these cases we are speaking of a bourgeoisie having definite parasitic features."[1]

Still another circumstance had its effect. Until the last decades of the nineteenth century the creditor countries of Latin America were Great Britain, and, to a lesser degree, France. Not until the end of the nineteenth century and the first decades of the twentieth century did the United States become a factor of real significance in the economy and finances of the Latin American countries and begin to win away one position after another from the European powers. While of course this meant increased conflict between the Anglo-American, Franco-American, and German-American interests, at the same time it strengthened the feeling of class community with other imperialist countries within the business and political circles of the United States, as against Latin America, and the bond between the usurer countries vis-à-vis the people they exploited.

It is characteristic that President Theodore Roosevelt had acknowledged the European powers' right to recover debts and even their "right" to punish Latin American nations. In this connection, he issued his own interpretation of the Monroe Doctrine, proclaiming that it was "in no measure inimical to any of the Old World states," and that the United States "does not guarantee a single one of the American countries against punishment" by European states "in case of misbehavior, provided that such punishment does not take the form of territorial seizure."[2]

These "new" trends found their expression particularly in the ideas set forth in the well-known book by Herbert Croly. American foreign policy ideas, he points out, had been formerly based on "the absolute incompatibility between the political institutions of America and Europe . . . . At the pre-

sent moment, an assertion of such incompatibility could be only the fruit of obtuse or ill-intentioned American democratic tyranny."[3]

Not until Wilson was the idea of the American nations' "spiritual brotherhood" again taken up. The attempt to create a Pan American league was accompanied by repeated declarations from Wilson and Lansing referring to the "common democratic ideals" and traditions inherent in the American nations. Thus, in December 1915, Lansing, while addressing the delegates of the Second Pan American Scientific Congress, emphasized that the American countries are distinguished by "an identity of political institutions" and that they "share a common concept of human rights."[4]

The promotion of these ideas was part and parcel of the pseudodemocratic phraseology of the Wilson period. Outwardly, the concepts of Lansing and Wilson are no different from the ideas of "spiritual unity" proposed earlier by Clay. But actually, in the twentieth century, when the domination by monopolies became established, the doctrine of "spiritual unity" assumed a new meaning—a new ring. Characteristic of the policy at that time of the imperialist powers, including the United States, was a transition from bourgeois democracy to reactionism. V. I. Lenin pointed out that "it was the turn *from* democracy *toward* political reaction that became the political superstructure over the new economy, over monopolistic capitalism (since imperialism is monopol-

[1]V. I. Lenin, "Imperializm, kak vysshaia stadiia kapitalizma," *Sochineniia*, vol. 22, p. 287.
[2]See S. F. Bemis, *The Latin American Policy of the United States* (New York, 1967), p. 147.
[3]H. Croly, *The Promise of American Life* (Cambridge, Mass., 1965), p. 297.
[4]See J. B. Moore, *The Principles of American Diplomacy* (New York, 1918), p. 406.

istic capitalism)."[5] The support of reactionary forces in Latin America reflected this shift.

It was precisely in Wilson's time that the reactionary imperialist nature of American capitalism was manifested especially strongly. "The idealized democratic republic of Wilson," wrote V. I. Lenin, "*turned out to be* actually a form of the fiercest imperialism of the most shameless oppression and stifling of weak and small peoples."[6]

On the other hand, while the former basic control groups in Latin American countries were connected economically and ideologically mainly with the European countries, in the twentieth century there began for these groups a reorientation toward their more powerful master, the United States, which was much better able to assure these groups of control within their own countries than could any European power. This was the basis on which the true political and "spiritual" unity began to take shape between American imperialism and the reactionary latifundista and comprador circles of Latin America. The sharp edge of this unity was aimed against bourgeois-democratic movements.

The reactionary imperialism of the United States became an obstacle in the path of Latin American bourgeois democracy. Already during the Mexican bourgeois-democratic revolution, American imperialism had operated on the side of Mexican feudal reactionism as opposed to Mexican bourgeois democracy.

The role that the Washington government and, in particular, American ambassador Henry Lane Wilson played in the overthrow of the bourgeois-democratic government of Madero in 1913 and the establishment of General Huerta's reactionary dictatorship is a well-known fact. As the American historian Gruening wrote: "The United States . . . played a decisive role in the overthrow of the government of Francisco Madero. Huerta's treason would never have been conceived without the militant encouragement and support of the ambassador."[7]

In 1916 the United States decided upon open armed intervention against the Mexican revolution. Only the prospect of prolonged guerrilla warfare by the Mexican people and sharp protests in other Latin American countries caused the withdrawal of General Pershing's army from Mexico in 1917.[8]

Even after the failure of this intervention, the United States categorically refused to recognize the revolutionary government of the country and its constitution that was proclaimed in 1917, which, in the opinion of W. Foster, was "the most democratic constitution" of that time among all the constitutions of bourgeois countries.[9]

Thus it was that in the twentieth century, in the age of imperialism, the "spiritual unity" of the American peoples began to acquire a very specific and real meaning. It was unity between U.S. imperialism and the reactionary, feudalistic, clerical-military elements of Latin America.

The idea of "spiritual unity" among the American nations came to its real flowering during the era of the "Good Neighbor Policy." In his speech before the administrative council of the Pan American Union on April 14, 1933, Franklin Roosevelt had already laid special stress on, among other factors, certain "common ideals" on which "Pan-Americanism is constructed."

[5]V. I. Lenin, "O karikature na marksizm i o 'imperialisticheskoi ekonomizme,'" *Sochineniia*, vol. 23, p. 31.

[6]V. I. Lenin, "Tsennye priznaniia Pitirima Sorokina," *Sochineniia*, vol. 28, p. 169.

[7]E. Gruening, *Mexico and Its Heritage* (New York, 1930), p. 576.

[8]M. Al'perovich and B. Rudenko, *Meksikanskaia revoliutsiia 1910–1917 gg. i politika S. Sh. A.* (Sotsekgiz, 1958), pp. 237–265.

[9]W. Z. Foster, *Ocherk politicheskoi istorii Ameriki* (Moskva, 1953), p. 426.

Franklin Roosevelt said, "I regard the Pan American Union as an expression of the spiritual unity of the American countries."[10] A few years later, this idea was fixed in the basic document of the Eighth Pan American Conference, the Lima Declaration, advertised in the United States as "the constitution of the Western Hemisphere."

"The peoples of America," says the Declaration of Lima, "have established their spiritual unity as a result of the identity of their republican institutions and the humanism and tolerance inherent in the American peoples, thanks to their total devotion to the principles ... of personal freedom without religious and racial prejudice."[11]

As a matter of fact, Franklin Roosevelt, Hull, and Welles stamped all the measures taken in the area of Latin American policy with the doctrine of the "spiritual unity" of the American nations. It must be noted that particularly favorable conditions had arisen for promoting this doctrine in the 1930's and 1940's.

First, Franklin Roosevelt's domestic policy was permeated by the principles of a "New Deal," with Roosevelt acting as a "defender" of the common people and as the "enemy" of monopolies. The aura of a "people's president" surrounded Franklin Roosevelt—and was assiduously cultivated by his supporters. Attacks on the President from the camp of extreme reaction, trying to paint him as virtually a socialist, only helped to build this halo.

These specific features of the political situation of the "New Deal" period aided the propagandizing of "spiritual brotherhood" that Franklin Roosevelt addressed to the Latin American countries. According to Welles, Roosevelt's foreign policy ideas were "permeated by 'New Deal' principles." He appeared as a "symbol of positive democracy, a friend of the disinherited."[12]

While these factors of a domestic nature facilitated Franklin Roosevelt's preaching of American "brotherhood," the international situation aided him even more. The 1930's were the years of high flowering of fascist ideology. Germany, Italy, and Japan come forward with frankly racist doctrines, the refutation of bourgeois democracy, and the denial of human rights. Under such conditions, the advancing of bourgeois democratic slogans—old ideas of freedom, equality, and brotherhood that had characterized the foreign policy doctrine of Franklin Roosevelt —had no little success in the Western Hemisphere countries. To proclaim a "free" unified America in contrast to nazified Europe could not help but impress large elements of Latin America's population.

Of course, the crux of the matter was not in the struggle between the two ideologies. German and Japanese imperialism by that time had become the basic and most dangerous adversary of the American monopolies. The U.S. foreign policy ideology was subordinated to the task of liquidating this menace and, in particular, of driving competitors out of the Western Hemisphere. Nevertheless, in this case the aims of the American monopolies, very luckily for them, coincided with the unpopularity of the political ideas of their principal imperialist rivals.

Even in this period, however, the formula of the "spiritual unity" of the American countries could have been applied in its real significance only to certain social groups of Latin America. These were, first, the upper comprador and financial bourgeoisie and

[10]*Addresses and Messages of F. D. Roosevelt*, pp. 5–6.
[11]*The International Conferences of American States.* First Supplement, 1933–1940, p. 308.
[12]S. Welles, *Where Are We Heading?*, p. 184.

some of the industrial bourgeoisie also, especially those parts of it involved in mixed corporations.

The activity of Franklin Roosevelt had the effect of somewhat broadening the social base that supported U.S. policy, but it could in no case succeed in creating any kind of unity between the American capitalists and the Latin American working people. As before, the "spiritual" brethren of the American monopolists were, in the main, the latifundistas, traders, and bankers of Latin America. During its "Good Neighbor" period, the United States continued to be the prop of reactionary forces in the Western Hemisphere. As examples of this, we might cite the support of ultrareactionary puppet regimes (Somoza in Nicaragua, Trujillo in the Dominican Republic, Carías in Honduras); interference in Cuban affairs aimed at crushing the Grau San Martín government, which had the support of democratic elements; and other activities.

After the Second World War, the concept of the "spiritual unity" of the American countries underwent considerable changes. Owing to the further worsening of the general crisis of capitalism, the reactionary character of U.S. imperialism became intensified. In 1947 the antilabor Taft-Hartley Act was passed. The reactionaries obtained the passage in 1950 of the so-called McCarran-Wood "internal security" bill, which annulled to a considerable degree the Bill of Rights and other mainstays of American bourgeois democracy.

The next step on that road was the McCarran-Walter Act of 1952, under which any alien can be arrested, deported, and deprived of all rights. The same idea of eliminating bourgeois democracy underlies the organization of committees (in the U.S. House and Senate) to investigate un-American activities. These committees hold un-

limited powers of questioning, investigation, and even arrest. The same spirit underlies the effort, begun in 1947, to check up on the "loyalty" of six million government employees, the expansion of the scope of the FBI's activity, and similar acts.

Correspondingly with the growing strength of reaction at home, the Washington ruling circles also made a transition in Latin America from a more or less disguised support of reactionary forces to widespread establishment of militarist regimes. This reactionary wave took the form of active support of General Odría in Peru; the military coup of 1948 in Venezuela, the main organizer of which, according to the official statement of Venezuelan President Gallegos, was the American attaché Colonel Adams; aid in the rise to power of General Rojas Pinilla in Colombia; and encouragement to dictator Batista in Cuba. The same course was manifested in the armed intervention against the bourgeois-democratic Árbenz government in Guatemala.

The creation of a foundation for this course of action and for the spiritual unity of American imperialism and Latin American reaction became the goal of Pan American ideology. The ideological trick at this point becomes complicated in that the preachers of Pan-Americanism have to explain somehow the "spiritual unity" of the openly reactionary Latin American regimes with the ruling groups of the United States who, as always, are being proclaimed as fighters for "democracy," "freedom," and so on. During the era of the "Good Neighbor Policy" of Franklin Roosevelt, the ideologists of Pan-Americanism preferred mostly to keep modestly silent about this side of their policy. In the postwar period, however, a different method was used that corresponds more closely to the deeply reactionary nature of American imperialist ideology.

This approach is based on the claim that no regime other than a military-police dictatorship can be stable in Latin America. American bourgeois historians and jurists try strenuously to prove this thesis.

Professor Tannenbaum aserts that "hopes for democratic government in Latin America are truly small."[13] In his book *Latin American Politics and Government,* Professor Macdonald categorically states that "Latin Americans have for a long time been sympathetic to caudillos...[14][and] have been inclined to follow colorful leaders. They have always been more interested in their statesmen than in their government policies."[15]

As "grounds" for such categorical pronouncements, American historians and journalists use two basic arguments: The first is a reference to "authoritarian traditions of the Spanish colonial system,"[16] in other words, the colonial past of Latin America. The second argument is of a racist nature. The main conclusion at which American "scholars" aim is to confirm the belief that Latin Americans naturally possess specific qualities that render them "incapable" of any form of government other than reactionary militarist dictatorships.

Professors Bannon and Dunne of the Catholic University of St. Louis attempt to prove that such traits of "Latin American character" as "individualism" and "emotionalism" lead to the lack of "a spirit of compromise," and "cooperation," which are indispensable for "normal legal order."[17]

The most outspoken of the racists even declare that the Indians and mestizos, who form the majority of the population in the Latin American countries, have an "innate" lack of political ability. Thus, the *Wall Street Journal* states without much ado that "the mestizo lacks the necessary intelligence to assume responsibility for dem-

ocratic government and needs someone else to do his thinking."[18]

From these insane theories, a logical conclusion is then made to the effect that the military-police dictatorships of [Pérez] Jiménez, Batista, and [Castillo] Armas are of a profoundly "national" nature.

The above-mentioned Professor Macdonald arrives at the following conclusion from his speculations: "The Latin American nations have given sufficient proof of their preference for dictatorial regimes."[19] Another American historian, Stokes, also asserts that "in most cases, public opinion supports the caudillo."[20]

The absurdity of the reactionary ravings of American "scholarship," which distort the true state of things, is quite obvious. Of course, the moldy Spanish colonial atmosphere had a negative effect on the development of the Latin American countries. However, this negative force was not an abstract category. It was embodied in definite social strata: the latifundistas, the clericals, and the upper layer of the military caste. The dominance of these strata under conditions of formal recognition of bourgeois-democratic principles was what brought to life the political institution of *caudillismo*—the dictatorship of some agent of large landowners, usually a demagogue and a poser who beat his breast, declaring his "devotion to the cause of democracy," but in practice mercilessly robbed and

[13]*Foreign Affairs,* No. 2, 1955, p. 439.
[14]*Caudillo* is a Spanish term meaning leader, head of some political group.
[15]A. Macdonald, *Latin American Politics and Government* (New York, 1954), p. 2.
[16]*Ibid.,* p. 13. See also J. M. Cabot, *Toward Our Common American Destiny* (Medford, Mass., 1955), p. 110.
[17]J. F. Bannon and P. M. Dunne, *Latin America: An Historical Survey* (Milwaukee, 1950), pp. 432, 434.
[18]*The Wall Street Journal,* September 2, 1952.
[19]A. Macdonald, *Latin American Politics and Government,* p. 13.
[20]See *United Nations World,* December 1951.

oppressed the people while crushing every protest against the dominance of the true masters of nineteenth-century Latin America: the landowning aristocracy.

In appraising the social essence of *caudillismo*, Mariátegui quotes an admission characteristic of the Mexican reactionary philosopher, historian, and defender of the interests of landowning aristocracy, Vasconcelos: "From the economic aspect, the caudillo is a reliable supporter of the latifundista.... There is scarcely one caudillo who has not himself become a landowner.... Even a superficial check of the property rights of our large landowners suffices to show that they owe nearly everything to the Spanish crown, ... or to gifts obtained from influential generals . . ."[21]

Nevertheless, there is no doubt that the blight of *caudillismo* would have been eliminated long ago had it not enjoyed the support of American imperialism, which is the chief prop of the constellation, so to speak, of today's Latin American caudillos. Writes W. Foster: "The Latin American dictators after the turn of the century differ sharply from their predecessors.... Most of today's dictators . . . are to some degree or other the puppets of U.S. imperialists . . ."[22]

In our day, statements about the "innate" inability of certain peoples to have any legal system other than that of servitude under the heel of the current imperialist puppet and latifundista oligarchs sound monstrous. W. Foster remarks in this connection that "it is stupid to explain *caudillismo*, as many bourgeois authors do, as being due to the fiery temperament of the Latin American people."[23]

Indeed, the growing unrest of the Latin American nations, sweeping away the dwarfish imitators of Mussolini or Franco, is the best disproof of the ravings of American racists. Conjectures about the "inability" of nationalities to govern themselves and about the fatal

influence of colonial traditions are needed by the ideologists of imperialism to help them picture U. S. encouragement and implantation of dictatorial regimes as "backing the national aspirations" of the Latin American peoples—as assistance to them without which they would lapse into anarchy. The American historian Macdonald writes precisely in this vein: "The ideal of freedom. . . . has too often been understood by ignorant masses as freedom from any limitations, and the anarchy resulting therefrom has made strong repressive measures indispensable."[24]

Preaching "strong" government is a typical feature of Pan American ideology in the postwar period. It is heard from American reactionary historians, jurists, and journalists, as well as from congressmen.

In this connection, the results of deliberations in 1957 in the U.S. Congress on a bill introduced by Representative Porter of Oregon are typical. This bill proposed to discontinue military aid to the Dominican dictator Trujillo—one of the bloodiest satraps of Latin America. The bill provoked a storm of protest from congressmen. Porter was accused of "communism," and the Trujillo regime was—without a trace of irony—extolled as one that "secured to the Dominican people material and spiritual welfare heretofore unknown."[25] House Democratic majority leader McCormack declared that Trujillo's policies were based upon "broad humanitarian" principles.[26] Porter's motion was defeated by a vote of 171 to 4.

[21]J. C. Mariátegui, *Siete ensayos de interpretación de la realidad peruana* (Lima, 1928), pp. 50–51.
[22]W. Z. Foster, *Ocherk politicheskoi istorii Ameriki*, p. 403.
[23]*Ibid.*, p. 411.
[24]A. Macdonald, *Latin American Politics and Government*, p. 13.
[25]*Inter-American Economic Affairs*, 11(3):36 (1957).
[26]*Ibid.*, p. 35.

Highly placed Washington statesmen also "caution" Latin Americans at every opportunity against the perils of social and political "democracy," while at the same time emphasizing the virtues of military-police regimes. Thus in 1958, after the fiasco of Vice-President Nixon's tour of the Latin American countries, Dulles asserted—slandering the Venezuelans who had overthrown the bloody [Pérez] Jiménez dictatorship— that after the elimination of this dictatorship "a political vacuum emerged," resulting in an absence of authority, "which always encourages anarchy." Dulles openly appealed for the creation of a regime of equal authority to that of [Pérez] Jiménez, for at the time "police forces are insufficient and do not know how to cope with organized extremists."[27]

All of this constitutes the ideological side of the U.S. course, in alliance with Latin American reaction—a course that is expressed politically in the support of reactionary dictatorships by every possible means. Of course, U.S. imperialism does not link its destiny exclusively with such regimes. This would be too risky nowadays, when they keep crumbling under the blows of the national-liberation movement. However, this does not alter the basic trend of Washington's policy—that of supporting the reactionary forces in Latin America and converting the area into an immense concentration camp.

Characterizing this trend, Luis Carlos Prestes wrote: "Coups have the aim of replacing . . . governments with a military-police dictatorship that would assure in the back yard of American imperialism the 'order' necessary to unleash new war, the creation of 'strong governments,' which, without regard for their own people, would grant any concessions desired by foreign monopolies, would agree to control by the [U.S.] State Department, would subordinate their armed forces to American

military command, [and] would hand over military and air bases."[28]

The apologia for reactionary dictatorships reflect the general trend of imperialistic forces during the period of further deepening of the crisis of the world capitalist system. This trend is characteristic in a greater or lesser measure of many capitalistic states.

In his report to the Twenty-first Congress of the Communist Party of the USSR, N. S. Khrushchev pointed out that "at present, the imperialists, even though they continue to speculate in slogans of liberty, equality, and fraternity, are moving increasingly toward open dictatorship . . . expanding their attacks on the democratic achievements of peoples who have gained their national independence."

Thus we face not separate facts but a clearly defined general trend typical of many countries in the capitalistic world. The reactionary forces are resorting to the old antipopular tactic: overthrowing democratic regimes and implanting "strong-arm" governments.[29] This trend, at present characteristic of the ideology of the "spiritual unity" of the American countries, is closely bound up with another feature in the modern interpretation of this "unity." In the nineteenth century, the basic premises of bourgeois-democratic ideology—liberty, equality, and popular rule—were promoted as general ideological principles supposedly uniting the peoples of the Western Hemisphere. At present, however, as the reactionary nature of imperialist ideological baggage has increased apace, something else is being advanced to the front rank more often

[27]*The Department of State Bulletin*, June 9, 1958, p. 943.
[28]*Pravda*, September 4, 1949.
[29]N. S. Khrushchev, "O kontrol'nykh tsifrakh razvitiia narodnogo khoziaistva SSSR na 1959-1965 gody," *Doklad na vneocherednom XXI s"ezde Kommunisticheskoi partii Sovetskogo Soiuza 27 ianvaria 1959 g* (Moskva: Gospolitizdat, 1959), p. 98.

as the common "spiritual force" uniting the American countries: religious morality and belief in an irrational principle.

When Assistant Secretary of State Cabot spoke at the official ceremony marking Pan American Day (April 14) in Bogota in 1953, he assigned first place among the "bonds" uniting Western Hemisphere nations to the "Christian religion."[30] This assertion was stated even more categorically by Assistant Secretary of State for Inter-American Affairs Rubottom. "The greatest possession of Latin America . . . ," he emphasized in late 1957, is "precisely this common spiritual faith [which] most intimately binds the United States with Latin America."[31] An active propagandist of this theory was Secretary of State John Foster Dulles, who invariably stressed the mystical "belief in the spiritual world" common to all American peoples.[32]

This propaganda of religious "unity" could not coincide more closely with the policy of the U.S. imperialists in an alliance with the reactionary-clerical circles of Latin America.

The tendency to appeal to religion as the foundation for the "spiritual unity" among the countries of the Western Hemisphere is in complete accord with the "new" trends within imperialistic ideology, which consist of a shift from the positions of philosophical rationalism characteristic of the bourgeoisie during its struggle for power, to irrationality and fideism during its decline.

The imperialist bourgeoisie has rejected rationalist philosophy, exactly as it has been treading underfoot the very slogans of liberty, equality, and fraternity that it had advanced during its struggle with feudalism. Actually, the bourgeoisie is now afraid of raising these principles upon its escutcheon, especially in semicolonial and dependent countries, since they could endanger its dominance. To propagate ideas of equality in Latin America,

caught up as it is with a movement to eliminate the feudal social structure, "threatens"—as acknowledged by U.S. Assistant Secretary of State Cabot—"to precipitate excesses and in some cases catastrophe."[33]

While, in their propaganda of "spiritual brotherhood," the advocates of Pan-Americanism give foremost place to elements of religious morality, they simultaneously decry as "anti-American" the very ideas of national self-determination that were formerly the banner of the progressive bourgeoisie, including the group in the United States. The preachers of Pan-Americanism decry defense of national independence and sovereignty as "nationalism which is a most dangerous betrayal of the most precious American ideals."[34]

In the OAS, the Washington representatives exert every effort to thwart passage of resolutions expressing solidarity with those nationalities of the Western Hemisphere under the yoke of European colonial powers. At the Tenth Pan American Conference in Caracas, the U.S. delegation was the only one to abstain from voting on the Argentinian resolution that expressed "the determination of the nations of America to put a final end to colonialism, which is maintained against the people's will," declared the "sympathy of American republics for the legitimate aspirations of oppressed peoples to obtain sovereignty," and indicated the solidarity of the American countries with the "just demands" for the libera-

[30]J. M. Cabot, *Toward Our Common American Destiny*, p. 24.
[31]*The Department of State Bulletin*, December 9, 1957, p. 923.
[32]The Inter-American Conference (Tenth), *Report of the Delegation of the USA*, p. 50.
[33]J. M. Cabot, *Toward Our Common American Destiny*, p. 111.
[34]From a speech by Rubottom in January 1958. See *The Department of State Bulletin*, February 3, 1958, p. 185.

tion of territories occupied by European powers.[35]

Only at the cost of great effort did the Washington delegation succeed in defeating Guatemala's proposal for the American republics to introduce in the UN General Assembly the question of immediately granting full independence to the colonies of European powers in the Western Hemisphere. Seven votes were for it and only four against, with nine delegations abstaining.

The United States voted against the proposal of Ecuador to convoke a special commission on "dependent territories" whenever "circumstances should require it."[36] This proposal called for mutual consultations between OAS members and the taking of necessary measures in case a power possessing colonies in the Western Hemisphere should try forcibly to suppress the national-liberation movement, as in British Guiana in 1954.

It would seem that, in keeping with the principles of Pan American "solidarity," the United States should support the struggle of the colonial peoples of the American continent against the European continental powers. Yet the class interests of the U.S. imperialist bourgeoisie in this case dictate an alliance with the European colonial powers so as to jointly stifle the national-liberation movement in America, as in Africa and Asia. Anathematizing national self-determination as a feature of the OAS preaching of "spiritual unity" is a reflection of the positions of American imperialism.

In the OAS the United States also opposes universal suffrage—one of the basic norms of democratic government. Thus, at the Tenth Pan American Congress the Washington delegation was the organizer of opposition to Bolivia's proposal that recommended the introduction of universal suffrage in all American countries.[37] This was merely further confirmation of the fact that the ideology of Pan-Americanism stands in complete contradiction to the democratic development of the Latin American nations, and that the Pan American "community" is a check on that development.

All the peculiarities of the ideas of Pan American "spiritual brotherhood" in its modern version focus on "anticommunism."

[35]The Inter-American Conference (Tenth). *Report of the Delegation of the USA,* appendix "B," pp. 159–160.
[36]*Ibid.,* p. 161.
[37]*Ibid.,* p. 30.

40. A Program for Latin American Economic Independence from U.S. Domination*

M. A. Grechev

The Latin American countries that have secured state independence as well as all economically backward lands are confronted with important and urgent tasks in developing their national economies, improving living conditions, and raising the cultural level of the masses. Resolving these problems is possible only through elimination of dependence on foreign imperialism. Economic independence is the major goal of the Latin American countries.

The yoke of American imperialism, which has converted many of the underdeveloped areas of the capitalist world into its tributaries, is felt with particular force in Latin America, which was the first target of U.S. imperialist expansion. Hence the struggle for economic independence in Latin American countries, regardless of the form it takes, is directed primarily at the elimination of imperialist domination by the United States.

The United States is the main exporter of capital to Latin America. Its share is over 80 percent of all foreign capital investment and it accounts for 50 percent of all commercial trade with the countries of this part of the world. From Latin America comes 97 percent

of the antimony, 70 percent of the brass, 52 percent of the lead, 62 percent of the zinc, 47 percent of the iron ore, and 83 percent of the oil imported by the United States. In addition, over 30 percent of all imports are conducted by affiliates of American companies.

The United States has subordinated the Latin American countries to its military-political domination. Serving this end are the Organization of American States (OAS), the Inter-American Defense Treaty of 1947, bilateral military agreements, military bases, and military missions.

Relying on its economic, political, and military posture, the United States intervenes in the internal affairs of the countries of Latin America and exerts pressure upon their foreign policies. Often it utilizes the votes of Latin American states in the OAS to secure adoption of decisions favorable to it.

The essential condition for overcoming economic backwardness and achieving economic independence is agrarian reform. More than half of the gainfully

*"Nekotorye problemy ekonomicheskoi nezavisimosti stran Latinskoi Ameriki," *Mirovaia ekonomika i mezhdunarodnye otnosheniia*, 10: 74–81 (October 1960).

employed population of Latin American countries is engaged in farming. The agriculture is of an extensive nature. Land resources are used unproductively. The yield is dropping. Technical progress is insignificant. For the years 1938 to 1958, the agricultural product rose by only 50 percent; however, per capita agricultural production dropped 6 percent below the prewar level. Latin America's share of world agricultural production shrank. The food problem is serious, both because of the fall in per capita production and because of the rapid growth of the urban population. Food exports fell 40 percent during the last twenty years and imports increased by 26 percent. The chief cause of agrarian backwardness is the existence of large landholdings with powerful traces of feudal forms of landholding and methods of land use.

Extremely inequitable distribution of land prevails in Latin America. According to the 1950 censuses, more than 50 percent of all the deeded acreage belonged to the 1.5 percent of all estates, over 6,000 hectares in area. Vast masses of land are concentrated in the hands of foreign companies. In Venezuela, oil companies control almost 7 million hectares of land. Of the 23 million hectares of the Paraguayan Chaco, 16 million have been given away as concessions to foreign companies. A similar picture may be observed in Argentina and Central America.

The overwhelming majority of the rural population is deprived of land. In Ecuador, 58 percent of the farmers are without land; in Chile, 74.7 percent; in Venezuela, 72 percent; in Colombia, 79 percent; in Guatemala, 80 percent; in Peru, 86 percent; in Paraguay, 93 percent. Over 75 percent of the arable land belongs to people who lease it. The rental costs are as high as 40 to 50 percent of the entire crop. Short-term rentals and precapitalist forms of rent (payment in kind), as well as the sharecrop-

ping and debt peonage systems, accentuate the backwardness of agriculture.

Agrarian reform is the most critical problem in Latin America. Distributing land to millions and millions of peasants would rapidly expand the internal market and at the same time would serve as a powerful stimulus for the development of productive forces in industry as well as agriculture. A radical land reform would mean the elimination of the latifundia system—including landownership by foreigners—the elimination of the system of debt peonage, and state aid to peasant farmers. Such a reform would lead to an expansion of arable land, the elimination of monoculture, technical progress in agriculture, and an increase in the standard of living of the peasantry. By doing away with the class of great landowners—the stronghold of internal reaction—land reform would clear the way for the democratization of society.

Except for the one in Cuba, the agrarian reforms that have been carried out in a few countries of Latin America have not been radical. The task they set for themselves was not the total elimination of landownership by the gentry but only a reduction of it. They have not brought about the eradication of feudal exploitation. The agrarian reforms in Mexico, begun as far back as the 1930's, have resulted in the distribution of 43 million hectares of land to the peasants, which led to a definite growth of agriculture. However, the agricultural problem in that country has not yet been resolved. Two million peons are landless, while 75 percent of the land is concentrated in the hands of the great landlords.

In Guatemala, as a result of the agrarian reforms of 1952 to 1954, 160,000 peasant families received 400,000 hectares of land. Of this total, 159,000 hectares were obtained (at a price) from the United Fruit Company. The puppet regime established through the intervention of the United States in 1954 actually restored the old landowning system.

The land reforms in Bolivia since 1952 have produced no tangible results, due to lack of organization and indecision of the democratic forces in the face of reaction. The government was unable to help the peasants who received land.

Venezuelan reactionary circles are actually trying to solve the agrarian problem without doing away with landlords and foreign ownership but by colonizing government-owned land.

The most radical land reform is being carried out in Cuba by the revolutionary Castro government. It is directed toward the elimination of large landholding properties and foreign ownership and the eradication of feudal methods of exploitation. The land is given to the peasants free of charge. The government aids the peasants with credit on easy terms. Agricultural cooperatives are developing. The reform is being carried out by the peasants themselves under the leadership of the people's government.

At present, no one in Latin America denies the need for agrarian reforms. However, there exist diametrically opposed views as to what they should consist of. Democratic, progressive elements demand radical measures that would break up the holdings of big landlords, distributing them among needy peasants and establishing strict control over the size of land allotments. Reactionary circles, on the other hand, propose to limit the reform to parcelling out government lands without touching private landowners. Characteristically, in discussions of Latin American land problems, the United States bourgeois press emphasizes that land reform must in no way undermine the principle of private property.

The basis for economic independence is the rapid development of the na-

tional economy and, primarily, industry. Industrialization is the most important means for overcoming economic backwardness and assuring a high rate of economic development. Due to a chain of circumstances, the industrial development of Latin America in the last two decades has proceeded at a more rapid pace than in other economically underdeveloped countries. The isolation of Latin America from European markets in the years of the Second World War, the absence at the time of foreign competition, and comparatively high prices for exportable raw materials[1] stimulated the development of national industry. (During the war years, the industrial production of Argentina rose 62 percent; of Chile, 48 percent; and of Mexico, 43 percent.)

In the first postwar years, Latin America profited from the high demand for raw materials and food products both from the European countries devastated by the war and from the United States, where intensive basic capital renewal was taking place. The Korean war and strategic stockpiling by the United States contributed to maintaining high prices for raw materials. All this activity promoted the relatively rapid pace of industrial development of the Latin American countries during the first postwar decade. Of course, the growth of industrial production was concentrated in enterprises owned or controlled by foreign capital.

From 1945 to 1958, the volume of industrial production in Latin America more than doubled. Oil production for this period tripled, steel-making increased sixfold, cement 3.5 times. In 1958, oil production in Latin America amounted to 176.7 million tons; steel production, 3.5 million tons; steel pro-

[1] It must be noted that the dollar currency accumulated in Latin American countries during the war was considerably depreciated after the war as a result of inflation of prices on imports.

duction, 3.5 million tons; electric power, 44 billion kilowatt hours; and cement, 14.5 million tons.

Some of the larger countries, such as Argentina, Brazil, Mexico, and to some extent Chile, have begun production of some types of machines and equipment for the textile, cellulose-paper, and food-processing industries; electric, gas, and diesel motors; freight-lifting machines; construction and, particularly, road construction equipment; railroad cars; and so on. New lines of industry have appeared, such as the production of ships, tractors, and chemicals.

While in 1940 the industries of the Latin American countries employed 6.4 million workers, in 1957 the number reached 12 million—including workers engaged in construction and transport.

Industrial development in the economies of these countries has caused structural dislocations. The relative volume of the manufacturing industry is increasing. In some countries, an increase in the volume of the major category is taking place. Thus, for instance, in Brazil, the relative volume of the major category increased from 20 percent of total industrial production in 1939 to 33 percent in 1956. For the period from 1920 to 1957, the number of workers increased sevenfold in Brazil, reaching 2 million persons, while the population had only doubled. In all the large Latin American countries, concentration of production and centralization of capital are increasing. The largest countries—Brazil, Argentina, Mexico, Chile—have set out on the path of conversion from agrarian to agroindustrial states. However, the present rates of industrial development of the Latin American countries are in sharp contrast with the vital need of overcoming their backwardness as fast as possible and achieving economic independence from foreign monopolies. These countries produce only 9 to 10 percent of the equipment they need. Argentina, Brazil, Mexico, and Chile account for up to 70 percent of the output of Latin America's manufacturing industries. From 1945 to 1958, the total economic product grew 80 percent, reaching approximately 54 billion dollars (in 1950 prices), while the industrial product for this period doubled. Taking into account the population growth, the average annual increase in industrial production per capita was 2 to 3 percent. Excluding Venezuela, the annual increase would be less than 2 percent.

At such rates of economic growth, in the face of narrow specialization, and under conditions where the key industries are controlled by foreign capital, it is impossible to count on rapidly overcoming ageold backwardness, achieving economic independence, and securing a high standard of living.

Representatives of the most diverse social groups of Latin America believe that industrialization is a matter of vital necessity. Even foreign monopolies, certainly not interested in industrialization, dare not openly oppose such a popular idea at this time.

Unable to check the process of industrial development that has become an objective necessity, the American monopolies, their ideologists and their statesmen are trying to divert it to their own advantage. That is, retaining the established international capitalist division of labor, developing light industry, and thereby preserving the one-sided dependence of Latin America on the United States, all with the aid of American capital, private and state. Serving this objective are the so-called theories of interdependence and mutually complementary economics, the basis of which is the spurious thesis of relative outlay for production, which supposedly determines the structure and direction of foreign trade in the capitalist world.

The rate of industrialization is of

decisive importance in overcoming backwardness and achieving economic independence. The rate of development, in turn, depends on the level of capital accumulation and the effectiveness of its utilization, labor productivity, and the labor force employed.

According to the data of the UN Economic Commission for Latin America, gross capital investment in this region amounts at this time to approximately 9 to 10 billion dollars a year, or 17 percent of the gross product (compared to 12 percent before the war). Despite a high level of accumulation, the average rate of growth of production was insignificant—from 2 to 3 percent. This is explained by a number of reasons. First, it must be noted that gross investment includes investment in the construction of homes, schools, hospitals, roads, means of communication, transport, irrigation, and reclamation expenditures, in addition to investment in new equipment. All of these items account for 60 to 70 percent of the gross investment, while the new equipment totals only 30 to 40 percent. On the other hand, the slow tempo of economic growth is explained by the low effectiveness of investment utilization. One of the most important indicators of the effectiveness of investment is the relation of expenditure for equipment to expenditure for construction. For example, according to the data of the Inter-American Economic and Social Council, for the years from 1950 to 1955, the relation in Argentina was 3:7; in Brazil, 1:1. Therefore, in Argentina, with a surplus level of 20 percent, the growth of the industrial product amounted to 2 percent; in Brazil, with a surplus level of 15.6 percent, growth was 5.5 percent.

The sources and methods of financing are of great significance for industrialization and obtaining economic independence. For the countries of Latin America, where the most important source of financing is foreign private capital, this problem assumes particular urgency.

According to our calculations, investment of foreign capital in the economy of the Latin American countries during the postwar years has amounted to an average of 1.2 billion dollars a year, including direct, private capital investment of 600 million dollars; private loans, 100 million dollars; government loans, 350 million dollars; loans by international financial institutions, 100 million dollars; and "aid" in the form of grants, 50 million dollars. Eighty percent of this latter sum comes from the United States. The share of foreign capital in gross investment comes to about 12 percent.

The subject of the role played by foreign capital investment as a source of financing economic development is one of lively debate in bourgeois literature. Imperialist propaganda insistently develops the thesis that foreign, especially private, capital has a beneficial influence on economic development, that without foreign capital any significant industrial development is altogether impossible. In January 1959, the voice of U.S. business circles, *Business Week*, wrote that "American private investments stimulate economic development in all the countries of the world—developed as well as underdeveloped ones." This thesis was also the leitmotif of Eisenhower's speeches during his tour of South America in February 1960.

The need to attract foreign capital, especially in the form of direct capital investment, is usually justified by the following considerations: Under conditions like those in Latin America, where the national income is low, the internal surplus inadequate, and the possibility limited for getting American government loans, (1) private capital may become practically the sole source of financing industrial development; (2) attracting foreign capital in the form of direct investment, as distinct from government loans, carries no obligation to pay interest and amortization; (3) taxation of foreign companies is an important source of budgetary revenue; (4) the problem of foreign exchange is eased; and (5) foreign capital stimulates the development of productive forces.

What is the actual situation? Is foreign capital the only source of financing? Facts do not support this view. The average annual growth of foreign private capital in Latin America in the postwar years amounts to about 600 to 700 million dollars, only from 4 to 5 percent of the gross investment. The explanation is mainly that the export of private capital depends on the establishment in Latin America of a so-called favorable investment climate, by which is meant freedom of foreign capital from taxes, the right to unrestricted dispersal of profits abroad, government guarantees against nationalization, and—most important—the prospect of high profits. In South America, the return on foreign direct capital investment amounts to 15 to 30 percent, which is three times the return within the United States.

Nor is there any validity to the claim that the taxes paid by American companies are an important item in budgetary revenue. First, they amount to no more than 5 percent of budgetary revenue of the countries of Latin America. Second, they comprise an insignificant part of the enormous profits, which come to about 1 billion dollars a year. Thus, the argument that greater advantage lies in attracting foreign private capital by direct investment than by government loans with their commitments of interest and amortization is also totally without foundation. Here the assmption is, of course, that the loans will be used effectively.

Equally false is the assertion that foreign private capital relieves the prob-

lem of foreign exchange. From 1946 to 1958, direct capital investment by the United States in Latin America increased by 5.7 billion dollars, which includes 4 billion in new investments and 1.7 billion in reinvestments. Total profits from all American direct investment for the period in question amounted to 9.8 billion dollars, of which 7.6 billion was taken to the United States. Thus, the outgo of foreign exchange by transfer of profits has outweighed the influx of foreign exchange as new direct investment by the sum of 3.6 billion dollars.

Productive forces are developed by foreign investments in directions not at all responsive to the interests of the national economy or economic independence. Foreign monopolies invest their capital, first of all, in the most profitable, exploitable industries, giving the development of the economy a one-sided, freakish character. Of the total sum of American private capital investment in Latin America,[2] the relative volume in the mining and oil industries for the years 1946 to 1958 increased from 39.5 percent to 50 percent. On the other hand, there is an outflow of capital in less profitable fields. For instance, the relative volume of investment in public service enterprises for the same period decreased from 25.6 percent to 13.4 percent.

True, in recent years foreign capital has also penetrated into the manufacturing industry; here the share of American investment has risen from 13 percent in 1946 to 20 percent in 1958. However, an analysis of these investments shows that basically they are in light industry, and, to some extent, in the chemical industry. The machine-building and metal industries account

[2]Of 12.8 billion dollars of American investments in Latin America in 1958, 85 percent was private, including about 70 percent direct, and approximately 13 percent government loans.

for only 5.3 percent of foreign capital investment.

Applying the most diverse methods of expansion—affiliations, subsidiaries, the system of incorporation, interlocking companies—foreign capital has gained control over key sectors of the Latin American economies.

For instance, in Brazil, American companies control 90 percent of the petrochemical industry, 81 percent of meat-packing plants, 65 percent of pharmaceuticals, and 55 percent of artificial fertilizer manufacturing. Manganese mining is in the hands of two American companies. The tobacco industry is controlled by one British company. Sixty percent of the total power of the biggest electric stations is in the hands of two foreign companies.

In Argentina, 360 American companies are in operation. They control over 40 percent of the meat-packing industries, 70 percent of wolfram production, 30 percent of cement, 90 percent of zinc, 50 percent of sulphur, 80 percent of electricity, and 50 percent of the chemical industry. In Mexico, 250 American companies control 90 percent of the production of zinc, lead, and copper; 50 percent of gold; and 60 percent of silver. In Venezuela there are 140 American companies, which control, among other things, 70 percent of the extraction and refining of oil. In Chile there are 80 American companies. They control 95 percent of the copper mining and 70 percent of nitrates. In Peru, 100 American companies are in operation, and they control the mining of 80 percent of copper, 70 percent of lead and zinc, and 50 percent of silver, and 100 percent of bismuth.

In Cuba, before the victorious revolution, American companies owned over 1.5 million hectares of land—primarily sugar cane plantations—and thirty-one sugar mills. They controlled 50 percent of the oil refineries, 95 percent of the output of electricity, and 40 percent of the railroads. The capital investment of the United States in Cuba amounted to approximately 1 billion dollars. By now, a considerable part of this investment has fallen under the control of the Cuban government.

Central America is dominated by the company of infamous name, United Fruit. It owns over 600,000 acres of the best land. Through its numerous affiliates, this monopoly controls the production of bananas, sugar, cocoa, and other agricultural products, primarily tropical in nature. In addition, the company owns a fleet of sixty-five ships and railroad trackage of over fifteen hundred miles. United Fruit also owns radio stations, a telegraph network, sugar-refining mills, and port facilities.

The oppressive role of foreign, primarily American, capital is the main cause of the narrow specialization of the Latin American countries and their transformation into monoculture countries and raw material appendages of the imperialist powers.

The aggressive actions of the United States against revolutionary Cuba serve as glaring examples of the way narrow specialization and monoculture are used by the imperialists for intervention in internal affairs to prevent the achievement of economic independence.

It is common knowledge that sugar production is the basic source of income for most of the Cuban population, as sugar accounts for 80 percent of the country's exports. Until recently, half the annual production of sugar—about 3 million tons—was exported by special arrangement to the United States.

The ruling circles of the United States decided to take advantage of Cuba's dependence on the North American sugar market and to force the Castro government to renounce revolutionary reforms. Early in June 1960, the U.S. government cut the Cuban sugar import quota by one-third, threatening to stop the import of Cuban sugar entirely. However, this act of economic aggression failed to bring Cuba to her knees. Today Cuba has friends able to give her active economic and political support. Surplus sugar has been purchased by the Soviet Union.

The United States also attempted to utilize the position of private capital in Cuba to undermine the mutually advantageous economic agreement between Cuba and the Soviet Union. The point is that almost all the oil imported by Cuba was being refined in three refineries, two American and one British. By order of their governments, these refineries refused to refine oil obtained by Cuba from the Soviet Union in exchange for sugar. The foreign monopolies tried to compel the Castro government to cease the importation of Soviet oil. In June 1960, however, the Castro government seized control of the refineries and put an end to sabotage by foreign monopolies.

In a situation where two politico-economic systems compete, the export of private capital has far-reaching political implications. Speaking on June 2, 1959, at Columbia University, Herter's assistant Dillon emphasized that the export of private capital is needed, first, to prove that private "initiative" can do more for economic progress than communist methods can and, second, that, in cooperating with domestic capital, the position of the latter is strengthened. He stated frankly that "the question of the export of capital is a problem in the struggle with communism." To encourage export of private capital to the countries of Latin America, such legislation as the Act of International Income of 1954 was passed to lower taxes on income from capital investment in the Western Hemisphere. Special bilateral agreements concluded by the American government with Colombia, Uruguay, and Haiti created a favorable "investment climate" in these countries. The U.S. government also employs so-called investment guarantees for capital exporters in case of expropriation of capital or difficulties with conversion of foreign exchange when taking profits out of the country. Such agreements have been concluded with Bolivia, Colombia, Costa Rica, Ecuador, Guatemala, and other countries.

Other incentives to export private capital are U.S. government loans through the Export-Import Bank, loans and subsidies in a variety of aid programs (e.g., the Mutual Security Program, [Public] Law R 480, and others), loans and credits of international financial institutions (the International Bank for Reconstruction and Development, the International Monetary Fund, and others) in which the United States has decisive influence.

The attitude of various Latin American social groups toward foreign capital differs. Democratic forces favor maximum limitation and strict control over foreign private capital. In the majority of Latin American countries legislation exists to limit, in varying degrees, the activity of foreign capital. In many countries, however, these restrictions take the form of higher or lower taxation, dictated by the interests of the state budget. In some countries, Venezuela and Brazil in particular, legislation stimulates foreign investment.

In the opinion of progressive circles, foreign government loans and credits, as well as aid in the form of subsidies, must be of a long-term nature, furnished at low interest rates with the right to amortization in national currency or goods of traditional export. Obviously, loans and credits must not be tied to political strings.

It is no accident that the loans of the Export-Import Bank are subjected to severe criticism by the Latin American press. The same attitude prevails toward loans by international financial institutions, because they are offered at high rates of interest and on the condition of acceptance of the so-called plan for stabilization of the economy, which actually means interference in the internal affairs of other countries.

That part of the national bourgeoisie which is to any degree tied to foreign capital takes an inconsistent stand on the question of foreign investment. Motivated by selfish interests, it frequently advocates attracting foreign—including private—capital, although not infrequently it demands restrictions aimed at protecting its interests.

The basic source of financing is internal accumulation. It is realized in the form of government capital investments in budgeted programs, resources of government life insurance corporations, and internal government loans, as well as in the form of investments from the private sector. The ratio between government and private investment is, on the average, 1:3. Government investment of capital in Mexico is from 45 to 50 percent of budgetary expenditures; in Brazil and Colombia, from 25 to 27 percent; and in Peru, Chile, and Argentina, from 17 to 18 percent.

The advantages of governmental capital investments are these: (1) they make possible the construction of large industrial projects that are beyond the capacity of national private capital; (2) they can be directed toward areas of enterprise that private capital would not enter but that are essential to the development of the national economy; (3) in government enterprises, greater resources can be allotted to expanding production and, at the same time, improving the conditions of the workers; and (4) state capitalism can become an effective instrument for squeezing out private capital.

In Latin America, state capitalism—the government sector especially—plays a basically progressive role, as the example of Cuba clearly demonstrates. The ruling circles of the United States are resolutely opposed to state capitalism and especially to the government sector in the economy of the Latin American countries. They fear that strengthening of it may weaken their positions and bring about undesirable social changes.

Meanwhile, foreign capital is trying to penetrate the government sector of the Latin American countries, mainly by creating "mixed companies." In this, it is making use of all the privileges enjoyed by government establishments, while the government assumes all the risks.

Not infrequently complaints may be heard in the Latin American press about inadequate internal capital accumulation, the cause of which bourgeois economists see to be the low per capita national income. The problem, however, lies not solely in the condition of the national income but also in its extremely inequitable distribution. The masses are deprived of the possibility to accumulate any savings that could be used as internal surplus. Native exploiting classes are not eager to invest their capital in industrial enterprises but prefer to put it into real estate or commerce, to use it for speculative purposes, or to transfer it abroad. While indirect taxation grows incessantly, weighing heavily on the shoulders of the broad consumer sector, insufficient taxation of the wealthy classes, as well as their numerous privileges, prevents a rise in the level of national accumulation.

Stability of foreign trade is of great importance for the economic development of the Latin American countries. Countries of narrow specialization, they export up to 25 percent of their gross product.

Foreign trade is the main source of foreign exchange with which to pay for equipment and one of the basic sources of revenue for the national treasury. In Venezuela, for example, oil export accounts for 97 percent of foreign exchange and 78 percent of treasury revenue; in Chile, export accounts for 50 percent of foreign exchange and 33 percent of treasury revenue.

The Latin American countries are interested in stable prices for traditional export items and also in stable markets, but the instability of the world capitalist economy and the foreign economic policy of the Western powers (particularly the United States) have a negative effect on the Latin American countries. The U.S. system of tariffs, quotas, and political dumping reflects perniciously on the trade and the balance of payments of the Latin American countries, causing inflation and a drain on foreign exchange reserves.

Certain elements of the national bourgeoisie hope to solve their countries' foreign trade problems through the formation of a Latin American "common market." This market, according to the scheme of its initiators, would lead to the extension of trade among the Latin American countries (at present, it comprises only 9 percent of all the foreign trade of this region), to the development of a public division of labor and the internal market, and to accelerated industrial growth.

Many persons view the regional Latin American market as a means of eliminating dependence on the United States. At present, however, the United States is also supporting the idea of a regional Latin American market, hoping to utilize it in the interest of its own monopolies. If a common market were created, American companies with industrial enterprises in Latin America could extract all the benefits from the abolition of economic and trade barriers.

The creation of a common market faces great difficulties, since many countries fear competition both from their own more powerful Latin American partners and from affiliates of North American monopolies. At present, agreements on the common market exist only among five Central American countries—El Salvador, Nicaragua, Guatemala, Honduras, and Costa Rica—while seven countries of South America—Argentina, Brazil, Chile, Bolivia, Paraguay, Peru, and Uruguay—have agreed on a free trade zone.

Thus, solving the problem of economic independence in the Latin American countries would require the following:

1. Implementation of a radical agrarian reform to end large landholdings and foreign landownership, which are the main obstacles to the development of productive forces
2. Limitation of the sphere of operation of foreign private capital and strict control over its activity until it is totally eliminated
3. The overcoming of narrow specialization, as a result of which the Latin American countries have become agrarian raw-material appendages of the industrially developed capitalist countries
4. The overcoming of economic and technical backwardness through maximum stimulation of industrial development and industrialization as a basis for rapid growth of the national economy
5. Establishment of economic and trade relations on equal and mutually beneficial terms with all countries of the world, but particularly with the socialist countries

Yet, the problem of economic independence should not be posed as an essentially technical-economic task. Technical progress and industrial development do not automatically lead to economic self-sufficiency.

Economic independence is inseparably connected with political independence and the democratization of internal political life. They are mutually dependent upon each other. The basis for state independence—that is, economic self-sufficiency—is, in turn, determined by the existing degree of political independence.

Striking proof of this is contemporary Cuba, which through the democratization of social life, the nationalization of the property of foreign companies on her territory, and the conduct of an independent foreign policy secured for herself the necessary conditions for **unprecedented economic progress.**

41. The Development of Postwar Soviet Political and Cultural Ties with Latin America*

Z. I. ROMANOVA

More than half the Latin American states maintain diplomatic relations with the Soviet Union. Among these are Argentina, Bolivia, the Dominican Republic, Guatemala, Costa Rica, Cuba, Mexico, Nicaragua, Uruguay, Ecuador, and Brazil. With Brazil, Argentina, Cuba, Mexico, and Uruguay there is also an exchange of diplomatic representatives. The USSR maintains trade representatives in Argentina and Cuba, while in Uruguay there is a commercial counselor. However, economic relations between the Latin American countries and the USSR extend far beyond the framework of diplomatic relations.

A growing cultural exchange movement greatly promotes rapprochement between the Latin American and the Soviet peoples. The implementation of cultural collaboration demonstrates the desire of both sides to know each other better and to learn of each other's achievements in music, theater, cinema, painting, and literature.

There has been a great response to the visits of Soviet cultural workers to Latin America. The visits by such representatives of Soviet culture as David Oistrakh, Emil Gilels, Zara Dolukhanova, Aram Khachaturian, Vakhtang Chabukiani, Violeta Bovt, Pavel Serebriakov, Konstantin Ivanov, and Mstislav Rostropovich have helped Latin Americans to become better acquainted with Soviet art. Plays by Russian authors—N. V. Gogol's *Mar-*

*Latinskaia Amerika: Kratkii politiko-ekonomicheskii spravochnik, ed. M. V. Danilevich, M. F. Kudachkina, and M. A. Okuneva (Moskva: Gosudarstvennoe izdatel'stvo politicheskoi literatury, 1962), pp. 116–117, 121–124.

riage, A. M. Gorky's *Vassa Zheleznova,* A. P. Chekhov's *The Cherry Orchard*—are successes in Latin America. Soviet films also enjoy great popularity.

The works of A. S. Pushkin, L. N. Tolstoy, A. P. Chekhov, A. M. Gorky, and others have become widely known in Latin America. Interest in Soviet literature has grown, and the publishing of Spanish translations of Soviet writers has increased. N. Ostrovskii's *Born of the Storm,* Alexei Tolstoy's *Road to Calvary,* M. Sholokhov's *Virgin Soil Upturned,* and others have also become well known. Latin American children and young people are fascinated by such works as N. Dubov's *Lights on the River,* L. Kassil's *Cheremysh, The Hero's Brother,* and N. Nosov's *Merry Little Family.*

The Latin Americans' burning desire to become better acquainted with Soviet culture has resulted in a need to learn the Russian language. Students, artists, physicians, engineers, and white-collar workers enthusiastically study Russian so that they may acquire a genuine acquaintance with Russian literature and science. In many Latin American cities, courses and schools for the study of Russian have been established.

Connections between learned institutions and individual scholars of the Soviet Union and Latin America are continually broadening and becoming more fruitful. Close working contact exists with learned institutions—including the universities—of Argentina, Bolivia, Brazil, Cuba, Venezuela, Colombia, Costa Rica, Mexico, Peru, Uruguay, Chile, and Ecuador. In scientific circles of the USSR, recognition has been given to the work of the Argentine paleontologist Florentino Ameguino, of Mexican and Cuban geographers, of Chilean ethnographers, and others. Scientific collaboration between Latin America and the USSR was furthered by the International Geographic Congress

of 1956 in Rio de Janeiro and by the International Physiological Congress of 1959 in Buenos Aires. The reports of Soviet delegates were received with great interest.

Extensive collaboration has been established between Soviet scholars and those of Argentina, Chile, and Mexico through the program of the International Geophysical Year of 1959. Latin American scientists participated in the Moscow congress of scientists on the findings of the International Geophysical Year, as did Soviet scientists in the 1959 Buenos Aires symposium on problems of Antarctic research.

The USSR orders a large number of books on sociology, politics, economics, and culture from the Latin American countries. The V. I. Lenin Library—largest in the USSR—exchanges books, pamphlets, periodicals, and newspapers with libraries, universities, and learned societies of most Latin American countries. Many books in science and the arts come to the All-Union State Library of Foreign Literature in Moscow. The creation of the Latin American Institute in Moscow in 1961 testifies to the deep interest of the Soviet people in the socio-economic and foreign-policy problems of the Latin American countries.

The organizations that have been created in Latin America for friendship and cultural collaboration with the USSR are making an immense contribution to the strengthening of ties between the countries. Included on the governing boards of these organizations are many outstanding cultural and scientific figures. By showing Soviet films, organizing meetings, lectures, and exhibits, and publishing the works of Soviet authors as well as those of Latin American writers who relate their impressions of visits to the Soviet Union, these organizations spread the truth about the country of Soviets. At the same time, they familiarize the Soviet people with life in their own counries by sending to the Soviet Union their own books, films and works of art and music.

An outstanding example of the desire of the Soviet people for closer ties with the people of Latin America was the creation in the USSR in January 1959 of the Association for Friendship and Cultural Collaboration with the Latin American Countries. The membership consists not only of individuals but also of entire collectives, such as theaters, institutes, museums, and publishing and industrial enterprises. This association has established new contacts with more than four hundred cultural and scholarly centers in fourteen Latin American countries.

In 1960 the nationalities composing the USSR observed a significant historical milepost—the 150th anniversary of the beginning of the struggle for national independence in Latin America. In Moscow, Leningrad, Erevan, Minsk, and other cities, special celebrations took place. A number of scholarly institutions held jubilee sessions.

The growth of collaboration and mutual understanding between countries is promoted by the exchange of official delegations. Latin American guests have had the opportunity to observe the work of the Supreme Soviet of the USSR and have visited collective farms, construction sites, schools, hospitals, and factories.

In the summer of 1956 the USSR for the first time was visited by parliamentary delegations from Uruguay and Brazil. In August of 1958 a delegation of the USSR Supreme Soviet visited Uruguay. Subsequently, the exchange of delegations between the two countries increased. A constructive role was played by the Conference of the Interparliamentary Union, held in Rio de Janeiro in 1958. Deputies of the Supreme Soviet not only broadened their contacts with Brazilian parliamentarians but also established new ones with parliamentary deputies from other Latin American countries. Parliamentary delegations from Venezuela, Colombia, Mexico, Argentina, Peru, Haiti, and other countries have visited the USSR. In turn, statesmen and delegates of the Supreme Soviet of the USSR have traveled to many of the Latin American nations. The visit to Mexico in 1959 and to Cuba in 1960 of First Deputy Chairman of the USSR Council of Ministers A. I. Mikoyan met with widespread response, as did the 1961 goodwill trip of a mission headed by M. P. Georgadze to several Latin American countries.

Latin American countries are resisting more and more actively the isolation that had been forcibly imposed upon them and are striving to expand economic and cultural collaboration with the USSR.

"Our relations with the countries of Latin America during the period of this report," said N. S. Khrushchev at the twenty-second Congress of the CPSU, "have also progressed despite the barriers artificially mounted by domestic reactionaries and by the American imperialist. After having broken down these barriers, the heroic people of Cuba are now establishing collaboration with foreign nations on the basis of full equality of rights. And although U.S. imperialists stop at nothing—including the overthrow of legitimate governments—to prevent the Latin American countries from following an independent policy, life will nevertheless assert itself."

42. The Significance of the Socialist System for the Future Economic Development of Latin America*

O. G. Klesmet

One of the conditions for securing economic independence in Latin America is the creation of genuine national industries capable of assuring the preferential growth of the means of production and thereby laying the foundation for an accelerated rate of economic development. History has shown the most effective method to be socialist industrialization, for it guarantees the most rational planned utilization of resources, based on the elimination of private ownership of the means of production. It was precisely the socialist industrialization and collectivization of agriculture that provided the rapid tempo of economic growth of the Soviet Union, which in a short period historically changed from a backward agricultural land into a mighty industrial power. Socialist industrialization has also been tested and proved in other socialist countries.

The program of the Communist Party of the Soviet Union states that socialism is the peoples' path to freedom and happiness. "It ensures rapid development of the economy and culture. In the lifetime of one generation, not in a millennium, it transforms a backward country into an industrial one. Socialism guarantees a high material and cultural

level of life for the working class and all toiling people. Socialism lifts the masses from darkness and ignorance and brings them within reach of contemporary culture."[1]

At present, when imperialism has ceased to play a dominant role in international affairs, the Latin American countries have an opportunity to secure their independent economic development. This opportunity is open to them because the world socialist system, an increasingly decisive factor in the development of human society, is always ready to aid underdeveloped countries.

The growth of the economic might of the socialist countries has led to the weakening of the monopoly of the imperialist powers in the area of industrial production and has deprived them of the possibility of perpetuating the economic backwardness of the underdeveloped countries by refusing

---

*"Voprosy ekonomicheskogo razvitiia stran Latinskoi Ameriki," in *Ekonomicheskie problemy stran Latinskoi Ameriki,* ed. V. Ia. Avarina and M. V. Danilevich (Moskva: Izdatel'stvo Akademii nauk SSSR, 1963), pp. 59-62.

[1] *Programma Kommunisticheskoi partii Sovetskogo Soiuza* (Moskva: Gospolitizdat, 1961), p. 48.

to supply them with the means of production.

Economic cooperation with socialist countries enables underdeveloped countries to obtain machines, equipment, and tools on favorable terms, in exchange for their export products. Loans and credits as well as technical aid are not conditional upon any kind of political demands and are issued at low interest rates. Economic relations with socialist countries permit underdeveloped countries to utilize the benefits of the international division of labor for the consolidation of their economy. The planned crisis-free nature of a socialist economy guarantees a constant market for underdeveloped countries, thereby stimulating the development of productive forces and promoting a higher rate of employment of the population. Furthermore, the development of economic relations with the socialist countries decreases the dependence of underdeveloped countries on imperialism and strengthens their political position.

The Latin American countries are still making little use of the opportunities inherent in economic cooperation with the socialist countries. However, the very existence of the socialist system, which consistently champions the independence and sovereignty of underdeveloped countries and is ready to render unselfish aid for their economic development, is conducive to strengthening the positions of the Latin American countries by impelling imperialist states to grant certain concessions.

The broad progressive community, as well as many ruling circles of Latin America, understands the enormous positive significance of establishing relations with the Soviet Union and the other socialist countries. This understanding is finding expression in the demands of the masses for the establishment of diplomatic and trade relations with countries of the socialist camp.

Concrete steps have been taken in this direction by certain countries, such as Brazil.

In particular, a number of works published in Latin America toward the end of the 1950's have pointed out the great positive significance that a rapprochement with the Soviet Union and other socialist countries could have for the Latin American countries. An article by the Chilean economist Pedro Ríos deserves attention.[2] The author compares the aid given the underdeveloped countries by the United States with the aid given by the socialist countries and arrives at conclusions unfavorable to the United States for the following reasons:

1. Socialist countries do not practice export of capital in the form of direct, private investment.
2. For technical aid, socialist countries send engineers and technicians, for the most part, while the United States sends mostly military advisers, bureaucrats, and others; the technical aid of socialist countries is frequently associated with the accomplishment of large projects involving loans, delivery of various equipment, and mutual trade, whereas U.S. aid is designed for petty, individual projects.
3. Socialist countries in rendering aid pay much attention to the development of natural resources, energy, transport, and the ferrous metals industry. Their activity is directed toward the creation of large industrial units designed to produce economic results quickly and to train domestic technical cadres. U.S. aid, however, is based on the principle of slow, gradual development and is directed primarily toward education and health.
4. Socialist countries extend loans on more favorable terms; rates of in-

[2]*Panorama Económico*, 224: 253–254 (September 1961).

terest are considerably lower and re-payment of loans can be made in local currency or in goods.

Concluding his article, Pedro Ríos notes that the foreign trade of the social-ist camp exerts a great economic in-fluence due to the fact that its transac-tions are centralized and that agree-ments are long term and calculated on a growing market.

Even representatives of the ruling circles of some Latin American coun-tries favor expansion of trade relations with the socialist countries. The Minis-ter of Foreign Affairs of Brazil, San-tiago Dantas, conferring with members of the diplomatic corps appointed to rep-resent Brazil in socialist countries, declared that, due to difficulties antic-ipated by official circles in the sale of export commodities in the European common market zone, "Brazil now, more than ever, is in need of strength-ening trade relations with the socialist countries."

The socialist countries are extending massive and effective support in rev-olutionary Cuba. In an interview with the editor-in-chief of *Pravda,* the Prime Minister of the revolutionary govern-ment of Cuba, Fidel Castro Ruz, de-clared, "Without the Soviet Union, without the socialist camp, without the help they are giving us, the victory of the revolution in a country as small as Cuba would be impossible, consider-ing the imperialist aggression."[3]

From the example of Cuba, the peoples of Latin America can be con-vinced that the world socialist system is "the reliable shield of an independ-ent national development of liberated peoples,"[4] and that the noncapitalist path of development is the best way to eliminate age-old backwardness and to improve the living conditions of the masses.

[3]*Pravda,* January 29, 1962.
[4]*Programmnye dokumenty bor'by za mir, demo-kratiiu i sotsializm* (Moskva: Gospolitizdat, 1961), p. 64.

X

The Cuban Revolution

The five selections incorporated here consider special aspects of the Cuban Revolution, unsurprisingly the subject of a large part of Soviet writings on Latin America.

The first selection (Item 43) presents a Soviet view of Cuban-American and Cuban-Soviet relations since the revolution. This unattributed selection clearly regards the settlement of the 1962 Cuban missile crisis as a victory for Soviet diplomacy.

In Item 44, A. M. Sivolobov surveys the course of agrarian reform in Cuba. Sivolobov considers the transition from latifundia through cooperatives to people's farms and state farms as inevitable, arising virtually spontaneously when the peasants understand that small owner-farmed plots are "uneconomical."

The third selection (Item 45), by N. N. Razumovich, details the procedures utilized by the revolutionary government in creating a state sector in the economy. Item 46 lists the aspects of the international significance of the Cuban Revolution that, in the Soviet view, are the most significant.

Finally, in Item 47, L. Iu. Slezkin reviews 1960 U.S. publications on the Cuban Revolution, concluding that C. Wright Mills' book was the only objective treatment to appear that year.

The volume of Soviet writings on the Cuban Revolution has diminished in recent years. A partial explanation for this phenomenon may be found in the following statement by M. S. Al'perovich, writing in *Sovetskaia istoriografiia stran Latinskoi Ameriki* (Moskva: Nauka, 1968), p. 48:

Research into the development of the revolutionary process in Cuba is an extremely complex problem. The difficulty is caused by the absence of materials and the contradictory nature of the data on a number of important problems; the presence of various and partially opposing evaluations of the motive forces of the revolution, the position and role of classes, social groups, and political parties; and the close interweaving of history with the present time. One must also take account of the fact that Cuban scholars themselves only relatively recently began to undertake a planned study of the history of the revolution. Thus it is not surprising that Soviet specialists have not yet supplied clear and exhaustive answers to many of the problems connected with the revolutionary events in Cuba, and that in a number of instances their opinions diverge considerably.

43. The Struggle to Defend Revolutionary Cuba against the Aggressive Policy of the United States*

The Revolution in Cuba and the Interventionist Course of the United States

Aggressive actions by the United States against Cuba began almost immediately after the victory of the people's revolution there, when it became clear that the revolutionary government was determined to uphold the political and economic independence of its country to the end.

The U.S. monopolies struck their first heavy blow in the summer of 1960, by sharply reducing the supply of oil to Cuba. Since highway transportation is the foundation of the country's transportation system, and the coastal shipping fleet also runs basically on oil, this step was tantamount to a declaration of economic war. An exceedingly difficult moment had arrived for the Cuban government. The only way out for it was to buy oil from the Soviet Union. Then the monopolies refused to refine Soviet oil at the refineries belonging to them in Cuba. It was again necessary to seek a way out of the situation. The pernicious results of the fact that all key branches of the economy of the country had been in the hands of foreign capitalists for many years became obvious.

On August 6, 1960, the revolutionary government of Cuba announced the nationalization of oil refineries, the elec-

tric and telephone companies, and thirty-six large sugar mills belonging to American capital.[1]

The economic war of U.S. imperialism against free Cuba continued in ever greater scope, up to the point of a total embargo on trade. Under U.S. pressure, the foreign ministers of the Latin American countries adopted the so-called Declaration of San José in August 1960, which was the beginning of a campaign for the diplomatic isolation of the Cuban Republic.[2] A secret war against Cuba conducted by the Central Intelligence Agency had begun earlier. Utilizing its agents on the island as well as émigrés, the CIA organized diversions, murders, and sabotage. The revolt in Camagüey, the conspiracy in Santa Clara, the formation of bands in the Escambray Mountains—these were all affairs of American intelligence, which had set itself the objective of forcible overthrow of the revolutionary government.

---

*Mezhdunarodnye otnosheniia posle Vtoroi mirovoi voiny, v. 3 (Moskva: Izdatel'stvo politicheskoi literatury, 1965), pp. 662–678.

[1]Revolución, August 7, 1960.

[2]New York Times, August 29, 1960.

By the second half of 1960, an armed invasion of Cuba by émigré gangs was occupying an ever larger place in the plans of the CIA. Strike forces of these gangs were being hammered together in special camps in Miami and other places. It was presupposed not only that the Americans would arm and train them and get them to Cuba, but also that auxiliary units of the U.S. armed forces would aid them. There was open talk about the plans for an invasion both in informed journalistic circles and among the émigré riffraff in Miami. Official personages in the United States did not even consider it necessary to conceal them. Such frankness can be explained by the total conviction of the hopelessness of Cuba's position and the fact that she was doomed to be the next victim of the "big stick" policy. The experience of the "Marine diplomacy" of the first half of the nineteenth [twentieth? Tr. note] century, plus the experience of 1954—when the CIA stifled the democratic revolution in Guatemala by using gangs of hirelings—sketched a picture of an inevitable and rapid defeat of free Cuba in the minds of the imperialists.

However, the international conditions under which the national-liberation struggle of oppressed peoples is taking place in our times have changed very substantially. As a result of the decisive change in the correlation of forces in the world, the socialist system—which rests first of all on the might of the Soviet Union—is creating favorable external conditions for the victory of the liberation struggle of the peoples. The Cuban Revolution is a brilliant example of this.

Cuban-Soviet contacts began with the Cuban purchase of oil products from the USSR and the sale of the basic Cuban export product—sugar—to the Soviet Union. These agreements were very important for the Cuban people's struggle for independence. The rapid development of trade relations between the two countries helped the Cuban people overcome the results of the embargo, which could have been catastrophic. Along with the other goods purchased in the socialist countries, Cuba also began to acquire arms, which were essential for raising the defensive capability of the army and the people's militia.

The commercial ties were soon supplemented by economic and technical aid. Some of the specific manifestations of the fraternal friendship that had been formed between the two peoples were credits and supplies of various goods, including weapons, participation in the construction of enterprises, training of Cubans in the Soviet Union, and the dispatch of Soviet technicians to Cuba.

American imperialism ever more insistently placed on the agenda forcible methods of subduing Cuba—that is, armed intervention. It attempted to take measures to prevent Cuba from acquiring arms abroad. American agents blew up the Belgian freighter Le Couvre, which had brought weapons made in Belgium to the Havana harbor.

Beginning with the second half of 1960, the revolutionary government in its statements repeatedly disclosed the aggressive plans of U.S. ruling circles. The Cuban representative to the United Nations drew the attention of the Security Council and the General Assembly to the threat of armed intervention from the United States.[3] In a passionate and well-reasoned speech before the Fifteenth Session of the General Assembly in New York, Fidel Castro dealt with the entire history of relations between the United States and Cuba and pointed out that U.S. imperialism did not wish to reconcile itself to the liberation of the island and was preparing aggression against it.

Notwithstanding the hypocritical denials, the ruling circles in Washington

[3] *Pravda,* July 13, 1960.

made no secret of the fact that an armed attack would be carried out against Cuba sooner or later. The practical organization of the invasion was entrusted to the Central Intelligence Agency during the Eisenhower administration.

The frame of reference in the preparation of the specific plan for the operation was the conception that the revolutionary government lacked solid support among the Cuban people. According to that conception, it would be enough to begin successful military operations on the islands with a contingent of well-armed and well-equipped interventionists, and there would be outbreaks of military actions everywhere, until the forces of counterrevolution could proclaim themselves to be a "government." After that, the United States would give it more aid. It was intended to make use of the existence of the American naval base at Guantánamo, on Cuban territory.

The story about the "precariousness" of the Fidel Castro government was widely distributed by émigré circles in Florida and by CIA agents in Cuba itself. This tale was circulated broadly not only in the press, but also in U.S. ruling circles. Taking wishes for reality, the strategists of the Pentagon counted on the sympathy—or at least the passiveness—of the majority of the population in case of intervention.

In working out the invasion plans, U.S. ruling circles set out from the point that the direct use of the U.S. army would arouse indignation throughout the Latin American part of the continent. Consequently, it was decided to conduct the invasion with émigré forces. The émigrés underwent special training under U.S. soldiers and were armed and equipped at the cost of the CIA and the armed forces at bases in Florida, as well as on the territory of Guatemala, Nicaragua, and other places. The U.S. air force and navy were supposed to help the invaders establish and con-

solidate themselves on the Cuban beaches.

The landing was made at dawn on April 17, 1961, at Playa Girón, on the Bay of Pigs. Operation "Pluto," worked out at the CIA, was supposed to look like an action undertaken by the so-called Cuban Revolutionary Council—an organization of counterrevolutionary rabble lodged in Miami. American journalists Meyer and Szulc, who wrote a book about the Playa Girón invasion, remarked on the "astonishment of the Cuban Revolutionary Council—the people in whose name the invasion was being conducted and who were being held in friendly isolation at the abandoned Ocaloca airfield—when they found out via a portable radio that their troops had made a landing."[4]

The interventionists, who numbered about five hundred men, were faced with a problem: to consolidate their beachhead and to initiate movement toward the northeast, toward the Escambray mountains, and to join up with individual counterrevolutionary gangs that were still operating there. If they were successful, the major means of communication between the western and eastern parts of the island would be cut. Reports slipped into the American press to the effect that after the interventionists had consolidated themselves on Cuban territory, official recognition by the United States of an émigré "government" headed by Miró Cardona could be expected, a government that would turn to Washington with a request for aid and general support.

In this hour of terrible danger, the entire Cuban people rallied about their government, which took decisive measures to crush the counterrevolutionaries quickly. The number of members of the people's milita and patriots who expressed a desire to head for Playa

[4]K. E. Meyer and T. Szulc, *The Cuban Invasion* (New York, 1962), p. 131.

Girón with weapons in hand was so great that the government had to call on everyone to remain at his post, except for the units dispatched to repel the aggression. Prime Minister Fidel Castro assumed command of these units.

Foreign Minister R. Roa spoke in protest against the U.S. aggression at the Security Council. The Cuban appeal was energetically supported by the Soviet Union. During the course of the discussions, high American officials flatly denied American participation in the invasion, in spite of the obvious facts. In their book, even Meyer and Szulc, who do not conceal their hostility toward the Cuban Revolution, say the following in this respect:

> While the tragic denouement of the invasion was being played out, the United States plunged ever more deeply into an obvious lie, contradictory assertions, and deception stemming from its own confusion and uncertainty. U. S. representative Adlai Stevenson unsuccessfully tried to convince the United Nations that the aircraft which had bombed Cuban airfields were Cuban, when it was becoming ever more evident that they had come from bases built by the United States in Guatemala. No less strange was the conduct of Secretary of State Dean Rusk, who announced on the day of the landing that this was a purely Cuban measure.[5]

The failure of this adventure is completely understandable. And even though there are still those in the United States who would seek the reasons for the failure in individual miscalculations and technical details, it is quite obvious to any clearheaded observer that the stake on the unpopularity of the revolutionary government was a failure and that the calculations on Cuban sympathy for the émigré gangs were built on sand. The echo of the shots on Playa Girón was heard around the world. The movement for solidarity with the heroic Cuban people embraced all Latin America and leaped to Europe, Asia, and Africa.

The defeat of the interventionists on the shores of the Bay of Pigs was an event of great political significance. Playa Girón became the symbol of the successful heroic struggle of a small nation against the most powerful of the imperialist nations for freedom and for total and genuine—not just declared—sovereignty, for total and genuine independence.

The Kennedy administration inherited Operation Pluto from the Eisenhower government. And while it was easy to find personal responsibility for it in the person of CIA Director Allen Dulles, who was soon retired, the new President also was responsible—as a result of his "100 days"—for the shameful failure the United States had suffered.

It might have been expected that the Kennedy administration, which spoke out for realism in politics and for the achievement of "new frontiers," would draw the necessary conclusions from the Playa Girón catastrophe. The major one would have been refraining from any further interference in the internal affairs of Cuba. However, this did not happen.

The "brain trust" at the White House factually recognized that the Cuban Revolution rested on the support of the people, that a struggle against it would consequently be a struggle against the Cuban people. However, instead of declining such a struggle, it came to the conclusion that the military strategic plans directed against Cuba would have to be changed.

After Playa Girón, the U.S. propaganda machine mounted a hysterical campaign about the socialist transformations in Cuba. In addition, every major episode in the class struggle in the other countries of the continent was pre-

[5]*Ibid.*, p. 134.

sumed to be the result of the activity of "Castroite agents." The Washington politicians believed that this would make it easier to frighten the national bourgeois circles in South America and to isolate free Cuba from the other countries of the continent.

A meeting of the foreign ministers of the OAS countries—the Latin American countries and the United States— was held on January 20, 1962, in the small resort village of Punta del Este, Uruguay. The State Department had been working hard on preparations for this conference, so as to secure passage of a resolution about breaking relations with Cuba and adopting sanctions against her. However, it became clear even before the meeting had begun that these plans were destined for failure. Mexico, Chile, Ecuador, and Argentina opposed sanctions. In a special notice (actually a reply to a secret letter of the State Department that had been distributed to all participants except Cuba on January 12), the Brazilian government stated on January 18 that it was not disposed to break relations with the Cuban Republic and it categorically rejected the proposal on sanctions.[6]

Dean Rusk, the head of the U.S. delegation, decided to exert new efforts for the purpose of securing support for his line. The official opening of the conference was delayed two days, during which intensive behind-the-scenes work among other delegations took place. As an American author testifies, the United States resorted to threats, declaring that "countries which do not recognize the danger of Cuban communism cannot count on participating in the distribution of the large sums of money within the framework of the Alliance for Progress."[7]

Even the reactionary press voiced its concern about the results of the pressure on the Latin American countries. The newspaper *New York World Tele-gram and Sun,* which spoke out on Cuban matters only with unrestrained malice, wrote as follows on the day the conference opened:

Doubts are arising with respect to the amount of help which the United States can expect from those countries which in the end will cooperate in extirpating communism in Cuba. The position of many of these countries either is unstable or is dictated by doubtful motives. Nicaragua, Haiti, and Paraguay are governed by dictators who see communism more as a personal than as an ideological threat.

Venezuela and Colombia, it seems, are sincerely full of determination to take measures against Castro. However, they must keep a careful watch on those at home who express a certain amount of sympathy for the "agrarian reforms" and "social revolution" of Castro.[8]

The Punta del Este conference was attended by a Cuban delegation headed by President Osvaldo Dorticós Torrado, which laid bare U.S. policy, which, in fact, was threatening the freedom and sovereignty of all the nations of Latin America.

Having understood that not even a majority of fourteen votes would go along with them, the U.S. representatives, headed by Secretary of State Dean Rusk, were forced to alter their proposals during the course of events. Withdrawing the proposal for sanctions, the North American delegation thrust on the conference (by means of pressure and threats) a resolution of "moral censure" of "communism in Cuba" and on the incompatibility of communism with membership in the OAS.[9]

It is characteristic that not all the governments represented at the Punta del Este meeting submitted to Washing-

[6]See *Pravda,* January 19, 1962.
[7]E. C. Stein, *Castro and Communism* (New York, 1962), p. 163.
[8]*New York World Telegram and Sun,* February 20, 1962.
[9]*New York Times,* February 1, 1962.

ton's thumb. The delegations of the largest states—Mexico, Argentina, Brazil, and others, in which three-fourths of the entire population of Latin America lives—did not support the resolution expelling Cuba "from participation in the Inter American system." With respect to the peoples of Latin America, they resolutely condemned the anti-Cuban actions of the imperialists. The movement of solidarity with the "free territory of America" continued to embrace ever more extensive sectors of the population and took on organized forms.

STRENGTHENING OF CUBAN-SOVIET FRIENDSHIP

Diplomatic relations between Cuba and the USSR were broken by dictator Batista's government in 1952. This stooge of U.S. ruling circles tried in every possible way to isolate the Cuban people from the socialist camp.

A completely different situation took shape after the victory of the Cuban Revolution. Taking consideration of the desire of the Cuban people for the establishment of durable friendly relations with the Soviet Union, the government of Fidel Castro in February 1960 signed an agreement with the USSR on commercial exchange, providing a Soviet credit of 100 million dollars to Cuba.[10] The Soviet Union agreed to buy during the course of five years 5 million tons of sugar from Cuba, which had at the time already experienced certain difficulties as a result of U.S. trade policy.

On May 8, 1960, a communique on the formal establishment of diplomatic relations was released. It pointed out that "these relations had been established de facto by the recognition of the Cuban revolutionary government by the government of the Union of Soviet Socialist Republics in January 1959."

While the trade agreement and the credit agreement helped Cuba to withstand economic pressure from American imperialism, the establishment of diplomatic relations with the Soviet Union signified that Cuba now had the possibility of relying on the solidarity of the Soviet people in political and diplomatic relations also. This situation was of primary importance in view of the ever increasing aggression from the north.

In early July 1960, one of the candidates for the presidency of the United States, millionaire Nelson Rockefeller, called for a more active struggle against Cuba and for stifling her by means of an economic blockade. Actually, all the other candidates and President Eisenhower also took the same position.

In this connection, the Soviet Union warned that if the U.S. imperialists took any aggressive actions against the Cuban people, who were defending their national independence, it would extend support to the Cuban people. The Soviet government thereby broadened Soviet-Cuban cooperation in a direction that had decisive importance for Cuba.

During his visit to the Soviet Union in July 1960, Cuban Minister of the Armed Forces Raúl Castro received renewed assurances from the leaders of the Soviet government to the effect that the Soviet Union would utilize any means in order to prevent U.S. armed intervention against the Cuban Republic. The position of the Soviet government vis-à-vis Cuba was highly valued by the Cuban leaders. In July 1960, Cuban Minister of the Armed Forces Raúl Castro stated that "the Cuban people will never forget the generous actions and aid of the Soviet Union, which will forever be part of the history of our country and of the history of all the Latin American nations."[11]

[10]See *Pravda*, February 15, 1960.
[11]*Narody SSSR i Kuby naveki vmeste, Dokumenty sovetsko-kubinskoi druzhby*, p. 55.

The economic and trade relations between Cuba and the USSR became ever closer and gradually became the basic factor in the foreign trade relations of the Cuban Republic. At a time of incredible difficulties caused by the American economic blockade, the Cuban people, thanks to these ties, were able to wage a successful battle for the reconstruction of their economy, for overcoming the ugly traces of a colonial economy, and for developing a diversified and rational economy.

Following agreements on supplementary deliveries of goods concluded by a Cuban foreign trade mission in April –May 1962, the newspaper *Noticias de Hoy* wrote: "In view of the difficulties in consumer goods caused by the imperialist blockade, the drought, and the inexperience and shortcomings of our economic organizations, our people were delighted to learn of the new deliveries of food, equipment, and raw materials from the Soviet Union and the other socialist countries." The volume of foreign trade between the two countries rose from 170 million dollars in 1960 to 500 million in 1961, and to about 700 million in 1962.

Economic and technical collaboration with the Soviet Union is extremely important for Cuba, reflected as it is in credits, in the dispatch of Soviet specialists to Cuba, and in the training of Cubans in the Soviet Union. In 1962 alone, over three thousand Cuban workers, agricultural workers, and engineers studied in the Soviet Union. Economic collaboration with the USSR facilitates the establishment of a developed industry in Cuba (the construction of chemical and mechanical plants, the expansion of the metallurgical basis, and so on) and also improvement in supplying the people of the island with food products (by making available a modern fishing fleet and the construction of ports for it with cold-storage facilities and other equipment, by supplying cane harvesting machines, and so on).

Cuba has similar relations with the other socialist countries. Aid to Cuba and the construction of socialism in that country have led to the development and consolidation of her economy.

Armaments designed to increase the country's defensive capability also occupied an important position among Soviet supplies to heroic Cuba. At the time of the battles at Playa Girón, the patriots who crushed the invaders were equipped with Soviet weapons. In late August 1962, a delegation of the national directorate of the Unified Revolutionary Organizations that was in the USSR, headed by Ernesto Guevara and Emilio Aragones, requested the Soviet government to extend additional aid in the form of armaments and the corresponding technical specialists for training Cuban soldiers. An agreement was reached on this matter.[12] In the face of the growing threat of aggression against Cuba from the U.S. armed forces (in which case the arms that had already been supplied to the Cuban army would, of course, have been insufficient for successful defense against the gigantic military machine of the United States), the governments of Cuba and the USSR reached agreement on the installation on Cuban territory of powerful defensive weapons, including medium-range rockets and aircraft.

THE CARIBBEAN CRISIS IN THE FALL OF 1962

The aid of the Soviet Union to the Republic of Cuba and the uplifting of her defensive capability turned out to be opportune. In the fall of 1962, the anti-Cuban hysteria in the United States continued to intensify.

On September 26, the Senate and the House of Representatives adopted a

[12]See *Pravda*, September 3, 1962.

resolution that, after the corresponding references to the Monroe Doctrine and the 1947 Treaty of Rio de Janeiro, stated the United States was determined "to prevent by the use of any and all means that might be necessary, including the use of weapons, the Marxist-Leninist regime in Cuba from spreading by force or the threat of force its aggressive or subversive activities to any part of this hemisphere."[13] The resolution was sanctioned by the President's signature.

It is characteristic that this resolution was adopted in response to Fidel Castro's statement on the construction of a modern fishing port in Cuba! Even a blind man could hardly fail to see that it was not difficult for the aggressive forces to categorize any events on the Latin American continent as "aggressive or subversive actions" by Cuba.

There were different points of view among U.S. ruling circles as to what their further policy should be. The group of "madmen"—called "hawks" in the press—demanded stepping up the preparation of plans for intervention and immediately striking a blow with all kinds of weapons against the rocket installations being constructed, and then occupying the island. The "doves"—that is, those who realistically evaluated the situation and understood the extreme danger of reckless aggressive actions under the new circumstances—proposed either to put the question before the Security Council or to discuss it immediately with the government of the Soviet Union and to reach agreement on the dismantling of the rocket installations. There were also other proposals, especially those for imposition of a naval blockade of Cuba. After almost interminable discussions, which stretched out over several days, the government made the decisions set forth in President Kennedy's speech on October 22.[14] The basic action was a naval blockade of Cuba, put into effect immediately. The President simultan-

eously revealed that a meeting of the advisory council of the OAS had been called for the purpose of implementing clauses 6 and 8 of the Rio Treaty, relating to military measures for ensuring the "security" of the hemisphere.

The blockade is generally treated as a "middle path" in American literature. In the final analysis, however, a peaceful solution of this "middle path" was possible only as a result of the peace-loving efforts of the Soviet government. The policy of blockade of Cuba harbored within itself a serious threat of war. The extremist elements in the U.S. government and in the Pentagon regarded it as a measure of preparation for a mass strike and invasion. On October 23, the correspondent of the London Financial Times reported, "The majority of American military experts consider that the blockade of Cuba will escalate at least into limited war."[15]

Powerful naval, army, and air force contingents were hurriedly mobilized and put on alert. Units that actually looked like an expeditionary force with the specific, detailed objective of military operations against Cuba were concentrated in ports and bases in the southern United States. According to some sources, even the time for the invasion to begin was set, an invasion for which a favorable situation had been created, in the opinion of the aggressors, by the uproar about the "Soviet threat."

After Kennedy's speech, the permanent Cuban representative to the UN, Incháustegui, energetically protested the blockade to the Security Council as a warlike act.[16] On October 23, the Soviet government also condemned the imposition of the blockade and the inspection of ships headed for Cuba. It insisted on discussion in the

[13]Quoted in the book The Cuban Crisis: A Documentary Record (New York, 1962), p. 11.
[14]New York Times, October 23, 1962.
[15]Financial Times, October 23, 1962.
[16]See Izvestiia, October 24, 1962.

Security Council of its statement "On the Violation of the UN Charter and the Threat of Peace from the United States."[17]

UN Secretary-General U Thant began an exchange of messages with the heads of the U.S. and Soviet governments, calling on both sides to cooperate in a peaceful solution of the conflict. On October 25, he sent a message to the Chairman of the Council of Ministers of the USSR in which he expressed his concern over the movement of Soviet merchant ships in the blockade zone. He proposed that these ships should be given temporary instructions to remain outside the blockade zone, so that the necessary conversations on the matter could be held.[18] At this tension-filled moment, many people throughout the world were wondering with alarm how many miles separated the Soviet ships making their regular runs to Cuba from the U.S. Navy, which had implemented the blockade in the Caribbean.

On October 26, the head of the Soviet government sent a reply to U Thant, in which he agreed to the proposal on postponing the penetration of Soviet ships into the blockade zone. However, he emphasized that such a situation could be maintained only temporarily.[19]

On that same day, U Thant sent a message to the head of the Cuban government, Fidel Castro. In the message, he referred to the declaration of President Osvaldo Dorticós to the General Assembly on October 8, to the effect that Cuba was prepared not to increase its armaments if there were a guarantee "in word and in deed" from the United States of nonaggression.[20] In his reply of October 27, Fidel Castro denied the right of the United States to interfere in the sovereign affairs of Cuba, but he supported a peaceful solution of the problem. Fidel Castro invited U Thant to come to Havana for direct talks.[21]

The adventurist policy of imperialism had brought mankind to the very brink of the chasm of worldwide thermonuclear war. It was impossible to lose a single hour. Seeking a way out of the unusual situation that had been created, the Chairman of the USSR Council of Ministers and the President of the United States entered into direct contact. The position of the Soviet government was based on two fundamental and mutually related goals: in the first place, not to permit armed aggression against Cuba and to defend her freedom and independence; in the second place, to ensure mankind of the maintenance of peace and to prevent the escalation of this acute crisis into worldwide thermonuclear war.

The maintenance of peace was made possible by the resolute position of the Soviet Union, a position that was simultaneously imbued with a sense of responsibility for the fate of the world. The American ruling circles understood the extreme danger of the adventurist actions against Cuba, where Soviet rockets and auxiliary ground troops were located. The prospects of settlement of the question of these rockets by means of negotiations was also opening before them. At this critical moment, the Kennedy government did not yield to hysterical exhortations that were being sounded from the camp of the "madmen," but halted the U.S. military machine.

The President officially stated that if "offensive weapons" were removed from Cuban territory (having in mind medium-range rockets and bombers), the United States would not undertake any armed intervention against Cuba and would not permit any to be carried out by any other country belonging to the Organization of American States.[22]

[17]*Ibid.*, October 23, 1962.
[18]See *Ibid.*, October 26, 1962.
[19]See *Pravda*, October 26, 1962.
[20]*New York Times*, October 27, 1962.
[21]*Noticias de Hoy*, October 28, 1962.
[22]See *Pravda*, October 29, 1962.

Under these conditions, the Soviet Union declared its willingness to remove the medium-range rockets.[23] Soviet Deputy Foreign Minister V. V. Kuznetsov flew to New York for conversations with U Thant and also with the U.S. permanent representative to the UN, A. Stevenson, and J. McCloy, whom President Kennedy had entrusted with conducting negotiations on the matter.

With the threat of invasion of the U.S. armed forces hanging over their heads, the Cuban people and government headed by Fidel Castro did not waver in their determination to defend the Revolution and to fight for their freedom and independence and for their bright future to the last drop of blood. The prime minister of the Cuban Republic set forth five demands of the Cuban people, the fulfillment of which he considered essential for the establishment of peace and security in the Caribbean area and for respect of the sovereign right of Cuba:[24]

1. Cessation of the economic blockade and of all measures of economic and commercial pressure

2. Cessation of subversive activity, the organization of invasions by mercenaries, and similar activity

3. Cessation of pirate attacks from bases located in the United States and Puerto Rico

4. Cessation of intrusions by U.S. military aircraft and naval vessels into Cuban air space and territorial waters

5. Evacuation of the naval base on Cuban territory at Guantánamo

A. I. Mikoyan, the First Deputy Chairman of the Council of Ministers of the USSR, flew to Havana on November 1, 1962, for an exchange of opinions with the Cuban government on problems of the international situation. On his way, he stopped off in New York to confer with U Thant, who had just returned from Havana, and, on the request of the American side, met with A. Stevenson and J. McCloy.

On departing New York for Havana, A. I. Mikoyan declared that the Soviet government resolutely supported the five points of Fidel Castro—which had been broadcast on Cuban radio and published a few hours before by the New York newspapers—as fully corresponding to the norms of international law and to the UN charter. He emphasized the inviolability of the fraternal unity and solidarity of the Soviet Union and the Cuban Republic.[25] During the course of the exchange of opinions between A. I. Mikoyan and Fidel Castro and other Cuban leaders, agreement was reached on points of view concerning further measures for peaceful settlement of the conflict in the Caribbean area.

The Cuban people and government exhibited statesmanship and an understanding of the interests of international peace and security. The peoples of the entire world welcomed the joint contribution of the Cuban Republic and the Soviet Union, thanks to which it was possible to defend the inviolability of Cuba and rescue mankind from a thermonuclear catastrophe.

In the face of the unity of the USSR and Cuba and their resolute and yet reasonable policy, imperialism was forced to take the path of settlement of the Caribbean crisis. In the second half of November, agreement was reached between the United States, on the one hand, and the USSR and Cuba, on the other, on the following questions: cessation of the U. S. naval blockade of Cuba; a U.S. statement to the UN guaranteeing not to attack Cuba; the withdrawal from Cuban territory of Soviet

[23]*Ibid.*
[24]*Revolución*, October 28, 1962.
[25]See *Pravda*, November 2, 1962.

medium-range weapons capable of carrying nuclear weapons; and granting the American side the possibility to carry out visual observation of the withdrawal by Soviet ships of the weapons mentioned above.

The events in the Caribbean proved once more that the forces of peace can successfully oppose the aggressive and adventuristic policy of imperialism.

THE SITUATION IN THE CARIBBEAN REGION SINCE THE CRISIS

The solution of the crisis demonstrated the possibility and necessity of settling international conflicts through negotiations. The peoples of the entire world joyfully greeted the peaceful settlement of the crisis.

However, the anti-Cuban hysteria cooked up by the U.S. reactionary circles did not cease. On the contrary, throughout 1963 the "madmen" continued their extremely sharp attacks on the government for "inactivity" and demanded military intervention. Moreover, in connection with the approaching presidential elections, the prospective Republican candidates made the "Cuban problem" ever more manifestly one of the cornerstones of their preelection campaigns.

Thus, Richard Nixon said the following in an interview on the forthcoming elections: "Cuba and Latin America alone can lead to the defeat of the present administration, if this problem is used effectively."[26] Arizona Senator B. Goldwater acted precisely in accordance with this recipe and incessantly demanded that the United States "use all its power" against Cuba. However, a relatively "moderate" point of view prevailed in the ruling circles following the crisis. This consisted of the idea that all means except direct intervention by U.S. armed forces should be used against Cuba. This entailed first of all a trade embargo—which the United

States wanted to bring all NATO countries into—economic and diplomatic isolation of the Island of Freedom, and the conduct of subversive activities among the people.

Rules put into effect in early 1963 prohibited the loading in U.S. ports of cargos financed by the government onto ships making runs to Cuba. Nevertheless, when this matter was investigated in Congress in September, it turned out that the "blacklist" contained the names of 181 ships, many of them belonging to the merchant marines of England, France, Greece, Morocco, Norway, and other countries.[27] On September 17, legislation was introduced in the House of Representatives to forbid entrance into U.S. ports of "any ship which has called at any Cuban port." And on October 16, 1963, the Senate Committee on Foreign Relations adopted a resolution demanding that the United States withdraw aid from those countries whose ships and aircraft supply Cuba with "military or strategic materials."

In February 1964, the American rulers organized an incident with the seizure of several Cuban fishing boats. Soon afterwards, a law on withdrawing aid to all countries that maintain trade relations with the Cuban Republic was passed.

In the spring of 1964, the U.S. government extended the trade embargo to food and medicines, thus decisively throwing off the mask of "humanitarianism" toward the Cuban people. During that same period, counterrevolutionary gangs carried out bandit attacks on a sugar mill and other coastal installations that would not have been possible without at least passive approval from Washington. It is a well-known fact that the activities of the émigrés are totally con-

[26]*U.S. News and World Report*, October 14, 1963, p. 88.
[27]*New York Herald Tribune*, September 27, 1963.

trolled by the Central Intelligence Agency. Thus, it is a matter of calculated provocations, of a renewal of aggressive sorties against Cuba. Serious apprehensions were also aroused among progressive society by the release into the "reserves" in May 1964 of several thousand Cuban émigrés who had formerly been part of the U. S. Army. On June 2, 1964, President Johnson declared that reconnaissance flights over Cuba by U-2 aircraft would continue.

Free Cuba terrifies the ruling circles of her northern neighbor first of all as a beacon for the national-liberation movements of all the other Latin American countries, as an example for solving the internal economic and social problems of those countries. And while the charges against Cuba of conducting "subversive activities" are totally false, the ideas of the Cuban Revolution unquestionably exert a great moral influence on the political situation on the continent. Thanks to the Cuban Revolution, the struggle of the Latin American peoples against imperialist oppression is attaining a new level. The events in Panama in early 1964 are a brilliant example of this. The entire Panamanian people resolutely demanded a re-examination of the oppressive treaty on the canal, which belongs to the same category as the treaty on the base at Guantánamo. It is characteristic that for the first time in history, a majority of the members of the OAS expressed censure of U.S. actions.

In March 1963, the Latin American Congress of Solidarity with Cuba was held under the sign of growing support of the Cuban people by the fraternal peoples of Latin America. Ever more people on the continent began to take note that the defense of the freedom of the Cuban people and their right to choose their own socioeconomic system is not just a struggle for the interests of the Cuban people, but also a struggle for the right of the other peoples of Latin America to determine their own fate by themselves. This is why the idea of non-interference in the internal affairs of Cuba embraces bourgeois sectors also.

The governments of a number of the largest Latin American countries have for some time refused to carry out Washington's demand for discontinuing trade and cultural relations with Cuba and for breaking diplomatic relations with her. Very significant in this connection is the position of Brazil, which prior to the coup in March 1964 had resolutely refused to accept the dictates of U.S. diplomacy. Immediately after the coup, Brazil broke relations with Cuba. Heavy pressure from the United States led to the Brazilian example's being followed in mid-1964 by Uruguay and Bolivia. In February 1964, President L. Johnson met with Mexican President López Mateos. The press indicated that Mexican-Cuban relations occupied an important place in the conversations, but Mexico retained her previous position.

The Caribbean crisis demonstrated the durability of the relations between USSR and Cuba, which are based on the principles of proletarian internationalism. Disappointment awaited those who overtly and covertly counted on this friendship being undermined.

The first visit of Prime Minister Fidel Castro to the Soviet Union took place in April–May 1963, under conditions of sincerity and fraternity between the two nations. A joint Soviet-Cuban declaration was signed in Moscow on May 23, 1963, which noted the results of the manifold exchange of opinions on questions of further consolidation and development of the relations of fraternal friendship and cooperation between the two countries.[28]

With respect to the situation in the Caribbean area, the parties noted that, "although the immediate threat of a military invasion of Cuba has been re-

[28]See *Pravda*, May 25, 1963.

moved, tension still continues to grow ever more in the Caribbean area." The statement read as follows with respect to the five points advanced by Premier Fidel Castro: "The Soviet government resolutely supports these principles, since they conform fully to the UN charter and reflect the efforts of the Cuban revolutionary government to find a peaceful solution to the unsolved problems that create tension in this area of the world." Further on, during the course of the conversations "it was confirmed that if an attack is carried out against Cuba in violation of the obligations assumed by the President of the United States with respect to non-invasion of Cuba, the Soviet Union will honor its international obligation to the fraternal Cuban people and extend to them with all the means at its disposal all necessary aid for defending the freedom and independence of the Republic of Cuba."

The parties also examined problems connected with the implementation of Soviet-Cuban agreements on commercial, technical, economic, scientific, and cultural collaboration. Agreement was reached on measures for their further development. Extremely important for the Cuban economy was the initiative of the Soviet government on amending the existing agreement to raise the price of Cuban raw sugar bought during 1963, so as to bring this price into line with the increases in the level of world prices during the period. The statement confirmed the complete agreement of the two sides on basic questions of the international situation, including the efforts of the Soviet government toward achieving disarmament and the cessation of nuclear testing.

Prime Minister Fidel Castro again visited the USSR in early 1964, and the visit was marked by further consolidation of Soviet-Cuban relations. One of the results of this visit was the long-term agreement on Cuban supplies of sugar to the USSR.[29] According to this agreement, Cuba will supply the Soviet Union with the following amounts of raw sugar during the period 1965–1970: 1965, 2.1 million tons; 1966, 3 million tons: 1967, 4 million tons; and in the following three years, 5 million tons annually. The establishment of a fixed price for the sugar over the period was extremely important for Cuba herself and also served as an example of the principles of a new approach to trade relations with countries that are dependent on the export of raw materials.[30]

Appearing on Moscow television on January 21, 1964, Fidel Castro noted that it was due precisely to the fraternal aid of the Soviet Union that the destructive hurricane Flora, the like of which had not been seen for many centuries, did not bring catastrophic consequences for the Cuban people.

Nevertheless, the country is experiencing no few difficulties in the field of economic construction and strengthening of the economic situation. The Cuban people declared 1964 to be the "Year of the Economy," and in so doing manifested their determination to concentrate their forces and attention on this key question in the development of the country. The joint Soviet-Cuban communique states that the Cuban revolutionary government "regards the successes achieved by the Soviet Union in the struggle to ban nuclear testing and its agreement not to launch satellites carrying weapons as a step forward toward peace and disarmament."[31]

The communique reiterates that militant U.S. military circles are stubbornly continuing to conduct an aggressive policy with respect to Cuba, in connection with which the Soviet Union again asserted its readiness to do everything

[29]See Pravda, January 23, 1964.
[30]The price was fixed at 6 American cents a pound, that is, more than the United States pays the Latin American countries for sugar.
[31]See Pravda, January 23, 1964.

possible to establish good-neighbor relations between the Republic of Cuba and the United States on the basis of the principles of peaceful coexistence of states with different social structures.

The anti-Cuban policy of the United States, which leads to increased international tension, is an obstacle to complete normalization of the situation in the Caribbean area. This situation requires the solidarity, vigilance, and unity of peace-loving forces and a resolute rebuff on their part of the aggressive activities of imperialism.

44. The Agrarian Reform in Cuba*

A. M. SIVOLOBOV

The popular movement against the pro-American dictatorship of Batista that developed in Cuba in 1956 took the form of a profound popular revolution and terminated on January 1, 1959, with the victory of the people and the establishment of a revolutionary government of the working class, peasantry, and working intelligentsia.

The Cuban Revolution smashed the bonds of North American domination in Latin America, elevated the national-liberation movement to a higher plane, and inspired the Latin American peoples with faith in their own strength and in the possibility for rapid liberation from the domination of imperialism and latifundism. With the victory of the Cuban Revolution, a "front of active struggle against imperialism was opened in Latin America."[1] The Cuban People's revolution "gave a powerful stimulus to the struggle of the peoples of Latin America for total national liberation."[2]

DISTINGUISHING FEATURES OF THE CUBAN REVOLUTION

In distinction from the revolutionary manifestations that have taken place in a number of Latin American countries, the people's revolution in Cuba has its distinguishing features.

In the first place, it radically solved the basic question of social revolution—the question of power. As the result of the popular revolt in Cuba, the overthrow of a dictatorial regime was accompanied for the first time in the history of the revolutionary movement in Latin America by the crushing defeat and expulsion from power of the reactionary classes connected with imperial-

*Ekonomicheskie problemy soiuza rabochego klassa i krest'ianstva stran Latinskoi Ameriki (Moskva: Universitet druzhby narodov imeni Patrisa Lumumbi, 1966), pp. 317–340.
[1] Dokumenty Soveshchaniia predstavitelei kommunisticheskikh i rabochikh partii (Moskva: Gospolitizdat, 1960), p. 34.
[2] Ibid., p. 32.

ism, by the smashing of the old state apparatus of control of the tyranny, and by the creation of new revolutionary organs of power by the Cuban people from the bottom up.

The revolution put an end to the economic and political dependence of Cuba on imperialist states. The revolutionary government established national sovereignty and has steadfastly defended it. The country acquired genuine independence. By expelling the imperialist monopolies, the Cuban people restored their sovereign rights and national resources to themselves. The further development of the revolution led to the country's setting out on the path of construction of a new, genuinely democratic society—socialism.

In the second place, the political foundation of revolutionary power in Cuba was the people's juntas (councils)—rural, municipal, and provincial juntas created during the course of the national-liberation struggle of the people. Until general elections are held, the Council of Ministers and the President of the Republic wield executive and legislative powers. The basic law of the Cuban Republic is the Havana Declaration, which supplements the constitution and which was adopted on September 2, 1960, by the National General Assembly. It establishes the rights and duties of the people and proclaims genuine popular rule. The declaration states that the people have empowered the government to implement the confiscation of the property of counterrevolutionaries, to expropriate without prior payment the excess land of latifundists and foreign landowners, and to nationalize the enterprises of enemies of the Cuban people and American monopolies.

In the third place, the decisive and reliable power of the revolutionary government in Cuba is the people's army, which was formed during the course of the national-liberation struggle of the

Cuban people on the basis of unification of partisan groups and detachments in a unitary Rebel Liberation Army under the command of Fidel Castro. The creation of a revolutionary army consisting of peasants, workers, and white-collar workers favored the successful development of the Cuban Revolution. At the same time, the revolutionary government organized general military training of the population and established a worker-peasant militia that numbers several hundred thousand persons. Thus socialist Cuba has become a unitary, militant, revolutionary camp prepared to defend and uphold the gains of the socialist revolution.

The guerrilla war in Cuba was one of the most important forms of struggle against imperialist domination and feudalism and for the establishment of a government of the toiling masses. The guerrilla movement was also effective because of its support of active mass demonstrations and strikes by workers and students, sabotage, boycotts of elections, and international solidarity.

Notwithstanding the repressions of the dictatorship and the treason of the corrupt trade-union leadership, the struggle of the Cuban working class did not cease. The general nationwide political strike in December 1955, the strike of railway workers in the eastern provinces of Oriente and Camagüey in 1956, the general strike in August 1957, and the strike in April 1958 played an important role in the preparation of the conditions for the elimination of the dictatorial regime in the country and aided the activization of partisan detachments in the countryside.

The constant threat of strikes by industrial workers forced Dictator Batista to keep the majority of his police and armed forces in the cities. Troops were sent into regions where guerrilla detachments were operating, which facilitated the development of armed struggle in the countryside. The revolutionary actions of the working class would have been more impressive had it not been for the traitorous policy of the leaders of the state trade unions, who tried in every possible way to prevent the working class from developing a struggle against the military-police dictatorship. Nevertheless, the working class played an important role in the overthrow of the dictatorship and the establishment of revolutionary power of the workers and peasants. Toward the end of December of 1958, when the people's army of Fidel Castro was approaching Havana, the imperialists and reactionaries, using their old and tested method of splitting the revolutionary forces, hurriedly established a puppet military junta government. However, a general strike of the Havana proletariat was proclaimed on January 1, 1959, on the call of the democratic forces and, first of all, the Cuban Communists. The strike paralyzed the activities of the reactionaries and swept away the government, creating the conditions for consolidation of revolutionary power by the Cuban people headed by F. Castro. "It was precisely the working class," said F. Castro, "which, with its general strike, put an end along with the Rebel Army to the plans of reaction, which had intended to snatch victory from the hands of the people at the last moment, as it had happened previously. . . . The general strike transferred power to the hands of the revolution."[3]

Thus, the driving forces of the Cuban Revolution were the workers, the peasants, and the revolutionarily inclined intelligentsia. During the process of development of the national-liberation struggle, the peasants and the middle sectors of the population broke loose from the influence of the bourgeois-landowner parties and groups, while those petty bourgeois and bourgeois circles which were frightened by the difficulties of the struggle were left outside the revolutionary forces and thus could

not exert decisive influence on them and were neutralized or isolated from the masses. The experience of the Cuban Revolution shows that the armed form of struggle and guerrilla warfare could be conducted just as successfully in other Latin American countries. It proves that, for a backward country in heavy economic and political dependence on foreign monopolies and in which power is held by dictatorial henchmen of monopolies, armed struggle and the creation of liberated guerrilla zones and the establishment of a national-liberation rebel army is one of the most important forms of the struggle for total national liberation.

One of the forms for the origination of guerrilla detachments—and, in the future, the people's revolutionary army —is for the rural population, with the support of the working class and the democratic and patriotic forces in the cities, to make the transition from the struggle for satisfaction of their demands to armed struggle against the landlords—to take up arms and organize detachments. Another form is the transfer of units of government troops over to the side of the revolutionary masses. The most favorable conditions for guerrilla warfare exist where there are extensive mountainous regions and forests, as well as connections with industrial centers.

The experience of the Cuban Revolution has shown that the guerrilla movement is most effective when it is combined with revolutionary manifestations of the workers in the cities and with general political and economic strikes. The strike movement of workers and white-collar workers in all forms of transportation is especially important under these conditions, since general strikes by these units of the proletariat can at the decisive moment paralyze the

[3]Fidel Castro, *Rechi i vystupleniia* (Moskva, 1960), p. 162.

activity of the reactionary government and thus support the guerrilla war in the most decisive manner.

It is a well-known fact that, in their effort to split the liberation movement, the reactionary forces often resort to maneuvering and attempt to replace one dictatorship with another, or, if that effort fails, try to retain the old army under the command of some pseudo-revolutionary in order to use it against the revolution. In the early days of the Cuban Revolution, the rightist elements among the revolutionary forces insisted on the formation of a transitional government that would consist basically of representatives of the national bourgeoisie. The left wing believed that the government from the very first should be a revolutionary, anti-imperialist, people's government, capable of proceeding to the implementation of a radical agrarian reform and other socio-economic transformations. The victory of the position of the leftist forces determined a rapid transition of the revolution from the stage of smashing the domination of imperialism and latifundism to its second stage, in which all power was placed in the hands of the working class and the peasantry.

The work of winning over, mobilizing, organizing, and politically awakening the peasantry—and especially agricultural workers, who are the basic nucleus of the guerrilla detachments and national-liberation forces—is extremely important in the struggle against imperialism and the domination of the latifundists, independently of whether the revolution takes the form of guerrilla warfare.

The experience of the Cuban Revolution has shown once more that the presence of a political crisis in the country is necessary for the victory of the national-liberation revolution—that is, such a situation in which the government suffers a loss of prestige among the majority of the population and for-

feits its ability to govern, or when the government shows itself to be so weak that it cannot mount serious resistance to the revolutionary national-liberation movement headed by a national front.

Another important accomplishment of the revolutionary struggle is the establishment of unity of the revolutionary, anti-imperialist, and antifeudal forces. The genuine unity of the people is achieved in action. Its foundation is a powerful alliance of the working class and the peasantry, with the working class playing the leading role.

Such is the significance of the Cuban Revolution in the matter of leadership of the rebel revolutionary movement. This experience shows that "where the paths are closed to the people, where the oppression of the workers and peasants is of an especially harsh nature, and where the domination of U.S. monopolies is especially strong... it is incorrect to divert the people with arid, time-serving illusions to the effect that power can be seized from the ruling classes—which are dug into all state positions, have education in their control, control all communications media, and have huge financial resources available to them—by means of legal methods that do not exist and will never exist, since the monopolies and the domestic oligarchies will defend their control with fire and sword, with the aid of the police and the army."[4] It has become obvious that the experience of the Cuban Revolution has a direct, practical significance for many Latin American countries.

REVOLUTIONARY SOCIOECONOMIC TRANSFORMATIONS

One of the most important features of the Cuban people's revolution is the fact that from the very first days the

[4]"Vtoraia Gavanskaia deklaratsiia," *Pravda*, February 6, 1962.

revolutionary government, headed by Fidel Castro and deriving its support from the working class and the peasantry, proceeded to the implementation of basic socioeconomic transformations. The nationalization of industrial enterprises belonging to American monopolies, as well as those belonging to big Cuban capitalists, was proclaimed. By early 1965, over 95 percent of the total industry of the country belonged to the state. In addition, all private and foreign banks were nationalized.

As a result of these revolutionary transformations, the government acquired complete control of the sugar, oil-refining, mining, chemical, metallurgical, and textile industries, as well as other branches of industry, in addition to railway, maritime, air, and a considerable portion of highway transportation. A state monopoly on foreign trade was established. A large part of the largest commercial enterprises in the country were nationalized. The state also established a monopoly in foreign exchange. Thus, the political and economic conditions essential for a planned economy were established.

The government has recently carried out a number of measures in the field of reorganization of the organs of state and economic management in order to improve management of the state sector and supervision of the private sector. In February 1961, the Ministries of Industry, Domestic Trade, and Foreign Trade were established. With a view to the formulation of short-term and long-term plans for the economic development of the country, a Central Council (Junta) for Economic Planning was established and a long-range plan for the economic development of Cuba in the period 1961–1965 was worked out.

The aid of the Soviet Union and the other socialist countries played a decisive role in ensuring the operation of the basic branches of the Cuban economy.

Thus, for example, supplies of Soviet oil assured the operation of Cuban oil refineries at full capacity and an uninterrupted supply of electric power to industrial and communal enterprises. The annual purchase of four million tons of Cuban sugar by the Soviet Union and other socialist countries created favorable conditions for the operation of the Cuban sugar industry. Soviet deliveries of chemical products (such as liquid ammonia and sulphur) to Cuba permitted an increase in the output of the nickel plant at Nicaro and a guaranteed supply of raw materials to plants producing sulphuric acid.

The economic and technical aid of the Soviet Union and the other socialist countries will permit Cuba in the coming years to increase the capacity of her metallurgical, oil-refining, machine-tool, chemical, and other plants, as well as the capacity of electric power stations, which will create favorable conditions for the further development of the entire Cuban economy.

The basic form of Cuban cooperation with the socialist countries is that of foreign trade. It objectively facilitates the coordination of the plans for the economic development of Cuba with the economic plans of the USSR and the other socialist countries. Soviet deliveries to Cuba of tractors; agricultural machinery; trucks; Diesel engines; mining, hoisting, and road construction equipment; airplanes for crop-spraying; motorcycles; oil and petroleum products; fertilizers; ferrous and non-ferrous metals; wheat, wheat flour, and other food products; lumber; and cotton played a leading role in the satisfaction of the urgent requirements of the Cuban economy and also in supplying the population with goods.

The great aid extended to Cuba by the USSR, at a time when imperialism was exerting every effort to isolate Cuba economically by means of a systematic blockade and every kind of incessant aggressive action, is becoming more important and arouses the deep gratitude of the Cuban people and government toward the Soviet people and the Soviet government.[5]

The government is now investigating the ways and means for assuring the regular supply of industry with raw and other materials and of the people with food. Technical councils have been established at the country's enterprises and are beginning operation. The administrations of nationalized enterprises turn to them for the solution of a number of practical matters connected with ensuring the normal work of enterprises and increased output. The trade unions extend effective aid to the government in the search for substitutes for raw materials, in repairing equipment, and in making and repairing spare parts with their own efforts through rationalization suggestions from the workers and technicians. With the support of the revolutionary organizations, the government has conducted an extensive campaign in the country for increasing labor productivity and for conserving raw materials. Very important in this respect is the competition begun in 1961 among enterprises in the sugar industry for better production indicators and for the production of 10 million tons of sugar in coming years (by 1970). An important role in the harvesting of a record sugar crop is played by the volunteer brigades of workers and white-collar workers from the cities who go out to the sugar plantations, the mechanization of sugar cane harvesting, and especially the aid of the USSR in producing combines for cutting cane.

On the appeal of the Communist Party of Cuba, the unified revolutionary trade-union organizations, and the Revolutionary Government, the Cuban working class is manifesting a high degree of consciousness under conditions

of a deterioration in the economic situation. This is reflected in the voluntary contribution of 4 percent of their wages to the country's industrialization fund, in voluntary work without pay, in substitutions for workers who have been mobilized into the ranks of the people's militia, and in active participation in the work of renovating sugar mills.

Along with the implementation of measures directed at the improvement of the work of nationalized branches of industry, the Cuban government is devoting great attention to the development of agriculture, achieving a constant supply of food for the urban population. The government has set a course of further expansion of the harvests of various agricultural crops and an increase in livestock and poultry, with a view of future reduction in imported agricultural products. However, the increases registered in agriculture and livestock still do not meet the demand. The measures taken by the government in the field of agriculture, especially in stock-raising, began to yield perceptible results by 1962–1963.

AGRARIAN REFORM

The greatest conquest of the Cuban Revolution is the agrarian reform, which Cubans call the "holiest of the holy" aspects of the revolution. The agrarian reform is destined to alter the fate not only of the peasantry, but of the entire country. The Cuban people are correctly connecting their plans for economic and cultural development, for the industrialization of the country, and for the elimination of unemployment, hunger, and poverty with the elimination of the latifundia and the semifeudal relations in the countryside. Ever since the moment that the law on agrarian reform was adopted on May 17, 1959, basic socioeconomic changes have taken

[5]*Pravda* May 15, 1962.

place in the life of the Cuban peasantry and the premises have been created for the introduction of socialist relations in the countryside.

As early as the eve of the general offensive of the Rebel People's Liberation Army, Fidel Castro on October 10, 1958, officially approved Law No. 3, "On the Right of the Peasants to Land," in the liberated region of the Sierra Maestra. This law had been first proclaimed by Castro in October 1956. "The first and second articles of this law granted the right of free ownership of lands up to two *caballerías* in size to the persons who occupied and cultivated it, regardless of the tenure conditions."[6] Law No. 3 was of a temporary nature and was in effect until the publication of the law on agrarian reform of May 17, 1959.[7]

The implementation of agrarian reform while the liberation struggle was still under way was a step forward, and it facilitated the active mobilization of the peasantry,[8] conferred an antifeudal, anti-imperialist nature on the liberation struggle, drew new sectors of the rural population into the broad movement, and thus hastened the fall of the dictatorship and the victory of the people. According to Law No. 3, the revolutionary organs of power—the councils of people's representatives—were entrusted with the task of dividing the land among the peasants; the construction of schools, housing, and medical care centers in rural areas; and the extension of aid to the peasants. Thousands of peasant tenants and *precaristas* (peasants who occupied landlord lands) received according to the terms of this law plots of land that had been confiscated from latifundist owners, and over 100,000 tenants were freed from bondage-type leasing agreements.[9]

A provincial peasant congress attended by over one thousand delegates representing all sectors of the peasant population of the eastern regions was held in the city of Santiago, in the province of Oriente, on February 23–24, 1959, immediately following the victory of the people's revolution in Cuba.[10] The congress was held in the most populous province, where peasant demonstrations against the Batista dictatorship had been especially active and where peasant organizations had been established even during the course of the revolutionary struggle. The congress elected a permanent executive organ. At the same time, another peasant congress was held in the province of Las Villas, in which more than two hundred delegates from sixty peasant organizations participated.[11]

In March 1959, peasant congresses were held in the provinces of Camagüey and Havana. The basic decision of the congresses was the transfer of land as their property to all tenants, subtenants, and agricultural laborers. A demand was advanced for the elimination of latifundia and the establishment of the maximum amount of land that one person could own. Excess land was to be divided among the peasants, agricultural workers, and members of the rebel army. The elimination of all forms of feudal exploitation of the peasants by landowners was provided for.[12]

On the "Day of the Peasant" on May 17, 1959, in response to the peasant wishes advanced at the peasant congresses, the government of Fidel Castro proclaimed a new law on agrarian reform, to be effective throughout the country. The executive agency for implementing the agrarian reforms was to be the National Institute for Agrarian Reform (INRA).

[6]A. Jiménez, *Agrarnaia reforma na Kube* (Moskva, 1960), pp. 31–32.
[7]A. Jiménez, *Geografiia Kuby* (Moskva, 1960), p. 225.
[8]A. Jiménez, *Agrarnaia reforma na Kube*, p. 32.
[9]*Noticias de Hoy*, November 28, 1961.
[10]*Fundamentos*, May 1959, p. 17.
[11]*Ibid.*   [12]*Ibid.*, pp. 17–18.

The law on agrarian reform prohibited the existence of latifundia. A maximum size of thirty *caballerías* was established for plots of land. Land exceeding this amount and belonging to a single person was subject to expropriation and distribution among landless and virtually landless peasants and agricultural workers. The maximum size of plots of land in the vicinity of cities was considerably smaller. The former landowner himself had to cultivate the plot. The law prohibited hiring labor.

Articles 3 and 4 of the law provided that state lands were also subject to distribution among the peasants. An exception were the lands devoted to social purposes, for the distribution of industry, lands rich in natural resources that could be exploited, state forests, lands of agricultural communes, and lands assigned for purposes of health care, education, and social services.[13]

Lator on, when it became obvious that owners of plots of land over five *caballerías* in size had begun to get involved in speculation with agricultural products, to sabotage the development of agricultural production, and were using nonlabor income for counterrevolutionary activities, the Cuban government in October 1963 adopted a decision on the nationalization of the lands of owners who had more than five *caballerías*. This law dealt a blow to the rural bourgeoisie.[14]

Only Cubans have the right to own land. All estates of foreign monopolies and stock companies were confiscated and the land was divided among the peasants. Well-organized agricultural plantations—sugar cane, tobacco, hemp, and especially stock farms—were not subject to distribution. They were converted into state property for the establishment of state farms or cooperatives.

The law of May 17, 1959, embraced a land area of 6 million hectares, out of a total of 9 million hectares belonging to various groups of landowners in the country. Article 29-A provided that the Cuban government would compensate landowners for their losses. The compensation for confiscated lands was to be paid in the form of bonds to be liquidated over a period of twenty years with annual interest of 4.5 percent. Land appraisals were established in accordance with the value of the property set in municipal documents at tax payment time on October 10, 1958. An examination of the largest agricultural establishments showed that their owners paid very low taxes, even though they owned huge expanses of land.[15]

A "minimum livelihood" plot of two *caballerías* (about 27 hectares) was established for a peasant family consisting of five persons, and this plot was made available to the family gratis in accordance with Article 16 of the law.

Peasant tenants and sharecroppers and the owners of small plots received documents giving them the right to free use of the land they cultivated, under the condition that its size not exceed two *caballerías*. Peasants who owned land up to five *caballerías* were exempted from tax payments on the two *caballerías* they received gratis. Progressively increasing taxes were levied above that norm. Article 21 of the law provided that, if the land area cultivated by tenants, colonists, or agricultural workers exceeded two *caballerías* but not five *caballerías*, in addition to the "minimum livelihood" plot received,

[13]*Ibid.*, p. 18.

[14]*Pravda*, November 6, 1963.

[15]The Atlántica del Golfo had 500,000 acres of land in Cuba; Rionda, 480,000; Cuban American, 330,000; and United Fruit Company, 266,000 acres. The latter paid taxes on an assessed value of 6 million pesos rather than 30 million. Consequently, it will be paid only 6 million pesos for the confiscated land.

Thirteen U.S. sugar companies held 47.4 percent of all the arable land in Cuba. Their plants produced 43 percent of the total sugar production, and their invested capital was estimated at 275 million dollars. In accordance with the law, all the land of these foreign monopolies was confiscated and became the property of the people.

the workers would have the right to acquire the remaining land cultivated by them from the government.

The law prohibited the buying and selling of land. Land received on the basis of the law "cannot be transferred to individuals or commercial firms, but can be transferred to a spouse or to agricultural cooperatives," and "can be willed to a single heir."

In order to carry out the agrarian reform in a more organized fashion, the country was divided into twenty-eight zones of agricultural development. State extension stations, experimental farms, schools, credit institutions, and state agricultural machinery stations were established in each zone.

COOPERATIVE CONSTRUCTION AND THE ESTABLISHMENT OF SOCIALIST RELATIONS IN THE COUNTRYSIDE

A broad peasant movement for the establishment of agricultural cooperatives on the land of estates developed in the country immediately following the implementation of the agrarian reform.

At first, two kinds of cooperatives were formed. The first kind was established on the lands of latifundist plantations. Agricultural workers and a few poor peasants became members of these cooperatives. The government took measures to convert them into diversified farms for the purpose of ensuring employment of their members throughout the year, so that some of the cooperatives could be turned into state farms (or people's farms) later on. A simpler kind of cooperative was simultaneously established, one in which poor peasants and tenants joined together "to carry out certain projects or for the purpose of obliterating boundary lines and producing jointly."[16]

Taking into account the presence in Cuba of large sugar cane, hemp, and tobacco plantations and large stock-breeding farms, the agrarian reform law provided for the encouragement of formation of so-called people's farms. These farms become the property of the state and of the entire people and are being turned into model agricultural enterprises.[17]

Under conditions in which a considerable part of the rural population of Cuba was hired workers, the conversion of these agricultural workers into owners of small, broken-up farms after the distribution of the lands of the plantations on which they worked would have had negative results[18] and would have led to decreased labor productivity. Small peasant farms cannot be developed according to the laws of expanded production. They are unprofitable. "In a social sense, such actions—converting the worker into an owner—would have been a step backward."[19] The agricultural workers preferred to receive wages, and they did not manifest any desire to have plots of land or to become owners. The presence of large organized agricultural plantations and a large number of hired workers on them "made it necessary to form large cooperative farms, people's [state] farms for the production of sugar cane and rice." The formation of large cooperative or state farms on the lands of the former plantations is very advantageous in comparison with their division into small, scattered peasant farms. It made it possible to improve the standard of living of the agricultural workers considerably in a short period of time.

Stock farms with an area of 4 to 10 thousand hectares, and on which only a few dozen workers were employed, could not be converted immediately into cooperative farms. Consequently, following their confiscation, the government began to establish state farms

[16]*Problemy mira i sotsializma*, 1:67 (1961).
[17]*Revista Internacional*, 10:6 (1961).
[18]*Ibid.*
[19]*Ibid.*

—people's cattle farms—at them.[20] The financing was done through the National Institute for Agrarian Reform. The institute invested over 100,000 pesos in state farms in just the first three years.[21] These resources went for the development of new branches of production, with technical equipment and supplies, for the acquisition of breeding stock, for the construction of reservoirs and irrigation facilities, and for the payment of wages to the workers in the people's farms.

The people's farms assumed an important position in the production of a number of the most important crops. In particular, they produce over 60 percent of the rice; 70 percent of the corn, soy beans, and cotton; and 95 percent of the kenaf, and do extensive stock breeding. Almost three-fourths of the entire tractor park of the country is at their disposal.

In connection with the law on agrarian reform, the National Institute for Agrarian Reform in March 1961 adopted a resolution on the establishment of zones of agricultural development in the country. In accordance with its provisions, three hundred state farms were quickly established in the country. Placed at their disposal were 23 million hectares of land.[22] Afterwards, every state farm became a center for the dissemination of experience in the management of agriculture.

The land, the major means of production, and the fruits of production are the property of the entire people. The workers receive wages, housing, and free medical care, and their children receive education at the schools. The majority of the workers at the people's farms are members of the agricultural workers' trade unions.

The state farms are beginning to play a large role in the reconstruction of agricultural production on socialist foundations. For example, the site now occupied by the Granma state farm is a diversified farm. Not only is stock raised on it now, but grain, leguminous crops, and fruits are also cultivated.[23] The former Rosario stock farm has now become a highly developed state farm. Cotton raising has been initiated on it, the milk yield increased, and the animal herds increased. On an estate where only a few dozen workers lived before, several hundred workers are now engaged, and 120 dwellings, schools, and a hospital have been built for them.[24] More and more such people's farms are being created.

As the cooperatives were strengthened in an organizational and economic sense, especially the cooperatives for the production of sugar cane and hemp, and as they became diversified farms, the need for converting certain of them into people's farms arose. As we noted earlier, the Cuban agricultural workers who had worked on sugar cane, hemp, or rice plantations or on stock-raising farms and had formerly received their wages in cash, still did not express the desire to have a subsidiary economy on the cooperative and to receive payment in kind for their work. In connection with this, a movement for the conversion of certain cooperatives into people's (state) farms arose among the members of cooperatives in 1962. At meetings on 582 cooperatives, the majority of the members passed resolutions asking the government to convert the cooperatives into people's farms. In August 1962, a national congress of members of cooperatives was held, and it discussed the question of the work of sugar cane cooperatives. The congress came out for conversion into people's farms of those cooperatives which had been strengthened organizationally and economically. The basic

[20]Ibid.
[21]Revolución, March 10, 1964.
[22]Ibid., March 10, 1961.
[23]Ibid.
[24]Ibid.

goals of this conversion were the increase of production, the expansion of
land under cultivation, the improvement in the welfare of the workers, a
rapid development of agricultural production on diversified farms, and the
consolidation of socialism in the countryside.

Thus state farms and large cooperative farms began to be established on
the majority of the land of the former
latifundist owners and foreign monopolies. The other part of the land was
distributed among tenants, settlers, and
small landowners in the form of small
plots.

The following data testify to the scope
of the cooperative movement. In early
1961, the total number of cooperatives
and state farms—including those which
were in the process of being organized
—was 1,400, of which 550 were agricultural and 500 stock farms.[25] By 1962
the country already had about 2,000
cooperatives, including 634 for the production of sugar and 324 state farms
(people's farms).[26] Cooperatives are
being organized for the production of
hemp and tobacco, as well as truck
farms. In the ensuing years, the development of the cooperative movement
was chiefly along the lines of their organizational and economic consolidation, and the conversion of certain cooperatives—especially those for the
production of sugar—into people's
farms. There were some cases in which
individual people's farms were converted into cooperatives.

In 1962, the state farms and cooperatives had at their disposal 3.8 million
hectares of land.[27] Peasant farms with
plots of less than 5 caballerías each that
had not yet joined cooperatives had 3.5
million hectares.[28] The party and the
government are taking all possible measures toward their unification through
the National Association of Small Producers (ANAP). With the help of this
association, individual peasant farms

receive technical and financial help
from the government and market their
agricultural production at guaranteed
prices. Associations for the joint cultivation of land have been formed in a number of places with the help of the ANAP.[29]
Almost all the remaining agricultural
population of Cuba has been unified
in this manner.

Thus, by 1962 the cooperative and
state agricultural sectors in Cuba had
41 percent of the total land at their disposal.[30] A large part of the agricultural
workers are employed on the land of
cooperatives and people's farms. The
state farms are headed by administrators appointed by INRA, while the
management of cooperatives is elected.

On the basis of the state plan formulated by the Central Planning Commission and taking into account the requirements of the cooperative and its members, the general meeting of members of
a cooperative determines the amount of
land to be sown in sugar cane and other
crops, the amount and direction of
capital investments, labor expenditures,
and other indicators, setting out in all
this from the point of view of the most
intensive possible use of the land and
an increase in agricultural production.

The working implements on the cooperative (tractor, plows, agricultural
equipment, and draught animals), the
brood livestock, the farm structures, and
the produce of the cooperative are the
property of all its members. As a rule,
the members of a cooperative receive
payment for their work in cash advances
twice a month. The cooperatives settle
accounts with their members after

[25]A. Jiménez, Agrarnaia reforma na Kube, p. 36.
[26]Noticias de Hoy, May 17, 1962.
[27]Revista Internacional, 10:6 (1961).
[28]Ibid.
[29]At the Second Congress of the ANAP, held in
August 1962, it was reported that the ANAP unites
2,600 local peasant associations, over 300 agricultural societies, and about 600 credit-granting cooperatives.
[30]Revista Internacional, 10:7 (1961).

liquidating indebtedness to the state for credits and technical aid received from it, after payment of taxes, and after deducting resources for the further development of the cooperative. Out of the total income, 20 to 30 percent is divided up among the members of the cooperative, and the remainder goes into the cooperative's indivisible fund. Part of the resources is assigned to the construction of houses, hospitals, and schools.

Scientific methods of land cultivation are used on the cooperatives. In Cuba, they have increasingly become agricultural educational institutions for the training of different kinds of specialists and in the organization of agricultural production. In a number of cities, courses for training specialists in the organization of agricultural production have been established in schools or universities. Thousands of students from the cooperatives and people's farms study at the schools for mechanization of agriculture, and several thousand young people have taken or are taking courses at institutes, agricultural schools, cooperative farms, and state farms in the Soviet Union,[31] where they master advanced methods of farm operation.

The agrarian reform provides measures for the improvement of the peasants' standard of living. Cooperative village centers are being built, and peasant housing is being reconstructed. On the sites of the old, brokendown shacks are rising thousands of well-constructed dwellings.[32] Extensive construction of schools, hospitals, and cultural-recreational establishments is going on everywhere in the Cuban countryside. While 1960 was the year of the cultural revolution, the succeeding years have been years for the elimination of illiteracy, for the reconstruction of cities and the countryside on a socialist basis, and for the establishment of new branches of industry.

CONSOLIDATION OF THE ALLIANCE OF WORKERS AND PEASANTS

The agrarian reform has strengthened the alliance of the working class and the peasantry. The landless peasants who received land were not in a position to cultivate it. They did not have the necessary implements or the resources for acquiring seed. The workers went to the assistance of the peasants. On their own initiative, they consigned part of their wages to a fund for the industrialization of the country and for the agrarian reform. These funds were essential to the revolutionary government for the purpose of adopting decisive measures for improving the situation of the urban and rural workers. Even in the first year, the government drew over 150,000 unemployed people into production. The establishment of cooperatives and people's farms permitted the essential elimination of agrarian overpopulation. Previously, under conditions of the single-crop nature of the Cuban economy, sugar production gave birth to an army of rural unemployed. "However, with the appearance in the country of new sources of work, with the development of other branches of agriculture, a shortage of workers for harvesting cane began to be manifested," F. Castro noted in his speech at the national meeting of workers in sugar production in 1962.[33] The workers from many enterprises often went out to work on their day off, spending their Sundays this way, and assigned their wages for those days to the peasants. Sometimes they collected money, bought agricultural machinery and equipment with it, and

[31]Speaking at the FAO meeting in November 1962, A. Jiménez reported that over 3,000 Cuban young people had already been trained in various agricultural specialties in the Soviet Union (*Renaschità*, 1962, No. 3).

[32]"In the last year alone, 12,500 dwellings and 500 schools and hospitals were built for the peasants" (*Revolución*, May 17, 1961).

[33]*Ibid.*, May 15, 1962.

turned it over to the government to be forwarded to the peasants. Campaigns to collect donations for implementing the agrarian reform were held throughout the country.

An extensive movement for the organization of patronage of cooperatives developed among the country's industrial workers in 1961. "The trade unions began to send their specialists in repair of agricultural machinery, electricity, radio, and the training of technical cadres to the cooperatives."[34] At the same time, they began to invite peasants to courses in production training, where the members of the cooperatives study metal working and the operation of tractors. Women study dressmaking and sewing, become acquainted with electric technology, and master agricultural technology.[35]

In the years that have passed since the Cuban Revolution, the technological agricultural foundation of the cooperatives has been considerably strengthened. Combines that were sent from the USSR for harvesting sugar cane have played an important role in this. They have made it possible to accelerate harvesting time and to raise labor productivity. This will make it possible to achieve production of 10 million tons of sugar in 1970.

The Cuban peasants and agricultural workers have been truly touched by the assistance of the revolutionary government and the country's working class. No longer are poverty-stricken farm workers and poor peasants characteristic of the modern Cuban countryside. Now the workers on the developing state farms and the members of agricultural cooperatives are the masters of the land and a bulwark of the Cuban Revolution and the people's power. The establishment of state farms and production cooperatives has determined the chief direction of development of Cuban agriculture, changed the socioeconomic face of Cuban society, and given birth to new socialist production relations in the countryside. Agriculture has become planned and is based on modern machinery, and new men who master the new technology are being shaped in the countryside.

The implementation of the agrarian reform and the cooperativization of the countryside have facilitated a considerable reconstruction of Cuban agriculture, turning it into a diversified enterprise capable not only of fully ensuring the supply of food to the population and of raw materials to industry, but also of producing a large quantity of goods for the foreign market.

The cooperativization of the countryside is creating the conditions for utilizing all the members of the cooperative on various projects throughout the year. That sector of the peasantry that received land and engages in small-scale farming but which seeks work on cooperatives during the time they have free from their own farm will be drawn into cooperatives to the degree that their diversified economies develop further and they become more strongly organized and technologically based.

The party and the government have taken a number of measures for a considerable expansion of the area sown in rice and other food products, for the purpose of overcoming the one-crop nature of agriculture and ensuring the requirements of the population for basic food products and those of industry for raw materials.

The social nature of cooperatives has also changed. Former agricultural workers who are thoroughly familiar with production processes have been placed in charge of them. About half the members of a cooperative are workers and half peasants. The *milicianos*— members of the people's militia—take an active part in the work of coopera-

---

[34]*Noticias de Hoy,* July 6, 1962.
[35]*Ibid.,* July 14, 1961.

tives. The efficient organization of work, the mechanization and financing of the cooperatives, and the improvement in the material living standards of the workers have yielded positive results. The development of a national food-processing industry is being stimulated.

The measures taken by the Cuban party and government for the development of land tenure have made it possible to increase the production of the basic kinds of food and technical products within a short period. The elimination of the latifundia and other feudal institutions, the transfer of land to the peasants and agricultural workers, the organization of people's stores, and the actions taken to develop various branches of agricultural production in accordance with the country's requirements and the need to overcome a one-sided development of agriculture have been accompanied by a constant rise in the standard of living of the workers, peasants, and entire population.[36] This cements even more strongly the alliance between the workers and the peasants. A new stage in the life of the peasantry and in the history of the entire Cuban people began with the adoption of the law on agrarian reform. The worker-peasant alliance has been strengthened. For the peasants, this signified freedom from bondage tenure, the transfer of land to them as their property, the elimination of illiteracy, the construction of schools, hospitals, and roads, a general rise in the standard of living, and the constant and many-faceted aid of the working class. The workers and the peasants are now genuine friends, brothers, and allies.[37]

While the Cuban people greeted the law on agrarian reform with joy and took up its implementation in the most resolute manner, the latifundist landowners and U.S. monopolies greeted the law with bayonets and tried to undermine it in every possible way, resorting to intimidations, threats, and sabotage. How-

ever, these plans were not destined to be carried out. Relying on the peasant organizations, INRA immediately undertook the confiscation of the lands of the saboteurs and deprived them of the right to use lands offered to them by the law.

In the end, the most important feature of the Cuban Revolution is the unity of the revolutionary forces consolidated about the revolutionary government of Fidel Castro. The unity of the revolutionary forces is a guarantee of the success and invincibility of the revolution. The foundation of this unity is a powerful alliance between the workers and the peasants. This arose during the years of struggle against the pro-imperialist Batista dictatorship and became a factor unifying all national, patriotic, and antifeudal forces in a unitary national front. The alliance was strengthened during the implementation of the agrarian reform, as well as during the defense of the republic from foreign intervention in April 1961 and October 1962 and in the battle with domestic counterrevolution for the peaceful construction of a new society.

A new stage in the development of the national-liberation and anti-imperialist movement in the Latin American countries began with the victory of the Cuban Revolution. The significance of the revolution lies above all in the fact that it is taking place under economic and political conditions that to a greater or lesser degree are identical in all the Latin American countries. The Cuban people have been the first to smash a link in the bonds of American colonialism, to topple the old and false suppositions about the omnipotence of American imperialism on the American continent.

The revolution broke out in the back

[36]Blas Roca, *Kuba—svobodnaia territoriia Ameriki* (Moskva, 1961), p. 64.
[37]*Revolución*, May 18, 1962.

yard of the citadel of imperialism, in the back yard of U.S. imperialism, and by so doing "toppled all the theories about geographic fatalism, that is, a theory to the effect that the Latin American countries, since they are in close geographic proximity to the United states . . . must strive not for political and economic independence, but rather for improving their position within the bounds of that dependence."[38] The Cuban Revolution has proven the falsity of that theory, "which serves as a veil for cowardice and treachery."[39]

The Cuban Revolution has proven that with the present correlation of forces on the international scene, a socialist victory in a country located far from the boundaries of the Soviet Union and the socialist camp is possible. The revolution broke out in a continent that speaks Spanish (and the related Portuguese), which will greatly facilitate the unification of national-liberation forces in a unified anti-imperialist Latin American front and favor the increased solidarity of the struggling peoples. The defense of the Cuban Revolution has become the basic concern of all Latin American toilers. Any revolutionary manifestation in any part of America meets with solidarity on the entire continent.

The direct U.S aggression against the Cuban Revolution in April 1961, the threat of intervention in October–November 1962, and the organization of a military and economic blockade by the United States aroused a storm of protests and a broad movement of solidarity in the Latin American countries. Almost everywhere, committees for the defense of the Cuban Revolution and its achievements were created. Worker and peasant organizations, many governmental and social figures, and representatives of bourgeois sectors came out in defense of Cuba. The affairs of the Cuban Revolution became a matter of vital interest not only to the democratic forces, but also to the extensive anti-imperialist forces of Latin America and all progressive mankind.

The crisis created by aggressive U.S. circles in the Caribbean was the most acute one of the postwar period. The policy of the imperialists consisted of carrying out an invasion of Cuba, stifling the Cuban Revolution, and starting a new, third world war.

As a result of the firm and flexible actions of the Soviet Union, which manifested consciousness of historical responsibility and a lofty understanding of the interests of peace and socialism and of all mankind, and thanks to the heroism of the Cuban people supported by all progressive mankind, the aggression against Cuba was forestalled, peace was salvaged, and the Cuban people fully retained their revolutionary gains and protected their right to proceed along the path of socialism.

Under the conditions of an upsurge in the national-liberation movement in the Latin American countries and its transition to a new stage of development, and when ever more extensive sectors of the population are being drawn into the common national movement, the agrarian question became one of the most important questions of the anti-imperialist, national-liberation, democratic movement. Every class and every party is forced to determine its program, tactics, and line in the peasant problem. The most characteristic features and traits in the activities of the parties and various classes in the national-liberation movement may be summarized as follows:

1. In the first place, certain representatives of bourgeois nationalistic parties have proposed a number of halfway agrarian reforms that are supposed to ward off the revolutionary explosion

---

[38]Blas Roca, *Kuba—svobodnaia territoriia Ameriki*, pp. 59–60.
[39]*Ibid.*, p. 60.

and at the same time give them political power, even if it is at the cost of a deal with the latifundist. They favor the retention of their countries in the orbit of the world capitalist system, and even a certain improvement in the situation of the toiling masses, and a gradual formation of capitalist relations in agriculture.

To these ends, the bourgeois nationalistic parties have advanced a number of theories, the essence of which can be boiled down to justification of the measures taken by bourgeois-landowner governments (Bolivia, Colombia, Venezuela, Mexico, Argentina, and other countries) and directed not at the confiscation of latifundia and the elimination of feudal traces, but at the opening of uninhabited government lands that are unsuitable for agriculture and are located far from industrial centers and cities. They apply only a technical-economic sense to the understanding of agrarian reform.

2. In the second place, the democratic forces of Latin America are demanding radical socioeconomic transformations in the countryside. They support the elimination of latifundia and other large estates, sharecropping, *corvée,* payment in kind, and indentured slavery, and back the predominant role of the working class and the peasantry in the implementation of agrarian transformations with the neutralization of the national bourgeoisie. They associate the struggle for the radical resolution of the agrarian problem with the struggle against foreign imperialist domination, for an independent economy, and for the noncapitalist path of development of the country.

These demands of the democratic forces and the basic mass of the peasantry are spelled out in the program documents adopted in recent years by the majority of the Communist parties of Latin America. The agrarian reform in Cuba helped the Communist parties

make their programmatic demands more concrete and clarified their perspectives and the forms and paths of making them a reality.

3. In the third place, the programs of the Communist parties of Argentina, Chile, Colombia, Ecuador, Venezuela, Mexico, Brazil, and a number of other countries have common characteristics, but they also take into consideration local conditions and the demands of the other parties that take part in united-front movements.

In view of the presence in Latin America of a widely developed plantation economy, the programs of the Communist parties foresee two approaches to the solution of the agrarian problem. On the one hand, it is considered that many large farms and plantations belonging to foreign monopolies will be transferred to the state for the establishment of state farms (people's farms) or cooperatives, and, on the other hand, the confiscation of latifundist lands and transfer of the ownership to the peasants are contemplated. Consequently, the transition to nationalization of land and socialist transformation in agriculture will be implemented gradually, through an intermediate period. Later on, the working peasantry—which constitutes the majority of the peasants—will become aware on the basis of their own experience and after the victory of the agrarian revolution of the need to unite and to combine their working implements on large cooperative farms. With respect to the nationalization of land, this can be carried out in a special way, by adopting a number of individual laws limiting the right to private ownership of land and making difficult —and later on totally forbidding—the buying and selling of land. The implementation of the agrarian reform in Cuba fully confirms this premise.

4. In the fourth place, the implementation of agrarian reforms on a democratic basis in Guatemala (1952–1954)

and especially in Cuba has completely confirmed the supposition that representatives of the national and even the petty bourgeoisie who have taken part in the national-liberation movement will change their attitude as soon as the peasantry, with the support of the democratic forces, proceeds to practical implementation of the agrarian reform. They will stretch out its implementation by all possible means, so as to prevent a revolutionary shattering of the agrarian relations that have been established in the Latin American countryside.

45. The Nationalization of Cuban Industry*

N. N. RAZUMOVICH

The attainment of full national independence made it necessary to disengage the Cuban economy from foreign monopolies, to normalize the national economy, and, finally, to put the economy into the service of the masses, giving full play to the development of productive forces. The only possible way to fulfill these goals, under conditions of sharpening international and class struggle, was the expropriation of the basic means of production and the use of the state as the chief tool in rebuilding the entire economy.

Along with agrarian reform, the first steps taken by the Cuban revolutionary government in improving the national economy included confiscation of the enterprises of criminal elements connected with the Batista régime, protection of natural resources, establishment of state control over industrial production in order to protect the interests of workers and employees, and expansion of international economic relationships. Successful introduction of this complex of measures made it possible for the revolutionary government to put an end to speculation with national wealth—which had been an occupation of the ruling upper classes—and to draw the working class into the task of radical social-economic reforms.

Confiscation of the property of state criminals who had usurped power as a result of the coup of 1952 was provided for in Article 24 of the Fundamental Law. In developing this constitutional situation, the revolutionary government in 1959 adopted laws[1] under which the

*Gosudarstvennye preobrazovaniia revoliutsionnoi Kuby (Moskva: Izdatel'stvo Mezhdunarodnye otnosheniia, 1964), pp. 55-72.
[1]Law No. 112 of February 27, 1957 (See Leyes del Gobierno Provisional de la Revolución, III, 240); Law No. 151 of March 17, 1959 (See Osnovnye zakonodatel'nye akty Kubinskoi Respubliki, pp. 157–163).

wealth plundered by Batista and his henchmen was returned to the people. All their property was classified as property illegally acquired as a result of holding power, and economic aid to the dictatorial régime was classified as a crime against the state. As a result, the state acquired without any indemnity the total possessions of Fulgencio Batista; of the officers who took part in the 1952 coup; of the dictatorial government's ministers, senators, deputies, governors of provinces, mayors of cities, and members of the advisory council; of the presidents of the National Bank and the Bank for Agricultural and Industrial Development; of the general secretaries of the Cuban Confederation of Labor; and of other persons guilty of collaborating with the tyranny.

Reports in the Cuban press make it possible to estimate the extent of property confiscated from Batista. The value of his confiscated possessions alone amounted to 400 million dollars. The property of 302 enemies of the revolution—former ministers, members of Congress, governors, and other persons who supported the Batista régime—confiscated by the Cuban government on January 19, 1960, was estimated by the press at 150 million dollars. On March 10 of the same year, the government confiscated twenty-one industrial and transportation firms with property amounting to about 35 million dollars. All these firms formerly belonged to the Burke brothers and James Hodges, Americans by descent who had grown rich through the dictator's protection.

Confiscation of property from persons guilty of illegal enrichment was carried out by the Ministry for Indemnifying the Losses of the State.[2] It carried out investigations for the purpose of indemnifying losses caused to the state, froze bank accounts, sealed or opened safe deposit boxes in banks and other private establishments, intervened in the real estate or commercial business of any person or organization, and, finally, expropriated property. It is characteristic that the law establishing this ministry included this criterion for illegal enrichment: the increase of property or capital in excess of established norms by means of concessions or contracts obtained from state institutions, and concessions granted without observing legally prescribed rules.

All confiscated property was handed over to the Ministry for Indemnifying the Losses of the State as well as to the National Institute for Agrarian Reform (INRA), or other state agencies that organized the disposition of such property. Thus, after confiscating the match trust, which had been created by high officials with money obtained fraudulently from the treasury, the government handed over all its ten factories to the INRA, which then appointed administrators for these factories.

While confiscating the capital of treasury thieves, the revolutionary government also took the necessary measures to protect national wealth from the plundering of foreign monopolies. Taking the position that exploitation of natural resources should serve the entire society and should aid the industrial development of the country, the revolutionary government decided to review mining concessions and introduce a new system for exploiting mineral resources. According to Law 617 of October 27, 1959,[3] all concessions were to be reregistered in the newly created Department of Mining and Oil Resources, with obligatory notice of the physical and legal identity of persons actually exploiting such resources. This latter condition was especially important, since foreign companies usually operated through Cuban concessioners. In case of refusal to reregister, the conces-

[2]See *Leyes del Gobierno Provisional de la Revolución*, III, 98–107.
[3]See *Osnovnye zakonodatel'nye akty Kubinskoi Respubliki*, pp. 175–178.

sion reverted under the law to the state and it was occupied by representatives of the state who thereupon organized its further exploitation.

To obtain financial security for state regulation of the extractive industries, a special fund was created for the development of the mining industry. This fund was established from taxes on concessions and payments for new claims on any mine. Moreover, concessioners were required to pay a certain percentage of their income to the state, either in cash or in kind, as determined by the state. If the ores or concentrates were to be exported, this percentage could be as much as one-fourth of all production.

In this manner the government not only returned to the people the national wealth seized by imperialists but also created the necessary conditions for using this wealth to develop the national economy.

Having taken the course of creating a state sector from the enterprises expropriated from private owners and from a few concessions, the revolutionary government also established state control over all capitalist enterprises in the country. On November 24, 1959, it adopted Law 647, concerning the right of the Ministry of Labor to intervene in private business,[4] declaring that the government has the following obligation and inalienable functions: to regulate economic relations between the various branches of production; to guarantee normal functioning of enterprises so as to assure full employment and development of the country's economy; to cooperate in the reorganization and improvement of the leadership in enterprises working at less than full capacity; and to mobilize the necessary resources for solving economic problems in the interest of production as well as of the people employed in it. For this purpose the Ministry of Labor was granted the right to intervene in the affairs of those enterprises in which the normal course

of production was obviously impaired and to appoint its representatives to such enterprises for stated periods of time.

In adopting this law, the revolutionary government set out first of all from the interests of the workers. This is convincingly shown by the reasons given for state intervention: lockouts, temporary or permanent closures, serious labor conflicts, mass discharges, and failure to carry out court decisions and decrees of the Ministry of Labor in cases of labor conflicts. Moreover, the revolutionary government aimed at developing industrial production and accordingly provided for state financial aid, upon request of their representatives, to those enterprises where state control was being established.

At first state intervention in the affairs of industrial enterprises was intended to be limited to a period of six months. The legislators considered the possibility of the government's sharing in the profits of capitalist enterprises as compensation for the capital invested and also considered the possibility of return of the credits granted, reserving only the right to be the privileged creditor. However, practice took a different course. As the class struggle grew more acute, the private entrepreneurs refused to make concessions to the workers, and finally, since sabotage was being organized by U.S. monopolies and by the domestic upper bourgeoisie, the revolutionary government was forced to accelerate the transition from state control to regulated industrial production and then to state management of industry. Under these circumstances the Institute for Revolutionary State Intervention in Private Business proved to be the best transitional form toward the expropriation of private industrial property. It enabled the state to control industry without cur-

[4]See ibid., pp. 179–183.

tailing production and to organize its management by making use of the experience of business leadership, the active support of labor and labor organizations, and the existing facilities for accounting, control, and financial regulation.

The resistance of American monopolies to all the economic measures of the Cuban government began with the first days of the revolution. They considered their main weapon to be their dominant position in Cuban foreign trade and the dependence of her monocultural economy on the U.S. market. While inciting the local counterrevolutionary agents by all possible means to engage in sabotage, diversion, and open resistance, the monopolies began to organize an economic blockade. At their request, the U.S. government addressed the Cuban government with the direct threat of curtailing purchases of sugar and deliveries of oil—a threat to deprive the country of foreign exchange receipts and her industry and transportation of fuel. At the same time there began a campaign for immediate transfer to the United States of foreign currency, curtailment of tourism (an important source of income), and the shutdown of plants owned by American firms.

The Cuban revolutionary government responded to the economic aggression of the United States by establishing control over foreign commercial and currency operations and turning to other countries with proposals for a general expansion of commercial relations. On November 3, 1959, the Cuban government adopted a resolution under which all exporters of Cuban products as well as persons paid in foreign currency for their services were required to surrender same to the National Bank of Cuba. This measure, along with others directed toward stopping the outflow of foreign currency, yielded positive results. By July 1960, net reserves of foreign currency amounted to 219 million dollars.[5] State control of foreign trade, restrictions placed on foreign currency, transactions and state intervention in industry were the first measures the revolutionary government took to overcome the economic isolation of the country, which had been artificially created by American monopolies.

In a search for new markets for both sales and purchases of vital commodities, the Cuban government turned to the countries of the socialist camp with an offer to sell sugar and to purchase crude oil, machinery, and industrial equipment. True to the principles of the solidarity of nations struggling for national independence, the Soviet Union and the other socialist countries responded favorably to the proposals of revolutionary Cuba. They made mutually advantageous trade agreements with her without any political strings attached, thereby giving needed help and wrecking the economic blockade of the United States. Following this, the imperialist monopolies went over to open struggle against Cuba. They did not stop at direct interference in internal affairs or the conscious organization of disruption of the country's economic life. In particular, they tried to block the delivery of Soviet crude oil to Cuba.

Through the National Bank, the Cuban government invited two American companies and one English company Esso Standard, Texaco, and Shell) to refine the Soviet oil at their Cuban plants. The Cuban government undertook to provide the necessary market for the production. However, the foreign firms categorically refused to refine crude oil from the Soviet Union and decided to close down their refineries. Thereupon the revolutionary government decided on state intervention in the work of these plants. In June 1960,

[5]See *National Guardian*, August 22, 1960.

armed guards were sent to the Texaco plant, and the Cuban Oil Institute was appointed temporary administrator. Several days later the same measure was applied to the other refineries. Cuban engineers, technicians, and workers without any foreign administration ensured uninterrupted production in the oil industry, while resolute action by the revolutionary government defeated the sabotage of the American oil magnates who sought to deprive Cuba of fuel and to paralyze her industry and transportation.

The serious threat that hung over Cuba as the result of U.S. economic aggression demanded extremely resolute actions from the government, and these followed immediately. A meeting of the Council of Ministers under the chairmanship of Fidel Castro adopted a resolution in July 1960 to begin the nationalization of industrial establishments belonging to U.S. monopolies. Law 851 was adopted in order to protect the national interests, empowering the government to make decisions and issue decrees concerning nationalization through compulsory expropriation of properties and enterprises owned by U.S. physical and juridical persons, as well as of enterprises in which such interests were financially involved even if they had been set up in compliance with Cuban law.[6]

The law on nationalization provided compensation for expropriated property by special bank bonds that the government undertook to pay off in thirty years at 2 percent annual interest. For making payments on these bank bonds, a special state fund was created, which was to be financed by surpluses of foreign currency obtained from sales of sugar to the United States over and above the established quota of three million tons.

Thus, acting as a sovereign state with full jurisdiction to determine the nature of property rights on its territory and to establish the conditions of property transfer, Cuba responded to U.S. economic aggression by expropriating industrial enterprises belonging to U.S. citizens. As to compensation, the Cuban government, without refusing to compensate for losses, related the period for compensation payments and their amount directly to observance by the United States of existing agreements and of principles of mutual respect for rights and interests of independent states, as accepted generally in international practice.

The United States did not heed the warning of the Cuban government. On the day the nationalization law was adopted, President Eisenhower signed into law a sugar quota that excluded imports of Cuban sugar to the United States for all of 1960. Such was the official expression of U.S. economic aggression against Cuba.

On August 6, a special decree of the Cuban revolutionary government announced the compulsory nationalization of twenty-six American companies.[7] With the exception of banks, these companies represented the entire American property in Cuba. In particular, this nationalization affected the largest power plants, the telephone network, oil refineries, thirty-six sugar refineries, and many other industrial and marketing enterprises. The value of this property was approximately half a billion dollars.

The nationalization of American banks was carried out by the Cuban government on September 17, 1960. A special government resolution announced that properties, rights, and shares of the American banks on Cuban soil, as well as their branches, were to be expropriated in favor of the state.[8]

While carrying out compulsory expropriation of American property, the

[6]See *Osnovnye zakonodatel'nye akty Kubinskoi Respubliki*, pp. 184–190.
[7]*Ibid.*, pp. 187–190.
[8]*Ibid.*, pp. 191–194.

revolutionary government exhaustively explained the reasons that forced it to take such stringent measures and made clear the premises for such action. The preamble to the law on the nationalization of American banks specifically pointed out that the activity of these banks, these bulwarks of imperialism in Cuba, was an obstacle in the path of national liberation. Their financial policy, the law said, consisted of giving complete support to the North American enterprises draining off Cuban raw materials, of assuring increased importation of North American industrial goods, of interfering with the development of national industry, and of keeping the Cuban economy dependent upon the United States. Their usurious credits would not allow the Cuban economy to grow, while periodic crises kept devouring the country's wealth. As for U.S. economic policy, the law described it as interference in Cuba's domestic affairs and stated that, after cutting the sugar quota, the United States and the American monopolists were continuing their aggressive policy with respect to trade between the two nations. "That a considerable portion of the National Bank should be perpetually held by the imperialists who cut our sugar quota cannot be tolerated. That is a criminal act of economic aggression." Such was the general conclusion of the preamble to the law on the nationalization of American banks.

Nationalization of all American property, which had a total value of one billion dollars, was an essential and unavoidable measure that ensured Cuba's liberation from imperialist exploitation. Not until monopoly capital had lost every opportunity to participate in the country's economic life did the people's independence become a reality based on the durable foundation of state ownership of the basic mass of means of production. From this moment on, broad horizons opened before the Cuban Revolution for reconstructing the country's social-economic relationships so as to place all productive forces in the service of all the Cuban people.

The working people of Cuba greeted this resolute step of the revolutionary government with great enthusiasm. Meetings attended by many thousands of workers, peasants, and salaried employees were held all over the country under the banner of complete solidarity with their revolutionary government. These meetings were brilliant testimony to the Cuban people's determination to put an end to oppression by American monopolies. The special greeting extended to Fidel Castro by the National Committee of the Cuban Popular Socialist Party on the occasion of the nationalization of the twenty-six American companies stated: "We greet with immense enthusiasm and support the historic resolution signed by yourself and President Dorticós on the nationalization of the majority of American enterprises. This act of such tremendous importance makes qualitative changes in the revolutionary process and opens the way to a new phase of national development. We have here a genuine act of economic independence. Our country is now completely free!"[9]

After the nationalization of American industrial enterprises and banks and after confiscation of the properties of Batista and his henchmen, the state sector of Cuba's national economy became the predominant one in production capacity. The state-cooperative sector in agriculture followed, built as a result of the agrarian reform and capable of assuring the needed raw materials for the manufacturing industry. Thus the necessary material premises were created in the country for a transition to a planned economy developed independently of foreign capital and in the interests of the entire population.

[9]*Noticias de Hoy*, August 9, 1960.

The realization of these premises depended in many ways on the position taken by the national industrial and commercial bourgeoisies. The latter, however, instead of cooperating with the people's revolution, preferred to orient their economic and political activity toward the American monopolies. As long as nationalization of electric and telephone companies, of banks, and especially of the oil refineries owned by American monopolies, was in progress—that is, as long as the domestic bourgeoisie, including the upper layer, derived certain profits from the lower cost of electric power, fuel, and means of communication—they accepted nationalization. But when the sugar industry and the majority of large industrial and commercial enterprises began to revert to the state, this bourgeoisie moved against the revolution and started to engage in active economic sabotage.

Considering the revolutionary government's economic policy as a threat to their class interests, the upper bourgeoisie of Cuba embarked upon betrayal of the national interest and became an agent of the forces of international counterrevolution. In such a situation, the Cuban Revolution naturally found it necessary to crush the resistance of the upper bourgeoisie, to relieve it of ownership of the means of production so as to prevent the possibility of a restoration of the old order, and to assure the overall development of the revolutionary government's economic function.

In October 1960, when the threat of invasion by imperialism's hired bands hung over Cuba, and the upper bourgeoisie began to resist openly, the revolutionary government resolved to nationalize all large private plants, all railways, factories, power stations, and other enterprises. Law No. 890, of October 13,[10] transferred to the state 381 industrial, transportation, and commercial enterprises, including 105 sugar plants, 3 chemical factories, 6 metallurgical plants, 61 textile factories, and 19 construction enterprises. In addition, a government resolution of October 24 nationalized 166 other enterprises that had been owned by foreign and mixed capital.[11]

Law No. 890 stated directly that the creative work of the revolution was aimed at the economic development of the nation and that this development was impossible without planning, increasing, and rationalizing production and without national control over the basic branches of the country's industry. The law stated that many large enterprises in the country were not following the course of general revolutionary reforms but, on the contrary, were conducting a policy contrary to the interests of the revolution and economic development. Sabotage, failure to use capital investments rationally, abuse of state credits, acquisition of foreign currency by illegal means and its transfer abroad, abnormal functioning of enterprises, curtailing of production, and labor conflicts—all forced the Ministry of Labor to intervene in the affairs of private enterprise. Meanwhile, the antinational activities of the employers, including the financing of counterrevolutionary agents, compelled the government to resort to the strictest measures to halt the abuses. In view of the above, the law stated: "It is the duty of the revolutionary government to take measures to establish order, assuring the final elimination of the economic domination of those who act against the welfare of the people; to nationalize large industrial and commercial enterprises that could not and never can function under the new revolutionary conditions in our mother country; and, simultaneously, to assure the necessary

[10]*Osnovnye zakonodatel'nye akty Kubinskoi Respubliki*, pp. 195–199.
[11]*Ibid.*, pp. 206–209.

resources and effective guaranties for the normal activity of all those medium and small enterprises whose interests can and must coincide with the higher interests of the nation."[12]

In completing the nationalization of industry, the Cuban revolutionary government simultaneously carried out a reorganization of the entire banking system, which now was to be based on the expropriation of private property. On the same day that the law nationalized all large enterprises owned by domestic capital, October 13, 1960, the revolutionary government adopted Law No. 891 on the nationalization of banks.[13] Its preamble stated that issuance of money and granting of credits were to be handled by the state exclusively and must conform to the goals of economic planning. These functions must not remain in the hands of private enterprise, whose efforts are motivated by profit and subordinate public to private interests. Through this principle, all banking was declared by law to be public, and in the future the state alone was to engage in banking operations. Private banking institutions, such as deposit banks, credit and mortgage banks, banks for aid and development, as well as all properties, rights, and shares owned by banking institutions on Cuban soil and banking accounts and deposits located abroad, reverted to the state.

While nationalizing banks through forcible expropriation, the revolutionary government did not exclude the possibility of paying compensation to their former owners. But Law No. 891 introduced a new compensation principles that did not originate from any norms of bourgeois jurisprudence, which provide for "indemnification of losses," or at least for preserving the scope of the former owner's property rights, and alter only the form of participation in property relationships; the new principle set out from the need to assure a livelihood to the former enterprise

owners. Article 7 of the law established as a maximum compensation the sum of ten thousand pesos plus additional payments by special checks for a period of fifteen years. This principle was further developed in the law on urban reform of October 14, 1960, which designated the compensation as "monthly lifetime rent," which, together with any other income, must not exceed two hundred pesos a month.[14]

The revolutionary government's decision to eliminate capitalist ownership of housing and to solve the country's housing crisis, which during the Batista regime had become truly a national disaster, was of great importance to the working people. On October 14, 1960, the revolutionary government adopted a constitutional law on urban reform.[15] Based on the principle that every person is entitled to housing, that every working man's family is entitled to a well-equipped dwelling, the law provided for a total solution of the housing problem in three stages. In the first stage, which the government defined as "the present," the state assured every family of the opportunity to buy on the easiest terms the dwelling it occupied. In addition to freeing working people from having to pay high rent, the capitalist system of lease of urban property was abolished. During the second stage the state, by using available resources, was to carry out mass construction of housing that would be handed over to the workers for their complete use at a monthly rate not to exceed 10 percent of the family's total income. In the future, during the third stage, the state itself, according to the law, was to build housing and to transfer it into the possession of every family free of charge.

The concentration of an important

[12]*Ibid.*, pp. 196–197.
[13]*Ibid.*, pp. 200–205.
[14]*Ibid.*, p. 229.
[15]*Ibid.*, pp. 215–234.

part of foreign trade in the hands of the state and the establishment of state control over domestic trade were essential supplements to nationalization. These measures made it possible to prevent economic sabotage by foreign monopolies and the counterrevolutionary Cuban bourgeoisie.

The expropriation of industrial enterprises and the organization of production in them were carried out by the National Bank, the Department of Industrialization, and the National Institute for Agrarian Reform [INRA]. In addition, special institutions were formed for the administration of state enterprises. The Cuban Institute of Mineral Resources (responsible for exploration and exploitation of all the country's mineral wealth) and the National Institute for Electrification (in charge of the production and distribution of electric power for industry, agriculture, commerce, and domestic consumption) were created in August 1960.

Administrators appointed by government institutions took over the direct management of state enterprises. Moreover, the government adopted a decision to create advisory technical councils to help the administration with problems of production, organization of labor, and the administration's relationships with the workers.

The advisory technical council—which includes representatives from workers of each department, shop, or section of an enterprise—has the right to discuss, jointly with the administration of the enterprise, all questions regarding development of production, establishment of production norms, increase of productivity, improvement of working conditions, and short-term and long-term production plans. The advisory council may on its own initiative propose to the administration certain measures for technical improvement of production processes or increasing produc-

tivity of labor and improving the quality of production. The administration may decide to accept or reject the advisory council's proposals; however, the council may in turn address itself to higher administrative organs if it believes that its proposals are desirable for improving the work of the enterprise.

Besides granting workers and salaried employees the right to participate in the management of enterprises, the revolutionary government worked out a system of regulating working conditions at state and mixed-ownership enterprises in accordance with the workers' interests.

A decree of the Ministry of Labor on August 23, 1960,[16] provided for wages to be confirmed by the ministry in accordance with the interests of the workers and the needs of production, independently of whether they had been determined on the basis of a work agreement or by administrative action. In establishing wage rates, account was to be taken of wages paid in analogous enterprises of the same area or country and of the cost of production and profitability of the enterprise. In cases where wages might turn out to be lower than the minimum cost of living, the decree provides for payment of subsidies to the enterprises to guarantee a minimum living wage for the workers. To stimulate economic development and to provide for the workers' active participation in economic progress, production norms and standards were introduced; premium payments for overfulfillment of established norms were also allowed for. Permanent funds were created at enterprises for the purpose of premium payments, and the enterprises's income over and above the plan went into that fund.

The nationalization of industry and the banking and transportation systems,

---

[16]See *Leyes del Gobierno Provisional de la Revolución*, pp. 297–300.

the establishment of state monopoly of foreign trade, and the development of durable economic relations with countries of the socialist camp—all these afforded the young Cuban republic an opportunity to obliterate the consequences of American imperialist domination and made possible the construction of a new economy, based on domestic resources and a just division of labor, and developing in accordance with a unitary state plan.

In the summer of 1961, the revolutionary government worked out and adopted an initial plan for developing the national economy. This plan provided for the extensive construction of new enterprises and the modernization of old ones, as well as for building Cuba's own metallurgical and machine-tool industry. In accordance with the principle that the Cuban economy must satisfy the population's growing demands mainly through domestic production and not the expensive importation of goods, the first national economic plan provided for the development of light industry. The plan gave great attention to the general improvement of agriculture and the need for machinery, chemical fertilizers, and such. It included planning to satisfy the population's food supply needs and for the expansion of export.

All the measures taken by the revolutionary government for the development of the national economy were aimed primarily at raising the living and cultural standard of the working population. Within a short period of time, these measures succeeded in materially curtailing unemployment, and some branches of industry even experienced a labor shortage. In 1959, wages and various payments to the population amounted to 920 million pesos, an increase of 39 percent over 1958.[17] The entire Cuban economy began to develop along new lines. Its basic aim was the satisfaction of the growing needs of workers rather than the exploitation of man by man.

In the process of socializing the means of production, the revolutionary government laid the foundation of economic administration in accordance with a unitary state plan. Nationalization of industry finally permitted the organization of production and labor in such a manner that every worker could be paid equally for equal work and could be guaranteed protection against destitution and exploitation. In all this activity, the creative function of the Cuban Revolution became fully apparent as it transformed the means of production from means that exploited workers to an instrument of their increased welfare. A durable foundation was laid for the common national goal of the struggle for national independence and the free flourishing of the people.

The creation of state sector of property and industry freed Cuba's working class from the exploitation of monopolies and domestic capital. Socialization of the means of production not only changed the situation of the Cuban working people but also gave a new meaning to the question of their participation in the revolution. The alliance of the working class with the peasantry and with all laborers was now on a durable economic foundation. Henceforth, the most important weapon in the workers' class struggle became their active participation in developing production, achieving a high level of productivity, and, simultaneously, increasing the well-being of the entire nation.

[17]See *Kuba. Istoriko-etnograficheskie ocherki*, p. 84.

46. The Impact of the Cuban Revolution upon the Revolutionary Movements of Latin America and Its Significance as a Symbol of a New Era in Latin American History[*]

A. F. SHUL'GOVSKII

The Cuban Revolution has been indelibly recorded in the annals of history as one of the most important events in modern times. It signifies an important step in the development of the world-wide national-liberation and communist movement. The experience of the Cuban Revolution merits considerable attention from a practical as well as from a theoretical point of view.

Certain aspects of the international significance of the Cuban Revolution are attracting the greatest attention:

1. It is the first victorious, profoundly national revolution on the American continent. It solved once and for all the problems of the national-liberation and antifeudalistic stage. Cuba is the first country in America to be free of the fetters of imperialism on the political and, especially important, on the economic level. This is the first revolution accomplished in the colonial and semicolonial back yard of U.S. imperialism. Cuba has become the active vanguard of all the 200 million Latin Americans. In addition, the revolution is giving an impetus not only to the liberation forces in Latin America but also to the revolutionary forces in Spain and Portugal and their colonies.

It is important to recall once again that all of Latin America has long been ripe for a revolution of a deep social character. The revolution in Cuba serves as a powerful stimulus for such countries as Chile, Venezuela, Brazil, Ecuador, Argentina, Colombia, Guatemala, and others. As the Latin Americans put it: Cuba started "the second war for independence" on a continental scale.

Cuba destroyed the myth of geographical fatalism with respect to the United States and Latin America. Moreover, it first won victory in the War for Liberation of 1956–58 against the American henchman, Batista, and later successfully repulsed the intervention organized by the United States at Playa Girón in April of 1961.

2. The Cuban Revolution brilliantly confirms the fact that the world has entered a new era characterized by the dominant strength of communism and the socialist camp. It confirms the fact that imperialism can no longer do what-

---

[*] "Rasstanovka klassovikh sil v bor'be za osvobozhdenie," in *Ekonomicheskie problemy stran Latinskoi Ameriki*, ed. V. Ia. Avarina and M. V. Danilevich (Moskva: Izdatel'stvo Akademii nauk SSSR, 1963), pp. 482–484.

ever it wishes to, without taking stock of the alignment of forces in the world.

Cuba demonstrated that practically any country in the world, under favorable internal conditions, can achieve a profoundly national revolution and launch the construction of socialism, with the present alignment of world forces, and in view of the ever intensifying crises of capitalism.

As the *New York Times* bitterly complained recently, in order to understand this situation: "The United States had to learn some painful lessons in the Bay of Pigs in Cuba, in the conference rooms of the summit meetings in Paris and Vienna, at the walls separating Eastern and Western Berlin, in the valleys of Laos, in the halls of Punta del Este, and in the halls of the Geneva Palace of Nations. From these bitter experiences it was learned that there were not American decisions for everything—there were even none for Cuba, which is located a mere ninety miles from the United States." Thus, the success of the Cuban Revolution serves as a graphic expression of the new alignment of powers in the world.

3. The Cuban Revolution introduced vital clarifications into the understanding of the problems of attaining success in the national-liberation struggle and converting it into a socialist revolution. It showed that the genuine revolution will succeed only as a result of a combination of all forms of struggle, with one or another of the forms prevailing depending upon the conjuncture of forces, place, time, and conditions at the moment.

In the fight against the tyranny of Batista, the Cubans consistently used electoral methods, general political strikes, guerrilla warfare, boycott of elections, demonstrations, and finally insurrection. In the final analysis, armed conflict, headed by the rebel army and its leader, Fidel Castro, became the decisive form of the struggle. However, it should not be forgotten that preparations for the insurrection were aided greatly by the continual mobilization of the masses for a prolonged number of years, the general strike of the sugar workers in 1955, the general political strike in August 1957, the widespread and vigorous boycott of the farcical elections in November 1958, and finally the general revolutionary strike of December 31, 1958, and January 1, 1959.

The Cuban experience conclusively demonstrates that no national-reformist, conciliatory leadership can lead the Latin American countries to the attainment of national sovereignty, economic independence, and industrial development.

The example of the Cuban Revolution proves that the Latin American countries can unquestionably withstand all the pressures, all the economic aggressions and military threats of U.S. imperialism and its accomplices, if they conquer their fear of revolutionary measures; if power is based on the workers, peasants, and urban, radical petty bourgeoisie; and if they overcome the defamatory, anticommunist propaganda and establish proper relations with the socialist countries and the liberated countries of Asia and Africa.

4. The Cuban Revolution in its current second stage is the first socialist revolution on the American continent. The transition to the socialist revolution took place in Cuba under conditions of peaceful coexistence, without war. This fact deserves special attention.

The Cuban Socialist Revolution is delivering an extremely hard blow to imperialist propaganda, which has been disseminating fabrications to the effect that a socialist revolution and socialistic transformations of societies could take place only near the borders of the USSR. The very existence of the Cuban Revolution and its continuing development once more deeply reaffirm the truths that socialism is a science, that social reforms are not a consequence of geographical proximity of some country to another nor of military aid from some particular country, but a result of inevitable, inexorable evolution of history—above all, of the internal struggle of classes and political forces.

Cuba's contribution is that it demonstrated to the entire American continent the historical compatibility and indissolubility of the national democratic revolution and the victorious social revolution.

47. 1960 American Historiography of the Cuban Revolution*

L. IU. SLEZKIN

On January 1, 1959, the Cuban Revolution was victorious. Up to that very day, the United States had extended aid to the Cuban dictator Batista and the American press had sung praises of him. This was both a policy and a tradition. A policy because Batista proclaimed himself to be an enemy of communism and he faithfully served his American masters. A tradition because Batista had been canonized by American historiography as a model ruler for the Latin American countries.

When the Cuban Revolution triumphed Washington adopted toward it a position that American propaganda and historiography usually call a "wait-and-see" attitude. This term reflects the policy of Washington at the time very closely. "Waiting" was indissolubly linked with pressure on the revolutionary government of Cuba, for the purpose of subjecting it to the will and interests of the United States. It was a very short-term affair and lasted only as long as was needed for the transition from undercover coercion to open pressure. Nevertheless, the Washington maneuver left a certain impression on the nature of articles and books about the Cuban Revolution that appeared in the United States in 1959. In the majority of them, there was no open censure of the victorious revolution. There were even some kind words directed toward it, although there was no shortage of regrets about the passing of the "old Cuba." During the entire period of "waiting," the events of the revolution were set forth in such a way that at the necessary time, a book or an article that appeared during the period could be converted into an ideological weapon to conceal possible U.S. intervention in Cuban affairs. However, openly coun-

---

*"Kamen' broshen (Amerikanskaia istoriografiia Kubinskoi revoliutsii 1960 g.)," *Novaia i noveishaia istoriia*, 4:133–142 (1968).

terrevolutionary statements were still relatively rare.

The purpose of this article is to establish the basic features that characterize American historical and journalistic literature in 1960 dealing with the problems of the Cuban Revolution.

Anti-Cuban counterrevolutionary propaganda became especially active in the United States after February 1960. This coincided with the opening on the island of an exhibit on the achievements of the Soviet economy and the conclusion on the thirteenth of the month of a Soviet-Cuban trade treaty. The acts of friendship toward the country that had liberated itself from the bloody tyranny of Batista, which were normal for the Soviet Union, were received with hysterical hostility in the United States.

After the signing of the Soviet-Cuban trade treaty Earl Smith, the former American ambassador to Cuba who had once openly supported the dictator, stated, "I consider that the time has come to take measures against the Castro regime."[1] Vice-President Nixon proposed doing the same thing but in a subtler manner, invoking the Monroe Doctrine.[2] President Eisenhower undertook an urgent trip to the Latin American countries for the purpose of mobilizing them against the Cuban revolutionary government under the pretext of "the threat of communism." (There was even talk of "Cuban aggression.") On that same pretext, the U. S. Senate made its rostrum available to counterrevolutionaries who had fled from Cuba. On March 4, 1960, the French freighter La Couvre blew up in Havana harbor with its cargo of weapons for the Cuban army that had been purchased by the revolutionary government. The evidence indicates that the diversion was carried out by American agents. At the memorial service for the victims of the catastrophe, the Cuban cry that is known the world over— "Fatherland or Death"—was born.

And so the anti-Cuban policy of the United States lost the last traces of the elements of "waiting." Its aggressive features and anticommunist orientation were being revealed ever more obviously.

To U.S. ruling circles, it was as if the Cuban Revolution with its internal problems had ceased to exist. When there was talk about Cuba and the revolution, one would simultaneously hear the "frightening" words that were spoken by Batista in his time: "communist threat," and "agents of the Kremlin." These things were invoked not just from genuine fear of communism and its influence—especially in Cuba—but also in the obvious intention of preparing the ground for intervention on the revolutionary island. Concealing aggression by referring to the need for defense from "the threat of communism" is an old strategem of American imperialists.

"CUBA: DANGER AT THE THRESHOLD"

For over one hundred years the United States used the slogan of "defense" in order to annex nearby territories of the Latin American countries. In such cases the victim country was declared to be a source of danger to the United States, even when it was infinitely smaller and weaker. The "threat" arose whenever a country was located nearby and its territory for some reason whetted Washington's appetite, when it lay on an important trade route or at a place which the American generals considered strategically important. Disturbances in the Latin American countries were also reckoned as "threats," not to speak of revolutions, which were called "disorders" in the United States.

For a long time copious literature designed to justify and legalize U.S. in-

[1] E. Smith, The Fourth Floor (New York, 1962), cover.
[2] R. Nixon, The Challenges We Face (New York, 1960), pp. 102–103.

terventionist actions for reasons of "defense" and "security" has existed in American historiography. An article by Harry Schwartz published in March 1960 and entitled "Cuba: Danger at the Threshold" can immediately be seen to have been constructed on the lines of this literature. The subtitle recalled that Americans had invested about one billion dollars in enterprises on the island and that it is an important strategic point on the approaches to the United States. Not yet speaking of the revolution that was taking place there, the author revealed other "disorders" in Cuba: mass military training, the attacks on the United States by the Cuban press, the consolidation of the positions of the Cuban Communists, the land reform, and the delight that Havana residents showed toward the Soviet exhibit. The situation that was taking shape in Cuba, he declared, "is generating obvious problems of security."[3]

Time was when such opinions would have been more than enough to call for intervention or to justify intervention that had already occurred. A few months after the publication of Schwartz' article, such arguments would conclude with the call to "crush communist Cuba!" However, it was still only March of 1960. And although certain American political figures of the Earl Smith type called for open intervention, the ruling circles had not yet lost hope of directing Cuba along the lines of U.S. wishes. All of this, as well as Schwartz' rather hard look at the international situation and the relations of the United States with the Latin American countries, determined the unique nature of the article under review. Begun in the "classic" traditions of aggressive American propaganda and historiography, it gradually draws back from them.

The article explains that talks are going on in Washington about an inva-

sion of Cuba by American Marines, about the construction of a radio station in Miami for broadcasting anti-Cuban counterrevolutionary propaganda, and about economic sanctions against the island. The United States was not preventing take-offs from its territory of aircraft that were bombing Cuban cities. Washington was striving to block the implementation of reforms in Cuba or at least to express dissatisfaction with the fact that they were being implemented.

This entire dismal list manifestly testifies to the fact that it was not that tiny Cuba was threatening the United States, but the opposite—the greatest and most powerful state in the capitalist world was encroaching on the sovereign rights of Cuba. This does not prevent Schwartz from drawing a genuinely unexpected conclusion: "In the half-crazed atmosphere of today in Cuba, one can easily get the impression that the evil United States is preparing to impose its will on its small neighbor again."[4]

In other words, according to Schwartz, the facts of U.S. interventionist policy, which he himself brought out, did not force the Cubans to be vigilant. The reason for it was mistrust, expressed softly. But the aircraft flying from the United States to bomb Cuba are obvious facts and cannot be ascribed to mistrust. Reference to "insanity" does not help here. This is hardly a new method for vilifying the revolutionary enthusiasm of the people. And Schwartz backs up, although with some difficulty, clinging to the old arguments. In writing about the fact that the Cubans see in the flights against them a repetition of the actions that suppressed the Guatemalan revolution, Schwartz concludes: "There is much that is unjust in this Cuban charge. However, it

[3]*The New Leader*, March 14, 1960, p. 3.
[4]*Ibid.*, p. 4.

would be difficult—more correctly impossible—to reject this accusation as totally unfounded."[5]

Who is threatened with danger? Cuba? No. Schwartz continues to maintain that it is the United States. Not from the twelve and thirteen year-old children who, according to Schwartz, are allegedly receiving military training in Cuba? No, and the idea of the Cuban army invading U.S. territory is implausible in whatever form it is put.

The main thing that concerns Harry Schwartz is the danger of revolution at the threshold of the United States. Moreover, the author discloses, Cuba is "the center of attention of all Latin America."[6] Giving himself away in that account, Schwartz wants to check the hand of Washington, which was already poised for a blow at revolutionary Cuba. He is striving to convince the government of this country that the Cuban Revolution is not simply "disorders," that the socioeconomic conditions in Latin America are similar to those which drove the Cubans to revolution. Latin America and Cuba are in a state of complete solidarity. The times have changed: carrying out aggression with impunity according to the old formulas and without considering anything is not a simple matter today.

Harry Schwartz gives the White House three pieces of advice: (1) Do not resort to armed intervention, which, in his opinion, would be a "disastrous mistake."[7] In the first place, the United States would suffer a moral loss. In the second place, it would be facing a situation similar to that which the French encountered in Indochina and Algeria, since the Cubans are devoted to the revolution and would defend it resolutely. In the third place, the United States should consider the possibility of Soviet support of Cuba. (2) Do not adopt economic sanctions against Cuba. It is true that they would cause

a great sacrifice for the island, but the revolutionary government could take countermeasures that would cause the most harm to American businessmen. Cuba would really begin to seek support from the socialist countries. (3) Clearly declare the absence of any desire to carry out an attack on Cuba and stop the aerial flights to the island; enter into bilateral talks on economic problems, including the question of sugar trade; establish friendly relations with Cuba, acknowledging the historical responsibility of the United States for the anti-American feelings that exist in Cuba; and don't make a scarecrow out of Havana's "flirting" with Moscow.

Obviously, Harry Schwartz found the strength in himself to back away some distance from the leveled cannon. However, U.S. interests, as understood in Washington, lay not in acknowledging historical responsibility and in shedding light on the disposition toward revolution, but rather in preserving the investments mentioned by Schwartz, in the amount of one billion dollars, and, along with them, their predominance on the island and the unequal economic relations, advantageous to American businessmen. Schwartz' recommendations were unacceptable to these imperialist interests and the imperialist policy dictated by them. Under the conditions of those times, such recommendations, expressing the feelings of Americans who were repelled by overtly interventionist U.S. policy toward Cuba, simultaneously masked the real essence of that policy, advanced under the false cry of "Cuba: Danger on the Threshold of the United States."

[5]Ibid.
[6]Ibid., p. 6
[7]Ibid., p. 5.

Cuba and the Theory of a "Third Force" of Robert Alexander

Not only the advice of Schwartz, but also the suggestions of Robert Alexander, one of the pillars of American anticommunism, were unacceptable to those who determined Washington's foreign policy. One of the principal ideas of Robert Alexander was the formation in Latin America of a "third force," opposing reactionary dictators on the one hand, and communism on the other. Alexander argued that it was this "third force" which should become the U.S. ally in Latin America. The democratic United States together with the democratic "third force" would establish a rule of democracy in the Western Hemisphere that would not be terrified of any communism. Defending this idea, Alexander permits himself to criticize Washington policy, which supports Latin American dictators and unites the Communists and the representatives of the "third force" against the United States. Deceiving himself and others, Alexander appears as an alleged defender of democracy, but is actually a defender of U.S. imperialism. His idea of a "third force" conceals the essence of U.S. imperialist policy with the illusion of the "common" democratic interests of the Western Hemisphere.

It was precisely from this position that Alexander examined Cuban-American relations in the spring of 1960 in the article "Cuba and the Sugar Quota," published just one week after Harry Schwartz' article.

Robert Alexander reports that certain influential circles in the United States are carrying out a campaign to limit the quota for sale of Cuban sugar on the American market. The supporters of this measure brought out the following arguments to justify it: it was neces-

sary to punish Cuba for the agrarian reform and for the conclusion of a trade treaty with the USSR; and, it was necessary to preclude the danger of U.S. trade with the "communist regime" that had been established in Cuba. Alexander says that these arguments, with a view to defending U. S. interests, are basically vicious. People who advance them do not consider the influence of the proposed measure on Cuba and on all Latin America.

"Genuine state wisdom," Alexander maintains, "requires of our Congressmen that they oppose any kind of pressure aimed at 'punishing' Cuba. Those who are obliged to sign the new sugar agreement should remember that the present Cuban leaders are carrying out a profound revolution that is extremely belated and welcomed by the overwhelming majority of Cubans."[8] Developing his idea further, the author declared that land reform is the prerogative of any sovereign state. Concerning the Soviet-Cuban trade treaty, it is advantageous to Cuba and reflects her desire to be independent of the United States, whose economic sway in the country had lasted too long.

In conclusion Alexander wrote:

A reduction in the Cuban quota would be viewed by the Cubans as an effort to place an obstacle in the way of their revolution. . . . This would play into the hands of those in the Castro government who would like to take Cuba into the neutral camp, as well as those who—like the Communists—would like for Cuba to switch sides in the protracted cold war. . . . Extensive circles in Latin America would regard reduction of the quota as the beginning of U.S. intervention against Castro, which would increase the already deep mistrust of U.S. policy. . . . Cuba's advantageous position in the U.S. sugar market should be retained.[9]

[8]*Ibid.*, March 21, 1960, p. 3.
[9]*Ibid.* pp. 4–5.

Like Schwartz' recommendation, this conclusion sounds very convincing at first glance. Behind it, however, lies not concern for the Cubans, for their revolution, or for good relations between Cuba and the United States. Alexander wants to see revolutionary Cuba as a "third force," which would become a U. S. ally in the "cold war." As we can see from the excerpt above, he would not be satisfied even with a neutral Cuba. He requires an anticommunist Cuba. His quarrel with backers of a reduction in the Cuban quota is not a quarrel to the advantage of Cuba. It is a quarrel about how best to prevent the development of the Cuban Revolution and the influence of communist ideas on it, and how to turn Cuba into an anticommunist U.S. ally. This is why Robert Alexander considered that it would be worthwhile to refrain from "punishing" Cuba.

However, it is characteristic of imperialism to "punish" those who try to break away from its grip and conduct an independent policy. The quota was reduced and later on completely eliminated.

BUSINESS AND DIPLOMACY

The first extensive and serious work about the Cuban Revolution came from the pen of Robert Freeman Smith, who teaches history at a Texas college and is a member of the American Historical Association.

Smith is extremely critical of U.S. actions in Cuba from 1917 to 1959. He remarks on the self-interest of American economic policy and the improper role of American diplomacy, which is so characterized by "errors and shortsightedness." According to Smith, "the entire Cuban economy was controlled by 'King Sugar' and the U.S. market."[10] The period of Batista rule was "a honeymoon" for American businessmen. Advancing data on the colossal income of American firms in Cuba, Smith simul-taneously emphasizes that the over-whelming majority of Cubans were very poor, that corruption prevailed in Cuban governmental circles, and that the people were humiliated by the arrogant rule of the Americans.

Smith acknowledges U.S. responsibility for the unbearable situation that forced the Cubans to take to arms. He rightly concludes that the Cuban revolution "was not a typical Caribbean-type political revolution."[11] "The problem of the Castro revolution in Cuba is a new chapter in the annals of political and economic relations of this century," he says in the foreword to his book.

A profound analysis of the economic relations between the United States and Cuba and a broad historical perspective embracing fifty years make Smith's opinions weighty and convincing. Unfortunately, however, that is true only as long as he is talking about the past. In analyzing current events, Smith stands on the same shaky ground as the authors of the articles reviewed above.

It develops that the former U.S. mistakes "should be analyzed in depth, so that it will be possible to take positive measures to ward off the spread of communist influence in the Western Hemisphere." Then follow the usual stock phrases: "interests of defense," "understandable fear of the communist threat," "Castro's fanaticism," and "Cuban attacks on the United States." And most important, the United States "is basically not an imperialist country."[12] And from there to the conclusion of the book: "We must show the sincerity of our national ideals, as otherwise there will be an increase in the chronic suspicion that we are an empire striving to rule the entire world."[13]

[10]R. F. Smith, *The United States and Cuba: Business and Diplomacy, 1917–1960* (New York, 1960), p. 175.
[11]*Ibid.*, p. 176.
[12]*Ibid.*, preface.
[13]*Ibid.*, p. 186.

Any unbiased reader who studied the history of Cuban-American relations in Smith's book would doubtless be strengthened in the above-mentioned "chronic suspicion" and would inevitably come to the conclusion that U.S. policy is not in any way guided by abstract ideals, but by imperialist business interests. The United States withdrew the Cuban sugar quota even before the appearance of his book. This hostile act in no way corresponded to "sincere national ideals." As we have seen, Robert Alexander termed this measure "punishment" for Cuba's desire to be independent. The United States would soon hurl mercenaries against her for the purpose of "punishing" her even more severely. Washington's policy with respect to Cuba proves quite clearly that the United States is attempting to subject the world to itself, and not with the help of diplomacy alone.

THEODORE DRAPER'S THEORY OF "BETRAYAL"

Setting aside Robert Smith's book, we return again to the journal *The New Leader*. In the issue of July 4–11, 1960, an article by Theodore Draper entitled "Cuba and the Revolution of Our Times" was published. Not long before that, Draper had visited Cuba and recounted his impressions in the journal *The Reporter*. Thus, the July article was the fruit of reflection. But first, a few words about the author.

Like Robert Alexander, Draper is a veteran anti-Communist and enemy of the Soviet Union. His earlier ties with the communist movement, which he betrayed, as well as his "knowledge" of the teachings of Marxism, permit him to play in the Western world the role of a man who is "intimately" familiar with the "mysteries" of communism and to pass for a great authority on questions of the international labor movement.

In order to appraise his remarks on the Cuban problem, it is necessary to review the events in the history of Cuban-American relations from March —when Harry Schwartz' article appeared—to June 1960, when Draper's article was published.

Following the explosion of the *La Couvre* in the spring of 1960, Cuba had to live through a new experience. American and English oil firms, and the American-owned Cuban Electricity Company ceased operations on the island. In violation of their contracts, the oil companies refused to refine crude oil acquired abroad by the Cuban government. The country was faced with the threat of deprivation of basic sources of electrical energy and fuel, which would have virtually paralyzed all production.

In order to save the Cuban economy, which had been deprived of electricity and fuel, the revolutionary government on June 29 issued a law nationalizing the oil refineries belonging to American companies. Attempting to thwart this measure, the American oil men put pressure on ship owners to refuse to supply Cuba with oil. On July 6, the subversive actions against the Cuban economy were supplemented by a considerable reduction of U.S. intake of Cuban sugar, the principal product of the island and one that was sold almost exclusively to the United States. Thus, under conditions of U.S. anti-Cuban policy, the prior economic dependence of Cuba on the United States was becoming an inexorably tightening noose for the Island of Freedom.

The Cuban government was faced with a dilemma: to retreat in the face of the U.S. attack, giving up its sovereignty and the revolutionary gains, or to take measures to defend them. Under the circumstances, there was no other path for the Cuban Republic than that of smashing the bonds of economic dependence that remained. On the day that Eisenhower disclosed the reduction of the Cuban quota, the Cuban revolutionary government issued a law nationalizing all enterprises belonging to Americans. The law took effect on August 6.

These defensive measures, provoked by U.S. economic aggression directed at disorganizing the Cuban economy with a view to crushing the revolution, were declared by American propaganda to be communist, and the "danger on the threshold of the United States" to be extreme. However, the nationalization of foreign companies is a measure that is frequently taken even in capitalist countries. To set aside this possible objection, American propaganda seized on the earlier slanderous accusation against Fidel Castro of having "betrayed" the revolution.

The essence of this boils down to the following. Fidel Castro is an old Communist who concealed the fact during his struggle with Batista and is now handing the island over to "Moscow." Thus, the communist nature of the nationalization is without any doubt. This was the approach that the Batista-ites who fled to the United States used from the very first, and, after them, the renegades of the Revolution who also found refuge there. The more or less objective listener can easily detect the false notes in the joint chorus of American propaganda and Cuban counterrevolutionaries. In order to muffle these notes, Theodore Draper undertook the construction of a theory of "betrayal." His article cited above is the first draft of that theory.

Its basic postulate is that "the Cuban Revolution was not a revolt of the workers and peasants. It was a revolt of the sons and daughters of the middle class in the name of the workers and peasants. At present, it is the peasants who have gained most from the revolution, while the workers have gained little or nothing at all, and the middle class is marked for total elimination."[14]

As proof that the revolution was carried out by the "middle class" alone, Draper brings out his only "argument." In April 1960, the Cuban revolutionary government was made up of intelligentsia. No one ever denied the participation of the "middle class" in the revolution. However, it does not follow either from this or from the fact that the revolution was headed by representatives of the Cuban intelligentsia that the revolution was carried out only by them. It is a well-known fact that the social origin of the ideologists and leaders of a revolution is not a sign that permits determining its nature or motivating forces. The Cuban Revolution was a genuine people's revolution. Extensive peasant and workers' masses took part in it, and not just "sons and daughters of the middle class," as Draper claims.

At the time the article appeared, agrarian reform was being carried out on the island, a reform that dealt a blow to latifundism, the rule of which had always been counter to the interests of the "middle class." The law nationalizing American property, which was disclosed at the same time, freed that class from the oppression of American imperialist monopolies. The law lowering rent payments did harm to homeowners, but it was of great aid to the majority of the Cuban bourgeoisie and intelligentsia, who generally rented apartments, not to speak of the poor people. Thus, at the time of the appearance of Draper's article, those who identified their interests with the interests of U.S. monopolies had without any doubt benefitted from the revolution. The social processes during which the fate of the "middle class" was to undergo changes would come later, and they would be given impetus—as in the case of the

[14]*The New Leader*, July 4–11, 1960.

nationalization of American companies —by renewed attacks on the revolution from its domestic and foreign enemies. Is it the "middle" class that Draper is concerned about? No. It is, in the first place, those billion dollars in American investments, the fate of which also worries Schwartz, in other words, the retention of U.S. domination in Cuba. Draper tried to find an ally in the struggle against the Cuban Revolution (let us recall the theory of the "third force"). It is for this reason that the entire implementation of the revolution is attributed to the "middle class," or to put it more accurately, its renegades of the ilk of Cardona and Urrutia, who fled to the United States and headed the counterrevolutionary emigration there.

What does Castro's "betrayal" consist of? Of his disinclination to follow the path of retreating from the revolutionary changes into which he was nudged by the representatives of that very "middle class." Isn't that betrayal? Moreover, in Draper's opinion, Castro had brought about "the construction of socialism on an isolated island," and even "by Communist methods."

Draper does not mention the word "betrayal" in this article. He does not claim—as others at the time did—that Castro was an "old Communist" and a "secret agent of Moscow." However, it was precisely Draper who, having constructed his scheme, gave grounds to those who hung this label on Castro, shouting about his double and even triple "betrayal": of the revolution of the "middle class" (which he allegedly destroyed), of "democracy" (since he was building socialism), and of his colleagues (since he was an "old Communist," but concealed it). Draper spread this primitive slander by Cuban counterrevolutionaries and dirty American propaganda and clothed it in "theoretical" garb.

We have been present at the first

example. In the succeeding years, Draper was to become one of the leading anti-Cuban counterrevolutionary theoreticians.

"Noninterference—the Failure of American Foreign Policy"

Draper wrote his article prior to the issuance of the Cuban law on the nationalization of American property. This measure of the revolutionary government—as well as the Soviet statement on July 26, 1960, promising her aid in case of aggression—aroused a furious anti-Cuban campaign in the United States. This was accompanied by an intensification of economic aggression against Cuba, which turned into an economic blockade of the island in the winter of 1960. The "Guatemalan variant" of invasion of the island with forces of Cuban counterrevolutionaries with U.S. support was simultaneously developed.

Centers for training mercenaries for the invasion army were established in Florida and in certain Latin American countries. Aspirants for government jobs in "liberated Cuba" appeared among the old politicians and renegades of the revolution who had fled the island. The White House assigned one million dollars to the Cuban émigrés for their counterrevolutionary activities. Powerful forces of the American army, navy, and air force were concentrated at the base in Guantánamo. Diplomatic preparations for the invasion were made. Washington utilized the forum of the OAS and the UN for this purpose.

In the United States, the voices of those who (like the Earl Smith mentioned above) advised an invasion of Cuba sounded ever more loudly. However, there were still those like Harry Schwartz, who considered that intervention to be harmful to U.S. interest. After Cuba adopted the law on nationalization, a clamorous propaganda campaign began in the United States under the slogan "noninterference by the United States in Cuban affairs was a mistake from the very beginning."

This slogan had been used earlier, but, as in the case of the theory of "betrayal," a man to give it some weight was needed. A. Berle offered his services. He was a diplomat, a specialist in Latin American affairs who had occupied high posts at various times: assistant Secretary of State, ambassador to Brazil, and others.

In July 1960, Berle called Cuba a "communist satellite" and called for fighting her "with all available resources." "This is in no way a violation of the principles of noninterference.... I submit not intervention, but defense," he wrote.[15] That such a "defense" would be conducted by using "all available resources" against another state did not arouse any doubts. It implied intervention. Berle added this supplement to his previous judgments in the article "The Cuban Crisis: The Failure of American Foreign Policy," published in October 1960.

This article is remarkable, first of all, because it indicates a refusal of the more-or-less semiofficial U.S. press to acknowledge (declared earlier with difficulty) that the egoistic American policy in Cuba created the conditions and was one of the reasons for the revolution. Berle asserts that relations between the United States and Cuba had always been "mutually advantageous." Only "irresponsible intellectuals" in the United States and "certain persons in Latin America" spoke about "dollar diplomacy," and later about "imperialism," which, the author declares, is "naked propaganda." "Actually, Cuba was free to defend her way of life and moral principles and to create new social forms."[16] This is a return to the terminology and the maneuver of expostulation, which was characteristic of American historiography and journal-

ism during the years when Batista ruled Cuba.

Berle did not dare to praise the bloody Batista regime directly, although he attempts to present the dictator—who was known for his machinations and who fled the country with treasury funds—as a completely disinterested man. This was a return to the traditions of American historiography, which had presented "a sergeant named Batista" as a model Cuban ruler.[17]

Thus, the restorationist trends of the American imperialists found expression in Berle's article. The theory of the "third force" and the theory of "betrayal" also figured into it. Anticommunism was its chief inspirational force. Its basic idea lay in the call to put an end to the policy of noninterference, which, Berle asserted, the United States had conducted in Latin America and particularly in Cuba. It was precisely this policy, he showed, which had suffered failure, particularly in the face of the Cuban Revolution.

According to Berle, the United States should have gone into action when the revolution had still been "democratic, antidictatorial, and anticommunist." Such a revolution should be "supported and guided, and given all aid at the moment of its success."[18] According to Berle's calculations, that stage of the revolution lasted approximately until the spring-summer of 1959.

In order to understand what is concealed behind this terminology and periodization, let us recall that the spring and summer of 1959 were the time when the agrarian reform began to be implemented in Cuba, the first basic

[15] See J. North, *Kuba—nadezhda kontinenta* (Moskva, 1961), p. 87.
[16] *Foreign Affairs*, 39(1): 41 (October 1960).
[17] This is the title of a book by E. Chester, one of the principal American apologists for Batista (E. Chester, *A Sergeant Named Batista* [New York, 1954]).
[18] *Foreign Affairs*, 39(1): 50–51 (October 1960).

social transformation on the island; the time when the premier of the Cuban government, Miró Cardona, and the President of the Republic, Manuel Urrutia, were replaced. Thus, the revolution that Berle sets up is a revolution without reforms, led by people who viewed the United States as their master and found there refuge and support in their struggle against the people of their country.

But why did Berle call the Cuban Revolution anticommunist? This allegation is absurd. He did it so as to kill two birds with one stone: namely, Castro's "betrayal" of the "anticommunist revolution" and "democracy" and the sincerity of the "democratic and anti-dictatorial revolution" of Cardona and Urrutia, on whom he bestows the laurels of warriors against communism. Berle adds that the "majority of Cubans" want a return to "liberal democracy."

Berle is not a historian, but a professional diplomat. He needs his opinions on the failure of the policy of "non-interference" and on an "anticommunist revolution" for shadowy speculations. His article begins with the words, "The deepening crisis in Cuba indisputably reflects the bankruptcy of American foreign policy."[19] Further on, the author gives some practical advice: only a rejection of the policy of noninterference can correct the situation. This was a call for intervention expressed in diplomatic terms.

However, Berle did not speak only of the necessity for intervention in Cuba. He clearly formulated watchwords for the intervention being prepared. In April 1961, when the Cuban mercenaries carried out an invasion of Cuba organized and directed by the United States, both parties pronounced the slogan of struggle for an "anticommunist, antidictatorial, and democratic revolution." Both sides put their

faith in the fact that "the majority of Cubans," dreaming of "liberal democracy," would join the invading army.

The decisive and rapid defeat of the interventionists by the courageous Cuban people testified to the failure of American foreign policy, a policy of intervention and aggression that Berle had called for in opposition to "non-interference."

Having called for intervention and having formulated its ideological credo, Berle was actually asserting that desire for revenge which American historiography of the Cuban Revolution had harbored in its bosom during the first months following the victory of the revolution. Conversations about a possible intervention in Cuba were held at that time also, but these talks were "in any case" just "for intimidation." The Berle article under review here was a part of an aggression that had already been prepared.

LISTEN, YANKEE!

In the fall of 1960, the anti-Cuban counterrevolutionary campaign took on particularly acute forms. And it was just at this time that there broke into the militant chorus the voice of a man who attempted to cool the violent and burning passions and to place an obstacle in the way of the stream of fantasies and provocations. He called his book *Listen, Yankee!*[20] On the jacket were the words "this is a deeply sobering book which must be read at the present turning point." The author of the book was the well-known American sociologist Wright Mills, who wrote it soon after a return from Cuba.

Mills set himself the task of showing Americans what the Cuban Revolution had brought. Even the most liberal American authors, as a rule, did not

[19]*Ibid.*, p. 40.
[20]W. Mills, *Listen, Yankee!* (New York, 1960).

write about that, but about how the revolution had harmed U.S. interests and the fact that these interests had to be protected. Mills emphasized that the revolution on the island was above all a revolution of Cubans and for Cubans. It was up to them to decide how and where to direct the revolution. They had a right to choose their friends and allies for the solution of the problems facing them and to defend the country and the revolution from enemies. No one under any pretext whatever had any right to interfere in their internal affairs.

Since American propaganda had concealed the nature of the processes that had taken place in Cuba and the nature of the relations between Cuba and the socialist countries, Mills attempted to sketch the true picture of life on the island and to communicate in the words of Cubans themselves their understanding of the events taking place. Mills wrote that Americans should listen to the voice of Cuba, the voice of all oppressed nations, a voice that is stifled by preconceived American propaganda. "If we do not listen," Americans are warned by the author, "if we do not listen carefully, then we shall face all the dangers engendered of ignorance, and that means the threat of grievous mistakes."[21]

In the name of the Cubans, Mills tells his countrymen: You never knew the real Cuba, its needs, or its aspirations. You were only interested in business on the island. In making your profits, you oppressed us Cubans. You fear communism and intimidate us with it. However, the revolution in Cuba took place not because of the intrigues of Cuban Communists or the plots of world communism, which you continually repeat to us. Hunger—that is the chief reason for it.

You call Cuba a country that is communist or under the influence of communism. The first part is not true. Concerning the second part, communist influence is present throughout the world today. Cuba is feeling its beneficent influence, in the form of the aid and support of the socialist countries. Is this influence reprehensible? The more you threaten and harm us, the greater that influence will be. It has nothing in common with the pressure that you are trying to exert on us. Moreover, isn't it our right to choose our path, even if it should be a communist one? Yankees, hands off Cuba! Fatherland or death!

Having expressed the point of view of the Cubans, Mills very clearly sets forth his own position: "I am for the Cuban Revolution. It does not worry me. I worry about it and with it."[22]

It is a well-known fact that in Washington they did not want to listen to Mills' voice, to the voice of revolutionary Cuba. In Washington, they disregarded recommendations that excluded intervention as a means of coercion of the Cuban Revolution. And Washington suffered a shameful failure at Playa Girón.

Characteristic of American historiography of the Cuban revolution during the period under examination was the coalescence of counterrevolutionary thrusts of Batista-ites and renegades of the revolution with the "theoretical" calculations of American ideologists of the anti-Cuban counterrevolutionary campaign (Draper, Berle), the obliteration of the boundary between open interventionism—the leading figure in which was former U.S. ambassador to Cuba Earl Smith—and the more surreptitious interventionism of former ambassador to Brazil Adolf Berle. This historiography will soon have to experience its shameful Playa Girón also.

[21]*Ibid.*, p. 7.
[22]*Ibid.*, p. 179.

Bibliographical Index of Items

Al'perovich, M. S.
1964 "Issledovanie problem istorii Latinskoi Ameriki," *Vestnik Akademii nauk SSSR*, 12:24–26. [Item 2]

Antiasov, M. V.
1960 *Sovremennyi panamerikanizm*. Moskva: Izdatel'stvo Instituta mezhdunarodnykh otnoshenii. Pp. 196–209. [Item 39]

Byl'skaia, M. I.
1964 "Studenchestvo v osvoboditel'noi bor'be narodov Latinskoi Ameriki." In *Osvoboditel'noe dvizhenie v Latinskoi Amerike*, ed. S. S. Mikhailov. Moskva: Izdatel'stvo Nauka. Pp. 236–239, 265–268. [Item 9]

Danilevich, M. V.
1960 "Zemlevladenie i zemlepol'zovanie v stranakh Latinskoi Ameriki." In *Latinskaia Amerika v proshlom i nastoiashchem*. Moskva: Izdatel'stvo sotsial'no-ekonomicheskoi literatury. Pp. 79–84. [Item 22]; Pp. 90–94, 96–97. [Item 23]

1962 *Rabochii klass v osvoboditel'nom dvizhenii narodov Latinskoi Ameriki*. Moskva: Gosudarstvennoe izdatel'stvo politicheskoi literatury. Pp. 22–35. [Item 17]; Pp. 49–51, 53–55. [Item 12]; Pp. 257–258, 260–273, 279–281. [Item 19]

1964 *Osvoboditel'noe dvizhenie v Latinskoi Amerike*, ed. S. S. Mikhailov. Moskva: Izdatel'stvo Nauka. Pp. 144, 170–180. [Item 8]

Grechev, M. A.
1960 "Nekotorye problemy ekonomicheskoi nezavistimosti stran Latinskoi Ameriki," *Mirovaia ekonomika i mezhdunarodnye otnosheniia*, 10:74–81 (October). [Item 40]

Grigor'ian, Iu.

1967 "Latin America: The industrialisation problem," *International Affairs* (Moscow) 6:29–34 (June). [Item 27]

Grigulevich, I. R.
1965 "Tserkov' i klerikalizm v Chili posle Vtoroi Mirovoi Voiny," *Voprosy istorii*, 11:85–89 (November). [Item 16]

Guber, A. A.
1963 Foreword to *Bor'ba za edinyi rabochii i anti-imperialisticheskii front v stranakh Latinskoi Ameriki*. Moskva: Izdatel'stvo VPSh i AON pri TsK KPSS. Pp. 7–15. [Item 7]

Gvozdarev, Boris Ivanovich
1964 *Soiuz radi progressa i ego sushchnost'*. Moskva: Izdatel'stvo Nauka. Pp. 118–122, 134–136. [Item 38]

Klesmet, O. G.
1963 "Razvitie obrabatyvaiushchei promyshlennosti." In *Ekonomicheskie problemy stran Latinskoi Ameriki*, ed. V. Ia. Avarina and M. V. Danilevich. Moskva: Izdatel'stvo Akademii nauk SSSR. [Pp. 163–165, 212–214. [Item 32]

1963 "Voprosy ekonomicheskogo razvitiia stran Latinskoi Ameriki." In *Ekonomicheskie problemy stran Latinskoi Ameriki*, ed. V. Ia. Avarina and M. V. Danilevich. Moskva: Izdatel'stvo Akademii nauk SSSR. Pp. 39–48. [Item 29]; Pp. 49–50, 56–59. [Item 30]; Pp. 59–62. [Item 42]

Konstantinov, O.
1963 *Voprosy mezhdunarodnogo rabochego i natsional'no-osvoboditel'nogo dvizheniia na sovremennom etape*, ed. A. A. Guber and V. V. Lenin. Moskva: Izdatel'stvo VPSh i AON. Pp. 91–94, 95–97. [Item 20]

Kovalev, E.
1966 "Agrarnaia reforma v Bolivii: klas-

sovaia sushchnost' i znachenie,"
*Mirovaia ekonomika i mezhdu-
narodnye otnosheniia,* 6:56–64.
[Item 25]

Koval'skii, N. A.
1964   "Politika katolicheskoi tserkvi v
       rabochem dvizhenii Latinskoi
       Ameriki." In *Osvoboditel'noe
       dvizhenie v Latinskoi Amerike,*
       ed. S. S. Mikhailov. Moskva:
       Izdatel'stvo Nauka. Pp. 191–206.
       [Item 14]

1964   *Vatikan i mirovaia politika.* Mosk-
       va: Izdatel'stvo Mezhdunarodnye
       otnosheniia. Pp. 202–204, 208–
       209, 211–212, 214. [Item 13]

Kudachkin, M., and N. Mostovets
1964   "Osvoboditel'noe dvizhenie v La-
       tinskoi Ameriki," *Kommunist* (Mos-
       cow), 11:121–130 (July). [Item 4]

Mashbits, Ia.
1966   "Latinskaia Amerika: Urbaniza-
       tsiia i sotsial'no-ekonomicheskoe
       razvitie," *Mirovaia ekonomika i
       mezhdunarodnye otnosheniia,* 10:
       43–51. [Item 26]

*Mezhdunarodnoe revoliutsionnoe dvizhenie
rabochego klassa.*
1966   3rd ed. Moskva: Izdatel'stvo poli-
       ticheskoi literatury. Pp. 333–343.
       [Item 6]

*Mezhdunarodnye otnosheniia posle Vtoroi
mirovoi voiny.*
1965   v. 3. Moskva: Izdatel'stvo politi-
       cheskoi literatury. Pp. 662–678.
       [Item 43]

Mikhailov, S. S.
1962   "Izuchenie problem Latinskoi
       Ameriki," *Vestnik Akademii nauk
       SSSR,* 5:54–59. [Item 1]

1964   "Osnovnye cherty natsional'no-
       osvoboditel'nogo dvizheniia v
       Latinskoi Amerike na sovremen-
       nom etape." In *Osvoboditel'noe
       dvizhenie v Latinskoi Amerike.*
       Moskva: Izdatel'stvo Nauka. Pp.
       5–19. [Item 5]

Onufriev, Iu. G.
1963   *Ekonomicheskie problemy stran
       Latinskoi Ameriki,* ed. V. Ia. Avar-
       ina and M. V. Danilevich. Moskva:
       Izdatel'stvo Akademii nauk SSSR.
       Pp. 289–296. [Item 24]

Razumovich, N. N.
1964   *Gosudarstvennye preobrazovaniia*

revoliutsionnoi Kuby. Moskva:
Izdatel'stvo Mezhdunarodnye otnosheniia. Pp. 55–72. [Item 45]

Romanova, Z. I.
1962   *Latinskaia Amerika: Kratkii poli-
       tiko-ekonomicheskii spravochnik,*
       ed. M. V. Danilevich, M. F.
       Kudachkina, and M. A. Okuneva.
       Moskva: Gosudarstvennoe iz-
       datel'stvo politicheskoi literatury.
       Pp. 116–117, 121–124. [Item 41]

1963   *Ekonomicheskaia ekspansiia SShA
       v Latinskoi Amerike.* Moskva: Iz-
       datel'stvo sotsial'no-ekonomiche-
       skoi literatury. Pp. 54–61. [Item
       36]; Pp. 87–96. [Item 37]

1965   *Problemy ekonomicheskoi inte-
       gratsii v Latinskoi Amerike.* Mosk-
       va: Izdatel'stvo Nauka. Pp. 243–
       250. [Item 33]

Semenov, S. I.
1964   *Osvoboditel'noe dvizhenie v Latin-
       skoi Amerike,* ed. S. S. Mikhailov.
       Moskva: Izdatel'stvo Nauka. Pp.
       207, 208–217. [Item 15]

Sheremet'ev, I. K.
1963   *Ekonomicheskie problemy stran
       Latinskoi Ameriki,* ed. V. Ia. Avar-
       ina and M. V. Danilevich. Moskva:
       Izdatel'stvo Akademii nauk SSSR.
       Pp. 398–401, 404–408. [Item 31]

1966   "Latin America's thorny path of
       industrial development," *Inter-
       national Affairs* (Moscow), 12:21–
       26 (December). [Item 28]

Shul'govskii, A. F.
1961   "Imperializm i ideologiia natsio-
       nal-reformizma v Latinskoi Ame-
       rike," *Mirovaia ekonomika i me-
       zhdunarodnye otnosheniia,* 8:45–
       59. [Item 11]

1963   "Rasstanovka klassovikh sil v
       bor'be za osvobozhdenie." In
       *Ekonomicheskie problemy stran
       Latinskoi Ameriki,* ed. V. Ia.
       Avarina and M. V. Danilevich.
       Moskva: Izdatel'stvo Akademii
       nauk SSSR. Pp. 482–484. [Item 46]

1964   *Osvoboditel'noe dvizhenie v Latin-
       skoi Amerike,* ed. S. S. Mikhailov.
       Moskva: Izdatel'stvo Nauka. Pp.
       98–121. [Item 10]

Sivolobov, A. M.
1964   "Krestian'skoe dvizhenie v Latin-
       skoi Amerike," *Kommunist* (Mos-

cow), 12:100–107 (August). [Item 21]

1966   *Ekonomicheskie problemy soiuza rabochego klassa i krest'ianstva stran Latinskoi Ameriki.* Moskva: Universitet druzhby narodov imeni Patrisa Lumumbi. Pp. 317–340. [Item 44]

Slezkin, L. Iu
1968   "Kamen' broshen (Amerikanskaia istoriografiia Kubinskoi revoliutsii 1960 g.)," *Novaia i noveishaia istoriia,* 4:133–142. [Item 47]

Spirin, V. G.
1967   "Vragi profsoiuznogo edinstva v Latinskoi Ameriki." In *Ot Aliaski do Ognennoi Zemli.* Moskva: Nauka. Pp. 347–360. [Item 18]

Vol'skii, Victor V.
1967   "The study of Latin America," *Latin American Research Review,* 3/1:77–87. [Item 3]

Zholobov, V.
1966   "Valiutnye problemy Latinskoi Ameriki," *Mirovaia ekonomika i mezhdunarodnye otnosheniia,* 5:79 –88. [Item 34]

Zubritskii, Iu. A.
1961   "Latinidad i ego sushchnost'," *Vestnik istorii mirovoi kul'tury,* 25/1:112–117 (January–February). [Item 35]